Python GUI Programming - A Complete Reference Guide

Develop responsive and powerful GUI applications with PyQt and Tkinter

Alan D. Moore
B. M. Harwani

BIRMINGHAM - MUMBAI

Python GUI Programming - A Complete Reference Guide

First Published: June 2019

Production Reference: 1200619

Published by Packt Publishing Ltd.
Livery Place, 35 Livery Street
Birmingham, B3 2PB, U.K.

ISBN 978-1-83898-847-0

www.packtpub.com

Contributors

About the Authors

Alan D. Moore is a data analyst and software developer who has been solving problems with Python since 2006. He's developed both open source and private code using frameworks like Django, Flask, Qt, and Tkinter. He contributes to various open source Python and Javascript projects. Alan maintains a blog by the name alandmoore, where he writes mainly about Python, Linux, free software, and his home studio recordings. Alan lives in Franklin, Tennessee, where he works for the county government, and with his wife, Cara, raises a crew of children who are just as geeky as their dad.

B. M. Harwani is founder and owner of Microchip Computer Education based in Ajmer, India that provides computer education in all programming and web developing platforms. Being involved in the teaching field for over 20 years, he has developed the art of explaining even the most complicated topics in a straightforward and easily understandable fashion. His latest books published include jQuery Recipes published by Apress, Introduction to Python Programming and Developing GUI Applications with PyQT published by Cengage Learning, The Android Tablet Developer's Cookbook published by Addison-Wesley Professional, UNIX & Shell Programming published by Oxford University Press, Qt5 Python GUI Programming Cookbook published by Packt.

Packt Is Searching for Authors Like You

If you're interested in becoming an author for Packt, please visit `authors.packtpub.com` and apply today. We have worked with thousands of developers and tech professionals, just like you, to help them share their insight with the global tech community. You can make a general application, apply for a specific hot topic that we are recruiting an author for, or submit your own idea.

Table of Contents

Preface

A responsive graphical user interface (GUI) helps you interact with your application, improves user experience, and enhances the efficiency of your applications. With Python, you'll have access to elaborate GUI frameworks that you can use to build interactive GUIs that stand apart from the rest.

This Learning Path begins by introducing you to Tkinter and PyQt, before guiding you through the application development process. As you expand your GUI by adding more widgets, you'll work with networks, databases, and graphical libraries that enhance its functionality. You'll also learn how to connect to external databases and network resources, test your code, and maximize performance using asynchronous programming. In later chapters, you'll understand how to use the cross-platform features of Tkinter and Qt5 to maintain compatibility across platforms. You'll be able to mimic the platform-native look and feel, and build executables for deployment across popular computing platforms.

By the end of this Learning Path, you'll have the skills and confidence to design and build high-end GUI applications that can solve real-world problems.

This Learning Path includes content from the following Packt products:

- *Python GUI Programming with Tkinter* by Alan D. Moore
- *Qt5 Python GUI Programming Cookbook* by B. M. Harwani

Who This Book Is For

If you're an intermediate Python programmer looking to enhance your coding skills by writing powerful GUIs in Python using PyQT and Tkinter, this is an ideal Learning Path for you. A strong understanding of the Python language is a must to grasp the concepts explained in this book.

What This Book Covers

`Chapter 1`, *Introduction to Tkinter*, introduces you to the basics of the Tkinter library and walks you through creating a Hello World application. It will also introduce you to IDLE as an example of a Tkinter application.

`Chapter 2`, *Designing GUI Applications with Tkinter,* goes through the process of turning a set of user requirements into a design that we can implement.

`Chapter 3`, *Creating Basic Forms with Tkinter and ttk Widgets,* shows you how to create a basic data entry form that appends data to a CSV file.

`Chapter 4`, *Reducing User Error with Validation and Automation,* demonstrates how to automatically populate and validate data in our form's inputs.

`Chapter 5`, *Planning for the Expansion of Our Application,* familiarizes you with how to break a small script into multiple files and build a Python module that you can import. It also contains some general advice on how to manage a larger code base.

`Chapter 6`, *Creating Menus with Menu and Tkinter Dialogs,* outlines the creation of a main menu using Tkinter. It will also show the use of several built-in dialog types to implement common menu functionality.

`Chapter 7`, *Navigating Records with Treeview,* details the construction of a records navigation system using the Tkinter Treeview and the conversion of our application from append-only to full read, write, and update capabilities.

`Chapter 8`, *Improving the Look with Styles and Themes,* informs you of how to change the colors, fonts, and widget styles of your application, and how to use them to make your application more usable.

`Chapter 9`, *Creating Automated Tests with unittest,* discusses how to verify your code with automated unit tests and integration tests.

`Chapter 10`, *Improving Data Storage with SQL,* takes you through the conversion of our application from the CSV flat-files to SQL data storage. You'll learn all about SQL and relational data models as well.

`Chapter 11`, *Connecting to the Cloud,* covers how to work with cloud services such as web services and FTP to download and upload data.

`Chapter 12`, *Visualizing Data Using the Canvas Widget,* teaches you how to work with the Tkinter `Canvas` widget to create visualizations and animations.

`Chapter 13`, *Creating a User Interface with Qt Components,* teaches you to use certain basic widgets of Qt Designer and how to display a welcome message along with the username. You will learn how to choose one out of several options using radio buttons and choose more than one out of several options by making use of checkboxes.

`Chapter 14`, *Event Handling – Signals and Slots*, covers how to execute specific tasks on the occurrence of certain events on any widget, as well as how to copy and paste text from one Line Edit widget to another, convert data types and make a small calculator, and use spin boxes, scrollbars, and sliders. You will also learn to perform multiple tasks using the List Widget.

`Chapter 15`, *Understanding OOP Concepts*, discusses object-oriented programming concepts such as how to use classes, single inheritance, multilevel inheritance in GUI applications, and multiple inheritance.

`Chapter 16`, *Understanding Dialogs*, explores the use of certain dialogs, where each dialog is meant for fetching a different kind of information. You will also learn to take input from the user using input dialog.

`Chapter 17`, *Understanding Layouts*, explains how to arrange widgets horizontally, vertically, and in different layouts by making use of Horizontal Layout, Vertical Layout, Grid Layout, as well as how to arrange widgets in two column layout using Form Layout.

`Chapter 18`, *Networking and Managing Large Documents*, demonstrates how to make a small browser, establish a connection between client and server, create a dockable and floatable sign in form, and manage more than one document using MDI. Also, you will learn how to display information in sections using the Tab widget, and how to create a custom menu bar that invokes different graphics tools when a specific menu item is chosen.

`Chapter 19`, *Database Handling*, outlines how to manage a SQLite database to keep information for future use. Using the knowledge gained, you will learn to make a signin form that checks whether a user's email address and password are correct or not.

`Chapter 20`, *Using Graphics*, explains how to display certain graphics in the application. You will also learn how to create a toolbar of your own that contains certain tools that can be used to draw different graphics.

`Chapter 21`, *Implementing Animation*, features how to display a 2D graphical image, make a ball move down on the click of a button, make a bouncing ball, and make a ball animate as per the specified curve.

`Chapter 22`, *Using Google Maps*, showcases how to use the Google API to display location and other information. You will learn to derive the distance between two locations and display location on Google Maps on the basis of longitude and latitude values that are entered.

To Get the Most out of This Book

This book expects that you know the basics of Python 3. You should know how to write and run simple scripts using built-in types and functions, how to define your own functions and classes, and how to import modules from the standard library.

You can follow this book if you run Windows, macOS, Linux, or even BSD. Ensure that you have Python 3 and Tcl/Tk installed and that you have an editing environment with which you are comfortable (we suggest IDLE since it comes with Python and uses Tkinter). In the later chapters, you'll need access to the internet so that you can install Python packages and the PostgreSQL database.

To run Python scripts on Android devices, you need to install QPython on your Android device. To package Python scripts into Android's APK using the Kivy library, you need to install Kivy, a Virtual Box, and Buildozer packager. Similarly, to run Python scripts on iOS devices, you need a macOS machine and some library tools, including Cython.

Download the Example Code Files

You can download the example code files for this book from your account at `www.packt.com`. If you purchased this book elsewhere, you can visit `www.packt.com/support` and register to have the files emailed directly to you.

You can download the code files by following these steps:

1. Log in or register at `www.packt.com`.
2. Select the **SUPPORT** tab.
3. Click on **Code Downloads & Errata**.
4. Enter the name of the book in the **Search** box and follow the onscreen instructions.

Once the file is downloaded, please make sure that you unzip or extract the folder using the latest version of:

- WinRAR/7-Zip for Windows
- Zipeg/iZip/UnRarX for Mac
- 7-Zip/PeaZip for Linux

The code bundle for the book is also hosted on GitHub at `https://github.com/PacktPublishing/Python-GUI-Programming-A-Complete-Reference-Guide`. In case there's an update to the code, it will be updated on the existing GitHub repository.

We also have other code bundles from our rich catalog of books and videos available at `https://github.com/PacktPublishing/`. Check them out!

Conventions Used

There are a number of text conventions used throughout this book.

`CodeInText`: Indicates code words in text, database table names, folder names, filenames, file extensions, pathnames, dummy URLs, user input, and Twitter handles. Here is an example: "Determine the appropriate `input` widget for each data field."

A block of code is set as follows:

```
def has_five_or_less_chars(string):
    return len(string) <= 5

    wrapped_function = root.register(has_five_or_less_chars)
    vcmd = (wrapped_function, '%P')
    five_char_input = ttk.Entry(root, validate='key',
validatecommand=vcmd)
```

When we wish to draw your attention to a particular part of a code block, the relevant lines or items are set in bold:

```
[default]
exten => s,1,Dial(Zap/1|30)
exten => s,2,Voicemail(u100)
exten => s,102,Voicemail(b100)
exten => i,1,Voicemail(s0)
```

Any command-line input or output is written as follows:

```
pip install --user psycopg2-binary
```

Bold: Indicates a new term, an important word, or words that you see onscreen. For example, words in menus or dialog boxes appear in the text like this. Here is an example: "Once installed, launch pgAdmin and create a new admin user for yourself by selecting **Object** | **Create** | **Login/Group Role**."

Warnings or important notes appear like this.

Tips and tricks appear like this.

Get in Touch

Feedback from our readers is always welcome.

General feedback: If you have questions about any aspect of this book, mention the book title in the subject of your message and email us at `customercare@packtpub.com`.

Errata: Although we have taken every care to ensure the accuracy of our content, mistakes do happen. If you have found a mistake in this book, we would be grateful if you would report this to us. Please visit `www.packt.com/submit-errata`, selecting your book, clicking on the Errata Submission Form link, and entering the details.

Piracy: If you come across any illegal copies of our works in any form on the Internet, we would be grateful if you would provide us with the location address or website name. Please contact us at `copyright@packt.com` with a link to the material.

If you are interested in becoming an author: If there is a topic that you have expertise in and you are interested in either writing or contributing to a book, please visit `authors.packtpub.com`.

Reviews

Please leave a review. Once you have read and used this book, why not leave a review on the site that you purchased it from? Potential readers can then see and use your unbiased opinion to make purchase decisions, we at Packt can understand what you think about our products, and our authors can see your feedback on their book. Thank you!

For more information about Packt, please visit `packt.com`.

1
Introduction to Tkinter

Welcome, Python **coder**! If you've learned the basics of Python and want to start designing powerful GUI applications, this book is for you.

By now, you have no doubt experienced the power and simplicity of Python. Perhaps you've written web services, performed data analysis, or administered servers. Perhaps you've written a game, automated routine tasks, or simply played around with code. But now you're ready to tackle the GUI.

With so much emphasis on web, mobile, and server-side programming, the development of simple desktop GUI applications seems increasingly like a lost art; many otherwise experienced developers have never learned to create one. What a tragedy! Desktop computers still play a vital role in work and home computing, and the ability to build simple, functional applications for this ubiquitous platform should be a part of every software developer's toolbox. Fortunately, for Python coders, that ability is well within reach thanks to Tkinter.

In this chapter, you will cover the following topics:

- Discovering Tkinter—a fast, fun, and easy-to-learn GUI library built right into the Python standard library
- Learning about IDLE—an editor and development environment written in Tkinter and bundled with Python
- Creating two `Hello World` applications to learn the basics of writing a Tkinter GUI

Introducing Tkinter and Tk

The Tk widget library originates from the **Tool Command Language** (**Tcl**) programming language. Tcl and Tk were created by John Ousterman while he was a professor at Berkeley in the late 1980s as an easier way to program engineering tools being used at the university. Because of its speed and relative simplicity, Tcl/Tk rapidly grew in popularity among academic, engineering, and Unix programmers. Much like Python itself, Tcl/Tk originated on the Unix platform and only later migrated to macOS and Windows. Tk's practical intent and Unix roots still inform its design today, and its simplicity compared to other toolkits is still a major strength.

Tkinter is a Python interface to the Tk GUI library and has been a part of the Python standard library since 1994 with the release of Python version 1.1, making it the de facto GUI library for Python. Documentation for Tkinter, along with links for further study, can be found in the standard library documentation at `https://docs.python.org/3/library/tkinter.html`.

Choosing Tkinter

Python coders who want to build a GUI have several toolkit options to choose from; unfortunately, Tkinter is often maligned or ignored as a legacy option. To be fair, it's not a glamorous technology that you can describe in trendy buzzwords and glowing hype. However, Tkinter is not only adequate for a wide variety of applications, it also has the following advantages that can't be ignored:

- **It's in the standard library**: With few exceptions, Tkinter is available wherever Python is available. There is no need to install `pip`, create virtual environments, compile binaries, or search the web for installation packages. For simple projects that need to be done quickly, this is a clear advantage.
- **It's stable**: While Tkinter development has not stopped, it is slow and evolutionary. The API has been stable for years, the changes mainly being additional functionality and bug fixes. Your Tkinter code will likely run unaltered for years or decades to come.
- **It's only a GUI toolkit**: Unlike some other GUI libraries, Tkinter doesn't have its own threading library, network stack, or filesystem API. It relies on regular Python libraries for such things, so it's perfect for applying a GUI to existing Python code.

- **It's simple and no-nonsense**: Tkinter is straightforward, old-school object-oriented GUI design. To use Tkinter, you don't have to learn hundreds of widget classes, a markup or templating language, a new programming paradigm, client-server technologies, or a different programming language.

Tkinter is not perfect, of course. It also has the following disadvantages:

- **Look and feel**: It's often derided for its look and feel, which still bear a few artifacts from the 1990s Unix world. This has improved a great deal in the last few years, thanks to updates in Tk itself and the addition of themed widget libraries. We'll learn how to fix or avoid some of Tkinter's more archaic defaults throughout the book.
- **Complex widgets**: It also lacks more complex widgets, like rich text or HTML rendering widgets. As we'll see later in this book, Tkinter gives us the ability to create complex widgets by customizing and combining its simple ones.

Tkinter might be the wrong choice for a game UI or slick commercial application; however, for data-driven applications, simple utilities, configuration dialogs, and other business logic applications, Tkinter offers all that is needed and more.

Installing Tkinter

Tkinter is included in the Python standard library for the Windows and macOS distributions. That means that, if you have Python on these platforms, you don't need to do anything to install Tkinter.

However, we're going to be exclusively focused on Python 3.x for this book; so, you need to make sure that this is the version you've got installed.

Installing Python 3 on Windows

You can obtain Python 3 installers for Windows from the `python.org` website by performing the following steps:

1. Go to `http://www.python.org/downloads/windows`.
2. Select the latest Python 3 release. At the time of writing, the latest version is 3.6.4, with 3.7 promising to be out by publishing time.

3. Under the **Files** section, select the Windows executable installer appropriate to your system's architecture (x86 for 32-bit Windows, x86_64 for 64-bit Windows).
4. Launch the downloaded installer.
5. Click on **Customize installation**. Make sure the **tcl/tk and IDLE** option is checked (it should be by default).
6. Continue through the installer with all defaults.

Installing Python 3 on macOS

As of this writing, macOS ships with Python 2 and Tcl/Tk 8.5 built in. However, Python 2 is scheduled to be deprecated in 2020, and the code in this book will not work with it, so macOS users will need to install Python 3 to follow this book.

Let's perform the following steps to install Python3 on macOS:

1. Go to `http://www.python.org/downloads/mac-osx/`.
2. Select the latest Python 3 release. At the time of writing, the latest version is 3.6.4, but 3.7 should be out by publication time.
3. Under the **Files** section, select and download `macOS 64-bit/32-bit installer`.
4. Launch the `.pkg` file that you've downloaded and follow the steps of the install wizard, selecting defaults.

There is currently no recommended way to upgrade to Tcl/Tk 8.6 on macOS, though it can be done with third-party tools if you wish. Most of our code will work with 8.5, though special mention is made when something is 8.6 only.

Installing Python 3 and Tkinter on Linux

Most Linux distributions include both Python 2 and Python 3, however, Tkinter is not always bundled with it or installed by default.

To find out if Tkinter is installed, open a Terminal and try the following command:

```
python3 -m tkinter
```

This should open a simple window showing some information about Tkinter. If you get `ModuleNotFoundError` instead, you will need to use your package manager to install your distribution's Tkinter package for Python 3. In most major distributions, including Debian, Ubuntu, Fedora, and openSUSE, this package is called `python3-tk`.

Introducing IDLE

IDLE is an integrated development environment that is bundled with the Windows and macOS Python distributions (it's readily available in most Linux distributions as well, usually as IDLE or IDLE3). IDLE is written in Python using Tkinter, and it provides us with not only an editing environment for Python, but also a great example of Tkinter in action. So, while IDLE's rudimentary feature set may not be considered professional grade by many Python coders, and while you may already have a preferred environment for writing Python code, I encourage you to spend some time using IDLE as you go through this book.

Let's get familiar with IDLE's two primary modes: **shell** mode and **editor** mode.

Using the shell mode of IDLE

When you launch IDLE, you begin in shell mode, which is simply a Python **Read-Evaluate-Print-Loop** (**REPL**) similar to what you get when you type `python` in a terminal window.

Take a look at the shell mode in the following screenshot:

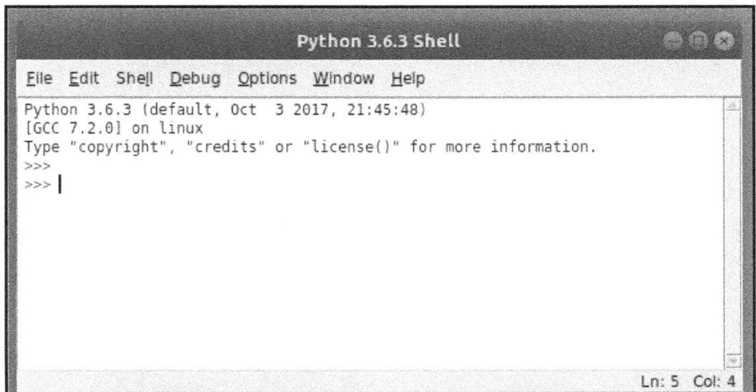

IDLE's shell has some nice features that you don't get from the command-line REPL, like syntax highlighting and tab-completion. The REPL is essential to the Python development process, as it gives you the ability to test code in real time and inspect classes and APIs without having to write complete scripts. We'll use the shell mode in later chapters to explore the features and behaviors of modules. If you don't have a shell window open, you can open one by clicking on **Start**, then selecting **Run**, and searching for Python shell.

Using the editor mode of IDLE

Editor mode is for creating Python script files, which you can later run. When the book tells you to create a new file, this is the mode you'll use. To open a new file in the editor mode, simply navigate to **File | New File** in the menu or hit *Ctrl* + *N* on the keyboard.

The following is a window where you can start typing a script:

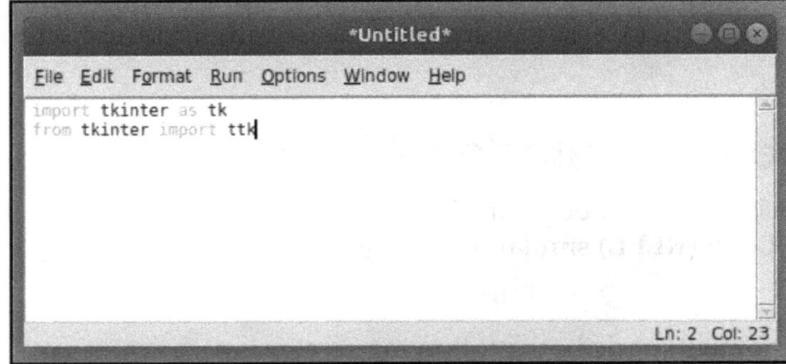

You can run your script without leaving IDLE by hitting *F5* in the editor mode; the output will show up in a shell window.

IDLE as a Tkinter example

Before we start coding with Tkinter, let's take a quick look at what you can do with it by inspecting some of IDLE's UI. Navigate to **Options | Configure IDLE** from the main menu to open IDLE's configuration settings, where you can change IDLE's fonts, colors and theme, keyboard shortcuts, and default behaviors, as shown in the following screenshot:

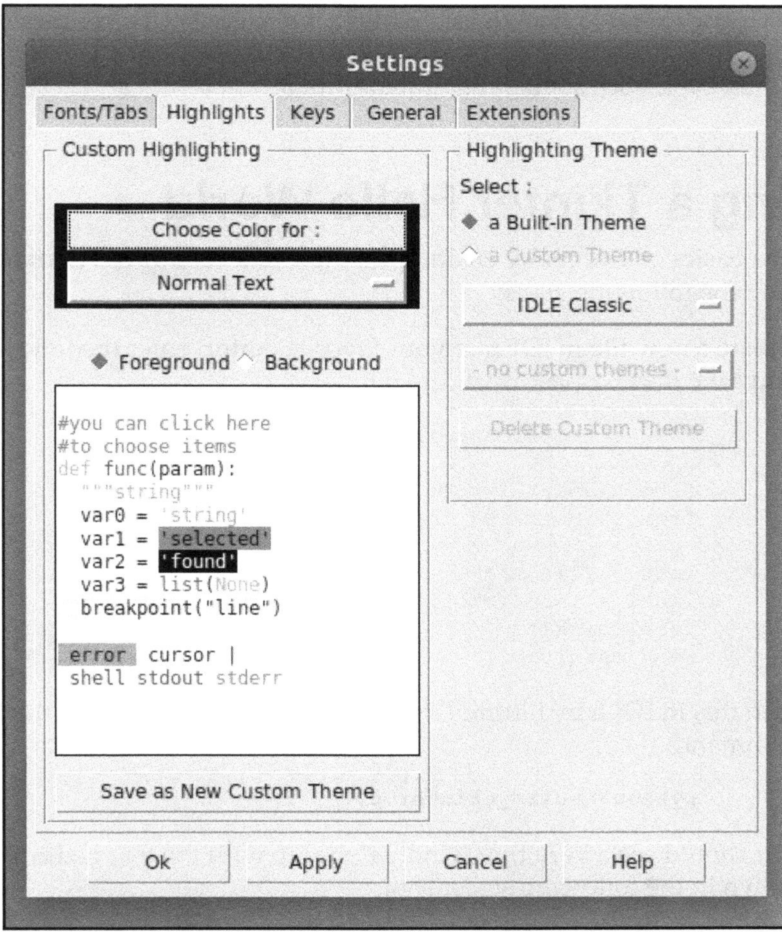

Consider some of the following components that make up this user interface:

- There are drop-down lists and radio buttons that allow you to select between different options
- There are many push buttons that you can click on to execute actions
- There is a text window that can display multi-colored text
- There are labeled frames that contain groups of components

Each of these components is known as a **widget**; we're going to meet these widgets and more throughout this book and learn how to use them as they've been used here. We'll begin, however, with something much simpler.

Creating a Tkinter Hello World

Let's learn the basics of Tkinter by creating a simple `Hello World` script for Tkinter by performing the following steps:

1. Create a new file in IDLE or your favorite editor, enter the following code, and save it as `hello_tkinter.py`:

```
"""Hello World application for Tkinter"""

from tkinter import *
from tkinter.ttk import *

root = Tk()
label = Label(root, text="Hello World")
label.pack()
root.mainloop()
```

2. Run this in IDLE by hitting *F5* or in your terminal by typing the following command:

```
python3 hello_tkinter.py
```

You should see a very tiny window pop up with the text **Hello World** as shown in the following screenshot:

3. Close the window and return to your editor screen. Let's break down this code and talk about what it does:
    - `from tkinter import *`: This imports the Tkinter library into the global namespace. This isn't best practice, because it fills your namespace with a lot of classes, which you might accidentally overwrite, but it's okay for very small scripts.
    - `from tkinter.ttk import *`: This imports the `ttk` or **themed** Tk widget library. We'll be using this library throughout the book, as it adds a number of useful widgets and improves the look of existing widgets. Since we're doing the star import here, our Tk widgets will be replaced by the better-looking `ttk` widgets wherever applicable (for instance, our `Label` object).
    - `root = Tk()`: This creates our root or master application object. This represents the primary top-level window and main execution thread of the application, so there should be one and only one instance of Tk for every application.
    - `label = Label(root, text="Hello World")`: This creates a new `Label` object. As the name implies, a `Label` object is just a widget for displaying text (or images). Looking closer at this line, we see the following:
        - The first argument we pass to `Label()` is the `parent` or master widget. Tkinter widgets are arranged in a hierarchy starting with the root window, each widget being contained by another. Any time you create a widget, your first argument will be the widget object that contains the new widget. In this case, we're placing our `Label` object on the main application window.
        - The second argument is a keyword argument that specifies the text to be displayed on the `Label` object.
        - We store the new `Label` instance in a variable, `label`, so that we can do more to it later.

- `label.pack()`: This places the new label widget onto its `parent` widget. In this case, we're using the `pack()` method, which is the simplest of three **geometry manager** methods you can use. We'll learn about these in more detail in future chapters.
- `root.mainloop()`: This final line starts our main event loop. This loop is responsible for processing all the events—keystrokes, mouse clicks, and so on—and it will run until the program is quit. This is usually the last line of any Tkinter script, since any code after it won't run until the main window is closed.

Take a few moments and play around with this script by adding more widgets before the `root.mainloop()` call. You can add more `Label` objects or try `Button` (which creates a clickable button) or `Entry` (which creates a text entry field). Just like `Label`, these widgets are initialized with a `parent` object (use `root`) and a `text` parameter. Don't forget to call `pack()` on your widget to add them to the window.

You can also try commenting out the `ttk` import, to see if you notice a difference in the look of the widgets. Depending on your OS, it may look different or not.

Creating a better Hello World Tkinter

Creating a GUI the way we just did works okay for very small scripts, but a much more scalable approach is to subclass Tkinter widgets to create component widgets that we will then assemble into a completed application.

Subclassing is simply a way of creating a new class based on an existing one, adding or changing only what is different in the new class. We will use subclassing extensively in this book to extend the functionality of Tkinter widgets.

Let's build a more robust `Hello World` script that demonstrates some patterns we'll use throughout the remainder of the book. Take a look at the following steps:

1. Create a file called `better_hello_tkinter.py` and begin with the following lines:

```
"""A better Hello World for Tkinter"""
import tkinter as tk
from tkinter import ttk
```

   This time, we aren't doing the star imports; instead, we'll keep Tkinter and the `ttk` objects in their own namespaces. This keeps our global namespace from being cluttered up and eliminates a potential source of bugs.

Star imports (`from module import *`) are seen often in Python tutorials and example code, but in production code they should be avoided. Python modules can contain any number of classes, functions, or variables; when you do a star import, you import all of them, which can lead to one import overwriting the objects imported from another module. If you find a module name cumbersome to type over and over, alias it to something short, as we've done with Tkinter.

2. Next, we create a new class called `HelloView`, as follows:

```
class HelloView(tk.Frame):
    """A friendly little module"""

    def __init__(self, parent, *args, **kwargs):
        super().__init__(parent, *args, **kwargs)
```

Our class is subclassed from `Tkinter.Frame`. The `Frame` class is a generic Tk widget that is typically used as a container for other widgets. We can add any number of widgets to the `Frame` class, then treat the whole thing as though it were a single widget. This is a lot simpler in the long run than individually placing every last button, label, and input on a single master window. The first order of business in the constructor is to call `super().__init__()`. The `super()` function gives us a reference to the super class (the class we've subclassed, in this case, `tk.Frame`). By calling the super class constructor and passing along `*args` and `**kwargs`, our new `HelloWidget` class can take any arguments that `Frame` can take.

In older versions of Python, `super()` had to be invoked with the name of the child class and a reference to the current instance, such as `super(MyChildClass, self)`. Python 3 allows you to call it with no arguments, but you will probably encounter code that uses the older invocation.

3. Next, we're going to create two Tkinter variable objects to store the name and greeting strings, as follows:

```
self.name = tk.StringVar()
self.hello_string = tk.StringVar()
self.hello_string.set("Hello World")
```

Tkinter has a collection of variable types including `StringVar`, `IntVar`, `DoubleVar`, and `BooleanVar`. You might wonder why we'd use these when Python has perfectly good data types for all of these (and more!). Tkinter variables are more than just containers for data: they have special functionality that regular Python variables lack, such as the ability to automatically propagate changes to all the widgets that reference them or trigger an event when they're changed. Here we'll use them as a way to access the data in a widget without having to keep or pass around references to the widget itself.

Notice that setting a value to a Tkinter variable requires use of the `set()` method, rather than direct assignment. Likewise, retrieving the data requires use of a `get()` method. Here, we set the value of `hello_string` to `Hello World`. We start building our view by creating a `Label` object and `Entry`, as follows:

```
name_label = ttk.Label(self, text="Name:")
name_entry = ttk.Entry(self, textvariable=self.name)
```

The `Label()` invocation looks familiar, but the `Entry` object gets a new argument: `textvariable`. By passing a Tkinter `StringVar` variable to this argument, the contents of the `Entry` box will be bound to the variable, and we can access it without needing to reference the widget. Whenever a user enters text in the `Entry` object, `self.name` will immediately be updated wherever it appears.

4. Now, let's create `Button`, as follows:

```
ch_button = ttk.Button(self, text="Change",
    command=self.on_change)
```

In the preceding code, we again have a new argument, `command`, which takes a reference to a Python function or method. We call a function or method passed this way a callback, and, as you might expect, this callback will be called when the button is clicked. This is the simplest way to bind functions to a widget; later, we'll learn a more flexible method that will allow us to bind various keystrokes, mouse clicks, and other widget events to function or method calls.

Make sure you don't actually call your callback at this point—it should be `self.on_change`, not `self.on_change()`. The callback should be a reference to the function or method, not the output from it.

5. Let's create another `Label`, as follows, this time to display our text:

```
hello_label = ttk.Label(self, textvariable=self.hello_string,
    font=("TkDefaultFont", 64), wraplength=600)
```

Here we've passed our other `StringVarvariable` variable, `self.hello_string` to the `textvariable` argument; on a label, the `textvariable` variable determines what will be displayed. By doing this, we can change the text on the label by simply changing `self.hello_string`. We'll also set a much larger font by using the `font` argument, which takes a tuple in the format `(font_name, font_size)`.

You can enter any font name you want here, but it must be installed on the system to work. Tk has some built-in aliases that map to sensible fonts on every platform, such as `TkDefaultFont` used here. We'll learn more about using fonts in Tkinter in `Chapter 8`, *Improving the Look with Styles and Themes*.

The `wraplength` argument specifies how wide the text can be before it wraps to the next line. We want our text to wrap when it reaches the edge of the window; by default, label text does not wrap, so it would be cut off at the edge of the window. By setting the wrap length to 600 pixels, our text will wrap at the width of the screen.

6. So far, our widgets have been created, but not yet placed on `HelloView`. Let's arrange our widgets as follows:

```
name_label.grid(row=0, column=0, sticky=tk.W)
name_entry.grid(row=0, column=1, sticky=(tk.W + tk.E))
        ch_button.grid(row=0, column=2, sticky=tk.E)
        hello_label.grid(row=1, column=0, columnspan=3)
```

In this case, we're adding our widgets using the `grid()` geometry manager, rather than the `pack()` geometry manager we used before. As the name implies, `grid()` allows us to position widgets on their `parent` object using rows and columns, much like a spreadsheet or HTML table. Our first three widgets are arranged across three columns in row `0`, while `hello_label` will be on the second row (row `1`). The `sticky` argument takes a cardinal direction (`N`, `S`, `E`, or `W`—you can either use strings or the Tkinter constants), which specifies which side of the cell the contents must stick to. You can add these together to stick the widget to multiple sides; for example, by sticking the `name_entry` widget to both the east and west sides, it will stretch to fill the whole width of the column. The `grid()` call for `hello_label` uses the `columnspan` argument. As you might expect, this causes the widget to span three grid columns. Since our first row established three columns for the grid layout, we need to span all three if we want this widget to fill the width of the application. Finally, we'll finish the `__init__()` method by adjusting the grid configuration:

```
self.columnconfigure(1, weight=1)
```

In the preceding code, the `columnconfigure()` method is used to make changes to a widget's grid columns. Here, we're telling it to weight column `1` (the second column) more than the others. By doing this, the second column of the grid (where our entry lives) will expand horizontally and squash surrounding columns to their minimum widths. There is also a `rowconfigure()` method for making similar changes to grid rows.

7. Before we finish our `HelloModule` class, we have to create the callback for `ch_button`, as follows:

```
def on_change(self):
    if self.name.get().strip():
        self.hello_string.set("Hello " + self.name.get())
    else:
        self.hello_string.set("Hello World")
```

To get the value of the text entry, we call the `get()` method of its text variable. If this variable contains any characters (notice we strip the white space), we'll set our hello text to greet the name entered; otherwise, we'll just greet the whole world.

Notice by using the `StringVar` objects we don't have to interact directly with the widgets. This saved us from having to keep a lot of widget references in our class, but, more importantly, our variable could be updated from any number of sources or update any number of destinations without us having to explicitly write code to do so.

8. With `HelloView` created, we move onto the actual application class, as follows:

```
class MyApplication(tk.Tk):
    """Hello World Main Application"""

    def __init__(self, *args, **kwargs):
        super().__init__(*args, **kwargs)
        self.title("Hello Tkinter")
        self.geometry("800x600")
        self.resizable(width=False, height=False)
```

This time, we subclass `Tk`, which will represent our main application object. There is some debate in the Tkinter world whether or not this is best practice. Since there can be only one `Tk` object in the application, it could theoretically create problems if we want multiple `MyApplication` objects somewhere down the line; for simple, single-window applications, it's perfectly fine.

9. As with our module, we call `super().__init__()` and pass along any arguments. Notice we don't need a `parent` widget this time, since the `Tk` object is the root window and has no `parent`. Then there are the following three calls to configure our application window:
    - `self.title()`: This call sets the window title, which usually appears in the task list and/or window bar in our OS environment.
    - `self.geometry()`: This call sets the size of our window in pixels, in the format `x * y` (width x height).
    - `self.resizable()`: This call sets whether the program window can be resized. We're disabling resizing here, both in width and height.
10. We finish our application class by adding our view to the main window, as follows:

```
HelloView(self).grid(sticky=(tk.E + tk.W + tk.N + tk.S))
self.columnconfigure(0, weight=1)
```

Notice that we create and place `HelloView` in a single line of code. We do this in situations where we don't need to keep a reference to the widget, but since `grid()` does not return a value, you'll have to stick to the two-statement version if you want to access the widget later in your code.

Because we want the view to fill the application window, our `grid()` call sticks it to all sides of its cell, and our `columnconfigure()` call causes the first column to expand. Note that we've omitted the `row` and `column` arguments without them, and `grid()` simply uses the first column of the next available row (in this case, `0`, `0`).

11. With our classes defined, we'll start the actual execution of the code, as follows:

```
if __name__ == '__main__':
    app = MyApplication()
    app.mainloop()
```

In Python, `if __name__ == '__main__':` is a common idiom to check if a script is being run directly, such as when we type `python3 better_hello_world.py` at a terminal. If we were to import this file as a module into another Python script, this check would be false and the code after would not be run. It's a good practice to put your program's main execution code below this check so that you can safely reuse your classes and functions in larger applications.

Remember that `MyApplication` is a subclass of `Tk`, so it acts as the root window. We only need to create it and then start its main loop. Take a look at the following screenshot:

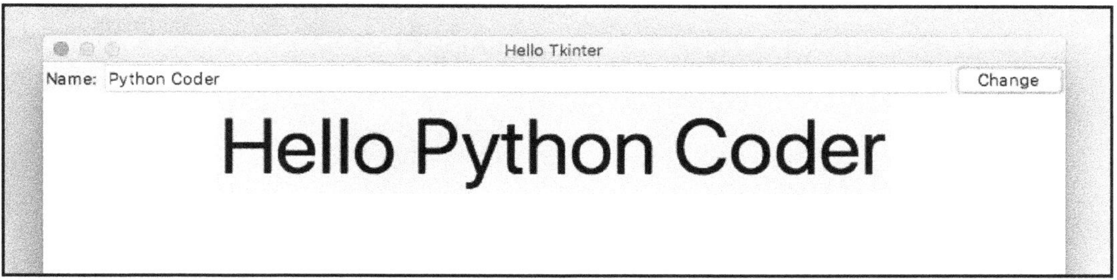

This was certainly overkill for a `Hello World` application, but it demonstrates the use of subclassing to segment our application into modules, which will vastly simplify layouts and code organization as we build larger programs.

Summary

Now that you've installed Python 3, learned to use IDLE, gotten a taste of the simplicity and power of Tkinter, and have seen how to begin structuring it for more complicated applications, it's time to start writing a real application.

In the next chapter, you'll start your new job at ABQ AgriLabs and be presented with a problem that will need to be solved with your programming skills and Tkinter. You will learn how to dissect this problem, develop a program specification, and design a user-friendly application that will be part of the solution.

2
Designing GUI Applications with Tkinter

Software applications are developed in three repeating phases: understanding a problem, designing a solution, and implementing the solution. These phases repeat throughout the life of an application, refining and honing it until it is either optimal or obsolete.

In this chapter, we'll learn about the following topics:

- Introducing and analyzing a scenario in the workplace that will need a software solution
- Documenting the requirements of the solution
- Developing a design for a piece of software that implements the solution

A problem at ABQ AgriLabs

Congratulations! Your Python skills have landed you a great data analyst job at ABQ AgriLabs. So far, your job is fairly simple: collating and doing simple data analysis on the CSV files sent to you daily from the lab's data entry staff.

There is a problem, though. You've noted with frustration that the quality of the CSV files from the lab is sadly inconsistent. Data is missing, typos abound, and often the files have to be re-entered in a time-consuming process. The lab director has noticed this as well and, knowing that you are a skilled Python programmer, she thinks you might be able to help.

You've been enlisted to program a solution that will allow the data entry staff to enter lab data into a CSV file with fewer mistakes. Your application needs to be simple and allow as little room for error as possible.

Assessing the problem

Spreadsheets are often the first stop for computer users who need to keep track of data. Their table-like layouts and computational features seem to make them ideal for the task. However, as a set of data grows and is added to by multiple users, the shortcomings of spreadsheets become apparent: they don't enforce data integrity, their table-like layout can be visually confusing when dealing with long rows of sparse or ambiguous data, and users can easily delete or overwrite data if they aren't being careful.

To improve this situation, you propose to implement a simple GUI data entry form that appends data to a CSV file in the format we need. Forms can help to improve data integrity in several ways:

- Allowing only the correct type of data to be entered (for example, only allowing numerals in a number field)
- Limiting choices to only valid options
- Auto-filling information like current dates, times, and so on
- Verifying that entered data is within expected ranges or matches expected patterns
- Ensuring that all data has been filled in

By implementing such a form, we can greatly reduce the number of errors being entered by the data entry staff.

Gathering information about the problem

To build the data entry form application, you need to gather details about what it needs to accomplish. Fortunately, you already know the output part of the equation: you need a CSV file containing data about the plants growing in the plots of each laboratory and the environmental conditions at each plot. You work with these files every day, so you're pretty familiar with the field layout.

However, you don't know everything about the data or the process of entering it; you'll need to talk to the other staff involved to find out more information.

First, you'll need to find out more detail about the data being recorded. This isn't always as easy as it sounds. The software needs absolute, black-and-white rules when dealing with data; people, on the other hand, tend to think in generalities about their data, and they often don't consider the exact details of limits or edge cases without some prompting.

As a programmer, it's your job to come up with questions that will bring out the information you need.

You decide you should start with the lab technicians and learn more about the data they're collecting. You come up with the following questions:

- What values are acceptable for each field? Are any fields constrained to a set of values?
- What units are represented by each of the numeric fields?
- Are numeric fields truly number-only fields? Would they ever need letters or symbols?
- What range of numbers is acceptable for each numeric field?
- How do you record data and how long does it take?

Data isn't the only consideration. If we're making a program to help reduce user error, we also have to understand those users and how they work. In the case of this application, our users will be the data entry staff. We need to ask them questions about their needs and workflow to understand how to create an application that works well for them.

We come up with the following list of questions:

- In what format do you get the data you're entering?
- When is the data received and how soon is it entered? What's the latest it might be entered?
- Are there fields that could be automatically populated? Should users be able to override the auto values?
- What's the overall technical ability of the users?
- What do you like about the current solution? What do you dislike?
- Do users have visual or manual impairments that should be accommodated?

Finally, we need to understand the technology involved with operating our application—the computers, networks, servers, and platforms being used to accomplish the task.

You decide to add the following questions, which you'll assess yourself when you meet with the data entry staff:

- What kind of computer does data entry use?
- What platform does it run?
- How fast or powerful is it?
- Is Python available on these systems?
- Which Python libraries are available?

What you found out

You start by writing down the following basics about ABQ that you know:

- Your ABQ facility has five greenhouses, each operating with a different climate, marked A, B, C, D, and E
- Each greenhouse has 20 plots (labeled 1 through 20)
- There are currently four seed samples, each coded with a six-character label
- Each plot has 20 seeds of a given sample planted in it, as well as its own environmental sensor unit

Information about the data being collected

Your talk with the lab technicians revealed a lot about the data. Four times a day, at 8:00, 12:00, 16:00, and 20:00, each technician checks the plots in one or two labs. They use a paper form to record values at each plot, recording all values to two decimal places. This usually takes 30 to 40 minutes per lab, and the whole process typically takes 90 minutes.

Each plot has an environmental sensor that detects the light, temperature, and humidity at the plot. Unfortunately, these devices are prone to failure, indicated by an `Equipment Fault` light on the unit. Technicians record if this light is lit, since it invalidates the environmental data.

Finally, the technicians tell you about the units and acceptable ranges for the fields, which you record in the following chart:

Field	Data type	Notes
`Date`	`Date`	The data collection date. Almost always the current date
`Time`	`Time`	The start of the period during which measurements were taken. One of 8:00, 12:00, 16:00, or 20:00

Lab	Character	The lab ID, which will be A to E
Technician	Text	The name of the technician recording data
Plot	Int	The plot ID, which will be 1 through 20
Seed Sample	Text	ID string for seed sample. Always a six-character code containing digits 0 to 9 and capital letters A to Z
Fault	Boolean	True if environmental equipment registered a failure, otherwise false
Humidity	Decimal	Absolute humidity in g/m^3, roughly between 0.5 and 52.0
Light	Decimal	Amount of sunlight at the plot center in kilolux, between 0 and 100
Temperature	Decimal	Degrees C, should not go below 4 or above 40
Blossoms	Int	The number of blossoms in the plot must be 0 or more, but unlikely to ever approach 1,000
Fruit	Int	The number of fruits in the plot must be 0 or more, but unlikely to ever approach 1,000
Plants	Int	The number of growing plants, between 0 and 20.
Max height	Decimal	The height of the tallest plant in cm. At least 0, unlikely to approach 1,000.
Median height	Decimal	The median height of plants in the plot, in cm. At least 0, unlikely to approach 1,000
Min height	Decimal	The height of the smallest plant in cm. At least 0, unlikely to approach 1,000
Notes	Long Text	Additional observations about the plant, data, instruments, and so on

Information about the users of the application

Your session with the data entry staff yielded good information about their workflow, requirements, and technology.

The lab technicians drop off their paper forms as they're completed. The data is typically entered right away and usually on the same day as it's handed in.

The technicians are currently using LibreOffice on a Debian Linux workstation to enter the data. Using copy and paste, they can bulk-fill fields with repeated data like date, time, and technician. The autocompletion feature of LibreOffice is often helpful in text fields, but sometimes causes accidental data errors in the number fields.

The workstation being used is several years old, but performs adequately. You get a chance to look at it and find that Python and Tkinter are already installed.

There are four data entry clerks in total, but only one working at any one time; while interviewing the clerks, you learn that one has red-green color blindness, and another has trouble using a mouse due to RSI issues. All are reasonably computer literate.

Documenting specification requirements

Now that you've assembled your data about the application, it's time to write up a **specification**. Software specifications can range from very formal, contractual documents that include time estimates and deadlines, to a simple set of descriptions of what the programmer intends to build. The purpose of the specification is to give everyone involved in the project a point of reference for what the developer will create. It spells out the problem to be solved, the functionality required, and the scope of what the program should and shouldn't do.

Your scenario is rather informal and your application is simple, so you do not need a detailed formal specification in this case. However, a basic write-up of what you know will make sure that you, your boss, and the users are all on the same page.

Contents of a simple specification

We'll start our specification with the following outline of the items we need to write:

- **Description**: This is one or two sentences that describe the primary purpose, function, and goals of the application. Think of it as the program's mission statement.
- **Functionality required**: This section is a list of specific things the program needs to be able to do to be minimally functional. It can include both hard requirements, such as detailed output and input formats, and soft requirements—goals that are not quantifiably attainable, but that the program should strive toward (for example, "reduce user errors as much as possible").
- **Functionality not required**: This section is a list of things the program does not need to do; it exists to clarify the scope of the software and make sure nobody expects unreasonable things from the application.
- **Limitations**: This is a list of constraints under which the program must operate, both technological and human.

- **Data dictionary**: This is a detailed list of the data fields the application will deal with and their parameters. These can get quite lengthy but are a critical reference as the application expands and the data gets utilized in other contexts.

Writing the ABQ data entry program specification

You could write a specification in your favorite word processor, but ideally the specification is a part of your code; it will need to be kept with the code and synchronized with any changes to the application. For that reason, we're going to write it in our text editor using the **reStructuredText** markup language.

For Python documentation, reStructuredText, or reST, is the official markup language. The Python community encourages the use of reST to document Python projects, and many packaging and publication tools used in the Python community expect the reST format. We'll cover reST in more depth in `Chapter 5`, *Planning for the Expansion of Our Application*, but you can find the official documentation at `http://docutils.sourceforge.net/rst.html`.

Let's begin writing our specification, one section at a time as follows:

1. Begin the specification with the name of the application and a short description. This should contain a summary of the program's purpose, as follows:

```
======================================
 ABQ Data Entry Program specification
======================================

Description
-----------
The program is being created to minimize data entry errors
for laboratory measurements.
```

2. Now, let's list the requirements. Remember that hard requirements are objectively attainable goals—input and output requirements, calculations that must be done, features that must be present, whereas our soft requirements are subjective or best-effort goals. Look through your findings from the last section, and consider which needs are which.

You should come up with something like the following:

```
Functionality Required
----------------------

The program must:

* allow all relevant, valid data to be entered, as per the
field chart
* append entered data to a CSV file
  - The CSV file must have a filename
    of abq_data_record_CURRENTDATE.csv, where
    CURRENTDATE is the date of the checks in
    ISO format (Year-month-day)
  - The CSV file must have all the fields as per the chart
* enforce correct datatypes per field

The program should try, whenever possible, to:

* enforce reasonable limits on data entered
* Auto-fill data
* Suggest likely correct values
* Provide a smooth and efficient workflow
```

3. Next, we'll reign in the scope of the program with the `Functionality Not Required` section. Remember that this is only an entry form for now; editing or deletion will be handled in the spreadsheet application. We'll clarify this as follows:

```
Functionality Not Required
--------------------------

The program does not need to:

* Allow editing of data. This can be done in LibreOffice
if necessary.
* Allow deletion of data.
```

4. For the `Limitations` section, remember that we have some users with physical constraints, as well has hardware and operating system constraints. Add it as follows:

```
Limitations
-----------

The program must:
```

```
* Be efficiently operable by keyboard-only users.
* Be accessible to color blind users.
* Run on Debian Linux.
* Run acceptably on a low-end PC.
```

5. Finally, the data dictionary, this is essentially the table we've made previously, but we'll break out range, data types, and units for quick reference, as follows:

```
+------------+----------+------+--------------+---------------
------+
|Field       | Datatype | Units| Range        |Descripton
|
+============+==========+======+==============+===============
======+
|Date        |Date      |      |              |Date of record
|
+------------+----------+------+--------------+---------------
------+
|Time        |Time      |      |8, 12, 16, 20 |Time period
|
+------------+----------+------+--------------+---------------
------+
|Lab         |String    |      | A - E        |Lab ID
|
+------------+----------+------+--------------+---------------
------+
|Technician  |String    |      |              |Technician name
|
+------------+----------+------+--------------+---------------
------+
|Plot        |Int       |      | 1 - 20       |Plot ID
|
+------------+----------+------+--------------+---------------
------+
|Seed        |String    |      |              |Seed sample ID
|
|sample      |          |      |              |
|
+------------+----------+------+--------------+---------------
------+
|Fault       |Bool      |      |              |Fault on sensor
|
+------------+----------+------+--------------+---------------
------+
|Light       |Decimal   |klx   | 0 - 100      |Light at plot
|
+------------+----------+------+--------------+---------------
```

```
------+
|Humidity    |Decimal   |g/m^3 | 0.5 - 52.0   |Abs humidity at
plot |
+------------+----------+------+-------------+---------------
------+
|Temperature |Decimal   |°C    | 4 - 40       |Temperature at
plot  |
+------------+----------+------+-------------+---------------
------+
|Blossoms    |Int       |      | 0 - 1000     |# blossoms in
plot   |
+------------+----------+------+-------------+---------------
------+
|Fruit       |Int       |      | 0 - 1000     |# fruits in
plot      |
+------------+----------+------+-------------+---------------
------+
|Plants      |Int       |      | 0 - 20       |# plants in
plot      |
+------------+----------+------+-------------+---------------
------+
|Max height  |Decimal   |cm    | 0 - 1000     |Ht of tallest
plant   |
+------------+----------+------+-------------+---------------
------+
|Min height  |Decimal   |cm    | 0 - 1000     |Ht of shortest
plant |
+------------+----------+------+-------------+---------------
------+
|Median      |Decimal   |cm    | 0 - 1000     |Median ht of
plants   |
|height      |          |      |              |
|
+------------+----------+------+-------------+---------------
------+
|Notes       |String    |      |              |Miscellaneous
notes   |
+------------+----------+------+-------------+---------------
------+
```

That's our specification for now! The specification is very likely to grow, change, or evolve in complexity as we discover new needs.

Designing the application

With our specification in hand and our requirements clear, it's time to start designing our solution. We'll start with the form GUI component itself.

We're going to create a basic design for our form in the following three steps:

1. Determine the appropriate `input` widget for each data field
2. Group together related items to create a sense of organization
3. Layout our widgets in their groups on a form sheet

Exploring Tkinter input widgets

Like all toolkits, Tkinter offers a variety of `input` widgets for different kinds of data. However, `ttk` offers additional widget types and enhances some (but not all!) of Tkinter's native widgets. The following table offers advice on which widgets are most appropriate for different kinds of data entry:

Widget	Description	Used for
`ttk.Entry`	Basic text entry	Single-line strings
`ttk.Spinbox`	Text entry with increment/decrement arrows	Numbers
`Tkinter.Listbox`	Box with a list of choices	Choice between several values
`Tkinter.OptionMenu`	Drop-down list with choices	Choice between several values
`ttk.Combobox`	Drop-down list with optional text entry	Choice between several values plus text entry
`ttk.Checkbutton`	Checkbox with label	Boolean values
`ttk.Radiobutton`	Like checkbox, but only one of a set can be selected	Choice between small set of values
`Tkiner.Text`	Multiline text entry box	Long, multiline strings
`Tkinter.Scale`	Mouse-operated slider	Bounded number data

Let's consider which of these widgets are appropriate for the data that needs to be entered:

- There are several `Decimal` fields, many with clear boundary ranges with `Min height`, `Max height`, `Median height`, `Humidity`, `Temperature`, and `Light`. You could use a `Scale` widget for these, but it's not really appropriate for precise data entry, since it requires careful positioning to get an exact value. It's also mouse-operated and that violates your specification requirements. Instead, use the `Spinbox` widget for these.
- There are also some `Int` fields, such as `Plants`, `Blossoms`, and `Fruit`. Again, the `Spinbox` widget is the right choice.
- There are a couple of fields with a limited set of possible values—`Time` and `Lab`. The `Radiobutton` or `Listbox` widgets could work for these, but both take up a lot of space and are less keyboard-friendly as they require selection with arrow keys. There is also `OptionMenu`, but it is also mouse or arrow keys only. For these, use the `Combobox` widget instead.
- Plot is a tricky case. At face value, it looks like an `Int` field, but think about it. The plots could just as well be identified by letters, or symbols, or names. Numbers just happen to be an easy set of values with which to assign arbitrary identifiers. The `Plot ID`, like the `Lab ID`, is a constrained set of values; so, it would make more sense to use a `Combobox` widget here.
- The `Notes` field is multiline text, so the `Text` widget is appropriate here.
- There is one `Boolean` field, `Fault`. It could be handled with `Radiobutton` or `Combobox`, but `Checkbutton` is the optimal choice—it's compact and reasonably keyboard-friendly.
- The remaining lines are simple, one-line character fields. We'll use `Entry` for those fields.
- You might be wondering about the `Date` field. Tkinter has no special widget for dates; so, we'll use a generic `Entry` widget here for the time being.

Our final analysis will be as follows:

Field	**Widget type**
`Blossoms`	`ttk.Spinbox`
`Date`	`ttk.Entry`
`Fault`	`ttk.Checkbutton`
`Fruit`	`ttk.Spinbox`
`Humidity`	`ttk.Spinbox`

Lab	ttk.Combobox
Light	ttk.Spinbox
Max height	ttk.Spinbox
Median height	ttk.Spinbox
Min height	ttk.Spinbox
Notes	Tkinter.Text
Plants	ttk.Spinbox
Plot	ttk.Combobox
Seed Sample	ttk.Entry
Technician	ttk.Entry
Temperature	ttk.Spinbox
Time	ttk.Combobox

Grouping our fields

Humans tend to get confused when staring at a huge wall of inputs in no particular order. You can do your users a big favor by breaking up the input form into sets of related fields. Of course, that assumes that your data has related sets of fields, doesn't it?

After looking over your fields, you identify the following related groups:

- The `Date`, `Lab`, `Plot`, `Seed Sample`, `Technician`, and `Time` fields are identifying data or metadata about the record itself. You could group these together under a heading like `Record information`.
- The `Blossoms`, `Fruit`, three `Height` fields, and `Plants` fields are all measurements that have to do with the plants in the `Plot` field. You could group these together as `Plant data`.
- The `Humidity`, `Light`, `Temperature`, and `Equipment Fault` fields, are all information from the environmental sensor. You could group these as `Environmental data`.
- The `Notes` field could be related to anything, so it's in a category of its own.

To group the preceding fields in Tkinter, we could just insert labels between each set of fields, but it's worth exploring the various options we have for grouping widgets together:

Widget	Description
`ttk.LabelFrame`	Frame with label text and an optional border
`ttk.NoteBook`	Tabbed widget that allows multiple pages
`Tkinter.PanedWindow`	Allows for multiple re-sizable frames in horizontal or vertical arrangement

We don't want our form on multiple pages, nor will users need to resize the sections, but the `LabelFrame` widget sounds perfect for our needs.

Laying out the form

So far, we know that we have 17 inputs, which are grouped as follows:

- Six fields under `Record information`
- Four fields under `Environmental data`
- Six fields under `Plant data`
- One large `Notes` field

We want to group the preceding inputs using `LabelFrame`.

Notice that two of the first three sections have widgets in multiples of three. That suggests that we could arrange them in a grid with three items across. How should we order the fields within each group?

Ordering of fields seems like a trivial item, but for the user it can make a significant difference in usability. Users who have to jump around a form haphazardly to match their workflow are more likely to make mistakes.

As you learned, the data is entered from paper forms filled out by the lab technicians. You obtained a copy of the form, as shown in the following screenshot:

Date: ________ Time (circle): 8:00 12:00 16:00 20:00 Lab (circle): A B C D E Tech: ____________

Plot	Seed	hum (g/m^3)	light (klux)	temp (°C)	Fault Y/N	Plants	Bloss	Fruit	min ht (cm)	max ht (cm)	med ht (cm)	Notes
1												
2												
3												
4												
5												
6												
7												
8												
9												
10												
11												
12												
13												
14												
15												
16												
17												
18												
19												
20												

It looks like items are mostly grouped the way our records are grouped, so we'll use the ordering on this form to order our fields. That way, data entry clerks can zip right through the form without having to bounce around the screen.

When designing a new application to replace some part of an existing workflow, it's important to learn and respect that workflow. While we'll have to adjust that workflow to actually improve it, we don't want to make another part of someone's job harder just to make the part we're working on simpler.

One last consideration in our design is where to place field labels in relation to the fields. There is a good deal of debate in the UI design community over the best placement of labels, but the consensus is that one of the following two options is best:

- Labels above fields
- Labels to the left of fields

You might try sketching out both to see which you prefer, but for this application labels above fields will probably work better for the following reasons:

- Since both fields and labels are rectangular in shape, our form will be more compact by stacking them
- It's a lot easier to make the layout work, since we don't have to find a label width that works for all the labels without distancing them too far from the fields

The one exception is the check button field; check buttons are typically labeled to the right of the widget.

Take a moment to make a mockup of your form, using paper and pencil, or a drawing program. Your form should look as follows:

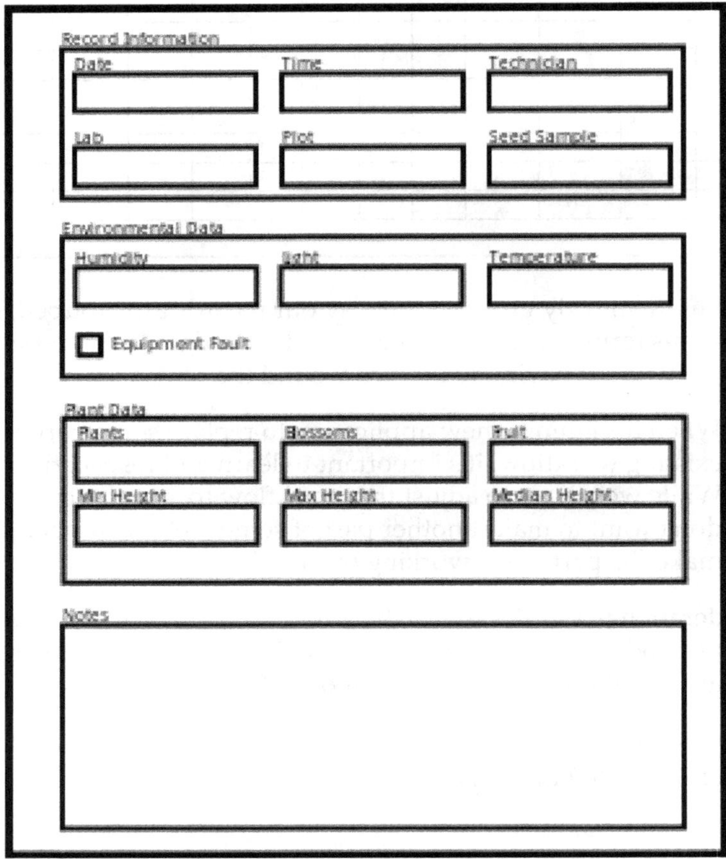

Laying out the application

With your form designed, it's time to consider the rest of the application's GUI:

- You'll need a save button to trigger storage of the entered data
- Sometimes, we might need to provide status information to the user; applications typically have a status bar that displays these kinds of messages
- Finally, it might be good to have a header indicating what the form is

Adding the following things to our sketch, we have something like the following screenshot:

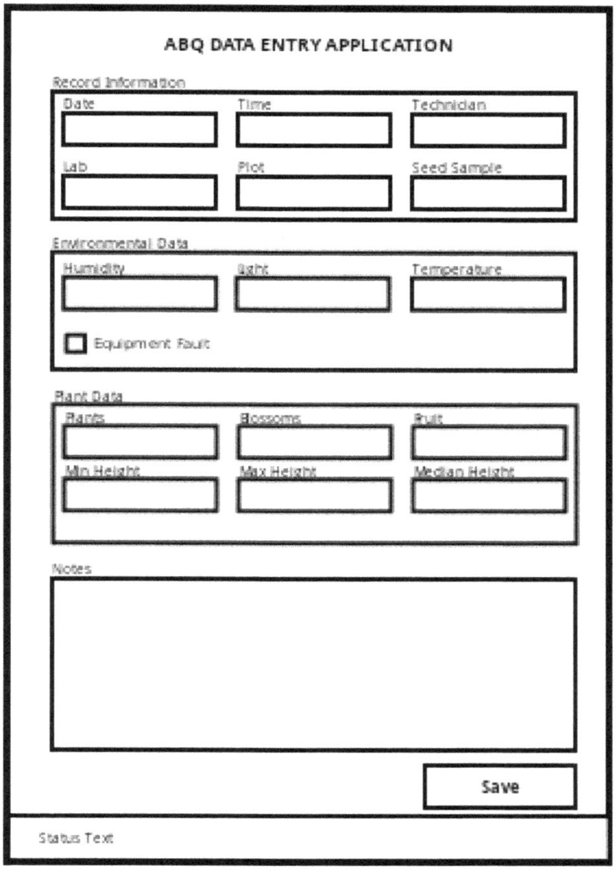

Looks good! This is definitely a form we can implement in Tkinter. Your final step is to show these designs to your users and the director for any feedback or approval.

Keep stakeholders involved as much as possible in your application design process. This reduces the possibility that you'll have to go back and redesign your application later.

Summary

In this chapter, you worked through the first two phases of application development: understanding the problem and designing a solution. You learned how to develop an application specification by interviewing users and examining the data and requirements, creating an optimal form layout for your users, and learned which widgets are available in Tkinter for dealing with different kinds of input data. Most importantly, you learned that developing an application doesn't begin with code, but with research and planning.

In the next chapter, you'll create a basic implementation of your designs with Tkinter and Python. We will get familiar with the Tkinter widgets required to create our form, build the form, and place the form within the application. We'll also learn how to make our form trigger callback actions and discover how to structure our code to ensure efficiency and consistency.

3
Creating Basic Forms with Tkinter and ttk Widgets

Good news! Your design has been reviewed and approved by the director. Now it's time to start implementing it!

In this chapter, you'll cover the following topics:

- Evaluating your technology choices in light of the design
- Getting to know our selected Tkinter and `ttk` widgets
- Implementing and testing the form and application

Let's get coding!

Evaluating our technology choices

Our first implementation of the design will be a very simple application that delivers the core functionality of the specification and little else. This is known as a **minimum viable product** or **MVP**. Once we've established an MVP, we'll have a better understanding of how to develop it into a final product.

Before we get to that, let's take a moment to evaluate our technology choices.

Choosing a technology

Naturally, we're going to build this form using Python and Tkinter. However, it's worth asking whether Tkinter is really a good choice of technology for the application. We need to take the following things into consideration when choosing the GUI toolkit used to implement this form:

- **Your current expertise and knowledge**: Your expertise is in Python, but you have little experience in creating GUIs. For the fastest time to deliver, you need an option that works well with Python and isn't complicated to learn. You also want something established and stable, as you won't have time to keep up with new developments in the toolkit. Tkinter works here.
- **The target platforms**: You will be developing the application on a Windows PC, but it will need to run on Debian Linux, so the choice of GUI should be cross-platform. The computer it will run on is old and slow, so your program needs to be frugal with resources. Tkinter also works here.
- **Application functionality**: Your application needs to be able to display basic form fields, validate the data entered, and write it to CSV. Tkinter can handle these frontend requirements, and Python can handle the CSV file easily.

Given the options available for Python, Tkinter is a good choice. It's got a short learning curve, it's lightweight, it's readily available on both your development and target platforms, and it contains the functionality necessary for the form.

Python has other options for GUI development, including **PyQT**, **Kivy**, and **wxPython**. These have different strengths and weaknesses compared to Tkinter, but if you find Tkinter doesn't fit well for a project, one of these might be a better option.

Exploring Tkinter widgets

When we designed our application, we picked out a widget class that most closely matched each field we needed. These were the `Entry`, `Spinbox`, `Combobox`, `Checkbutton`, and `Text` widgets. We also determined that we'd need the `Button` and `LabelFrame` widgets to implement the application layout. Before we start writing our class, let's take a look at each of these widgets.

Some of our widgets are in Tkinter, others are in the `ttk` themed widget set, and a few are in both libraries. We prefer the `ttk` versions wherever they exist, since they look better across platforms. Pay careful attention to the library from which we import each widget.

The Entry widget

The `ttk.Entry` widget is a basic, one-line character entry, as shown in the following screenshot:

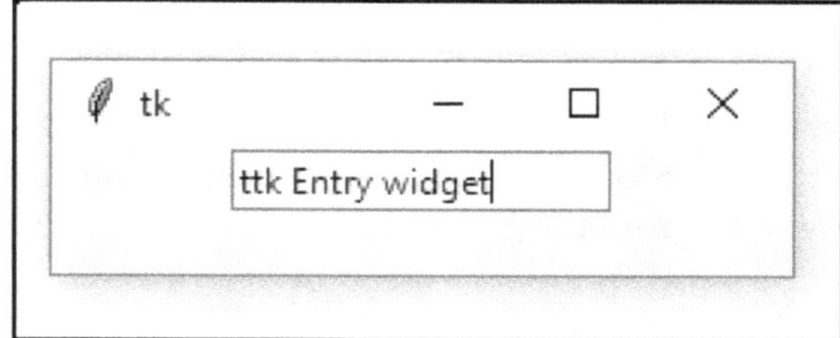

You can create an entry by executing the following code:

```
my_entry = ttk.Entry(parent, textvariable=my_text_var)
```

In the preceding code, the commonly used arguments to `ttk.Entry` are as follows:

- `parent`: This argument sets the `parent` widget for the entry.
- `textvariable`: This is a Tkinter `StringVar` variable whose value will be bound to this `input` widget.
- `show`: This argument determines which character will be displayed when you type into the box. By default, it's the character you type, but this can be replaced (for example, for password entry you might specify `*` or dot to be shown instead).
- `Entry`: This widget, like all the `ttk` widgets, supports additional formatting and styling options.

Among all the preceding arguments, use of the `textvariable` argument is optional; without it, we can extract the value in the `Entry` widget, using its `get()` method. Binding a variable to our `input` widget has some advantages, however. First, we don't have to keep or pass around a reference to the widget itself. This will make it easier to reorganize our software into separate modules in later chapters. Also, changes to the value of the input are automatically propagated to the variable and vice versa.

The Spinbox widget

The `ttk.Spinbox` widget adds increment and decrement buttons to a regular `Entry` widget, making it suitable for numerical data.

Prior to Python 3.7, `Spinbox` was only available in Tkinter, not `ttk`. If you're using Python 3.6 or an older version, use the `Tkinter.Spinbox` widget instead. The sample code uses the Tkinter version for compatibility.

A `Spinbox` widget is created as follows:

```
my_spinbox = tk.Spinbox(
    parent,
    from_=0.5,
    to=52.0,
    increment=.01,
    textvariable=my_double_var)
```

As seen in the preceding code, the `Spinbox` widget takes some extra constructor arguments to control the increment and decrement button behavior, as follows:

- `from_`: This argument determines the lowest value to which the arrows decrement. The ending underscore is needed because `from` is a Python keyword; in Tcl/`Tk` it's just `from`.
- `to`: This argument determines the highest value to which the arrows increment.
- `increment`: This argument represents the amount at which arrows increment or decrement.
- `values`: This argument takes a list of string or number values that can be incremented through.

Note that both `from_` and `to` are required if you use either; that is, you cannot just specify a lower limit, doing so will either cause an exception or strange behavior.

Take a look at the `Spinbox` widget in the following screenshot:

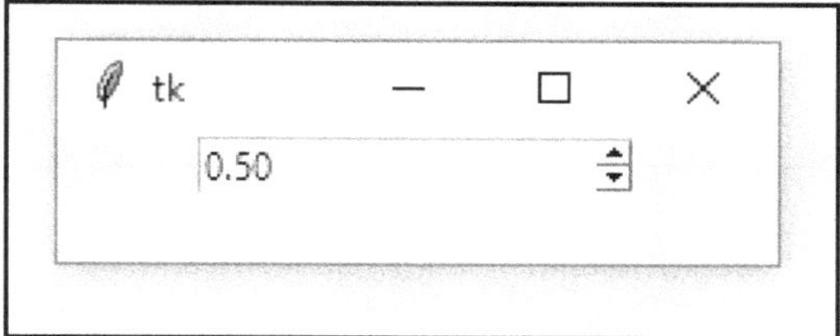

The `Spinbox` widget is not just for numbers, even though that's primarily how we'll be using it. It can also take a list of strings, which can be selected using the arrow buttons. Because it can be used for strings or numbers, the `textvariable` argument takes the `StringVar`, `IntVar`, or `DoubleVar` data types.

Be aware that none of these parameters actually limit what can be typed into a `Spinbox` widget. It's nothing more than an `Entry` widget with buttons tacked on, and you can type not only values outside the valid range, but letters and symbols as well. Doing so can cause an exception if you've bound the widget to a non-string variable.

The Combobox widget

The `ttk.Combobox` argument is an `Entry` widget that adds a drop-down select menu. To populate the drop-down menu, simply pass in a `values` argument with a list of the strings, which the user can select.

You can execute the following code to create a `Combobox` widget:

```
combobox = ttk.Combobox(
    parent, textvariable=my_string_var,
    values=["Option 1", "Option 2", "Option 3"])
```

The preceding code will generate the following widget:

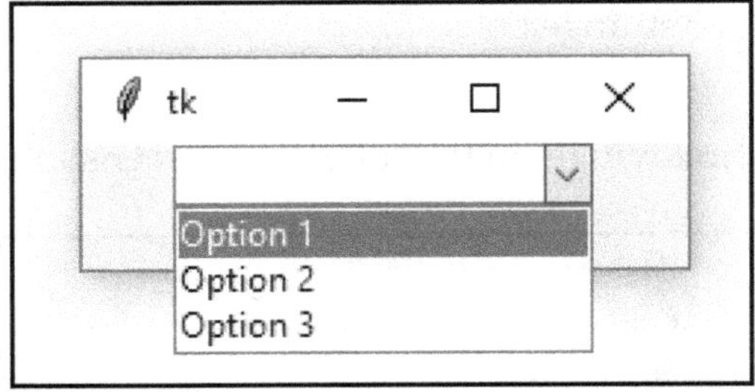

If you're used to HTML `<SELECT>` widgets or drop-down widgets in other toolkits, the `ttk.Combobox` widget may seem strange to you. It's really an `Entry` widget with a drop-down menu to select some preset strings. Just like the `Spinbox` widget, it doesn't limit the values that can be typed in.

The Checkbutton widget

The `ttk.Checkbutton` widget is a labeled checkbox for entering boolean data. Unlike `Spinbox` and `Combobox`, it is not derived from the `Entry` widget and its arguments are different as follows:

- `text`: This argument sets the label for the widget.
- `variable`: This argument is `BooleanVar`, to which the checked status is bound.
- `textvariable`: Unlike the `Entry` based widgets, this argument can be used to bind a variable to the label text of the widget. You won't use this often, but you should know it exists in case you mistakenly assign your variable to it.

You can execute the following code to create a `Checkbutton` widget:

```
my_checkbutton = ttk.Checkbutton(
    parent, text="Check to make this option True",
    variable=my_boolean_var)
```

The `Checkbox` widget appears as a clickable box with a label by it, as shown in the following screenshot:

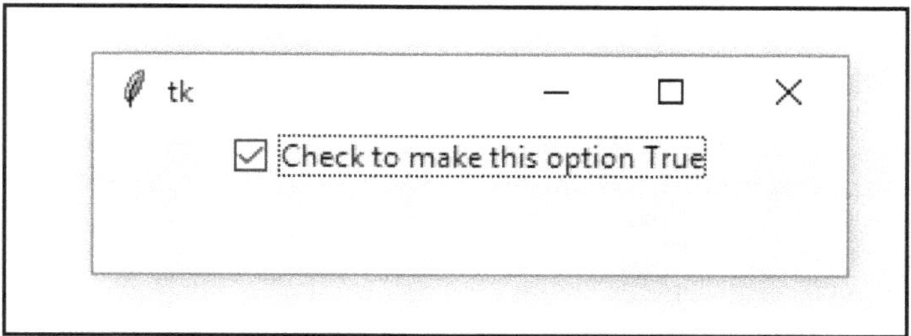

The Text widget

The `Text` widget is much more than just a multiline `Entry` widget. It has a powerful tagging system that allows you to implement multicolored text, hyperlink-style clickable text, and more. Unlike other widgets, it can't be bound to a Tkinter `StringVar`, so setting or retrieving its contents needs to be done through its `get()`, `insert()`, and `delete()` methods.

When reading or modifying with these methods, you are required to pass in one or two **index** values to select the character or range of characters that you're operating on. These index values are strings that can take any of the following formats:

- The line number and character number separated by a dot. Lines are numbered from 1 and characters from 0, so the first character on the first line is `1.0`, while the twelfth character on the fourth line would be `4.11`.
- The `end` string or Tkinter constant `END`, indicating the end of the field.
- A numerical index plus one of the words `linestart`, `lineend`, `wordstart`, and `wordend`, indicating the start or end of the line or word relative to the numerical index. For example, `6.2 wordstart` would be the start of the word containing the third character on line 6; `2.0 lineend` would be the end of line 2.
- Any of the preceding, a plus or minus operator, and a number of characters or lines. For example, `2.5 wordend - 1 chars` would be the character before the end of the word containing the sixth character on line 2.

The following example shows the basics of working with a `Text` widget:

```
# create the widget.  Make sure to save a reference.
mytext = tk.Text(parent)

# insert a string at the beginning
mytext.insert('1.0', "I love my text widget!")

# insert a string into the current text
mytext.insert('1.2', 'REALLY ')

# get the whole string
mytext.get('1.0', tk.END)

# delete the last character.
# Note that there is always a newline character
# at the end of the input, so we backup 2 chars.
mytext.delete('end - 2 chars')
```

If you run the preceding code, you'll get the following output:

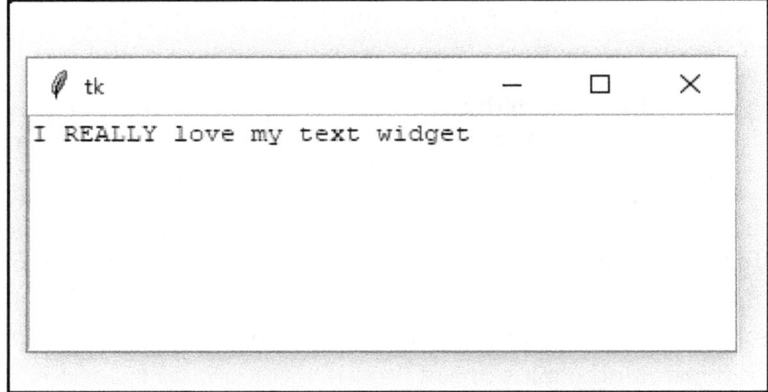

For the `Notes` field in this form, we just need a simple multiline `Entry`; so, we'll only be using the most basic functionality of the `Text` widget for now.

The Button widget

The `ttk.Button` widget should also be familiar. It's just a straightforward button that you click with the mouse or spacebar, as shown in the following screenshot:

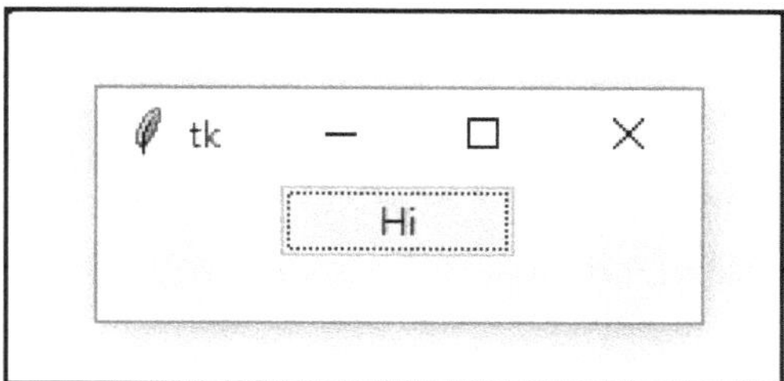

Just like the `Checkbutton` widget, this widget uses the `text` and `textvariable` configuration options to control the label on the button. The `Button` objects don't take `variable`, but they do take a `command` argument, which specifies a Python function to run when the button is clicked.

The following example shows the use of a `Button` object:

```
tvar = tk.StringVar()
def swaptext():
    if tvar.get() == 'Hi':
        tvar.set('There')
    else:
        tvar.set('Hi')

my_button = ttk.Button(parent, textvariable=tvar, command=swaptext)
```

The LabelFrame widget

We have chosen the `ttk.LabelFrame` widget to group the fields in our application. As the name implies, it's `Frame` with `Label` (and a box around it, usually). The `LabelFrame` widget takes a `text` argument in the constructor that sets the label, positioned in the top-left of the frame.

Tkinter and ttk contain many more widgets, some of which we'll encounter later in this book. Python also ships with a widget library called tix, which contains several dozen widgets. However, tix is very outdated, and we won't be covering it in this book. You should know that it exists, though.

Implementing the application

To start our application script, create a folder called ABQ data entry and a file inside it called data_entry_app.py.

We'll start with the following boilerplate code:

```
import tkinter as tk
from tkinter import ttk

# Start coding here


class Application(tk.Tk):
    """Application root window"""

if __name__ == "__main__":
    app = Application()
    app.mainloop()
```

Running this script should give you a blank Tk window.

Saving some time with a LabelInput class

Every input widget on our form has a label associated with it. In a small application, we can just create the label and input separately, then add each to the parent frame as follows:

```
form = Frame()
label = Label(form, text='Name')
name_input = Entry(form)
label.grid(row=0, column=0)
name_input.grid(row=1, column=0)
```

That works fine and you could do it that way for your application, but it also creates a lot of tedious, repetitious code, and moving inputs around means changing twice as much code. Since the label and input widgets belong together, it would be smart to create a small wrapper class to contain both and establish some universal defaults.

When coding, be on the lookout for sections that contain a lot of repetitive code. You can often abstract this code into a class, function, or loop. Doing so won't just save your fingers some typing, it will ensure consistency and reduce the total amount of code you have to maintain.

Let's take a look at the following steps:

1. We'll call this class LabelInput and define it at the top of our code, just under the Start coding here comment:

```
"""Start coding here"""
class LabelInput(tk.Frame):
    """A widget containing a label and input together."""

    def __init__(self, parent, label='',
input_class=ttk.Entry,
             input_var=None, input_args=None, label_args=None,
             **kwargs):
            super().__init__(parent, **kwargs)
            input_args = input_args or {}
            label_args = label_args or {}
            self.variable = input_var
```

2. We'll base the class on Tkinter.Frame, just as we did with HelloWidget. Our constructor takes a number of the following arguments:

    - parent: This argument is a reference to the parent widget; all widgets we create will take this as the first argument.
    - label: This the text for the label part of the widget.
    - input_class: This is the class of the widget we want to create. It should be an actual callable class object, not a string. If left blank, ttk.Entry will be used.
    - input_var: This is a Tkinter variable to assign to the input. It's optional, since some widgets don't use variables.
    - input_args: This is an optional dictionary of any additional arguments for the input constructor.

- `label_args`: This is an optional dictionary of any additional arguments for the `label` constructor.
- `**kwargs`: Finally, we catch any additional keyword arguments in `**kwargs`. These will be passed to the `Frame` constructor.

3. The first thing we do in the constructor is call `super().__init__()` and pass in the `parent` and extra keyword arguments. We then make sure that both `input_args` and `label_args` are dictionaries, and save a reference to our input variable as `self.variable`.

Don't be tempted to use an empty dictionary (`{}`) as a default value for a method's keyword arguments. If you did so, a dictionary would be created when the method definition is evaluated and shared by all objects in the class. This would have some very strange effects on your code! The accepted practice is to pass `None` for mutable types like dictionaries and lists, then replacing `None` with an empty container in the method body.

4. We want to be able to take any kind of `input` widget and deal with it appropriately in our class; unfortunately, as we learned previously, there are small differences between the constructor arguments and behavior in different widget classes, such as the way `Combobox` and `Checkbutton` use their `textvariable` argument. At the moment, we just need to differentiate between the way button widgets like `Button` and `Checkbutton` handle variables and label text. To deal with this, we'll add the following code:

```
if input_class in (ttk.Checkbutton, ttk.Button,
ttk.Radiobutton):
    input_args["text"] = label
    input_args["variable"] = input_var
else:
    self.label = ttk.Label(self, text=label, **label_args)
    self.label.grid(row=0, column=0, sticky=(tk.W + tk.E))
    input_args["textvariable"] = input_var
```

5. For button-type widgets, we do the following tasks differently:
    - Instead of adding a label, we just set the `text` argument. All buttons use this argument to add a `label` to the widget.
    - Instead of assigning our variable to `textvariable`, we assign it to `variable`.

6. In the case of other `input` classes, we set `textvariable` and create a `Label` widget, adding it to the first row of the `LabelInput` class.
7. Now we need to create the `input` class, as follows:

```
self.input = input_class(self, **input_args)
self.input.grid(row=1, column=0, sticky=(tk.W + tk.E))
```

8. This is pretty straightforward: we call the `input_class` class passed into the constructor with the `input_args` dictionary expanded to keyword arguments. Then, we add it to the grid at row `1`.
9. Lastly, we configure the `grid` layout to expand our lone column across the entire widget, as follows:

```
self.columnconfigure(0, weight=1)
```

10. One nice thing we can do when creating custom widgets that will save us a lot of coding is to add defaults to its geometry manager methods. For example, we're going to want all our `LabelInput` objects to fill the entire grid cell that they're placed within. Instead of adding `sticky=(tk.W + tk.E)` to every `LabelInput.grid()` call, we can add it as a default value by overriding the method:

```
    def grid(self, sticky=(tk.E + tk.W), **kwargs):
        super().grid(sticky=sticky, **kwargs)
```

By defining it as a default parameter, we can still override it as usual. The `input` widgets all have a `get()` method that returns their current value. To save some redundant typing later, we'll implement a `get()` method in our `LabelInput` class that will simply pass along the request to the input or its variable. Add this method next:

```
    def get(self):
        try:
            if self.variable:
                return self.variable.get()
            elif type(self.input) == tk.Text:
                return self.input.get('1.0', tk.END)
            else:
                return self.input.get()
        except (TypeError, tk.TclError):
            # happens when numeric fields are empty.
            return ''
```

We're using a `try` block here, because Tkinter variables will throw an exception if you call `get()` under certain conditions, such as when a numeric field is empty (blank strings can't convert to a numeric value). In such a case, we'll simply return an empty value from the form. Also, we need to handle the `tk.Text` widgets differently, since they require a range to retrieve text. We're always going to want all the text from this form, so we'll just specify that here. As a complement to `get()`, we'll implement a `set()` method that passes the request to the variable or `widget`, as follows:

```
    def set(self, value, *args, **kwargs):
        if type(self.variable) == tk.BooleanVar:
                self.variable.set(bool(value))
        elif self.variable:
                self.variable.set(value, *args, **kwargs)
        elif type(self.input) in (ttk.Checkbutton,
        ttk.Radiobutton):
            if value:
                self.input.select()
            else:
                self.input.deselect()
        elif type(self.input) == tk.Text:
            self.input.delete('1.0', tk.END)
            self.input.insert('1.0', value)
        else: # input must be an Entry-type widget with no
variable
            self.input.delete(0, tk.END)
            self.input.insert(0, value)
```

The `.set()` method abstracts away some of the differences between how various Tkinter widgets set their values:

- If we have a variable of class `BooleanVar`, cast `value` to `bool` and set it. `BooleanVar.set()` will only take a `bool`, not other falsy or truthy values. This ensures our variable only gets an actual boolean value.
- If we have any other kind of variable, just pass `value` to its `.set()` method.
- If we have no variable, and a button-style class, we use the `.select()` and `.deselect()` methods to select and deselect the button based on the truthy value of the variable.
- If it's a `tk.Text` class, we can use its `.delete` and `.insert` methods.

- Otherwise, we use the `.delete` and `.insert` methods of `input`, which work on the `Entry`, `Spinbox`, and `Combobox` classes. We have to do this separately from the `tk.Text` inputs, because the indexing values work differently.

This may not account for every possible `input` widget, but it covers the ones we plan to use and a few more we may need later. While building the `LabelInput` class took a lot of work, we'll see that defining the form is much simpler now.

Building the form

Instead of building our form directly on the main application window, we're going to build our form as its own object. Initially, this makes it easier to maintain a nice layout, and later down the road it will make it easier for us to expand our application. Let's perform the following steps for building our form:

1. Once again, we'll subclass `Tkinter.Frame` to build this module. After the `LabelInput` class definition, begin a new class as follows:

```
class DataRecordForm(tk.Frame):
    """The input form for our widgets"""

    def __init__(self, parent, *args, **kwargs):
        super().__init__(parent, *args, **kwargs)
```

   This should be familiar by now. We subclass `Frame`, define our constructor, and call `super().__init__()` to initialize the underlying `Frame` object.

2. Now we're going to create a structure to hold references to all the form's `input` widgets, as follows:

```
# A dict to keep track of input widgets
self.inputs = {}
```

   As we create the `input` widgets, we'll store references to them in the dictionary, using the field name as a key. This will make it easier later to retrieve all our values.

Adding LabelFrame and other widgets

Our form is divided into sections with a label for and a box around each section. For each section, we'll create a `LabelFrame` widget and start adding our `LabelInput` widgets to it by performing the following steps:

1. Let's start with the record information frame by executing the following code:

```
recordinfo = tk.LabelFrame(self, text="Record Information")
```

Remember that the `text` argument to `LabelFrame` defines the text of the label. This widget will be passed as the `parent` widget to all the inputs in the record information group.

2. Now, we'll add the first line of the `input` widgets, as follows:

```
self.inputs['Date'] = LabelInput(recordinfo, "Date",
    input_var=tk.StringVar())
self.inputs['Date'].grid(row=0, column=0)

self.inputs['Time'] = LabelInput(recordinfo, "Time",
    input_class=ttk.Combobox, input_var=tk.StringVar(),
    input_args={"values": ["8:00", "12:00", "16:00",
"20:00"]})
self.inputs['Time'].grid(row=0, column=1)

self.inputs['Technician'] = LabelInput(recordinfo,
"Technician",
    input_var=tk.StringVar())
self.inputs['Technician'].grid(row=0, column=2)
```

3. The `Date` and `Technician` inputs are simple text entries; we only need to pass the `parent`, `label`, and `input` variables into our `LabelInput` constructor. For the `Time` entry, we specify a list of possible values that will be used to initialize the `Combobox` widget.
4. Let's work on line 2, as follows:

```
# line 2
self.inputs['Lab'] = LabelInput(recordinfo, "Lab",
    input_class=ttk.Combobox, input_var=tk.StringVar(),
    input_args={"values": ["A", "B", "C", "D", "E"]})
self.inputs['Lab'].grid(row=1, column=0)

self.inputs['Plot'] = LabelInput(recordinfo, "Plot",
```

```
        input_class=ttk.Combobox, input_var=tk.IntVar(),
       input_args={"values": list(range(1, 21))})
    self.inputs['Plot'].grid(row=1, column=1)

    self.inputs['Seed sample'] = LabelInput(
        recordinfo, "Seed sample", input_var=tk.StringVar())
    self.inputs['Seed sample'].grid(row=1, column=2)

    recordinfo.grid(row=0, column=0, sticky=tk.W + tk.E)
```

5. Here, we have two more `Combobox` widgets and another `Entry`. These are created similarly to those in line 1. The values for `Plot` just need to be a list of numbers from 1 through 20; we can create that with Python's built-in `range()` function. Finished with the record information, we add its `LabelFrame` to the form widget with a call to `grid()`. The remaining fields are defined in essentially the same way. For example, our environmental data will look as follows:

```
    # Environment Data
    environmentinfo = tk.LabelFrame(self, text="Environment Data")
    self.inputs['Humidity'] = LabelInput(
        environmentinfo, "Humidity (g/m³)",
        input_class=tk.Spinbox, input_var=tk.DoubleVar(),
        input_args={"from_": 0.5, "to": 52.0, "increment": .01})
    self.inputs['Humidity'].grid(row=0, column=0)
```

6. Here, we've added the first of our `Spinbox` widgets, specifying the valid ranges and increment amount; you can add in the `Light` and `Temperature` inputs in the same way. Notice that our `grid()` coordinates have started over with `0, 0`; that's because we're starting a new parent object, so the coordinates begin all over again.

All of these nested grids can get confusing. Remember that whenever you call `.grid()` on a widget, the coordinates are relative to the top-left corner of the widget's parent. The parent's coordinates are relative to its parent, and so on, back up to the root window.

This section also contains the lone `Checkbutton` widget:

```
    self.inputs['Equipment Fault'] = LabelInput(
        environmentinfo, "Equipment Fault",
        input_class=ttk.Checkbutton,
        input_var=tk.BooleanVar())
    self.inputs['Equipment Fault'].grid(
        row=1, column=0, columnspan=3)
```

7. There are no real arguments to use with the `Checkbutton`, though note that we're using a `BooleanVar` to store its value. Now, we move on to the plant data section:

```
plantinfo = tk.LabelFrame(self, text="Plant Data")

self.inputs['Plants'] = LabelInput(
    plantinfo, "Plants",
    input_class=tk.Spinbox,
    input_var=tk.IntVar(),
    input_args={"from_": 0, "to": 20})
self.inputs['Plants'].grid(row=0, column=0)

self.inputs['Blossoms'] = LabelInput(
    plantinfo, "Blossoms",
    input_class=tk.Spinbox,
    input_var=tk.IntVar(),
    input_args={"from_": 0, "to": 1000})
self.inputs['Blossoms'].grid(row=0, column=1)
```

Notice that, unlike our decimal `Spinboxes`, we're not setting the increment for the integer fields; that's because it defaults to `1.0`, which is what we want for integer fields.

8. We're also using `1000` as a maximum for `Blossoms` although it technically shouldn't have a maximum; our `Lab Technicians` assured us that it would never approach 1,000. Since `Spinbox` requires both `to` and `from_`, if we use either, we'll go ahead and use this value.

You can also specify the strings `infinity` or `-infinity` as values. These can be cast to the `float` values, which behave appropriately.

9. The `Fruit` field and three `Height` fields will be mostly identical to these. Go ahead and create them, making sure to follow your data dictionary for the appropriate `input_args` values and `input_var` types. We finish our form fields by adding the following notes:

```
        # Notes section
        self.inputs['Notes'] = LabelInput(
            self, "Notes",
            input_class=tk.Text,
            input_args={"width": 75, "height": 10}
        )
        self.inputs['Notes'].grid(sticky="w", row=3, column=0)
```

10. There's no need for `LabelFrame` here, so we're just adding the note's `LabelInput` frame directly to the form. The `Text` widget takes the `width` and `height` arguments to specify the size of the box. We'll give it a nice generous size for note entry.

Retrieving data from our form

Now that we're finished with the form, we need a way to retrieve data from it so it can be processed by the application. We'll create a method that returns a dictionary of the form's data and, as we did with our `LabelInput` objects, maintain the Tkinter convention of calling it `get()`.

Add the following method to your form class:

```
    def get(self):
        data = {}
        for key, widget in self.inputs.items():
            data[key] = widget.get()
        return data
```

The code is simple: we loop through our instance's `inputs` object containing our `LabelInput` objects and build a new dictionary by calling `get()` on each variable.

This code demonstrates the power of both iterable objects and consistent naming schemes. If we had stored our inputs as discrete properties of the form, or neglected to normalize the `get()` method, our code would be a lot less elegant.

Resetting our form

We're almost done with our form class, but there's one more method needed. After each save of the form, we're going to need to reset it to empty fields; so, let's add a method to do that by performing the following steps:

1. Add this method to the end of the form class:

```
def reset(self):
    for widget in self.inputs.values():
        widget.set('')
```

2. As with our `get()` method, we're iterating through the `input` dictionary and setting each `widget` to an empty value.
3. To make sure our application behaves consistently, we should call `reset()` immediately after the application loads, clearing out any `Tk` defaults that we might not want.
4. Back up to the last line of `__init__()` and add the following code line:

```
self.reset()
```

Building our application class

Let's take a look at the following steps for building our application class:

1. Move down under the `Application` class doc string (the line that reads `Application root window`) and start an `__init__()` method for `Application`, as follows:

```
def __init__(self, *args, **kwargs):
    super().__init__(*args, **kwargs)

    self.title("ABQ Data Entry Application")
    self.resizable(width=False, height=False)
```

2. Once again we make the familiar call to `super().__init__()`, passing along any arguments or keyword arguments.

Note that we don't pass in a `parent` widget here, since `Application` is the root window.

3. We call `.title()` to set our application's title string; this isn't required, but it will certainly help users who are running multiple applications to find our application quickly in their desktop environment.
4. We also prohibit resizing of the window with a call to `self.resizable`. This also isn't strictly necessary, but it makes it simpler for us to control our layout for the time being. Let's start adding our application components as follows:

```
ttk.Label(
    self,
    text="ABQ Data Entry Application",
    font=("TkDefaultFont", 16)
).grid(row=0)
```

5. The application will start at the top with a `Label` object showing the name of the application in a larger than normal font. Notice that we don't specify `column` here; our main application layout will only have one column, so it's not strictly necessary to specify `column`, as it defaults to `0`. Next, we'll add our `DataRecordForm` as follows:

```
self.recordform = DataRecordForm(self)
self.recordform.grid(row=1, padx=10)
```

6. We're adding 10 pixels of padding on the left and right using the `padx` argument to `grid`. This just adds a little whitespace around the edges of the form, making it a bit more readable.
7. Let's add in the save button next, as follows:

```
self.savebutton = ttk.Button(self, text="Save",
command=self.on_save)
self.savebutton.grid(sticky=tk.E, row=2, padx=10)
```

8. We've given the button a `command` value of `self.on_save`; we haven't written that method yet, so we'll need to do that before we can run our code.

When writing methods or functions to be callbacks for a GUI event, it's conventional to use the format `on_EVENTNAME`, where `EVENTNAME` is a string describing the event triggering it. We could also name this method `on_save_button_click()`, but for now `on_save()` is adequate.

9. Finally, let's add in the status bar, as follows:

```
# status bar
self.status = tk.StringVar()
self.statusbar = ttk.Label(self, textvariable=self.status)
self.statusbar.grid(sticky=(tk.W + tk.E), row=3, padx=10)
```

10. We start by creating a string variable called `self.status` and use this as `textvariable` for `ttk.Label`. All our application will need to do to update the status is call `self.status.set()` anywhere inside the class. Our GUI is completed by adding the status bar to the bottom of the application widget.

Saving to CSV

When a user clicks on save, the following chain of events needs to take place:

1. A file called `abq_data_record_CURRENTDATE.csv` is opened
2. If the file doesn't exist, it will be created, and field headers will be written to the first line
3. The data dictionary is retrieved from `DataEntryForm`
4. The data is formatted as a CSV row and appended to the file
5. The form is cleared, and the user is notified that the record was saved

We're going to need a few more Python libraries to help us out with this:

1. First, we'll need a date string for our filename. Python's `datetime` library can help us here.
2. Next, we'll need to be able to check if a file exists. Python's `os` library has a function for this.
3. Finally, we need to be able to write to a CSV file. Python has a CSV library in the standard library that would be perfect here.

Let's take a look at the following steps:

1. Back up to the top of the file and add the following imports above the Tkinter imports:

   ```
   from datetime import datetime
   import os
   import csv
   ```

2. Now, go back to the `Application` class and start the `on_save()` method, as follows:

   ```
   def on_save(self):
        datestring = datetime.today().strftime("%Y-%m-%d")
        filename = "abq_data_record_{}.csv".format(datestring)
        newfile = not os.path.exists(filename)
   ```

3. The first thing we do is create our date string. The `datetime.today()` method returns a `datetime` at midnight of the current day; we then format this using `strftime()` to an ISO date string in the form year-month-day (using numbers 01 through 12 for the month). This gets plugged into the filename template from our specification and saved as `filename`.
4. Next, we need to determine whether the file already exists; `os.path.exists()` will return a boolean value indicating if the file exists; we negate this value and store it as `newfile`.
5. Now, let's get the data from `DataEntryForm`:

   ```
   data = self.recordform.get()
   ```

6. With the data acquired, we need to open our file and write the data into it. Add in the following code:

   ```
   with open(filename, 'a') as fh:
       csvwriter = csv.DictWriter(fh, fieldnames=data.keys())
       if newfile:
           csvwriter.writeheader()
       csvwriter.writerow(data)
   ```

The `with open(filename, 'a') as fh:` statement opens our generated filename in append mode and gives us a file handle called `fh`. Append mode means we can't read or edit any existing lines in the file, just add to the end of it, which is exactly what we want.

The `with` keyword works with **context manager** objects, which our call to `open()` returns. Context managers are special objects that define code to run before and after the `with` block. By opening files using this method, they'll automatically be closed correctly at the end of the block.

7. Next, we create a `csv.DictWriter` object using the file handle. This object will allow us to write dictionaries of data to the CSV file, matching up the dictionary keys with the CSV's header row labels. This will work better for us in the long run than the default CSV writer object, which would require the fields in the correct order every time.
8. To configure this, we have to first pass in the `fieldnames` argument to the `DictWriter` constructor. Our field names are the keys of the `data` dictionary that we get from the form. If we're working on a new file, we need to write those field names to the first row, which we do by calling `DictWriter.writeheader()`.
9. Finally, we write our `data` dictionary to a new row, using the `.writerow()` method of our `DictWriter` object. At the end of the code block, the file is automatically closed and saved.

Finishing and testing

At this point, you should be able to run the application, enter data, and save it to the CSV file. Try it out! You should see something similar to the following screenshot:

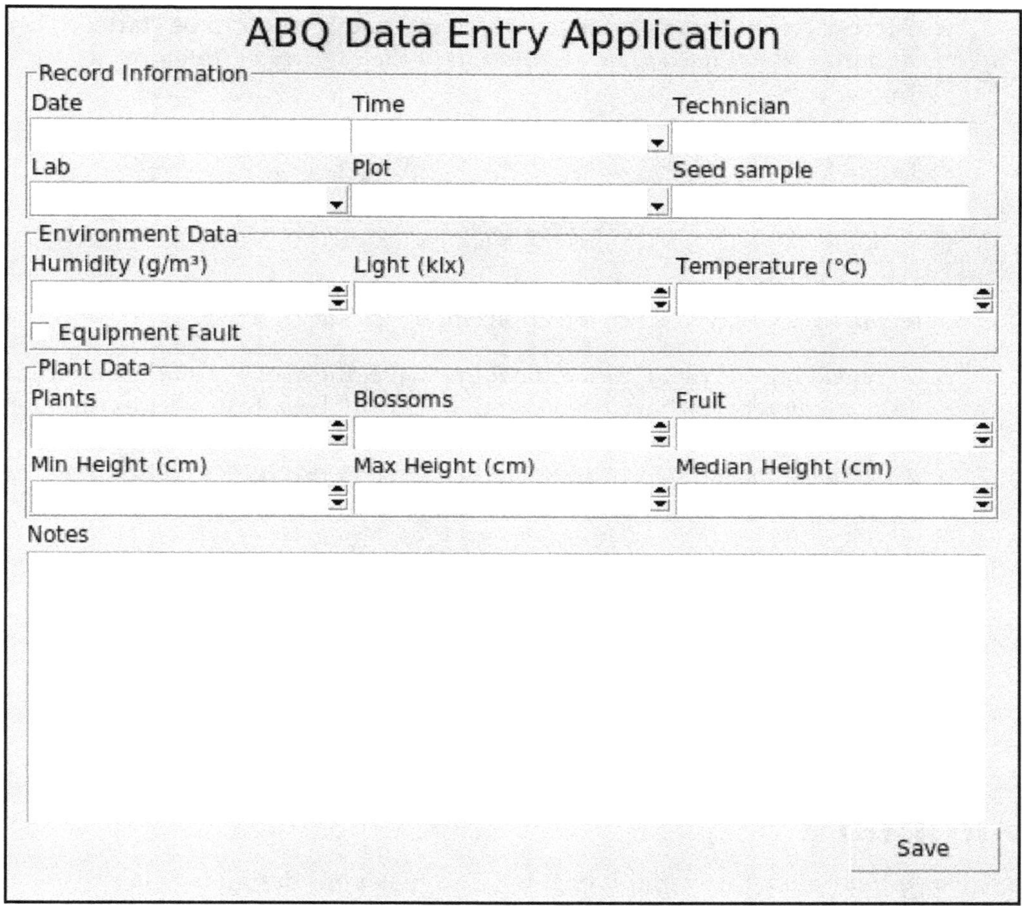

Perhaps the first thing you notice is that clicking **Save** has no noticeable effect. The form stays populated, and there's no indication that anything was done. We should fix this.

We'll perform the following two things to help here:

1. First, put a notification in our status bar that the record was saved and how many records have been saved this session. For the first part, add the following code line to the end of the `Application` constructor, as follows:

   ```
   self.records_saved = 0
   ```

2. Second, clear the form after saving, so the next record can be started. Then add the following code line to the end of the `on_save()` method, as follows:

```
        self.records_saved += 1
        self.status.set(
            "{} records saved this
session".format(self.records_saved))
```

   This code sets up a counter variable that will keep track of the number of records we've saved since the application was started.

3. After saving the file, we increment the value, then set our status to indicate how many records have been saved. Users will be able to see this number increase and know that their button click has done something.
4. Next, we'll reset the form after saving. Append this code to the end of `Application.on_save()`, as follows:

```
        self.recordform.reset()
```

   That will zero out the form and ready it for the next record to be entered.

5. Now, run the application again. It should clear out and give you a status indication on saving a record.

Summary

Well, we've come a long way in this chapter! You took your design from a specification and some drawings to a running application that already covers the basic functionality you need. You learned to work with basic Tkinter and `ttk` widgets, and create custom widgets to save yourself a lot of repetitive work.

In the next chapter, we're going to address the issues with our `input` widgets. We'll learn to customize the behavior of our `input` widgets, prevent erroneous keystrokes, and validate the data to make sure it's within the tolerances laid out in our specification. Along the way, we'll dig deeper into Python classes and learn more techniques for efficient and elegant code.

4
Reducing User Error with Validation and Automation

Our form works, and both the director and data entry personnel are thrilled with the form design, but we're not ready for production yet! Our form doesn't yet perform the promised task of preventing or discouraging user errors. Number boxes still allow letters, combo boxes aren't limited to the choices given, and dates have to be filled in by hand. In this chapter, we're going to cover the following topics:

- Deciding on the best approach for validating user input
- Learning how to use Tkinter's validation system
- Creating custom widgets for our form that validate entered data
- Automating default values where appropriate in our form

Let's get started!

Validating user input

At first glance, Tkinter's selection of the input widgets seems a little disappointing. It doesn't give us a true number entry that only allows digits, nor a true drop-down selector that only allows items from the drop-down list to be selected. We have no date inputs, email inputs, or other specially-formatted input widgets.

But these weaknesses can become strengths. Because these widgets assume nothing, we can make them behave in a way that's appropriate to our specific needs, rather than some generic way that may or may not work optimally. For example, letters may seem inappropriate in a number entry, but are they? In Python, strings such as `NaN` and `Infinity` are valid float values; having a box that could increment numerals but also handle those string values may be very useful in some applications.

We're going to learn how to shape our widgets to our needs, but before we learn how to control this behavior, let's think about what we want to do.

Strategies to prevent data errors

There is no universal answer to how a widget should react to a user trying to enter bad data. The validation logic found in various graphics toolkits can differ greatly; when bad data is entered, an input widget might validate the user input as follows:

- Prevent the invalid keystrokes from registering at all
- Accept the input, but return an error or list of errors when the form is submitted
- Show an error when the user leaves the entry field, perhaps disabling form submission until it's corrected
- Lock the user in the entry field until valid data is entered
- Silently correct the bad data using a best-guess algorithm

The correct behavior in a data entry form (which is filled out hundreds of times a day by users who may not even be looking at it) may be different from an instrument control panel (where values absolutely must be correct to avoid a disaster) or an online user registration form (which is filled out once by a user who has never seen it before). We need to ask ourselves and our users about which behavior will best minimize errors.

After discussing this with your users on the data entry staff, you come to the following set of guidelines:

- Whenever possible, meaningless keystrokes should be ignored (for example, letters in a number field)
- An empty field should register an error (all fields are required), with the exception of `Notes`
- Fields containing bad data should be marked in some visible way with an error describing the problem
- Form submission should be disabled if there are fields with errors

Let's add the following requirements to our specification before moving on. Under the `Required Features` section, update the hard requirements as follows:

```
The program must:
...
* have inputs that:
```

```
    - ignore meaningless keystrokes
    - require a value for all fields, except Notes
    - get marked with an error if the value is invalid on focusout
  * prevent saving the record when errors are present
```

So, how do we implement this?

Validation in Tkinter

Tkinter's validation system is one of those parts of the toolkit that is less than intuitive. It relies on the following three configuration options that we can pass into any input widget:

- `validate`: This option determines which type of event will trigger the validation callback
- `validatecommand`: This option takes the command that will determine if the data is valid
- `invalidcommand`: This option takes a command that will run if `validatecommand` returns `False`

This seems pretty straightforward, but there are some unexpected curves.

The values we can pass to `validate` are as follows:

Validates string	Triggers when
`none`	It is none that turns off validation
`focusin`	The user enters or selects the widget
`unfocus`	The user leaves the widget
`focus`	Either `focusin` or `focusout`
`key`	The user enters text in the widget
`all`	`focusin`, `focusout`, and `key`

The `validatecommand` argument is where things get tricky. You might think this takes the name of a Python function or method, but that's not quite it. Instead, we need to give it a tuple containing a reference to a Tcl/`Tk` function, and optionally some **substitution codes** that specify information about the triggering event that we want to pass into the function.

How do we get a reference to a Tcl/`Tk` function? Fortunately, this isn't too hard; we just pass a Python callable to the `.register()` method on any Tkinter widget. This returns a string that we can use with `validatecommand`.

Of course, validation functions aren't very useful unless we pass in some data to be validated. To do this, we add one or more substitution codes to our `validatecommand` tuple.

These codes are as follows:

Code	Value passed
`%d`	A code indicating the action being attempted: `0` for `delete`, `1` for insert, and `-1` for other events. Note that this is passed as a string, and not as an integer.
`%P`	The proposed value that the field would have after the change (key events only).
`%s`	The value currently in the field (key events only).
`%i`	The index (from `0`) of the text being inserted or deleted on key events, or `-1` on non-key events. Note that this is passed as a string, not as an integer.
`%S`	For insertion or deletion, the text that is being inserted or deleted (key events only).
`%v`	The widget's `validate` value.
`%V`	The event that triggered validation: `focusin`, `focusout`, `key`, or `forced` (indicating the text variable was changed).
`%W`	The widget's name in Tcl/`Tk`, as a string.

The `invalidcommand` option works exactly the same way, requiring the use of the `.register()` method and substitution codes.

To see what this looks like together, consider the following code for an `Entry` widget that only accepts five characters:

```
def has_five_or_less_chars(string):
    return len(string) <= 5

wrapped_function = root.register(has_five_or_less_chars)
vcmd = (wrapped_function, '%P')
five_char_input = ttk.Entry(root, validate='key',
validatecommand=vcmd)
```

Here, we've created a function that simply returns whether or not the length of a string is less than or equal to five characters. We then register this function with `Tk` using the `register()` method, saving its reference string as `wrapped_function`. Next, we build our `validatecommand` tuple using the reference string and the `'%P'` substitution code, which represents the proposed value (the value that the entry would have if the key event was accepted).

You can pass in as many substitution codes as you wish, and in any order, as long as your function is written to accept those arguments. Finally, we'll create our `Entry` widget, setting the validation type to `key` and passing in our validation command tuple.

Notice we did not define an `invalidcommand` method in this case; when validation is triggered by a keystroke, returning `False` from the `validate` command will cause the keystroke to be ignored. This is not the case when triggering validation from a focus or other event type; in that case, there is no default behavior defined and an `invalidcommand` method is necessary.

Consider the following alternate, class-based version of `FiveCharEntry`, which allows you to type as much as you want, but truncates your text when you leave the field:

```
class FiveCharEntry2(ttk.Entry):
    """An Entry that truncates to five characters on exit."""

    def __init__(self, parent, *args, **kwargs):
        super().__init__(parent, *args, **kwargs)
        self.config(
            validate='focusout',
            validatecommand=(self.register(self._validate), '%P'),
            invalidcommand=(self.register(self._on_invalid),)
        )

    def _validate(self, proposed_value):
        return len(proposed_value) <= 5

    def _on_invalid(self):
        self.delete(5, tk.END)
```

This time, we've implemented validation by subclassing `Entry` and defining our validation logic in a method rather than an external function. This simplifies access to the widget in our validation methods.

The underscores at the beginning of `_validate()` and `_on_invalid()` indicate that these are internal methods meant to be accessible only within the class. While it's not necessary to make this code work correctly, and Python does not treat it any differently from a normal method, it lets other programmers know that these methods are for internal use and shouldn't be called outside the class.

We've also changed the validate argument to focusout and added an _on_invalid() method that truncates the value in Entry. Whenever the widget loses focus, the _validate() method will be called with the entered text. If it fails, _on_invalid() will be called, causing the contents to be truncated using the Entry widget's delete() method.

Creating a DateEntry widget

Let's try creating a validating version of our Date field. We'll make a DateEntry widget that prevents most erroneous keystrokes, then checks for date validity on focusout. If the date is invalid, we'll mark the field in some way and display an error. Let's perform the following steps to do the same:

1. Open a new file called DateEntry.py and begin with the following code:

```
from datetime import datetime

class DateEntry(ttk.Entry):
    """An Entry for ISO-style dates (Year-month-day)"""

    def __init__(self, parent, *args, **kwargs):
        super().__init__(parent, *args, **kwargs)
        self.config(
            validate='all',
            validatecommand=(
                self.register(self._validate),
                '%S', '%i', '%V', '%d'
            ),
        invalidcommand=(self.register(self._on_invalid), '%V')
    )
    self.error = tk.StringVar()
```

2. Since we'll need datetime for our validation method, we import it here at the top.
3. We subclass ttk.Entry, then start our constructor method with a call to super().__init__() as usual.
4. Next, we use self.config() to alter the configuration of the widget. You might wonder why we don't pass these arguments into the super().__init__() call; the reason is that the self.register() method doesn't exist until the underlying Entry widget has been initialized.

5. We're registering the following two methods: `self._validate` and `self._on_invalid`, which we'll write shortly:

    - `_validate()`: This method will get the inserted text (`%S`), the index of insertion (`%i`), the type of event (`%V`), and the action performed (`%d`).
    - `_on_invalid()`: This method will only get the event type. Since we want to validate on both keystrokes and `focusout`, we'll set `validate` to `all`. Our validation methods can figure out which event is taking place by looking at the event type (`%V`).

6. Finally, we create `StringVar` to hold our error text; this will be accessed outside the class, so we don't use the leading underscore in its name.
7. The next method we create is `_toggle_error()`, as follows:

```
def _toggle_error(self, error=''):
    self.error.set(error)
    if error:
        self.config(foreground='red')
    else:
        self.config(foreground='black')
```

8. We're using this method to consolidate the widget's behavior in the case of an error. It starts by setting our `error` variable to the string provided. If the string is not blank, we turn on the error marking (in this case, turning the text red); if it's blank, we turn off the error marking. The `_validate()` method is as follows:

```
    def _validate(self, char, index, event, action):

        # reset error state
        self._toggle_error()
        valid = True

        # ISO dates, YYYY-MM-DD, only need digits and hyphens
        if event == 'key':
            if action == '0':  # A delete event should always
validate
                valid = True
            elif index in ('0', '1', '2', '3',
                           '5', '6', '8', '9'):
                valid = char.isdigit()
            elif index in ('4', '7'):
                valid = char == '-'
            else:
                valid = False
```

9. The first thing we do is toggle off our error status and set a `valid` flag to `True`. Our input will be `innocent until proven guilty`.
10. Then, we'll look at keystroke events. `if action == '0':` tells us if the user is trying to delete characters. We always want to allow this so that the user can edit the field.

The basic format of an ISO date is: four digits, a dash, two digits, a dash, and two digits. We can test whether the user is following this format by checking whether the inserted characters match our expectation at the inserted `index`. For example, `index in ('0', '1', '2', '3', '5', '6', '8', '9')` will tell us if the character being inserted is one of the positions that requires a digit, and if so we check that the character is a digit. An index of `4` or `7` should be a dash. Any other keystroke is invalid.

Although you might expect them to be integers, Tkinter passes the action codes and indexes them as strings. Keep this in mind when writing your comparisons.

While this is a hopelessly naive heuristic for a correct date, since it allows for complete nonsense dates like `0000-97-46` or right-looking-but-still-wrong dates like `2000-02-29`, it at least enforces the basic format and removes a large number of invalid keystrokes. A completely accurate partial date analyzer is a project unto itself, so for now this will do.

Checking our date for correctness on `focusout` is simpler and much more foolproof, as follows:

```
elif event == 'focusout':
    try:
        datetime.strptime(self.get(), '%Y-%m-%d')
    except ValueError:
        valid = False
return valid
```

Since we have access to the final value the user meant to enter at this point, we can use `datetime.strptime()` to try to convert the string to a Python `datetime` using the format `%Y-%m-%d`. If this fails, we know the date is invalid.

To end the method, we return our `valid` flag.

Validation methods must always return a Boolean value. If, for some reason, your validation method doesn't return a value (or returns `None`), your validation will silently break without any error. Be careful to make sure your methods will always return a Boolean value, especially if you're using multiple `return` statements.

As you saw previously, for invalid keystrokes, it's sufficient to return `False` and prevent the character from being inserted, but for errors on focus events, we'll need to respond in some way.

Take a look at the `_on_invalid()` method in the following code:

```
    def _on_invalid(self, event):
        if event != 'key':
            self._toggle_error('Not a valid date')
```

We pass only the event type into this method, which we'll use to ignore keystroke events (they're already adequately handled by the default behavior). For any other event type, we'll use our `_toggle_error()` method to display the error.

To test our `DateEntry` class, add the following test code to the bottom of the file:

```
if __name__ == '__main__':
    root = tk.Tk()
    entry = DateEntry(root)
    entry.pack()
    tk.Label(textvariable=entry.error).pack()

    # add this so we can unfocus the DateEntry
    tk.Entry(root).pack()
    root.mainloop()
```

Save the file and run it to try the new `DateEntry` class. Try entering various bad dates or invalid keystrokes, and see what happens.

Implementing validated widgets in our form

Now that you know how to validate your widgets, you have your work cut out for you! We have 16 input widgets, and you'll have to write code like that shown in the previous section for all of them to get the behavior we need. Along the way, you'll need to make sure the widgets respond consistently to errors and present a consistent API to the application.

If that sounds like something you'd like to put off indefinitely, I can't blame you. Maybe there's a way we can cut down the amount of code we need to write.

Exploiting the power of multiple inheritance

So far, we have learned that Python allows us to create new classes by subclassing, inheriting features from the super class, and only adding or changing what's different about our new class. Python also supports **multiple inheritance**, where a subclass can inherit from multiple superclasses. We can exploit this feature to our advantage by creating what's called a **mixin** class.

Mixin classes contain only a specific set of functionalities that we want to be able to mix in with other classes to compose a new class.

Take a look at the following example code:

```
class Displayer():

    def display(self, message):
        print(message)

class LoggerMixin():

    def log(self, message, filename='logfile.txt'):
        with open(filename, 'a') as fh:
            fh.write(message)

    def display(self, message):
        super().display(message)
        self.log(message)

class MySubClass(LoggerMixin, Displayer):

    def log(self, message):
```

```
        super().log(message, filename='subclasslog.txt')


subclass = MySubClass()
subclass.display("This string will be shown and logged in
subclasslog.txt.")
```

We implement a basic class called `Displayer` with a `display()` method that prints a message. Then, we create a mixin class called `LoggerMixin`, which both adds a `log()` method to write a message to a text file and overrides the `display()` method to add a call to `log()`. Finally, we create a subclass by inheriting from both `LoggerMixin` and `Displayer`. The subclass then overrides the `log()` method and sets a different filename.

When we create a class using multiple inheritance, the rightmost class we specify is called the **base class**, and mixin classes should be specified before it. There's no special syntax for a mixin class as opposed to any other class, but pay attention to the use of `super()` in the mixin's `display()` method. Technically, `LoggerMixin` inherits from Python's built-in `object` class, which has no `display()` method. How, then, can we call `super().display()` here?

In a multiple inheritance situation, `super()` does something a little more complex than just standing in for the superclass. It looks up the chain of inheritance using something called the **Method Resolution Order** and determines the nearest class that defines the method we're calling. Thus, when we call `MySubclass.display()`, a series of method resolutions occurs, as follows:

- `MySubClass.display()` is resolved to `LoggerMixin.display()`.
- `LoggerMixin.display()` calls `super().display()`, which is resolved to `Displayer.display()`.
- It also calls `self.log()`. Since `self`, in this case, is a `MySubClass` instance, it resolves to `MySubClass.log()`.
- `MySubClass.log()` calls `super().log()`, which is resolved back to `LoggerMixin.log()`.

If this seems confusing, just remember that `self.method()` will look for `method()` in the current class first, then follow the list of inherited classes from left to right until the method is found. The `super().method()` will do the same, except that it skips the current class.

The method resolution order of a class is stored in its `__mro__` property; you can inspect this method in a Python shell or debugger if you're having trouble with inherited methods.

Note that `LoggerMixin` is not usable on its own: it only works when combined with a class that has a `display()` method. This is why it's a mixin class because it's meant to be mixed in to enhance other classes.

A validating mixin class

Let's apply our knowledge of multiple inheritance to build a mixin that will give us some boilerplate validation logic by performing the following steps:

1. Open `data_entry_app.py` and start the class before your `Application` class definition:

```
class ValidatedMixin:
    """Adds a validation functionality to an input widget"""

    def __init__(self, *args, error_var=None, **kwargs):
        self.error = error_var or tk.StringVar()
        super().__init__(*args, **kwargs)
```

2. We start this class as usual, though we're not subclassing anything this time. The constructor also has an extra argument called `error_var`. This will allow us to pass in a variable to use for the error message; if we don't, the class creates its own. The call to `super().__init__()` will cause the base class that we mix with to execute its constructor.
3. Next, we set up validation, as follows:

```
vcmd = self.register(self._validate)
invcmd = self.register(self._invalid)

self.config(
    validate='all',
    validatecommand=(vcmd, '%P', '%s', '%S', '%V', '%i',
'%d'),
    invalidcommand=(invcmd, '%P', '%s', '%S', '%V', '%i',
```

```
'%d')
        )
```

4. We're setting up our `validate` and `invalid` methods here. We'll go ahead and pass in all the substitution codes (except `'%w'`, the widget name, since it's fairly useless inside a class context). We're running validation on all conditions, so we can capture both focus and keystroke events.
5. Now, we'll define our error condition handler:

```
    def _toggle_error(self, on=False):
        self.config(foreground=('red' if on else 'black'))
```

6. This will just change the text color to red if there's an error, or black otherwise. We don't set the error in this function, since we'll want to set the actual error text in the validate method as follows:

```
  def _validate(self, proposed, current, char, event, index,
  action):
        self._toggle_error(False)
        self.error.set('')
        valid = True
        if event == 'focusout':
            valid = self._focusout_validate(event=event)
        elif event == 'key':
            valid = self._key_validate(proposed=proposed,
                current=current, char=char, event=event,
                index=index, action=action)
        return valid

    def _focusout_validate(self, **kwargs):
        return True

    def _key_validate(self, **kwargs):
        return True
```

Our `_validate()` method just handles a few setup chores like toggling off the error and clearing the error message. Then, it runs an event-specific validate method, depending on the event type passed in. We only care about the `key` and `focusout` events right now, so any other event just returns `True`.

Notice that we call the individual methods using keywords; when we create our subclasses, we'll be overriding these methods. By using keyword arguments, our overridden functions can just specify the needed keywords or extract individual arguments from `**kwargs`, rather than having to get all the arguments in the right order. Also notice that all the arguments are passed into `_key_validate()`, but only `event` is passed into `_focusout_validate()`. Focus events don't return anything useful for any of the other arguments, so there's no point in passing them along.

7. The ultimate idea here is that our subclasses only need to override the validation method or methods we care about for that widget. If we don't override them, they just return `True`, so validation passes. Now, we need to handle an invalid event:

```
def _invalid(self, proposed, current, char, event, index,
action):
     if event == 'focusout':
          self._focusout_invalid(event=event)
     elif event == 'key':
          self._key_invalid(proposed=proposed,
               current=current, char=char, event=event,
               index=index, action=action)

 def _focusout_invalid(self, **kwargs):
     self._toggle_error(True)

 def _key_invalid(self, **kwargs):
     pass
```

8. We take an identical approach to these methods. Unlike the validate methods, though, our invalid data handlers don't need to return anything. For invalid keys, we do nothing by default, and for invalid data on `focusout`, we toggle our error status on.

9. Keystroke validation only really makes sense in the context of entering keys, but there may be times when we want to manually run the `focusout` checks, since it effectively checks a completely entered value. For this reason, we'll implement the following method:

```
def trigger_focusout_validation(self):
    valid = self._validate('', '', '', 'focusout', '', '')
    if not valid:
        self._focusout_invalid(event='focusout')
    return valid
```

10. We're just duplicating the logic that occurs when a `focusout` event happens: run the validation function, and if it fails, run the invalid handler. This is all we need for `ValidatedMixin`, so let's start applying it to some of our widgets and see how it works.

Building our widgets

Let's think through what classes we need to implement with our new `ValidatedMixin` class, as follows:

- All our fields except `Notes` are required, so we'll need a basic `Entry` widget that registers an error if there's no input.
- We have one `Date` field, so we need an `Entry` widget that enforces a valid date string.
- We have a number of the `Spinbox` widgets for decimal or integer input. We'll need to make sure these only accept valid number strings.
- We have a few `Combobox` widgets that don't behave quite the way we want them to.

Let's get started!

Requiring data

All of our fields are required, so let's start with a basic `Entry` widget that requires data. We can use these for fields: `Technician` and `Seed sample`.

Add the following code under the `ValidatedMixin` class:

```
class RequiredEntry(ValidatedMixin, ttk.Entry):

    def _focusout_validate(self, event):
        valid = True
        if not self.get():
            valid = False
            self.error.set('A value is required')
        return valid
```

There's no keystroke validation to do here, so we just need to create `_focusout_validate()`. If the entered value is empty, we just set an error string and return `False`.

That's all there is to it!

A Date widget

Now, let's apply the mixin class to the `DateEntry` class we made before, keeping the same validation algorithm as follows:

```
class DateEntry(ValidatedMixin, ttk.Entry):

    def _key_validate(self, action, index, char, **kwargs):
        valid = True

        if action == '0':
            valid = True
        elif index in ('0', '1', '2', '3', '5', '6', '8', '9'):
            valid = char.isdigit()
        elif index in ('4', '7'):
            valid = char == '-'
        else:
            valid = False
        return valid

    def _focusout_validate(self, event):
        valid = True
        if not self.get():
            self.error.set('A value is required')
            valid = False
        try:
            datetime.strptime(self.get(), '%Y-%m-%d')
        except ValueError:
            self.error.set('Invalid date')
```

```
            valid = False
        return valid
```

Again, pretty simple, all we need to do is specify the validation logic. We've added the logic from our RequiredEntry class too, since the Date value is required.

Let's move on to something a bit more intricate.

A better Combobox widget

The drop-down widgets in different toolkits behave fairly consistently when it comes to mouse operation, but the response to keystrokes varies, as follows:

- Some do nothing
- Some require the use of arrow keys to select items
- Some move to the first entry that begins with any key pressed, and cycle through entries beginning with that letter on subsequent presses
- Some narrow down the list to entries that match what's typed

We need to think about what behavior our Combobox widget should have. Since our users are accustomed to doing data entry with the keyboard, and some have difficulty with the mouse, the widget needs to work with the keyboard. Making them use repeated keystrokes to select options is not very intuitive, either. After talking with the data entry staff, you decide on this behavior:

- If the proposed text matches no entries, it will be ignored
- When the proposed text matches a single entry, the widget is set to that value
- A delete or backspace clears the entire box

Add this code under the DateEntry code:

```
class ValidatedCombobox(ValidatedMixin, ttk.Combobox):

    def _key_validate(self, proposed, action, **kwargs):
        valid = True
        # if the user tries to delete, just clear the field
        if action == '0':
            self.set('')
            return True
```

The `_key_validate()` method starts out by setting up a `valid` flag and doing a quick check to see if this is a delete action. If it is, we set the value to a blank string and return `True`.

Now, we'll add the logic to match the proposed text to our values:

```
        # get our values list
        values = self.cget('values')
        # Do a case-insensitive match against the entered text
        matching = [
            x for x in values
            if x.lower().startswith(proposed.lower())
        ]
        if len(matching) == 0:
            valid = False
        elif len(matching) == 1:
            self.set(matching[0])
            self.icursor(tk.END)
            valid = False
        return valid
```

A copy of the widget's list of values is retrieved using its `.cget()` method. Then, we use list comprehension to reduce this list to only the entries that match the proposed text, calling `lower()` on both the values in the list item and the proposed text so that our match is case-insensitive.

Every Tkinter widget supports the `.cget()` method. It can be used to retrieve any of the widget's configuration values by name.

If the length of the matching list is `0`, we reject the keystroke. If it's `1`, we've found our match, so we'll set the variable to that value. If it's anything else, we need to let the user keep typing. As a final touch, we'll send the cursor to the end of the field using the `.icursor()` method if a match is found. This isn't strictly necessary, but it looks better than leaving the cursor in the middle of the text. Now, we'll add the `focusout` validator, as follows:

```
    def _focusout_validate(self, **kwargs):
        valid = True
        if not self.get():
            valid = False
            self.error.set('A value is required')
        return valid
```

We don't have to do much here, because the key validation method ensures that the only possible values are a blank field or an item in the values list, but since all fields are required to have a value, we'll copy the validation from `RequiredEntry`.

That takes care of our `Combobox` widget. Next, we'll deal with the `Spinbox` widget.

A range-limited Spinbox widget

A number entry seems like it shouldn't be too complicated to deal with, but there are a number of subtleties to work through to make it bulletproof. In addition to limiting the field to valid number values, you'll want to enforce the `from`, `to`, and `increment` arguments as the minimum, maximum, and precision of the input, respectively.

The algorithm needs to implement the following rules:

- Deletion is always allowed
- Digits are always allowed
- If `from` is less than `0`, a minus is allowed as the first character
- If `increment` has a decimal component, one dot is allowed
- If the proposed value is greater than the `to` value, ignore the keystroke
- If the proposed value requires more precision than `increment`, ignore the keystroke
- On `focusout`, make sure the value is a valid number string
- Also on `focusout`, make sure the value is greater than the `from` value

Take a look at the following steps:

1. Here's how we'll code, regarding the preceding rules:

```
class ValidatedSpinbox(ValidatedMixin, tk.Spinbox):

    def __init__(self, *args, min_var=None, max_var=None,
                 focus_update_var=None, from_='-Infinity',
                 to='Infinity', **kwargs):
        super().__init__(*args, from_=from_, to=to, **kwargs)
        self.resolution = Decimal(str(kwargs.get('increment',
        '1.0')))
        self.precision = (
            self.resolution
            .normalize()
```

```
            .as_tuple()
            .exponent
        )
```

2. We'll start by overriding the `__init__()` method so that we can specify some defaults and grab the `increment` value from the constructor arguments for processing.
3. The `Spinbox` arguments can be passed in as floats, integers, or strings. Regardless of how you pass them in, Tkinter converts them to floats. Determining the precision of a float is problematic, because of floating-point error, so we want to convert it to a Python `Decimal` before it becomes a float.

Floats attempt to represent decimal numbers in binary form. Open a Python shell and enter `1.2 / .2`. You might be surprised to find the answer is `5.999999999999999` rather than `6`. This is known as a **floating-point error**, and it's a source of computation error in nearly every programming language. Python offers us the `Decimal` class, which takes a numeric string and stores it in a way that makes mathematical operations safe from floating-point errors.

4. Before we can use `Decimal`, we need to import it. Add the following code to your imports at the top of the file:

```
from decimal import Decimal, InvalidOperation
```

5. `InvalidOperation` is an exception thrown when `Decimal` is given a string it cannot interpret. We'll be using it later on.

Notice that we cast `increment` to `str` before passing it to `Decimal`. Ideally, we should pass `increment` in as a string to ensure it will be interpreted correctly, but in case we need to pass in a float for some reason, `str` will do some sensible rounding first.

6. We also set defaults for `to` and `from_`: `-Infinity` and `Infinity`. Both `float` and `Decimal` will happily accept these values and treat them as you'd expect them to do. The default `to` and `from_` values for `Tkinter.Spinbox` are `0`; if they're left there, Tkinter treats it as no limit, but this creates a problem if we specify one but not the other.

7. We extract `precision` of the `resolution` value as an exponent of the smallest valid decimal place. We'll use this value in the validation class.
8. Our constructor is settled, so let's write the validate methods. The key validate method is a bit tricky, so we'll walk through it chunk by chunk. First, we start the method:

```
    def _key_validate(self, char, index, current,
                      proposed, action, **kwargs):
        valid = True
        min_val = self.cget('from')
        max_val = self.cget('to')
        no_negative = min_val >= 0
        no_decimal = self.precision >= 0
```

9. To begin, we retrieve the `from` and `to` values, then assign flag variables to indicate if negatives and decimals should be allowed, as follows:

```
if action == '0':
    return True
```

Deletion should always work, so if it's a deletion, return `True`.

We've broken our no multiple returns guideline here, because the same logic with only one `return` would be nested quite deeply. When trying to write readable, maintainable code, sometimes one has to pick the lesser of two evils.

10. Next, we test if the keystroke is a valid character, as follows:

```
# First, filter out obviously invalid keystrokes
  if any([
          (char not in ('-1234567890.')),
          (char == '-' and (no_negative or index != '0')),
          (char == '.' and (no_decimal or '.' in current))
  ]):
      return False
```

Valid characters are digits plus `-` and `.`. The minus sign is only valid at index `0`, and the dot can only appear once. Anything else returns `False`.

The built-in `any` function takes a list of expressions and returns `True` if any one of the expressions in the list are true. There's also an `all` function that returns `True` if all the expressions are true. These functions allow you to condense a long chain of boolean expressions.

We're almost guaranteed at this point to have a valid `Decimal` string, but not quite; we might have just `-`, `.`, or `-.` characters.

11. The following are valid partial entries, so we just return `True` for them:

```
# At this point, proposed is either '-', '.', '-.',
# or a valid Decimal string
if proposed in '-.':
    return True
```

12. At this point, the proposed text can only be a valid `Decimal` string, so we'll make a `Decimal` from it and do some more tests:

```
# Proposed is a valid Decimal string
# convert to Decimal and check more:
proposed = Decimal(proposed)
proposed_precision = proposed.as_tuple().exponent

if any([
    (proposed > max_val),
    (proposed_precision < self.precision)
]):
    return False

return valid
```

13. Our last two tests check to see if the proposed text is either greater than our maximum value, or has more precision than the `increment` that we specified (the reason we use a < operator here is because `precision` is given as a negative value for decimal places). In case nothing has been returned yet, we return the `valid` value as a safeguard. Our `focusout` validator is much simpler, as follows:

```
def _focusout_validate(self, **kwargs):
    valid = True
    value = self.get()
    min_val = self.cget('from')

    try:
        value = Decimal(value)
```

```
        except InvalidOperation:
            self.error.set('Invalid number string:
{}'.format(value))
            return False

        if value < min_val:
            self.error.set('Value is too low (min
{})'.format(min_val))
            valid = False
        return valid
```

14. With the entire intended value, we only need to make sure it's a valid `Decimal` string and greater than the minimum value.

With that, our `ValidatedSpinbox` is ready to go.

Dynamically adjusting the Spinbox range

Our `ValidatedSpinbox` method seems adequate for most of our fields. But consider the `Height` fields for a moment. It would not make any sense for the `Mini height` value to be more than the `Max height` value, or for the `Median height` value not to be between them. Is there some way we can work this kind of interdependent behavior into our class?

We can! To do this, we'll rely on the **tracing** feature of Tkinter variables. A trace is essentially a hook into the `.get()` and `.set()` methods of variables that allows you to trigger any Python function or method when a variable is read or changed.

The syntax is as follows:

```
sv = tk.StringVar()
sv.trace('w', some_function_or_method)
```

The first argument to `.trace()` indicates which event we want to trace. Here, `w` indicates a write (`.set()`), `r` indicates a read (`.get()`), and `u` indicates an undefined variable or deletion of the variable.

Our strategy will be to allow optional `min_var` and `max_var` variables into the `ValidatedSpinbox` method and set a trace on these variables to update the `ValidatedSpinbox` method's min or max value whenever this variable is changed. We'll also have a `focus_update_var` variable that will be updated with the `Spinbox` widget value at `focusout` time.

Let's take a look at the following steps:

1. To start, we'll update our `ValidatedSpinbox` constructor as follows:

```
    def __init__(self, *args, min_var=None, max_var=None,
        focus_update_var=None, from_='-Infinity',
to='Infinity',
    **kwargs
    ):
        super().__init__(*args, from_=from_, to=to, **kwargs)
        self.resolution = Decimal(str(kwargs.get('increment',
'1.0')))
        self.precision = (
            self.resolution
            .normalize()
            .as_tuple()
            .exponent
        )
        # there should always be a variable,
        # or some of our code will fail
        self.variable = kwargs.get('textvariable') or
tk.DoubleVar()

        if min_var:
            self.min_var = min_var
            self.min_var.trace('w', self._set_minimum)
        if max_var:
            self.max_var = max_var
            self.max_var.trace('w', self._set_maximum)
        self.focus_update_var = focus_update_var
        self.bind('<FocusOut>', self._set_focus_update_var)
```

2. First, note that we've added a line to store our variable in `self.variable`, and we create one if the program doesn't pass one in explicitly. Some of the code we need to write will depend on a text variable existing, so we'll force this, just in case.
3. If we pass in either a `min_var` or `max_var` argument, the value is stored and a trace is configured. The `trace()` method points to an appropriately named method.
4. We also store a reference to the `focus_update_var` argument and bind the `<FocusOut>` event to a method that will be used to update it.

The `bind()` method can be called on any Tkinter widget, and it's used to connect widget events to a Python callable. Events can be keystrokes, mouse movements or clicks, focus events, window management events, and more.

5. Now, we need to add the callback methods for our `trace()` and `bind()` commands. Start with `_set_focus_update_var()`, as follows:

```
def _set_focus_update_var(self, event):
        value = self.get()
        if self.focus_update_var and not self.error.get():
            self.focus_update_var.set(value)
```

This method simply gets the widget's current value and, if there is a `focus_update_var` argument present in the instance, sets it to the same value. Note that we don't set the value if there's an error currently present on the widget. It wouldn't make sense to update the value to something invalid.

When Tkinter calls a `bind` callback, it passes in an event object that contains information about the event that triggered the callback. Even if you aren't going to use this information, your function or method needs to be able to take this argument.

6. Now, let's create the callback for setting the minimum, as follows:

```
def _set_minimum(self, *args):
    current = self.get()
    try:
        new_min = self.min_var.get()
        self.config(from_=new_min)
    except (tk.TclError, ValueError):
        pass
    if not current:
        self.delete(0, tk.END)
    else:
        self.variable.set(current)
    self.trigger_focusout_validation()
```

7. The first thing we do is retrieve the current value. `Tkinter.Spinbox` has the slightly annoying behavior of correcting its value when the `to` or `from` values are changed, moving too-low values to the `from` value and too-high values to the `to` value. This kind of silent auto-correction might slip past the attention of our user and cause bad data to be saved. What we want is to leave the value out of range and mark it as an error; so to work around Tkinter, we're going to save the current value, change the configuration, and then put the original value back in the field.
8. With the current value saved, we attempt to get the value of the `min_var` and set our widget's `from_` value from it. There are several things that could go wrong here, such as a blank or invalid value in whatever field controls our minimum and maximum variables, all of which should throw either a `tk.TclError` or a `ValueError`. In either case, we'll just do nothing.

It's generally a bad idea to just silence exceptions; however, in this case, there's nothing we can reasonably do if the variable is bad except ignore it.

9. Now, we just need to write the current value that we saved back into the field. If it's empty, we just delete the field; otherwise, we set the input's variable. The method ends with a call to the `trigger_focusout_validation()` method to re-check the value in the field against the new minimum.
10. The `_set_maximum()` method will be identical to this method, except that it will update the `to` value using `max_var` instead. You can write it yourself, or see the sample code included with the book.
11. There is one last change we need to make to our `ValidatedSpinbox` class. Since our maximum can potentially change after entry, and we're relying on our `focusout` validation to detect that, we'll need to add some conditions to check the maximum.
12. We need to add this to the `_focusout_validate()` method:

```
        max_val = self.cget('to')
        if value > max_val:
            self.error.set('Value is too high (max
{})'.format(max_val))
```

13. Add those lines just before the `return` statement to check the maximum value and set the error, as appropriate.

Updating our form

Now that our widgets are all made, it's time to make the form use them by performing the following steps:

1. Scroll down to the `DataRecordForm` class constructor, and we'll start updating our widgets one row at a time. Line 1 is fairly straightforward:

```
self.inputs['Date'] = LabelInput(
    recordinfo, "Date",
    input_class=DateEntry,
    input_var=tk.StringVar())
self.inputs['Date'].grid(row=0, column=0)
self.inputs['Time'] = LabelInput(
    recordinfo, "Time",
    input_class=ValidatedCombobox,
    input_var=tk.StringVar(),
    input_args={"values": ["8:00", "12:00", "16:00",
"20:00"]})
self.inputs['Time'].grid(row=0, column=1)
self.inputs['Technician'] = LabelInput(
    recordinfo, "Technician",
    input_class=RequiredEntry,
    input_var=tk.StringVar())
self.inputs['Technician'].grid(row=0, column=2)
```

2. It's as simple as swapping out the `input_class` value in each `LabelInput` for our new class. Go ahead and run your application and try out the widgets. Try some different valid and invalid dates, and see how the `Combobox` widget works (`RequiredEntry` won't do much at this point, since the only visible indication is red text, and there's no text to mark red if it's empty; we'll address that later on). Now, on to line 2, first add the `Lab` widget, as follows:

```
self.inputs['Lab'] = LabelInput(
    recordinfo, "Lab",
    input_class=ValidatedCombobox,
    input_var=tk.StringVar(),
    input_args={"values": ["A", "B", "C", "D", "E"]})
```

3. Next, add the `Plot` widget, as follows:

```
self.inputs['Plot'] = LabelInput(
    recordinfo, "Plot",
    input_class=ValidatedCombobox,
    input_var=tk.IntVar(),
    input_args={"values": list(range(1, 21))})
```

   Fairly straightforward again, but if you run it, you'll find there's a problem with `Plot`. It turns out that our `ValidatedComobox` method doesn't work right when the values are integers since the characters the user types are always strings (even if they're digits); we can't compare strings and integers.

4. If you think about it, `Plot` shouldn't really be an integer value. Yes, the values are technically integers, but as we decided back in `Chapter 3`, *Creating Basic Forms with Tkinter and ttk Widgets,* they could as well be letters or symbols; you wouldn't do maths on a plot number. So, we'll change `Plot` to use a `StringVar` variable and make the values of the widget strings as well. Change the `Plot` widget creation, as follows:

```
self.inputs['Plot'] = LabelInput(
    recordinfo, "Plot",
    input_class=ValidatedCombobox,
    input_var=tk.StringVar(),
    input_args={"values": [str(x) for x in range(1, 21)]})
```

5. Here, we're just changing the `input_var` to a `StringVar` and using a list comprehension to cast every `values` item to a string. Now, `Plot` works as expected.
6. Continue through the form, replacing the default `ttk` widgets with your newly validated versions. For the `Spinbox` widget, make sure you're passing in the `to`, `from_`, and `increment` values as strings rather than integers. For instance, the `Humidity` widget should be as follows:

```
self.inputs['Humidity'] = LabelInput(
    environmentinfo, "Humidity (g/m³)",
    input_class=ValidatedSpinbox,
    input_var=tk.DoubleVar(),
    input_args={"from_": '0.5', "to": '52.0', "increment":
    '.01'})
```

7. When we get to the `Height` boxes, it's time to put our `min_var` and `max_var` features to the test. First, we need to set up variables to store the minimum and maximum height, as follows:

```
# Height data
# create variables to be updated for min/max height
# they can be referenced for min/max variables
min_height_var = tk.DoubleVar(value='-infinity')
max_height_var = tk.DoubleVar(value='infinity')
```

   We create two new `DoubleVar` objects to hold the current minimum and maximum heights, setting them to infinite values to begin with. This ensures there will be effectively no minimum or maximum height to start with.

Note that our widgets won't be affected by these values until they actually change, so they won't nullify the original `to` and `from_` values passed in.

8. Now, we create the `Min Height` widget, as follows:

```
self.inputs['Min Height'] = LabelInput(
    plantinfo, "Min Height (cm)",
    input_class=ValidatedSpinbox,
    input_var=tk.DoubleVar(),
    input_args={
        "from_": '0', "to": '1000', "increment": '.01',
        "max_var": max_height_var, "focus_update_var":
         min_height_var})
```

9. We'll use `max_height_var` to set the maximum here, ensuring that our minimum will never go above the maximum value, and set the `focus_update_var` to `min_height_var` values so that it will be updated whenever this field is changed. Now, the `Max Height` widget is as follows:

```
self.inputs['Max Height'] = LabelInput(
    plantinfo, "Max Height (cm)",
    input_class=ValidatedSpinbox,
    input_var=tk.DoubleVar(),
    input_args={
        "from_": 0, "to": 1000, "increment": .01,
        "min_var": min_height_var, "focus_update_var":
        max_height_var})
```

10. This time, we use our `min_height_var` variable to set the widget's minimum value and update the `max_height_var` from the widget's current value. Finally, the `Median Height` field is as follows:

```
self.inputs['Median Height'] = LabelInput(
    plantinfo, "Median Height (cm)",
    input_class=ValidatedSpinbox,
    input_var=tk.DoubleVar(),
    input_args={
        "from_": 0, "to": 1000, "increment": .01,
        "min_var": min_height_var, "max_var": max_height_var})
```

11. Here, we're setting the minimum and maximum values for the field from the `min_height_var` and `max_height_var` variables, respectively. We're not updating any variables from the `Median Height` field, although we could add additional variables and code here to make sure that `Min Height` couldn't go above it or `Max Height` below it. In most cases, it won't matter if the user is entering data in order since `Median Height` is last.
12. You might wonder why we don't just use the `input_var` variables from `Min Height` and `Max Height` to hold these values instead. If you try this, you'll discover the reason: the `input_var` updates as you type, which means your partial value instantly becomes the new maximum or minimum value. We'd rather wait until the user has committed the value to assign this, and thus we created a separate variable that is only updated on `focusout`.

Displaying errors

If you run the application, you may notice that while fields with the `focusout` errors turn red, we don't get to see the actual error. We need to fix this by performing the following steps:

1. Locate your `LabelInput` class, and add the following code to the end of the constructor method:

```
self.error = getattr(self.input, 'error', tk.StringVar())
self.error_label = ttk.Label(self, textvariable=self.error)
self.error_label.grid(row=2, column=0, sticky=(tk.W + tk.E))
```

2. Here, we check to see if our input has an error variable, and if not, we create one. We save a reference to it as `self.error`, then create a `Label` with the error as `textvariable`.
3. Finally, we place this under the input widget.
4. Now, when you try the application, you should be able to see the field errors.

Preventing form submission on error

The final step in preventing errors from getting into our CSV file is to stop the application from saving if the form has known errors. Let's perform the following steps to do this:

1. The first step in implementing this is to provide a way for the `Application` object (which handles saving the data) to retrieve the error status from the `DataRecordForm` object.
2. At the end of the `DataRecordForm` class, add the following method:

```
        def get_errors(self):
            """Get a list of field errors in the form"""

            errors = {}
            for key, widget in self.inputs.items():
                if hasattr(widget.input,
'trigger_focusout_validation'):
                    widget.input.trigger_focusout_validation()
                if widget.error.get():
                    errors[key] = widget.error.get()

            return errors
```

3. Similar to how we handled getting the data, we just loop through the `LabelFrame` widgets. We look for inputs that have the `trigger_focusout_validation` method and call it, just to be sure that all values have been checked. Then, if the widget's `error` variable has any value, we add it to an `errors` dictionary. This way, we can retrieve a dictionary of field names and the errors on each field.
4. Now, we need to add this behavior to the `Application` class's save logic.

5. Add the following code to the beginning of `on_save()`, under `docstring`:

```
# Check for errors first

errors = self.recordform.get_errors()
if errors:
    self.status.set(
        "Cannot save, error in fields: {}"
        .format(', '.join(errors.keys()))
    )
    return False
```

   This logic is straightforward: get the errors, if we find any, and alert the user in the status area and return from the function (thus not saving anything).

6. Start the application and try it out by trying to save a blank form. You should get error messages in all fields and a message at the bottom telling you which fields have errors.

Automating input

Preventing users from entering bad data is one way to help users enter better data; another approach is to automate. Using our understanding of how the forms are likely to be filled out, we can insert values that are very likely to be correct for certain fields.

Remember from `Chapter 2`, *Designing GUI Applications with Tkinter,* that the forms are nearly always recorded the same day that they're filled out, and that they're filled out one at a time from `Plot` 1 to `Plot` 20 in order. Also remember that the `Date`, `Lab`, and `Technician` values remain the same for each form which is filled in. Let's automate this for our users.

Inserting a date

Inserting the current date is an easy place to start. The place to do this is in the `DataRecordForm.reset()` method, which sets up the form for entering a new record.

Update that method as follows:

```
def reset(self):
    """Resets the form entries"""

    # clear all values
    for widget in self.inputs.values():
        widget.set('')

    current_date = datetime.today().strftime('%Y-%m-%d')
    self.inputs['Date'].set(current_date)
```

Just as we do in the `Application.save()` method, we get the current date from `datetime.today()` and format it as an ISO date. Then, we set the `Date` widget's input to that value.

Automating Lab, Time, and Technician

Something which is slightly more complex is our handling of `Lab`, `Time`, and `Technician`. Let's review the logic as follows:

1. Before clearing the data, save the `Lab`, `Time`, and `Technician` values.
2. If `Plot` is less than the last value (`20`), we'll put those values back after clearing all the fields, then increment to the next `Plot` value.
3. If `Plot` is the last value or no value, leave those fields blank. The code is as follows:

```
def reset(self):
    """Resets the form entries"""

    # gather the values to keep for each lab
    lab = self.inputs['Lab'].get()
    time = self.inputs['Time'].get()
    technician = self.inputs['Technician'].get()
    plot = self.inputs['Plot'].get()
    plot_values = self.inputs['Plot'].input.cget('values')

    # clear all values
    for widget in self.inputs.values():
        widget.set('')

    current_date = datetime.today().strftime('%Y-%m-%d')
    self.inputs['Date'].set(current_date)
    self.inputs['Time'].input.focus()
```

```
            # check if we need to put our values back, then do it.
            if plot not in ('', plot_values[-1]):
                self.inputs['Lab'].set(lab)
                self.inputs['Time'].set(time)
                self.inputs['Technician'].set(technician)
                next_plot_index = plot_values.index(plot) + 1
    self.inputs['Plot'].set(plot_values[next_plot_index])
                self.inputs['Seed sample'].input.focus()
```

Because `Plot` looks like an integer, it might be tempting to increment it like one, but it's better to work with it as though it were not. We use the indexes of the values list instead.

4. One last tweak, the focus of the form always starts in the first field, but this means the user has to tab through fields that are already filled in. It would be nice if the next empty inputs were focused at the start instead. Tkinter inputs have a `focus()` method, which gives them keyboard focus. Depending on which fields we've filled in, this will either be `Time` or `Seed sample`. Under the line that sets the `Date` value, add the following code line:

```
        self.inputs['Time'].input.focus()
```

5. And under the line that sets the `Plot` value, inside the conditional block, add the following line of code:

```
    self.inputs['Seed sample'].input.focus()
```

Our form is now ready for a trial run with our users. It's definitely an improvement over the CSV entry at this point, and will help data entry to make quick work of those forms.

Summary

The application has really come a long way. In this chapter, we learned about Tkinter validation, created a validation mixin class, and used it to create validated versions of the `Entry`, `Combobox`, and `Spinbox` widgets. We validated different kinds of data on keystrokes and focus events, and created fields that dynamically update their constraints based on the value of related fields.

In the next chapter, we're going to prepare our code base for expansion and learn how to organize a large application for easier maintenance. More specifically, we'll learn about the MVC pattern and how to structure our code in multiple files for simpler maintenance. We'll also learn more about RST and and version control software.

5
Planning for the Expansion of Our Application

The application is a real hit! After some initial testing and orientation, the data entry staff have been utilizing your new form for a few weeks now. The reduction in errors and data entry time is dramatic, and there's a lot of excited talk about what other problems this program might solve. With even the director joining in on the brainstorming, you have a strong suspicion that you'll be asked to add some new features soon. There's a problem, though; the application is already a script of several hundred lines, and you're worried about its manageability as it grows. You need to take some time to organize your codebase in preparation for future expansion.

In this chapter, we'll learn about the following topics:

- How to separate the concerns of your application using the **Model-View-Controller** pattern
- How to organize your code into a Python package
- To create the basic files and directories for your package structure
- How to use the Git version control system to track your changes

Separating concerns

Proper architectural design is essential for any project that needs to scale. Anyone can prop up some studs and build a garden shed, but a house or skyscraper takes careful planning and engineering. Software is no different; simple scripts can get away with shortcuts such as global variables or manipulating class properties directly, but as the program grows, our code needs to isolate and encapsulate different functionalities in a way that limits the amount of complexity we need to understand at any given moment.

We call this **separation of concerns**, and it's accomplished through the use of architectural patterns that describe different application components and how they interact.

The MVC pattern

Probably the most enduring of these patterns is the MVC pattern, which was introduced in the 1970s. While this pattern has evolved and spun off variations over the years, the basic gist remains: keep the data, the presentation of the data, and the application logic in separate, independent components.

Let's take a deeper look at these components and understand them in the context of our application as it stands.

What is a model?

The **model** in MVC represents the data. This includes the storage of the data, but also the various ways data can be queried or manipulated. Ideally, the model is not concerned or affected by how data will be presented or what UI controls will be granted, but rather presents a high-level interface that only minimally concerns other components with its inner workings. In theory, if you decided to completely change the UI of the program (say, from a Tkinter application to a web application), the model should be totally unaffected.

Some examples of functionality or information you find in the model include the following:

- Preparation and writing of program data to a persistent medium (data file, database, and so on)
- Retrieval of data from a file or database into a format useful to the program
- An authoritative list of the fields in a set of data, along with their data types and limits
- Validation of data against the data types and limits defined
- Calculations on stored data

We don't have a model class in our application currently; the data layout is defined in the form class, and the `Application.on_save()` method is the only code concerned with data persistence so far. We're going to need to split this logic off into a separate object that will define the data layout and handle all the CSV operations.

What is a view?

A **view** is an interface for presenting data and controls to the user. Applications may have many views, often on the same data. Views don't talk to the model directly, and ideally contain only enough logic to present the UI and communicate user actions back to the controller.

Some examples of code you find in a view include the following:

- GUI layout and widget definitions
- Form automations, such as auto-completion of fields, dynamic toggling of widgets, or display of error dialogs
- Formatting of raw data for presentation

Our `DataRecordForm` class is our main view: it contains most of the code for our application's user interface. It also currently defines the structure of our data records. This logic can stay in the view, because the view does need a way to store the data temporarily before handing it off to the model, but it won't be defining our data record from here on out.

We'll be adding more views to our application as we move forward.

What is a controller?

The **controller** is the Grand Central station for the application. It handles requests from the user and takes care of routing data between the views and the model. Most variations of MVC change the role (and sometimes the name) of the controller, but the important thing is that it acts as the intermediary between the view and the model. Our controller object will need to hold references to the views and models used by our application and be responsible for managing interactions between them.

Examples of code you find in the controller include the following:

- Startup and shutdown logic for the application
- Callbacks for user interface events
- Creation of model and view instances

Our `Application` object is currently acting as the controller for our application, though it has some view and model logic in it as well. As the application evolves, we'll be moving more presentation logic into the views and more data logic into the models, leaving mainly connecting code in our `Application` object.

Why complicate our design?

Initially, it may seem like a lot of needless overhead to split up the application this way. We'll have to shuttle data around between different objects and ultimately write more code to do exactly the same thing. Why would we do this?

Put simply, we're doing it to make expansion manageable. As the application grows, the complexity will also grow. Isolating our components from one another limits the amount of complexity that any one component has to manage; for example, when we restructure the layout of our form view, we shouldn't need to worry about how the model will structure the data in the output file. Those two aspects of the program should be independent of one another.

It also helps us to be consistent about where we put certain types of logic. For example, having a discrete model object helps us to avoid littering our UI code with ad hoc data queries or file access attempts.

The bottom line is, without some guiding architectural strategy, our program is in danger of becoming a hopeless tangle of spaghetti logic. Even without adhering to a strict definition of MVC design, consistently following even a loose MVC pattern will save a lot of headaches as the application becomes more complex.

Structuring our application directory

Just as logically breaking our program into separate concerns helps us manage the logical complexity of each component, physically breaking the code into multiple files helps us keep the complexity of each file manageable. It also reinforces more isolation between components; for example, you can't share global variables, and if your models file imports `tkinter`, you know you're doing something wrong.

Basic directory structure

There is no official standard for laying out a Python application directory, but there are some common conventions that will help us keep things tidy and make it easier to package our software later on. Let's set up our directory structure as follows:

1. To begin, create a directory called `ABQ_Data_Entry`. This is the **root directory** of our application, so whenever we refer to the **application root**, this is it.

2. Under the application root, create another directory called `abq_data_entry`. Notice it's in lowercase. This is going to be a Python package that will contain all the code for the application; it should always be given a fairly unique name so that it won't be confused with existing Python packages. Normally, you wouldn't have a different casing between the application root and this main module, but it doesn't hurt anything either; we're doing it here to avoid confusion.

Python modules should always be named using all lowercase names with underscores. This convention is spelled out in PEP 8, Python's official style guide. See `https://www.python.org/dev/peps/pep-0008` for more information about PEP 8.

3. Next, create a `docs` folder under the application root. This folder will be for documentation files about the application.
4. Finally, create two empty files in the application root: `README.rst` and `abq_data_entry.py`. Your directory structure should look as follows:

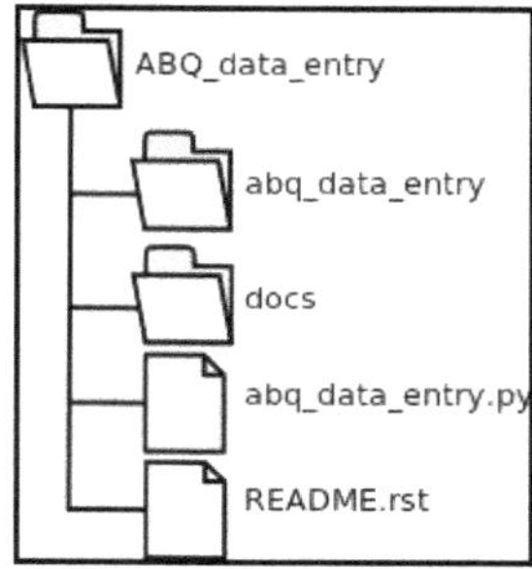

The abq_data_entry.py file

Just as before, `abq_data_entry.py` is the main file that gets executed to start the program. Unlike before, though, it won't contain the bulk of our program. In fact, this file should be as minimal as possible.

Open the file and enter the following code:

```
from abq_data_entry.application import Application

app = Application()
app.mainloop()
```

Save and close the file. The only purpose of this file is to import our `Application` class, make an instance of it, and run it. The remainder of the work will happen inside the `abq_data_entry` package. We haven't created that yet, so this file won't run just yet; before we do, let's deal with our documentation.

The README.rst file

Since as far back as the 1970s, programs have included a short text file called `README` containing a condensed summary of the program's documentation. For small programs, it may be the only documentation; for larger programs, it usually contains essential pre-flight instructions for users or administrators.

There's no prescribed set of contents for a `README` file, but as a basic guideline, consider the following sections:

- **Description**: A brief description of the program and its function. We can reuse the description from our specification, or something like it. This might also contain a brief list of the main features.
- **Author information**: The names of the authors and copyright date. This is especially important if you plan to share your software, but even for something in-house it's useful for future maintainers to know who created the software and when.
- **Requirements**: A list of the software and hardware requirements for the software, if any.
- **Installation**: Instructions for installing the software, its prerequisites, dependencies, and basic setup.
- **Configuration**: How to configure the application and what options are available. This is generally aimed at the command-line or configuration file options, not options set interactively in the program.
- **Usage**: A description of how to launch the application, command-line arguments, and other notes a user would need to know to use the basic functionality of the application.
- **General notes**: A catch-all for notes or critical information users should be aware of.
- **Bugs**: A list of known bugs or limitations in the application.

Not all of these sections will apply to every program; for example, ABQ data entry doesn't currently have any configuration options, so there's no reason to have a configuration section. You might add other sections as well, depending on the situation; for example, publicly distributed software may have a FAQ section, or open source software might have a contributing section with instructions on how to submit patches.

The `README` file is written in plain ASCII or Unicode text, either free-form or using a markup language. Since we're doing a Python project, we'll use reStructuredText, the official markup for Python documentation (which is why our file uses an `rst` file extension).

ReStructuredText

The reStructuredText markup language is part of the Python `docutils` project, and a complete reference can be found at the Docutils website: `http://docutils.sourceforge.net`. The `docutils` project also provides utilities for converting RST to formats like PDF, ODT, HTML, and LaTeX.

The basics can be grasped fairly quickly, so let's go through them:

- Paragraphs are created by leaving a blank line between blocks of text.
- Headings are created by underlining a single line of text with a non-alphanumeric symbol. The exact symbol doesn't matter; whichever one you use first will be treated as a level one heading for the rest of the document, whichever you use second as a level two, and so on. Conventionally, `=` is usually used for level one, `-` for level two, `~` for level three, and `+` for level four.
- Titles and subtitles are created like headings, except with a line of symbols above and below.
- Bullet lists are created by starting a line with any of `*`, `-`, or `+` and a space. Switching symbols will create a sub-list, and multiline points are created by indenting subsequent lines to where the text starts at the first bullet point.
- Numbered lists are created like bullet lists, but using either digits (which don't need to be correctly ordered) or the `#` symbol as a bullet.
- Code examples can be specified inline by enclosing them in double backtick characters (``` `` ```), or in a block by ending a lead-in line with a double colon and indenting the code block.

- Tables can either be created by surrounding columns of text with = symbols, separated by spaces to indicate the column breaks, or by constructing ASCII-art tables from |, -, and +. Tables can be tedious to create in a plain text editor, but some programming tools have plugins to generate the RST tables.

We've used RST already in `Chapter 2`, *Designing GUI Applications with Tkinter*, to create our program specification; there, you saw the use of titles, headers, bullets, and a table. Let's walk through creating our `README.rst` file:

1. Open the file and start with the title and description, as follows:

```
============================
 ABQ Data Entry Application
============================

Description
===========

This program provides a data entry form for ABQ Agrilabs
laboratory data.

Features
--------

* Provides a validated entry form to ensure correct data
* Stores data to ABQ-format CSV files
* Auto-fills form fields whenever possible
```

2. Next, we'll list the authors by adding the following code:

```
Authors
=======

Alan D Moore, 2018
```

Add yourself, of course. Eventually, other people might work on your application; they should add their names here with the dates they worked on it. Now, add the requirements as follows:

```
Requirements
============

* Python 3
* Tkinter
```

Right now, we only need Python 3 and Tkinter, but as our application grows we may be expanding this list. Our application doesn't really need to be installed, and has no configuration options, so for now we can skip those sections. Instead, we'll skip to `Usage` as follows:

```
Usage
=====

To start the application, run::

  python3 ABQ_Data_Entry/abq_data_entry.py
```

There really isn't much to know about running the program other than this command; no command-line switches or arguments. We don't know of any bugs, so we'll just leave some general notes at the end as follows:

```
General Notes
=============

The CSV file will be saved to your current directory in
the format "abq_data_record_CURRENTDATE.csv", where
CURRENTDATE is today's date in ISO format.

This program only appends to the CSV file.  You should
have a spreadsheet program installed in case you need to
edit or check the file.
```

It seems prudent to tell the user where the file will be saved and what it will be called, since that's hardcoded into the program right now. Also, we should mention the fact that the user should have some kind of spreadsheet, since the program can't edit or view the data. That finishes the `README.rst` file. Save it and let's move on to the `docs` folder.

Populating the docs folder

The `docs` folder is where documentation goes. This can be any kind of documentation: user manuals, program specifications, API references, diagrams, and so on.

For now, you copy in the program specification we wrote in previous chapters, your interface mockups, and a copy of the form used by the technicians.

At some point, you might need to write a user manual, but for now the program is simple enough not to need it.

Making a Python package

Creating your own Python package is surprisingly easy. A Python package consists of the following three things:

- A directory
- One or more Python files in that directory
- A file called `__init__.py` in the directory

Once you've done this, you can import your package in whole or in part, just like you would import standard library packages, provided your script is in the same parent directory as the package directory.

Note that `__init__.py` in a module is somewhat analogous to what `self.__init__()` is for a class. Code inside it will run whenever the package is imported. The Python community generally discourages putting much code in this file, though, and since no code is actually required, we'll leave this file empty.

Let's start building our application's package. Create the following six empty files under `abq_data_entry`:

- `__init__.py`
- `widgets.py`
- `views.py`
- `models.py`
- `application.py`
- `constants.py`

Each of those Python files is called a **module**. A module is nothing more than a Python file inside a package directory. Your directory structure should now look like this:

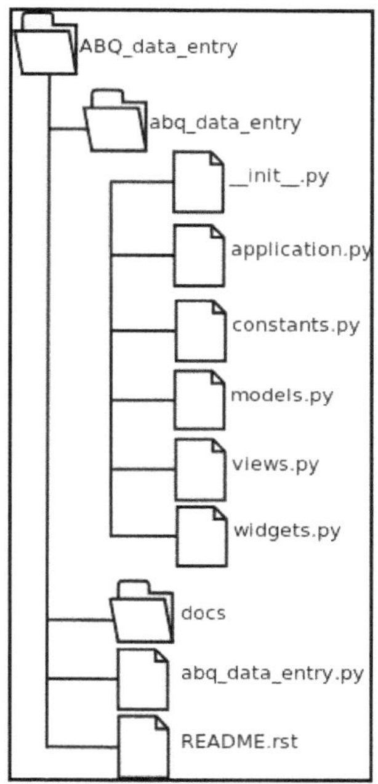

At this point, you have a working package, albeit with no actual code in it. To test this, open a Terminal/command-line window, change to your `ABQ_Data_Entry` directory, and start a Python shell.

Now, type the following command:

```
from abq_data_entry import application
```

This should work without error. Of course, it doesn't do anything, but we'll get to that next.

Don't confuse the term package here with the actual distributable Python packages, such as those you download using `pip`.

Splitting our application into multiple files

Now that our directory structure is in order, we need to start dissecting our application script and splitting it up into our module files. We'll also need to create our model class. Open up your `abq_data_entry.py` file from `Chapter 4`, *Reducing User Error with Validation and Automation,* and let's begin!

Creating the models module

When your application is all about data, it's good to begin with the model. Remember that the job of a model is to manage the storage, retrieval, and processing of our application's data, usually with respect to its persistent storage format (in this case, CSV). To accomplish this, our model should contain all the knowledge about our data.

Currently, our application has nothing like a model; knowledge about the application's data is scattered into the form fields, and the `Application` object simply takes whatever data the form contains and stuffs it directly into a CSV file when a save operation is requested. Since we aren't yet retrieving or updating information, our application has no actual knowledge about what's inside the CSV file.

To move our application to an MVC architecture, we'll need to create a model class that both manages data storage and retrieval, and represents the authoritative source of knowledge about our data. In other words, we have to encode the knowledge contained in our data dictionary here in our model. We don't really know what we'll *do* with this knowledge yet, but this is where it belongs.

There are a few ways we could store this data, such as creating a custom field class or a `namedtuple` object, but we'll keep it simple for now and just use a dictionary, mapping field names to field metadata.

The field metadata will likewise be stored as a dictionary of attributes about the field, which will include:

- Whether or not the field is required

- The type of data stored in the field
- The list of possible values, if applicable
- The minimum, maximum, and increment of values, if applicable

To store the data type for each field, let's define some data types. Open the `constants.py` file and add the following code:

```
class FieldTypes:
    string = 1
    string_list = 2
    iso_date_string = 3
    long_string = 4
    decimal = 5
    integer = 6
    boolean = 7
```

We've created a class called `FieldTypes` that simply stores some named integer values, which will describe the different types of data we're going to store. We could just use Python types here, but it's useful to differentiate between certain types of data that are likely to be the same Python type (such as `long`, `short`, and `date` strings). Note that the integer values here are basically meaningless; they just need to be different from one another.

Python 3 has an `Enum` class, which we could have used here, but it adds very little that we actually need in this case. You may want to investigate this class if you're creating a lot of constants such as our `FieldTypes` class and need additional features.

Now, open `models.py`, where we'll import `FieldTypes` and create our model class and field definitions as follows:

```
import csv
import os
from .constants import FieldTypes as FT

class CSVModel:
    """CSV file storage"""
    fields = {
        "Date": {'req': True, 'type': FT.iso_date_string},
        "Time": {'req': True, 'type': FT.string_list,
                 'values': ['8:00', '12:00', '16:00', '20:00']},
        "Technician": {'req': True, 'type':  FT.string},
        "Lab": {'req': True, 'type': FT.string_list,
                'values': ['A', 'B', 'C', 'D', 'E']},
        "Plot": {'req': True, 'type': FT.string_list,
```

```
            'values': [str(x) for x in range(1, 21)]},
        "Seed sample":  {'req': True, 'type': FT.string},
        "Humidity": {'req': True, 'type': FT.decimal,
                     'min': 0.5, 'max': 52.0, 'inc': .01},
        "Light": {'req': True, 'type': FT.decimal,
                  'min': 0, 'max': 100.0, 'inc': .01},
        "Temperature": {'req': True, 'type': FT.decimal,
                        'min': 4, 'max': 40, 'inc': .01},
        "Equipment Fault": {'req': False, 'type': FT.boolean},
        "Plants": {'req': True, 'type': FT.integer,
                   'min': 0, 'max': 20},
        "Blossoms": {'req': True, 'type': FT.integer,
                     'min': 0, 'max': 1000},
        "Fruit": {'req': True, 'type': FT.integer,
                  'min': 0, 'max': 1000},
        "Min Height": {'req': True, 'type': FT.decimal,
                       'min': 0, 'max': 1000, 'inc': .01},
        "Max Height": {'req': True, 'type': FT.decimal,
                       'min': 0, 'max': 1000, 'inc': .01},
        "Median Height": {'req': True, 'type': FT.decimal,
                          'min': 0, 'max': 1000, 'inc': .01},
        "Notes": {'req': False, 'type': FT.long_string}
    }
```

Notice the way we import `FieldTypes`: `from .constants import FieldTypes`. The dot in front of `constants` makes this a **relative import**. Relative imports can be used inside a Python package to locate other modules in the same package. In this case, we're in the `models` module, and we need to access the `constants` module inside the `abq_data_entry` package. The single dot represents our current parent module (`abq_data_entry`), and thus `.constants` means the `constants` module of the `abq_data_entry` package.

Relative imports also distinguish our custom modules from modules in `PYTHONPATH`. Thus, we don't have to worry about any third-party or standard library packages conflicting with our module names.

In addition to field attributes, we're also documenting the order of fields here. In Python 3.6 and later, dictionaries retain the order they were defined by; if you're using an older version of Python 3, you'd need to use the `OrderedDict` class from the `collections` standard library module to preserve the field order.

Now that we have a class that understands which fields need to be stored, we need to migrate our save logic from the application class into the model.

The code in our current script is as follows:

```
datestring = datetime.today().strftime("%Y-%m-%d")
filename = "abq_data_record_{}.csv".format(datestring)
newfile = not os.path.exists(filename)

data = self.recordform.get()

with open(filename, 'a') as fh:
    csvwriter = csv.DictWriter(fh, fieldnames=data.keys())
    if newfile:
        csvwriter.writeheader()
    csvwriter.writerow(data)
```

Let's go through this code and determine what goes to the model and what stays in the controller (that is, the `Application` class):

- The first two lines define the filename we're going to use. This could go into the model, but thinking ahead, it seems that the users may want to be able to open arbitrary files or define the filename manually. This means the application will need to be able to tell the model which filename to work with, so it's better to leave the logic that determines the name in the controller.
- The `newfile` line determines whether the file exists or not. As an implementation detail of the data storage medium, this is clearly the model's problem, not the application's.
- `data = self.recordform.get()` pulls data from the form. Since our model has no knowledge of the form's existence, this needs to stay in the controller.
- The last block opens the file, creates a `csv.DictWriter` object, and appends the data. This is definitely the model's concern.

Now, let's begin moving code into the `CSVModel` class:

1. To start the process, let's create a constructor for `CSVModel` that allows us to pass in a filename:

```
def __init__(self, filename):
    self.filename = filename
```

The constructor is pretty simple; it just takes a `filename` parameter and stores it as a property. Now, we'll migrate the save logic as follows:

```
def save_record(self, data):
    """Save a dict of data to the CSV file"""

    newfile = not os.path.exists(self.filename)

    with open(self.filename, 'a') as fh:
        csvwriter = csv.DictWriter(fh,
            fieldnames=self.fields.keys())
        if newfile:
            csvwriter.writeheader()
        csvwriter.writerow(data)
```

This is essentially the logic we chose to copy from `Application.on_save()`, but with one difference; in the call to `csv.DictWriter()`, the `fieldnames` parameter is defined by the model's `fields` list rather than the keys of the `data` dict. This allows our model to manage the format of the CSV file itself, and not depend on what the form gives it.

2. Before we're done, we need to take care of our module imports. The `save_record()` method uses the `os` and `csv` libraries, so we need to import them. Add this to the top of the file as follows:

```
import csv
import os
```

With the model in place, let's start working on our view components.

Moving the widgets

While we could put all of our UI-related code in one `views` file, we have a lot of widget classes that should really be put in their own file to limit the complexity of the `views` file.

So instead, we're going to move all of the code for our widget classes into the `widgets.py` file. Widgets include all the classes that implement reusable GUI components, including compound widgets like `LabelInput`. As we develop more of these, we'll add them to this file.

Open `widgets.py` and copy in all of the code for `ValidatedMixin`, `DateInput`, `RequiredEntry`, `ValidatedCombobox`, `ValidatedSpinbox`, and `LabelInput`. These are our widgets.

The `widgets.py` file will need to import any module dependencies used by the code being copied in. We'll need to look through our code and find what libraries we use and import them. Obviously, we need `tkinter` and `ttk`, so add those at the top as follows:

```
import tkinter as tk
from tkinter import ttk
```

Our `DateInput` class uses the `datetime` class from the `datetime` library, so import that too, as follows:

```
from datetime import datetime
```

Finally, our `ValidatedSpinbox` class makes use of the `Decimal` class and `InvalidOperation` exception from the `decimal` library as follows:

```
from decimal import Decimal, InvalidOperation
```

This is all we need in `widgets.py` for now, but we'll revisit this file as we refactor our view logic.

Moving the views

Next, we need to create the `views.py` file. Views are larger GUI components, like our `DataRecordForm` class. Currently it's our only view, but we'll be creating more views in later chapters, and they'll be added here.

Open the `views.py` file and copy in the `DataRecordForm` class, then go back to the top to deal with the module imports. Again, we'll need `tkinter` and `ttk`, and our file saving logic relies on `datetime` for the filename.

Add them to the top of the file as follows:

```
import tkinter as tk
from tkinter import ttk
from datetime import datetime
```

We aren't done, though; our actual widgets aren't here and we'll need to import them. Since we're going to be doing a lot of importing of objects between our files, let's pause for a moment to consider the best way to handle these imports.

There are three ways we could import objects:

- Use a wildcard import to bring in all the classes from `widgets.py`
- Explicitly import all the needed classes from `widgets.py` using the `from ... import ...` format
- Import `widgets` and keep our widgets in their own namespace

Let's consider the relative merits of those ways:

- The first option is by far the easiest, but it can cause us headaches as the application expands. A wildcard import will bring in every name defined at the global scope within the module. That includes not just the classes we defined, but any imported modules, aliases, and defined variables or functions. This can lead to unintended consequences and subtle bugs as the application expands in complexity.
- The second option is cleaner, but means we'll need to maintain the list of imports as we add new classes and use them in different files, and this leads to a long and ugly imports section that is hard for humans to parse.
- The third option is by far the best, as it keeps all names within a namespace and keeps the code elegantly simple. The only downside is that we'll need to update our code so that all references to widget classes include the module name as well. To keep this from being unwieldy, let's alias the `widgets` module to something short, like `w`.

Add the following code to your imports:

```
from . import widgets as w
```

Now, we just need to go through the code and prepend `w.` to all instances of `LabelInput`, `RequiredEntry`, `DateEntry`, `ValidatedCombobox`, and `ValidatedSpinbox`. This should be easy enough to do in IDLE or any other text editor using a series of search and replace actions.

For example, `line 1` of the form is as follows:

```
# line 1
self.inputs['Date'] = w.LabelInput(
    recordinfo, "Date",
    input_class=w.DateEntry,
    input_var=tk.StringVar()
)
self.inputs['Date'].grid(row=0, column=0)
self.inputs['Time'] = w.LabelInput(
    recordinfo, "Time",
```

```
        input_class=w.ValidatedCombobox,
        input_var=tk.StringVar(),
        input_args={"values": ["8:00", "12:00", "16:00", "20:00"]}
    )
    self.inputs['Time'].grid(row=0, column=1)
    self.inputs['Technician'] = w.LabelInput(
        recordinfo, "Technician",
        input_class=w.RequiredEntry,
        input_var=tk.StringVar()
    )
    self.inputs['Technician'].grid(row=0, column=2)
```

Before you go through and change that everywhere, though, let's stop and take a moment to refactor some of the redundancy out of this code.

Removing redundancy in our view logic

Look at the field definitions in the view logic: they contain a lot of information that is also in our model. Minimums, maximums, increments, and possible values are defined both here and in our model code. Even the type of the input widget is related directly to the type of data being stored. Ideally, this should only be defined one place, and that place should be the model. If we needed to update the model for some reason, our form would be out of sync.

What we need to do is to pass the field specification from our model into the view class and let the widgets' details be defined from that specification.

Since our widget instances are being defined inside the `LabelInput` class, we're going to enhance that class with the ability to automatically work out the `input` class and arguments from our model's field specification format. Open up the `widgets.py` file and import the `FieldTypes` class, just as you did in `model.py`.

Now, locate the `LabelInput` class and add the following code before the `__init__()` method:

```
    field_types = {
        FT.string: (RequiredEntry, tk.StringVar),
        FT.string_list: (ValidatedCombobox, tk.StringVar),
        FT.iso_date_string: (DateEntry, tk.StringVar),
        FT.long_string: (tk.Text, lambda: None),
        FT.decimal: (ValidatedSpinbox, tk.DoubleVar),
```

```
        FT.integer: (ValidatedSpinbox, tk.IntVar),
        FT.boolean: (ttk.Checkbutton, tk.BooleanVar)
    }
```

This code acts as a key to translate our model's field types into a widget type and variable type appropriate for the field type.

Now, we need to update `__init__()` to take a `field_spec` parameter and, if given, use it to define the input widget as follows:

```
    def __init__(self, parent, label='', input_class=None,
         input_var=None, input_args=None, label_args=None,
         field_spec=None, **kwargs):
        super().__init__(parent, **kwargs)
        input_args = input_args or {}
        label_args = label_args or {}
        if field_spec:
            field_type = field_spec.get('type', FT.string)
            input_class = input_class or
            self.field_types.get(field_type)[0]
            var_type = self.field_types.get(field_type)[1]
            self.variable = input_var if input_var else var_type()
            # min, max, increment
            if 'min' in field_spec and 'from_' not in input_args:
                input_args['from_'] = field_spec.get('min')
            if 'max' in field_spec and 'to' not in input_args:
                input_args['to'] = field_spec.get('max')
            if 'inc' in field_spec and 'increment' not in input_args:
                input_args['increment'] = field_spec.get('inc')
            # values
            if 'values' in field_spec and 'values' not in input_args:
                input_args['values'] = field_spec.get('values')
        else:
            self.variable = input_var
        if input_class in (ttk.Checkbutton, ttk.Button,
ttk.Radiobutton):
            input_args["text"] = label
            input_args["variable"] = self.variable
        else:
            self.label = ttk.Label(self, text=label, **label_args)
            self.label.grid(row=0, column=0, sticky=(tk.W + tk.E))
            input_args["textvariable"] = self.variable
        # ... Remainder of __init__() is the same
```

Let's break down the changes:

1. First, we've added `field_spec` as a keyword argument with `None` as a default. We might want to use this class in a situation where there isn't a field specification, so we keep this parameter optional.
2. If there is `field_spec` given, we're going to do the following things:
    - We'll grab the `type` value and use that with our class's field key to get `input_class`. In case we want to override this, an explicitly passed `input_class` will override the detected one.
    - We'll determine the appropriate variable type in the same way. Once again, if `input_var` is explicitly passed, we'll prefer that, otherwise we'll use the one determined from the field type. We'll create an instance either way and store it in `self.variable`.
    - For `min`, `max`, `inc`, and `values`, if the key exists in the field specification, and the corresponding `from_`, `to`, `increment`, or `values` argument has not been passed in explicitly, we'll set up the `input_args` variable with the `field_spec` value.
3. If `field_spec` wasn't passed in, we need to assign `self.variable` from the `input_var` argument.
4. We're using `self.variable` now instead of `input_var` for assigning the input's variable, since those values might not necessarily be the same anymore and `self.variable` will contain the correct reference.

Now, we can update our view code to take advantage of this new ability. Our `DataRecordForm` class will need access to the model's `fields` dictionary, which it can then use to send a field specification to the `LabelInput` class.

Back in the `views.py` file, edit the method signature so that we can pass in a dictionary of field specifications:

```
def __init__(self, parent, fields, *args, **kwargs):
```

With access to the `fields` dictionary, we can just get the field specification from it and pass that into the `LabelInput` class instead of specifying the input class, input variable, and input arguments.

Now, the first line looks like this:

```
        self.inputs['Date'] = w.LabelInput(
            recordinfo, "Date",
            field_spec=fields['Date'])
        self.inputs['Date'].grid(row=0, column=0)
```

```
self.inputs['Time'] = w.LabelInput(
    recordinfo, "Time",
    field_spec=fields['Time'])
self.inputs['Time'].grid(row=0, column=1)
self.inputs['Technician'] = w.LabelInput(
    recordinfo, "Technician",
    field_spec=fields['Technician'])
self.inputs['Technician'].grid(row=0, column=2)
```

Go ahead and update the rest of the widgets the same way, replacing `input_class`, `input_var`, and `input_args` with `field_spec`. Note that when you get to the height fields, you'll need to keep the part of `input_args` that defines `min_var`, `max_var`, and `focus_update_var`.

For example, the following is the `Min Height` input definition:

```
self.inputs['Min Height'] = w.LabelInput(
    plantinfo, "Min Height (cm)",
    field_spec=fields['Min Height'],
    input_args={"max_var": max_height_var,
                "focus_update_var": min_height_var})
```

That does it. Now, any changes to our field specification can be made solely in the model, and the form will simply do the correct thing.

Creating the application file

Finally, let's create our controller class, `Application`, by following these steps:

1. Open the `application.py` file and copy in the `Application` class definition from the script.
2. The first thing we'll fix is our imports. At the top of the file, add the following code:

```
import tkinter as tk
from tkinter import ttk
from datetime import datetime
from . import views as v
from . import models as m
```

We need tkinter and ttk, of course, and datetime to define our filename. Although we only need one class each from views and models, we're going to keep them in their own namespaces anyway. It's likely we're going to have many more views as the application expands, and possibly more models.

3. We need to update the call to DataRecordForm in __init__() for the new namespace and make sure we pass in the required field specification dictionary as follows:

```
        self.recordform = v.DataRecordForm(self,
m.CSVModel.fields)
```

4. Finally, we need to update Application.on_save() to use the model, as follows:

```
def on_save(self):
    """Handles save button clicks"""

    errors = self.recordform.get_errors()
    if errors:
        self.status.set(
            "Cannot save, error in fields: {}"
            .format(', '.join(errors.keys())))
        return False

    # For now, we save to a hardcoded filename
    with a datestring.
    datestring = datetime.today().strftime("%Y-%m-%d")
    filename = "abq_data_record_{}.csv".format(datestring)
    model = m.CSVModel(filename)
    data = self.recordform.get()
    model.save_record(data)
    self.records_saved += 1
    self.status.set(
        "{} records saved this session".
        format(self.records_saved)
    )
    self.recordform.reset()
```

As you can see, using our model is pretty seamless; we just created a `CSVModel` class by passing in the filename, and then passed the form's data to `save_record()`.

Running the application

The application is now completely migrated to the new data format. To test it, navigate to the application root folder, `ABQ_Data_Entry`, and execute the following command:

```
python3 abq_data_entry.py
```

It should look and act just like the single script from `Chapter 4`, *Reducing User Error with Validation and Automation,* and run without errors, as shown in the following screenshot:

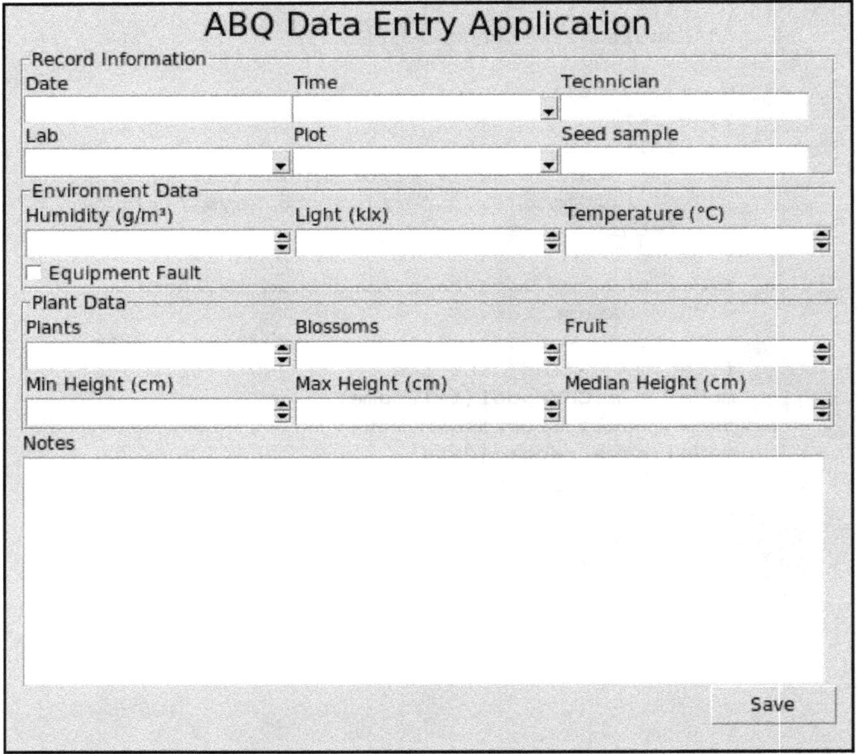

Success!

Using version control software

Our code is nicely structured for expansion, but there's one more critical item we should address: **version control**. You may already be familiar with a **version control system** (**VCS**), sometimes called **revision control** or **source code management**, but if not, it's an indispensable tool for dealing with a large and changing codebase.

When working on an application, we sometimes think we know what needs to be changed, but it turns out we're wrong. Sometimes we don't know exactly how to code something, and it takes several attempts to find the correct approach. Sometimes we need to revert to code that was changed a long time back. Sometimes we have multiple people working on the same piece of code, and we need to merge their changes together. Version control systems were created to address these issues and more.

There are dozens of different version control systems, but most of them work essentially the same:

- You have a working copy of the code that you make changes to
- You periodically select changes to commit back to the master copy
- You can checkout older versions of the code at any point, then revert back to the master copy
- You can create branches of the code to experiment with different approaches, new features, or large refactors
- You can later merge these branches back into the master copy

VCS provides a safety net that gives you the freedom to change your code without the fear that you'll hopelessly ruin it: reverting to a known working state is just a few quick commands away. It also helps us to document changes to our code, and collaborate with others if the opportunity arises.

There are dozens of VC systems available, but by far the most popular for many years now is **Git**.

A super-quick guide to using Git

Git was created by Linus Torvalds to be the version control software for the Linux kernel project, and has since grown to be the most popular VC software in the world. It is utilized by source sharing sites like GitHub, Bitbucket, SourceForge, and GitLab. Git is extremely powerful, and mastering it can take months or years; fortunately, the basics can be grasped in a few minutes.

First, you'll need to install Git; visit `https://git-scm.com/downloads` for instructions on how to install Git on macOS, Windows, Linux, or other Unix operating systems.

Initializing and configuring a Git repository

Once Git is installed, we need to initialize and configure our project directory as a Git repository by following these steps:

1. Run the following command in the application's root directory (`ABQ_Data_Entry`):

   ```
   git init
   ```

   This command creates a hidden directory under our project root called `.git` and initializes it with the basic files that make up the repository. The `.git` directory will contain all the data and metadata about our saved revisions.

2. Before we add any files to the repository, we need to instruct Git to ignore certain kinds of files. For example, Python creates bytecode (`.pyc`) files whenever it executes a file, and we don't want to save these as part of our code. To do this, create a file in your project root called `.gitignore` and put the following lines in it:

   ```
   *.pyc
   __pycache__/
   ```

Adding and committing code

Now that our repository is initialized, we can add files and directories to our Git repository using the following commands:

```
git add abq_data_entry
git add abq_data_entry.py
git add docs
git add README.rst
```

At this point, our files are staged, but not yet committed to the repository. You can check the status of your repository and the files in it at any time by entering `git status`.

You should get the following output:

```
On branch master

No commits yet

Changes to be committed:
  (use "git rm --cached <file>..." to unstage)

        new file:   README.rst
        new file:   abq_data_entry.py
        new file:   abq_data_entry/__init__.py
        new file:   abq_data_entry/application.py
        new file:   abq_data_entry/models.py
        new file:   abq_data_entry/views.py
        new file:   abq_data_entry/widgets.py
        new file:   docs/Application_layout.png
        new file:   docs/abq_data_entry_spec.rst
        new file:   docs/lab-tech-paper-form.png

Untracked files:
  (use "git add <file>..." to include in what will be committed)

        .gitignore
```

This shows you that all the files under `abq_data_entry` and `docs`, as well as the files you specified directly, are staged to be committed to the repository.

Let's go ahead and commit the changes as follows:

```
git commit -m "Initial commit"
```

The `-m` flag here passes in a commit message, which is stored with the commit. Each time you commit code to the repository, you will be required to write a message. You should always make these messages as meaningful as possible, detailing what changes you made and the rationale behind them.

Viewing and using our commits

To view your repository's history, run the `git log` command as follows:

```
alanm@alanm-laptop:~/ABQ_Data_Entry$ git log
commit df48707422875ff545dc30f4395f82ad2d25f103 (HEAD -> master)
Author: Alan Moore <alan@example.com>
Date:   Thu Dec 21 18:12:17 2017 -0600

    Initial commit
```

As you can see, the `Author`, `Date`, and `commit` message is displayed for our last commit. If we had more commits, they would be listed here as well, from newest to oldest. The long hexadecimal value you see in the first line of output is the **commit hash**, a unique value that identifies the commit. This value can be used to refer to the commit in other operations.

For example, we can use it to reset our repository to a past state, as follows:

1. Delete the `README.rst` file, and verify that it's completely gone.
2. Now, enter the command `git reset --hard df48707`, replacing `df48707` with the first seven characters of your commit's hash.
3. Check your file listing again: the `README.rst` file is back.

What happened here is that we altered our repository, then told Git to hard reset the state of the repository to our first commit. If you don't want to reset your repository, you can also checkout an old commit temporarily, or create a branch using a particular commit as the base. As you can see already, this gives us a powerful safety net for experimentation; no matter how much you tinker with the code, any commit is just a command away!

Git has many more features that are beyond the scope of this book. If you'd like to learn more, the Git project provides a free online manual at `https://git-scm.com/book` where you can learn about advanced features like branching and setting up remote repositories. For now, the important thing is to commit changes as you go, so that you maintain your safety net and document the history of changes.

Summary

In this chapter, you learned to prepare your simple script for some serious expansion. You learned how to divide your application's areas of responsibility into separate components, and how to split your code into separate modules. You learned how to document your code using reStructuredText and track all your changes with version control.

In the next chapter, we're going to put our new project layout to the test by implementing some new features. You'll learn how to work with Tkinter's application menu widgets, how to implement file opening and saving, and how to use message popups to alert users or confirm actions.

6
Creating Menus with Menu and Tkinter Dialogs

As an application grows, organizing access to its features becomes increasingly important. Traditionally, applications have addressed this with a **menu system**, which is typically located at the top of the application window or (on some platforms) in a global desktop menu. While these menus are application-specific, certain organizational conventions have been developed that we should follow in order to make our software user-friendly.

In this chapter, we're going to cover the following topics:

- Analyzing some reported problems and deciding on a solution
- Exploring some of Tkinter's dialog classes, and using them for implementing common menu functionality
- Learning how to work with Tkinter's Menu widget and using it to create a menu for our application
- Creating some options for our application and saving them to disk

Solving problems in our application

Your boss has brought you the first set of problems that need to be addressed in your application. First, in situations where the last reports of the day aren't able to be entered until the following day, the hardcoded date string in the filename is a problem. The data entry staff need a way to manually choose which file they'll be appending to.

Also, the data entry staff have mixed feelings about the auto-populate features in the form. Some find it very helpful, but others would really like to see it disabled. You'll need a way to allow users to turn this feature on and off.

Finally, some users have a hard time noticing the status bar text at the bottom, and would like the application to be more conspicuous when it fails to save data due to errors.

Deciding how to address these problems

It's clear you need to implement a way to select a file and toggle the auto-populate features of the form. First, you consider just adding controls to the main application for both of these, and make this quick mock-up:

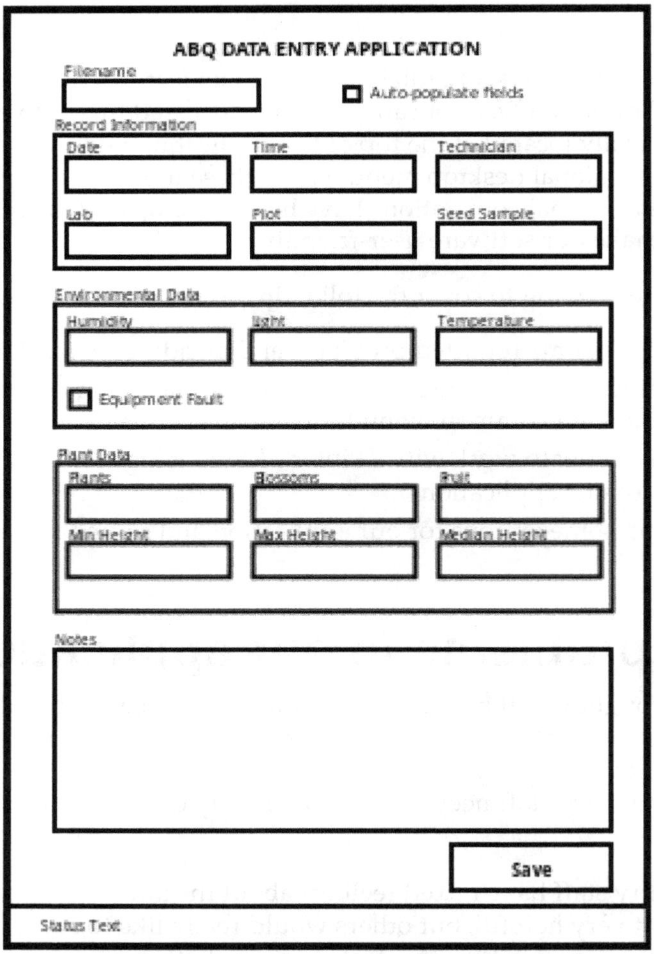

It doesn't take long for you to realize that this is not a great design, and certainly not one that will accommodate growth. Your users don't want to have to type a file path and filename blindly into the box, nor do they want a lot of extra fields cluttering up the UI.

Fortunately, Tkinter offers some tools that will help us to solve these problems:

- **File dialogs**: Tkinter's `filedialog` library will help make file selection simple
- **Error dialogs**: Tkinter's `messagebox` library will let us display error messages more noticeably
- **Main menu**: Tkinter's `Menu` class can help us organize common functionality for easy access

Implementing simple Tkinter dialogs

The status bar is fine for incidental information that shouldn't interrupt a user's workflow, but for errors that prevent work from continuing as expected, users should be alerted in a more assertive way. An **error dialog** that halts the program until it's acknowledged with a mouse click is fairly assertive and seems like a good way to address the issue of users not seeing errors. In order to implement these, you'll need to learn about Tkinter's `messagebox` library.

Tkinter messagebox

The best way to display simple dialog boxes in Tkinter is by using the `tkinter.messagebox` library, which contains several convenient functions that allow you to quickly create common dialog types. Each function displays a preset icon and a selection of buttons with a message and detail text that you specify, and returns a value depending on which button the user clicked.

The following table shows some of the `messagebox` functions with their icons and return values:

Function	Icon	Button / return value
`askokcancel`	Question	**Ok** (`True`), **Cancel** (`False`)
`askretrycancel`	Warning	**Retry** (`True`), **Cancel** (`False`)
`askyesno`	Question	**Yes** (`True`), **No** (`False`)
`askyesnocancel`	Question	**Yes** (`True`), **No** (`False`), **Cancel** (`None`)

`showerror`	Error	**Ok** (`ok`)
`showinfo`	Information	**Ok** (`ok`)
`showwarning`	Warning	**Ok** (`ok`)

We can pass the following three text arguments into any `messagebox` function:

- `title`: This argument sets the title of the window, which is displayed in the title bar and/or task bar in your desktop environment.
- `message`: This argument sets the main message of the dialog. It's usually in a heading font and should be kept fairly short.
- `detail`: This argument sets the body text of the dialog, which is usually displayed in the standard window font.

Here is a basic call to `showinfo()`:

```
messagebox.showinfo(
    title='This is the title',
    message="This is the message",
    detail='This is the detail')
```

In Windows 10, it results in a dialog box (on other platforms, it may look a bit different), as shown in the following screenshot:

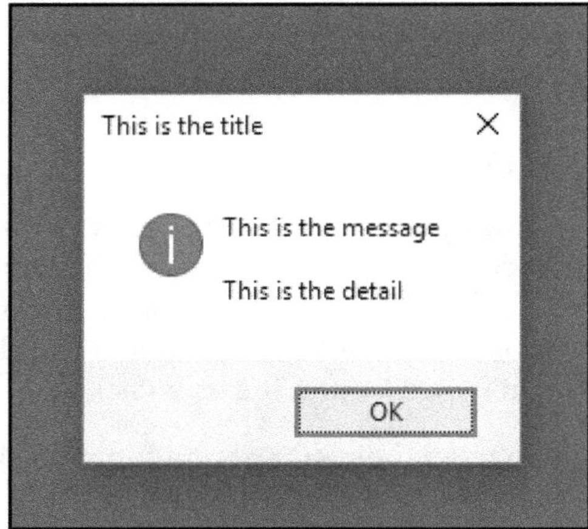

Tkinter `messagebox` dialog boxes are **modal**, which means that the program execution pauses and the rest of the UI is unresponsive while the dialog box is open. There is no way to change this, so only use them in situations where it's acceptable for the program to pause execution while the box is open.

Let's create a small example to show the use of the `messagebox` functions:

```
import tkinter as tk
from tkinter import messagebox
```

To use `messagebox`, we need to import it from Tkinter; you can't simply use `tk.messagebox` because it's a submodule and must be explicitly imported.

Let's create a yes-no message box as follows:

```
see_more = messagebox.askyesno(title='See more?',
    message='Would you like to see another box?',
    detail='Click NO to quit')
if not see_more:
    exit()
```

This creates a dialog with **Yes** and **No** buttons; if **Yes** is clicked, the function returns `True`. If **No** is clicked, the function returns `False` and the application exits.

In case our user wants to see more boxes, let's display an information box:

```
messagebox.showinfo(title='You got it',
    message="Ok, here's another dialog.",
    detail='Hope you like it!')
```

Note the difference between the way `message` and `detail` are displayed on your platform. On some platforms, there is no difference; on others, `message` is large and bold, which is appropriate for short texts. For cross-platform software, it's best to use `detail` for extended output.

Showing the error dialogs

Now that you understand how to use `messagebox`, error dialogs should be easy to implement. The `Application.on_save()` method already displays errors in the status bar; we just need to make this error display in an error message box as well by performing the following steps:

1. First, we'll need to import it in `application.py` as follows:

```
from tkinter import messagebox
```

2. Now, in the `on_save()` method after the check for errors, we'll set up the message for the error dialog. We'll make a bullet list of the fields with errors by joining them with `"\n  *"`. Unfortunately, `messagebox` doesn't support any sort of markup, so constructs like bullet lists need to be built manually using regular characters, as in the following:

```
message = "Cannot save record"
detail = "The following fields have errors: \n  * {}".format(
    '\n  * '.join(errors.keys()))
```

3. Now, we can call `showerror()`, just after the call to `status()` as follows:

```
    messagebox.showerror(title='Error', message=message,
detail=detail)
```

4. Now, open the program and hit **Save**; you'll see a dialog box alerting you to the errors in the application, as shown in the following screenshot:

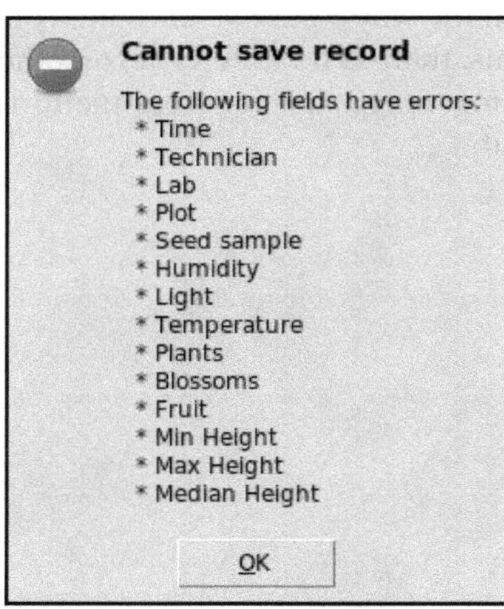

This error should be hard for anyone to miss!

One shortcoming of the `messagebox` dialogs is that they don't scroll; a long error message will create a dialog that may fill (or extend beyond) the screen. If this is a potential problem, you'll want to create a custom dialog containing a scrollable widget.

Designing our menu

Most applications organize functionality into a hierarchical **menu system**, typically displayed at the top of the application or screen (depending on the OS). While the organization of this menu varies between operating systems, certain items are fairly common across platforms.

Of these common items, our application will need the following:

- A file menu containing file operations such as open/save/export, and often an option to quit the application. Our users will need this menu to select a file and quit the program.
- An options, preferences, or settings menu where users can configure the application. We'll need this menu for our toggle settings; we'll call it options for now.
- A help menu, which contains links to help documentation, or, at the very least, an about message giving the basic information about the application. We'll implement this menu for the about dialog.

Apple, Microsoft, and the Gnome Project publish guidelines for macOS, Windows, and Gnome desktops (used on Linux and BSD), respectively; each set of guidelines addresses the layout of menu items specific to that platform.

Before we can implement our menu, we'll need to understand how menus work in Tkinter.

Creating menus in Tkinter

The `tkinter.Menu` widget is used to implement menus in Tkinter applications; it's a fairly simple widget that acts as a container for any number of menu items.

The menu items can be one of the following five types:

- `command`: These items are labeled buttons that, when clicked, run a callback.
- `checkbutton`: These items are just like `Checkbutton` in our forms, and can be used to toggle `BooleanVar`.
- `radiobutton`: These items are similar to `Checkbutton`, but can be used to switch any kind of Tkinter variable between several mutually exclusive options.
- `separator`: These items are used to segment the menu into sections.
- `cascade`: These items allow you to add a submenu to the menu. The submenu is just another `tkinter.Menu` object.

Let's write the following small program to demonstrate the use of Tkinter menus:

```
import tkinter as tk

root = tk.Tk()
main_text = tk.StringVar(value='Hi')
label = tk.Label(root, textvariable=main_text)
label.pack()

root.mainloop()
```

This application sets up a label whose text is controlled by a string variable, `main_text`. If you run this application, you'll see a simple window that says **Hi**. Let's start adding the menu components.

Right above `root.mainloop()`, add the following code:

```
main_menu = tk.Menu(root)
root.config(menu=main_menu)
```

This creates a main menu and then sets it as the main menu of our application.

Currently, that menu is empty, so let's add an item by adding the following code:

```
main_menu.add('command', label='Quit', command=root.quit)
```

We've added a command to quit the application. The `add` method allows us to specify an item type and any number of attributes to create a new menu item. In the case of a command, we need to at least have a `label` argument specifying the text that will show in the menu and a `command` argument pointing to a Python callback.

Some platforms, such as macOS, don't allow a command in the top-level menu.

Let's try creating a submenu as follows:

```
text_menu = tk.Menu(main_menu, tearoff=False)
```

Creating a submenu is just like creating a menu, except that we specify the `parent` menu as the widget's `parent`. Notice the `tearoff` argument; by default, submenus in Tkinter are tearable, which means they can be pulled off and moved around as independent windows. You don't have to disable this option, but it is a rather archaic UI feature that is rarely used on modern platforms. Users will likely just find it confusing, so it's best to disable it whenever you create submenus.

Add some commands to the menu as follows:

```
text_menu.add_command(label='Set to "Hi"',
              command=lambda: main_text.set('Hi'))
text_menu.add_command(label='Set to "There"',
              command=lambda: main_text.set('There'))
```

We're using the `lambda` functions here for convenience, but you can pass any Python callable. The `add_command` method used here is simply a shortcut for `add('command')`. There are analogous methods for adding other items as well (cascade, separator, and so on).

Let's use the `add_cascade` method to add our menu back to its `parent` widget as follows:

```
main_menu.add_cascade(label="Text", menu=text_menu)
```

When adding a submenu to its `parent` menu, we simply have to provide the label for the menu and the menu itself.

We can add the `Checkbutton` and `Radiobutton` widgets to the menu as well. To demonstrate this, let's create another submenu to alter the label's appearance.

First, we need the following setup code:

```
font_bold = tk.BooleanVar()
font_size = tk.IntVar()

def set_font(*args):
    font_spec = 'TkDefaultFont {size} {bold}'.format(
        size=font_size.get(),
        bold='bold' if font_bold.get() else '')
    label.config(font=font_spec)

font_bold.trace('w', set_font)
font_size.trace('w', set_font)
```

Here, we're just creating variables to store the state of the bold option and font size, then a callback method that actually sets the label's font from these variables when called. Then, we set up a trace on both variables to call the callback whenever their values are changed.

Now, we just need to create the menu options to change the variables by adding the following code:

```
# appearance menu
appearance_menu = tk.Menu(main_menu, tearoff=False)
main_menu.add_cascade(label="Appearance", menu=appearance_menu)

# bold text button
appearance_menu.add_checkbutton(label="Bold", variable=font_bold)
```

Like a regular `Checkbutton` widget, the `add_checkbutton` method takes `BooleanVar`, which is passed to the `variable` argument that will be bound to its checked status. Unlike a regular `Checkbutton` widget, use the `label` argument, rather than the `text` argument, to assign the label text.

To demonstrate the radio buttons, let's add a submenu to our submenu, like so:

```
size_menu = tk.Menu(appearance_menu, tearoff=False)
appearance_menu.add_cascade(label='Font size', menu=size_menu)
for size in range(8, 24, 2):
    size_menu.add_radiobutton(label="{} px".format(size),
        value=size, variable=font_size)
```

Just as we added a submenu to our main menu, we can add submenus to submenus. In theory, you could nest submenus indefinitely, but most UI guidelines discourage more than two levels. To create the items for our size menu, we're just iterating a generated list of even numbers between 8 and 24; for each one, we add a `radiobutton` item with a value equal to that size. Just like with regular `Radiobutton` widgets, the variable given in the `variable` argument will be updated with the value given in the `value` argument when the button is selected.

Launch the application and try it out, as shown in the following screenshot:

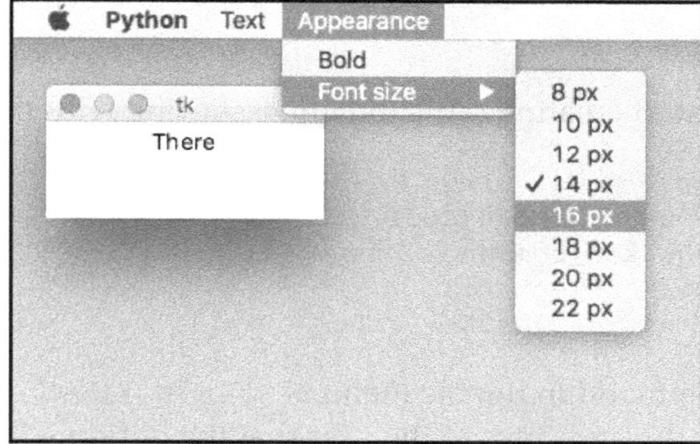

Now that you understand the `Menu` widget, let's add one to our application.

Implementing our application menu

As a major component of the GUI, our menu is clearly a view, and should be implemented in the `views.py` file. However, it's also going to need to set options that affect other views (such as the form options we're implementing now) and run functions that affect the application (like quitting). We need to implement it in such a way that we keep controller functions in the `Application` class but still keep the UI code in `views.py`. Let's take a look at the following steps:

1. Let's start out by opening `views.py` and creating a `MainMenu` class that subclasses `tkinter.Menu`:

```
class MainMenu(tk.Menu):
"""The Application's main menu"""
```

Our overridden `__init__()` method will take two dictionaries, a `settings` dictionary and a `callbacks` dictionary, as follows:

```
def __init__(self, parent, settings, callbacks, **kwargs):
    super().__init__(parent, **kwargs)
```

We'll use these dictionaries to communicate with the controller: `settings` will contain Tkinter variables that can be bound to our menu controls, and `callbacks` will be controller methods that we can bind to menu commands. Naturally, we'll need to make sure to populate these dictionaries with the expected variables and callables in our `Application` object.

2. Now, let's start creating our submenus, starting with the file menu as follows:

```
file_menu = tk.Menu(self, tearoff=False)
file_menu.add_command(
    label="Select file...",
    command=callbacks['file->open'])
```

Our first command in the file menu is `Select file...`. Notice the ellipses in the label: this indicates to the user that the option will open another window that will require further input. We're setting `command` to a reference from our `callbacks` dictionary using the `file->open` key. This function doesn't exist yet; we'll implement it shortly. Let's add our next file menu command, `file->quit`:

```
file_menu.add_separator()
file_menu.add_command(label="Quit",
        command=callbacks['file->quit'])
```

Once again, we've pointed this command to an as yet undefined function in our `callbacks` dictionary. We've also added a separator; since quitting the program is a fundamentally different sort of operation from selecting a target file, it makes sense to separate them, and you'll see this in most application menus.

3. This completes the file menu, so we need to add it to the main `menu` object as follows:

```
self.add_cascade(label='File', menu=file_menu)
```

4. The next submenu we need to create is our `options` menu. Since we only have two menu options, we'll just add them directly to the submenu as `Checkbutton`. The option menu looks as follows:

```
options_menu = tk.Menu(self, tearoff=False)
options_menu.add_checkbutton(label='Autofill Date',
    variable=settings['autofill date'])
options_menu.add_checkbutton(label='Autofill Sheet data',
    variable=settings['autofill sheet data'])
self.add_cascade(label='Options', menu=options_menu)
```

   The variables bound to these `Checkbutton` widgets are in the `settings` dictionary, so our `Application` class will populate `settings` with two `BooleanVar` variables: `autofill date` and `autofill sheet data`.

5. Last of all, we'll create a `help` menu, featuring an option to show an `About` dialog:

```
help_menu = tk.Menu(self, tearoff=False)
help_menu.add_command(label='About...', command=self.show_about)
self.add_cascade(label='Help', menu=help_menu)
```

   Our `About` command points to an internal `MainMenu` method called `show_about`, which we'll implement next. The `About` dialog is going to be pure UI code with no actual application functionality in it, so we can implement it entirely within the view.

Showing an About dialog

We've already seen how to use `messagebox` to create error dialogs. Now, we can apply that knowledge to create our `About` box by performing the following steps:

1. Start a new method definition after `__init__()`:

```
def show_about(self):
    """Show the about dialog"""
```

2. The `About` dialog can show any information you feel is relevant, including your contact information, support information, version information, or even the entire `README` file. In our case, we'll keep it fairly short. Let's specify the `message` header text and `detail` body text:

```
about_message = 'ABQ Data Entry'
about_detail = ('by Alan D Moore\n'
    'For assistance please contact the author.')
```

We're just using the application name for the header, and a short message about our name and who to contact for support for the detail. Feel free to put whatever text you wish in your `About` box.

There are several ways you can deal with long, multiline strings in Python code; the approach used here is to place multiple strings between parenthesis with only whitespace between them. Python automatically concatenates strings separated by only whitespace, so to Python this looks like a single long string inside a set of parentheses. In contrast to other methods, such as triple-quoting, this allows you to maintain clean indents and control new lines explicitly.

3. Finally, we need to display our `About` box as follows:

```
messagebox.showinfo(title='About', message=about_message,
    detail=about_detail)
```

In the preceding code, the `showinfo()` function is clearly the most appropriate, since we are in fact showing information. This finishes our `show_about()` method and our `MainMenu` class. Next, we need to make the necessary modifications to `Application` to make it work.

Adding the menu functionality in the controller

Now that our menu class is defined, our `Application` object needs to create an instance and add it into the main window. Before we can do that, we'll need to define some things that our `MainMenu` class needs.

Remember the following things from the previous section:

- We need a `settings` dictionary that contains Tkinter variables for our two settings options
- We need a `callbacks` dictionary that points to callbacks for `file->select` and `file->quit`
- We need the actual functions that implement file selection and quitting

Let's define some things that our `MainMenu` class needs.

Open `application.py` and let's start adding code just before the creation of `self.recordform`:

```
        self.settings = {
            'autofill date': tk.BooleanVar(),
            'autofill sheet data': tk.BooleanVar()
        }
```

This will be our global settings dictionary that stores the boolean variables for our two configuration options. Next, we'll create the `callbacks` dictionary:

```
        self.callbacks = {
            'file->select': self.on_file_select,
            'file->quit': self.quit
        }
```

Here, we're pointing our two callbacks to the methods of the `Application` class that will implement the functionality. Fortunately for us, Tkinter already implements `self.quit`, which does exactly what you'd expect it to do, so we only need to implement `on_file_select` ourselves. We will finish up here by creating our `menu` object and add it to the application as follows:

```
            menu = v.MainMenu(self, self.settings, self.callbacks)
            self.config(menu=menu)
```

Handling file selection

When a user needs to enter a file or directory path, the preferred way to do this is to display a dialog containing a miniature file browser, commonly called a file dialog. Like most toolkits, Tkinter provides us with dialogs for opening files, saving files, and selecting a directory. These are all part of the `filedialog` module.

Just like `messagebox`, `filedialog` is a Tkinter submodule that needs to be explicitly imported to be used. Also like `messagebox`, it contains a set of convenience functions that create file dialogs that are appropriate for different scenarios.

The following table lists the functions, what they return, and their UI features:

Function	Return value	Features
`askdirectory`	Directory path as string	Only shows directories, no files
`askopenfile`	File handle object	Only allows selection of existing files
`askopenfilename`	File path as string	Only allows selection of existing files
`askopenfilenames`	File paths as list of strings	Like `askopenfilename`, but allows multiple selections
`askopenfiles`	List of file handle objects	Like `askopenfile`, but allows multiple selections
`asksaveasfile`	File handle object	Allows creation of new files, prompts for confirmation on existing files
`asksaveasfilename`	File path as string	Allows creation of new files, prompts for confirmation on existing files

As you can see, each file selection dialog comes in two versions: one that returns a path as a string, and one that returns an open file object.

Each function can take the following common arguments:

- `title`: This argument specifies the dialog window title.
- `parent`: This argument specifies the (optional) `parent` widget. The file dialog will appear over this widget.
- `initialdir`: This argument is the directory in which the file browser should start.

- `filetypes`: This argument is a list of tuples, each with a label and matching pattern, which will be used to create files of the filter drop-down type typically seen under the filename entry. This is used to filter the visible files to only those supported by the application.

The `asksaveasfile` and `asksaveasfilename` methods take the following two additional options:

- `initialfile`: This option is a default file path to select
- `defaultextension`: This option is a file extension string that will be automatically appended to the filename if the user doesn't do it

Finally, the methods that return a file object take a `mode` argument that specifies the file-open mode; these are the same one- or two-character strings used by Python's `open` built-in function.

Which dialog do we need to use in our application? Let's consider our needs:

- We need a dialog that allows us to select an existing file
- We also need to be able to create a new file
- Since opening the file is the responsibility of the model, we just want to get a filename to pass to the model

These requirements clearly point to the `asksaveasfilename` function. Let's take a look at the following steps:

1. Start a new method on the `Application` object:

```
def on_file_select(self):
"""Handle the file->select action from the menu"""

filename = filedialog.asksaveasfilename(
    title='Select the target file for saving records',
    defaultextension='.csv',
    filetypes=[('Comma-Separated Values', '*.csv *.CSV')])
```

   The method first asks the user to select a file with a `.csv` extension; using the `filetypes` argument, the selection of existing files will be limited to those ending in `.csv` or CSV. When the dialog exits, the function will return the path to the selected file as a string to `filename`. Somehow, we have to get this path to our model.

2. Currently, the filename is generated in the `Application` object's `on_save` method and passed into the model. We need to move `filename` to a property of the `Application` object so that we can override it from our `on_file_select()` method.
3. Back in the `__init__()` method, add the following code line before the `settings` and `callbacks` definitions:

```
self.filename = tk.StringVar()
```

4. The `self.filename` property will keep track of the currently selected save file. Previously, we set up our hardcoded filename inside the `on_save()` method; there's no good reason to keep doing this every time `on_save()` is called, particularly since we're only using it if the user hasn't selected a file otherwise. Instead, move those lines from `on_save()` to just above the `self.filename` definition:

```
datestring = datetime.today().strftime("%Y-%m-%d")
default_filename = "abq_data_record_{}.csv".
format(datestring)
self.filename = tk.StringVar(value=default_filename)
```

5. With the default filename defined, we can supply it as a default value for `StringVar`. The value will be updated by `on_file_select()` whenever the user selects a filename. This is accomplished by the following lines at the end of `on_file_select()`:

```
if filename:
    self.filename.set(filename)
```

6. The reason for the `if` statement is that we only want to set a value if a file was actually selected by the user. Remember that the file dialogs will return `None` if the user cancels the operation; in this case, a user would expect that the currently set filename will remain the target.
7. Lastly, we need to make our `on_save()` method use this value when it's set instead of the hardcoded default.
8. Down in the `on_save()` method, locate the line where `filename` is defined and change it to the following line:

```
filename = self.filename.get()
```

9. That completes the code changes to make filename selection work. At this point, you should be able to run the application and test out the file selection functionality. Save a few records and note that they indeed save to the file you selected.

Making our settings work

While the file saving works, the settings do not. The `settings` menu items should work as expected, remaining checked or unchecked, but they don't yet change the behavior of the data entry form. Let's make this work.

Recall that both autofill features are implemented in the `DataRecordForm` class's `reset()` method. To use our new settings, we need to give our form access to the `settings` dictionary by performing the following steps:

1. Open `views.py` and update the `DataRecordForm.__init__()` method as follows:

```
def __init__(self, parent, fields, settings, *args, **kwargs):
    super().__init__(parent, *args, **kwargs)
    self.settings = settings
```

2. We've added an additional positional argument, `settings`, and then set that to `self.settings` so that all of the methods in the class can access it. Now, look at the `reset()` method; currently, the date autofill code is as follows:

```
current_date = datetime.today().strftime('%Y-%m-%d')
self.inputs['Date'].set(current_date)
self.inputs['Time'].input.focus()
```

3. We just need to make sure this happens only when `settings['autofill date']` is `True`:

```
if self.settings['autofill date'].get():
    current_date = datetime.today().strftime('%Y-%m-%d')
    self.inputs['Date'].set(current_date)
    self.inputs['Time'].input.focus()
```

Autofilling the sheet data is already under a conditional statement, as you can see here:

```
if plot not in ('', plot_values[-1]):
    self.inputs['Lab'].set(lab)
    self.inputs['Time'].set(time)
   ...
```

4. To make the setting effective, we just need to add another condition to the `if` statement:

```
if (self.settings['autofill sheet data'].get() and
    plot not in ('', plot_values[-1])):
    ...
```

The last piece of the puzzle is to make sure we're sending our `settings` dictionary to `DataRecordForm` when it's created.

5. Back in the `Application` code, update our call to `DataRecordForm()` to include `self.settings` as follows:

```
self.recordform = v.DataRecordForm(self,
    m.CSVModel.fields, self.settings)
```

6. Now, if you run the program, you should find that the settings are respected; try checking and unchecking them and see what happens after you save a record.

Persisting settings

Our settings work, but there's a major annoyance: they don't persist between sessions. Shut down the application and start it up again, and you'll see that the settings are back to their defaults. It's not a major problem, but it's a rough edge we shouldn't leave for our users.

Python gives us a variety of ways to persist data in files. We've already experienced CSV, which is designed for tabular data; there are other formats designed with different capabilities in mind.

The following table shows just a few of the options for storing data available in the Python standard library:

Library	Data type	Suitable	Benefits	Drawbacks
`pickle`	Binary	Any kind of object	Fast, easy, small files	Not safe, files aren't human-readable, whole file has to be read
`configparser`	Text	`key->value` pairs	Fast, easy, human-readable files	Can't handle sequences or complex objects, limited heirarchy
`json`	Text	Simple values and sequences	Widely used, easy, human-readable files	Can't serialize complex objects without modification
`xml`	Text	Any kind of Python object	Powerful, flexible, mostly human-readable files	Not safe, complex to use, verbose file syntax
`sqlite`	Binary	Relational data	Fast and powerful files	Requires SQL knowledge, objects must be translated to tables

If this weren't enough, there are even more options available in the third-party libraries. Almost any of them would be suitable for storing a couple of boolean values, so how do we choose?

- SQL and XML are powerful, but far too complex for our simple needs here.
- We'd like to stick to a text format in case we need to debug a corrupt settings file, so `pickle` is out.
- `configparser` would work now, but its inability to handle lists, tuples, and dictionaries may be limiting in the future.
- That leaves `json`, which is a good option. While it can't handle every kind of Python object, it can handle strings, numbers, and booleans, as well as lists and dictionaries. That should cover our configuration needs just fine.

What does it mean when we say that a library is "not safe"? Some data formats are designed with powerful capabilities, such as extensibility, linking, or aliasing, which parser libraries must implement. Unfortunately, those capabilities can be exploited for malicious purposes. For example, the billion laughs XML vulnerability combines three XML capabilities to craft a file that, when parsed, expands to a massive size (usually causing the program or, in some cases, the system, to crash).

Building a model for settings persistence

As with any kind of data persistence, we need to start by implementing a model. As with our CSVModel class, the settings model needs to save and load the data, as well as define the layout of the settings data.

In the models.py file, let's start a new class as follows:

```
class SettingsModel:
    """A model for saving settings"""
```

Just as we did with our CSVModel class, we'll need to define our model's schema:

```
    variables = {
        'autofill date': {'type': 'bool', 'value': True},
        'autofill sheet data': {'type': 'bool', 'value': True}
     }
```

The variables dictionary will store both the schema and the values for each item. Each setting has a dictionary listing the data type and default value (we could list other attributes here if they are needed, such as minimum, maximum, or possible values). The variables dictionary will be the data structure we save to disk and load from disk to persist the program's settings.

The model needs a location to save the configuration file too, so our constructor will take the filename and path as arguments. For now, we'll just provide and use reasonable defaults, but in the future we may want to change these.

We can't just provide a single file path, though; we have different users on the same computer who will want to save different settings. We need to make sure that the settings are saved in the individual user's home directory rather than a single common location.

Therefore, our __init__() method is as follows:

```
    def __init__(self, filename='abq_settings.json', path='~'):
        # determine the file path
        self.filepath = os.path.join(
            os.path.expanduser(path), filename)
```

As users of the Linux or macOS Terminal will know, the ~ symbol is a Unix shortcut that points to the user's home directory. Python's `os.path.expanduser()` function translates this character into an absolute path (even on Windows), so that the file will be saved in the home directory of the user running the program. `os.path.join()` appends the filename to the expanded path, giving us a full path to a user-specific configuration file.

As soon as the model is created, we'll want to load the user's saved options from disk. Loading data from disk is a pretty basic model operation that we should be able to control outside the class, so we'll make this a public method.

We'll call this method `load()`, and call it here:

```
        self.load()
```

`load()` will expect to find a JSON file containing a dictionary in the same format as the `variables` dictionary. It will need to load that data from the file and replace its own copy of `variables` from the file copy.

A simplistic implementation is as follows:

```
    def load(self):
        """Load the settings from the file"""

        with open(self.filepath, 'r') as fh:
            self.variables = json.loads(fh.read())
```

The `json.loads()` function reads in a JSON string and converts it to a Python object, which we're saving directly to our `variables` dictionary. Of course, there are some problems with this method. First of all, what happens if the settings file doesn't exist? In that case, `open` will throw an exception and the program will crash. Not good!

So, before we try to open the file, let's test to see if it exists as follows:

```
        # if the file doesn't exist, return
        if not os.path.exists(self.filepath):
            return
```

If the file doesn't exist, the method simply returns and does nothing. It's perfectly reasonable for the file not to exist, especially if the user has never run the program or edited any of the settings. In this case, the method would leave `self.variables` alone and the user would end up with the defaults.

The second problem is that our settings file might exist, but contain no data or invalid data (such as keys not present in the variables dictionary), resulting in a crash. To prevent this, we'll pull in the JSON data to a local variable; we'll then update variables by asking raw_values for only those keys that exist in variables, providing a default value if they aren't present.

The new, safer code is as follows:

```
        # open the file and read in the raw values
        with open(self.filepath, 'r') as fh:
            raw_values = json.loads(fh.read())

        # don't implicitly trust the raw values,
        # but only get known keys
        for key in self.variables:
            if key in raw_values and 'value' in raw_values[key]:
                raw_value = raw_values[key]['value']
                self.variables[key]['value'] = raw_value
```

Since variables is created with default values already in place, we just need to ignore raw_values if it doesn't have a given key or if the dictionary in that key doesn't contain a values item.

Now that load() is written, let's write a save() method to write our values to the file:

```
    def save(self, settings=None):
        json_string = json.dumps(self.variables)
        with open(self.filepath, 'w') as fh:
            fh.write(json_string)
```

The json.dumps() function is the inverse of loads(): it takes a Python object and returns a JSON string. Saving our settings data is as simple as converting the variables dictionary to a string and writing it to the specified text file.

The final method our model needs is a way for external code to set values; they could manipulate variables directly, but in the interest of protecting our data integrity, we'll do it through a method call. Keeping with Tkinter convention, we'll call this method set().

A basic implementation of the set() method is as follows:

```
    def set(self, key, value):
        self.variables[key]['value'] = value
```

This simple method just takes a key and value and writes them to the `variables` dictionary. Once again, though, this opens up some potential problems; what if the value provided isn't valid for the data type? What if the key isn't in our `variables` dictionary? This could create a situation that would be hard to debug, so our `set()` method should safeguard against this.

Change the code as follows:

```
        if (
            key in self.variables and
            type(value).__name__ == self.variables[key]['type']
        ):
            self.variables[key]['value'] = value
```

By using the `type` strings that correspond to the names of actual Python types, we can match it against the value's type name using `type(value).__name__` (we could have used the actual type objects themselves in our `variables` dictionary, but those can't be serialized to JSON). Now, an attempt to write an unknown key or incorrect variable type will fail.

However, we shouldn't let it fail silently; we should immediately raise `ValueError` to alert us to the problem as follows:

```
        else:
            raise ValueError("Bad key or wrong variable type")
```

Why raise an exception? If the test fails, it can only mean a bug in the calling code. With an exception, we'll know immediately if calling code is sending bad requests to our model. Without it, requests would fail silently, leaving a hard-to-find bug.

The idea of raising an exception on purpose often seems strange to beginners; after all, exceptions are something we're trying to avoid, right? This is true in the case of small scripts where we're mainly users of existing modules; when writing your own module, however, exceptions are the correct way for your module to communicate problems to the code using it. Trying to handle—or worse, silence—bad behavior by external calling code will, at best, break modularity; at worst, it will create subtle bugs that are difficult to track down.

Using the settings model in our application

Our application needs to load in the settings when it starts, then save them automatically whenever they are changed. Currently, the application's `settings` dictionary is created manually, but our model should really be telling it what kind of variables to create. Let's perform the following steps for using the `settings` model in our application:

1. Replace the code that defines `Application.settings` with the following code:

```
self.settings_model = m.SettingsModel()
self.load_settings()
```

   First, we create a `settings` model and save it to our `Application` object. Then, we're going to run a `load_settings()` method. This method will be responsible for setting up the `Application.settings` dictionary based on `settings_model`.

2. Now, let's create `Application.load_settings()`:

```
def load_settings(self):
    """Load settings into our self.settings dict."""
```

3. Our model stores the type and value for each variable, but our application needs Tkinter variables. We need a way to translate the model's representation of the data into a structure that `Application` can use. A dictionary provides a handy way to do this as follows:

```
vartypes = {
    'bool': tk.BooleanVar,
    'str': tk.StringVar,
    'int': tk.IntVar,
   'float': tk.DoubleVar
}
```

Notice that each name matches the type name of a Python built-in function. We could add more entries here, but this should cover most of our future needs. Now, we can combine this dictionary with the model's `variables` dictionary to construct the `settings` dictionary:

```
        self.settings = {}
        for key, data in
self.settings_model.variables.items():
            vartype = vartypes.get(data['type'], tk.StringVar)
            self.settings[key] = vartype(value=data['value'])
```

4. The main reason for using Tkinter variables here is so that we can trace any changes the user makes to the values via the UI and respond immediately. Specifically, we want to save our settings whenever the user makes a change as follows:

```
        for var in self.settings.values():
            var.trace('w', self.save_settings)
```

5. Of course, this means we need to write a method called `Application.save_settings()`, which will run whenever the values are changed. `Application.load_settings()` is complete, so let's do that next:

```
    def save_settings(self, *args):
        """Save the current settings to a preferences file"""
```

6. The `save_settings()` method just needs to get the data back from `Application.settings` to the model and then save it:

```
        for key, variable in self.settings.items():
            self.settings_model.set(key, variable.get())
        self.settings_model.save()
```

It's as simple as looping through `self.settings` and calling our model's `set()` method to pull in the values one at a time. Then, we call the model's `save()` method.

7. Now, you should be able to run the program and observe that the settings are saved, even when you close and re-open the application. You'll also find a file in your home directory called `abq_settings.json`.

Summary

In this chapter, our simple form has taken a big step forward towards being a fully-blown application. We've implemented a main menu, option settings that are persisted between executions, and an `About` dialog. We've added the ability to select a file where records are saved, and improved the visibility of form errors with an error dialog. Along the way, you learned about Tkinter menus, file dialogs, and message boxes, as well as the various options for persisting data in the standard library.

In the next chapter, we're going to be asked to make the program read and write. We'll learn about Tkinter's tree widget, how to switch between main views, and how to make our `CSVModel` and `DataRecordForm` classes capable of reading and updating existing data.

7
Navigating Records with Treeview

You've received another request for features in the application. Now that your users can open arbitrary files, they'd like to be able to see what's in those files and correct old records using the data entry form they've grown accustomed to, rather than having to switch over to a spreadsheet. In a nutshell, it's finally time to implement read and update capabilities in our application.

In this chapter, we're going to cover the following topics:

- Modifying our CSV model for read and update capabilities
- Discovering the ttk `Treeview` widget, and building a list of records with it
- Implementing record loading and updating in our data record form
- Redesigning the menu and application with read and update in mind

Implementing read and update in the model

Our entire design up to this point has been centered around a form that only appends data to a file; adding read and update capabilities is a fundamental change that will touch nearly every portion of the application. It may seem like a daunting task, but by taking it one component at a time, we'll see that the changes are not so overwhelming.

The first thing we should do is update our documentation, starting with the `Requirements` section:

```
The program must:

* Provide a UI for reading, updating, and appending data to the CSV
file
* ...
```

And, of course, also update the part that is not required that follows:

```
The program does not need to:

* Allow deletion of data.
```

Now, it's a simple matter of making the code match with the documentation.

Adding read and update to our model

Open `models.py` and consider what's missing from the `CSVModel` class:

- We'll need a method that can retrieve all records in a file so we can display them. We'll call it `get_all_records()`.
- We'll need a method to fetch individual records from the file by row number. We can call this `get_record()`.
- We'll need to save records in a way that can not only append new records, but update existing records as well. We can update our `save_record()` method to accommodate this.

Implementing get_all_records()

Start a new method called `get_all_records()`:

```
    def get_all_records(self):
        if not os.path.exists(self.filename):
            return []
```

The first thing we've done is check if the model's file exists yet. Remember that when our application starts, it generates a default filename pointing to a file that likely doesn't exist yet, so `get_all_records()` will need to handle this situation gracefully. It makes sense to return an empty list in this case, since there's no data if the file doesn't exist.

If the file does exist, let's open it in read-only mode and get all the records:

```
        with open(self.filename, 'r') as fh:
            csvreader = csv.DictReader(fh)
            records = list(csvreader)
```

While not terribly efficient, pulling the entire file into memory and converting it into a list is acceptable in our case, since we know that our largest files should be limited to a mere 401 rows: 20 plots times 5 labs plus a header row. This code is just a little too trusting, however. We should at least do some sanity checks to make sure that the user has actually opened a CSV file containing the proper fields and not some other arbitrary file.

Let's check that the file has the correct field structure:

```
        csvreader = csv.DictReader(fh)
        missing_fields = (set(self.fields.keys()) -
                          set(csvreader.fieldnames))
        if len(missing_fields) > 0:
            raise Exception(
                "File is missing fields: {}"
                .format(', '.join(missing_fields))
            )
        else:
            records = list(csvreader)
```

Here, we first find any missing fields by converting a list of our `fields` dictionary `keys` and the CSV file's `fieldnames` to Python `set` objects. We can subtract the `fieldnames` set from `keys` and determine which fields, if any, are missing in the file. If there are any, we'll raise an exception; otherwise, we convert the CSV data to `list`.

Python `set` objects are very useful for comparing the content of the `list`, `tuple`, and other sequence objects. They provide an easy way to get information such as the difference (items in `x` that are not in `y`) or intersection (items in both `x` and `y`) between two sets, or allow you to compare sequences without respect to order.

Before we can return the `records` list, we need to correct one issue; all data in a CSV file is stored as text, and read by Python as a string. Most of this is not a problem, since Tkinter will take care of converting strings to `float` or `int` as necessary, but `bool` values are stored in the CSV file as the strings `True` and `False`, and coercing these values directly back to `bool` doesn't work. `False` is a non-empty string, and all non-empty strings evaluate to `True` in Python.

To fix this, let's first define a list of strings that should be interpreted as `True`:

```
trues = ('true', 'yes', '1')
```

Any values not in this list will be considered `False`. We'll do a case-insensitive comparison, so there are only lowercase values in our list.

Next, we create a list of fields that are `boolean` fields using a list comprehension as follows:

```
bool_fields = [
    key for key, meta
    in self.fields.items()
    if meta['type'] == FT.boolean]
```

We know that `Equipment Fault` is our only boolean field, so technically we could just hardcode that here, but it's a good idea to design your model so that any changes to the schema will be automatically handled appropriately by the logic portions.

Now, let's check these boolean fields in each row by adding the following code:

```
for record in records:
    for key in bool_fields:
        record[key] = record[key].lower() in trues
```

For every record, we iterate through our list of the boolean fields and check its value against our list of truthy strings, setting the value of the item accordingly.

With the boolean values fixed, we can return our `records` list as follows:

```
return records
```

Implementing get_record()

Our get_record() method needs to take a row number and return a single dictionary containing the data for that row.

This is pretty simple if we leverage our get_all_records() method as follows:

```
def get_record(self, rownum):
    return self.get_all_records()[rownum]
```

Since our files are small and there's very little overhead to pulling all the records, we can simply do that and then dereference the record we need.

Keep in mind that it's possible to pass rownum that doesn't exist in our records list; in this case, we'd get IndexError; our calling code will need to catch this error and deal with it appropriately.

Adding update to save_record()

To convert our save_record() method so that we can update records, the first thing we'll need to do is provide the ability to pass in a row number to update. The default will be None, which will indicate that the data is a new row that should be appended.

The new method signature looks like this:

```
def save_record(self, data, rownum=None):
    """Save a dict of data to the CSV file"""
```

Our existing logic doesn't need to change, but it should only be run if rownum is None.

So, the first thing to do in the method is check rownum:

```
if rownum is not None:
    # This is an update, new code here
else:
    # Old code goes here, indented one more level
```

For relatively small files, the simplest way to update a single row is to load the entire file into a list, change the row in the list, and then write the entire list back to a clean file.

Under the `if` block, we'll add the following code:

```
records = self.get_all_records()
records[rownum] = data
with open(self.filename, 'w') as fh:
    csvwriter = csv.DictWriter(fh,
        fieldnames=self.fields.keys())
    csvwriter.writeheader()
    csvwriter.writerows(records)
```

Once again, we leverage our `get_all_records()` method to fetch the CSV file's content into a list. We then replace the dictionary in the requested row with the `data` dictionary provided. Finally, we open the file in write mode (`w`), which will clear its content and replace it with whatever we write to the file, and write the header and all records back to the file.

The approach we're taking makes it unsafe for two users to work in the save CSV file simultaneously. Creating software that allows for multiple users editing a single file is notoriously difficult, and many programs simply opt to prevent it in the first place using lock files or other protection mechanisms.

This method is finished, and that's all we need to change in our model to enable updating and viewing. Now, it's time to add the necessary features to our GUI.

Implementing a record list view

The record list view will allow our users to browse the content of the file and open records for viewing or editing. Our users are accustomed to seeing this data in a spreadsheet, laid out in a table-like format, so it makes sense to design our view in a similar fashion. Since our view mainly exists for finding and selecting individual records, we don't need to display all the information; just enough for the users to distinguish one record from another.

A quick analysis shows that we need CSV row number, `Date`, `Time`, `Lab`, and `Plot`.

For building table-like views with selectable rows, Tkinter gives us the ttk `Treeview` widget. To build our record list view, we'll need to learn about `Treeview`.

The ttk Treeview

The `Treeview` is a ttk widget designed to show columns of data in a hierarchical structure.

Perhaps the best example of this kind of data is a filesystem tree:

- Each row can represent a file or directory
- Each directory can contain additional files or directories
- Each row can have additional data properties, such as permissions, size, or ownership information

To explore how `Treeview` works, we'll create a simple file browser with some help from `pathlib`.

In previous chapters, we used `os.path` to work with file paths. `pathlib` is a new addition to the Python 3 standard library that provides a more object-oriented approach to paths.

Open a new file called `treeview_demo.py` and start with this template:

```
import tkinter as tk
from tkinter import ttk
from pathlib import Path

root = tk.Tk()
# Code will go here

root.mainloop()
```

We'll start by getting a list of all the file paths under the current working directory. `Path` has a method called `glob` that will give us such a list as follows:

```
paths = Path('.').glob('**/*')
```

`glob()` expands wildcard characters like `*` and `?` against a filesystem tree. The name goes back to a very early Unix command, though the same wildcard syntax is now used across most modern operating systems.

`Path('.')` creates a path object referencing the current working directory, and `**/*` is a special wildcard syntax that recursively grabs all objects under the path. The result is a list of the `Path` objects that include every directory and file under our current directory.

With that done, we can create and configure our `Treeview` widget by executing the following code:

```
tv = ttk.Treeview(root, columns=['size', 'modified'],
                  selectmode='None')
```

Like any Tkinter widget, the first argument to `Treeview` is its `parent` widget. Each column in the `Treeview` widget is given an identifying string; by default, there is always one column named `"#0"`. This column represents the basic identifying information about each item in the tree, such as a name or ID number. To add more columns, we specify them using the `columns` argument. This list contains any number of strings that will be used to identify the subsequent columns.

Finally, we set `selectmode`, which determines how users can select items in the tree.

The following table shows the options for `selectmode`:

Value	Behavior
`selectmode`	Selections can be made
`none` (as a string, not the `None` object)	No selections can be made
`browse`	User can select one item only
`extended`	User can select multiple items

In this case, we're preventing selection, so we set it to `none`.

To show how we use the column names, we'll set some headings for the columns:

```
tv.heading('#0', text='Name')
tv.heading('size', text='Size', anchor='center')
tv.heading('modified', text='Modified', anchor='e')
```

The `Treeview` heading method is for manipulating the column `heading` widget; it takes the column name, and then any number of attributes you want to assign to the column's `heading` widget.

Those attributes can include:

- `text`: The text displayed for the heading. By default, it's blank.
- `anchor`: The alignment of the text; it can be any of eight cardinal directions or `center`, specified as strings or Tkinter constants.
- `command`: A command to run when the heading is clicked. This might be used to order the rows by that column, or select all the values in the column, for example.
- `image`: An image to display in the heading.

Finally, we pack the column into the `root` widget and expand it to fill the widget:

```
tv.pack(expand=True, fill='both')
```

In addition to configuring the headers, we can configure some attributes of the column itself using the `Treeview.column` method.

For example, we can add the following code:

```
tv.column('#0', stretch=True)
tv.column('size', width=200)
```

In this example, we've set `stretch` to `True` in the first column, which will cause it to expand to fill available; and we've set the `width` value on the `size` column to `200` pixels.

The column parameters that can be set include:

- `stretch`: Whether or not to expand this column to fill the available space.
- `width`: The width of the column in pixels.
- `minwidth`: The minimum width to which the column can be resized, in pixels.
- `anchor`: The alignment of the text in the column. Can be any of eight cardinal directions or center, specified as strings or Tkinter constants.

With the tree view configured, it now needs to be filled with data. Populating a `Treeview` with data is done one row at a time using the `insert` method.

The `insert` method looks like this:

```
mytreeview.insert(parent, 'end', iid='item1',
          text='My Item 1', values=['12', '42'])
```

The first argument specifies the `parent` item for the inserted row. This is not the `parent` widget, but rather the `parent` row under which the inserted row belongs in the hierarchical structure. The value is a string that refers to the `iid` of the `parent` item. For top-level items, this value should be an empty string.

The next argument specifies where the item should be inserted. It's either a numerical index or `end`, which places the item at the end of the list.

After this, we specify keyword arguments, which can include:

- `text`: This is the value to be shown in the first column.
- `values`: This is a list of values for the remaining columns.
- `image`: This is an image object to display in the far left of the column.
- `iid`: The item ID string. This will be automatically assigned if you don't specify it.
- `open`: Whether or not the row is open (displaying child items) at the start.
- `tags`: A list of tag strings.

To insert our paths into the `Treeview`, let's iterate our `paths` list as follows:

```
for path in paths:
    meta = path.stat()
    parent = str(path.parent)
    if parent == '.':
        parent = ''
```

Before calling `insert`, we need to extract and prepare some data from the path object. `path.stat()` will give us an object containing various file information. `path.parent` provides us the containing path; however, we need to change the name of the `root` path (currently a single dot) to an empty string, which is how `Treeview` represents the `root` node.

Now, we add the `insert` call as follows:

```
        tv.insert(parent, 'end', iid=str(path),
            text=str(path.name), values=[meta.st_size, meta.st_mtime])
```

By using the path string as the item ID, we can then specify it as a parent for its child objects. We use only the object `name` (without the containing path) as our display value, then `st_size` and `st_mtime` for populating the size and modification time columns.

Run this script and you should see a simple file tree browser that looks something like this:

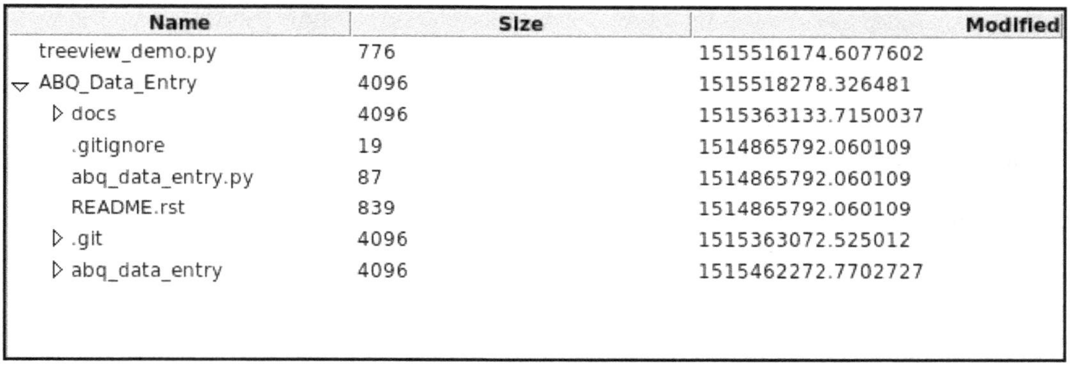

Name	Size	Modified
treeview_demo.py	776	1515516174.6077602
▽ ABQ_Data_Entry	4096	1515518278.326481
▷ docs	4096	1515363133.7150037
.gitignore	19	1514865792.060109
abq_data_entry.py	87	1514865792.060109
README.rst	839	1514865792.060109
▷ .git	4096	1515363072.525012
▷ abq_data_entry	4096	1515462272.7702727

The `Treeview` widgets doesn't offer any kind of sorting functionality by default, but we can add it fairly easily.

First, let's create a sorting function by adding the following code:

```
def sort(tv, col):
    itemlist = list(tv.get_children(''))
    itemlist.sort(key=lambda x: tv.set(x, col))
    for index, iid in enumerate(itemlist):
        tv.move(iid, tv.parent(iid), index)
```

In the preceding code snippet, the `sort` function takes a `Treeview` widget and the ID of a column in which we'll sort. It starts by getting a list of all the `iid` values using the `get_children()` method of `Treeview`. Next, it sorts the various `iid` values using the value of `col` for each item as a key; rather confusingly, the `set()` method of `Treeview` is used to retrieve the value of the column (there is no `get()` method). Finally, we iterate the list and use the `move()` method to move each item to a new index under its parent (which is retrieved using the `parent()` method).

To make our columns sortable, add this function as a callback to the headers using the `command` argument as follows:

```
tv.heading('#0', text='Name', command=lambda: sort(tv, '#0'))
tv.heading('size', text='Size', anchor='center',
           command=lambda: sort(tv, 'size'))
tv.heading('modified', text='Modified', anchor='e',
           command=lambda: sort(tv, 'modified'))
```

Implementing our record list with Treeview

Now that we understand how to use the `Treeview` widget, let's start building our record list widget.

We'll begin by subclassing `tkinter.Frame`, just as we did with our record form:

```
class RecordList(tk.Frame):
    """Display for CSV file contents"""
```

To save ourselves from some repetitious code, we'll define our column properties and defaults in class constants. This also makes it easier to tweak them to suit our needs.

Start out your class with the following properties:

```
    column_defs = {
        '#0': {'label': 'Row', 'anchor': tk.W},
        'Date': {'label': 'Date', 'width': 150, 'stretch': True},
        'Time': {'label': 'Time'},
        'Lab': {'label': 'Lab', 'width': 40},
        'Plot': {'label': 'Plot', 'width': 80}
        }
    default_width = 100
    default_minwidth = 10
    default_anchor = tk.CENTER
```

Recall that we're going to be displaying `Date`, `Time`, `Lab`, and `Plot`. For the first default column, we'll show the CSV row number. We've also set the `width` and `anchor` values for some columns, and configured the `Date` field to stretch. We'll use these values when configuring the `Treeview` widget in `__init__()`.

Let's start our `__init__()` definition as follows:

```
def __init__(self, parent, callbacks, *args, **kwargs):
    super().__init__(parent, *args, **kwargs)
    self.callbacks = callbacks
```

As with other views, we're going to accept a dictionary of callback methods from the `Application` object, and save it as an instance property.

Configuring a Treeview widget

Now, let's create our `Treeview` widget by executing the following code snippet:

```
        self.treeview = ttk.Treeview(self,
            columns=list(self.column_defs.keys())[1:],
            selectmode='browse')
```

Note that we're excluding the `#0` column from our `columns` list; it should never be specified here since it's automatically created. We're also choosing the `browse` select mode, so that users can select individual rows of the CSV file.

Let's go ahead and add our `Treeview` widget to `RecordList` and make it fill the widget:

```
        self.columnconfigure(0, weight=1)
        self.rowconfigure(0, weight=1)
        self.treeview.grid(row=0, column=0, sticky='NSEW')
```

Now, configure the columns and headings of `Treeview` by iterating through the `column_defs` dictionary:

```
        for name, definition in self.column_defs.items():
```

For each set of items, let's extract the configuration values we need as follows:

```
            label = definition.get('label', '')
            anchor = definition.get('anchor', self.default_anchor)
            minwidth = definition.get(
                'minwidth', self.default_minwidth)
            width = definition.get('width', self.default_width)
            stretch = definition.get('stretch', False)
```

Finally, we'll use those values to configure the heading and columns:

```
self.treeview.heading(name, text=label, anchor=anchor)
self.treeview.column(name, anchor=anchor,
    minwidth=minwidth, width=width, stretch=stretch)
```

Adding a scrollbar

The ttk `Treeview` does not have a scrollbar by default; it *can* be scrolled, using the keyboard or mouse-wheel controls, but users would reasonably expect a scrollbar on a scrollable area to help them visualize the size of the list and their current position in it.

Fortunately, ttk provides us with a `Scrollbar` object that can be connected to our `Treeview` widget:

```
self.scrollbar = ttk.Scrollbar(self,
    orient=tk.VERTICAL, command=self.treeview.yview)
```

Here, `Scrollbar` takes the following two important arguments:

- `orient`: This argument determines whether it is a horizontal or vertical scroll
- `command`: This argument provides a callback for scrollbar move events

In this case, we set the callback to the tree view's `yview` method, which is used to make the `Treeview` scroll up and down. The other option would be `xview`, which would be used for horizontal scrolling.

We also need to connect our `Treeview` back to the scrollbar:

```
self.treeview.configure(yscrollcommand=self.scrollbar.set)
```

If we don't do this, our `Scrollbar` won't know how far down the list we've scrolled or how long the list is, and can't set the size or location of the bar widget appropriately.

With our `Scrollbar` configured, we need to place it on the widget—conventionally, just to the right of the widget being scrolled.

We can use our `grid` layout manager for this:

```
self.scrollbar.grid(row=0, column=1, sticky='NSW')
```

Notice we set sticky to north, south, and west. North and south make sure the scrollbar stretches the entire height of the widget, and west makes sure it's snug against the Treeview widget to the left of it.

Populating the Treeview

Now that we have our Treeview widget, we'll create a populate() method to populate it with data:

```
def populate(self, rows):
    """Clear the treeview & write the supplied data rows to it."""
```

The rows argument will take a list of the dict data types, such as what is returned from model. The idea is that the controller will fetch a list from the model and then pass it to this method.

Before refilling Treeview, we need to empty it:

```
for row in self.treeview.get_children():
    self.treeview.delete(row)
```

The get_children() method of Treeview returns a list of every row's iid. We're iterating this list, passing each iid to the Treeview.delete() method, which, as you'd expect, deletes the row.

With the Treeview cleared, we can iterate through the rows list and populate the table:

```
valuekeys = list(self.column_defs.keys())[1:]
for rownum, rowdata in enumerate(rows):
    values = [rowdata[key] for key in valuekeys]
    self.treeview.insert('', 'end', iid=str(rownum),
                         text=str(rownum), values=values)
```

The first thing we do here is create a list of all the keys we actually want to fetch from each row; this is just the list of keys from self.column_defs minus the "#0" column.

Next, we iterate through the rows using the enumerate() function to generate a row number. For each row, we'll create a list of values in the proper order using a list comprehension, then insert the list to the end of the Treeview widget with the insert() method. Notice that we're just using the row number (converted to a string) as both iid and text for the row.

The last thing we need to do in this function is a small usability tweak. To make our `Treeview` keyboard friendly, we need to focus the first item so that keyboard users can immediately start to navigate it via the arrow keys.

Doing this in a `Treeview` widget actually takes three method calls as follows:

```
if len(rows) > 0:
    self.treeview.focus_set()
    self.treeview.selection_set(0)
    self.treeview.focus('0')
```

First, `focus_set` moves focus to `Treeview`. Next, `selection_set(0)` selects the first record in the list. Finally, `focus('0')` focuses the row with `iid` of `0`. And, of course, we only do this if there are any rows at all.

Responding to record selection

The purpose of this widget is for users to select and open records; therefore, we need a way to do that. It would be nice to be able to trigger this from an event like a double-click or keyboard selection.

The `Treeview` widget has three special events which we can use to trigger a callback as shown in the following table:

Event string	Triggered when
`<<TreeviewSelect>>`	A row is selected, such as by clicking it with a mouse
`<<TreeviewOpen>>`	A row is opened by a double-click or by selecting it and hitting *Enter*
`<<TreeviewClose>>`	An open row is closed

`<<TreeviewOpen>>` sounds like the event we want; even though we're not using a hierarchical list, the user is still conceptually opening the record, and the triggering action (double-click) seems intuitive. We'll bind this event to a method that will open the selected record.

Add this code at the end of `__init__()`:

```
self.treeview.bind('<<TreeviewOpen>>', self.on_open_record)
```

The `on_open_record()` method is quite simple; add this code to the class:

```
    def on_open_record(self, *args):
        selected_id = self.treeview.selection()[0]
        self.callbacks['on_open_record'](selected_id)
```

It's as simple as retrieving the selected ID from `Treeview`, then calling a function provided by our controller in the `callbacks` dictionary with the selected ID. It will be up to the controller to do something appropriate here.

The `RecordList` class is now complete, but some of our other view classes need attention.

Modifying the record form for read and update

As long as we're editing views, we'll need to look at our `DataRecordForm` view and adjust it to make it capable of updating records.

Take a moment and consider the following changes we'll need to make:

- The form will need some way to load in a record provided by the controller.
- The form will need to keep track of what record it's editing, or if it's a new record.
- Our user will need some visual indication of what record is being edited.
- Our **Save** button is currently in the application. It doesn't really make sense in any context other than the form, so it should probably be part of the form.
- This means our form will need a callback to call when the save button is clicked. We'll need to provide it with a `callbacks` dictionary like we did with our other views.

Updating __init__()

Let's start working through these with our `__init__()` method:

```
def __init__(self, parent, fields,
             settings, callbacks, *args, **kwargs):
    self.callbacks = callbacks
```

We're adding a new argument, `callbacks`, and storing it as an instance property. This will give the controller a way to provide methods for the view to call.

Next, our `__init__()` method should set up a variable in which to store the current record:

```
        self.current_record = None
```

We'll use `None` to indicate that no record is loaded and the form is being used to create a new record. Otherwise, this value will be an integer referencing a row in the CSV data.

We could use a Tkinter variable here, but there's no real advantage in this case, and we wouldn't be able to use `None` as a value.

At the top of the form, before the first form fields, let's add a label that will keep track of which record we're editing:

```
        self.record_label = ttk.Label()
        self.record_label.grid(row=0, column=0)
```

We're placing this in row `0`, column `0`, but the first `LabelFrame` is also in that location. You'll need to go through each `LabelFrame` and increment the `row` value in its call to `grid`.

We'll make sure this label gets updated whenever a record is loaded into the form.

At the very end of the widget, after the `Notes` field, let's add our new **Save** button as follows:

```
        self.savebutton = ttk.Button(self,
            text="Save", command=self.callbacks["on_save"])
        self.savebutton.grid(sticky="e", row=5, padx=10)
```

The button will call an on_save() method from the callbacks dictionary when clicked. We'll need to make sure to provide this method when creating DataRecordForm in Application.

Adding a load_record() method

The last thing to add in our view is a method for loading in a new record. This method will need to set up our form with a given row number and data dictionary from the controller.

Let's call it load_record() as follows:

```
    def load_reccrd(self, rownum, data=None):
```

The first thing we should do is set the form's current_record value from the rownum provided:

```
        self.current_record = rownum
```

Recall that rownum could be None, indicating that this is a new record.

Let's check for that by executing the following code:

```
        if rownum is None:
            self.reset()
            self.record_label.config(text='New Record')
```

If we're going to be inserting a new record, we simply want to reset the form, then set the label to indicate that this is a new record.

Note that our if condition here checks specifically whether rownum is None; we can't just check the truth value of rownum, since 0 is a valid rownum for updating!

If we do have a valid rownum, we'll need it to act differently:

```
        else:
            self.record_label.config(text='Record #{}'.format(rownum))
            for key, widget in self.inputs.items():
                self.inputs[key].set(data.get(key, ''))
                try:
                    widget.input.trigger_focusout_validation()
                except AttributeError:
                    pass
```

In this block, we first set the label appropriately with the row number we're editing.

Then, we cycle through the keys and widgets of our `inputs` dictionary and pull in the matching values from the `data` dictionary. We also attempt to call the `trigger_focusout_validation()` method on each widget's input, since it's possible that the CSV file contains invalid data. If the input has no such method (that is, if we used a regular Tkinter widget rather than one of our custom ones, such as with `Checkbutton`), we just do nothing.

Updating the rest of the application

Before our changes to the form can take effect, we need to update the remaining portions of our application for the new functionality. Our main menu needs some navigation items so that users can switch between the record list and the form, and controller methods need to be created or updated in `Application` to bring together our new model and view functionality.

Main menu changes

Since we're already in the `views.py` file, let's start by updating our main menu view with some commands to switch between the record list and record form. We'll add a `Go` menu containing two more options to our menu that will allow switching between the record list and a blank record form.

Add the following lines between the `Options` and `Help` menus:

```
go_menu = tk.Menu(self, tearoff=False)
go_menu.add_command(label="Record List",
                    command=callbacks['show_recordlist'])
go_menu.add_command(label="New Record",
                    command=callbacks['new_record'])
self.add_cascade(label='Go', menu=go_menu)
```

As before, we're binding these menu commands to functions in the `callbacks` dictionary, which we'll need to add in our `Application` class.

Connecting the pieces in Application

Let's quickly take stock of the following changes we're going to need to make in our `Application` class:

- We need to add an instance of our `RecordList` view
- We'll need to update our use of `CSVModel` so that we can access data from it
- We'll need to implement or refactor several callback methods used by our views

Adding the RecordList view

We'll create the `RecordList` object in `__init__()`, just after `DataRecordForm`, by executing the following code snippet:

```
self.recordlist = v.RecordList(self, self.callbacks)
self.recordlist.grid(row=1, padx=10, sticky='NSEW')
```

Notice that when we call `grid()`, we're adding the `RecordList` view to the grid cell that already contains `DataRecordForm`. **This is intentional**. When we do this, Tkinter just stacks the second widget on top of the first, like laying one piece of paper on top of another; we'll add code in a moment to control which view is visible by raising one or the other to the top of the stack. Notice that we also stick the widget to all sides of the cell. Without this code, bits of one widget might be visible behind the other.

Similarly, we need to update the `grid` call for the record form as follows:

```
self.recordform.grid(row=1, padx=10, sticky='NSEW')
```

Moving the model

Currently, our data model object is only created in the `on_save()` method, and is recreated every time the user saves. Some of the other callbacks we're going to write will need access to the model as well, so instead we'll create a single data model instance that can be shared by all the methods when the `Application` class is started or whenever a new filename is chosen. Let's take a look at the following steps:

1. First, edit the `Application.__init__()` method right after the `default_filename` is created:

   ```
   self.filename = tk.StringVar(value=default_filename)
   self.data_model = m.CSVModel(filename=self.filename.get())
   ```

2. Next, the `on_file_select()` method needs to recreate the `data_model` object whenever the filename is changed.
3. Change the end of `on_file_select()` to the following code:

   ```
   if filename:
       self.filename.set(filename)
       self.data_model = m.CSVModel(filename=self.filename.get())
   ```

   Now, `self.data_model` will always point to a current data model and all our methods can use it for saving or reading data.

Populating the record list

The `Treeview` widget is added to our application, but we need a way to fill it with data.

We'll create a method called `populate_recordlist()` by executing the following code:

```
def populate_recordlist(self):
```

The logic is simple enough: just get all the rows from the model and send them to the record list's `populate()` method.

We could write it as simply as this:

```
rows = self.data_model.get_all_records()
self.recordlist.populate(rows)
```

Remember, though, that in the event of a problem with the file, `get_all_records()` will raise an `Exception`; we need to catch that exception and let the user know things are wrong.

Update the code with the `try` and `except` blocks as follows:

```
try:
    rows = self.data_model.get_all_records()
except Exception as e:
    messagebox.showerror(title='Error',
        message='Problem reading file',
        detail=str(e))
else:
    self.recordlist.populate(rows)
```

In this case, if we get an exception from `get_all_records()`, we'll display an error dialog showing the `Exception` text.

The `RecordList` view should be repopulated any time a new model gets created; currently, that happens in `Application.__init__()` and `Application.on_file_select()`.

Update `__init__()` just after the record list is created:

```
self.recordlist = v.RecordList(self, self.callbacks)
self.recordlist.grid(row=1, padx=10, sticky='NSEW')
self.populate_recordlist()
```

Update `on_file_select()` at the very end, inside the `if filename:` block as follows:

```
if filename:
    self.filename.set(filename)
    self.data_model = m.CSVModel(filename=self.filename.get())
    self.populate_recordlist()
```

Adding the new callbacks

Looking over our view code, the following callback functions need to be added to our `callbacks` dictionary:

- `show_recordlist()`: This function is called when the user clicks the **Record List** option in the menu, it should cause the record list to be visible
- `new_record()`: This function is called when the user clicks **New Record** in the menu, it should show a reset `DataRecordForm`
- `on_open_record()`: This function is called when a record list item is opened, it should show `DataRecordForm` which is populated with the ID and data of the record
- `on_save()`: This function is called when the **Save** button (now part of `DataRecordForm`) is clicked, it should cause the data in the record form to be updated or inserted in the model

We'll start with `show_recordlist()`:

```
def show_recordlist(self):
    """Show the recordform"""
    self.recordlist.tkraise()
```

Remember that when we laid out the main application, we stacked `recordlist` on top of the data entry form, so that one obscured the other. The `tkraise()` method can be called on any Tkinter widget to raise it to the top of a stack of widgets. Calling it here will raise our `RecordList` widget to the top and obscure the data entry form.

Don't forget to add the following content to the `callbacks` dictionary:

```
self.callbacks = {
    'show_recordlist': self.show_recordlist,
    ...
```

Both the `new_record()` and `on_open_record()` callbacks cause `recordform` to be displayed; one is called without a row number, and the other is called with a row number. We can easily answer both of these in a single method.

Let's call that method `open_record()`:

```
def open_record(self, rownum=None):
```

Remember that our `DataRecordForm.load_record()` method takes a row number and a `data` dictionary, and that if the row number is `None`, it resets the form for a new record. So, all we need to do is set the row number and record accordingly and pass them into the `load_record()` method.

First, we'll handle `rownum` being `None`:

```
        if rownum is None:
            record = None
```

Without a row number, there is no record. Easy enough.

Now, if there is a row number, we need to attempt to fetch that row from the model and use that for `record`:

```
        else:
            rownum = int(rownum)
            record = self.data_model.get_record(rownum)
```

Note that Tkinter may be passing in `rownum` as a string, since the `iid` values of `Treeview` are strings. We'll do a safety cast to `int`, since that's what our model expects.

Remember that in the event of a problem reading the file, the model throws an `Exception`, so we should catch this.

Place the call to `get_record()` inside a `try` block:

```
        try:
            record = self.data_model.get_record(rownum)
        except Exception as e:
            messagebox.showerror(title='Error',
                message='Problem reading file',
                detail=str(e))
            return
```

In the event of an `Exception`, we'll display an error dialog and return from the function without changing anything.

With `rownum` and `record` set correctly, we can now pass them to `DataRecordForm`:

```
        self.recordform.load_record(rownum, record)
```

Finally, we need to raise the `form` widget so that it's on top of the record list:

```
self.recordform.tkraise()
```

Now, we can update our `callbacks` dictionary to point those keys to the new method:

```
self.callbacks = {
    'new_record': self.open_record,
    'on_open_record': self.open_record,
    ...
```

You could argue that we shouldn't have the same method in here twice, and just have our views pull the same key; however, it makes sense to let the views refer to callbacks semantically—that is, in terms of what they intend to accomplish, rather than how it's accomplished—and then letting the controller determine which piece of code best meets that semantic need. If, at some point, we need to separate these into two methods, we'll only need to do that in `Application`.

We already have a method for `on_save()`, so that's simple enough to add to our callbacks:

```
self.callbacks = {
    ...
    'on_save': self.on_save
}
```

However, our current `on_save()` method only handles inserting new records. We'll need to fix that.

First, we can remove the two lines that fetch the filename and create the model, since we can just use the `Application` object's `data_model` property.

Now, replace the next couple of lines with this:

```
data = self.recordform.get()
rownum = self.recordform.current_record
try:
    self.data_model.save_record(data, rownum)
```

We simply need to get the data and current record from `DataRecordForm`, then pass them to the model's `save_record()` method. Remember that if we send `rownum` of `None`, the model will insert a new record; otherwise it will update the record at that row number.

Because `save_record()` can throw a couple of different exceptions, it's under a `try` block here.

First, if we try to update a row number that doesn't exist, we'll get `IndexError`, so let's catch that:

```
        except IndexError as e:
            messagebox.showerror(title='Error',
                message='Invalid row specified', detail=str(e))
            self.status.set('Tried to update invalid row')
```

In the event of the problem, we're going to show an error dialog and update the status text.

The `save_record()` method can also throw a generic `Exception`, since it calls the model's `get_all_records()` method.

We'll catch this as well and show an appropriate error:

```
        except Exception as e:
            messagebox.showerror(title='Error',
                message='Problem saving record', detail=str(e))
            self.status.set('Problem saving record')
```

The remaining code in this method should only be run if no exceptions were thrown, so move it under an `else` block:

```
    else:
        self.records_saved += 1
        self.status.set(
            "{} records saved this session".format(self.records_saved)
        )
        self.recordform.reset()
```

Since inserting or updating records will usually cause a change in the record list, we should also repopulate the record list after a successful file save.

Add the following line under the `if` block:

```
self.populate_recordlist()
```

Finally, we only want to reset the record form if we're inserting new files; if not, we should do nothing.

Put the call to `recordform.reset()` under an `if` block:

```
if self.recordform.current_record is None:
    self.recordform.reset()
```

Cleaning up

Before coming out of `application.py`, make sure to remove the **Save** button code, since we've moved that piece of UI to the `DataRecordForm`.

Look for these lines in `__init__()` to remove them:

```
self.savebutton = ttk.Button(self, text="Save",
                             command=self.on_save)
self.savebutton.grid(sticky="e", row=2, padx=10)
```

You can also move the `statusbar` position up one row:

```
self.statusbar.grid(sticky="we", row=2, padx=10)
```

Testing our program

At this point, you should be able to run the application and load in a sample CSV file as shown in the following screenshot:

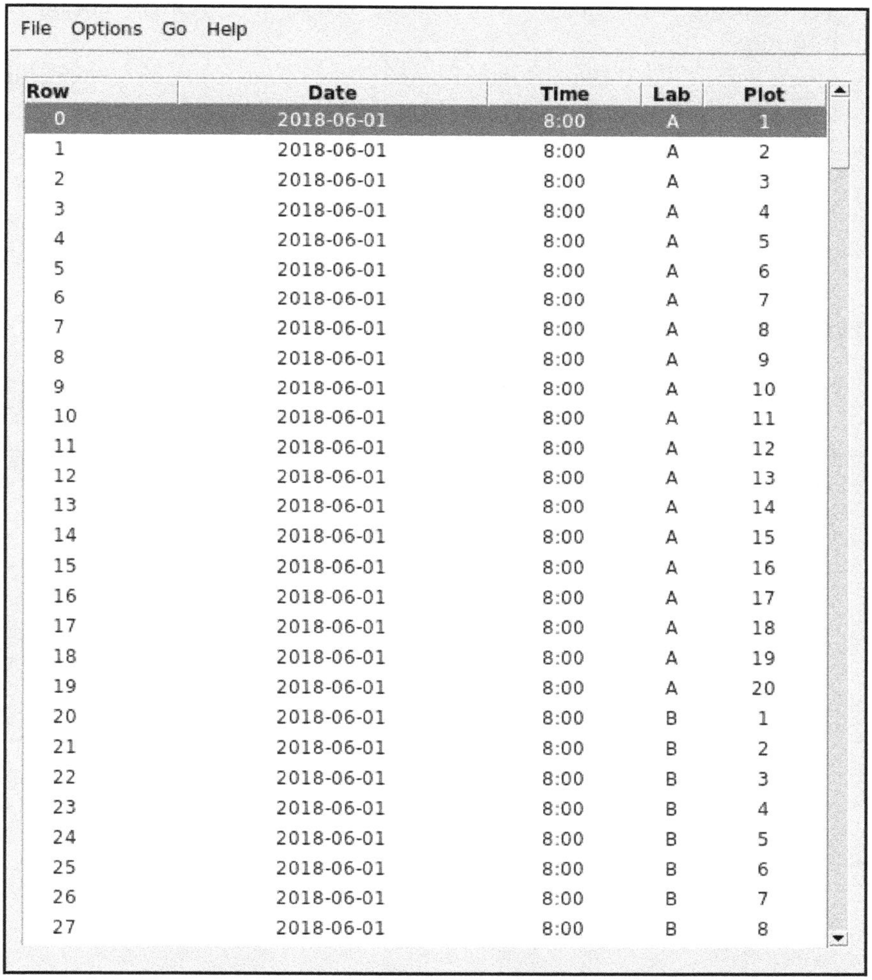

File Options Go Help

Row	Date	Time	Lab	Plot
0	2018-06-01	8:00	A	1
1	2018-06-01	8:00	A	2
2	2018-06-01	8:00	A	3
3	2018-06-01	8:00	A	4
4	2018-06-01	8:00	A	5
5	2018-06-01	8:00	A	6
6	2018-06-01	8:00	A	7
7	2018-06-01	8:00	A	8
8	2018-06-01	8:00	A	9
9	2018-06-01	8:00	A	10
10	2018-06-01	8:00	A	11
11	2018-06-01	8:00	A	12
12	2018-06-01	8:00	A	13
13	2018-06-01	8:00	A	14
14	2018-06-01	8:00	A	15
15	2018-06-01	8:00	A	16
16	2018-06-01	8:00	A	17
17	2018-06-01	8:00	A	18
18	2018-06-01	8:00	A	19
19	2018-06-01	8:00	A	20
20	2018-06-01	8:00	B	1
21	2018-06-01	8:00	B	2
22	2018-06-01	8:00	B	3
23	2018-06-01	8:00	B	4
24	2018-06-01	8:00	B	5
25	2018-06-01	8:00	B	6
26	2018-06-01	8:00	B	7
27	2018-06-01	8:00	B	8

Make sure to try opening a record, editing and saving it, as well as inserting new records and opening different files.

You should also test the following error conditions:

- Try opening a file that isn't a CSV file, or a CSV with incorrect fields. What happens?
- Open a valid CSV file, select a record for editing, then, before clicking **Save**, select a different or empty file. What happens?
- Open two copies of the program and point them to the saved CSV file. Try alternating edit or update actions between the programs. Note what happens.

Summary

We have changed our program from being an append-only form to an application capable of loading, viewing, and updating data from existing files. You learned how to make a read-write model, work with the ttk `Treeview`, and modify the existing views and controller to read and update records.

In our next chapter, we'll be learning how to modify the look and feel of our application. We'll learn about using widget attributes, styles, and themes, as well as working with bitmapped graphics.

8
Improving the Look with Styles and Themes

While programs can be perfectly functional with plain text in shades of black, white, and gray, the subtle use of colors, fonts, and images can enhance the visual appeal and usability of even the most utilitarian applications. Your data entry application is no exception. Your boss and your users have brought several issues to your attention, which seem to require the use of Tkinter's styling capabilities. Your boss has informed you that corporate HQ requires all in-house software to prominently display the company logo, while the data entry staff have mentioned a variety of issues with the readability and overall look of the application.

In this chapter, we're going to learn about some features of Tkinter that will help us to solve these issues:

- We'll learn how to add images to our Tkinter GUI
- We'll learn how to adjust the fonts and colors in our Tkinter widgets, both directly and with tags
- We'll learn how to adjust the look of Ttk widgets using styles and themes

Working with images in Tkinter

The first requirement we're going to handle is adding the company logo. As a result of corporate policy, your application is supposed to have the company logo embedded in it, and you've been asked to make your application comply if possible.

To add this image to our application, you'll need to learn about Tkinter's `PhotoImage` class.

Tkinter PhotoImage

Several Tkinter widgets, including `Label` and `Button`, can take an `image` argument, which allows them to display an image. We can't simply put a path to an image file in those cases; instead, we have to create a `PhotoImage` object.

Making a `PhotoImage` object is fairly simple:

```
myimage = tk.PhotoImage(file='my_image.png')
```

`PhotoImage` is typically called with the keyword argument `file`, which is pointed to a file path. Alternatively, you can use the `data` argument to point to a `bytes` object containing image data.

A `PhotoImage` can be used wherever an `image` argument is accepted, such as a `Label`:

```
mylabel = tk.Label(root, image=myimage)
```

It's critical to note that your application must retain a reference to the `PhotoImage` object that will stay in scope for as long as the image is shown; otherwise, the image will not appear.

Consider the following example:

```
import tkinter as tk
class App(tk.Tk):
    def __init__(self):
        super().__init__()
        smile = tk.PhotoImage(file='smile.gif')
        tk.Label(self, image=smile).pack()
App().mainloop()
```

If you run this example, you'll notice that no image gets displayed. That's because the `smile` variable is destroyed as soon as `__init__()` exits; with no reference to the `PhotoImage` object, the image vanishes, even though we've packed it into the layout. To fix this, you would need to store the `image` object in an instance variable such as `self.smile`, which will continue to exist after the method returns.

Image support in Tkinter is limited to GIF, PGM, PPM, and (as of version 8.6) PNG files. To use other file formats, such as JPEG or BMP, you'll need to use an image manipulation library such as Pillow to convert them into a format that Tkinter understands.

At the time of writing, Python 3 for macOS ships with Tkinter 8.5. To use PNG on macOS, you'll need to upgrade to Tkinter 8.6 or later, or use Pillow. Please see `https://www.python.org/download/mac/tcltk/` for more information about Tcl/Tk and macOS. Pillow is not in the Python standard library. To install it, follow the instructions at `http://python-pillow.org`.

Adding the company logo

With our knowledge of `PhotoImage`, adding the company logo to our program should be simple; however, we have to solve the problem of how to determine the image file's path. The path can be either absolute or relative to the working directory, but we don't know what those will be on another system. Fortunately, there's a way to figure it out.

Under the `abq_data_entry` directory, create a new directory called `images`, and within it place an appropriately-sized PNG file that we can use in our application (the image has an 8x5 aspect ratio, so in this case, we're using `32x20`). To get an absolute path to the image, we're going to rely on a built-in variable in Python called `__file__`. In any Python script, the `__file__` variable will contain the absolute path to the current script file, which we can use to locate our image files.

For example, from our `application.py` file, we could find our image using this code:

```
from os import path
image_path = path.join(path.dirname(__file__),
                       'images/abq_logo_32x20.png')
```

In this example, we first find the directory that contains the `application.py` file by calling `path.dirname(__file__)`. This gives us an absolute path to `abq_data_entry`, from which we know the relative path to the image. We can join these two paths and have an absolute path to the image, no matter where the program is installed on the filesystem.

This approach works fine, but consider that we may want to access images from a variety of modules in our application, and having to import `path` and repeat this logic in multiple files is less than optimal. A cleaner approach is to treat our `images` folder like a Python package and create constants in it that point to image paths.

Start by creating an `__init__.py` file inside the `images` folder and add the following code:

```
from os import path

IMAGE_DIRECTORY = path.dirname(__file__)

ABQ_LOGO_32 = path.join(IMAGE_DIRECTORY, 'abq_logo-32x20.png')
ABQ_LOGO_64 = path.join(IMAGE_DIRECTORY, 'abq_logo-64x40.png')
```

Now, our `application.py` module can simply do this:

```
from .images import ABQ_LOGO_32
```

`Application.__init__()` can then create a `PhotoImage` object using the path in `ABQ_LOGO_32`:

```
        self.logo = tk.PhotoImage(file=ABQ_LOGO_32)
        tk.Label(self, image=self.logo).grid(row=0)
```

After creating the `PhotoImage` object, we display it using a `Label`. If you run the application, you should see the logo show up at the top.

Setting our Window icon

We can also add the logo as our Window icon, which makes more sense than leaving the default Tkinter logo. This way, the logo will show up in both the window decorations and in the operating system's taskbar.

As a subclass of Tk, our `Application` object has a method called `iconbitmap` which should, given a path to an icon file, set the icon appropriately. Unfortunately, this method is fairly finicky about the type of file it's given and does not work well across platforms. We can work around this using `PhotoImage` and the special Tk `call()` method.

The `call` method allows us to directly call Tcl/Tk commands, and can be useful to access Tk capabilities that Tkinter wraps poorly or not at all.

The code looks like this:

```
        self.taskbar_icon = tk.PhotoImage(file=ABQ_LOGO_64)
        self.call('wm', 'iconphoto', self._w, self.taskbar_icon)
```

The first line creates another `PhotoImage` object, referencing a larger version of the logo. Next, we execute `self.call()`, passing in the individual tokens of the Tcl/Tk command. In this case, we're calling the `wm iconphoto` command. `self._w` returns the Tcl/Tk name for our `Application` object; and, last of all, we pass in the `PhotoImage` object we created.

Hopefully, you won't need to use `call` often, but if you do, you can find documentation about Tcl/Tk commands at: `https://www.tcl.tk/doc/`.

Run your application and notice how the icon has changed.

Styling Tkinter widgets

Tkinter has essentially two styling systems: the old Tkinter widgets system, and the newer Ttk system. Since we still need to work with both Tkinter and Ttk widgets, we'll have to look at both systems. Let's take a look first at the older Tkinter system and apply some styling to the Tkinter widgets in our application.

Widget color properties

Basic Tkinter widgets allow you to change two colors: **foreground**, meaning mainly the text and borders, and **background**, meaning the rest of the widget. These can be set using the `foreground` and `background` arguments, or their aliases `fg` and `bg`.

This example shows the use of colors on a `Label`:

```
l = tk.Label(text='Hot Dog!', fg='yellow', bg='red')
```

The values for the colors can be color name strings or CSS-style RGB hex strings.

For example, this code produces the same effect:

```
l2 = tk.Label(text='Also Hot Dog!',
              foreground='#FFFF00',
              background='#FF0000')
```

There are over 700 named colors recognized by Tkinter, roughly corresponding to those recognized by the X11 display server used on Linux and Unix, or the CSS named colors used by web designers. For a complete list, see https://www.tcl.tk/man/tcl8.6/TkCmd/colors.htm.

Using widget properties on our form

One request you received from the data entry staff is to increase the visual separation between the sections on the data entry form. Our LabelFrame widgets are simple Tkinter widgets (not Ttk), so we can accomplish this fairly simply by giving the sections colored backgrounds.

After some thought and discussion, you decide to color-code the sections as follows:

- Record information will use khaki, suggesting the classic manila folders used for paper records
- Environment information will use lightblue, symbolic of water and air
- Plant information will have a lightgreen background, symbolic of plants
- Notes are distinctive enough, so it will remain the same

Open up views.py and edit the LabelFrame calls in DataRecordForm.__init__():

```
        recordinfo = tk.LabelFrame(
            self, text="Record Information",
            bg="khaki", padx=10, pady=10)
...
        environmentinfo = tk.LabelFrame(
            self, text="Environment Data",
            bg='lightblue', padx=10, pady=10)
...
        plantinfo = tk.LabelFrame(
            self, text="Plant Data",
            bg="lightgreen", padx=10, pady=10)
```

Notice that we've added a bit of padding here as well, to make the color more visible around the widgets and to also create more separation in the form.

We should add similar padding around the Notes widget:

```
        self.inputs['Notes'].grid(sticky="w", row=4, column=0,
                                  padx=10, pady=10)
```

In this case, we add the padding to the `grid` call, so that the entire `LabelInput` gets shifted over.

The result, at least on Debian Linux, looks something like this:

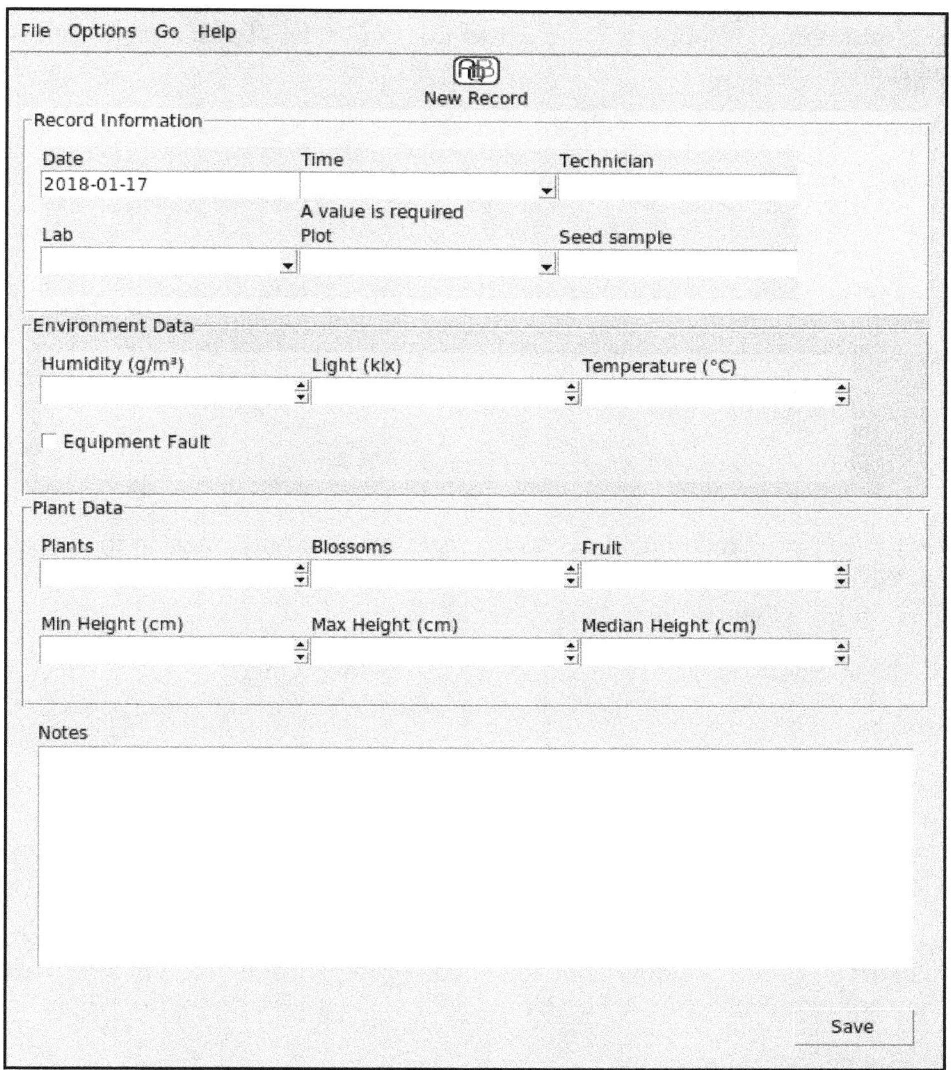

Hardly a visual masterpiece yet, but we have some separation and color coding between form sections.

Using tags

Foreground and background are sufficient for simple widgets such as buttons, but more complex Tkinter widgets like the `Text` widget or the Ttk `Treeview` rely on a system of **tags**. A tag in Tkinter is a named region of a widget's content to which color and font settings can be applied. To see how this works, let's build a crude, but pretty, Python shell.

We'll start by creating a `Text` widget:

```
import tkinter as tk
text = tk.Text(width=50, height=20, bg='black', fg='lightgreen')
text.pack()
```

Here, we've used the `fg` and `bg` arguments to set up a green-on-black theme, popular with programmers. Rather than have only green text, though, let's configure different colors for our prompt and our interpreter output.

To do this, we'll define some tags:

```
text.tag_configure('prompt', foreground='magenta')
text.tag_configure('output', foreground='yellow')
```

The `tag_configure` method allows us to create and configure tags on the `Text` widget. We've created one called `'prompt'` for our shell prompt, and another called `'output'` for the Python output.

To `insert` text with a given tag applied, we do the following:

```
text.insert('end', '>>> ', ('prompt',))
```

As you may remember, the `Text.insert` method takes an index and string as its first two arguments. Notice the third argument: this is a tuple of the tags with which we want to mark the inserted text. This value must be a tuple, even if you're only using one tag.

If you add `text.mainloop()` to the end of the code and run it, you'll see that we have a black text entry window with a magenta prompt, but if you type your text, it will show up in green. So far so good; now, let's make it execute some Python.

Create a function just before the `mainloop()` call:

```
def on_return(*args):
    cmd = text.get('prompt.last', 'end').strip()
```

When retrieving text from a Text widget, we're required to supply start and end indices for the text we want to retrieve. Notice that we've used our tag name in the index. prompt.last tells Tkinter to fetch the text starting after the end of the region tagged prompt.

Next, let's execute cmd:

```
    if cmd:
        try:
            output = str(eval(cmd))
        except Exception as e:
            output = str(e)
```

If our cmd actually contains anything, we'll try to execute it with eval, then store a string of the response value as output. If it throws an exception, we'll get our exception as a string and set that as the output.

Then, we'll just show our output:

```
    text.insert('end', '\n' + output, ('output',))
```

We insert our output text, prepended with a newline and tagged as output.

We'll finish off the function by giving the user back a prompt:

```
    text.insert('end', '\n>>> ', ('prompt',))
    return 'break'
```

We also return the string break here to tell Tkinter to ignore the original event that triggered the callback. Since we're going to trigger this from a Return/Enter keystroke, we want to ignore that keystroke after we're finished. If we don't, the keystroke will be executed after our function returns and the user will be on the line under the prompt.

Finally, we need to bind our function to the Return key:

```
text.bind('<Return>', on_return)
```

Note that the event for the Enter/Return key is always <Return>, even on non-Apple hardware (where the key is more commonly labeled Enter).

Your application should look something like this:

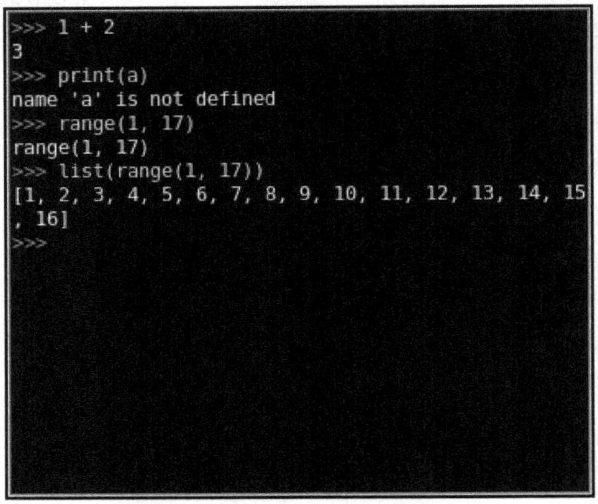

While this shell won't be supplanting IDLE any time soon, it does look rather nice, don't you think?

Styling our record list with tags

Although `Treeview` is a Ttk widget, it uses tags to control the styling of individual rows. We can use this to answer another of the requests you've gotten from the data entry staff: they'd like the record list to highlight records updated and inserted during the current session.

The first thing we'll need to do is have our `Application` object keep track of which rows have been updated or inserted during the session.

In `Application.__init__()`, we'll create the following instance variables:

```
self.inserted_rows.clear()
self.updated_rows.clear()
```

When a record is saved, we'll need to update one or the other of these lists with its row number. We'll do this in `Application.on_save()`, after the record is saved, but before we repopulate the record list.

First, we'll check for an updated record:

```
        if rownum is not None:
            self.updated_rows.append(rownum)
```

Updates have `rownum` which do not have a `None` value, so if this is the case, we'll append it to the list. If a record is continually updated, there will be duplicates in our list, but that's not really of any consequence in the scale at which we're operating.

Now, we need to deal with inserts:

```
        else:
            rownum = len(self.data_model.get_all_records()) - 1
            self.inserted_rows.append(rownum)
```

Inserted records are a little more troublesome in that we don't have a row number readily available to record. We do know that inserts are always appended to the end of the file, though, so it should be one less than the number of rows in the file.

Our inserted and updated records will be kept until the end of the program session (when the user exits the program), but we need to manually delete them in the case where a user selects a new file.

We can handle that by clearing the lists in `on_file_select()`:

```
        if filename:
             ...
             self.inserted_rows = []
             self.updated_rows = []
```

Now, our controller knows about inserted and updated records. Our record list does not, however; we need to fix that.

Find the `RecordList` call in `Application.__init__()` and add the variables to its arguments:

```
        self.recordlist = v.RecordList(
             self, self.callbacks,
             self.inserted_rows,
             self.updated_rows)
```

Now, we'll need to go back into `views.py` and tell the `RecordList` what to do with this information.

We'll start by updating its argument list and saving the lists to instance variables:

```
def __init__(self, parent, callbacks,
             inserted, updated,
             *args, **kwargs):
    self.inserted = inserted
    self.updated = updated
```

Next, we'll need to configure tags with appropriate colors. Our data entry staff feels that `lightgreen` would be a sensible color for inserted records, and `lightblue` for updated.

Add this code in `__init__()` after the `self.treeview` configuration:

```
self.treeview.tag_configure('inserted', background='lightgreen')
self.treeview.tag_configure('updated', background='lightblue')
```

Just as we did with the `Text` widget earlier, we call `tag_configure` to connect background color settings with our tag names. Note that you aren't restricted to just one configuration setting here; we could conceivably add `foreground`, `font`, or other configuration settings to the same call.

To add the tags to our `TreeView` rows, we'll need to update the `populate` method.

Inside the `for` loop, just before inserting the row, we'll add this code:

```
if self.inserted and rownum in self.inserted:
    tag = 'inserted'
 elif self.updated and rownum in self.updated:
    tag = 'updated'
 else:
    tag = ''
```

We want `tag` to equal `'inserted'` if the `inserted` list exists and our `rownum` is in it; we want it to be `'updated'` if the `updated` list exists and our `rownum` is in it. Otherwise, we leave it blank.

Now, our `treeview.insert` call just needs to be amended with this `tag` value:

```
self.treeview.insert('', 'end', iid=str(rownum),
                     text=str(rownum), values=values,
                     tag=tag)
```

Run the application and try inserting and updating some records.

You should get something like this:

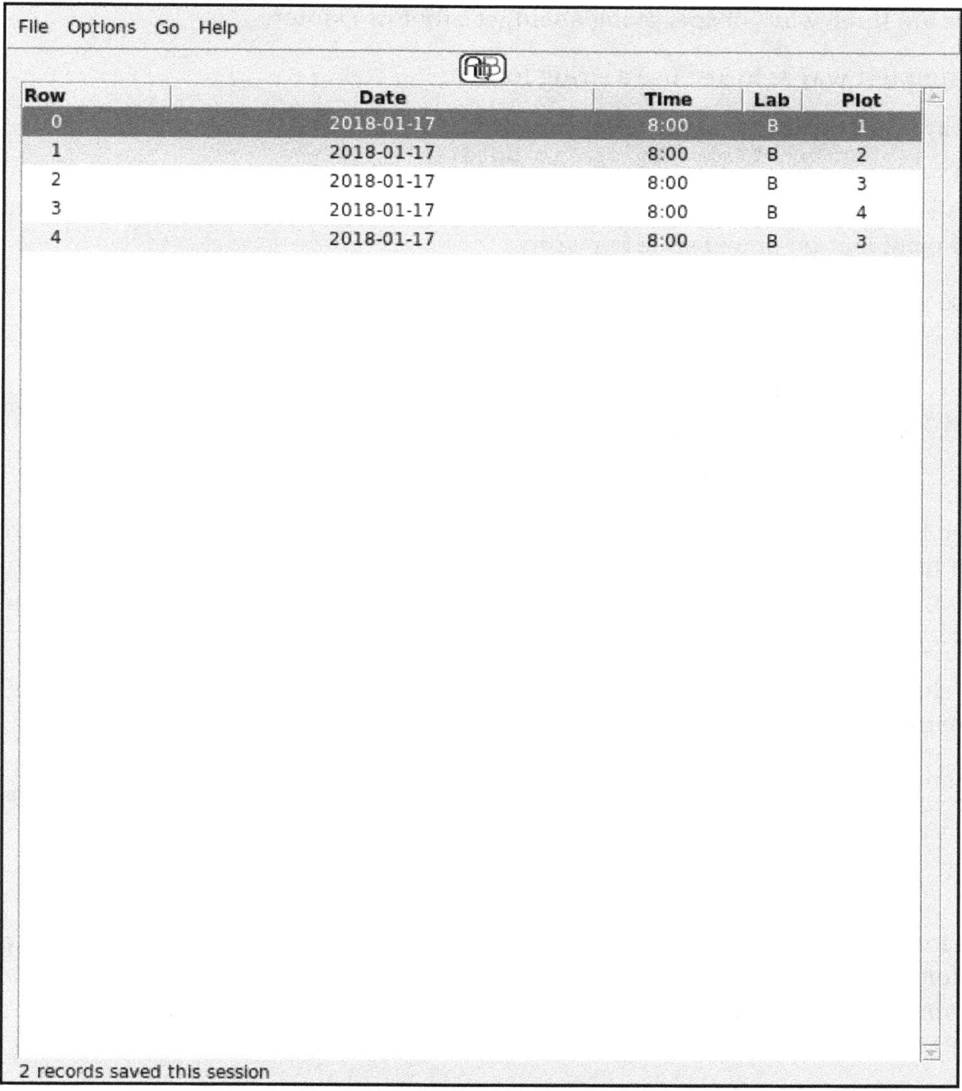

Tkinter fonts

There are three ways of specifying a widget's font in Tkinter.

The simplest way is to just use a string format:

```
tk.Label(text="Direct font format",
         font="Times 20 italic bold")
```

The string takes the format `Font-family size styles`, where `styles` can be any valid combination of text style keywords.

Those words include:

- `bold` for boldface text, or `normal` for normal weight
- `italic` for italized text, or `roman` for regular slant
- `underline` for underlined text
- `overstrike` for struck-out text

Everything but the font family is optional, though you need to specify a `size` if you want to specify any of the styling keywords. The ordering of style keywords doesn't matter, but the weight and slant keywords are mutually exclusive (that is, you can't have `bold normal` or `italic roman`).

One shortcoming of the string approach is that it cannot handle fonts with spaces in the name.

To handle these, you can use the tuple format for fonts:

```
tk.Label(
    text="Tuple font format",
    font=('Droid sans', 15, 'overstrike'))
```

This format is exactly like the string format except that the different components are written as items in a tuple. The `size` component can be an integer or a string containing digits, which provides some flexibility depending on where the value comes from.

This approach works fine for setting up a handful of font changes at launch time, but for situations that need to dynamically manipulate font settings, Tkinter has a feature called **named fonts.** This approach uses a `Font` class that can be assigned to widgets and then dynamically changed.

To use `Font`, it must be imported from the `tkinter.font` module:

```
from tkinter.font import Font
```

Now, we can create a custom `Font` object and assign it to widgets:

```
labelfont = Font(family='Courier', size=30,
                 weight='bold', slant='roman',
                 underline=False, overstrike=False)
tk.Label(text='Using the Font class', font=labelfont).pack()
```

As you can see, the `Font` constructor arguments correlate the keywords used in string and tuple font specifications.

Once this font is assigned, we can dynamically alter aspects of it at runtime:

```
def toggle_overstrike():
    labelfont['overstrike'] = not labelfont['overstrike']

tk.Button(text='Toggle Overstrike', command=toggle_overstrike).pack()
```

In this example, we're providing a `Button` that will toggle the `overstrike` attribute on and off.

Tk comes with several named fonts already configured; we can create Python `Font` objects from them using the `nametofont` function from the `tkinter.font` module.

This table shows some of the named fonts included in Tkinter:

Font name	**Defaults to**	**Used for**
`TkCaptionFont`	System title font	Window and dialog caption bars
`TkDefaultFont`	System default font	Items not otherwise specified
`TkFixedFont`	System fixed-width font	Nothing
`TkHeadingFont`	System heading font	Column headings in lists and tables
`TkIconFont`	System icon font	Icon captions
`TkMenuFont`	System menu font	Menu labels
`TkSmallCaptionFont`	System title	Subwindows, tool dialogs
`TkTextFont`	System input font	Input widgets: Entry, Spinbox, and so on
`TkTooltipFont`	System tooltip font	Tooltips

If you're curious as to what fonts Tkinter is using on your operating system, you can use the `tkinter.font.names()` function to retrieve a list of them.

To change the overall look of the application, we can override these named fonts and the changes will get applied across all widgets that don't otherwise have a font set.

For example:

```
import tkinter as tk
from tkinter.font import nametofont

default_font = nametofont('TkDefaultFont')
default_font.config(family='Helvetica', size=32)

tk.Label(text='Feeling Groovy').pack()
```

In this example, we use the `nametofont` function to retrieve an object for `TkDefaultFont`, the default named font class for Tkinter applications. After retrieving it, we can set its font `family` and `size`, changing those values for all widgets using `TkDefaultFont`.

The `Label` then shows the result of this adjustment:

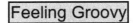

Feeling Groovy

Giving users font options

Some of our data entry users have complained that the font of the application is just a little too small to read easily, but others dislike the idea of you increasing it because it makes the application too big for the screen. To accommodate all the users, we can add a configuration option that allows them to set a preferred font size.

We need to begin by adding a `'font size'` option to our settings model.

Open `models.py` and append the `SettingsModel.variables` dictionary as follows:

```
    variables = {
        ...
        'font size': {'type': 'int', 'value': 9}
```

Next, we'll add a set of radio buttons to our options menu so that the user can set the value.

Open `views.py` and let's start creating a menu just before the options menu gets added to the main menu:

```
font_size_menu = tk.Menu(self, tearoff=False)
for size in range(6, 17, 1):
    font_size_menu.add_radiobutton(
        label=size, value=size,
        variable=settings['font size'])
options_menu.add_cascade(label='Font size',
                         menu=font_size_menu)
```

This should look familiar, since we created a nearly identical font size menu when learning about the Tkinter `Menu` widget. We're allowing fonts from `6` to `16`, which should provide plenty of range for our users.

In the `Application` class, let's create a method that will apply the font setting to our application's fonts:

```
def set_font(self, *args):
```

We include `*args` because `set_font` will be called as a `trace` callback, so we need to capture any arguments being sent in, even though we won't use them.

Next, we'll get the current `'font size'` value:

```
font_size = self.settings['font size'].get()
```

There are several named fonts we're going to need to change, not just `TkDefaultFont`. For our application, `TkDefaultFont`, `TkTextFont`, and `TkMenuFont` should be sufficient.

We'll just loop through these, retrieving the classes and setting the size on each one:

```
font_names = ('TkDefaultFont', 'TkMenuFont', 'TkTextFont')
for font_name in font_names:
    tk_font = nametofont(font_name)
    tk_font.config(size=font_size)
```

The last thing we need to do is to make sure this callback gets called.

Just after the `load_settings()` call in `Application.__init__()`, add this:

```
self.set_font()
self.settings['font size'].trace('w', self.set_font)
```

We call `set_font()` once to activate any saved `font size` settings and then set a `trace` to run it whenever the value is changed.

Run the application and try out the font menu. It should look something like this:

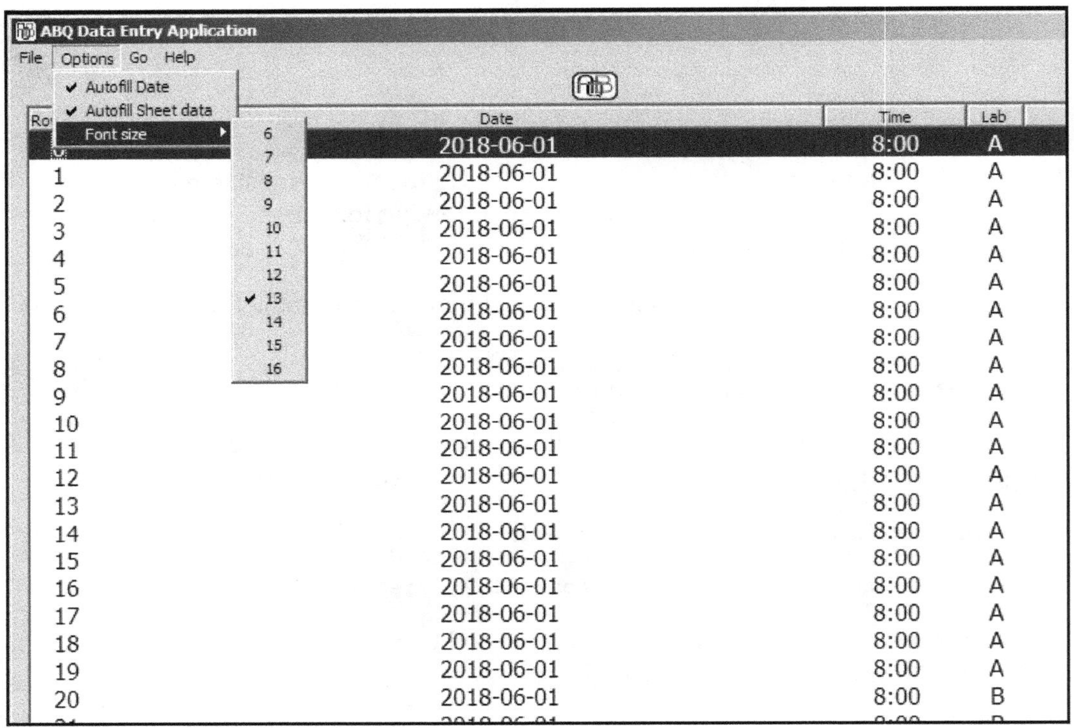

Styling Ttk widgets

Ttk widgets represent a major improvement over standard Tkinter widgets in terms of the power and flexibility with which they can be styled. This flexibility is what gives Ttk widgets the ability to mimic native UI controls across platforms, but it comes at a cost: Ttk styling is confusing, poorly documented, and occasionally inconsistent.

To understand Ttk styling, let's start with some vocabulary, from the most basic elements to the most complex:

- Ttk starts with **elements**. An element is one piece of a widget, such as a border, an arrow, or a field where text can be typed.
- Elements are composed using **layouts** into a complete widget (a `Combobox` or `Treeview`, for example).
- **Styles** are collections of properties that define color and font settings:
    - Each style has a name, usually T, plus the name of the widget, such as `TButton` or `TEntry`. There are some exceptions to this.
    - Each element in a layout references one or more style properties to define its appearance.
- Widgets have a number of **states**, which are flags that can be turned on or off:
    - Styles can be configured with a **map** that connects property values to states or combinations of states
- A collection of styles is called a **theme**. Tkinter ships with different themes on different platforms.:
    - A theme might define not only different styles, but different layouts as well. For example, a `ttk.Button` on the default macOS theme may contain a different set of elements, applying style settings differently compared to a `ttk.Button` using the default theme in Windows.

If you're confused at this point, that's okay. Let's take a deep dive into the anatomy of a `ttk.Combobox` to get a better feel for these ideas.

Exploring a Ttk widget

To get a better picture of how a Ttk widget is built, open a shell in IDLE and import `tkinter`, `ttk`, and `pprint`:

```
>>> import tkinter as tk
>>> from tkinter import ttk
>>> from pprint import pprint
```

Now, create a root window, `Combobox`, and `Style` object:

```
>>> root = tk.Tk()
>>> cb = ttk.Combobox(root)
>>> cb.pack()
>>> style = ttk.Style()
```

The `Style` object is, perhaps, slightly misnamed; it doesn't point to a single style, but rather gives us a handle to examine and alter the styles, layouts, and maps for the current theme.

In order to examine our `Combobox`, we'll first get its `stylename` using the `winfo_class()` method:

```
>>> cb_stylename = cb.winfo_class()
>>> print(cb_stylename)
TCombobox
```

We can then inspect the layout of the `Combobox` using the `Style.layout()` method:

```
>>> cb_layout = style.layout(cb_stylename)
>>> pprint(cb_layout)
[('Combobox.field',
  {'children':  [('Combobox.downarrow',
                {'side': 'right', 'sticky': 'ns'}),
                ('Combobox.padding',
                {'children': [('Combobox.textarea',
                {'sticky': 'nswe'})],
                'expand': '1',
                'sticky': 'nswe'})],
                'sticky': 'nswe'})]
```

By passing the style name (in this case, `TCombobox`) to the `style.layout()` method, we get back a layout specification that shows the hierarchy of elements used to construct this widget.

The elements, in this case, are `"Combobox.field"`, `"Combobox.downarrow"`, `"Combobox.padding"`, and `"Combobox.textarea"`. As you can see, each element has associated positioning properties similar to what you'd pass into `pack()`.

The `layout` method can also be used to replace a style's layout by passing in a new layout specification. Unfortunately, this requires replacing the entire layout specification—you can't just adjust or replace a single element in place.

To see how the style connects to the elements, we can use the `style.element_options()` method. This method takes an element name and returns a list of options that can be used to alter it.

For example:

```
>>> pprint(style.element_options('Combobox.downarrow'))
('background', 'relief', 'borderwidth', 'arrowcolor', 'arrowsize')
```

This tells us that the `downarrow` element of the `Combobox` uses these style properties to determine its appearance. To change these properties, we'll have to use the `style.configure()` method.

Let's change the color of the arrow to `red`:

```
>>> style.configure('TCombobox', arrowcolor='red')
```

You should see that the `arrowcolor` has changed to `red`. This is all we need to know to configure widgets for static changes, but what about dynamic changes?

To make dynamic changes, we'll need to understand our widget's state.

We can inspect or alter the state of our `Combobox` using the `state` method:

```
>>> print(cb.state())
()
>>> cb.state(['active', 'invalid'])
('!active', '!invalid')
>>> print(cb.state())
('active', 'invalid')
```

`Combobox.state()` with no arguments will return a tuple with the currently set state flags; when used with an argument (which must be a sequence of strings), it will set the corresponding state flags.

To turn off a state flag, prepend a `!` to the flag name:

```
>>> cb.state(['!invalid'])
('invalid',)
>>> print(cb.state())
('active',)
```

When you call `state()` with an argument to change the value, the return value is a tuple containing a set of states that would, if applied, undo the state change you just set. This might be useful in a situation where you want to temporarily set a widget's state, then return it to its previous (unknown) state.

You can't just use any strings for `state()`; they must be one of the following:

- `active`
- `disabled`
- `focus`
- `pressed`
- `selected`
- `background`
- `readonly`
- `alternate`
- `invalid`

Exactly how different widgets use each of these states depends on the widget; not every `state()` is configured to have an effect by default.

Widget states interact with the widget style through the use of a map. We use the `style.map()` method to inspect or set the map for each style.

Take a look at the default map for `TCombobox`:

```
>>> pprint(style.map(cb_stylename))
{'arrowcolor': [('disabled', '#a3a3a3')],
 'fieldbackground': [('readonly', '#d9d9d9'),
                     ('disabled', '#d9d9d9')]}
```

As you can see, `TCombobox` has a style map for the `arrowcolor` and `fieldbackground` properties by default. Each style map is a list of tuples, and each tuple is one or more state flags followed by a value for the setting. When all of the state flags match the current state of the widget, the value takes effect.

The default map turns the arrow color to a light gray color when the `disabled` flag is set, and turns the field background to a different light gray color when either the `disabled` or `readonly` flags are set.

We can set our own style mapping using the same method:

```
>>> style.map('TCombobox', arrowcolor=[('!invalid',  'blue'),
('invalid', 'focus', 'red')])
{}
>>> pprint(style.map('TCombobox'))
{'arrowcolor': [('!invalid', 'blue'), ('invalid', 'focus', 'red')],
 'fieldbackground': [('readonly', '#d9d9d9'), ('disabled',
'#d9d9d9')]}
```

Here, we've configured the `arrowcolor` property to be `blue` when the `invalid` flag is not set, and `red` when both the `invalid` and `focus` flags are set. Notice that while our call to `map` completely overwrote the `arrowcolor` style map, the `fieldbackground` map was unaffected. This means you can replace style mappings individually, but you can't simply append to the existing map for a given property.

So far, we've been operating on the `TCombobox` style, which is the default style for all `Combobox` widgets. Any changes we made would impact every `Combobox` in the application. We can also create custom styles derived from the existing style by prepending a name and a dot to an existing style name.

For example:

```
>>> style.configure('Blue.TCombobox', fieldbackground='blue')
>>> cb.configure(style='Blue.TCombobox')
```

`Blue.TCombobox` inherits all of the properties of `TCombobox` (including the `blue downarrow` we previously configured), but can add or override them with settings of its own that don't affect `TCombobox`. This allows you to create custom styles for some widgets without affecting other widgets of the same type.

We can alter the look of all the Ttk widgets at once by changing the theme. Remember that a theme is a collection of styles, so by changing the theme, we'll be replacing all the built-in styles and layouts.

Different themes are shipped on different platforms; to see the themes available on your platform, use the `theme_names()` method:

```
>>> style.theme_names()
('clam', 'alt', 'default', 'classic')
```

(These are the themes available on Debian Linux; yours may differ.)

To query the current theme, or to set a new theme, use the `theme_use()` method:

```
>>> style.theme_use()
'default'
>>> style.theme_use('alt')
```

Notice how the previous styling is gone when you change the theme. If you switch back to the default, however, you'll see that your changes were retained.

Styling our form labels

The first thing we can tackle with our knowledge of styling is our form widgets. Our colorization of the form is rather ugly and incomplete due to the `LabelInput` widgets retaining their default, drab color. We'll need to style each of those widgets to match the color of its `LabelInput`.

In the `views.py` file, add this near the start of the `DataRecordForm.__init__()` method:

```
        style = ttk.Style()
```

We're creating our `Style` object so that we can start working with our Ttk styles. What styles do we need?

- We need a style for Ttk `Label` widgets for each section, since we'll need different colors for the widgets in `RecordInfo`, `EnvironmentInfo`, and `Plant Info`.
- We'll need to style our Ttk `Checkbutton`, since it uses its own built-in label rather than a separate label widget. Since there's only one right now, we only need one style for it.

Let's create those styles:

```
        style.configure('RecordInfo.TLabel', background='khaki')
        style.configure(
            'EnvironmentInfo.TLabel',
             background='lightblue')
        style.configure(
            'EnvironmentInfo.TCheckbutton',
            background='lightblue')
        style.configure('PlantInfo.TLabel', background='lightgreen')
```

As you can see, we're creating a custom style based on `TLabel`, but this is prefixed for each individual section. For each style, we're just setting the `background` color appropriately.

Now comes the tedious task of adding this style to each widget:

```
self.inputs['Date'] = w.LabelInput(
     recordinfo, "Date",
     field_spec=fields['Date'],
     label_args={'style': 'RecordInfo.TLabel'})
```

In each `LabelInput` call, you'll need to add a `label_args` argument that sets the `style` to the appropriate `TLabel` style for the section. Go through and do this for all the widgets.

For the `Checkbutton`, you'll need to do it differently:

```
self.inputs['Equipment Fault'] = w.LabelInput(
     environmentinfo, "Equipment Fault",
     field_spec=fields['Equipment Fault'],
     label_args={'style': 'EnvironmentInfo.TLabel'},
     input_args={'style': 'EnvironmentInfo.TCheckbutton'})
```

Here, we've set `input_args`, since the style applies to the `Checkbutton` rather than the label (leave `label_args`; we'll need that in a minute).

If you run the program at this point, you'll see a marked improvement, but it's not quite there yet; the error labels are still the old, default color.

To fix this, we just need to edit our `LabelInput` widget to use the `label_args` for the error label as well.

Open `widgets.py` and fix the `self.error_label` assignment in `LabelInput.__init__()`:

```
self.error_label = ttk.Label(self, textvariable=self.error,
                             **label_args)
```

Now, your application should have consistent colors and look a lot more attractive:

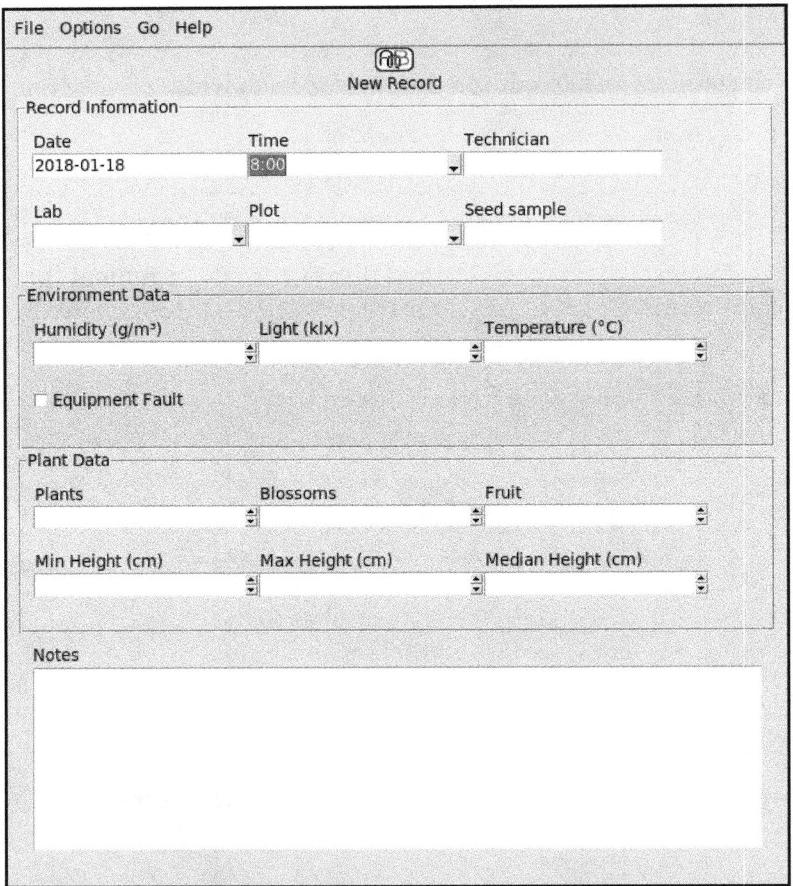

Styling input widgets on error

Our data entry staff has complained that the error-styling in our fields is not terribly noticeable. Currently, we're just setting the `foreground` color to `red`.

This has a couple of problems:

- For empty fields, there's nothing to actually color `red`
- Our color blind user has trouble distinguishing the `red` from the normal text color

We'll use our styling knowledge to improve the error styling and make invalid fields more noticeable.

Before we can do that, though, you may have to fix a minor issue with one of our widgets.

Making our Spinbox a Ttk widget

If you're using Python 3.6 or earlier, the `Spinbox` widget is only available in `tkinter`, and not `ttk`. We'll need to fix this so that our error-styling can be consistent.

At the time of writing this book, the author has submitted a patch to Python 3.7 to include the Ttk `Spinbox`. If you're using Python 3.7 or later, you can just use `ttk::spinbox` and skip this section.

Since `Spinbox` is already in the Tcl/Tk Ttk library, creating a Python class for it is surprisingly easy.

Add this code near the top of `widgets.py`:

```
class TtkSpinbox(ttk.Entry):

    def __init__(self, parent=None, **kwargs):
        super().__init__(parent, 'ttk::spinbox', **kwargs)
```

This is all that's needed to create a Ttk `Spinbox` for this application. We're simply subclassing `ttk.Entry`, but changing the Ttk widget being used in the `__init__` statement. If we needed any `Spinbox` methods that `Entry` lacks, we'd need to provide those; for this application, we don't need anything else.

Now, we only need to update our `ValidatedSpinbox` class to inherit `TtkSpinbox` rather than `tk.Spinbox`:

```
class ValidatedSpinbox(ValidatedMixin, TtkSpinbox):
```

Updating ValidatedMixin

Now that we're working with all Ttk widgets, we can update our `ValidatedMixin` class with some dynamic styling.

We'll begin in the `__init__()` method by creating a `Style` object:

```
style = ttk.Style()
```

Since this is a mixin class, we don't know the original style name of the widget we're mixing with, so we'll have to fetch that.

Remember that we can do this with `winfo_class()`:

```
        widget_class = self.winfo_class()
        validated_style = 'ValidatedInput.' + widget_class
```

After getting the widget class, we're creating a derivative style by prepending `ValidatedInput` to it. In order to toggle our input appearance between error and non-error appearances, we'll create a style map that switches with the state of the `invalid` state flag.

You can do this with a call to `style.map()`:

```
        style.map(
            validated_style,
            foreground=[('invalid', 'white'), ('!invalid', 'black')],
            fieldbackground=[('invalid', 'darkred'), ('!invalid',
'white')]
        )
```

We're still using red, since it's an established "error color", but this time we're inverting the field from dark-on-light to light-on-dark. This should help our colorblind user to distinguish errors, even though they are red.

Finally, we need to update our call to `self.config` to include setting the widget's style to our new validated style:

```
        self.config(
            style=validated_style,
            validate='all',
            ...
```

Ttk widgets automatically set their `invalid` flags as part of the built-in validation system. Currently, we have a method called `_toggle_error()`, which is called whenever validation begins or fails and sets the error state on and off. We can remove that method completely, and all references to it.

If you try the application now, you'll see that fields with errors now turn a dark red color with white text:

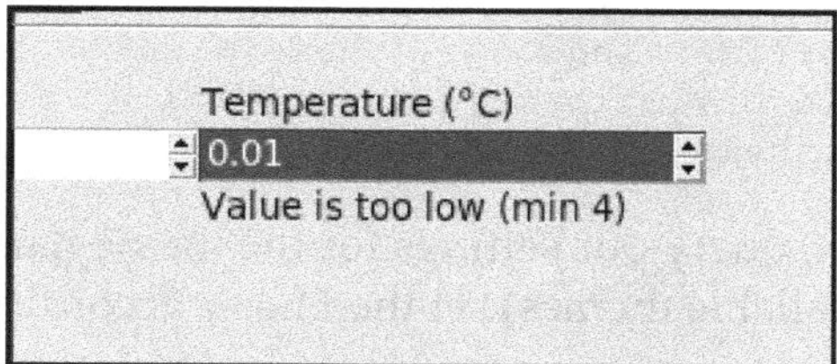

Setting themes

Generally speaking, the default Ttk theme on any given platform is probably the best one to use on that platform, but looks are subjective and sometimes we might feel that Tkinter gets it wrong. Having a way to adjust the theme might help to smooth out some rough edges and make some users feel more comfortable with the look of the application.

As we've already seen, querying available themes and setting a new theme is fairly simple. Let's create a configuration option to change the theme of our application.

Building a theme selector

Themes aren't something users are going to need to change often, and as we've seen, changing the theme can undo style changes we've made to our widgets. In light of this, we'll play it safe by designing our theme changer in such a way that it requires a restart of the program to make the actual change.

We'll start by adding a theme option to our `SettingsModel`:

```
variables = {
    ...
    'theme': {'type': 'str', 'value': 'default'}
}
```

Every platform has a theme aliased to default, so this is a safe and sensible default value.

Next, our Application.__init__() method will need to check this value and set the theme accordingly.

Add this code just after the call to load_settings():

```
style = ttk.Style()
theme = self.settings.get('theme').get()
if theme in style.theme_names():
    style.theme_use(theme)
```

We create a Style object, query our settings for the theme name, then (assuming the saved theme is in the available themes) set the theme accordingly.

What remains now is to create the UI.

In the views.py file, we'll create a new submenu for the options_menu:

```
style = ttk.Style()
themes_menu = tk.Menu(self, tearoff=False)
for theme in style.theme_names():
    themes_menu.add_radiobutton(
        label=theme, value=theme,
        variable=settings['theme']
    )
options_menu.add_cascade(label='Theme', menu=themes_menu)
```

Here, we simply loop through the available themes and add a Radiobutton for each theme, tying it to our settings['theme'] variable.

It may not be obvious to users that changing the theme requires a restart, so let's make sure to let them know.

We'll add a trace to the variable:

```
settings['theme'].trace('w', self.on_theme_change)
```

The on_theme_change method will just display a warning dialog informing the user that a restart will be needed to realize the change.

Add it to the end of the `MainMenu` class:

```
def on_theme_change(self, *args):
    """Popup a message about theme changes"""
    message = "Change requires restart"
    detail = (
        "Theme changes do not take effect"
        " until application restart")
        messagebox.showwarning(
        title='Warning',
        message=message,
        detail=detail)
```

Now, you can run the application and try changing the `theme`. Which theme looks best on your platform?

You might find that some themes on your platform break the widget styling in the form. Remember that themes don't just change default colors and fonts, they change the layout and contents of the widget elements themselves. Sometimes, a style setting doesn't carry across different themes due to this change of property names.

Summary

In this chapter, we overhauled the look and feel of our application for both aesthetic and usability improvements. You learned how to work with color and font settings for Tkinter widget, and the intricate world of Ttk styles.

9
Creating Automated Tests with unittest

With the size and complexity of your application rapidly expanding, you've become nervous about making changes. What if you break something? How will you know? You need a reliable way to make sure your program is working properly as the code changes.

Fortunately, we have a way: automated testing. In this chapter, you'll cover the following topics:

- Learning the basics of automated testing
- Learning specific strategies for testing Tkinter applications
- Applying this knowledge to our data entry application

Automated testing basics

Up until now, testing our application has been a process of launching it, running it through a few basic procedures, and verifying that it did what we expected it to do. This approach works acceptably on a very small script, but, as our application grows, it becomes an increasingly time-consuming and error-prone process to verify the application's behavior. Using automated testing, we can consistently verify our application logic within seconds.

There are several forms of automated testing, but the two most common are **unit testing** and **integration testing**. Unit tests work with discrete pieces of code in isolation, allowing us to quickly verify the behavior of specific sections. Integration tests verify the interactions of multiple units of code. We'll be writing both kinds of tests to verify the behavior of our application.

A simple unit test

At its most basic, a unit test is just a short program that runs a unit of code under different conditions and compares its output against expected results.

Consider the following calculation class:

```
import random

class MyCalc:

    def __init__(self, a, b):
        self.a = a
        self.b = b

    def add(self):
        return self.a + self.b

    def mod_divide(self):
        if self.b == 0:
            raise ValueError("Cannot divide by zero")
        return (int(self.a / self.b), self.a % self.b)

    def rand_between(self):
        return ((random.random() * abs(self.a - self.b)) +
        min(self.a, self.b))
```

This class is initialized with two numbers and can then perform a variety of arithmetic methods on them.

Let's create a naive test for this function as follows:

```
from mycalc import MyCalc

mc1 = MyCalc(1, 100)
mc2 = MyCalc(10, 4)

try:
    assert mc1.add() == 101, "Test of add() failed."
    assert mc2.mod_divide() == (2, 2), "Test of mod_divide() failed."
except AssertionError as e:
    print("Test failed: ", e)
else:
    print("Tests succeeded!")
```

Our test code creates a `MyCalc` object and then uses `assert` statements to check the output of `add()` and `mod_divide()` against expected values. The `assert` keyword in Python is a special statement that raises an `AssertionError` exception if the statement that follows it evaluates to `False`. The message string after the comma is the error string that will be passed to the `AssertionError` exception.

The code `assert statement, "message"` is essentially equivalent to this:

```
if not statement:
    raise AssertionError("message")
```

Currently, all tests pass if you run the test script for `MyCalc`. Let's try changing the `add()` method as follows to make it fail:

```
    def add(self):
        return self.a - self.b
```

Now, running the test gives this error:

```
Test failed:  Test of add() failed.
```

What is the value of such tests? Suppose someone decides to refactor our `mod_divide()` method as follows:

```
    def mod_divide(self):
        ...
        return (self.a // self.b, self.a % self.b)
```

Since this passes our tests, we can be pretty sure this algorithm is correct, even if we didn't understand the code. If there were a problem with the refactor, our tests should show that fairly quickly.

Testing pure mathematical functions is fairly simple; unfortunately, testing real application code presents us with some challenges that demand a more sophisticated approach.

Consider these issues:

- Code units often rely on a pre-existing state that must be set up before the test and cleared up afterwards.
- Code may have side effects that change objects outside the code unit.
- Code may interact with resources that are slow, unreliable, or unpredictable.

- Real applications contain many functions and classes that require testing, and ideally we'd like to be alerted to all problems at once. Our tests, as written, would stop on the first failed assertion, so we'd only get alerted to one problem at a time.

To address these issues and others, programmers rely on **testing frameworks** to make writing and executing automated tests as simple and reliable as possible.

The unittest module

The `unittest` module is the Python standard library's automated testing framework. It provides us with some powerful tools to make testing our code reasonably easy.

`unittest` is based on these standard unit testing concepts found in many test frameworks:

- **Test**: A **test** is a single method that will either finish or raise an exception. Tests generally focus on one unit of code, such as a function, method, or process. A test can either pass, meaning the test was successful; fail, meaning the code failed the test; or error, meaning the test itself encountered a problem
- **Test case**: A test case is a collection of tests which should be run together and contain similar setup and tear-down requirements, typically corresponding to a class or module. Test cases can have fixtures, which are items that need to be set up before each test and torn down after each test to provide a clean, predictable environment in which the test can run
- **Test suite**: A test suite is a collection of test cases which cover all the code for an application or module.
- **Mock**: A mock is an object that stands in for an external resource, such as a file or database. Mocks are patched over those resources during the test.

To explore these concepts in depth, let's test our `MyCalc` class using `unittest`.

Writing a test case

Let's create a test case for the MyCalc class in the test_mycalc.py as follows:

```
from mycalc import MyCalc
import unittest

class TestMyCalc(unittest.TestCase):
    def test_add(self):
        mc = MyCalc(1, 10)
        assert mc.add() == 11

if __name__ == '__main__':
    unittest.main()
```

The names of both your test modules and your test methods should be prefixed with test_. Doing so allows the unittest runner to automatically find test modules and distinguish test methods from other methods in your test case classes.

As you probably guessed, the TestCase class represents a test case. To make our test case for MyCalc, we subclass TestCase and start adding the test_ methods to test various aspects of our class. Our test_add() method creates a MyCalc object, then makes an assertion about the output of add(). To run the test case, we add a call to unittest.main() at the end of the file.

If you run your test file at the command line, you should get the following output:

```
.
----------------------------------------------------------------------
Ran 1 test in 0.000s

OK
```

The single dot on the first line represents our test (test_add()). For each test method, unittest.main() will output a dot for passing, F for failure, or E for error. At the end, we get a summary of what happened.

To see what happens when a test fails, let's alter our test to be incorrect:

```
    def test_add(self):
        mc = mycalc.MyCalc(1, 10)
        assert mc.add() == 12
```

Now when you run the test module, you should see a failure as follows:

```
F
======================================================================
FAIL: test_add (__main__.TestMyCalc)
----------------------------------------------------------------------
Traceback (most recent call last):
  File "test_mycalc.py", line 8, in test_add
    assert mc.add() == 12
AssertionError
----------------------------------------------------------------------
Ran 1 test in 0.000s

FAILED (failures=1)
```

Note the single `F` at the top, representing our failed test. After all the tests have run, we get the full traceback of any failed tests, so that we can easily locate the failing code and correct it. This traceback output isn't very ideal, though; we can see that `mc.add()` didn't equal `12`, but we don't know what it was equal to. We could add a comment string to our `assert` call, but `unittest` provides a nicer method.

TestCase assertion methods

`TestCase` objects have a number of assertion methods that provide a cleaner and more robust way to run various tests on our code output.

For example, there is the `TestCase.assertEqual()` method to test equality, which we can use as follows:

```
    def test_add(self):
        mc = mycalc.MyCalc(1, 10)
        self.assertEqual(mc.add(), 12)
```

When we run our tests with this code, you can see that the traceback is improved:

```
Traceback (most recent call last):
  File "test_mycalc.py", line 11, in test_add
    self.assertEqual(mc.add(), 12)
AssertionError: 11 != 12
```

Now, we can see the value that `mc.add()` created, which is much more helpful for debugging. `TestCase` contains more than 20 assertion methods that can simplify testing for a variety of conditions such as class inheritance, raised exceptions, and sequence membership.

Some more commonly used ones are listed in the following table:

Method	Tests
`assertEqual(a, b)`	`a == b`
`assertTrue(a)`	`a` is `True`
`assertFalse(a)`	`a` is `False`
`assertIn(item, sequence)`	`item` is in `sequence`
`assertRaises(exception, callable, args)`	`callable` called with `args` raises `exception`
`assertGreater(a, b)`	`a` is greater than `b`
`assertLess(a, b)`	`a` is less than `b`

You can easily add your own custom assertion methods to your test case as well; it's simply a matter of creating a method that raises an `AssertionError` exception under some condition.

Let's use an assertion method to test that `mod_divide()` raises `ValueError` when `b` is `0`:

```
    def test_mod_divide(self):
        mycalc = mycalc.MyCalc(1, 0)
        self.assertRaises(ValueError, mycalc.mod_divide)
```

`assertRaises` passes if the function raises the given assertion when called. If we need to pass any arguments into the tested function, they can be specified as additional arguments to `assertRaises()`.

`assertRaises()` can also be used as a context manager like so:

```
        mycalc = MyCalc(1, 0)
        with self.assertRaises(ValueError):
            mycalc.mod_divide()
```

This code accomplishes the exact same thing, but is a little clearer and more flexible.

Fixtures

Rather than perform the tedious task of creating the `MyCalc` objects in every test, our `TestCase` object can have a `setUp()` method that automatically creates any resources our tests need.

For example, take a look at the following code:

```
def setUp(self):
    self.mycalc1_0 = mycalc.MyCalc(1, 0)
    self.mycalc36_12 = mycalc.MyCalc(36, 12)
```

Now, every test case can use these objects to run its tests. The `setUp()` method will be rerun before every test, so these objects will always be reset between test methods. If we have items that need to cleaned up after each test, we can define a `tearDown()` method, which will be run after each test (in this case, it's not necessary).

Now, for example, our `test_add()` method can be much simpler:

```
def test_add(self):
    self.assertEqual(self.mycalc1_0.add(), 1)
    self.assertEqual(self.mycalc36_12.add(), 48)
```

In addition to the instance methods `setUp()` and `tearDown()`, `TestCase` has class methods for setup and tear down as well, namely `setUpClass()` and `tearDownClass()`. These can be used for slower operations that can be run when the test case is created and destroyed, rather than needing to be refreshed between each test method.

Using Mock and patch

The `rand_between()` method generates a random number between `a` and `b`. Because we can't possibly predict its output, we can't provide a fixed value to test it against. How can we test this method?

A naive approach is as follows:

```
def test_rand_between(self):
    rv = self.mycalc1_0.rand_between()
    self.assertLessEqual(rv, 1)
    self.assertGreaterEqual(rv, 0)
```

This test passes if our code is correct, but it doesn't necessarily fail if the code is wrong; in fact, if the code is wrong, it may pass or fail unpredictably. For example, if `MyCalc(1, 10).rand_between()` was incorrectly returning values between 2 and 11, there is only a 10% chance that the test would fail on each run.

We can safely assume that a standard library function such `random()` works correctly, so our unit test should really test whether our method correctly handles the number provided to it by `random()`. If we could temporarily replace `random()` with a function that returns a fixed value, it would be simple to test the correctness of our subsequent calculations.

The `unittest.mock` module provides us with the `Mock` class for this purpose. `Mock` objects can be used to predictably simulate the behavior of another class, method, or library. We can give our `Mock` objects return values, side effects, properties, methods, and other features needed to fake the behavior of another object, then drop it in place of that object before running our tests.

Let's create a fake `random()` function using `Mock` as follows:

```
from unittest.mock import Mock

#... inside TestMyCalc
    def test_rand_between(self):
        fakerandom = Mock(return_value=.5)
```

The `Mock` object's `return_value` argument allows us to hard code a value to be returned whenever it's called as a function. Here, `fakerandom` will always return `0.5`.

Now we can put `fakerandom` in place of `random()` as follows:

```
        orig_random = mycalc.random.random
        mycalc.random.random = fakerandom
        rv = self.mycalc1_0.rand_between()
        self.assertEqual(rv, 0.5)
        mycalc.random.random = orig_random
```

We start by saving a reference to `mycalc.random.random` before replacing it. Note that we're specifically replacing only the version of `random` being used in `mycalc.py` so that we don't affect `random` anywhere else. It's a best practice to be as specific as possible when patching libraries to avoid unforeseen side effects.

With `fakerandom` in place, we call our method and test the output. Because `fakerandom` will always return `0.5`, we know that the answer should be (0.5 × 1 + 0) or `0.5` when `a` is `1` and `b` is `0`. Any other value would indicate an error in our algorithm. Last of all, we revert `random` to the original function so that other tests don't accidentally use the mock.

Having to store or revert the original library each time is an annoyance we can do without, so `unittest.mock` provides a cleaner approach using `patch`.
The `patch` command can be used as either a context manager or a decorator, and either approach makes patching a `Mock` object into our code much cleaner.

Using our mock `random()` using `patch` as a context manager looks like this:

```
from unittest.mock import patch

    #... inside TestMyCalc
    def test_rand_between(self):
       with patch('mycalc.random.random') as fakerandom:
            fakerandom.return_value = 0.5
            rv = self.mycalc1_0.rand_between()
            self.assertEqual(rv, 0.5)
```

`The patch()` command takes an import path string and provides us with a `Mock` object that it has patched in. We can set methods and properties on the `Mock` object and run our actual tests in the block, and the patched library will be reverted when the block ends.

Using `patch()` as a decorator is similar:

```
    @patch('mycalc.random.random')
    def test_rand_between2(self, fakerandom):
        fakerandom.return_value = 0.5
        rv = self.mycalc1_0.rand_between()
        self.assertEqual(rv, 0.5)
```

In this case, the mock object created by `patch` is passed as an argument to our test method and will remain patched for the duration of the decorated function.

Running multiple unit tests

While we can run our unit tests by including a call to `unittest.main()` at the end, that approach doesn't scale well. As our application grows, we're going to write many test files, which we'll want to run in groups or all at once.

Fortunately, `unittest` can discover and run all tests in a project with one command:

```
python -m unittest
```

So long as you have followed the recommended naming scheme of prefixing your test modules with `test_`, running this command in your project's root directory should run all your tests.

Testing Tkinter code

Testing Tkinter code presents us with a few particular challenges. First, Tkinter handles many callbacks and methods **asynchronously**, meaning that we can't count on the results of some code to be apparent immediately. Also, testing GUI behaviors often relies on external factors such as window management or visual cues that our tests cannot detect.

We're going to learn some tools and strategies that will help you craft tests for your Tkinter code.

Managing asynchronous code

Whenever you interact with a Tkinter UI—whether it's clicking a button, typing in a field, or raising a window, for example—the response is not executed immediately in-place. Instead, these actions are placed in a to-do list, called an **event queue**, to be handled later while your code execution continues. While these actions seem instant to users, test code cannot count on a requested action being completed before the next line of code.

To solve this problem, we can use these special widget methods that allow us to manage the event queue:

- `wait_visibility()`: This method causes the program to wait until a widget is fully drawn on-screen before executing the next line of code.
- `update_idletasks()`: This method forces Tkinter to process any idle tasks currently outstanding on the widget. Idle tasks are low-priority tasks such as drawing and rendering.
- `update()`: This method forces Tkinter to process all events which are outstanding on a widget, including calling callbacks, redraws, and geometry management. It includes everything that `update_idletasks()` does and more.

Simulating user actions

When automating GUI tests, we may wish to know what happens when a user clicks on a certain widget, or types a certain keystroke. When these actions happen in the GUI, Tkinter generates an `Event` object for the widget and passes it to the event queue. We can do the same thing in code, using a widget's `event_generate()` method.

Specifying an event sequence

To create an event with `event_generate()`, we need to pass in an event sequence string, in the format `<EventModifier-EventType-EventDetail>`.

Event type specifies the kind of event we're sending, such as a keystroke, mouse click, windowing event, and so on.

Tkinter has around 30 event types, but you will typically only need to work with the following:

Event types	Description
`ButtonPress`	Also `Button`, represents a mouse button click
`ButtonRelease`	Represents lifting off a mouse button
`KeyPress`	Also `Key`, represents pressing a keyboard key
`KeyRelease`	Represents lifting off a keyboard key
`FocusIn`	Represents giving focus to a widget
`FocusOut`	Represents exiting a widget
`Enter`	Represents the mouse cursor entering a widget
`Leave`	Represents the mouse cursor moving off a widget
`Configure`	Called when the widget's configuration changes, either by a `.config()` call or user action (resize, for example)

Event modifiers are optional words that can alter the event type; for example, `Control`, `Alt`, and `Shift` can be used to indicate that one of those modifier keys is held down; `Double` or `Triple` can be used to indicate a double or triple click of the described button. Multiple modifiers can be strung together if required.

Event detail, only valid for keyboard or mouse events, describes which key or button was pressed. For example, `<Button-1>` refers to the left mouse button, while `<Button-3>` refers to the right. For letter and number keys, the literal letter or number can be used; most symbols, however, are described by a word (`minus`, `colon`, `semicolon`, and so on) to avoid syntactic clashes.

For button presses and key presses, the event type is technically optional; however, it's probably a good idea to leave it in for the sake of clarity. For example, `<1>` is a valid event, but does it refer to the left mouse button or typing the `1` key? You may be surprised to find that it's the mouse button.

The following table shows some examples of valid event sequences:

Sequence	Meaning
`<Double-Button-3>`	Double-clicking the right mouse button
`<Alt-KeyPress-exclam>`	Holding `Alt` and typing an exclamation point
`<Control-Alt-Key-m>`	Holding `Control` and `Alt` and pressing the `m` key
`<KeyRelease-minus>`	Lifting off a pressed minus key

In addition to the sequence, we can pass other arguments to `event_generate()` which describe various aspects of the event. Many of these are redundant, but, in some cases, we need to provide extra information for the event to have any meaning; for example, mouse button events need to include the `x` and `y` arguments that specify the coordinates of the click.

Managing focus and grab

Focus refers to the widget or window which is currently receiving keyboard input. Widgets can also grab focus, preventing mouse movements or keystrokes outside their bounds.

Tkinter gives us these widget methods for managing focus and grab, some of which are useful for running tests:

Method	Description
`focus_set()`	Focuses the widget whenever its window next gains focus
`focus_force()`	Focuses a widget and the window it's in, immediately
`grab_set()`	The widget grabs all events for the application
`grab_set_global()`	The widget grabs all screen events
`grab_release()`	The widget relinquishes its grab

In a test environment, we can use these methods to make sure that our generated keyboard and mouse events are going to the correct widget or window.

Getting widget information

Tkinter widgets have a set of `winfo_` methods that give us access to information about the widget. While this set of methods leaves much to be desired, it does provide a few methods we can use in tests to provide feedback about the state of a given widget.

The following are a few `winfo_` methods that we will find useful:

Method	Description
`winfo_height()`, `winfo_width()`	Get the height and width of the widget
`winfo_children()`	Get a list of child widgets
`winfo_geometry()`	Get the size and location of the widget
`winfo_ismapped()`	Determine whether the widget is mapped, meaning it's been added to a layout using `pack()` or `grid()`, for instance
`winfo_viewable()`	Determine whether a widget is viewable, meaning it and all its parents have been mapped
`winfo_x()`, `winfo_y()`	Get the `x` or `y` coordinate of the widget's top left corner

Writing tests for our application

Let's put our knowledge of `unittest` to work and write some tests for our application. To get started, we need to create a test module for our application. Make a directory called `test` inside the `abq_data_entry` package, and create the customary empty `__init__.py` file inside. We'll create all of our test modules inside this directory.

Testing our model

Our `CSVModel` code is fairly self-contained apart from its need to read and write files. Since file operations are one of the more common things that need to be mocked out in a test, the `mock` module provides `mock_open`, a `Mock` subclass ready-made to replace Python's `open` method. When called, a `mock_open` object returns a `mock` file handle object, complete with support for the `read()`, `write()`, and `readlines()` methods.

Let's begin creating our test case class in `test/test_models.py` as follows:

```
from .. import models
from unittest import TestCase
from unittest import mock

class TestCSVModel(TestCase):
    def setUp(self):
        self.file1_open = mock.mock_open(
            read_data=(
                "Date,Time,Technician,Lab,Plot,Seed
sample,Humidity,Light,"
                "Temperature,Equipment Fault,Plants,Blossoms,Fruit,"
                "Min Height,Max Height,Median Height,Notes\r\n"
                "2018-06-01,8:00,J Simms,A,2,AX478,
                 24.47,1.01,21.44,False,14,"
                "27,1,2.35,9.2,5.09,\r\n"
                "2018-06-01,8:00,J Simms,A,3,AX479,
                24.15,1,20.82,False,18,49,"
                "6,2.47,14.2,11.83,\r\n"))
        self.file2_open = mock.mock_open(read_data='')
        self.model1 = models.CSVModel('file1')
        self.model2 = models.CSVModel('file2')
```

The mock_open and read_data arguments allows us to specify a string that will be returned when its file handle is read. We've created two mock_open objects, one containing a CSV header and two lines of data, and the other containing nothing.

We've also created two CSVModel objects, one with a filename of file1 and the other with a filename of file2. It's worth mentioning that there's no actual connection between our models and our mock_open objects. The choice of the mock_open object, rather than the filename, will determine what data will be returned

Testing file reading in get_all_records()

To see how we use these, let's start a test for the get_all_records() method as follows:

```
@mock.patch('abq_data_entry.models.os.path.exists')
def test_get_all_records(self, mock_exists):
    mock_exists.return_value = True
```

Since our filenames don't actually exist, we're using the decorator version of patch to patch os.path.exists with a mock function that always returns True. We can later change the return_value value if we want to test a scenario where the file doesn't exist.

To run the get_all_records() method, we'll use the context manager form of patch() as follows:

```
        with mock.patch('abq_data_entry.models.open',
self.file1_open):
            records = self.model1.get_all_records()
```

Any call to open() inside the models.py file which has been initiated inside the context manager block will be replaced by our mock_open object, and the file handle returned will contain read_data we specified. However, before we can go on, there's an unfortunate shortcoming in mock_open that we'll need to work around. While it implements most file methods, it doesn't implement the iterator methods that the csv library requires to read data from the file handler.

A slight alteration to our models.py code will fix this:

```
def get_all_records(self):
    ...
    with open(self.filename, 'r', encoding='utf-8') as fh:
        csvreader = csv.DictReader(list(fh.readlines()))
```

Instead of simply passing `fh` into `DictReader`, we need to call `readlines()` and cast it to `list`. This won't affect the program in any way, but it will allow `mock_open()` to work correctly.

There's nothing wrong with making adjustments to your code to accommodate tests; in many cases, the code will even be better for it! However, if you make an unintuitive change such as the previous one, be sure to add a comment to your code to explain why. Otherwise, someone is likely to factor it out at some point in the future.

Now we can start making assertions about the records which have been returned:

```
self.assertEqual(len(records), 2)
self.assertIsInstance(records, list)
self.assertIsInstance(records[0], dict)
```

Here, we're checking that `records` contains two lines (since our read data contained two `csv` records), that it's a `list` object, and that its first member is a `dict` object (or subclass of `dict`).

Next, let's make sure all our fields made it through and that our Boolean conversion worked:

```
fields = (
   'Date', 'Time', 'Technician', 'Lab', 'Plot',
   'Seed sample', 'Humidity', 'Light',
   'Temperature', 'Equipment Fault', 'Plants',
   'Blossoms', 'Fruit', 'Min Height', 'Max Height',
   'Median Height', 'Notes')
for field in fields:
    self.assertIn(field, records[0].keys())
self.assertFalse(records[0]['Equipment Fault'])
```

By iterating a tuple of all our field names, we can check that all our fields are present in the record output. Don't be afraid to use loops in a test this way to check a large amount of content quickly.

A `Mock` object can do more than just stand in for another class or function; it also has its own assertion methods that can tell us if it's been called, how many times, and with what arguments.

For example, we can check our `mock_open` object to make sure it was called with the expected arguments:

```
        self.file1_open.assert_called_with('file1', 'r',
encoding='utf-8')
```

`assert_called_with()` takes a set of arguments and checks if the last call to the `mock` object used those arguments. We expected `file1_open` to be called with the filename `file1`, a mode of `r`, and an encoding of `utf-8`. By confirming that a mocked function was called with the correct arguments, and assuming the correctness of the real function (the built-in `open()` function, in this case), we can avoid having to test the actual outcome.

Testing file saving in save_record()

To demonstrate how to test file-writing with `mock_open`, let's test `save_record()`:

```
    @patch('abq_data_entry.models.os.path.exists')
    def test_save_record(self, mock_exists):
```

To test the conversion from a `dict` to a `csv` string, we'll need a sample record in both formats:

```
        record = {
            "Date": '2018-07-01', "Time": '12:00',
            "Technician": 'Test Tech', "Lab": 'E',
             "Plot": '7', "Seed sample": 'test',
            "Humidity": '10', "Light": '99',
            "Temperature": '20', "Equipment Fault": False,
            "Plants": '10', "Blossoms": '200', "Fruit": '250',
            "Min Height": '40', "Max Height": '50',
            "Median Height": '55', "Notes": 'Test Note\r\nTest
Note\r\n'}
        record_as_csv = (
            '2018-07-01,12:00,Test Tech,E,17,test,10,99,20,False,'
            '10,200,250,40,50,55,"Test Note\r\nTest Note\r\n"\r\n')
```

You may be tempted to generate either the record or its expected output using code, but it's always better to stick to literals in tests; doing so makes the expectations of the test explicit and avoids logic errors in your tests.

For our first scenario, let's simulate writing to an empty but existing file by using `file2_open` and `model2` as follows:

```
        mock_exists.return_value = True
        with patch('abq_data_entry.models.open', self.file2_open):
            self.model2.save_record(record, None)
```

Setting our `mock_exists.return_value` to `True` to tell our method that the file already exists, we then patch over `open()` with our second `mock_open` object and call the `save_record()` method. Since we passed in a record with no row number (which indicates a record insert), this should result in our code trying to open `file2` in append mode and writing in the CSV-formatted record.

`assert_called_with()` will test that assumption as follows:

```
            self.file2_open.assert_called_with('file2', 'a',
                encoding='utf-8')
```

`file2_open` can tell us that it was called with the expected parameters, but how do we access its file handler so that we can see what was written to it?

It turns out we can just call our `mock_open` object and retrieve the `mock` file handle object:

```
            file2_handle = self.file2_open()
            file2_handle.write.assert_called_with(record_as_csv)
```

Once we have the `mock` file handle (which is itself a `Mock`), we can run test methods on it to find out if it was called with the CSV data as expected. In this case, the file handle's `write` method should have been called with the CSV-format record string.

Let's do a similar set of tests, passing in a row number to simulate a record update:

```
        with patch('abq_data_entry.models.open', self.file1_open):
            self.model1.save_record(record, 1)
            self.file1_open.assert_called_with('file1', 'w',
            encoding='utf-8')
```

Checking that our update was done correctly presents a problem: `assert_called_with()` only checks the last call made to the mock function. When we update our CSV file, the entire CSV file is updated, with one `write()` call per row. We can't just check that the last call was correct; we need to make sure the `write()` calls for all the rows were correct. To accomplish this, `Mock` provides us with `assert_has_calls()`, to which we can pass a list of `Call` objects to compare against the object's call history.

We create `Call` objects using the `mock.call()` function as follows:

```
        file1_handle = self.file1_open()
        file1_handle.write.assert_has_calls([
            mock.call('Date,Time,Technician,Lab,Plot,Seed sample,'
                 'Humidity,Light,Temperature,Equipment Fault,'
                 'Plants,Blossoms,Fruit,Min Height,Max Height,'
                 'Median Height,Notes\r\n'),
            mock.call('2018-06-01,8:00,J
Simms,A,2,AX478,24.47,1.01,'
                 '21.44,False, '14,27,1,2.35,9.2,5.09,\r\n'),
            mock.call('2018-07-01,12:00,Test
Tech,E,17,test,10,99,20,'
                 'False,10,200,250,'40,50,55,'
                 '"Test Note\r\nTest Note\r\n"\r\n')
        ])
```

The arguments to `call()` represent the arguments that were passed to the function call. The list of `Call` objects we pass to `assert_has_calls()` represents each call that should have been made to `write()` in order. The keyword argument `in_order` can also be set to `False`, in which case the order won't need to match. In this case, order matters, since a wrong order would result in a corrupt CSV file.

More tests

Testing the remainder of the `CSVModel` class and the `SettingsModel` class methods should be essentially along the same lines as these two methods. A few more tests are included in the sample code, but see if you can come up with some of your own as well.

Testing our application

We've implemented our application as a `Tk` object that acts not only as a main window but as a controller, patching together models and views defined elsewhere in the application. As you may expect, `patch()` is going to figure heavily into our testing code as we mock out all of those other components to isolate `Application`. Let's take a look at how this is done:

1. In a new file called `test_application.py`, import `unittest` and `application`. Now start a test case as follows:

```
class TestApplication(TestCase):
    records = [
        {'Blossoms': '21', 'Date': '2018-06-01',
         'Equipment Fault': 'False', 'Fruit': '3,
         'Humidity': '24.09', 'Lab': 'A', 'Light': '1.03',
         'Max Height': '8.7', 'Median Height': '2.73',
         'Min Height': '1.67','Notes': '\n\n', 'Plants':
'9',
         'Plot': '1', 'Seed sample': 'AX477',
         'Technician': 'J Simms', 'Temperature': '22.01',
         'Time': '8:00'},
        {'Blossoms': '27', 'Date': '2018-06-01',
         'Equipment Fault': 'False', 'Fruit': '1',
         'Humidity': '24.47', 'Lab': 'A', 'Light': '1.01',
         'Max Height': '9.2', 'Median Height': '5.09',
         'Min Height': '2.35', 'Notes': '', 'Plants':
'14',
         'Plot': '2', 'Seed sample': 'AX478',
         'Technician': 'J Simms', 'Temperature': '21.44',
         'Time': '8:00'}]
    settings = {
        'autofill date': {'type': 'bool', 'value': True},
        'autofill sheet data': {'type': 'bool', 'value':
True},
        'font size': {'type': 'int', 'value': 9},
        'theme': {'type': 'str', 'value': 'default'}}
```

Our `TestApplication` class will be using mocks in place of our data and settings models, so we've created some class properties to store samples of the data which `Application` expects to retrieve from those models. The `setUp()` method is going to patch out all the external classes with mocks, configure the mocked models to return our sample data, and then create an `Application` instance that our tests can use.

2. Let's start by using `patch()` as a context manager to replace all the external resources as follows:

```
    def setUp(self):
        with \
            patch('abq_data_entry.application.m.CSVModel')\
                as csvmodel,\
            patch('abq_data_entry.application.m.SettingsModel')
\
                as settingsmodel,\
patch('abq_data_entry.application.v.DataRecordForm'), \
            patch('abq_data_entry.application.v.RecordList'),\
patch('abq_data_entry.application.get_main_menu_for_os')\
        :
```

Here, we've created a `with` block using five `patch()` context managers, one for each library we're mocking out. Notice that we're only creating aliases for the model mocks, since we'll want to do some extra configuration on them. The view mocks won't really need to do much except be imported or called, and we can access them as properties of our `Application` object anyway.

Since Python 3.2, you can create a block with multiple context managers by separating each context manager call with a comma. Unfortunately, you can't put them in parenthesis, so we're using the comparatively ugly escaped-newline method of breaking this gigantic call into multiple lines.

3. Inside the block, we'll need to configure our model mocks to return the appropriate data as follows:

```
    settingsmodel().variables = self.settings
    csvmodel().get_all_records.return_value = self.records
```

Notice that we're instantiating our `settingsmodel` and `csvmodel` objects and configuring methods on the return values rather than the mocks themselves. Remember that our mocks are replacing the *classes*, not the *objects*, and it is the objects which will contain the methods our `Application` object will be calling. Therefore, we need to call them to access the actual `Mock` object that will be used by `Application` as the data or settings model.

Unlike the actual class that it stands in for, a `Mock` object called as a function will return the same object every time it's called. Thus, we don't have to save a reference to the object created by calling a mocked class; we can just call the mocked class repeatedly to access that object. Note, however, that the `Mock` class will return a unique `Mock` object each time.

4. This takes care of our mocks, so let's create an `Application` object:

```
self.app = application.Application()
```

5. Because `Application` is a subclass of Tk, it's a good idea for us to safely dispose of it after each use; even though we're reassigning its variable name, it will go on existing and cause problems with our tests. To solve this, create a `tearDown()` method:

```
def tearDown(self):
    self.app.update()
    self.app.destroy()
```

Notice the call to `app.update()`. If we don't call this before destroying `app`, there may be tasks in the event queue that will try to access it after it's gone. This won't break our code, but it will clutter up our test output with error messages.

6. Now that our fixtures are taken care of, let's write a test:

```
def test_show_recordlist(self):
    self.app.show_recordlist()
    self.app.update()
    self.app.recordlist.tkraise.assert_called()
```

`Application.show_recordlist()` contains one line of code, which is merely a call to `recordlist.tkraise()`. Because we made `recordlist` a mock object, `tkraise` is also a mock object, and we can check to see that it was called. `assert_called()` merely checks that a method was called, without checking arguments, which is appropriate in this case because `tkraise()` takes none.

7. We can use a similar technique to check `populate_recordlist()` as follows:

```
    def test_populate_recordlist(self):
        self.app.populate_recordlist()
        self.app.data_model.get_all_records.assert_called()
self.app.recordlist.populate.assert_called_with(self.records)
```

8. Under some circumstances, `get_all_records()` can raise an exception, in which case we're supposed to show an error message box. But since we've mocked out our data model, how can we get it to raise an exception? The solution is to use mock's `side_effect` property as follows:

```
self.app.data_model.get_all_records.side_effect =
Exception('Test message')
```

`side_effect` can be used to simulate more complex functionality in a mocked callable. It can be set to a function, in which case the mock will run that function and return the results when called; it can be set to an iterable, in which case the mock will return the next item in the iterable each time it's called; or, as in this case, it can be set to an exception, which will be raised when the mock is called.

9. Before we can use this, we'll need to patch out `messagebox` as follows:

```
with patch('abq_data_entry.application.messagebox'):
    self.app.populate_recordlist()
    application.messagebox.showerror.assert_called_with(
        title='Error', message='Problem reading file',
        detail='Test message')
```

10. This time when we call `populate_recordlist()`, it throws an exception, prompting the method to call `messagebox.showerror()`. Since we've mocked `showerror()`, we can assert that it was called with the expected arguments.

Clearly, the hardest part of testing our `Application` object is patching in all the mocked components and making sure they behave enough like the real thing to satisfy `Application`. Once we've done that, writing the actual tests is fairly straightforward.

Testing our widgets

So far, we've done well with `patch`, `Mock`, and the default `TestCase`, but testing our widgets module is going to present some new challenges. To begin with, our widgets will need a `Tk` instance to be their root window. We can create this in each case's `setUp()` method, but this will slow down the tests considerably, and it isn't really necessary; our tests aren't going to modify the root window, so one root window will suffice for each test case. We can take advantage of the `setUpClass()` method to create a single instance of Tk just once at class instantiation. Secondly, we have a large number of widgets to test, which means we have a large number of test cases requiring the same boilerplate `Tk()` setup and tear down.

To address this, let's start our `test_widgets.py` module with a custom `TestCase` class as follows:

```
class TkTestCase(TestCase):
    """A test case designed for Tkinter widgets and views"""
    @classmethod
    def setUpClass(cls):
        cls.root = tk.Tk()
        cls.root.wait_visibility()

    @classmethod
    def tearDownClass(cls):
        cls.root.update()
        cls.root.destroy()
```

The `setUpClass()` method creates the `Tk()` object and calls `wait_visibility()` just to make sure our window is visible before our tests start working with it. Just as we did with our `Application` test, we also supply a complimentary tear-down method that updates the Tk instance and destroys it.

Unit testing the ValidatedSpinbox widget

`ValidatedSpinbox` is one of the more complicated widgets we created for our application, so it's a good place to start writing tests.

Subclass the `TkTestCase` class to create a test case for `ValidatedSpinbox` as follows:

```
class TestValidatedSpinbox(TkTestCase):

    def setUp(self):
        self.value = tk.DoubleVar()
        self.vsb = widgets.ValidatedSpinbox(
            self.root,
            textvariable=self.value,
            from_=-10, to=10, increment=1)
        self.vsb.pack()
        self.vsb.wait_visibility()

    def tearDown(self):
        self.vsb.destroy()
```

Our setup method creates a variable in which to store the widget's value, then creates an instance of the `ValidatedSpinbox` widget with some basic settings: a minimum value of -10, a maximum of 10, and an increment of 1. After creating it, we pack it and wait for it to become visible. For our tear-down method, we simply destroy the widget.

There are a couple of approaches we can take in testing our widget. The first approach is a unit testing-oriented approach, in which we focus on the actual method code, simply mocking out any external functionality.

Let's try that with the `_key_validate()` method as follows:

```
    def test__key_validate(self):
        # test valid input
        for x in range(10):
            x = str(x)
            p_valid = self.vsb._key_validate(x, 'end', '', '', x, '1')
            n_valid = self.vsb._key_validate(
                x, 'end', '-', '-' + x, '1')
            self.assertTrue(p_valid)
            self.assertTrue(n_valid)
```

We're simply iterating from 0 to 9 and testing both the positive and negative of the number against `_key_validate()`, which should return `True` for all of these values. The `_key_validate()` method takes a lot of positional arguments, and most of them are redundant; it might be nice to have a wrapper method that makes it easier to call, since our test case is potentially going to call it dozens of times.

Let's call that method `key_validate()` and add it to our `TestValidatedSpinbox` class as follows:

```
    def key_validate(self, new, current=''):
        # args are inserted char, insertion index, current value,
        # proposed value, and action code (where '1' is 'insert')
        return self.vsb._key_validate(new, 'end', current,
        current + new, '1')
```

This will make future calls to the method shorter and less error-prone.

Let's use it now to test some invalid input as follows:

```
        # test letters
        valid = self.key_validate('a')
        self.assertFalse(valid)

        # test non-increment number
        valid = self.key_validate('1', '0.')
        self.assertFalse(valid)

        # test too high number
        valid = self.key_validate('0', '10')
        self.assertFalse(valid)
```

In the first example, we're entering `a`; in the second, `1` when `0.` is already in the box, resulting in `0.1`; in the third, `0` when `10` is in the box, resulting in `100`. All of these scenarios should fail the validation method.

Integration testing the ValidatedSpinbox widget

In the preceding tests, we weren't actually entering any data into the widget; we were simply calling the key validation method directly and evaluating its output. This is good unit testing, but it isn't quite satisfying as a test of this code. Since our custom widget is so deeply dependent on Tkinter's validation API, we'd like to test that we've actually implemented this API correctly. After all, that aspect of the code was more challenging than the actual logic in our validation methods.

We can accomplish this by creating some integration tests that simulate actual user actions and then check the results of those actions. To do this cleanly, we'll first need to create some supporting methods.

Start by adding a new method to the `TkTestCase` class as follows:

```
def type_in_widget(self, widget, string):
    widget.focus_force()
    for char in string:
        char = self.keysyms.get(char, char)
```

This class will take a widget and a string and attempt to simulate a user typing the string into the widget. The first thing we do is force the focus to the widget; we need to use `focus_force()` because our test Tk window is unlikely to be in focus when the test is being run.

Once we have focus, we'll iterate through the characters in the string and translate the raw character into the appropriate key symbols for our event sequence. Recall that some characters, particularly symbols, must be represented as strings, such as `minus` or `colon`.

To make this work, we'll need a class property called `dict` to translate between characters and their key symbols as follows:

```
keysyms = {'-': 'minus', ' ': 'space', ':': 'colon', ...}
```

More key symbols can be found at `http://www.tcl.tk/man/tcl8.4/TkCmd/keysyms.htm`, but these should do for now.

Once our character is translated to the appropriate key symbol, we can create our event sequences and generate our key events. Back in the `type_in_widget()` method, we can create and call a key event sequence as follows:

```
        self.root.update()
        widget.event_generate('<KeyPress-{}>'.format(char))
        self.root.update()
```

Note that we call `self.root.update()` both before and after generating the keypress event. This ensures the widget is prepared for input, and that the inputs register after being generated. `update_idletasks()` will not do here, by the way; try it and you'll find that the tests will fail.

We can create a similar method for simulating mouse button clicks as follows:

```
    def click_on_widget(self, widget, x, y, button=1):
        widget.focus_force()
        self.root.update()
        widget.event_generate("<ButtonPress-
{}>".format(button),
        x=x, y=y)
        self.root.update()
```

Just as we did with our keystroke method, we first force focus, update the application, generate our events, then update again. In this method, however, we also need to specify the `x` and `y` coordinates for the mouse click. These are coordinates relative to the upper-left corner of the widget. We can also specify a button number, but we'll default to the left button (`1`).

With these methods in place, return to `TestValidatedSpinbox` and write a new test:

```
    def test__key_validate_integration(self):
        self.vsb.delete(0, 'end')
        self.type_in_widget(self.vsb, '10')
        self.assertEqual(self.vsb.get(), '10')
```

This method starts by clearing the widget, then simulates some valid input with `type_in _widget()` and checks that it was accepted by the widget. Note that in these integration tests we'll need to clear the widget each time because we are simulating keystrokes in an actual widget and triggering all the side effects of that action.

Next, let's test some invalid input by executing the following code:

```
self.vsb.delete(0, 'end')
self.type_in_widget(self.vsb, 'abcdef')
self.assertEqual(self.vsb.get(), '')

self.vsb.delete(0, 'end')
self.type_in_widget(self.vsb, '200')
self.assertEqual(self.vsb.get(), '2')
```

We can use our mouse click method to test the functionality of the `Spinbox` arrow buttons as well. To make this simpler, let's create a helper method in our test case class to click on the arrow we want. Add this to `TestValidatedSpinbox`:

```
def click_arrow(self, arrow='inc', times=1):
    x = self.vsb.winfo_width() - 5
    y = 5 if arrow == 'inc' else 15
    for _ in range(times):
        self.click_on_widget(self.vsb, x=x, y=y)
```

We can target the increment arrow by clicking `5` pixels from the right and `5` from the top of the widget. The decrement arrow can be found at `5` pixels from the right and `15` from the top. This may need some adjustment depending on the theme or screen settings, of course. Now, we can test our arrow key functionality easily as follows:

```
def test_arrows(self):
    self.value.set(0)
    self.click_arrow(times=1)
    self.assertEqual(self.vsb.get(), '1')

    self.click_arrow(times=5)
    self.assertEqual(self.vsb.get(), '6')

    self.click_arrow(arrow='dec', times=1)
    self.assertEqual(self.vsb.get(), '5')
```

By setting the value of the widget, then clicking the appropriate arrow a specified number of times, we can test that the arrows did their jobs according to the rules of our widget class.

Testing our mixin class

One additional challenge we haven't approached yet is testing our mixin class. Unlike our other widget classes, our mixin cannot really exist on its own: it depends on methods and properties found in the `ttk` widget which it's combined with.

One approach to testing this class would be to mix it with a `Mock` object which mocks out any inherited methods. This approach has merit, but a simpler (if less ideal) approach is to subclass it with the simplest possible `ttk` widget and test the resulting child class.

That approach looks like this:

```
class TestValidatedMixin(TkTestCase):

    def setUp(self):
        class TestClass(widgets.ValidatedMixin, ttk.Entry):
            pass
        self.vw1 = TestClass(self.root)
```

Here, we've created just a basic child class using `ttk.Entry` and modified nothing else. Then, we created an instance of the class.

Let's test our `_validate()` method as follows:

```
    def test__validate(self):
        args = {'proposed': 'abc', 'current': 'ab', 'char': 'c',
        'event': 'key', 'index': '2', 'action': '1'}
        self.assertTrue(self.vw1._validate(**args))
```

Because we're sending a key event to `_validate()`, it routes the request to `_key_validate()`, which simply returns `True` by default. We'll need to verify that `_validate()` does what is needed when `_key_validate()` returns `False` as well.

We'll employ `Mock` to do this:

```
        fake_key_val = Mock(return_value=False)
        self.vw1._key_validate = fake_key_val
        self.assertFalse(self.vw1._validate(**args))
        fake_key_val.assert_called_with(**args)
```

We test that `False` is returned and that `_key_validate` was called with the correct arguments.

By updating the `event` value in `args`, we can check that `focusout` events also work:

```
        args['event'] = 'focusout'
        self.assertTrue(self.vw1._validate(**args))
        fake_focusout_val = Mock(return_value=False)
        self.vw1._focusout_validate = fake_focusout_val
        self.assertFalse(self.vw1._validate(**args))
        fake_focusout_val.assert_called_with(event='focusout')
```

We've taken an identical approach here, just mocking out `_focusout_validate()` to make it return `False`.

As you can see, once we've created our test class, testing `ValidatedMixin` is like testing any other widget class. There are other test method examples in the included source code; these should be enough to get you started with creating a complete test suite.

Summary

In this chapter, we learned about automated testing and the capabilities provided by Python's `unittest` library. We wrote both unit tests and integration tests against portions of our application, and you learned methods for tackling a variety of testing challenges.

In the next chapter, we'll upgrade our backend to use a relational database. You'll also learn about relational databases, SQL, and database normalization. You'll learn to work with the PostgreSQL database server and Python's `psycopg2` PostgreSQL interface library.

10
Improving Data Storage with SQL

As weeks have passed by, there is a growing problem at the lab: the CSV files are everywhere! Conflicting copies, missing files, records getting changed by non-data entry staff, and other CSV-related frustrations are plaguing the project. It's clear that individual CSV files are not working out as a way to store data for the experiments. Something better is needed.

The facility has an older Linux server with a PostgreSQL database installed. You've been asked to update your program so that it stores data in the PostgreSQL database rather than in the CSV files. This promises to be a major update to your application!

In this chapter, you'll learn the following topics:

- Installing and configuring the PostgreSQL database system
- Structuring data in a database for good performance and reliability
- The basics of SQL queries
- Using the `psycopg2` library to connect your program to PostgreSQL

PostgreSQL

PostgreSQL (usually pronounced post-gress) is a free, open source, cross-platform relational database system. It runs as a network service with which you can communicate using client programs or software libraries. At the time of writing, the project has just released version 10.0.

Although ABQ has provided a PostgreSQL server which is already installed and configured, you'll need to download and install the software on your workstation for development purposes.

Shared production resources such as databases and web services should never be used for testing or development. Always set up a separate development copy of these resources on your own workstation or a separate server machine.

Installing and configuring PostgreSQL

To download PostgreSQL, visit `https://www.postgresql.org/download/`. Installers are provided for Windows, macOS, and Linux by the EnterpriseDB company, a commercial entity that provides paid support for PostgreSQL. These packages include the server, command-line client, and pgAdmin graphical client all in one package.

To install the software, launch the installer using an account with administrative rights and follow the screens in the installation wizard.

Once installed, launch pgAdmin and create a new admin user for yourself by selecting **Object** | **Create** | **Login/Group Role**. Make sure to visit the **Privileges** tab to check **Superuser**, and the **Definition** tab to set a password. Then, create a database by selecting **Object** | **Create** | **Database**. Make sure to set your user as an owner. To run SQL commands on your database, select your database and click **Tools** | **Query Tool**.

MacOS or Linux users who prefer the command line can also use the following these commands:

```
sudo -u postgres createuser -sP myusername
sudo -u postgres createdb -O myusername mydatabasename
psql -d mydatabasename -U myusername
```

Although Enterprise DB provides binary installers for Linux, most Linux users will prefer to use packages supplied by their distribution. You may end up with a slightly older version of PostgreSQL, but that won't matter for most basic use cases. Be aware that pgAdmin is usually part of a separate package, and that the latest version (pgAdmin 4) may not be available. Regardless, you should have no trouble following this chapter with the older version.

Connecting with psycopg2

To make SQL queries from our application, we'll need to install a Python library that can talk directly to our database. The most popular choice is `psycopg2`.
The `psycopg2` library is not a part of the Python standard library. You can find the most current installation instructions at `http://initd.org/psycopg/docs/install.html`; however, the preferred method is to use `pip`.

For Windows, macOS, and Linux, the following command should work:

```
pip install --user psycopg2-binary
```

If that doesn't work, or if you'd rather install it from the source, check the requirements on the website. The `psycopg2` library is written in C, not Python, so it requires a C compiler and a few other development packages. Linux users can usually install `psycopg2` from their distribution's package management system. We'll get in-depth with the use of `psycopg2` later in the chapter.

SQL and relational database basics

Before we can start using PostgreSQL with Python, you'll need to have at least a basic understanding of SQL. If you already have one, you can skip to the next section; otherwise, brace yourself for a super-short crash course on relational databases and SQL.

For over three decades, relational database systems have remained a de-facto standard for storing business data. They are more commonly known as **SQL databases**, after the **Structured Query Language** (**SQL**) used to interact with them.

SQL databases are made up of tables. A table is something like our CSV file, in that it has rows representing individual items and columns representing data values associated with each item. A SQL table has some important differences from our CSV file. First, each column in the table is assigned a data type which is strictly enforced; just as Python will produce an error when you try to use `abcd` as an `int`, a SQL database will complain if you try to insert letters into a numeric or other non-string column. SQL databases typically support data types for text, numbers, dates and times, boolean values, binary data, and more.

SQL tables can also have constraints, which further enforce the validity of data inserted into the table. For example, a column can be given a unique constraint, which prevents two rows having the same value, or a not null constraint, which means that every row must have a value.

SQL databases commonly contain many tables; these tables can be joined together to represent much more complicated data structures. By breaking data into multiple linked tables, it can be stored in a way that is much more efficient and resilient than our two-dimensional plaintext CSV files.

Basic SQL operations

SQL is a powerful and expressive language for doing mass manipulations of tabular data, but the basics can be grasped quickly. SQL is executed as individual queries which either define or manipulate data in the database. SQL dialects vary somewhat between different relational database products, but most of them support ANSI/ISO-standard SQL for core operations. While we'll be using PostgreSQL in this chapter, most of the SQL statements we write will be portable to different databases.

To follow this section, connect to an empty database on your PostgreSQL database server, either using the `psql` command-line tool, the pgAdmin 4 graphical tool, or another database client software of your choosing.

Syntax differences from Python

If you've only ever programmed in Python, SQL may feel odd at first, as the rules and syntax are very different.

We'll be going over the individual commands and keywords, but the following are some general differences from Python:

- **SQL is (mostly) case-insensitive**: Although it's conventional for readability purposes to type the SQL keywords in all-caps, most SQL implementations are not case-sensitive. There are a few small exceptions here and there, but, for the most part, you can type SQL in whatever case is easiest for you.
- **Whitespace is not significant**: In Python, new lines and indentation can change the meaning of a piece of code. In SQL, whitespace is not significant and statements are terminated with a semicolon. Indents and new lines in a query are only there for readability.

- **SQL is declarative**: Python could be described as an imperative programming language: we tell Python what we want it to do by telling it how to do it. SQL is more of a declarative language: we describe what we want, and the SQL engine figures out how to do it.

We'll encounter additional syntax differences as we look at specific SQL code examples.

Defining tables and inserting data

SQL tables are created using the `CREATE TABLE` command as shown in the following SQL query:

```
CREATE TABLE musicians (id SERIAL PRIMARY KEY, name TEXT NOT NULL,
born DATE, died DATE CHECK(died > born));
```

In this example, we're creating a table called `musicians`. After the name, we specify a list of column definitions. Each column definition follows the format `column_name data_type constraints`.

In this case, we have the following four columns:

- The `id` column will be an arbitrary row ID. It's type is `SERIAL`, which means it will be an autoincrementing integer field, and its constraint is `PRIMARY KEY`, which means it will be used as the unique identifier for the row.
- The `name` field is of type `TEXT`, so it can hold a string of any length. Its constraint of `NOT NULL` means that the `NULL` values are not allowed in this field.
- The `born` and `died` fields are the `DATE` fields, so they can only hold a date value. The `born` field has no constraints, but `died` has a `CHECK` constraint enforcing that its value must be greater than the value of `born` for any given row.

Although it's not required, it's a good practice to specify a primary key for each table. Primary keys can be one field, or a combination of fields, but the value must be unique for any given row. For example, if we made `name` the primary key field, we couldn't have two musicians with the same name in our table.

To add rows of data to this table, we use the `INSERT INTO` command as follows:

```
INSERT INTO musicians (name, born, died) VALUES ('Robert Fripp',
'1946-05-16', NULL),   ('Keith Emerson', '1944-11-02', '2016-03-11'),
('Greg Lake', '1947-11-10', '2016-12-7'),   ('Bill Bruford',
'1949-05-17', NULL), ('David Gilmour', '1946-03-06', NULL);
```

The `INSERT INTO` command takes a table name and an optional list specifying the fields to receive data; other fields will receive their default value (`NULL` if not otherwise specified in the `CREATE` statement). The `VALUES` keyword indicates that a list of data values to be followed, formatted as a comma-separated list of tuples. Each tuple corresponds to one table row and must match the field list specified after the table name.

Note that strings are delimited by the single quote character. Unlike Python, single quotes and double quotes have different meanings in SQL: a single quote indicates a string literal, while double quotes are used for object names that include spaces or need to preserve case. Had we used double quotes here, it would have resulted in an error.

Let's create and populate an `instruments` table:

```
CREATE TABLE instruments (id SERIAL PRIMARY KEY, name TEXT NOT NULL);
INSERT INTO instruments (name) VALUES ('bass'), ('drums'), ('guitar'),
('keyboards');
```

Note that the `VALUES` lists must always use parentheses around each row, even if there's only one value per row.

Tables can be changed after they are created using the `ALTER TABLE` command as follows:

```
ALTER TABLE musicians ADD COLUMN main_instrument INT REFERENCES
instruments(id);
```

The `ALTER TABLE` command takes a table name, then a command altering some aspect of the table. In this case, we're adding a new column called `main_instrument`, which will be an integer. The `REFERENCES` constraint we've specified is known as a **foreign key** constraint; it limits the possible values of `main_instrument` to existing ID numbers in the `instruments` table.

Retrieving data from tables

To retrieve data from tables, we use the `SELECT` statement as follows:

```
SELECT name FROM musicians;
```

The `SELECT` command takes a column or comma-separated list of columns followed by a `FROM` clause, which specifies the table or tables containing the specified columns. This query asks for the `name` column from the `musicians` table.

Its output is as follows:

name
Bill Bruford
Keith Emerson
Greg Lake
Robert Fripp
David Gilmour

Instead of a list of columns, we can also specify an asterisk, which means all columns as shown in the following query:

```
SELECT * FROM musicians;
```

The preceding SQL query returns a following table of data:

ID	name	born	died	main_instrument
4	Bill Bruford	1949-05-17		
2	Keith Emerson	1944-11-02	2016-03-11	
3	Greg Lake	1947-11-10	2016-12-07	
1	Robert Fripp	1946-05-16		
5	David Gilmour	1946-03-06		

To filter out rows we don't want, we can specify a `WHERE` clause as follows:

```
SELECT name FROM musicians WHERE died IS NULL;
```

The `WHERE` command must be followed by a conditional statement; rows that satisfy the condition are shown, while rows that do not are left out. In this case, we have asked for the names of musicians who do not have a date of death.

We can specify complex conditions with the `AND` and `OR` operators as follows:

```
SELECT name FROM musicians WHERE born < '1945-01-01' AND died IS NULL;
```

In this case, we would only get musicians born before 1945 who have not died.

The `SELECT` command can also do operations on fields, or re-order the results by certain columns:

```
SELECT name, age(born), (died - born)/365 AS "age at death" FROM
musicians ORDER BY born DESC;
```

In this example, we're using the `age()` function to determine the age of the musicians from their birth dates. We're also doing math on the `died` and `born` dates to determine the age at death for those who have passed. Notice that we're using the `AS` keyword to rename, or alias, the generated column.

When you run this query, notice that `age at death` is `NULL` for those without a date of death. Mathematical or logical operations on a `NULL` value always return an answer of `NULL`.

The `ORDER BY` clause specifies a column or list of columns by which the results should be ordered. It also takes an argument of `DESC` or `ASC` to specify descending or ascending order. We have ordered the output here by date of birth in descending order. Note that each data type has its own rules for sorting data, just like in Python. Dates are ordered by their calendar position, strings by alphabetical order, and numbers by their numeric value.

Updating rows, deleting rows, and more WHERE clauses

To update or delete existing rows, we use the `UPDATE` and `DELETE FROM` keywords in conjunction with a `WHERE` clause to select the affected rows.

Deleting is fairly simple looks like this:

```
DELETE FROM instruments WHERE id=4;
```

The `DELETE FROM` command will delete any rows that match the `WHERE` conditions. In this case, we match the primary key to ensure only one row is deleted. If no rows match the `WHERE` conditions, no rows will be deleted. Note, however, that the `WHERE` clause is technically optional: `DELETE FROM instruments` will simply delete all rows in the table.

Updating is similar, except it includes a `SET` clause to specify new column values as follows:

```
UPDATE musicians SET main_instrument=3 WHERE id=1;
UPDATE musicians SET main_instrument=2 WHERE name='Bill Bruford';
```

Here, we are setting `main_instrument` to the corresponding `instruments` primary key value for two musicians. We can select our musician records to update by primary key, name, or any valid set of conditions. Like `DELETE`, omitting the `WHERE` clause would affect all rows.

Any number of columns can be updated in the `SET` clause:

```
UPDATE musicians SET main_instrument=4, name='Keith Noel Emerson'
WHERE name LIKE 'Keith%';
```

Additional column updates are just separated by commas. Note that we've also matched the record using the `LIKE` operator in tandem with the `%` wildcard character. `LIKE` can be used with text and string data types to match partial values. Standard SQL supports two wildcard characters: `%`, which matches any number of characters, and _, which matches a single character.

We can also match against transformed column values:

```
UPDATE musicians SET main_instrument=1 WHERE LOWER(name) LIKE '%lake';
```

Here, we've used the `LOWER` function to match our string against the lowercase version of the column value. This doesn't permanently change the data in the table; it just temporarily changes the value for the check.

Standard SQL specifies that `LIKE` is a case-sensitive match. PostgreSQL offers an `ILIKE` operator which does case-insensitive matching as well as a `SIMILAR TO` operator that matches using more advanced regular expression syntax.

Subqueries

Rather than using the raw primary key values of our `instruments` table each time, we can use a subquery as shown in the following SQL query:

```
UPDATE musicians SET main_instrument=(SELECT id FROM instruments WHERE
name='guitar') WHERE name IN ('Robert Fripp', 'David Gilmour');
```

A subquery is a SQL query within a SQL query. If your subquery can be guaranteed to return a single value, it can be used anywhere you would use a literal value. In this case, we're letting our database do the work of figuring out what the primary key of `guitar` is, and inserting that for our `main_instrument` value.

In the `WHERE` clause, we've also used the `IN` operator to match against a list of values. This allows us to match against a list of values.

`IN` can be used with a subquery as well as follows:

```
SELECT name FROM musicians WHERE main_instrument IN (SELECT id FROM
instruments WHERE name like '%r%')
```

Since `IN` is meant to be used with a list of values, any query that returns a single column with any number of rows is valid.

Subqueries that return multiple rows and multiple columns can be used anywhere a table can be used:

```
SELECT name FROM (SELECT * FROM musicians WHERE died IS NULL) AS
living_musicians;
```

Note that subqueries in a `FROM` clause require an alias; we've aliased the subquery as `living_musicians`.

Joining tables

Subqueries are one way of using multiple tables together, but a more flexible and powerful way is to use `JOIN`.

`JOIN` is used in the `FROM` clause of an SQL statement as follows:

```
SELECT musicians.name, instruments.name as main_instrument FROM
musicians JOIN instruments ON musicians.main_instrument =
instruments.id;
```

A `JOIN` statement requires an `ON` clause that specifies the conditions used to match rows in each table. The `ON` clause acts like a filter, much like the `WHERE` clause does; you can imagine that the `JOIN` creates a new table containing every possible combination of rows from both tables, then filters out the ones that don't match the `ON` conditions. Tables are typically joined by matching the values in common fields, such as those specified in a foreign key constraint. In this case, our `musicians.main_instrument` column contains the `id` values from the `instrument` table, so we can join the two tables based on this.

Joins are used to implement the following four types of table relationships:

- One-to-one joins match exactly one row in the first table to exactly one row in the second.
- Many-to-one joins match multiple rows in the first table to exactly one row in the second.
- One-to-many joins match one row in the first table to multiple rows in the second.
- Many-to-many joins match multiple rows in both tables. This kind of join requires the use of an intermediary table.

The earlier query shows a many-to-one join, since many musicians can have the same main instrument. Many-to-one joins are often used when a column's value should be limited to a set of options, such as fields that our GUI might represent with a `ComboBox` widget. The table joined is called a **lookup table**.

If we were to reverse it, it would be one-to-many:

```
SELECT instruments.name AS instrument, musicians.name AS musician FROM
instruments JOIN musicians ON musicians.main_instrument =
instruments.id;
```

One-to-many joins are commonly used when a record has a list of sub-records associated with it; in this case, each instrument has a list of musicians who consider it their main instrument. The joined table is often called a **detail table.**

The preceding SQL query will give you the following output:

instrument	musician
drums	Bill Bruford
keyboards	Keith Emerson
bass	Greg Lake
guitar	Robert Fripp
guitar	David Gilmour

Notice that `guitar` is duplicated in the instrument list. When two tables are joined, the rows of the result no longer refer to the same type of object. One row in the instrument table represents an instrument. One row in the `musician` table represents one musician. One row in this table represents an `instrument-musician` relationship.

But suppose we wanted to keep the output such that one row represented one instrument but could still include information about associated musicians in each row. To do this, we'll need to aggregate the matched musician rows using an aggregate function and the `GROUP BY` clause as shown in the following SQL query:

```
SELECT instruments.name AS instrument, count(musicians.id) as
musicians FROM instruments JOIN musicians ON musicians.main_instrument
= instruments.id GROUP BY instruments.name;
```

The `GROUP BY` clause specifies which column or columns describe what each row in the output table represents. Output columns not in the `GROUP BY` clause must then be reduced to single values using an aggregate function. In this case, we're using the `count()` function to count the total number of musician records associated with each instrument. Standard SQL contains several more aggregate functions, such as `min()`, `max()`, and `sum()`, and most SQL implementations extend this with their own functions as well.

Many-to-one and one-to-many joins don't quite cover every possible situation that databases need to model; quite often, a many-to-many relationship is required.

To demonstrate a many-to-many join, let's create a new table called `bands` as follows:

```
CREATE TABLE bands (id SERIAL PRIMARY KEY, name TEXT NOT NULL);
INSERT INTO bands(name) VALUES ('ABWH'), ('ELP'), ('King Crimson'),
('Pink Floyd'), ('Yes');
```

A band has multiple musicians, and musicians can be part of multiple bands. How can we create a relationship between musicians and bands? If we added a `band` field to the `musicians` table, this would limit each musician to one band. If we added a `musician` field to the `band` table, this would limit each band to one musician. To make the connection, we need to create a **junction table**, in which each row represents a musician's membership in a band.

By convention, we call this `musicians_bands`:

```
CREATE TABLE musicians_bands (musician_id INT REFERENCES
musicians(id), band_id INT REFERENCES bands(id), PRIMARY KEY
(musician_id, band_id));
INSERT INTO musicians_bands(musician_id, band_id) VALUES (1, 3), (2,
2), (3, 2), (3, 3), (4, 1), (4, 2), (4, 5), (5,4);
```

The `musicians_bands` table simply contains two foreign key fields, one to point to a musician's ID and one to point to the band's ID. Notice that instead of creating or specifying one field as the primary key, we use the combination of both fields as the primary key. It wouldn't make sense to have multiple rows with the same two values in them, so the combination makes an acceptable primary key. To write a query that uses this relationship, our `FROM` clause needs to specify two `JOIN` statements: one from `musicians` to `musicians_bands` and one from `bands` to `musicians_bands`.

For example, let's get the names of the bands each musician has been in:

```
SELECT musicians.name, array_agg(bands.name) AS bands FROM musicians
JOIN musicians_bands ON musicians.id = musicians_bands.musician_id
JOIN bands ON bands.id = musicians_bands.band_id GROUP BY
musicians.name ORDER BY musicians.name ASC;
```

This query ties `musicians` to `bands` using the junction table, then displays musician names next to an aggregated list of the bands they've been in, and orders it by the musician's name.

The preceding SQL query gives you the following output:

name	bands
Bill Bruford	{ABWH,"King Crimson",Yes}
David Gilmour	{"Pink Floyd"}
Greg Lake	{ELP,"King Crimson"}
Keith Emerson	{ELP}
Robert Fripp	{"King Crimson"}

The `array_agg()` function used here aggregates string values into an array structure. This method and the `ARRAY` data type are specific to PostgreSQL. There is no SQL standard function for aggregating string values, but most SQL implementations have a solution for it.

Learning more

This has been a quick overview of SQL concepts and syntax; we've covered most of what you need to know to write a simple database application, but there's much more to learn. The PostgreSQL manual, available at `https://www.postgresql.org/docs/manuals/`, is a great resource and reference for SQL syntax and the specific features of PostgreSQL.

Modeling relational data

Our application currently stores data in a single CSV file; a file like this is often called a **flat file**, because the data has been flattened to two dimensions. While this format works acceptably for our application and could be translated directly to an SQL table, a more accurate and useful data model requires more complexity.

Normalization

The process of breaking out a flat data file into multiple tables is called **normalization**. Normalization is a process involving a series of levels called **normal forms** which progressively remove duplication and create a more precise model of the data we're storing. Although there are many normal forms, most issues encountered in common business data can be handled by conforming to the first three.

Roughly speaking, that requires the following conditions:

- The **first normal form** requires that each field contains only one value, and that repeating columns must be eliminated.
- The **second normal form** additionally requires that every value must be dependent on the entire primary key. In other words, if a table has primary key fields `A`, `B`, and `C`, and the value of column of `X` depends solely on the value of column `A` without respect to `B` or `C`, the table violates the second normal form.
- The **third normal form** additionally requires every value in the table to be dependent only on the primary key. In other words, given a table with primary key `A`, and data fields `X` and `Y`, the value of `Y` can't depend on the value of `X`.

Conforming data to these forms eliminates the potential for redundant, conflicting, or undefined data situations.

The entity-relationship diagrams

One effective way to help normalize our data and prepare it for a relational database is to analyze it and create an **entity-relationship diagram**, or **ERD**. An ERD is a way of diagramming the things which our database is storing information about and the relationships between those things.

Those things are called **entities**. An **entity** is a uniquely identifiable object; it corresponds to a single row of a single table. Entities have attributes, which correspond to the columns of its table. Entities have relationships with other entities, which correspond to the foreign key relationships we define in SQL.

Let's consider the entities in our lab scenario with their attributes and relationships:

- There are labs. Each lab has a name.
- There are plots. Each plot belongs to a lab and has a number. A seed sample is planted in the plot.
- There are lab technicians, who each have a name.
- There are lab checks, which are performed by a lab tech at a given lab. Each one has a date and time.
- There are plot checks, which is the data gathered at a plot during a lab check. Each plot check has various plant and environmental data recorded on it.

The following diagram of these entities and relationships is as follows:

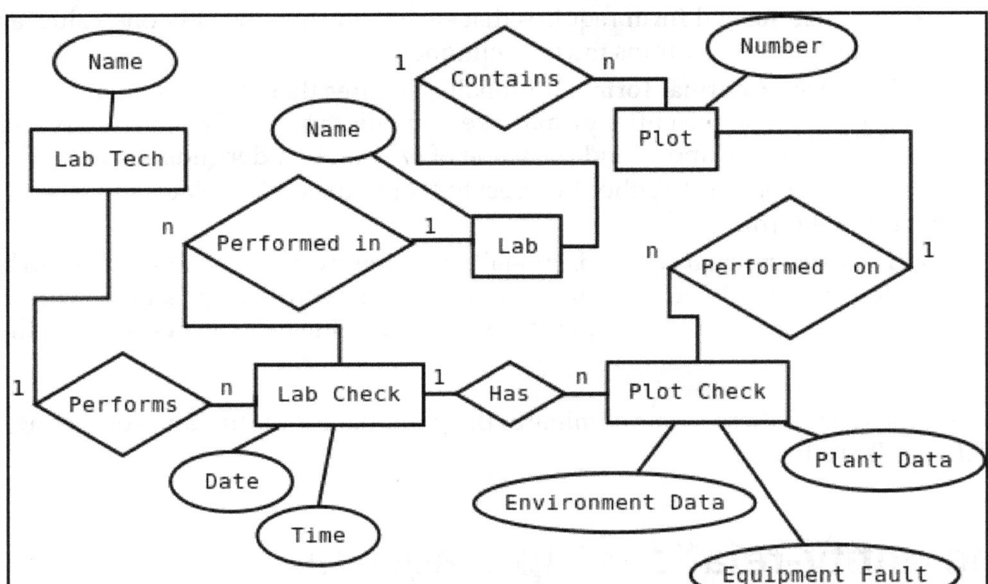

In the preceding diagram, the entities are represented by rectangles. We have five entities: **Lab**, **Plot**, **Lab Tech**, **Lab Check**, and **Plot Check**. Each entity has attributes, represented by the ovals. The relationships are represented by diamonds, with the words describing the left-to-right relationship. For example, **Lab Tech** performs **Lab Check**, and **Lab Check** is performed in **Lab**. Note the small **1** and **n** characters around the relationship: these show whether a relationship is one-to-many, many-to-one, or many-to-many.

This diagram represents a reasonably normalized structure for our data. To implement it in SQL, we'd just make a table for each entity, a column for each attribute, and a foreign key relationship (possibly including an intermediate table) for each relationship. Before we can do that, let's consider SQL data types.

Assigning data types

Standard SQL defines 16 data types, including types for integers and floating-point numbers of various sizes, ASCII or Unicode strings of either fixed or variable sizes, date and time types, and bit types. Nearly every SQL engine extends this with yet more types to accommodate binary data, special types of strings or numbers, and more. Many data types seem a little redundant, and several have aliases that may be different between implementations. Choosing data types for your columns can be surprisingly confusing!

For PostgreSQL, the following chart provides some reasonable choices:

Data being stored	Recommended type	Notes
Fixed-length strings	`CHAR`	Requires a length.
Short-to-medium strings	`VARCHAR`	Requires a max length argument, for example, `VARCHAR(256)`.
Long, freeform text	`TEXT`	Unlimited length, slower performance.
Smaller Integers	`SMALLINT`	Up to ±32,767.
Most Integers	`INT`	Up to around ±2.1 billion.
Larger Integers	`BIGINT`	Up to around ±922 quadrillion.
Decimals numbers	`NUMERIC`	Takes optional length and precision arguments.
Integer Primary Key	`SERIAL`, `BIGSERIAL`	Autoincrementing integer or big integers.
Boolean	`BOOLEAN`	
Date and time	`TIMESTAMP WITH TIMEZONE`	Stores date, time, and timezone. Accurate to 1 µs.
Date without time	`DATE`	
Time without date	`TIME`	Can be with or without time zone.

These types will probably meet the vast majority of your needs in most applications, and we'll be using a subset of these for our ABQ database. As we create our tables, we'll refer to our data dictionary and choose appropriate data types for our columns.

Be careful not to choose overly specific or restrictive data types. Any data can ultimately be stored in a `TEXT` field; the purpose of choosing more specific types is mainly to enable the use of operators, functions, or sorting specific to that type. If those aren't required, consider a more generic type. For example, phone numbers and U.S. Social Security numbers can be represented purely with digits, but that's no reason to make them `INTEGER` or `NUMERIC` fields; after all, you wouldn't do arithmetic with them!

Creating the ABQ database

Now that we've modeled our data and gotten a feel for the data types available, it's time to build our database. To begin, create a database on your SQL server called `abq` and make yourself the owner.

Next, under your project root folder, create a new directory called `sql`. Inside the `sql` folder, create a file called `create_db.sql`. We'll start writing our database creation code in this file.

Creating our tables

The order in which we create our tables is significant. Any table referred to in a foreign key relationship will need to exist before the relationship is defined. Because of this, it's best to start with your lookup tables and follow the chain of one-to-many relationships until all the tables are created. In our ERD, that takes us from roughly the upper-left to the lower-right.

Creating the lookup tables

We need to create the following three lookup tables:

- `labs`: This lookup table will contain the ID strings for our laboratories.
- `lab_techs`: This lookup table will have the names of the lab technicians, identified by their employee ID numbers.
- `plots`: This lookup table will have one row for each physical plot, identified by lab and plot numbers. It will also keep track of the current seed sample planted in the plot.

Add the SQL query for creating these tables to `create_db.sql` as follows:

```
CREATE TABLE labs (id CHAR(1) PRIMARY KEY);
CREATE TABLE lab_techs (id SMALLINT PRIMARY KEY, name VARCHAR(512)
UNIQUE NOT NULL);
CREATE TABLE plots (lab_id CHAR(1) NOT NULL REFERENCES labs(id),
    plot SMALLINT NOT NULL, current_seed_sample CHAR(6),
    PRIMARY KEY(lab_id, plot),
    CONSTRAINT valid_plot CHECK (plot BETWEEN 1 AND 20));
```

Before we can use our database, the lookup tables will need to be populated:

- `labs` should have values `A` through `E` for the five labs.
- `lab_techs` needs the name and ID number for our four lab technicians: `J Simms` (`4291`), `P Taylor` (`4319`), `Q Murphy` (`4478`), and `L Taniff` (`5607`).
- `plots` needs all 100 of the plots, numbers `1` through `20` for each lab. The seed sample rotates between four values such as `AXM477`, `AXM478`, `AXM479`, and `AXM480`.

You can populate these tables by hand using pgAdmin, or using the `db_populate.sql` script included with the example code.

The lab_checks table

The `lab_check` table is an instance of a technician checking all the plots of a lab at a given time on a given date as shown in the following SQL query:

```
CREATE TABLE lab_checks(
    date DATE NOT NULL, time TIME NOT NULL,
    lab_id CHAR(1) NOT NULL REFERENCES labs(id),
    lab_tech_id SMALLINT NOT NULL REFERENCES lab_techs(id),
    PRIMARY KEY(date, time, lab_id));
```

The `date`, `time`, and `lab_id` columns together uniquely identify a lab check, and so we designate them the primary key columns. The ID of the lab technician performing the check is the lone attribute in this table.

The plot_checks table

Plot checks are the actual data records collected at individual plots. These are part of a lab check, and so must refer back to an existing lab check.

We'll begin with the primary key columns:

```
CREATE TABLE plot_checks(date DATE NOT NULL, time TIME NOT NULL,
lab_id CHAR(1) NOT NULL REFERENCES labs(id), plot SMALLINT NOT NULL,
```

This is the primary key of a `lab_check` table plus a `plot` number; its key constraints look like this:

```
PRIMARY KEY(date, time, lab_id, plot),
FOREIGN KEY(date, time, lab_id)
    REFERENCES lab_checks(date, time, lab_id),
FOREIGN KEY(lab_id, plot) REFERENCES plots(lab_id, plot),
```

Now we can add the attribute columns:

```
seed_sample CHAR(6) NOT NULL,
humidity NUMERIC(4, 2) CHECK (humidity BETWEEN 0.5 AND 52.0),
light NUMERIC(5, 2) CHECK (light BETWEEN 0 AND 100),
temperature NUMERIC(4, 2) CHECK (temperature BETWEEN 4 AND 40),
equipment_fault BOOLEAN NOT NULL,
blossoms SMALLINT NOT NULL CHECK (blossoms BETWEEN 0 AND 1000),
plants SMALLINT NOT NULL CHECK (plants BETWEEN 0 AND 20),
fruit SMALLINT NOT NULL CHECK (fruit BETWEEN 0 AND 1000),
max_height NUMERIC(6, 2) NOT NULL CHECK (max_height BETWEEN 0 AND
1000),
min_height NUMERIC(6, 2) NOT NULL CHECK (min_height BETWEEN 0 AND
1000),
median_height NUMERIC(6, 2) NOT NULL
    CHECK (median_height BETWEEN min_height AND max_height),
notes TEXT);
```

Notice our use of data types and the `CHECK` constraint to duplicate the limits from our `data` dictionary. Using these, we've leveraged the power of the database to safeguard against invalid data.

Creating a view

Before we finish our database design, we're going to create a view that will simplify access to our data. A view behaves like a table in most respects, but contains no actual data; it's really just a stored `SELECT` query. Our view will format our data for easier interaction with the GUI.

Views are created using the `CREATE VIEW` command as follows:

```
CREATE VIEW data_record_view AS (
```

Inside the parentheses, we put the SELECT query that will return the table data for our view:

```
SELECT pc.date AS "Date", to_char(pc.time, 'FMHH24:MI') AS "Time",
    lt.name AS "Technician", pc.lab_id AS "Lab", pc.plot AS "Plot",
    pc.seed_sample AS "Seed sample", pc.humidity AS "Humidity",
    pc.light AS "Light", pc.temperature AS "Temperature",
    pc.plants AS "Plants", pc.blossoms AS "Blossoms", pc.fruit AS
    "Fruit",
    pc.max_height AS "Max Height", pc.min_height AS "Min Height",
    pc.median_height AS "Median Height", pc.notes AS "Notes"
FROM plot_checks AS pc JOIN lab_checks AS lc ON pc.lab_id = lc.lab_id
AND pc.date = lc.date AND pc.time = lc.time JOIN lab_techs AS lt ON
lc.lab_tech_id = lt.id);
```

We're selecting the plot_checks table, and joining it to lab_checks and lab_techs by way of our foreign key relationships. Notice that we've aliased these tables by using the AS keyword. Short aliases like this can help make a large query more readable. We're also aliasing each field to the name used in the application's data structures. These must be enclosed in double quotes to allow for the use of spaces and to preserve case. By making the column names match the data dictionary keys in our application, we won't need to translate field names in our application code.

SQL database engines such as PostgreSQL are highly efficient at joining and transforming tabular data. Whenever possible, leverage this power and make the database do the work of formatting the data for the convenience of your application.

This completes our database creation script. Run this script in your PostgreSQL client and verify that the four tables and the view have been created.

Integrating SQL into our application

Converting our application to a SQL backend will be no small task. The application was built around the assumption of the CSV files, and although we've taken care to separate our concerns, many things are going to need to change.

Let's break down the steps we'll need to take:

- We'll need to write a SQL model
- Our `Application` class will need to use the SQL model
- The record form will need to be reordered to prioritize our keys, use the new lookups, and autopopulate using the database
- The record list will need to be adjusted to work with the new data model and primary keys

Along the way, we'll need to fix other bugs or implement some new UI elements as needed. Let's get started!

Creating a new model

We'll start in `models.py` by importing `psycopg2` and `DictCursor`:

```
import psycopg2 as pg
from psycopg2.extras import DictCursor
```

`DictCursor` will allow us to fetch results in Python dictionary rather than the default tuples, which is easier to work with in our application.

Begin a new model class called `SQLModel` and copy over the `fields` property from the `CSVModel`.

Start by clearing the value lists from `Technician`, `Lab`, and `Plot`, and making `Technician` an `FT.string_list` type:

```
class SQLModel:
    fields = {
        ...
        "Technician": {'req': True, 'type': FT.string_list,
                       'values': []},
        "Lab": {'req': True, 'type': FT.string_list, 'values': []},
        "Plot": {'req': True, 'type': FT.string_list,'values': []},
```

These lists will be populated from our lookup tables rather than hardcoded into the model.

We'll do that in the `__init__()` method:

```
    def __init__(self, host, database, user, password):
        self.connection = pg.connect(host=host, database=database,
            user=user, password=password, cursor_factory=DictCursor)
        techs = self.query("SELECT * FROM lab_techs ORDER BY name")
        labs = self.query("SELECT id FROM labs ORDER BY id")
        plots = self.query(
        "SELECT DISTINCT plot FROM plots ORDER BY plot")
        self.fields['Technician']['values'] = [x['name'] for x in
        techs]
        self.fields['Lab']['values'] = [x['id'] for x in labs]
        self.fields['Plot']['values'] = [str(x['plot']) for x in
plots]
```

`__init__()` takes our basic database connection details and establishes a connection to the database using `psycopg2.connect()`. Because we passed in `DictCursor` as the `cursor_factory`, this connection will return lists of dictionaries for all data queries.

Then, we query the database for the pertinent columns in our three lookup tables and use a list comprehension to flatten the results of each query for the `values` list.

The `query` method used here is a wrapper that we need to write next:

```
    def query(self, query, parameters=None):
        cursor = self.connection.cursor()
        try:
            cursor.execute(query, parameters)
        except (pg.Error) as e:
            self.connection.rollback()
            raise e
        else:
            self.connection.commit()
            if cursor.description is not None:
                return cursor.fetchall()
```

Querying a database using psycopg2 involves generating a cursor object from the connection, then calling its execute() method with the query string and optional parameter data. By default, all queries are executed in a transaction, meaning they don't take effect until we commit the changes. If the query raises an exception for any reason (SQL syntax error, constraint violation, connection issue, and so on) the transaction enters a corrupt state and must be rolled back (reverted to the beginning state of the transaction) before we can use our connection again. Therefore, we will execute our queries in a try block and rollback the transaction using connection.rollback() in the event of any psycopg2-related exceptions (which all descend from pg.Error).

To retrieve data from a cursor after the query is executed, we're using the fetchall() method, which retrieves all results as a list. However, if the query wasn't a data-returning query (such as INSERT, for example), fetchall() will throw an exception. To avoid this, we first check cursor.description: if the query returned data (even an empty set of data), cursor.description will contain metadata about the returned table (column names, for example). If not, it will be None.

Let's test our query() method by writing the get_all_records() method:

```
    def get_all_records(self, all_dates=False):
        query = ('SELECT * FROM data_record_view '
            'WHERE NOT %(all_dates)s OR "Date" = CURRENT_DATE '
            'ORDER BY "Date", "Time", "Lab", "Plot"')
        return self.query(query, {'all_dates': all_dates})
```

Since our users are used to working with only the current day's data, we'll only show that data by default, but add an optional flag should we ever need to retrieve all data. We can get the current date in most SQL implementations using the CURRENT_DATE constant, which we've used here. To use our all_dates flag, we're employing a prepared query.

The syntax %(all_dates)s defines a parameter; it tells psycopg2 to check the included parameter dictionary for the key all_dates and substitute its value into the query. The psycopg2 library will automatically do this in a way that's both safe and works correctly with various data types like None or Boolean values.

Always use prepared queries to pass data into a SQL query. Never use string formatting or concatenation! Not only is it harder than you think to get it right, it can leave you open to accidental or malicious database corruption.

Next, let's create `get_record()`:

```
def get_record(self, date, time, lab, plot):
    query = ('SELECT * FROM data_record_view '
        'WHERE "Date" = %(date)s AND "Time" = %(time)s '
        'AND "Lab" = %(lab)s AND "Plot" = %(plot)s')
    result = self.query(
        query, {"date": date, "time": time, "lab": lab, "plot": plot})
    return result[0] if result else {}
```

We're no longer dealing in row numbers like our `CSVModel` did, so this method needs all four key fields to retrieve a record. Once again, we're using a prepared query, specifying parameters for the four fields. Take note of the `s` after the closing parenthesis of the parameter; this is a required format specifier, and should always be `s`.

Even with a single row, `query()` is going to return results in a list. Our application expects a single row dictionary from `get_record()`, so our `return` statement extracts the first item in `result` if the list is not empty, or an empty `dict` if it is.

Retrieving a lab check record is very similar:

```
    def get_lab_check(self, date, time, lab):
        query = ('SELECT date, time, lab_id, lab_tech_id, '
            'lt.name as lab_tech FROM lab_checks JOIN lab_techs lt '
            'ON lab_checks.lab_tech_id = lt.id WHERE '
            'lab_id = %(lab)s AND date = %(date)s AND time =
%(time)s')
        results = self.query(
            query, {'date': date, 'time': time, 'lab': lab})
        return results[0] if results else {}
```

In this query, we're using a join to make sure we have the technician name available and not just the ID. This method will come in handy in our `save_record()` method and form data autofill methods.

The `save_record()` method will need four queries: an `INSERT` and `UPDATE` query for each of `lab_checks` and `plot_checks`. To keep the method reasonably concise, let's create the query strings as class properties.

We'll start with the lab check queries:

```
lc_update_query = ('UPDATE lab_checks SET lab_tech_id = '
    '(SELECT id FROM lab_techs WHERE name = %(Technician)s) '
    'WHERE date=%(Date)s AND time=%(Time)s AND lab_id=%(Lab)s')
lc_insert_query = ('INSERT INTO lab_checks VALUES (%(Date)s,
    '%(Time)s, %(Lab)s,(SELECT id FROM lab_techs '
    'WHERE name=%(Technician)s))')
```

These queries are fairly straightforward, though note our use of a subquery to populate `lab_tech_id` in each case. Our application will have no idea what a lab tech's ID is, so we'll need to look the ID up by name. Also, take note that our parameter names match the names used in our application's fields. This will save us having to reformat the record data acquired from our form.

The plot check queries are longer but no more complicated:

```
pc_update_query = (
    'UPDATE plot_checks SET seed_sample = %(Seed sample)s, '
    'humidity = %(Humidity)s, light = %(Light)s, '
    'temperature = %(Temperature)s, '
    'equipment_fault = %(Equipment Fault)s, '
    'blossoms = %(Blossoms)s, plants = %(Plants)s, '
    'fruit = %(Fruit)s, max_height = %(Max Height)s, '
    'min_height = %(Min Height)s, median_height = '
    '%(Median Height)s, notes = %(Notes)s '
    'WHERE date=%(Date)s AND time=%(Time)s '
    'AND lab_id=%(Lab)s AND plot=%(Plot)s')

pc_insert_query = (
    'INSERT INTO plot_checks VALUES (%(Date)s, %(Time)s, %(Lab)s,'
    ' %(Plot)s, %(Seed sample)s, %(Humidity)s, %(Light)s,'
    ' %(Temperature)s, %(Equipment Fault)s, %(Blossoms)s,'
    ' %(Plants)s, %(Fruit)s, %(Max Height)s, %(Min Height)s,'
    ' %(Median Height)s, %(Notes)s)')
```

With the queries in place, we can start the `save_record()` method:

```
def save_record(self, record):
    date = record['Date']
    time = record['Time']
    lab = record['Lab']
    plot = record['Plot']
```

The `CSVModel.save_record()` method took a `record` dictionary and a `rownum`, but we no longer need the `rownum` since it's meaningless. All our key information is already in the record. For convenience, we'll extract those four fields and assign them local variable names.

There are three possibilities when we try to save a record in this database:

- Neither a lab check or plot check record exists. Both will need to be created.
- The lab check exists but the plot check does not. The lab check will need to be updated, in case the user wants to correct the technician value, and the plot check will need to be added.
- Both the lab check and plot check exist. Both will need to be updated with the submitted values.

To determine which possibility is true, we'll make use of our `get_` methods:

```
if self.get_lab_check(date, time, lab):
    lc_query = self.lc_update_query
else:
    lc_query = self.lc_insert_query
if self.get_record(date, time, lab, plot):
    pc_query = self.pc_update_query
else:
    pc_query = self.pc_insert_query
```

For both the lab check and plot check, we attempt to retrieve a record from the respective table using our key values. If one is found, we'll use our update queries; otherwise, we'll use our insert queries.

Now, we just run those queries with `record` as the parameter list:

```
self.query(lc_query, record)
self.query(pc_query, record)
```

Note that `psycopg2` has no problem with us passing a dictionary with extra parameters that aren't referenced in the query, so we don't need to bother with filtering unneeded items from `record`.

There is one more thing we need to do here: remember that our `Application` needs to keep track of updated and inserted rows. Since we are no longer dealing with row numbers, only the database model knows whether an insert or update was performed.

Let's create an instance property to share that information:

```
        if self.get_record(date, time, lab, plot):
            pc_query = self.pc_update_query
            self.last_write = 'update'
        else:
            pc_query = self.pc_insert_query
            self.last_write = 'insert'
```

Now `Application` can check the value of `last_write` after calling `save_record()` to determine which operation was done.

There is one last method this model needs; since our database knows what seed sample is currently in each plot, we want our form to populate this automatically for the user. We'll need a method that takes a `lab` and `plot_id` and returns the seed sample name.

We'll call it `get_current_seed_sample()`:

```
    def get_current_seed_sample(self, lab, plot):
        result = self.query('SELECT current_seed_sample FROM plots '
            'WHERE lab_id=%(lab)s AND plot=%(plot)s',
            {'lab': lab, 'plot': plot})
        return result[0]['current_seed_sample'] if result else ''
```

This time, our `return` statement is not just extracting the first row of results, but the value of the `current_seed_sample` column from that first row. If there's no `result`, we return an empty string.

That completes our model class; now let's incorporate it into the application.

Adjusting the Application class for the SQL backend

The first thing the `Application` class will need is the database connection information to pass to the model.

For the host and database name, we can just add settings to our `SettingsModel`:

```
variables = {
    ...
    'db_host': {'type': 'str', 'value': 'localhost'},
    'db_name': {'type': 'str', 'value': 'abq'}
```

These can be saved in our JSON `config` file, which can be edited to switch from development to production, but our username and password will need to be entered by the user. For that, we'll need to build a login dialog.

Building a login window

Tkinter does not provide us with a ready-made login dialog, but it does provide us with a generic `Dialog` class which can be subclassed to create custom dialogs.

Import this class from `tkinter.simpledialog` into our `views.py` file:

```
from tkinter.simpledialog import Dialog
```

Let's start with our class declaration and `__init__()` method:

```
class LoginDialog(Dialog):

    def __init__(self, parent, title, error=''):
        self.pw = tk.StringVar()
        self.user = tk.StringVar()
        self.error = tk.StringVar(value=error)
        super().__init__(parent, title=title)
```

Our class will take a `parent` as usual, a window `title`, and an optional `error`, which will be used in case we need to re-display the dialog with an `error` message (for example, if the password is wrong). The rest of `__init__()` sets up some Tkinter variables for the password, username, and `error` string; then, it finishes with the customary call to `super()`.

The form itself is not defined in `__init__()`; instead, we need to override the `body()` method:

```
    def body(self, parent):
        lf = tk.Frame(self)
        ttk.Label(lf, text='Login to ABQ', font='Sans 20').grid()
```

The first thing we do is make a frame and add a title label to the first row using a large font.

Next, we'll check for an `error` string and, if there is one, display it in an appropriate style:

```
        if self.error.get():
            tk.Label(lf, textvariable=self.error,
                     bg='darkred', fg='white').grid()
```

Now we'll add the username and password fields and `pack` our frame into the dialog:

```
        ttk.Label(lf, text='User name:').grid()
        self.username_inp = ttk.Entry(lf, textvariable=self.user)
        self.username_inp.grid()
        ttk.Label(lf, text='Password:').grid()
        self.password_inp = ttk.Entry(lf, show='*',
        textvariable=self.pw)
        self.password_inp.grid()
        lf.pack()
        return self.username_inp
```

Notice our use of the `show` option in the password entry, which replaces any typed text with the character we specify, to create a hidden text field. Also, note that we return the username input widget from the method. `Dialog` will focus whichever widget is returned here when it's displayed.

`Dialog` automatically supplies the **OK** and **Cancel** buttons; we'll want to know which button was clicked, and if it was the **OK** button, retrieve the entered information.

Clicking **OK** calls the `apply()` method, so we can override it to set up a `result` value:

```
        def apply(self):
            self.result = (self.user.get(), self.pw.get())
```

Dialog creates a property by default called result which is set to None. But now, if our user clicks **OK**, result will be a tuple containing a username and password. We'll use this property to determine what was clicked and what was entered.

Using the login window

To use the dialog, our application needs a method that will display the dialog in an infinite loop until either the user clicks **Cancel** or the provided credentials successfully authenticate.

Start a new database_login() method in Application:

```
    def database_login(self):
        error = ''
        db_host = self.settings['db_host'].get()
        db_name = self.settings['db_name'].get()
        title = "Login to {} at {}".format(db_name, db_host)
```

We begin by setting up an empty error string and a title string to pass to our LoginDialog class.

Now we'll start the infinite loop:

```
    while True:
        login = v.LoginDialog(self, title, error)
        if not login.result:
            break
```

Inside the loop, we create a LoginDialog, which will block until the user clicks one button or the other. After the dialog returns, if login.result is None, the user has clicked **Cancel**, so we break out of the loop and exit the method.

If we have a non-None login.result, we'll attempt to log in with it:

```
    else:
        username, password = login.result
        try:
            self.data_model = m.SQLModel(
             db_host, db_name, username, password)
        except m.pg.OperationalError:
            error = "Login Failed"
        else:
            break
```

After extracting the `username` and `password` from the `result` tuple, we try to create a `SQLModel` instance with it. If the credentials fail, `psycopg2.connect` will raise an `OperationalError`, in which case we'll simply populate our `error` string and let the infinite loop iterate again.

If the data model creation succeeded, we simply break out of the loop and exit the method.

Back in `__init__()`, just after setting up our settings, let's put `database_login()` to work:

```
self.database_login()
if not hasattr(self, 'data_model'):
    self.destroy()
    return
```

After our call to `self.database_login()`, `Application` either has a `data_model` attribute (because the login succeeded) or doesn't (because the user clicked **Cancel**). If it doesn't, we'll quit the application by destroying the main window and returning immediately from `__init__()`.

Of course, before this logic will work, we need to delete the creation of the `CSVModel`:

```
# Delete this line:
self.data_model = m.CSVModel(filename=self.filename.get())
```

Fixing some model incompatibilities

In theory, we should be able to swap in a new model with the same method calls and our application object will just work, but this isn't quite the case. There are a few small fixes we need to make to get `Application` working with our new model.

DataRecordForm creation

First, let's fix our `DataRecordForm` instantiation in `Application.__init__()`:

```
# The data record form
self.recordform = v.DataRecordForm(
    self, self.data_model.fields, self.settings,
    self.callbacks)
```

Previously, we'd pulled the `fields` argument from the static class property of `CSVModel`. We need to pull it from our data model instance instead, since the instance is setting up some values.

Fixing the open_record() method

Next, we need to fix our `open_record()` method. It takes a `rownum` currently, but we no longer have row numbers; we have `date`, `time`, `lab`, and `plot`.

To reflect this, replace all instances of `rownum` with `rowkey`:

```
def open_record(self, rowkey=None):
    if rowkey is None:
    # ...etc
```

Finally, expand `rowkey` in the `get_record()` call, since it expects four positional arguments:

```
        record = self.data_model.get_record(*rowkey)
```

Fixing the on_save() method

The error handling portion of `on_save()` is fine, but after the `if errors:` block, we'll start changing things:

```
data = self.recordform.get()
try:
    self.data_model.save_record(data)
```

We no longer need to extract the row number or pass it into `save_record()`, and we can delete the handling of `IndexError` since `SQLModel` will not raise that exception. We also need to rewrite the updating of `inserted_rows` and `updated_rows`.

Remove all the code in this method after the call to `self.status.set()`, and replace it with this:

```
key = (data['Date'], data['Time'], data['Lab'], data['Plot'])
if self.data_model.last_write == 'update':
    self.updated_rows.append(key)
else:
    self.inserted_rows.append(key)
self.populate_recordlist()
if self.data_model.last_write == 'insert':
    self.recordform.reset()
```

After building the primary key tuple from `data` passed into the method, we use the value of `last_write` to append it to the proper list. Finally, we reset the record form in the case of an insert.

Creating new callbacks

There are two callbacks we want to have for our record form. When the user enters a `lab` and `plot` value, we want to automatically populate the correct `seed` value that is currently planted in that `plot`. Also, when the `date`, `time`, and `lab` values have been entered, and we have an existing lab check that matches, we should populate the name of the lab tech who did that check.

Of course, if our user prefers not to have data autofilled, we shouldn't do either of these things.

Let's start with the `get_current_seed_sample()` method:

```
def get_current_seed_sample(self, *args):
    if not (hasattr(self, 'recordform')
        and self.settings['autofill sheet data'].get()):
        return
    data = self.recordform.get()
    plot = data['Plot']
    lab = data['Lab']
    if plot and lab:
        seed = self.data_model.get_current_seed_sample(lab, plot)
        self.recordform.inputs['Seed sample'].set(seed)
```

We begin by checking whether we have a record form object created, and whether the user wants data autofilled. If not, we exit the method. Next, we fetch the `plot` and `lab` from the form's current data. If we have both, we use them to fetch the `seed` sample value from the model and set the form's `Seed sample` value accordingly.

We'll do something similar with the lab tech value:

```
def get_tech_for_lab_check(self, *args):
    if not (hasattr(self, 'recordform')
        and self.settings['autofill sheet data'].get()):
        return
    data = self.recordform.get()
    date = data['Date']
    time = data['Time']
    lab = data['Lab']

    if all([date, time, lab]):
        check = self.data_model.get_lab_check(date, time, lab)
        tech = check['lab_tech'] if check else ''
        self.recordform.inputs['Technician'].set(tech)
```

This time, we need the `date`, `time`, and `lab` arguments to fetch the lab check record. Because we can't be sure if a check matching the values exists, we'll set `tech` to a blank string if we can't find a matching lab check.

Add these two methods to the `callbacks` dictionary and the `Application` class should be ready to go.

Updating our views for the SQL backend

Let's review the changes we need to make in our views:

- Re-arrange our fields to put all the primary keys upfront
- Fix our form's `load_record()` method to work with the new key structure
- Add triggers to our form to populate `Technician` and `Seed sample`
- Fix our record list to work with the new keys

Let's start with our record form.

The data record form

The first task we have is to move the fields around. This is really just a matter of cutting and pasting code and then fixing our `grid()` arguments. Place them in the proper key order: **Date**, **Time**, **Lab**, **Plot**. Then, leave **Technician** and **Seed sample** at the end of the **Record Information** section.

It should look like this:

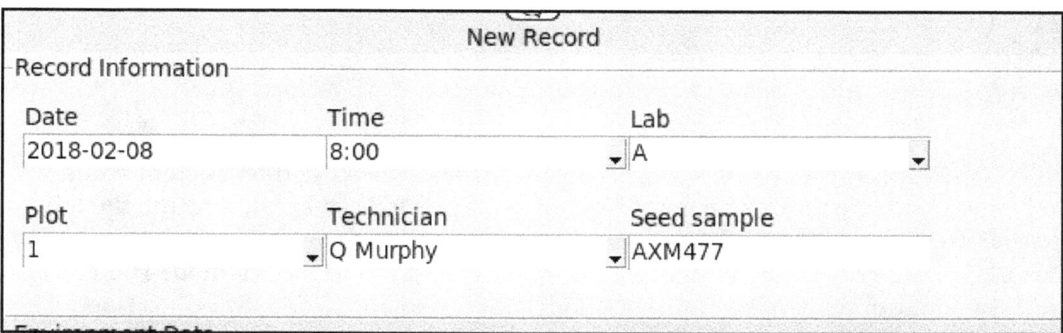

The reason for this change is so that all the fields which could trigger autofilling of **Technician** or **Seed sample** will come before those fields. If any of them came after, we'd be uselessly autofilling a field the user had already filled.

At the end of `__init__()`, let's add our triggers to populate **Technician** and **Seed sample**:

```
        for field in ('Lab', 'Plot'):
            self.inputs[field].variable.trace(
                'w', self.callbacks['get_seed_sample'])
        for field in ('Date', 'Time', 'Lab'):
            self.inputs[field].variable.trace(
                'w', self.callbacks['get_check_tech'])
```

We're putting a trace on the key variables for lab check and plot; should any of them change, we'll call the appropriate callback to auto-populate the form.

In `load_record()`, replace `rownum` with `rowkey` for clarity, then fix the label `text` so that it makes sense:

```
        self.record_label.config(
            text='Record for Lab {2}, Plot {3} at {0} {1}'
            .format(*rowkey))
```

The last change of all for `DataRecordForm` deals with a small usability issue. As we auto-populate the form, it gets more and more confusing to determine which field we need to focus next. We're going to address this by creating a method that finds and focuses the first empty field in the form.

We'll call it `focus_next_empty()`:

```
    def focus_next_empty(self):
        for labelwidget in self.inputs.values():
            if (labelwidget.get() == ''):
                labelwidget.input.focus()
                break
```

In this method, we're just iterating all the inputs and checking their current value. When we find one returns an empty string, we focus it, then break through the loop so that no more are checked. We can remove any calls to focus fields from `DataRecordForm.reset()` and replace them with a call to this method. You can also add it to our application's autofill methods, `get_current_seed_sample()` and `get_tech_for_lab_check()`.

The record list

In RecordList, the Row column no longer contains useful information we wish to display.

We can't remove it, but we can hide it with this code:

```
self.treeview.config(show='headings')
```

The show configuration option takes any or both of two values: tree and headings. The tree argument represents the #0 column since it's used to expand tree. The headings argument represents the remaining columns. By specifying only headings here, the #0 column is hidden.

We also need to deal with our populate() method, which relies heavily on rownum.

We'll start by changing the for loop that populates the values:

```
        for rowdata in rows:
            rowkey = (str(rowdata['Date']), rowdata['Time'],
            rowdata['Lab'], str(rowdata['Plot']))
            values = [rowdata[key] for key in valuekeys]
```

We can remove the enumerate() call and just deal with the row data, extracting the rowkey tuple from it by getting Date, Time, Lab, and Plot. These need to be cast to string, because they come out of the database as Python objects like date and int, and we need to match them against the keys in inserted and updated which are all string values (since they were pulled from our form).

Let's do that comparison and set our row tags:

```
            if self.inserted and rowkey in self.inserted:
                tag = 'inserted'
            elif self.updated and rowkey in self.updated:
                tag = 'updated'
            else:
                tag = ''
```

Now, we need to decide how to handle our row's iid value. The iid values must be strings; this wasn't a problem when our primary key was an integer (easily castable to and from a string), but our tuple must be serialized in some way that we can easily reverse.

A simple way to address this is to turn our tuple into a delimited string:

```
            stringkey = '{}|{}|{}|{}'.format(*rowkey)
```

Any character that isn't going to appear in the data will work fine as a delimiter; we've chosen to use the pipe character in this case.

Now we can use the string version of the key in `treeview`:

```
self.treeview.insert('', 'end', iid=stringkey,
    text=stringkey, values=values, tag=tag)
```

The last part of this method focuses the first row for keyboard users. To focus the first row before, we relied on the fact that the first `iid` was always `0`. Now it will be some data-dependent tuple, so we'll have to retrieve the first `iid` before we can set the selection and focus.

We can do this by using the `Treeview.identify_row()` method:

```
if len(rows) > 0:
    firstrow = self.treeview.identify_row(0)
    self.treeview.focus_set()
    self.treeview.selection_set(firstrow)
    self.treeview.focus(firstrow)
```

The `identify_row()` method takes a row number and returns the `iid` of that row. Once we have that, we can pass it to `selection_set()` and `focus()`.

Our final change is to the `on_open_record()` method. Since we've used our serialized tuple as an `iid` value, we obviously need to translate this back to a tuple that can be passed back to the `on_open_record()` method.

This is as easy as calling `split()`:

```
self.callbacks['on_open_record'](selected_id.split('|'))
```

That fixes all our view code, and our program is ready to run!

Last changes

Phew! That was quite a journey, but you're not quite done yet. As homework, you'll need to update your unit tests to accommodate the database and login. The best approach would be to mock out the database and login dialog.

There are also still some remnants of the CSV backend sitting around, such as the **Select target...** item in the file menu. You can delete those UI elements, but leave the backend code as it may come in handy in the near future.

Summary

In this chapter, you learned about relational databases and SQL, the language used to work with them. You learned to model and normalize data to reduce the possibility of inconsistencies, and how to convert flat files into relational data. You learned how to work with the `psycopg2` library, and went through the arduous task of converting the application to use a SQL backend.

In the next chapter, we'll be reaching out to the cloud. We'll need to contact some remote servers using different networking protocols to exchange data. You'll learn about the Python standard library's modules for working with HTTP and FTP, and use them to download and upload data.

11
Connecting to the Cloud

It seems that nearly every application needs to talk to the outside world sooner or later, and your `ABQ data entry` application is no exception. You've received some new feature requests that will require some interactions with remote servers and services. First, the quality assurance division is doing a study of how local weather conditions are impacting the environmental data in each lab; they've requested a way to download and store local weather data in the database on demand. The second request is from your boss, who is still required to upload daily CSV files to the central corporate servers. She would like this process streamlined and available at a mouse click.

In this chapter, you will learn the following topics:

- Connecting to web services and downloading data using `urllib`
- Managing more complex HTTP interactions using the `requests` library
- Connecting and uploading to FTP services using `ftplib`

HTTP using urllib

Every time you open a website in your browser, you're using the **Hyper Text Transfer Protocol, or HTTP**. HTTP was created over 25 years ago as a way for web browsers to download HTML documents, but has evolved into one of the most popular client-server communication protocols for any number of purposes. Not only can we use it to move everything from plain text to streaming video across the Internet, but applications can also use it to transfer data, initiate remote procedures, or distribute computing tasks.

A basic HTTP transaction includes a client and a server, which function as follows:

- **Client**: The client creates a request. The request specifies an operation called a **method**. The most common methods are `GET`, for retrieving data, and `POST`, for submitting data. The request has a URL, which specifies the host, port, and path to which the request is being made, and headers which include metadata like the data-type or authorization tokens. Finally, it has a payload, which may contain serialized data in key-value pairs.
- **Server**: The server receives the request and returns a response. The response has a header containing metadata such as the status code or content-type of the response. It also has a payload containing the actual content of the response, such as HTML, XML, JSON, or binary data.

In a web browser, these operations take place in the background, but our application will deal directly with request and response objects in order to talk to remote HTTP servers.

Basic downloading with urllib.request

The `urllib.request` module is a Python module for generating HTTP requests. It contains a number of functions and classes for generating HTTP requests, the most basic of which is the `urlopen()` function. The `urlopen()` function can create a `GET` or `POST` request and send it to a remote server.

Let's explore how `urllib` works; open a Python shell and execute the following commands:

```
>>> from urllib.request import urlopen
>>> response = urlopen('http://packtpub.com')
```

The `urlopen()` function takes, at a minimum, a URL string. By default, it makes a `GET` request to the URL and returns an object that wraps the response received from the server. This `response` object exposes metadata or content received from the server, which we can use in our application.

Much of the response's metadata is found in the header, which we can extract using `getheader()` as follows:

```
>>> response.getheader('Content-Type')
'text/html; charset=utf-8'
>>> response.getheader('Server')
'nginx/1.4.5'
```

Responses have a status, indicating the error conditions encountered (if any) during the request process; the status has both a number and a text explanation, called `reason`.

We can extract both from our `response` object as follows:

```
>>> response.status
200
>>> response.reason
'OK'
```

In the preceding code, a `200` status means the transaction was a success. Client-side errors, such as sending a bad URL or incorrect permissions, are indicated by statuses in the 400s, while server-side problems are indicated by statuses in the 500s.

The payload of the `response` object can be retrieved using an interface similar to a file handle as follows:

```
>>> html = response.read()
>>> html[:15]
b'<!DOCTYPE html>'
```

Just like a file handle, the response can only be read once, using the `read()` method; unlike a file handle, it can't be "rewound" using `seek()`, so it's important to save the response data in another variable if it needs to be accessed more than once. The output of `response.read()` is a bytes object, which should be cast or decoded into an appropriate object.

In this case, we have a `utf-8` string as follows:

```
>>> html.decode('utf-8')[:15]
'<!DOCTYPE html>'
```

In addition to the `GET` requests, `urlopen()` can also generate `POST` requests.

To do this, we include a `data` argument as follows:

```
>>> response = urlopen('http://duckduckgo.com', data=b'q=tkinter')
```

The `data` value needs to be a URL-encoded bytes object. The URL-encoded data string consists of key-value pairs separated by ampersand (`&`) symbols, with certain reserved characters encoded to URL-safe alternatives (for example, the space character is `%20`, or sometimes just `+`).

A string like this can be created by hand, but it's easier to use the `urlencode` function provided by the `urllib.parse` module. Take a look at the following code:

```
>>> from urllib.parse import urlencode
>>> data = {'q': 'tkinter, python', 'ko': '-2', 'kz': '-1'}
>>> urlencode(data)
'q=tkinter%2C+python&ko=-2&kz=-1'
>>> response = urlopen('http://duckduckgo.com',
data=urlencode(data).encode())
```

The `data` argument must be bytes, not a string, so `encode()` must be called on the URL-encoded string before `urlopen` will accept it.

Let's try downloading the weather data needed for our application. The site we'll be using is `http://weather.gov`, which provides weather data within the United States. The actual URL we'll be downloading is `http://w1.weather.gov/xml/current_obs/STATION.xml`, where `STATION` is replaced by the call-sign of the local weather station. In the case of ABQ, we'll be using KBMG, located in Bloomington, Indiana.

The QA team wants you to record the temperature (in degrees Celsius), relative humidity, air pressure (in millibars), and sky conditions (a string, like overcast or fair). They also need the date and time at which the weather was observed by the station.

Creating a download function

We're going to be creating several functions that access network resources for our application. These functions won't be tied to any particular class, so we'll just put them in their own file called `network.py`. Let's take a look at the following steps:

1. Create `network.py` in the `abq_data_entry` module directory.
2. Now, let's open `network.py` and start our weather download function:

```
from urllib.request import urlopen

def get_local_weather(station):
    url = (
        'http://w1.weather.gov/xml/current_obs/{}.xml'
        .format(station))
    response = urlopen(url)
```

Our function will take a `station` string as an argument, in case we need to change that later or if someone wants to use this application at a different facility. The function begins by building the URL for the weather data and requests it using `urlopen()`.

3. Assuming things went okay, we just need to parse out this `response` data and put it into a form the `Application` class can pass to the database model. To determine how we'll handle the response, let's go back to the Python shell and examine the data in it:

```
>>> response =
urlopen('http://w1.weather.gov/xml/current_obs/KBMG.xml')
>>> print(response.read().decode())
<?xml version="1.0" encoding="ISO-8859-1"?>
<?xml-stylesheet href="latest_ob.xsl" type="text/xsl"?>
<current_observation version="1.0"
         xmlns:xsd="http://www.w3.org/2001/XMLSchema"
xmlns:xsi="http://www.w3.org/2001/XMLSchema-instance"
xsi:noNamespaceSchemaLocation="http://www.weather.gov/view
/current_observation.xsd">
        <credit>NOAA's National Weather Service</credit>
        <credit_URL>http://weather.gov/</credit_URL>
....
```

4. As the URL indicated, the payload of the response is an XML document, most of which we won't need. After some searching, though, we can find the fields we're after as follows:

```
<observation_time_rfc822>Wed, 14 Feb 2018 14:53:00
-0500</observation_time_rfc822>
<weather>Fog/Mist</weather>
<temp_c>11.7</temp_c>
<relative_humidity>96</relative_humidity>
<pressure_mb>1018.2</pressure_mb>
```

Good, the data we need is there, so we just need to extract it from the XML string into a format our application can use. Let's take a moment to learn about parsing XML data.

Parsing XML weather data

The Python standard library contains an `xml` package, which consists of several submodules for parsing or creating XML data.
The `xml.etree.ElementTree` submodule is a simple, lightweight parser that should meet our needs.

Let's import `ElementTree` into our `network.py` file as follows:

```
from xml.etree import ElementTree
```

Now, back at the end of our function, we'll parse the XML data in our `response` object as follows:

```
    xmlroot = ElementTree.fromstring(response.read())
```

The `fromstring()` method takes an XML string and returns an `Element` object. To get at the data we need, we'll need to understand what an `Element` object represents, and how to work with it.

XML is a hierarchical representation of data; an element represents a node in this hierarchy. An element begins with a tag, which is a text string inside angle brackets. Each tag has a matching closing tag, which is just the tag with a forward-slash prepended to the tag name. Between the opening and closing tags, an element may have other child elements or it may have text. An element can also have attributes, which are key-value pairs placed inside the angle brackets of the opening tag, just after the tag name.

Take a look at the following example of XML:

```
<star_system starname="Sol">
  <planet>Mercury</planet>
  <planet>Venus</planet>
  <planet>Earth
    <moon>Luna</moon>
    </planet>
  <planet>Mars
    <moon>Phobos</moon>
    <moon>Deimos</moon>
    </planet>
  <dwarf_planet>Ceres</dwarf_planet>
</star_system>
```

This is an (incomplete) XML description of the solar system. The root element has a tag of `<star_system>` with an attribute of `starname`. Under this root element, we have four `<planet>` elements and a `<dwarf_planet>` element, each of which contains a text node with the planet's name. Some of the planet nodes also have child `<moon>` nodes, each containing a text node with the moon's name.

Arguably, this data could have been structured differently; for example, planet names could have been in a child `<name>` node inside the planet elements, or listed as an attribute of the `<planet>` tag. While XML syntax is well-defined, the actual structure of an XML document is up to the creator, so fully parsing XML data requires a knowledge of the way the data is laid out in the document.

If you look at the XML weather data that we downloaded in the shell earlier, you'll notice it's a fairly shallow hierarchy. Under the `<current_observations>` node, there are a number of child elements whose tags represent specific data fields like temperature, humidity, windchill, and so on.

To get at these child elements, `Element` offers us the following variety of methods:

Method	Returns
`iter()`	An iterator of all child nodes (recursively)
`find(tag)`	The first element matching the given tag
`findall(tag)`	A list of elements matching the given tag
`getchildren()`	A list of the immediate child nodes
`iterfind(tag)`	An iterator of all child nodes matching the given tag (recursive)

When we downloaded the XML data earlier, we identified five tags containing the data we want to extract from this document: `<observation_time_rfc822>`, `<weather>`, `<temp_c>`, `<relative_humidity>`, and `<pressure_mb>`. We'll want our `get_local_weather()` function to return a Python `dict` containing each of these keys.

Let's add the next lines in the `network.py` file as follows:

```
    xmlroot = ElementTree.fromstring(response.read())
    weatherdata = {
        'observation_time_rfc822': None,
        'temp_c': None,
        'relative_humidity': None,
        'pressure_mb': None,
        'weather': None
    }
```

Our first line extracts the raw XML from the response and parses it into an `Element` tree, returning the root node to `xmlroot`. Then, we've set up `dict` containing the tags we want to extract from our XML data.

Now, let's get the values by executing the following code:

```
    for tag in weatherdata:
        element = xmlroot.find(tag)
        if element is not None:
            weatherdata[tag] = element.text
```

For each of our tag names, we're going to use the `find()` method to try to locate the element with a matching tag in `xmlroot`. This particular XML document does not use duplicate tags, so the first instance of any tag should be the only one. If the tag is matched, we'll get back an `Element` object; if not, we get back `None`, so we need to make sure `element` is not `None` before trying to access its `text` value.

To finish the function just return `weatherdata` .

You can test this function in the Python shell; from a command line, navigate to the `ABQ_Data_Entry` directory and start a Python shell:

```
>>> from abq_data_entry.network import get_local_weather
>>> get_local_weather('KBMG')
{'observation_time_rfc822': 'Wed, 14 Feb 2018 16:53:00 -0500',
 'temp_c': '11.7', 'relative_humidity': '96', 'pressure_mb': '1017.0',
 'weather': 'Drizzle Fog/Mist'}
```

You should get back a `dict` with the current weather conditions in Bloomington, Indiana. You can find the station codes for other cities inside the U.S. at `http://w1.weather.gov/xml/current_obs/`.

Now that we have our weather function, we just need to build the table for storing the data and the interface for triggering the operation.

Implementing weather data storage

To store our weather data, we'll start by creating a table in the ABQ database to hold the individual observation data, then build a `SQLModel` method to store data in it. We don't need to worry about writing code to retrieve data from it, since our laboratory's QA team has their own reporting tools which they'll use to access it.

Creating the SQL table

Open the `create_db.sql` file, and add a new `CREATE TABLE` statement as follows:

```
CREATE TABLE local_weather (
        datetime TIMESTAMP(0) WITH TIME ZONE PRIMARY KEY,
        temperature NUMERIC(5,2),
        rel_hum NUMERIC(5, 2),
        pressure NUMERIC(7,2),
        conditions VARCHAR(32)
        );
```

We're using the `TIMESTAMP` data type on the record as a primary key; there's no point in saving the same timestamped observation twice, so this makes an adequate key. The `(0)` size after the `TIMESTAMP` data type indicates how many decimal places we need for the seconds' measurement. Since these measurements are taken approximately hourly, and we only need one every four hours or so (when the lab checks are done), we don't need fractions of seconds in our timestamp.

Notice that we're saving the time zone; always store time zone data with timestamps when it's available! It may not seem necessary, especially when your application will be run in a workplace that will never change time zones, but there are many edge cases such as daylight-saving time changes where the lack of a time zone can create major problems.

Run this `CREATE` query in your database to build the table, and let's move on to creating our `SQLModel` method.

Implementing the SQLModel.add_weather_data() method

Over in `models.py`, let's add a new method to the `SQLModel` class called `add_weather_data()`, which takes a data `dict` as its only argument.

Let's start this method by writing an `INSERT` query as follows:

```
    def add_weather_data(self, data):
        query = (
            'INSERT INTO local_weather VALUES '
            '(%(observation_time_rfc822)s, %(temp_c)s, '
            '%(relative_humidity)s, %(pressure_mb)s, '
            '%(weather)s)'
        )
```

This is a straightforward parameterized `INSERT` query using variable names that match the `dict` keys that the `get_local_weather()` function extracts from the XML data. We should only need to pass this query and the data `dict` into our `query()` method.

There is one problem, however; if we get a duplicate timestamp, our query will fail due to a duplicate primary key. We could do another query to check first, but that would be slightly redundant, since PostgreSQL itself checks for duplicate keys before inserting a new row. When it detects such an error, `psycopg2` raises an `IntegrityError` exception, so we just need to catch this exception and, if it gets raised, do nothing.

To do this, we'll wrap our `query()` call in the `try...except` blocks as follows:

```
try:
    self.query(query, data)
except pg.IntegrityError:
    # already have weather for this datetime
    pass
```

Now, our data entry staff can call this method as often as they wish, but it will only save a record when there is a fresh observation to save.

Updating the SettingsModel class

Before leaving `models.py`, we will need to add a new application setting to store the preferred weather station. Add a new entry in the `SettingsModel.variables` dictionary as follows:

```
variables = {
    ...
    'weather_station': {'type': 'str', 'value': 'KBMG'},
    ...
```

We won't add a GUI for this setting, since users won't need to update it. It'll be up to us, or the system admin at other lab sites, to make sure this is properly set on each workstation.

Adding the GUI elements for weather download

The `Application` object now needs to connect the weather download method from `network.py` to the database method in `SQLModel` with an appropriate callback method that the main menu classes can call. Follow these steps:

1. Open `application.py` and start a new method as follows:

```
def update_weather_data(self):

  try:
      weather_data = n.get_local_weather(
          self.settings['weather_station'].get())
```

2. Recall that in an error scenario, `urlopen()` can raise any number of exceptions, depending on what went wrong with the HTTP transaction. There isn't really anything the application can do to handle such exceptions other than inform the user and exit the method. Therefore, we'll catch the generic `Exception` and display the text in `messagebox` as follows:

```
        except Exception as e:
            messagebox.showerror(
                title='Error',
                message='Problem retrieving weather data',
                detail=str(e)
            )
            self.status.set('Problem retrieving weather
data')
```

3. In the event that `get_local_weather()` succeeds, we simply need to pass the data on to our model method as follows:

```
    else:
        self.data_model.add_weather_data(weather_data)
        self.status.set(
            'Weather data recorded for {}'
.format(weather_data['observation_time_rfc822']))
```

In addition to saving the data, we've notified the user in the status bar that the weather was updated and displayed the timestamp of the update.

4. With the callback method done, let's add it to our `callbacks` dictionary:

```
self.callbacks = {
    ...
    'update_weather_data': self.update_weather_data,
    ...
```

5. Now we can now add a command item for the callback in the main menu. On Windows, functionality like this goes in the `Tools` menu, and since neither the Gnome nor macOS guidelines seem to indicate a more appropriate location, we'll implement a `Tools` menu in the `LinxMainMenu` and `MacOsMainMenu` classes to hold this command, just to be consistent. In `mainmenu.py`, starting in the generic menu class, add a new menu as follows:

```
#Tools menu
tools_menu = tk.Menu(self, tearoff=False)
tools_menu.add_command(
    label="Update Weather Data",
    command=self.callbacks['update_weather_data'])
self.add_cascade(label='Tools', menu=tools_menu)
```

6. Add this same menu to the macOS and Linux menu classes, and add the command to the Windows main menu's `tools_menu`. After updating the menus, you can run the application and try the new command from the `Tools` menu. If all went well, you should see an indication in the status bar as shown in the following screenshot:

Weather data recorded for Wed, 14 Feb 2018 23:53:00 -0500

7. You should also connect to the database with your PostgreSQL client and check that the table contains some weather data now by executing the following SQL command:

```
SELECT * FROM local_weather;
```

That SQL statement should return output similar to the following:

datetime	temperature	rel_{hum}	pressure	conditions
2018-02-14 22:53:00-06	15.00	87.00	1014.00	Overcast

HTTP using requests

You've been asked to create a function in your program to upload a CSV extract of the daily data to ABQ's corporate web services, which uses an authenticated REST API. While `urllib` is easy enough to use for simple one-off `GET` and `POST` requests, complex interactions involving authentication tokens, file uploads, or REST services can be frustrating and complicated using `urllib` alone. To get this done, we'll turn to the `requests` library.

REST stands for **REpresentational State Transfer**, and is the name used for web services built around advanced HTTP semantics. In addition to `GET` and `POST`, REST APIs use additional HTTP methods like `DELETE`, `PUT`, and `PATCH`, along with data formats like XML or JSON, to present an API with a complete range of interactions.

The third-party `requests` library is highly recommended by the Python community for any serious work involving HTTP (even the `urllib` documentation recommends it). As you'll see, `requests` removes many of the rough edges and outdated assumptions left in `urllib`, and provides convenient classes and wrapper functions for more modern HTTP transactions. Complete documentation on `requests` can be found at `http://docs.python-requests.org`, but the next section will cover most of what you need to know to use it effectively.

Installing and using requests

The `requests` package is written in pure Python, so installing it with `pip` requires no compiling or binary downloads. Simply type `pip install --user requests` in the terminal and it will be added to your system.

Open your Python shell, and let's make some requests as follows:

```
>>> import requests
>>> response = requests.request('GET', 'http://www.alandmoore.com')
```

`requests.request` requires, at minimum, an HTTP method and a URL. Just like `urlopen()`, it constructs the appropriate request packet, sends it to the URL, and returns an object representing the server's response. Here, we're making a `GET` request to this author's website.

In addition to the `request()` function, `requests` has shortcut functions that correspond to the most common HTTP methods.

Thus, the same request can be made as follows:

```
response = requests.get('http://www.alandmoore.com')
```

The `get()` method requires only the URL and performs a `GET` request. Likewise, the `post()`, `put()`, `patch()`, `delete()`, and `head()` functions send requests using the corresponding HTTP method. All of the request functions take additional optional arguments.

For example, we can send data with a `POST` request as follows:

```
>>> response = requests.post(
    'http://duckduckgo.com',
    data={'q': 'tkinter', 'ko': '-2', 'kz': '-1'})
```

Notice that, unlike `urlopen()`, we can use a Python dictionary directly as a `data` argument; `requests` does the job of converting it to the proper bytes object for us.

Some of the more common arguments used with request functions are as follows:

Argument	Purpose
`params`	Like `data`, but added to the query string rather than the payload
`json`	JSON data to include in the payload
`headers`	A dictionary of header data to use for the request
`files`	A dictionary of `{fieldnames: file objects}` to send as a multipart form data request
`auth`	Username and password tuple to use for basic HTTP digest authentication

The requests.session() fucntion

Web services, particularly privately owned ones, are often password protected. Sometimes, this is done using the older HTTP digest authentication system, which we can address using the `auth` argument of the request functions. More commonly these days though, authentication involves posting credentials to a REST endpoint to obtain a session cookie or authentication token that is used to validate subsequent requests.

An endpoint is simply a URL that corresponds to data or functionality exposed by the API. Data is sent to or retrieved from an endpoint.

The `requests` method makes all of this simple by providing the `Session` class. A `Session` object allows you to persist settings, cookies, and connections across multiple requests.

To create a `Session` object, use the `requests.session()` factory function as follows:

```
s = requests.session()
```

Now, we can call request methods like `get()`, `post()`, and others on our `Session` object as follows:

```
# Assume this is a valid authentication service that returns an auth
token
s.post('http://example.com/login', data={'u': 'test', 'p': 'test'})
# Now we would have an auth token
response = s.get('http://example.com/protected_content')
# Our token cookie would be listed here
print(s.cookies.items())
```

Token and cookie handling like this happens in the background, without any explicit action from us. Cookies are stored in a `CookieJar` object stored as our `Session` object's `cookies` property.

We can also set values on our `Session` object that will persist across requests as in this example:

```
s.headers['User-Agent'] = 'Mozilla'
# will be sent with a user-agent string of "Mozilla"
s.get('http://example.com')
```

In this example, we've set the user-agent string to `Mozilla`, which will be used for all requests made from this `Session` object. We can also set default URL parameters using the `params` property or callback functions using the `hooks` property.

The response objects

The response objects returned from these request functions are not the same as those returned by `urlopen()`; they contain all the same data, but in a slightly different (and generally more convenient) form.

For example, the response headers are already translated into a Python `dict` for us, as follows:

```
>>> r = requests.get('http://www.alandmoore.com')
>>> r.headers
{'Date': 'Thu, 15 Feb 2018 21:13:42 GMT', 'Server': 'Apache',
 'Last-Modified': 'Sat, 17 Jun 2017 14:13:49 GMT',
 'ETag': '"20c003f-19f7-5945391d"', 'Content-Length': '6647',
 'Keep-Alive': 'timeout=15, max=200', 'Connection': 'Keep-Alive',
 'Content-Type': 'text/html'}
```

Another difference is that `requests` does not automatically raise an exception on HTTP errors. However, the `.raise_for_status()` response method can be called to do so.

For example, this URL will give an HTTP `404` error, as shown in the following code:

```
>>> r = requests.get('http://www.example.com/does-not-exist')
>>> r.status_code
404
>>> r.raise_for_status()
Traceback (most recent call last):
  File "<stdin>", line 1, in <module>
  File "/usr/lib/python3.6/site-packages/requests/models.py", line
935, in raise_for_status
    raise HTTPError(http_error_msg, response=self)
requests.exceptions.HTTPError: 404 Client Error: Not Found for url:
http://www.example.com/does-not-exist
```

This gives us the option of dealing with HTTP errors using exception handling or more traditional flow control logic.

Implementing API upload

To start implementing our upload function, we need to figure out what kind of requests we're going to send. We've been provided with some documentation from the corporate office that describes how to interact with the REST API.

The documentation tells us the following things:

- We first need to obtain an authentication token. We do this by submitting a `POST` request to the `/auth` endpoint. The parameters of the `POST` request should include `username` and `password`.
- With the authentication token acquired, we'll need to submit our CSV file. The request is a `PUT` request sent to the `/upload` endpoint. The file is uploaded as multipart form data specified in a `file` parameter.

We already know enough to implement our REST upload function using `requests`, but before we do, let's create a service that we can use to test our code against it.

Creating a test HTTP service

Developing code that interoperates with an outside service can be frustrating. We're going to need to send a lot of bad or test data to the service while writing and debugging our code; we don't want to do so against a production service, and a "test mode" is not always available. Automated tests can use a `Mock` object to patch out network requests altogether, but during development, it's nice to be able to see what's actually going to be sent out to the web service.

Let's implement a very simple HTTP server that will accept our requests and print out information about what it receives. We can do this using the Python standard library's `http.server` module.

The module documentation shows the following example of a basic HTTP server:

```
from http.server import HTTPServer, BaseHTTPRequestHandler
def run(server_class=HTTPServer,
handler_class=BaseHTTPRequestHandler):
    server_address = ('', 8000)
    httpd = server_class(server_address, handler_class)
    httpd.serve_forever()
run()
```

The server class, HTTPServer, defines an object that listens for HTTP requests on the configured address and port. The handler class, BaseHTTPRequestHandler, defines an object that receives the actual request data and returns response data. We'll use this code as a starting point, so save it outside the ABQ_Data_Entry directory in a file called sample_http_server.py.

If you run this code, you'll have a web service running on port 8000 on your local computer; however, if you make any requests to this service either using requests, a tool like curl, or just a web browser, you'll find it only returns an HTTP 501 (unsupported method) error. To make a server that works sufficiently, like our target API for testing purposes, we'll need to create our own handler class that can respond to the necessary HTTP methods.

To do that, we'll create our own handler class called TestHandler as follows:

```
class TestHandler(BaseHTTPRequestHandler):
    pass

def run(server_class=HTTPServer, handler_class=TestHandler):
    ...
```

Our corporate API uses the POST method to receive login credentials, and the PUT method to receive files, so both of those need to work. To make an HTTP method work in a request handler, we need to implement a do_VERB method, where VERB is our HTTP method name in all uppercase.

So, for PUT and POST add the following code:

```
class TestHandler(BaseHTTPRequestHandler):
    def do_POST(self, *args, **kwargs):
        pass

    def do_PUT(self, *args, **kwargs):
        pass
```

This alone doesn't address the problem, because these methods need to result in our handler sending some kind of response. We don't need any particular response for our purposes; just something with a status of 200 (OK) will do fine.

Since both methods need this, let's add a third method we can call from the other two as follows:

```
    def _send_200(self):
        self.send_response(200)
        self.send_header('Content-type', 'text/html')
        self.end_headers()
```

This is about the most minimal response required to satisfy most HTTP clients: a status of `200` and a header with a valid `Content-type`. This won't send any actual data back to the client, but will tell the client its request was received and successfully processed.

Something else we'd like to do in our methods is print out any data that was sent, so we can make sure our client is sending the right data.

We'll implement the following method that does this:

```
    def _print_request_data(self):
        content_length = self.headers['Content-Length']
        print("Content-length: {}".format(content_length))
        data = self.rfile.read(int(content_length))
        print(data.decode('utf-8'))
```

The handler object's `headers` property is a `dict` object containing the request headers, which includes the number of bytes sent (`content-length`). Apart from printing that information, we can also use it to read the data sent. The handler's `rfile` property is a file-like object containing the data; its `read()` method requires a length argument to specify how much data should be read, so we use our extracted `content-length` value. The returned data is a `bytes` object, so we decode it to `utf-8`.

Now that we have these two methods, let's update `do_POST()` and `do_PUT()` to call them as follows:

```
    def do_POST(self, *args, **kwargs):
        print('POST request received')
        self._print_request_data()
        self._send_200()

    def do_PUT(self, *args, **kwargs):
        print("PUT request received")
        self._print_request_data()
        self._send_200()
```

Now, each method will print out the length and data it receives to `POST` or `PUT` as well as any data. Run this script in a terminal window so you can monitor its output.

Now, open a shell and let's test it as follows:

```
>>> import requests
>>> requests.post('http://localhost:8000', data={1: 'test1', 2:
'test2'})
<Response[200]>
```

In the web server terminal, you should see the following output:

```
POST request received
Content-length: 15
1=test1&2=test2
127.0.0.1 - - [15/Feb/2018 16:22:41] "POST / HTTP/1.1" 200 -
```

We could implement additional functionality, like actually checking credentials and returning an authentication token, but for now this server does enough to help us write and test our client code.

Creating our network function

Now that our test service is up and running, let's start working on the network function that will interact with the REST API:

1. We'll start by creating a function in `network.py` that will take a path to the CSV file, the upload and authentication URLs, and a username and password:

```
import requests

...

def upload_to_corporate_rest(
    filepath, upload_url, auth_url, username, password):
```

2. Since we're going to have to deal with authentication tokens, the first thing we should do is create a session. We'll call it `session` as follows:

```
session = requests.session()
```

3. After creating the session, we post our username and password to the authentication endpoint like so:

```
response = session.post(
    auth_url,
    data={'username': username, 'password': password})
response.raise_for_status()
```

The `session` object will automatically store the token we receive if we're successful. In the event of a problem, we've called `raise_for_status()`, so that the function will abort and the calling code can handle any exceptions raised by network or data problems.

4. Assuming we haven't raised an exception, we must be authenticated at this point and can now submit the file. This will be done with a `put()` call as follows:

```
files = {'file': open(filepath, 'rb')}
response = session.put(
    upload_url,
    files=files
)
```

To send a file, we have to actually open it and pass it into `put()` as a file handle; notice we open it in binary-read mode (`rb`). The `requests` documentation recommends this as it ensures the correct `content-length` value will be calculated for the header.

5. After sending the request, we close the file and check again for a failed status before ending the function, like so:

```
files['file'].close()
response.raise_for_status()
```

Updating application

Before we can call our new function from `Application`, we need to implement a way to create a CSV extract of the daily data. This will be used by more than one function, so we'll implement it separately from the function that calls the upload code. Follow along with these steps:

1. To begin, we'll need a temporary location to store our generated CSV file. The `tempfile` module includes functions to work with temporary files and directories; we'll import `mkdtemp()`, which will give us a name for a platform-specific temporary directory.:

```
from tempfile import mkdtemp
```

Note that `mdktemp()` doesn't actually create a directory; it merely provides an absolute path to a randomly named directory in the platform's preferred `temp` file location. We'll have to create the directory ourselves.

2. Now, let's start our new `Application` method as follows:

```
    def _create_csv_extract(self):
        tmpfilepath = mkdtemp()
        csvmodel = m.CSVModel(
            filename=self.filename.get(),
filepath=tmpfilepath)
```

After creating a temporary directory name, we've created an instance of our `CSVModel` class; even though we're no longer storing our data in the CSV files, we can still use the model to export a CSV file. We've passed the `Application` object's default filename, which is still set to `abq_data_record-CURRENTDATE.csv`, and also the temporary directory's path as `filepath`. Of course, our `CSVModel` doesn't currently take a `filepath`, but we'll fix that in a moment.

3. After creating the CSV model, we'll extract our records from the database as follows:

```
        records = self.data_model.get_all_records()
        if not records:
            return None
```

   Remember that our `SQLModel.get_all_records()` method returns a list of all records for the current day by default. If we don't happen to have any records for the day, it's probably best to stop right away and alert the user, rather than sending an empty CSV file to corporate, so we return `None` from the method if there are no records. Our calling code can test for a `None` return value and display the appropriate warning.

4. Now all we need to do is iterate through the records and save each one to the CSV, then return the `CSVModel` object's filename, like this:

```
for record in records:
    csvmodel.save_record(record)

return csvmodel.filename
```

5. Now that we have a way to create a CSV extract file, we can write the callback method as follows:

```
    def upload_to_corporate_rest(self):

        csvfile = self._create_csv_extract()

        if csvfile is None:
            messagebox.showwarning(
                title='No records',
                message='There are no records to upload'
            )
            return
```

   To begin, we created a CSV extract file and checked if it's `None`. If it is, we'll display an error message and exit the method.

6. Before we can upload, we need to get a username and password from the user. Fortunately, we have the perfect class for this:

```
d = v.LoginDialog(
    self,
    'Login to ABQ Corporate REST API')
if d.result is not None:
    username, password = d.result
else:
    return
```

Our login dialog serves us well here. Unlike with our database login, we're not going to run this in an endless loop; if the password is wrong, the user can just rerun the command. Recall that `result` will be `None` if the user clicks **Cancel**, so we'll just exit the callback method in that case.

7. Now, we can execute our network function as follows:

```
try:
    n.upload_to_corporate_rest(
        csvfile,
        self.settings['abq_upload_url'].get(),
        self.settings['abq_auth_url'].get(),
        username,
        password)
```

We're executing `upload_to_corporate_rest()` in a `try` block since there are a number of exceptions it might raise. We're passing in the upload and authentication URLs from our settings object; we haven't added those yet, so that will need to happen before we're done.

8. Now, let's catch a few exceptions, starting with the `RequestException`. This exception would happen if there were some problem with the data we were sending to the API, most likely a wrong username and password. We'll attach the exception string to the message we show the user, like so:

```
except n.requests.RequestException as e:
    messagebox.showerror('Error with your request',
str(e))
```

9. Next we'll catch `ConnectionError`; this exception is going to be the result of a network problem, such as the internet connection at the lab being down, or the server not responding:

```
except n.requests.ConnectionError as e:
    messagebox.showerror('Error connecting', str(e))
```

10. Any other exception will just be displayed as `General Exception`, like so:

```
except Exception as e:
    messagebox.showerror('General Exception', str(e))
```

11. Let's wrap up the method with a success dialog as follows:

```
else:
    messagebox.showinfo(
        'Success',
        '{} successfully uploaded to REST API.'
        .format(csvfile))
```

12. Let's finish our changes to `Application` by adding this method to `callbacks` as follows:

```
self.callbacks = {
    ...
    'upload_to_corporate_rest':
   self.upload_to_corporate_rest,
    ...
```

Updating the models.py file

There are a couple of things to fix in the `models.py` file before we can test our new functionality. We'll go through these steps to address them:

1. First, our `CSVModel` class needs to be able to take `filepath`:

```
def __init__(self, filename, filepath=None):
    if filepath:
        if not os.path.exists(filepath):
            os.mkdir(filepath)
        self.filename = os.path.join(filepath, filename)
    else:
        self.filename = filename
```

If `filepath` is specified, we need to first make sure the directory exists. Since the `mkdtmp()` method called in the `Application` class does not actually create a temporary directory, we'll create it here. Once that's done, we'll join the `filepath` and `filename` values and store it in the `CSVModel` object's `filename` property.

2. The other thing we need to do in `models.py` is add our new settings. Scroll down to the `SettingsModel` class, and add two more `variables` entries as follows:

```
variables = {
    ...
    'abq_auth_url': {
        'type': 'str',
        'value': 'http://localhost:8000/auth'},
    'abq_upload_url': {
        'type': 'str',
        'value': 'http://localhost:8000/upload'},
     ...
```

We won't be building a GUI to set these settings they'll need to be manually created in a user's configuration file, though for testing, we can use the defaults.

Finishing up

The last thing to do is add the command to our main menu.

Add a new entry to the `tools_menu` in each menu class:

```
tools_menu.add_command(
    label="Upload CSV to corporate REST",
    command=self.callbacks['upload_to_corporate_rest'])
```

Now, run the application and let's try it out. To make it work, you'll need to have at least one data entry, and you'll need to start up the `sample_http_server.py` script.

If all goes well, you should get a dialog like this:

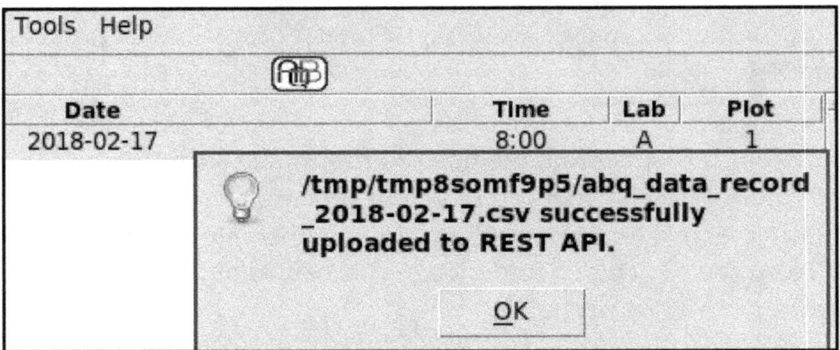

Your server should also have printed some output to the terminal similar to this:

```
POST request received
Content-length: 27
username=test&password=test
127.0.0.1 - - [16/Feb/2018 10:17:22] "POST /auth HTTP/1.1" 200 -
PUT request received
Content-length: 397
--362eadeb828747769e75d5b4b6d32f31
Content-Disposition: form-data; name="file";
filename="abq_data_record_2018-02-16.csv"

Date,Time,Technician,Lab,Plot,Seed
sample,Humidity,Light,Temperature,Equipment
Fault,Plants,Blossoms,Fruit,Min Height,Max Height,Median Height,Notes
2018-02-16,8:00,Q
Murphy,A,1,AXM477,10.00,10.00,10.00,,1,2,3,1.00,3.00,2.00,"
"

--362eadeb828747769e75d5b4b6d32f31--

127.0.0.1 - - [16/Feb/2018 10:17:22] "PUT /upload HTTP/1.1" 200 -
```

Notice the `POST` and `PUT` requests, as well as the raw text of the CSV file in the payload of `PUT`. We have successfully met the API requirements for this function.

FTP using ftplib

While HTTP and REST APIs are the current trend in client-server interactions, it's not unusual for businesses to rely on older, time tested, and sometimes obsolete technology to implement data transfers. ABQ is no exception: in addition to the REST upload, you need to implement support for ABQ corporate's legacy system that relies on FTP.

Basic concepts of FTP

File Transfer Protocol, or **FTP**, dates back to the early 1970s, predating HTTP by almost 20 years. Nevertheless, it's still commonly used by many organizations to exchange large files over the internet. FTP is considered somewhat obsolete in many circles due in part to the fact that it transmits data and credentials in clear text, though SSL-encrypted variants of FTP are also available.

Like HTTP, FTP clients send requests containing plain text commands similar to HTTP methods, and the FTP server returns a response packet containing header and payload information.

There are, however, many significant differences between the two protocols:

- FTP is a **stateful connection**, meaning the client and server maintain a constant connection over the course of the session. In other words, FTP is more like a live telephone call, whereas HTTP is like two people having a dialog over voicemail.
- FTP requires a session to be authenticated before any other commands or data are sent, even for anonymous users. FTP servers also implement a more complex set of permissions.
- FTP has separate modes for transferring text and binary data (the main difference being that text mode transfers automatically correct line endings and encoding for the receiving OS).
- FTP servers are less consistent in their implementation of commands.

Creating a test FTP service

Before we implement our FTP upload functionality, it's helpful to have a test FTP service, just as we did with our test HTTP service. You can, of course, download any of a number of free FTP servers such as FileZilla, PureFTPD, ProFTPD, or others.

Rather than going to the trouble of installing, configuring, and later removing an FTP service on your system just for testing one function of an application, we can instead build a rudimentary server in Python. The third-party `pyftpdlib` package offers us an easy way to implement a quick-and-dirty FTP server adequate for test needs.

Install `pyftpdlib` using `pip`:

```
pip install --user pyftpdlib
```

Just like our simple HTTP server, the FTP service consists of a *server* object and a *handler* object. It also needs an *authorizer* object to handle authentication and permissions.

We'll start our `basic_ftp_server.py` file by importing those:

```
from pyftpdlib.authorizers import DummyAuthorizer
from pyftpdlib.handlers import FTPHandler
from pyftpdlib.servers import FTPServer
```

To make sure our authentication code works properly, let's set up our `DummyAuthorizer` class with a test user:

```
auth = DummyAuthorizer()
auth.add_user('test', 'test', '.', perm='elrw')
```

The `perm` argument takes a string of characters, each of which represents a specific permission on the server. In this case, we have `e` (connect), `l` (list), `r` (read), and `w` (write new file). There are many other permissions available, all of which are off by default until granted, but this is sufficient for our needs.

Now, let's set up the handler:

```
handler = FTPHandler
handler.authorizer = auth
```

Notice we're not instantiating the handler, just aliasing the class. The server class will manage the creation of handler classes. We can, however, assign our `auth` object as the handler's `authorizer` class, so that any created handlers will use our authorizer.

Finally, let's set up and run the server portion:

```
address = ('127.0.0.1', 2100)
server = FTPServer(address, handler)

server.serve_forever()
```

This is simply a matter of instantiating an `FTPServer` object with an address tuple and handler class, then calling the object's `server_forever()` method. The address tuple is in the form `(ip_address, port)`, so a tuple of `('127.0.0.1', 2100)` means we'll be serving on our computer's loopback address on port `2100`. The default port for FTP is usually 21, but on most operating systems, starting a service that listens on a port under `1024` requires root or system-admin privileges. For simplicity's sake, we'll just use a higher port.

While it's possible to build production quality FTP servers with `pyftpdlib`, we haven't done that here. This script is adequate for testing, but please don't use it in production if you value security.

Implementing the FTP upload function

Now that the test server is up and running, let's build our FTP upload function and the logic for the GUI. While the standard library doesn't contain an FTP server library, it does contain an FTP client library in the form of the `ftplib` module.

Begin by importing `ftplib` into our `network.py` file:

```
import ftplib as ftp
```

An FTP session can be created using the `ftplib.FTP` class. Because this is a stateful session, it needs to be closed after we're done; to make sure we do this, `FTP` can be used as a context manager.

Let's start our function by connecting to the FTP server:

```
def upload_to_corporate_ftp(
        filepath, ftp_host,
        ftp_port, ftp_user, ftp_pass):

    with ftp.FTP() as ftp_cx:
        ftp_cx.connect(ftp_host, ftp_port)
        ftp_cx.login(ftp_user, ftp_pass)
```

The `upload_to_corporate()` function takes the CSV filepath and the `FTP` host, port, user, and password, much like our `upload_to_corporate_rest()` function did. We begin by creating our `FTP` object and calling `FTP.connect()` and `FTP.login`.

Next, `connect()` takes the host and port that we're going to talk to and starts a session with the server. We aren't yet authenticated at this point, but we do have a connection going.

Then, `login()` takes a username and password and attempts to authenticate our session. If our credentials check out, we're logged in to the server and can begin sending more commands; if not, an `error_perm` exception is raised. However, our session is still alive until we close it, and we can send additional login attempts if we wish.

To actually upload a file, we use the `storbinary()` method:

```
        filename = path.basename(filepath)
        with open(filepath, 'rb') as fh:
            ftp_cx.storbinary('STOR {}'.format(filename), fh)
```

To send the file, we have to open it in binary-read mode, then call `storbinary` (yes, it's "stor", not "store"—programmers in the 1970s had a thing about dropping letters from words).

The first argument to `storbinary` is a valid FTP `STOR` command, usually `STOR filename`, where "filename" is what you want the uploaded data to be called on the server. It seems a little counter-intuitive to have to include the actual command string; presumably this must be specified in case the server uses slightly different commands or syntax.

The second argument is the file object itself. This should be opened in binary mode since we're sending it as binary data. This may seem odd since the CSV file we're sending is essentially a plain text file, but sending it as binary data guarantees that the server won't change the file in any way during transit; this is nearly always what you want when transferring files, regardless of the nature of the data being exchanged.

This is all our network function needs to do for FTP upload. Although we only needed the `storbinary()` method for our program, it's worth noting a few other common `ftp` methods in case you find yourself having to work with an FTP server.

Listing files

There are three methods for listing files on an FTP server. The `mlsd()` method calls the `MLSD` command, which is typically the best and most complete output available. It can take an optional `path` argument, specifying the path to list (otherwise it lists the current directory), and a list of `facts` , such as "size", "type", or "perm", reflecting which data you'd like included with the filenames. The `mlsd()` command returns a generator object which can be iterated or cast to another sequence type.

`MLSD` is a newer command and not always available, so there are two other methods available, `nlst()` and `dir()`, which correspond to the older `NLST` and `DIR` commands. Both methods accept an arbitrary number of arguments that will be appended verbatim to the command string sent to the server.

Retrieving files

Downloading files from an FTP server involves either one of the `retrbinary()` or `retrlines()` methods, depending on whether we wish to use binary or text mode (as mentioned before, you should probably always use binary). Like `storbinary`, each method takes a command string as its first argument, but in this case it should be a valid `RETR` command (usually "RETR filename" will suffice).

The second argument is a callback function which will be called on every line (for `retrlines()`) or chunk (for `retrbinary()`). This callback can be used to store the downloaded data.

For example, take a look at the following code:

```
from ftplib import FTP
from os.path import join

filename = 'raytux.jpg'
path = '/pub/ibiblio/logos/penguins'
destination = open(filename, 'wb')
with FTP('ftp.nluug.nl', 'anonymous') as ftp:
    ftp.retrbinary(
        'RETR {}'.format(join(path, filename)),
        destination.write)
destination.close()
```

The return value of each function is a result string containing some statistics about the download as follows:

```
'226-File successfully transferred\n226 0.000 seconds (measured here),
146.96 Mbytes per second'
```

Deleting or renaming files

Deleting and renaming files using `ftplib` is mercifully simple by comparison. The `delete()` method takes only a filename and attempts to delete the given file on the server. The `rename()` method takes only a source and destination, and attempts to rename the source to the destination name.

Naturally, the success of either method depends on the permissions granted to the login account used.

Adding FTP upload to the GUI

Our FTP upload function is ready to go, so let's add the necessary bits to the rest of our application to make it all work together.

We'll start by adding the FTP host and port to the `SettingsModel` in `models.py`:

```
variables = {
    ...
    'abq_ftp_host': {'type': 'str', 'value': 'localhost'},
    'abq_ftp_port': {'type': 'int', 'value': 2100}
    ...
```

Remember that our test FTP uses port `2100`, not the usual port `21`, so we'll make `2100` the default for now.

Now, we'll move over to `application.py` and create the callback method that will create the CSV file and pass it to the FTP upload function.

Create a new method in the `Application` object:

```
def upload_to_corporate_ftp(self):
    csvfile = self._create_csv_extract()
```

The first thing we do is create our CSV file, using the method we created for the `REST` upload.

Next, we'll ask the user for the FTP username and password:

```
    d = v.LoginDialog(
        self,
        'Login to ABQ Corporate FTP')
```

And now, we'll call our network function:

```
    if d.result is not None:
        username, password = d.result
        try:
            n.upload_to_corporate_ftp(
                csvfile,
                self.settings['abq_ftp_host'].get(),
                self.settings['abq_ftp_port'].get(),
                username,
                password)
```

We call the FTP upload function in a `try` block because there are several exceptions that can be raised by our FTP process.

Rather than catching them individually, we can catch `ftplib.all_errors`:

```
        except n.ftp.all_errors as e:
            messagebox.showerror('Error connecting to ftp',
str(e))
```

Note that `ftplib.all_errors` is the base class for all exceptions defined in `ftplib`, which include, among other things, authentication errors, permission errors, and connectivity errors.

To end this method, we'll show a success message:

```
        else:
            messagebox.showinfo(
                'Success',
                '{} successfully uploaded to FTP'.format(csvfile))
```

With the callback method written, we need to add it to the `callbacks` dictionary:

```
self.callbacks = {
    ...
    'upload_to_corporate_ftp': self.upload_to_corporate_ftp
}
```

The last thing we need to do is to add our callback to the main menu classes.

Over in `mainmenu.py`, add a new command to the `tools_menu` in each class:

```
tools_menu.add_command(
    label="Upload CSV to corporate FTP",
    command=self.callbacks['upload_to_corporate_ftp'])
```

Launch the sample FTP server in a terminal, then run your application and try out the FTP upload. Remember to enter `test` for the username and password!

You should see a success dialog like this:

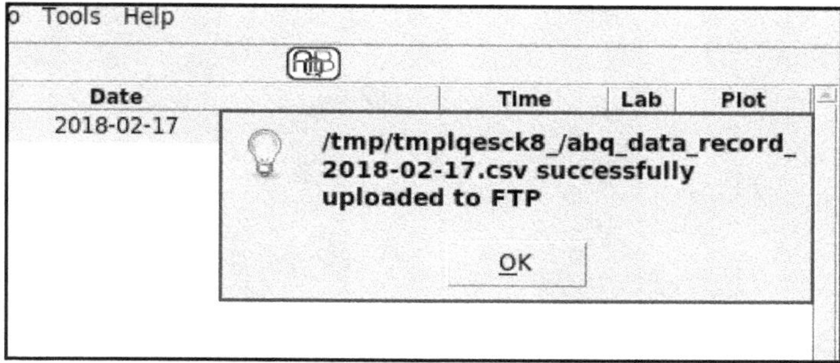

Likewise, there should be a new CSV file in whatever directory you ran the sample FTP server from.

The FTP server should have printed out some information like this:

```
127.0.0.1:32878-[] FTP session opened (connect)
127.0.0.1:32878-[test] USER 'test' logged in.
127.0.0.1:32878-[test] STOR
/home/alanm/FTPserver/abq_data_record_2018-02-17.csv completed=1
bytes=235 seconds=0.001
127.0.0.1:32878-[test] FTP session closed (disconnect).
```

Looks like our FTP upload works great!

Summary

In this chapter, we reached out to the cloud using HTTP and FTP. You learned how to download data using `urllib` and parse XML using `ElementTree`. You also discovered the `requests` library and learned the basics of interacting with a REST API. Finally, we learned how to download and upload files to FTP using Python's `ftplib`.

12
Visualizing Data Using the Canvas Widget

With months of experimental data logged in the database, it's time to begin the process of visualizing and interpreting it. Rather than exporting data into a spreadsheet to create charts and graphs, your fellow analysts have asked whether the program itself can create graphical data visualizations. To implement this feature, you're going to need to learn about Tkinter's `Canvas` widget.

In this chapter, you'll learn the following topics:

- Using the `Canvas` widget for drawing and animation
- Building a simple line graph using `Canvas`
- Incorporating more advanced graphs and charts using Matplotlib

Drawing and animation with Tkinter's Canvas

The `Canvas` widget is undoubtedly the most powerful widget available in Tkinter. It can be used to build anything from custom widgets and views to complete user interfaces. As the name implies, `Canvas` is a blank area on which figures and images can be drawn.

A `Canvas` object can be created like any other widget:

```
root = tk.Tk()
canvas = tk.Canvas(root, width=1024, height=768)
canvas.pack()
```

`Canvas` accepts the usual widget configuration arguments, as well as `width` and `height` for setting its size. Once created, we can start adding items to `canvas` using its many `create_()` methods.

For example, we can add a rectangle with this code:

```
canvas.create_rectangle(100, 100, 200, 200, fill='orange')
```

The first four arguments are the coordinates of the upper-left and lower-right corners, in pixels from the upper-left corner of the canvas. Each `create_()` method begins like this, with coordinates defining the shape. The `fill` option specifies the color of the inside of the object.

Coordinates can also be specified as tuple pairs, like so:

```
canvas.create_rectangle((600, 100), (700, 200), fill='#FF8800')
```

Although this is more characters, it improves readability considerably. Also note that, just like colors elsewhere in Tkinter, we can use names or hex codes.

We can also create ovals, as shown in the following:

```
canvas.create_oval((350, 250), (450, 350), fill='blue')
```

An oval, like a rectangle, takes the coordinates of the upper-left and lower-right corners of its **bounding box**. A bounding box is the smallest rectangle that will contain an item, so in the case of this oval, you can imagine a circle inside a square with corners at `(350, 250)` and `(450, 350)`.

We can create lines using `create_line()`, like so:

```
canvas.create_line((100, 400), (400, 500),
    (700, 400), (100, 400), width=5, fill='red')
```

Lines can consist of any number of points, between which Tkinter will connect the dots. We've specified the width of the line as well as its color (using the `fill` argument). Additional arguments can control the shape of corners and ends, the presence and style of arrows at each end of the line, whether and how the line is dashed, and whether the line is straight or curved.

In a similar fashion, we can create polygons, like this:

```
canvas.create_polygon((400, 150), (350,  300), (450, 300),
    fill='blue', smooth=True)
```

This is just like creating a line, except that Tkinter connects the last dot back to the first and fills in the interior. Setting `smooth` to `True` causes the corners to be rounded using Bezier curves.

In addition to simple shapes, we can also place text or images on the `canvas` object as follows:

```
canvas.create_text((400, 600), text='Smile!',
    fill='cyan', font='TkDefaultFont 64')
smiley = tk.PhotoImage(file='smile.gif')
image_item = canvas.create_image((400, 300), image=smiley)
```

The return value of any `create_()` method is a string that uniquely identifies the item in the context of the `Canvas` object. We can use that identification string to do things to the item after creation.

For example, we can bind events like so:

```
canvas.tag_bind(image_item, '<Button-1>', lambda e:
canvas.delete(image_item))
```

Here, we've used the `tag_bind` method to bind a left-mouse click on our image object to the canvas's `delete()` method, which (when given an item identifier) deletes the item.

Animating Canvas objects

Tkinter's `Canvas` widget doesn't have a built-in animation framework, but we can still create simple animations by combining its `move()` method with our understanding of the event queue.

To demonstrate this, we'll create a bug race simulator, in which two bugs (represented by colored circles) will race haphazardly toward a finish line on the other side of the screen. Like real bugs, they won't have any notion that they're in a race and will move randomly, the winner being whichever bug incidentally hits the finish line first.

To begin, open a new Python file and start with a basic boilerplate as follows:

```
import tkinter as tk

class App(tk.Tk):
    def __init__(self):
```

```
        super().__init__()

App().mainloop()
```

Creating our objects

Let's create the objects to be used in our game:

1. In `App.__init__()`, we'll simply create our `canvas` object and add it using `pack()`:

    ```
            self.canvas = tk.Canvas(self, background='black')
            self.canvas.pack(fill='both', expand=1)
    ```

2. Next, we'll create a `setup()` method as follows:

    ```
        def setup(self):
            self.canvas.left = 0
            self.canvas.top = 0
            self.canvas.right = self.canvas.winfo_width()
            self.canvas.bottom = self.canvas.winfo_height()
            self.canvas.center_x = self.canvas.right // 2
            self.canvas.center_y = self.canvas.bottom // 2

            self.finish_line = self.canvas.create_rectangle(
                (self.canvas.right - 50, 0),
                (self.canvas.right, self.canvas.bottom),
                fill='yellow', stipple='gray50')
    ```

    In the preceding code snippet, `setup()` begins by calculating some relative locations on the `canvas` object and saving them as instance properties, which will simplify the placement of objects on the `canvas` object. The finish line, which is a rectangle across the right edge of the window, uses the `stipple` argument to specify a bitmap that will overlay the solid color to give it some texture; in this case, `gray50` is a built-in bitmap that alternates black and transparent pixels.

3. Add a call to `setup()` at the end of `__init__()` as follows:

    ```
            self.after(200, self.setup)
    ```

    Because `setup()` relies on the `width` and `height` values of the `canvas` object, we need to make sure it isn't called until the operating system's window manager has drawn and sized the window. The simplest way of doing this is to delay the call by a few hundred milliseconds.

4. Next, we need to create our players. Let's create a class to represent them as follows:

```
class Racer:

    def __init__(self, canvas, color):
        self.canvas = canvas
        self.name = "{} player".format(color.title())
        size = 50
        self.id = canvas.create_oval(
            (canvas.left, canvas.center_y),
            (canvas.left + size, canvas.center_y + size),
            fill=color)
```

   The `Racer` class will be created with a reference to `canvas` and a `color` string, from which its color and name will be derived. We'll draw the racer initially at the middle-left of the screen and make it `50` pixels in size. Finally, we save a reference to its item ID string in `self.id`.

5. Now, back in `App.setup()`, we'll create two racers by executing the following code:

```
        self.racers = [
            Racer(self.canvas, 'red'),
            Racer(self.canvas, 'green')]
```

6. At this point, all the objects in our game are set up. Run the program and you should see a yellow-stippled finish line on the right and a green circle on the left (the red circle will be hidden under the green).

Animating the racers

To animate our racers, we're going to use the `Canvas.move()` method. `move()` takes an item ID, a number of `x` pixels, and a number of `y` pixels, and moves the item by that amount. By using `random.randint()` and some simple logic, we can generate a series of moves that will send each racer on a meandering path towards the finish line.

A simple implementation may look like this:

```
def move_racer(self):
    x = randint(0, 100)
    y = randint(-50, 50)
    t = randint(500, 2000)
    self.canvas.after(t, self.canvas.move, self.id, x, y)
```

```
        if self.canvas.bbox(self.id)[0] < self.canvas.right:
            self.canvas.after(t, self.move_racer)
```

This isn't really what we want, though; the problem is that `move()` happens instantaneously, causing the bug to jump across the screen; we want our moves to take place smoothly over a period of time.

To accomplish this, we're going to take the following approach:

1. Calculate a series of linear moves, each with a random delta `x`, delta `y`, and `time`, that will reach the finish line
2. Break each move into a number of steps determined by dividing the time into a regular interval
3. Add each step of each movement to a queue
4. At our regular interval, pull the next step from the queue and pass it to `move()`

Let's start by defining our frame interval and creating our animation queue:

```
from queue import Queue
...
class Racer:
    FRAME_RES = 50

    def __init__(...):
        ...
        self.animation_queue = Queue()
```

`FRAME_RES` (short for frame resolution) defines the number of milliseconds between each `Canvas.move()` call. `50` milliseconds gives us 20 frames per second and should be sufficient for smooth movements.

Now create a method to plot the course to the finish line:

```
    def plot_course(self):
        start_x = self.canvas.left
        start_y = self.canvas.center_y
        total_dx, total_dy = (0, 0)

        while start_x + total_dx < self.canvas.right:
            dx = randint(0, 100)
            dy = randint(-50, 50)
            target_y = start_y + total_dy + dy
            if not (self.canvas.top < target_y < self.canvas.bottom):
                dy = -dy
            time = randint(500, 2000)
```

```
            self.queue_move(dx, dy, time)
            total_dx += dx
            total_dy += dy
```

This method plots a course from the left-center of `canvas` to the right-side by generating random `x` and `y` movements until the total `x` is greater than the width of the `canvas` object. The change in `x` will always be positive, keeping our bugs moving towards the finish line, but the change in `y` can be positive or negative. To keep our bugs on the screen, we constrain the total `y` movements by negating any change in `y` that would put the player outside the top or bottom bound of the canvas.

In addition to `dx` and `dy`, we generate a random amount of `time` for the move to take, between half a second and two seconds, and send the generated values to a `queue_move()` method.

The `queue_move()` command will need to break the large move into individual frames that describe how much movement should happen in one `FRAME_RES` interval. To do this, we need a **partition function**: a mathematical function that will break an integer `n` into `k` approximately equal integers. For example, if we wanted to break -10 into four parts, our function should return a list like [-3, -3, -2, -2].

Create `partition()` as a static method on `Racer`:

```
    @staticmethod
    def partition(n, k):
        """Return a list of k integers that sum to n"""
        if n == 0:
            return [0] * k
```

We start with the easy case: when `n` is `0`, return a list of `k` zeros.

The rest of the code looks like this:

```
        base_step = int(n / k)
        parts = [base_step] * k
        for i in range(n % k):
                parts[i] += n / abs(n)
        return parts
```

First, we create a list of length `k` that is made up of `base_step`, that is, the integer portion of `n` divided by `k`. We use a cast of `int()` here rather than floor division because it behaves more appropriately with negative numbers. Next, we need to distribute the remainder among the list as evenly as we can. To accomplish this, we add `1` or `-1` (depending on the sign of the remainder) to the first `n % k` items in the parts list.

Follow the math here using our example of `n = -10` and `k = 4`:

- -10 / 4 = -2.5, truncated to -2.
- So we have a list: [-2, -2, -2, -2].
- -10 % 4 = 2, so we add -1 (that is, -10 / 10) to the first two items in the list.
- We arrive at an answer of [-3, -3, -2, -2]. Perfect!

Now we can write `queue_move()`:

```
def queue_move(self, dx, dy, time):
    num_steps = time // self.FRAME_RES
    steps = zip(
        self.partition(dx, num_steps),
        self.partition(dy, num_steps))

    for step in steps:
        self.animation_queue.put(step)
```

We first determine the number of steps in this move by dividing the time by `FRAME_RES` using floor division. We create a list of `x` moves and a list of `y` moves by passing `dx` and `dy` each to our `partition()` method. Those two lists are combined with `zip` to form a single list of `(dx, dy)` pairs, which then gets added to the animation queue.

To make the animation actually happen, we'll write an `animate()` method:

```
def animate(self):
    if not self.animation_queue.empty():
        nextmove = self.animation_queue.get()
        self.canvas.move(self.id, *nextmove)
    self.canvas.after(self.FRAME_RES, self.animate)
```

The `animate()` method checks the queue for a move. If there is one, `canvas.move()` is called with the racer's ID and the moves that need to be made. Finally, the `animate()` method is scheduled to run again in `FRAME_RES` milliseconds.

The last step in animating the racers is to call `self.plot_course()` and `self.animate()` at the end of `__init__()`. If you run the game now, your two dots should wander the screen from left to right. But nobody's winning just yet!

Detecting and handling a win condition

To detect a win condition, we're going to periodically check whether a racer is overlapping with the finish line item. When one of them is, we'll declare it the winner and offer the option to play again.

Collision detection between items is slightly awkward with the Tkinter `Canvas` widget. We have to pass a set of bounding box coordinates to `find_overlapping()`, which returns a tuple of item identifiers that overlap with the bounding box.

Let's create an `overlapping()` method for our `Racer` class:

```
    def overlapping(self):
        bbox = self.canvas.bbox(self.id)
        overlappers = self.canvas.find_overlapping(*bbox)
        return [x for x in overlappers if x!=self.id]
```

This method retrieves the bounding box of the `Racer` item using the canvas's `bbox()` method. It then fetches a tuple of items overlapping this bounding box using `find_overlapping()`. Next, we'll filter this tuple to remove the `Racer` item's ID, effectively returning a list of items overlapping with the `Racer` class.

Back in our `App()` method, we'll create a `check_for_winner()` method:

```
    def check_for_winner(self):
        for racer in self.racers:
            if self.finish_line in racer.overlapping():
                self.declare_winner(racer)
                return
        self.after(Racer.FRAME_RES, self.check_for_winner)
```

This method iterates our list of racers and checks whether the `finish_line` ID is in the list returned by the racer's `overlapping()` method. If it is, `racer` has hit the finish line and will be declared the winner.

If no player was declared the winner, we'll schedule the check to run again after `Racer.FRAME_RES` milliseconds.

We handle a win condition in the `declare_winner()` method:

```
    def declare_winner(self, racer):
        wintext = self.canvas.create_text(
            (self.canvas.center_x, self.canvas.center_y),
            text='{} wins!\nClick to play again.'.format(racer.name),
            fill='white',
            font='TkDefaultFont 32',
            activefill='violet')
        self.canvas.tag_bind(wintext, '<Button-1>', self.reset)
```

In this method, we've just created a `text` item declaring `racer.name` as the winner in the center of `canvas`. The `activefill` argument causes the color to appear violet when the mouse is hovered over it, indicating to the user that this text is clickable.

When that text is clicked, it calls the `reset()` method:

```
    def reset(self, *args):
        for item in self.canvas.find_all():
            self.canvas.delete(item)
        self.setup()
```

The `reset()` method needs to clear off the canvas, so it retrieves a list of all item identifiers using the `find_all()` method, then calls `delete()` on each one. Finally, we call `setup()` to reset the game.

The game is now complete, as you can see in the following screenshot:

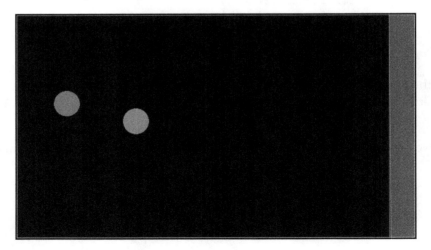

While not exactly simple, animation in Tkinter can provide smooth and satisfactory results with some careful planning and a bit of math.

Enough games, though; let's get back to the lab and figure out how to use the Tkinter `Canvas` widget to visualize data.

Creating simple graphs on the canvas

The first graph we want to produce is a simple line graph that shows the growth of our plants over time. Each lab has varying climate conditions, and we want to see how those conditions are affecting the growth of all plants, so the chart will have one line per lab showing the average of the median height measurements for all plots in the lab over the days of the experiment.

We'll start by creating a model method to return the raw data, then create a `Canvas`-based line-chart view, and finally create an application callback to pull the data and send it to the chart view.

Creating the model method

Suppose we have a SQL query that determines the day number of a plot check by subtracting its date from the oldest date in the `plot_checks` table, then pulls `lab_id` and the average of `median_height` for all plants in the given lab on the given day.

We'll run this query in a new `SQLModel` method called `get_growth_by_lab()`:

```
    def get_growth_by_lab(self):
        query = (
            'SELECT date - (SELECT min(date) FROM plot_checks) AS day,
'
            'lab_id, avg(median_height) AS avg_height FROM plot_checks
'
            'GROUP BY date, lab_id ORDER BY day, lab_id;')
        return self.query(query)
```

We'll get back a table of data that looks something like this:

Day	Lab ID	Average height
0	A	7.4198750000000000
0	B	7.3320000000000000
0	C	7.5377500000000000
0	D	8.4633750000000000
0	E	7.8530000000000000
1	A	6.7266250000000000
1	B	6.8503750000000000

We'll use this data to build our chart.

Creating the graph view

Head over to `views.py`, where we'll create the `LineChartView` class:

```
class LineChartView(tk.Canvas):

    margin = 20

    def __init__(self, parent, chart_width, chart_height,
                 x_axis, y_axis, x_max, y_max):
        self.max_x = max_x
        self.max_y = max_y
        self.chart_width = chart_width
        self.chart_height = chart_height
```

`LineChartView` is a subclass of `Canvas`, so we'll be able to draw items directly on it. We'll accept a parent widget, height, and width for the chart portion, labels for the `x` and `y` axes as arguments, and the maximum values for `x` and `y` to display. We'll save the chart dimensions and maximum values for later use, and set a class property of 20 pixels for the margin width.

Let's start setting up this `Canvas`:

```
        view_width = chart_width + 2 * self.margin
        view_height = chart_height + 2 * self.margin
        super().__init__(
            parent, width=view_width,
            height=view_height, background='lightgrey')
```

We calculate the `width` and `height` values of view by adding the margin to both sides, then call the superclass `__init__()` with them, also setting the background to `lightgrey`. We'll also save the chart `width` and `height` as instance properties.

Next, let's draw the axes:

```
        self.origin = (self.margin, view_height - self.margin)
        self.create_line(
            self.origin, (self.margin, self.margin), width=2)
        self.create_line(
            self.origin,
            (view_width - self.margin,
             view_height - self.margin))
```

Our chart's origin will be `self.margin` pixels from the bottom-left corner, and we'll draw the `x` and `y` axes as simple black lines moving left and up from it to the edge of the chart.

Next, we'll label the axes:

```
        self.create_text(
            (view_width // 2, view_height - self.margin),
            text=x_axis, anchor='n')
        # angle requires tkinter 8.6 -- macOS users take note!
        self.create_text(
            (self.margin, view_height // 2),
            text=y_axis, angle=90, anchor='s')
```

Here, we're creating the `text` items set to the labels for the `x` and `y` axes. There are a few new arguments in use here: `anchor` sets which side of the text's bounding box is attached to the coordinates provided, and `angle` rotates the text object by the given number of degrees. Note that `angle` is a Tkinter 8.6 feature, so it could be a problem for macOS users. Also, note that we've used south as `anchor` for the rotated text; even though it's rotated, the cardinal directions refer to the non-rotated sides, so south will always be the bottom of the text as it's normally printed.

Last of all, we need to create a second `Canvas` that will contain the actual chart:

```
        self.chart = tk.Canvas(
            self, width=chart_width, height=chart_height,
            background='white')
        self.create_window(
            self.origin, window=self.chart, anchor='sw')
```

While we could place widgets on `canvas` using a geometry manager like `pack()` or `grid()`, the `create_window()` method places a widget on `Canvas` as a `Canvas` item using coordinates. We're anchoring the lower-left corner of the chart to the origin point on our graph.

With the pieces in place, we'll now create a method to draw data on the chart:

```
    def plot_line(self, data, color):
        x_scale = self.chart_width / self.max_x
        y_scale = self.chart_height / self.max_y

        coords = [(round(x * x_scale),
            self.chart_height - round(y * y_scale))
            for x, y in data]

        self.chart.create_line(*coords, width=2, fill=color)
```

In `plot_line()`, we first have to convert the raw data into coordinates that can be drawn. We'll need to scale our `data` points so that they range from `0` to the height and width of the chart object. Our method calculates the scale of `x` and `y` (that is, how many pixels per unit `x` or `y`) by dividing the chart dimensions by the maximum values of `x` and `y`. We can then transform our data by using a list comprehension that multiplies each data point by the scale value.

Also, data is usually graphed with the origin in the bottom-left, but coordinates measure from the top-left, so we'll need to flip the `y` coordinates; this is done in our list comprehension as well by subtracting the new `y` value from the chart height. These coordinates can now be passed to `create_line()` along with a reasonable `width` and the `color` argument passed in by the caller.

One last thing we need is a **legend**, to tell the user what each color on the chart represents. Without legend, this chart would be meaningless.

Let's create a `draw_legend()` method:

```
        def draw_legend(self, mapping):
            y = self.margin
            x = round(self.margin * 1.5) + self.chart_width
            for label, color in mapping.items():
                  self.create_text((x, y), text=label, fill=color,
                  anchor='w')
                  y += 20
```

Our method takes a dictionary that maps labels to colors, which will be provided by the application. For each one, we simply draw a text item containing the `label` text with the associated `fill` color. Since we know our labels will be short (only a single character), we can get away with just putting this in the margin.

Updating the application

In the `Application` class, create a new method for showing our chart:

```
    def show_growth_chart(self):
        data = self.data_model.get_growth_by_lab()
        max_x = max([x['day'] for x in data])
        max_y = max([x['avg_height'] for x in data])
```

The first order of business is to fetch data from our `get_growth_by_lab()` method and calculate the maximum values for the `x` and `y` axes. We've done this by using list comprehensions to extract values into lists and calling the built-in `max()` function on it.

Next, we'll build a widget to hold our `LineChartView` object:

```
        popup = tk.Toplevel()
        chart = v.LineChartView(popup, 600, 300, 'day',
                                'centimeters', max_x, max_y)
        chart.pack(fill='both', expand=1)
```

We're using the `Toplevel` widget in this case, which creates a new window outside our main application window. We've then created `LineChartView` that is `600` by `300` pixels with the *x*-axis and *y*-axis labels and added it to `Toplevel` using `pack()`.

Next, we'll assign colors to each lab and draw `legend`:

```
        legend = {'A': 'green', 'B': 'blue', 'C': 'cyan',
                  'D': 'yellow', 'E': 'purple'}
        chart.draw_legend(legend)
```

The last thing to do is to draw the actual lines:

```
        for lab, color in legend.items():
            dataxy = [(x['day'], x['avg_height'])
                for x in data
                if x['lab_id'] == lab]
            chart.plot_line(dataxy, color)
```

Remember that our data contains values for all the labs together, so we're iterating through the labs in `legend` and using a list comprehension to extract only the data for that lab. Then our `plot_line()` method does the rest.

With this method complete, add it to the `callbacks` dictionary and add a menu item to the tools menu for each platform.

When you call your function, you should see something like this:

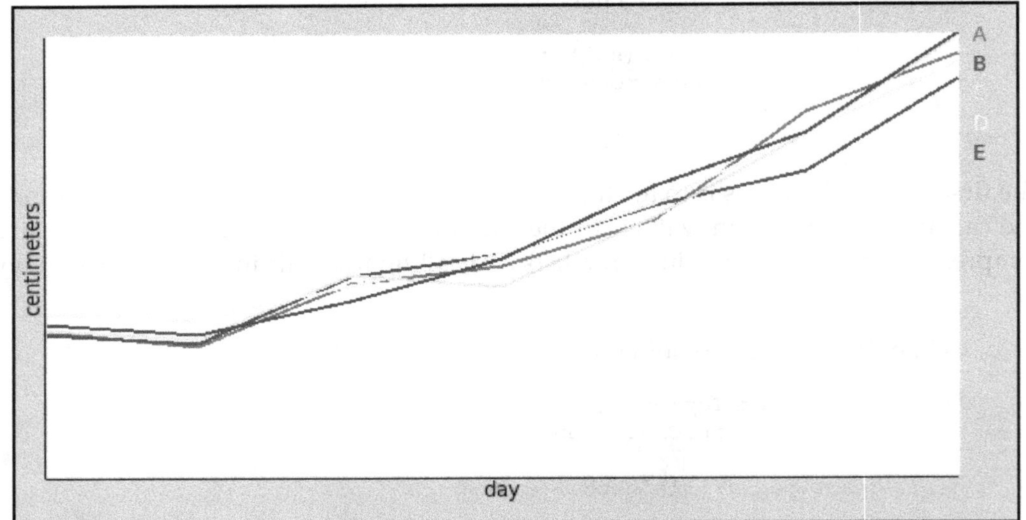

The graph won't look like much without some sample data. Unless you just like doing data entry, there is a script for loading sample data in the `sql` directory.

Advanced graphs using Matplotlib and Tkinter

Our line graph is pretty, but it still needs considerable work to be fully functional: it lacks a scale, grid lines, and other features that would make it a completely useful chart.

We could spend a lot of time making it more complete, but there's a faster way to get much more satisfactory graphs and charts in our Tkinter application: **Matplotlib**.

Matplotlib is a third-party library for generating professional-quality, interactive graphs of all types. It's a vast library with many add-ons, and we won't cover much of its actual usage, but we should look at how to integrate Matplotlib into a Tkinter application. To do this, we'll create a bubble chart showing the yield of each plot as it relates to `humidity` and `temperature`.

You should be able to install `matplotlib` using `pip` with the command `pip install --user matplotlib`. For complete instructions on installing, please see `https://matplotlib.org/users/installing.html`.

Data model method

Before we can make a chart, we'll need a `SQLModel` method to extract the data:

```
    def get_yield_by_plot(self):
        query = (
            'SELECT lab_id, plot, seed_sample, MAX(fruit) AS yield, '
            'AVG(humidity) AS avg_humidity, '
            'AVG(temperature) AS avg_temperature '
            'FROM plot_checks WHERE NOT equipment_fault '
            'GROUP BY lab_id, plot, seed_sample')
        return self.query(query)
```

The purpose of this chart is to find the sweet spot of `temperature` and `humidity` for each seed sample. Therefore, we need one row per `plot` that includes the maximum `fruit` measurement, average humidity and temperature at the `plot` column, and `seed_sample`. Since we don't want any bad data, we'll filter out rows that have `Equipment Fault`.

Creating the bubble chart view

To integrate MatplotLib into a Tkinter application, there are several imports we need to make.

The first is `matplotlib` itself:

```
import matplotlib
matplotlib.use('TkAgg')
```

It may seem odd to run code in the `import` section, and your editor may even complain about it. But before we import anything else from `matplotlib` we need to tell it which backend it should use. In this case, we want the `TkAgg` backend, which is made to integrate into Tkinter.

Now we can make a few more imports from `matplotlib`:

```
from matplotlib.figure import Figure
from matplotlib.backends.backend_tkagg import (
    FigureCanvasTkAgg, NavigationToolbar2TkAgg)
```

The `Figure` class represents the basic drawing area on which `matplotlib` charts can be drawn. The `FigureCanvasTkAgg` class is an interface between the `Figure` and the Tkinter `Canvas`, and `NavigationToolbar2TkAgg` allows us to place a pre-made toolbar for `Figure` on our graph.

To see how these fit together, let's start our `YieldChartView` class in `views.py`:

```
class YieldChartView(tk.Frame):
    def __init__(self, parent, x_axis, y_axis, title):
        super().__init__(parent)
        self.figure = Figure(figsize=(6, 4), dpi=100)
        self.canvas = FigureCanvasTkAgg(self.figure, master=self)
```

After calling `super().__init__()` to create the `Frame` object, we create a `Figure` object to hold our chart. Instead of a size in pixels, the `Figure` object takes a size in **inches** and a **dots per inch** (**dpi**) setting (in this case, resulting in a 600 by 400 pixel `Figure`). Next, we create a `FigureCanvasTkAgg` object to connect our `Figure` object with a Tkinter `Canvas`. The `FigureCanvasTkAgg` object is not itself a `Canvas` object or subclass, but it has a `Canvas` object we can place in our application.

Next, we'll add the toolbar and `pack()` to our `FigureCanvasTkAgg` object:

```
        self.toolbar = NavigationToolbar2TkAgg(self.canvas, self)
        self.canvas.get_tk_widget().pack(fill='both', expand=True)
```

Our toolbar is passed our `FigureCanvasTkAgg` object and the root window (`self` in this case), attaching it to our figure and it's canvas. To place the `FigureCanvasTkAgg` object on our `Frame` object, we need to call `get_tk_widget()` to retrieve its Tkinter `Canvas` widget, which we can then pack or grid as desired using `pack()` and `grid()`.

The next step is to set up the axes:

```
        self.axes = self.figure.add_subplot(1, 1, 1)
        self.axes.set_xlabel(x_axis)
        self.axes.set_ylabel(y_axis)
        self.axes.set_title(title)
```

In Matplotlib, an `axes` object represents a single set of `x` and `y` axes on which data can be graphed, and is created using the `add_subplot()` method. The three integers passed to `add_subplot()` establish that this is the first set of `axes` out of one row of one column of subplots. Our figure could conceivably contain multiple subplots arranged in a table-like format, but we only need one. After it's created, we set the labels on the `axes` object.

To create a bubble chart, we're going to use the **scatter plot** feature of Matplotlib, but use the size of each dot to indicate the fruit yield. We'll also color code the dots to indicate the seed sample.

Let's implement a method to draw our scatter plots:

```
    def draw_scatter(self, data, color, label):
        x, y, s = zip(*data)
        s = [(x ** 2)//2 for x in s]
        scatter = self.axes.scatter(
            x, y, s, c=color, label=label, alpha=0.5)
```

The data passed in should contain three columns per record, and we're breaking those out into three separate lists containing the `x`, `y`, and `size` values. Next, we're going amplify the differences between size values to make them more apparent by squaring each value then dividing it by half. This isn't strictly necessary, but it helps make the chart more readable when differences are relatively small.

Finally, we draw the data onto the `axes` object by calling `scatter()`, also passing along the `color` and `label` values for the dots, and making them semi-transparent with the `alpha` argument.

`zip(*data)` is a Python idiom for breaking a list of n-length tuples into n lists of values, essentially the reverse of `zip(x, y, s)`.

To draw legend for our `axes` object, we need two things: a list of our `scatter` objects and list of their labels. To get these, we'll have to create a couple of blank lists in `__init__()` and append them whenever `draw_scatter()` is called.

In `__init__()`, add some empty lists:

```
self.scatters = []
self.scatter_labels = []
```

Now, at the end of `draw_scatter()`, append the lists and update the `legend()` method:

```
self.scatters.append(scatter)
self.scatter_labels.append(label)
self.axes.legend(self.scatters, self.scatter_labels)
```

We can call `legend()` repeatedly and it will simply destroy and redraw the legend each time.

Application method

Back in `Application`, let's create the method to show our yield data.

Start by creating a `Toplevel` method and adding our chart view:

```
popup = tk.Toplevel()
chart = v.YieldChartView(popup,
    'Average plot humidity', 'Average Plot temperature',
    'Yield as a product of humidity and temperature')
chart.pack(fill='both', expand=True)
```

Now let's set up the data for our scatters:

```
data = self.data_model.get_yield_by_plot()
seed_colors = {'AXM477': 'red', 'AXM478': 'yellow',
    'AXM479': 'green', 'AXM480': 'blue'}
```

We've retrieved the yield `data` from the data model and created a dictionary that will hold the colors we want to use for each seed sample.

Now we just need to iterate through the seed samples and draw the scatters:

```
for seed, color in seed_colors.items():
    seed_data = [
        (x['avg_humidity'], x['avg_temperature'], x['yield'])
        for x in data if x['seed_sample'] == seed]
    chart.draw_dots(seed_data, color, seed)
```

Once again, we're formatting and filtering down our data using a list comprehension, providing average humidity for `x`, average temperature for `y`, and yield for `s`.

Add the method to the `callbacks` dictionary and create a menu item for it just under the growth chart option.

Your bubble chart should look something like this:

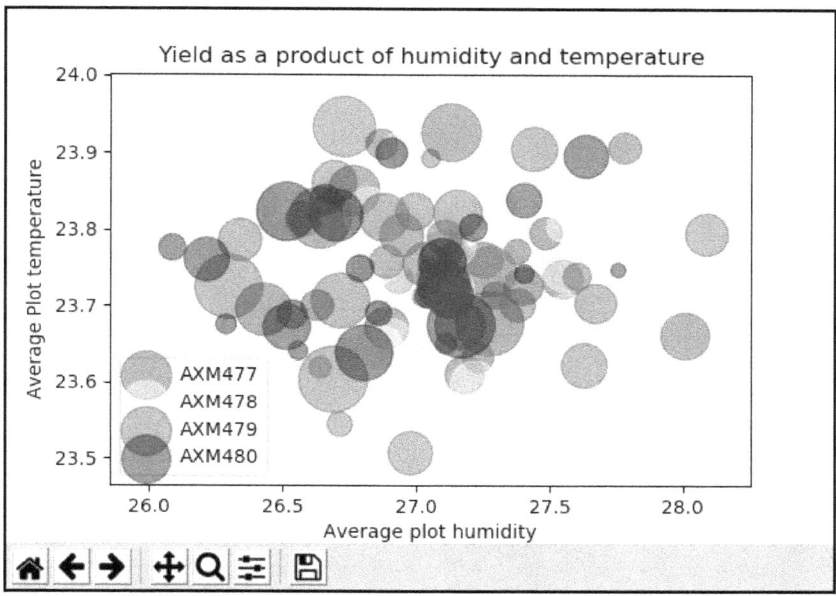

Take a moment to play with this chart using the navigation toolbar. Notice how you can zoom and pan, adjust the size of the chart, and save the image. These are powerful tools that Matplotlib provides automatically.

Summary

In this chapter, you learned about Tkinter's graphical capabilities. You learned how to draw and animate figures on the Tkinter `Canvas` widget, and how to use these capabilities to visualize data. You also learned how to integrate Matplotlib figures into your application, and we implemented two charts in our application by connecting SQL queries to our chart views.

13
Creating a User Interface with Qt Components

In this chapter, we will learn to use the following widgets:

- Displaying a welcome message
- Using the Radio Button widget
- Grouping radio buttons
- Displaying options in the form of checkboxes
- Displaying two groups of checkboxes

Introduction

We will be learning to create GUI applications using the Qt toolkit. The Qt toolkit, known simply as Qt, is a cross-platform application and UI framework developed by **Trolltech**, which is used for developing GUI applications. It runs on several platforms, including Windows, macOS X, Linux, and other UNIX platforms. It is also referred to as a widget toolkit because it provides widgets such as buttons, labels, textboxes, push buttons, and list boxes, which are required for designing a GUI. It includes a cross-platform collection of classes, integrated tools, and a cross-platform IDE. To create real-time applications, we will be making use of Python bindings for the Qt toolkit called, **PyQt5**.

PyQt

PyQt is a set of Python bindings for the cross-platform application framework that combines all the advantages of Qt and Python. With PyQt, you can include Qt libraries in Python code, enabling you to write GUI applications in Python. In other words, PyQt allows you to access all the facilities provided by Qt through Python code. Since PyQt depends on the Qt libraries to run, when you install PyQt, the required version of Qt is also installed automatically on your machine.

A GUI application may consist of a main window with several dialogs or just a single dialog. A small GUI application usually consists of at least one dialog. A dialog application contains buttons. It doesn't contain a menu bar, toolbar, status bar, or central widget, whereas a main window application normally has all of those.

Dialogs are of the following two types:

- **Modal**: This dialog is one that blocks the user from interacting with other parts of the application. The dialog is the only part of the application that the user can interact with. Until the dialog is closed, no other part of the application can be accessed.
- **Modeless**: This dialog is the opposite of a modal dialog. When a modeless dialog is active, the user is free to interact with the dialog and with the rest of the application.

Ways of creating GUI applications

There are the following two ways to write a GUI application:

- From scratch, using a simple text editor
- With Qt Designer, a visual design tool with which you can create a user interface quickly using drag and drop

You will be using Qt Designer to develop GUI applications in PyQt, as it is a quick and easy way to design user interfaces without writing a single line of code. So, launch Qt Designer by double-clicking on its icon on desktop.

On opening, Qt Designer asks you to select a template for your new application, as shown in the following screenshot:

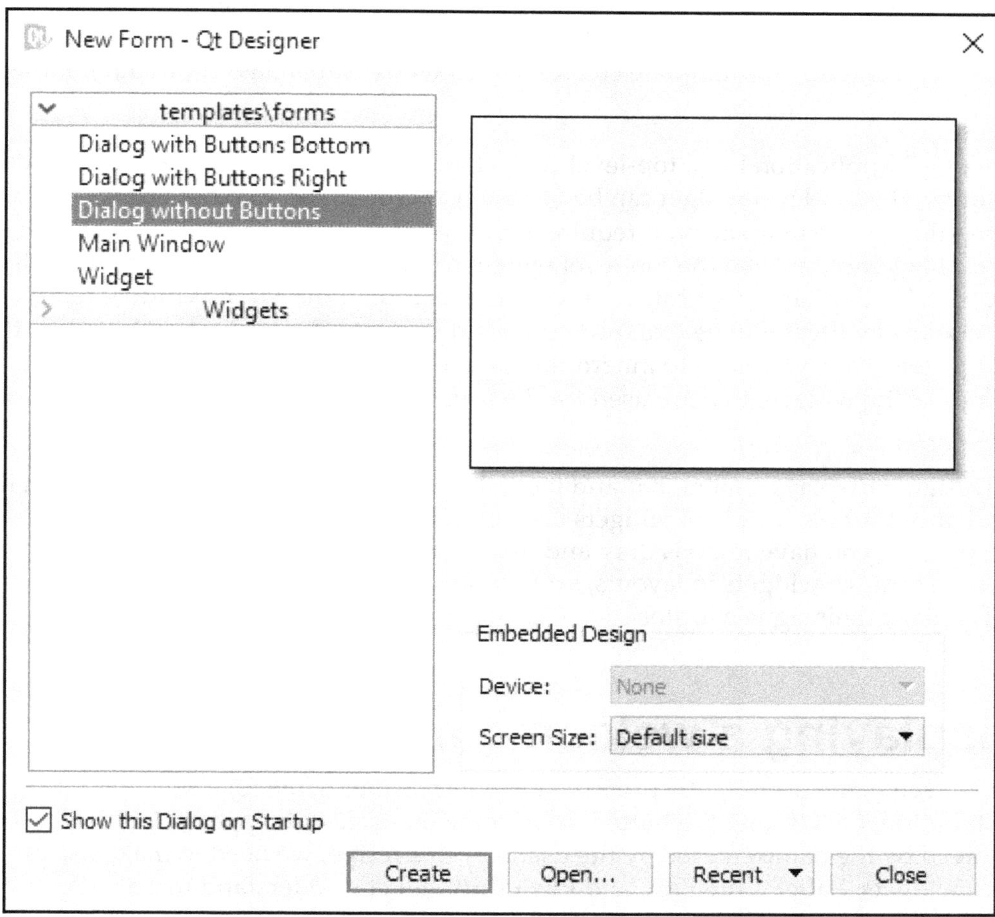

Qt Designer provides a number of templates that are suitable for different kinds of applications. You can choose any of these templates and then click the **Create** button.

Qt Designer provides the following predefined templates for a new application:

- **Dialog with Buttons Bottom**: This template creates a form with the **OK** and **Cancel** buttons in the bottom-right corner.
- **Dialog with Buttons Right**: This template creates a form with the **OK** and **Cancel** buttons in the top-right corner.

- **Dialog without Buttons**: This template creates an empty form on which you can place widgets. The superclass for dialogs is `QDialog`.
- **Main Window**: This template provides a main application window with a menu bar and a toolbar that can be removed if not required.
- **Widget**: This template creates a form whose superclass is `QWidget` rather than `QDialog`.

Every GUI application has a top-level widget and the rest of the widgets are called its children. The top-level widget can be `QDialog`, `QWidget`, or `QMainWindow`, depending on the template you require. If you want to create an application based on the dialog template, then the top-level widget or the first class that you inherit will be `QDialog`. Similarly, to create an application based on the **Main Window** template, the top-level widget will be `QMainWindow`, and to create the application based on the **Widget** template, you need to inherit the `QWidget` class. As mentioned previously, the rest of the widgets that are used for the user interface are called child widgets of the classes.

Qt Designer displays a menu bar and toolbar at the top. It shows a **Widget** box on the left that contains a variety of widgets used to develop applications, grouped in sections. All you have to do is drag and drop the widgets you want from the form. You can arrange widgets in layouts, set their appearance, provide initial attributes, and connect their signals to slots.

Displaying a welcome message

In this recipe, the user will be prompted to enter his/her name followed by clicking a push button. On clicking the button, a welcome message will appear, "Hello," followed by the name entered by the user. For this recipe, we need to make use of three widgets, **Label**, **Line Edit**, and **Push Button**. Let's understand these widgets one by one.

Understanding the Label widget

The **Label** widget is an instance of the `QLabel` class and is used for displaying messages and images. Because the **Label** widgets simply display results of computations and don't take any input, they are simply used for supplying information on the screen.

Methods

The following are the methods provided by the `QLabel` class:

- `setText()`: This method assigns text to the **Label** widget
- `setPixmap()`: This method assigns `pixmap`, an instance of the `QPixmap` class, to the **Label** widget
- `setNum()`: This method assigns an integer or double value to the **Label** widget
- `clear()`: This method clears text from the **Label** widget

The default text of `QLabel` is **TextLabel**. That is, when you add a `QLabel` class to a form by dragging a **Label** widget and dropping it on the form, it will display **TextLabel**. Besides using `setText()`, you can also assign text to a selected `QLabel` object by setting its **text** property in the **Property Editor** window.

Understanding the Line Edit widget

The **Line Edit** widget is that is popularly used for entering single-line data. The **Line Edit** widget is an instance of the `QLineEdit` class, and you can not only enter, but also edit the data too. Besides entering data, you can undo, redo, cut, and paste data in the **Line Edit** widget.

Methods

The following are the methods provided by the `QLineEdit` class:

- `setEchoMode()`: It sets the echo mode of the **Line Edit** widget. That is, it determines how the contents of the **Line Edit** widget are to be displayed. The available options are as follows:
    - `Normal`: This is the default mode and it displays characters the way they are entered
    - `NoEcho`: It switches off the **Line Edit** echo, that is, it doesn't display anything
    - `Password`: This option is used for password fields, no text will be displayed; instead, asterisks appear for the text entered by the user
    - `PasswordEchoOnEdit`: It displays the actual text while editing the password fields, otherwise it will display the asterisks for the text

- `maxLength()`: This method is used to specify the maximum length of text that can be entered in the **Line Edit** widget.
- `setText()`: This method is used for assigning text to the **Line Edit** widget.
- `text()`: This method accesses the text entered in the **Line Edit** widget.
- `clear()`: This method clears or deletes the complete content of the **Line Edit** widget.
- `setReadOnly()`: When the Boolean value true is passed to this method, it will make the **Line Edit** widget read-only, that is, non-editable. The user cannot make any changes to the contents displayed through the **Line Edit** widget, but can only copy.
- `isReadOnly()`: This method returns the Boolean value true if the **Line Edit** widget is in read-only mode, otherwise it returns false.
- `setEnabled()`: By default, the **Line Edit** widget is enabled, that is, the user can make changes to it. But if the Boolean value false is passed to this method, it will disable the **Line Edit** widget so the user cannot edit its content, but can only assign text via the `setText()` method.
- `setFocus()`: This method positions the cursor on the specified **Line Edit** widget.

Understanding the Push Button widget

To display a push button in an application, you need to create an instance of the `QPushButton` class. When assigning text to buttons, you can create shortcut keys by preceding any character in the text with an ampersand. For example, if the text assigned to a push button is `Click Me`, the character `C` will be underlined to indicate that it is a shortcut key, and the user can select the button by pressing *Alt* + *C*. The button emits the **clicked()** signal if it is activated. Besides text, an icon can also be displayed in the push button. The methods for displaying text and an icon in a push button are as follows:

- `setText()`: This method is used to assign text to the push button
- `setIcon()`: This method is used to assign an icon to the push button

How to do it...

Let's create a new application based on the **Dialog without Buttons** template. As said earlier, this application will prompt the user to enter a name and, on clicking the push button after entering a name, the application with display a hello message along with the entered name. Here are the steps to create this application:

1. The other Label with default text should have the objectName property of `labelResponse`
2. Drag one more **Label** widget from the **Display Widgets** category and drop it on the form. Do not change the **text** property of this **Label** widget and leave its **text** property to its default value, **TextLabel**. This is because the **text** property of this **Label** widget will be set through code, that is, it will be used to display the hello message to the user.
3. Drag one **Line Edit** from the **Input Widgets** category and drop it on the form. Set its **objectName** property to `lineEditName`.
4. Drag one **Push Button** widget from the **Buttons** category and drop it onto the form. Set its **text** property to `Click`. You can change the **text** property of the **Push Button** widget through any of three ways: by double-clicking the **Push Button** widget and overwriting the default text, by right-clicking the **Push Button** widget and selecting the **Change text...** option from the context menu that pops up, or by selecting the **text** property from the **Property Editor** window and overwriting the default text.
5. Set the **objectName** property of the **Push Button** widget to `ButtonClickMe`.

6. Save the application with the name `demoLineEdit.ui`. Now the form will appear, as shown in the following screenshot:

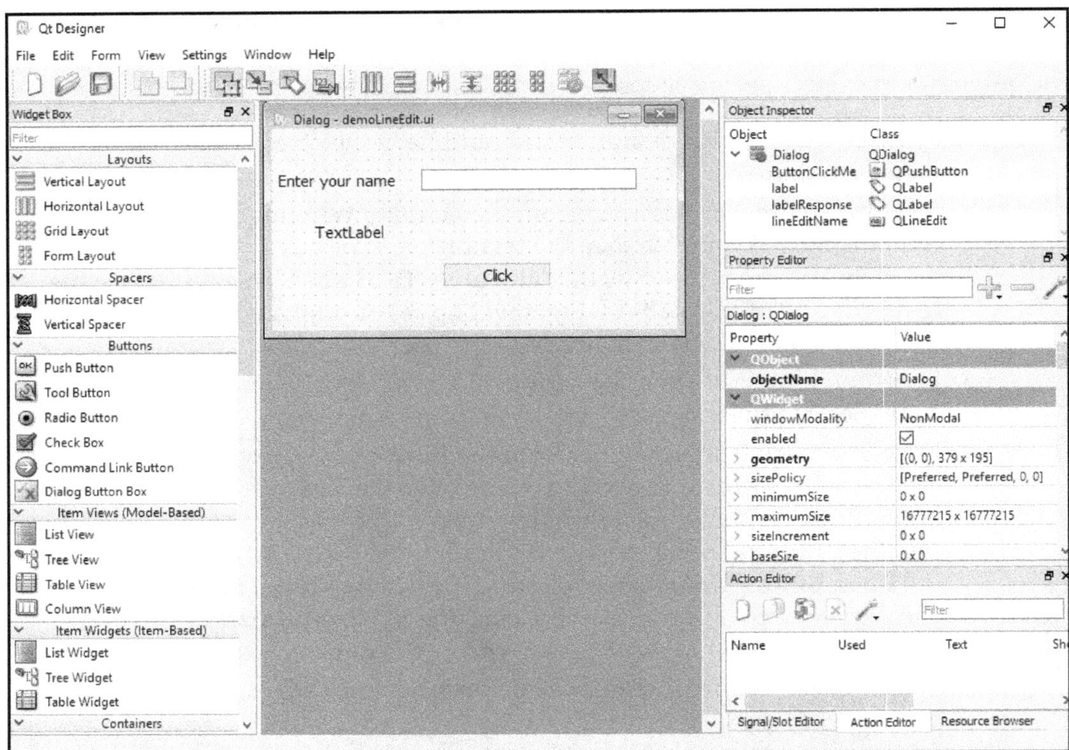

The user interface that you create with Qt Designer is stored in a `.ui` file that includes all the form's information: its widgets, layout, and so on. The `.ui` file is an XML file, and you need to convert it to Python code. That way, you can maintain a clear separation between the visual interface and the behavior implemented in code.

7. To use the `.ui` file, you first need to convert it into a Python script. The command utility that you will use for converting a `.ui` file into a Python script is `pyuic5`. In Windows, the `pyuic5` utility is bundled with PyQt. To do the conversion, you need to open a Command Prompt window and navigate to the folder where the file is saved and issue the following command:

```
C:\Pythonbook\PyQt5>pyuic5 demoLineEdit.ui -o demoLineEdit.py
```

Let's assume that we saved the form at this location: `C:\Pythonbook\PyQt5>`. The preceding command shows the conversion of the `demoLineEdit.ui` file into a Python script, `demoLineEdit.py`.

The Python code generated by this method should not be modified manually, as any changes will be overwritten the next time you run the `pyuic5` command.

The code of the generated Python script file, `demoLineEdit.py`, can be seen in the source code bundle of this book.

8. Treat the code in the `demoLineEdit.py` file as a header file, and import it to the file from which you will invoke its user interface design.

The header file is a term referred to those files which are imported into the current file. The command to import such files is usually written at the top in the script, hence named as header files.

9. Let's create another Python file with the name `callLineEdit.py` and import the `demoLineEdit.py` code into it as follows:

```
import sys
from PyQt5.QtWidgets import QDialog, QApplication
from demoLineEdit import *
class MyForm(QDialog):
    def __init__(self):
        super().__init__()
        self.ui = Ui_Dialog()
        self.ui.setupUi(self)
self.ui.ButtonClickMe.clicked.connect(self.dispmessage)
        self.show()
    def dispmessage(self):
        self.ui.labelResponse.setText("Hello "
        +self.ui.lineEditName.text())
if __name__=="__main__":
    app = QApplication(sys.argv)
    w = MyForm()
    w.show()
    sys.exit(app.exec_())
```

How it works...

The `demoLineEdit.py` file is very easy to understand. A class with the name of the top-level object is created, with `Ui_` prepended. Since the top-level object used in our application is `Dialog`, the `Ui_Dialog` class is created and stores the interface elements of our widget. That class has two methods, `setupUi()` and `retranslateUi()`. The `setupUi()` method sets up the widgets; it creates the widgets that you use while defining the user interface in Qt Designer. The method creates the widgets one by one and also sets their properties. The `setupUi()` method takes a single argument, which is the top-level widget in which the user interface (child widgets) is created. In our application, it is an instance of `QDialog`. The `retranslateUi()` method translates the interface.

Let's understand what `callLineEdit.py` does statement-wise:

1. It imports the necessary modules. `QWidget` is the base class of all user interface objects in PyQt5.
2. It creates a new `MyForm` class that inherits from the base class, `QDialog`.
3. It provides the default constructor for `QDialog`. The default constructor has no parent, and a widget with no parent is known as a window.
4. Event handling in PyQt5 uses signals and slots. A signal is an event, and a slot is a method that is executed on the occurrence of a signal. For example, when you click a push button, a `clicked()` event, also known as a signal, occurs. The `connect()` method connects signals with slots. In this case, the slot is a method: `dispmessage()`. That is, when the user clicks the push button, the `dispmessage()` method will be invoked. `clicked()` is an event here and an event handling loop waits for an event to occur and then dispatches it to perform some task. The event handling loop continues to work until either the `exit()` method is called or the main widget is destroyed.
5. It creates an application object with the name `app` through the `QApplication()` method. Every PyQt5 application must create `sys.argv` application object which contains a list of arguments from the command line, and it is passed to the method while creating the application object. The `sys.argv` parameter helps in passing and controlling the startup attributes of a script.

6. An instance of the `MyForm` class is created with the name `w`.
7. The `show()` method will display the widget on the screen.
8. The `dispmessage()` method performs event handling for the push button. It displays the **Hello** text, along with the name entered in the **Line Edit** widget.
9. The `sys.exit()` method ensures a clean exit, releasing memory resources.

The `exec_()` method has an underscore because `exec` is a Python keyword.

On executing the preceding program, you get a window with the **Line Edit** and **Push Button** widgets, as shown in the following screenshot. When the push button is selected, the `dispmessage()` method will be executed, displaying the **Hello** message along with the user's name that is entered in the **Line Edit** widget:

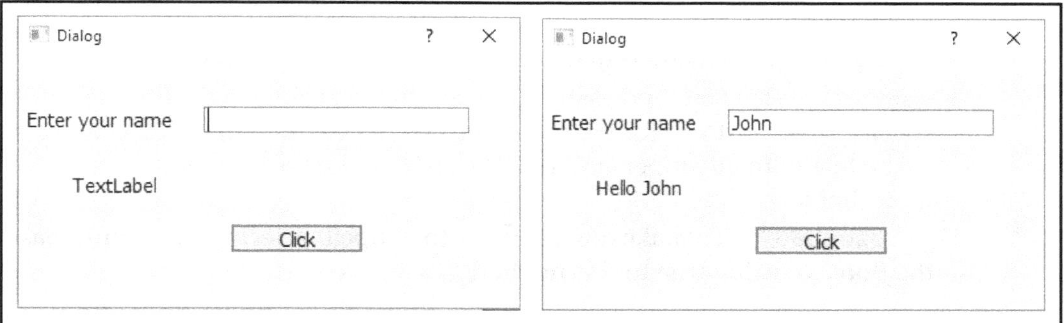

Using the Radio Button widget

This recipe displays certain flight types via **Radio Button** and when the user selects the radio button, the price associated with that flight will be displayed. We need to first understand the workings of **Radio Button**.

Understanding Radio Button

The **Radio Button** widgets are very popular when you want the user to select only one option out of the available options. Such options are known as mutually exclusive options. When the user selects an option, the previously selected option is automatically deselected. The **Radio Button** widgets are instances of the `QRadioButton` class. Every radio button has an associated text label. The radio button can be either in selected (checked) or unselected (unchecked) states. If you want two or more sets of radio buttons, where each set allows the exclusive selection of a radio button, put them into different button groups (instances of `QButtonGroup`). The methods provided by `QRadioButton` are shown next.

Methods

The `QRadioButton` class provides the following methods:

- `isChecked()`: This method returns the Boolean value true if the button is in the selected state.
- `setIcon()`: This method displays an icon with the radio button.
- `setText()`: This method assigns the text to the radio button. If you want to specify a shortcut key for the radio button, precede the preferred character in the text with an ampersand (`&`). The shortcut character will be underlined.
- `setChecked()`: To make any radio button appear selected by default, pass the Boolean value true to this method.

Signal description

Signals emitted by `QRadioButton` are as follows:

- **toggled()**: This signal is emitted whenever the button changes its state from checked to unchecked or vice versa
- **clicked()**: This signal is emitted when a button is activated (that is, pressed and released) or when its shortcut key is pressed
- **stateChanged()**: This signal is emitted when a radio button changes its state from checked to unchecked or vice versa

To understand the concept of radio buttons, let's create an application that asks the user to select the flight type and displays three options, **First Class**, **Business Class**, and **Economy Class**, in the form of radio buttons. On selecting an option through the radio button, the price for that flight will be displayed.

How to do it...

Let's create a new application based on the **Dialog without Buttons** template. This application will display different flight types along with their respective prices. When a user selects a flight type, its price will be displayed on the screen:

1. Drag and drop two **Label** widgets and three **Radio Button** widgets onto the form.
2. Set the **text** property of the first **Label** widget to `Choose the flight type` and delete the **text** property of the second **Label** widget. The **text** property of the second **Label** widget will be set through code; it will be used to display the price of the selected flight type.
3. Set the **text** property of the three **Radio Button** widgets to `First Class $150`, `Business Class $125`, and `Economy Class $100`.
4. Set the **objectName** property of the second **Label** widget to `labelFare`. The default object names of the three radio buttons are `radioButton`, `radioButton_2`, and `radioButton_3`. Change the **objectName** property of these three radio buttons to `radioButtonFirstClass`, `radioButtonBusinessClass`, and `radioButtonEconomyClass`.
5. Save the application with name `demoRadioButton1.ui`.

   Take a look at the following screenshot:

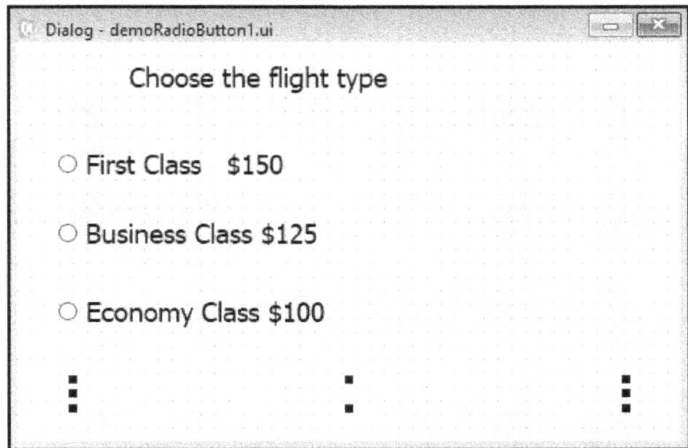

The `demoRadioButton1.ui` application is an XML file and needs to be converted into Python code through the `pyuic5` command utility. The generated Python code, `demoRadioButton1.py`, can be seen in the source code bundle of this book.

6. Import the `demoRadioButton1.py` file as a header file in the Python script that you are going to create next to invoke the user interface design.
7. In the Python script, write the code to display the flight type on the basis of the radio button selected by the user. Name the source file `callRadioButton1.py`; its code is shown here:

```
import sys
from PyQt5.QtWidgets import QDialog, QApplication
from demoRadioButton1 import *
class MyForm(QDialog):
    def __init__(self):
        super().__init__()
        self.ui = Ui_Dialog()
        self.ui.setupUi(self)
        self.ui.radioButtonFirstClass.toggled.connect(self.
        dispFare)
        self.ui.radioButtonBusinessClass.toggled.connect(self.
        dispFare)
        self.ui.radioButtonEconomyClass.toggled.connect(self.
        dispFare)
        self.show()
    def dispFare(self):
        fare=0
        if self.ui.radioButtonFirstClass.isChecked()==True:
            fare=150
        if self.ui.radioButtonBusinessClass.isChecked()==True:
            fare=125
        if self.ui.radioButtonEconomyClass.isChecked()==True:
            fare=100
        self.ui.labelFare.setText("Air Fare is "+str(fare))
if __name__=="__main__":
    app = QApplication(sys.argv)
    w = MyForm()
    w.show()
    sys.exit(app.exec_())
```

How it works...

The **toggled()** event of **Radio Button** is connected to the `dispFare()` function, which will display the price of the selected flight type. In the `dispFare()` function, you check the state of the radio buttons. Hence, if `radioButtonFirstClass` is selected, the value `150` is assigned to the fare variable. Similarly, if `radioButtonBusinessClass` is selected, the value `125` is assigned to the `fare` variable. Similarly, the value `100` is assigned to the `fare` variable when `radioButtonEconomyClass` is selected. Finally, the value in the `fare` variable is displayed via `labelFare`.

On executing the previous program, you get a dialog that displays three flight types and prompts the user to select the one that he/she wants to use for travel. On selecting a flight type, the price of the selected flight type is displayed, as shown in the following screenshot:

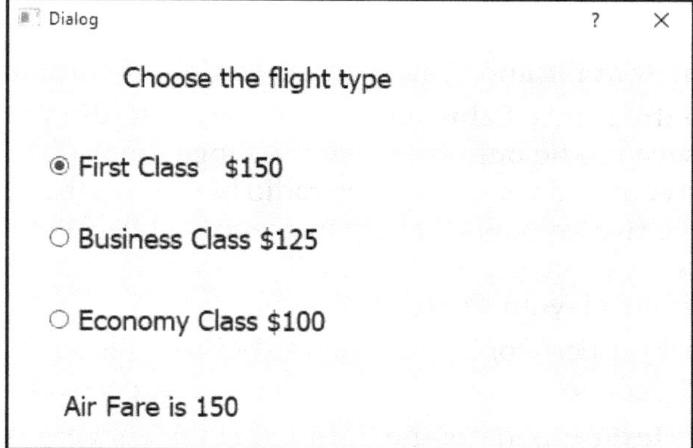

Grouping radio buttons

In this application, we will learn to create two groups of radio buttons. The user can select radio buttons from either group and accordingly the result or text will appear on the screen.

Getting ready

We will display a dialog that displays shirts of different sizes and different payment methods. On selecting a shirt size and a payment method, the selected shirt size and payment method will be displayed on the screen. We will create two groups of radio buttons, one of the shirt sizes and other payment methods. The shirt size group displays four radio buttons showing four different types of the size such as **M**, **L**, **XL**, and **XXL**, where **M** stands for medium size, **L** stands for large size, and so on. The payment method group displays three radio buttons, **Debit/Credit Card**, **NetBanking**, and **Cash On Delivery**. The user can select any radio button from either of the groups. When the user selects any of the shirt sizes or payment methods, the selected shirt size and payment method will be displayed.

How to do it...

Let's recreate the preceding application step by step:

1. Create a new application based on the **Dialog without Buttons** template.
2. Drag and drop three **Label** widgets and seven **Radio Button** widgets. Out of these seven radio buttons, we will arrange four radio buttons in one vertical layout and the other three radio buttons in the second vertical layout. The two layouts will help in grouping these radio buttons. Radio buttons being mutually exclusive will allow only one radio button to be selected from a layout or group.
3. Set the **text** property of the first two **Label** widgets to `Choose your Shirt Size` and `Choose your payment method` respectively.
4. Delete the **text** property of the third **Label** widget because we will display the selected shirt size and payment method through the code.
5. In the **Property Editor** window, increase the font size of all the widgets to increase their visibility in the application.
6. Set the **text** property of the first four radio buttons to `M`, `L`, `XL`, and `XXL`. Arrange these four radio buttons into one vertical layout.
7. Set the **text** property of the next three radio buttons to `Debit/Credit Card`, `NetBanking`, and `Cash On Delivery`. Arrange these three radio buttons into a second vertical layout. Remember, these vertical layouts help by grouping these radio buttons.
8. Change the object names of the first four radio buttons to `radioButtonMedium`, `radioButtonLarge`, `radioButtonXL`, and `radioButtonXXL`.

9. Set the **objectName** property of the first `VBoxLayout` layout to `verticalLayout`. The `VBoxLayout` layout will be used for aligning radio buttons vertically.
10. Change the object names of next three radio buttons to `radioButtonDebitCard`, `radioButtonNetBanking`, and `radioButtonCashOnDelivery`.
11. Set the **objectName** property of the second `QVBoxLayout` object to `verticalLayout_2`.
12. Set the **objectName** property of the third **Label** widget to `labelSelected`. It is through this **Label** widget that the selected shirt size and payment method will be displayed.
13. Save the application with the name `demoRadioButton2.ui`.
14. Now, the form will appear, as shown in the following screenshot:

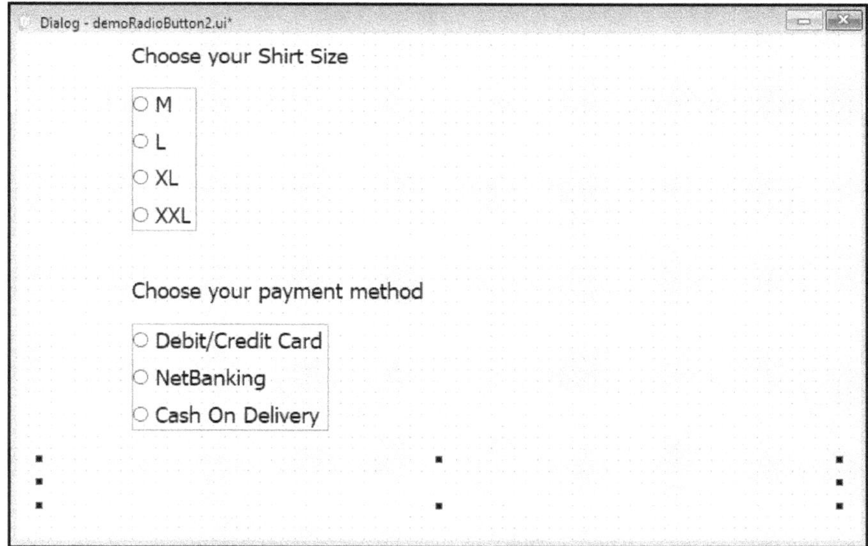

The `.ui` (XML) file is then converted into Python code through the `pyuic5` command utility. You can find the Python code, `demoRadioButton2.py`, in the source code bundle for this book.

15. Import the `demoRadioButton2.py` file, as a header file in our program to invoke the user interface design and to write code to display the selected shirt size and payment method through a **Label** widget when the user selects or unselects any of the radio buttons.

16. Let's name the program `callRadioButton2.pyw`; its code is shown here:

```
import sys
from PyQt5.QtWidgets import QDialog, QApplication
from demoRadioButton2 import *
class MyForm(QDialog):
    def __init__(self):
        super().__init__()
        self.ui = Ui_Dialog()
        self.ui.setupUi(self)
        self.ui.radioButtonMedium.toggled.connect(self.
        dispSelected)
        self.ui.radioButtonLarge.toggled.connect(self.
        dispSelected)
self.ui.radioButtonXL.toggled.connect(self.dispSelected)
        self.ui.radioButtonXXL.toggled.connect(self.
        dispSelected)
        self.ui.radioButtonDebitCard.toggled.connect(self.
        dispSelected)
        self.ui.radioButtonNetBanking.toggled.connect(self.
        dispSelected)
self.ui.radioButtonCashOnDelivery.toggled.connect(self.
        dispSelected)
        self.show()
    def dispSelected(self):
        selected1="";
        selected2=""
        if self.ui.radioButtonMedium.isChecked()==True:
            selected1="Medium"
        if self.ui.radioButtonLarge.isChecked()==True:
            selected1="Large"
        if self.ui.radioButtonXL.isChecked()==True:
            selected1="Extra Large"
        if self.ui.radioButtonXXL.isChecked()==True:
            selected1="Extra Extra Large"
        if self.ui.radioButtonDebitCard.isChecked()==True:
            selected2="Debit/Credit Card"
        if self.ui.radioButtonNetBanking.isChecked()==True:
            selected2="NetBanking"
        if
self.ui.radioButtonCashOnDelivery.isChecked()==True:
            selected2="Cash On Delivery"
        self.ui.labelSelected.setText("Chosen shirt size is
        "+selected1+" and payment method as " + selected2)
if __name__=="__main__":
    app = QApplication(sys.argv)
```

```
w = MyForm()
w.show()
sys.exit(app.exec_())
```

How it works...

The **toggled()** event of all the radio buttons is connected to the `dispSelected()` function, which will display the selected shirt size and payment method. In the `dispSelected()` function, you check the status of the radio buttons to find out whether they are checked or unchecked. On the basis of the selected radio button in the first vertical layout, the value of the `selected1` variable will be set to `Medium`, `Large`, `Extra Large`, or `Extra Extra Large`. Similarly, from the second vertical layout, depending on the radio button selected, the value of the `selected2` variable will be initialized to **Debit/Credit Card**, **NetBanking**, or **Cash On Delivery**. Finally, the shirt size and payment method assigned to the `selected1` variable and selected variables will be displayed via the `labelSelected` widget. On running the application, you get a dialog prompting you to select the shirt size and payment method. On selecting a shirt size and payment method, the selected shirt size and payment method are displayed via the **Label** widget, as shown in the following screenshot:

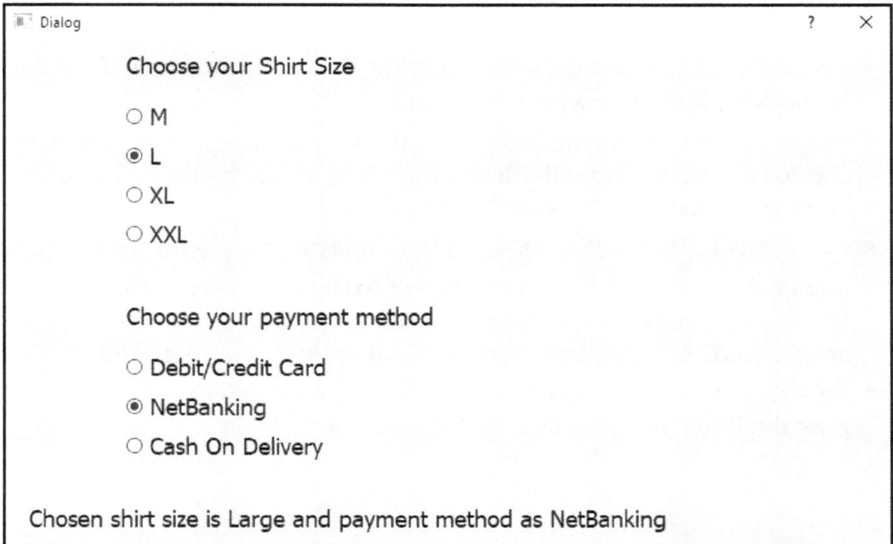

Displaying options in the form of checkboxes

While creating applications, you may come across a situation where you need to provide several options for the user to select from. That is, you want the user to select one or more than one option from a set of options. In such situations, you need to make use of checkboxes. Let's find out more about checkboxes.

Getting ready

Whereas radio buttons allow only one option to be selected in a group, checkboxes allow you to select more than one option. That is, selecting a checkbox will not affect other checkboxes in the application. Checkboxes are displayed with a text label as an instance of the `QCheckBox` class. A checkbox can be in any of three states: selected (checked), unselected (unchecked), or tristate (unchanged). Tristate is a no change state; the user has neither checked nor unchecked the checkbox.

Method application

The following are the methods provided by the `QCheckBox` class:

- `isChecked()`: This method returns the Boolean value true if the checkbox is checked, and otherwise returns false.
- `setTristate()`: If you don't want the user to change the state of the checkbox, you pass the Boolean value true to this method. The user will not be able to check or uncheck the checkbox.
- `setIcon()`: This method is used to display an icon with the checkbox.
- `setText()`: This method assigns text to the checkbox. To specify a shortcut key for the checkbox, precede the preferred character in the text with an ampersand. The shortcut character will appear as underlined.
- `setChecked()`: In order to make a checkbox appear as checked by default, pass the Boolean value true to this method.

Signal description

The signals emitted by `QCheckBox` are as follows:

- **clicked()**: This signal is emitted when a checkbox is activated (that is, pressed and released) or when its shortcut key is pressed
- **stateChanged()**: This signal is emitted whenever a checkbox changes its state from checked to unchecked or vice versa

To understand the **Check Box** widget, let's assume that you run a restaurant where several food items, such as pizzas, are sold. The pizza is sold along with different toppings, such as extra cheese, extra olives, and so on, and the price of each topping is also mentioned with it. The user can select a regular pizza with one or more toppings. What you want is that when a topping is selected, the total price of the pizza, including the selected topping, is displayed.

How to do it...

The focus of this recipe is to understand how an action is initiated when the state of a checkbox changes from checked to unchecked or vice versa. Following is the step-by-step procedure to create such an application:

1. Begin by creating a new application based on the **Dialog without Buttons** template.
2. Drag and drop three **Label** widgets and three **Check Box** widgets onto the form.
3. Set the **text** property of the first two **Label** widgets to `Regular Pizza $10` and `Select your extra toppings`.
4. In the **Property Editor** window, increase the font size of all three labels and checkboxes to increase their visibility in the application.
5. Set the **text** property of the three checkboxes to `Extra Cheese $1`, `Extra Olives $1`, and `Extra Sausages $2`. The default object names of the three checkboxes are `checkBox`, `checkBox_2`, and `checkBox_3`.
6. Change these to `checkBoxCheese`, `checkBoxOlives`, and `checkBoxSausages`, respectively.
7. Set the **objectName** property of the **Label** widget to `labelAmount`.

8. Save the application with the name `demoCheckBox1.ui`. Now, the form will appear as shown in the following screenshot:

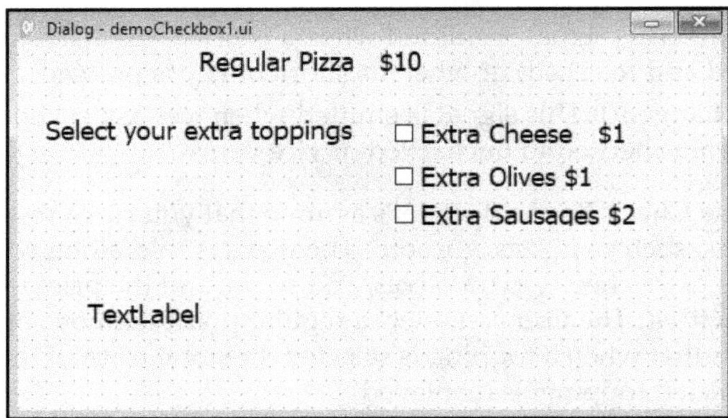

The `.ui` (XML) file is then converted into Python code through the `pyuic5` command utility. The Python code generated in the `demoCheckBox1.py` file can be seen in the source code bundle of this book.

9. Import the `demoCheckBox1.py` file, as a header file in our program to invoke the user interface design and to write code to calculate the total cost of regular pizza, along with the selected toppings, through a **Label** widget when the user selects or unselects any of the checkboxes.
10. Let's name the program `callCheckBox1.pyw`; its code is shown here:

```
import sys
from PyQt5.QtWidgets import QDialog
from PyQt5.QtWidgets import QApplication, QWidget, QPushButton
from demoCheckBox1 import *
class MyForm(QDialog):
    def __init__(self):
        super().__init__()
        self.ui = Ui_Dialog()
        self.ui.setupUi(self)
        self.ui.checkBoxCheese.stateChanged.connect(self.
        dispAmount)
        self.ui.checkBoxOlives.stateChanged.connect(self.
        dispAmount)
        self.ui.checkBoxSausages.stateChanged.connect(self.
        dispAmount)
        self.show()
    def dispAmount(self):
        amount=10
```

```
            if self.ui.checkBoxCheese.isChecked()==True:
                amount=amount+1
            if self.ui.checkBoxOlives.isChecked()==True:
                amount=amount+1
            if self.ui.checkBoxSausages.isChecked()==True:
                amount=amount+2
            self.ui.labelAmount.setText("Total amount for pizza is
            "+str(amount))
if __name__=="__main__":
    app = QApplication(sys.argv)
    w = MyForm()
    w.show()
    sys.exit(app.exec_())
```

How it works...

The **stateChanged()** event of checkboxes is connected to the `dispAmount` function, which will calculate the cost of the pizza along with the toppings selected. In the `dispAmount` function, you check the status of the checkboxes to find out whether they are checked or unchecked. The cost of the toppings whose checkboxes are checked is added and stored in the `amount` variable. Finally, the addition of the amount stored in the `amount` variable is displayed via `labelAmount`. On running the application, you get a dialog prompting you to select the toppings that you want to add to your regular pizza. On selecting any toppings, the amount of the regular pizza along with the selected toppings will be displayed on the screen, as shown in the following screenshot:

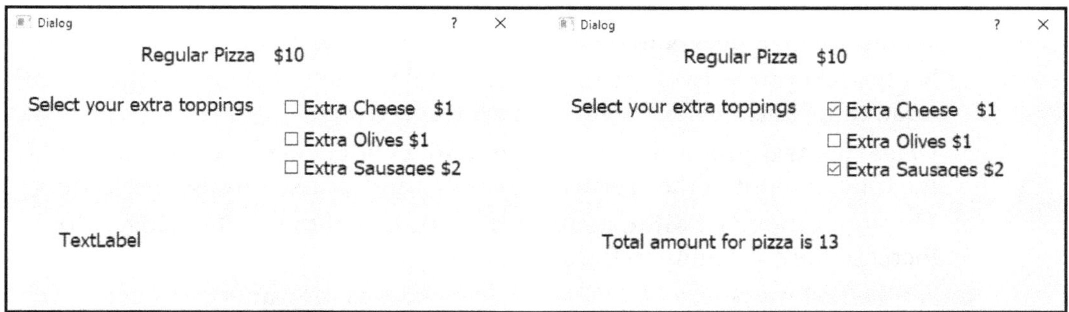

The `dispAmount` function will be invoked every time the status of any checkbox changes. As a result, the total amount will be displayed via the **Label** widget, as soon as any checkbox is checked or unchecked.

Displaying two groups of checkboxes

In this application, we will learn to make two groups of checkboxes. The user can select any number of checkboxes from either group and, accordingly, the result will appear.

Getting ready

We will try displaying a menu of a restaurant where different types of ice creams and drinks are served. We will create two groups of checkboxes, one of ice creams and the other of drinks. The ice cream group displays four checkboxes showing four different types of ice cream, mint chocolate chip, cookie dough, and so on, along with their prices. The drinks group displays three checkboxes, coffee, soda, and so on, along with their prices. The user can select any number of checkboxes from either of the groups. When the user selects any of the ice creams or drinks, the total price of the selected ice creams and drinks will be displayed.

How to do it...

Here are the steps to create an application, which explain how checkboxes can be arranged into different groups and how to take respective action when the state of any checkbox from any group changes:

1. Create a new application based on the **Dialog without Buttons** template.
2. Drag and drop four **Label** widgets, seven **Check Box** widgets, and two **Group Box** widgets onto the form.
3. Set the **text** property of the first three **Label** widgets to `Menu`, `Select your IceCream`, and `Select your drink` respectively.
4. Delete the **text** property of the fourth **Label** widget because we will display the total amount of the selected ice creams and drinks through the code.
5. Through **Property Editor**, increase the font size of the all the widgets to increase their visibility in the application.
6. Set the **text** property of the first four checkboxes to `Mint Choclate Chips $4`, `Cookie Dough $2`, `Choclate Almond $3`, and `Rocky Road $5`. Put these four checkboxes into the first group box.
7. Set the **text** property of the next three checkboxes to `Coffee $2`, `Soda $3`, and `Tea $1` respectively. Put these three checkboxes into the second group box.

8. Change the object names of the first four checkboxes to `checkBoxChoclateChips`, `checkBoxCookieDough`, `checkBoxChoclateAlmond`, and `checkBoxRockyRoad`.
9. Set the **objectName** property of the first group box to `groupBoxIceCreams`.
10. Change the **objectName** property of the next three checkboxes to `checkBoxCoffee`, `checkBoxSoda`, and `checkBoxTea`.
11. Set the **objectName** property of the second group box to `groupBoxDrinks`.
12. Set the **objectName** property of the fourth **Label** widget to `labelAmount`.
13. Save the application with the name `demoCheckBox2.ui`. It is through this **Label** widget that the total amount of the selected ice creams and drinks will be displayed, as shown in the following screenshot:

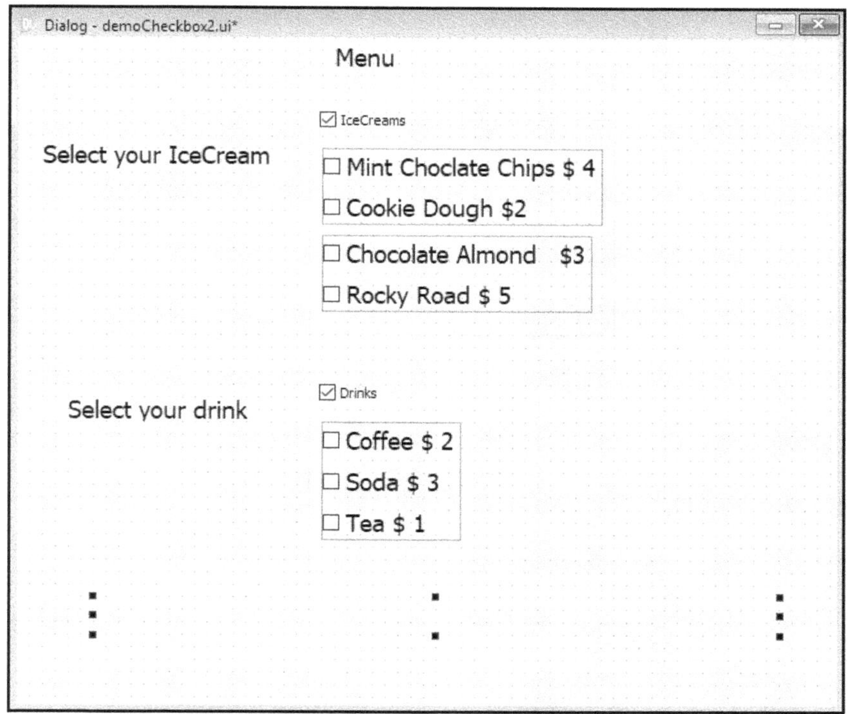

The `.ui` (XML) file is then converted into Python code through the `pyuic5` command utility. You can find the generated Python code, the `demoCheckbox2.py` file, in the source code bundle of this book.

14. Import the `demoCheckBox2.py` file as a header file in our program to invoke the user interface design, and to write code to calculate the total cost of ice creams and drinks through a **Label** widget when the user selects or unselects any of the checkboxes.
15. Let's name the program `callCheckBox2.pyw`; its code is shown here:

```
import sys
from PyQt5.QtWidgets import QDialog
from PyQt5.QtWidgets import QApplication, QWidget, QPushButton
from demoCheckBox2 import *
class MyForm(QDialog):
    def __init__(self):
        super().__init__()
        self.ui = Ui_Dialog()
        self.ui.setupUi(self)
        self.ui.checkBoxChoclateAlmond.stateChanged.connect
        (self.dispAmount)
self.ui.checkBoxChoclateChips.stateChanged.connect(self.
        dispAmount)
        self.ui.checkBoxCookieDough.stateChanged.connect(self.
        dispAmount)
        self.ui.checkBoxRockyRoad.stateChanged.connect(self.
        dispAmount)
        self.ui.checkBoxCoffee.stateChanged.connect(self.
        dispAmount)
        self.ui.checkBoxSoda.stateChanged.connect(self.
        dispAmount)
        self.ui.checkBoxTea.stateChanged.connect(self.
        dispAmount)
        self.show()
    def dispAmount(self):
        amount=0
        if self.ui.checkBoxChoclateAlmond.isChecked()==True:
            amount=amount+3
        if self.ui.checkBoxChoclateChips.isChecked()==True:
            amount=amount+4
        if self.ui.checkBoxCookieDough.isChecked()==True:
            amount=amount+2
        if self.ui.checkBoxRockyRoad.isChecked()==True:
            amount=amount+5
        if self.ui.checkBoxCoffee.isChecked()==True:
            amount=amount+2
        if self.ui.checkBoxSoda.isChecked()==True:
            amount=amount+3
        if self.ui.checkBoxTea.isChecked()==True:
            amount=amount+1
        self.ui.labelAmount.setText("Total amount is
```

```
            $"+str(amount))
if __name__=="__main__":
    app = QApplication(sys.argv)
    w = MyForm()
    w.show()
    sys.exit(app.exec_())
```

How it works...

The **stateChanged()** event of all the checkboxes is connected to the dispAmount function, which will calculate the cost of the selected ice creams and drinks. In the dispAmount function, you check the status of the checkboxes to find out whether they are checked or unchecked. The cost of the ice creams and drinks whose checkboxes are checked is added and stored in the amount variable. Finally, the addition of the amount stored in the amount variable is displayed via the labelAmount widget. On running the application, you get a dialog prompting you to select the ice creams or drinks that you want to order. On selecting the ice creams or drinks, the total amount of the chosen items will be displayed, as shown in the following screenshot:

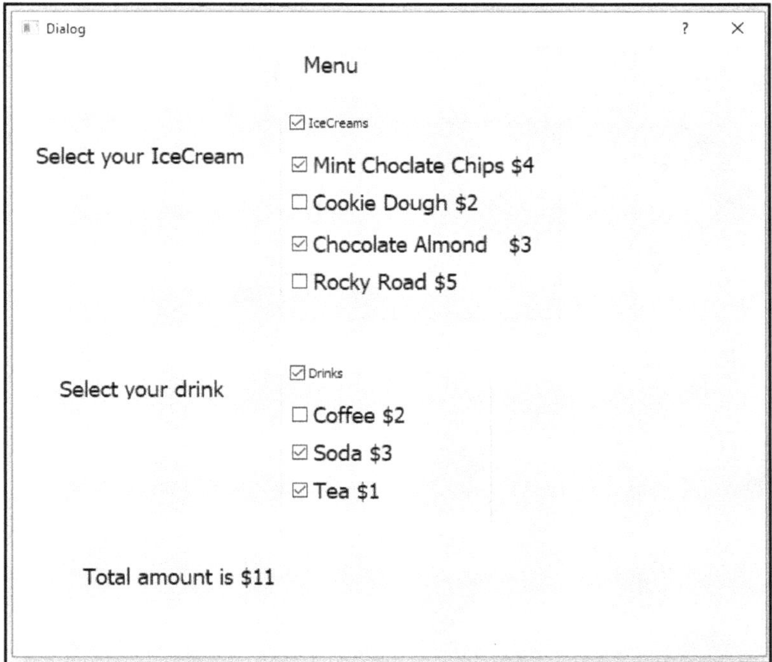

14
Event Handling - Signals and Slots

In this chapter, we will learn about the following topics:

- Using Signal/Slot Editor
- Copying and pasting text from one Line Edit widget to another
- Converting data types and making a small calculator
- Using the Spin Box widget
- Using scrollbars and sliders
- Using List Widget
- Selecting multiple list items from one List Widget and displaying them in another
- Adding items into List Widget
- Performing operations in List Widget
- Using the Combo Box widget
- Using the Font Combo Box widget
- Using the Progress Bar widget

Introduction

Event handling is an important mechanism in every application. The application should not only recognize the event, but must take the respective action to serve the event, too. The action taken on any event determines the course of the application. Each programming language has a different technique for handling or listening to events. Let's see how Python handles its events.

Using Signal/Slot Editor

In PyQt, the event handling mechanism is also known as **signals** and **slots**. An event can be in the form of clicking or double-clicking on a widget, or pressing the *Enter* key, or selecting an option from a radio button, checkbox, and so on. Every widget emits a signal when any event is applied on it and, that signal needs to be connected to a method, also known as a slot. A slot refers to the method containing the code that you want to be executed on the occurrence of a signal. Most widgets have predefined slots; you don't have to write code to connect a predefined signal to a predefined slot.

You can even edit a signal/slot by navigating to the **Edit** | **Edit Signals/Slots** tool in the toolbar.

How to do it...

To edit the signals and slots of different widgets placed on the form, you need to switch to signals and slots editing mode by performing the following steps:

1. You can press the *F4* key, navigate to the **Edit** | **Edit Signals/Slots** option, or select the **Edit Signals/Slots** icon from the toolbar. The mode displays all the signal and slot connections in the form of arrows, indicating the connection of a widget with its respective slot.

You can also create new signal and slot connections between widgets in this mode and delete an existing signal.

2. To establish a signal and slot connection between two widgets in a form, select a widget by left-clicking the mouse on the widget, dragging the mouse towards another widget to which you want to connect, and releasing the mouse button over it.
3. To cancel the connection while dragging the mouse, simply press the *Esc* key.
4. On releasing the mouse over the destination widget, a **Connection Dialog** box appears, prompting you to select a signal from the source widget and a slot from the destination widget.
5. After selecting the respective signal and slot, select **OK** to establish the signal and slot connection.

The following screenshot shows dragging a **Push Button** over a **Line Edit** widget:

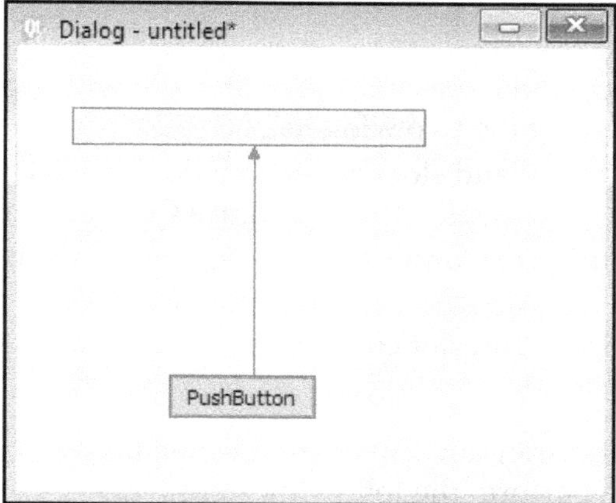

6. On releasing the mouse button on the **Line Edit** widget, you get the list of predefined signals and slots, as shown in the following screenshot:

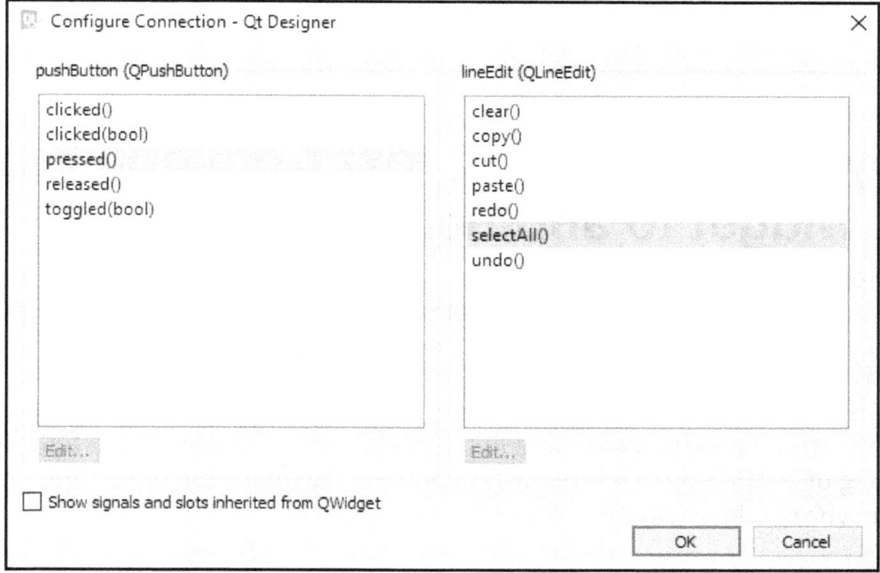

You can also select **Cancel** in the **Configure Connection** dialog box to cancel the signal and slot connection.

7. When connected, the selected signal and slot will appear as labels in the arrow, connecting the two widgets.
8. To modify a signal and slot connection, double-click the connection path or one of its labels to display the **Configure Connection** dialog box.
9. From the **Configure Connection** dialog, you can edit a signal or a slot as desired.
10. To delete a signal and slot connection, select its arrow on the form and press the *Delete* key.

The signal and slot connection can also be established between any widget and the form. To do so, you can perform the following steps:

1. Select the widget, drag the mouse, and release the mouse button over the form. The end point of the connection changes to the electrical ground symbol, representing that a connection has been established with the form.
2. To come out of signal and slot editing mode, navigate to **Edit** | **Edit Widgets** or press the *F3* key.

Copying and pasting text from one Line Edit widget to another

This recipe will make you understand how an event performed on one widget invokes a predefined action on the associated widget. Because we want to copy content from one **Line Edit** widget on clicking the push button, we need to invoke the `selectAll()` method on the occurrence of the **pressed()** event on push button. Also, we need to invoke the `copy()` method on occurrence of the **released()** event on the push button. To paste the content in the clipboard into another **Line Edit** widget on clicking of another push button, we need to invoke the `paste()` method on the occurrence of the **clicked()** event on another push button.

Getting ready

Let's create an application that consists of two **Line Edit** and two **Push Button** widgets. On clicking the first push button, the text in the first **Line Edit** widget will be copied and on clicking the second push button, the text copied from the first **Line Edit** widget will be pasted onto the second **Line Edit** widget.

Let's create a new application based on the **Dialog without Buttons** template by performing the following steps:

1. Begin by adding `QLineEdit` and `QPushButton` to the form by dragging and dropping the **Line Edit** and **Push Button** widgets from the **Widget** box on the form.

To preview a form while editing, select either **Form**, **Preview**, or use *Ctrl* + *R* .

2. To copy the text of the **Line Edit** widget when the user selects the push button on the form, you need to connect the push button's signal to the slot of **Line Edit**. Let's learn how to do it.

How to do it...

Initially, the form is in widget editing mode, and to apply signal and slot connections, you need to first switch to signals and slots editing mode:

1. Select the **Edit Signals/Slots** icon from the toolbar to switch to signals and slots editing mode.

2. On the form, select the push button, drag the mouse to the **Line Edit** widget, and release the mouse button. The **Configure Connection** dialog will pop up, allowing you to establish a signal and slot connection between the **Push Button** and the **Line Edit** widgets, as shown in the following screenshot:

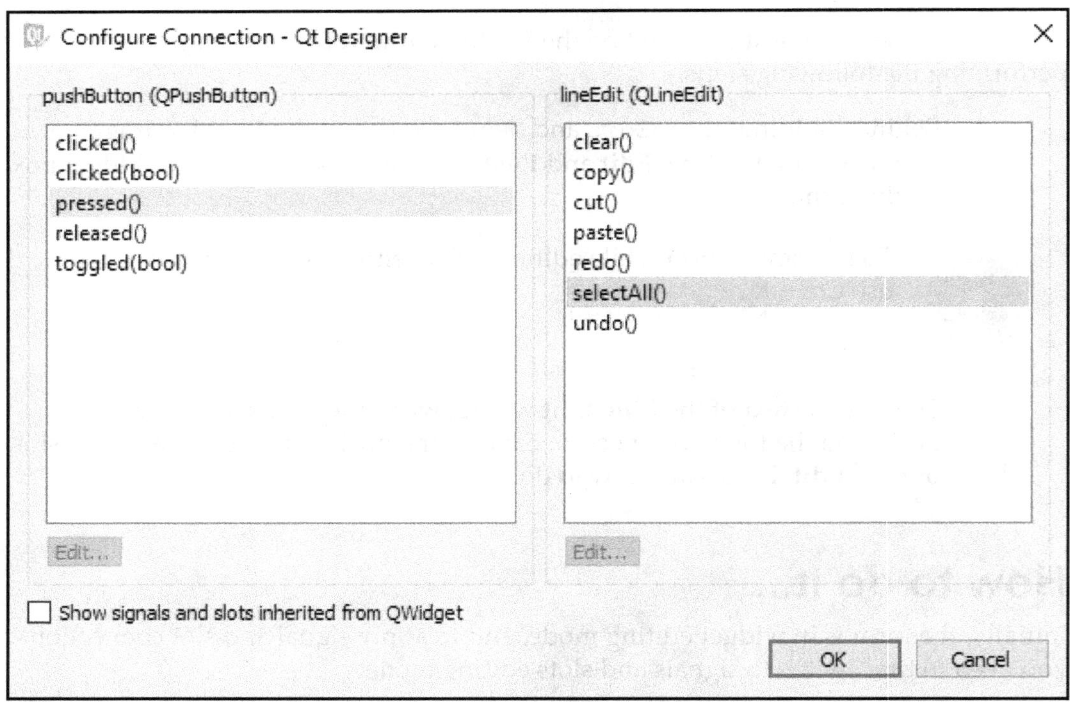

3. Select the **pressed()** event or signal from the **pushButton (QPushButton)** tab and the **selectAll()** slot for the **lineEdit (QLineEdit)** tab.

The connected signal of the **Push Button** widget with the slot of **Line Edit** will appear in the form of an arrow, representing the signal and slot connection between the two widgets, as shown in the following screenshot:

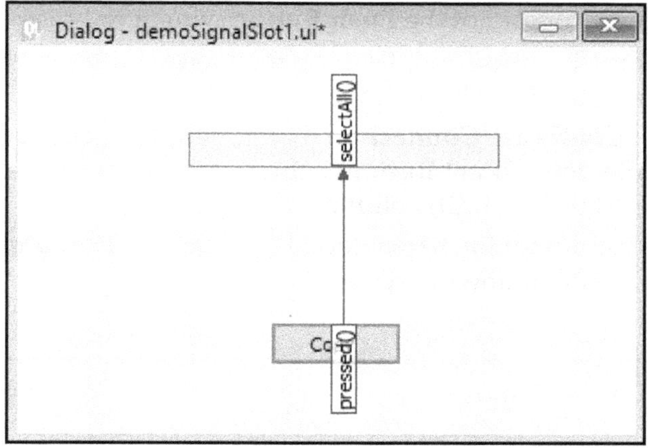

4. Set the **text** property of the **Push Button** widget to `Copy` to represent the fact that it will copy the text entered in the **Line Edit** widget.
5. Next, we will repeat the procedure of clicking the push button and dragging it to the **Line Edit** widget to connect the **released()** signal of the push button with the **copy()** slot of the **Line Edit** widget. On the form, you will see another arrow, representing the second signal and slot connection established between the two widgets, as is shown in the following screenshot:

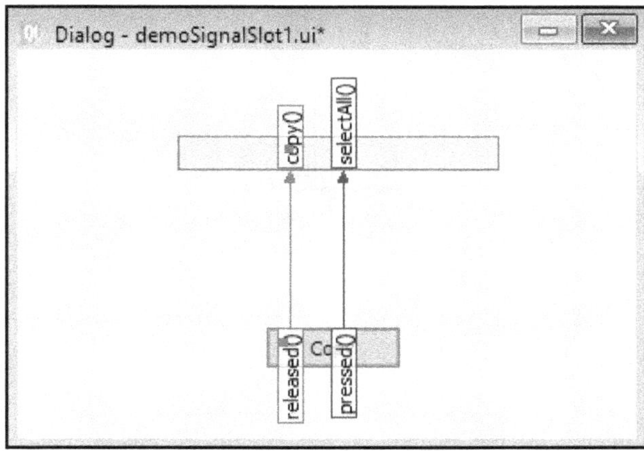

6. In order to paste the copied content, drag and drop one push button and one **Line Edit** widget on the form.

7. Set the **text** property of the **Push Button** widget to `Paste`.
8. Click the push button and, keeping the mouse button pressed, drag it and release it on the **Line Edit** widget.
9. From the **Configure Connection** dialog, select the **clicked()** event from the **pushButton (QPushButton)** column and the **paste()** slot from the **lineEdit (QLineEdit)** column.
10. Save the form with the name `demoSignal1.ui`. The form will now appear as shown in the following screenshot:

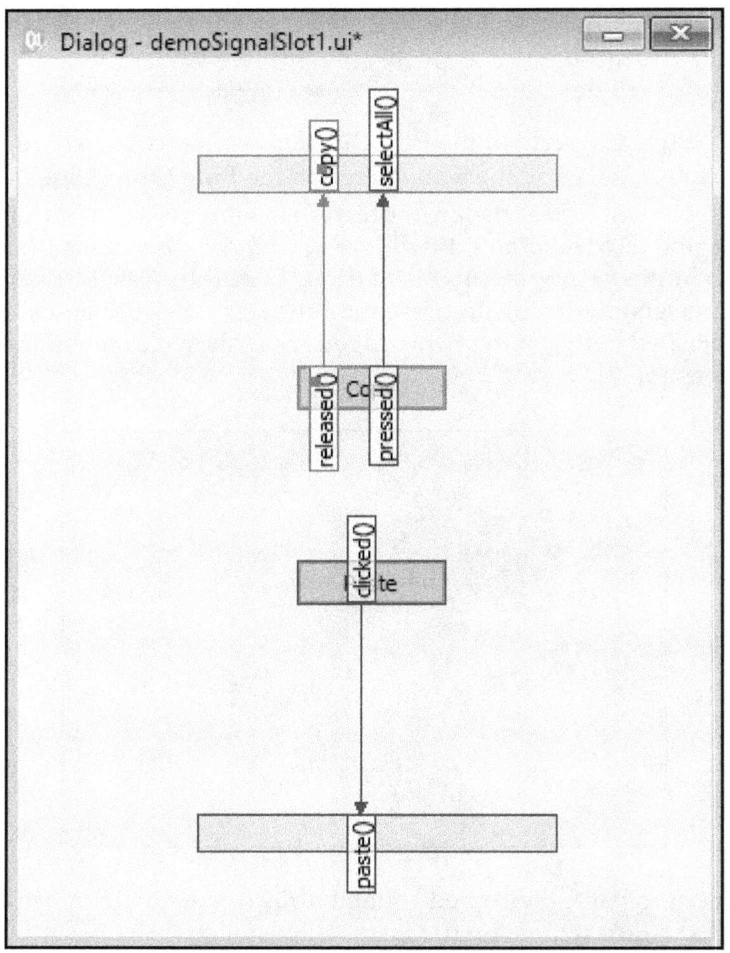

The form will be saved in a file with the .ui extension. The demoSignal1.ui file will contain all the information of the form, its widgets, layout, and so on. The .ui file is an XML file, and it needs to be converted into Python code by making use of the pyuic5 utility. The generated Python code file, demoSignal1.py, can be seen in the source code bundle of this book. In the demoSignal1.py file, you will find that it imports everything from both modules, QtCore and QtGui, as you will be needing them for developing GUI applications:

- QtCore: The QtCore module forms the foundation of all Qt-based applications. It contains the most fundamental classes, such as QCoreApplication, QObject, and so on. These classes do important tasks, such as event handling, implementing the signal and slot mechanism, I/O operations, handling strings, and so on. The module includes several classes, including QFile, QDir, QIODevice, QTimer, QString, QDate, and QTime.
- QtGui: As the name suggests, the QtGUI module contains the classes required in developing cross-platform GUI applications. The module contains the GUI classes, such as QCheckBox, QComboBox, QDateTimeEdit, QLineEdit, QPushButton, QPainter, QPaintDevice, QApplication, QTextEdit, and QTextDocument.

11. Treat the demoSignalSlot1.py file, as a header file and import it to the file from which you will invoke its user interface design.
12. Create another Python file with the name calldemoSignal1.pyw and import the demoSignal1.py code into it:

```
import sys
from PyQt5.QtWidgets import QDialog, QApplication
from demoSignalSlot1 import *
class MyForm(QDialog):
    def __init__(self):
        super().__init__()
        self.ui = Ui_Dialog()
        self.ui.setupUi(self)
        self.show()
if __name__=="__main__":
    app = QApplication(sys.argv)
    w = MyForm()
    w.show()
    sys.exit(app.exec_())
```

How it works...

The sys module is imported as it supplies access to the command-line arguments stored in the sys.argv list. This is because every PyQt GUI application must have a QApplication object to provide access to information such as the application's directory, screen size, and so on, so that you create an QApplication object. To enable PyQt to use and apply command-line arguments (if any), you pass the command-line arguments while creating a QApplication object. You create an instance of MyForm and call its show() method, which adds a new event to the QApplication object's event queue. This new event is used to display all the widgets specified in the MyForm class. The app.exec_ method is called to start the QApplication object's event loop. Once the event loop begins, the top-level widget used in the class, MyForm, is displayed, along with its child widgets. All the system-generated events, as well as user interaction events, are added to the event queue. The application's event loop continuously checks to see whether an event has occurred. On the occurrence of an event, the event loop processes it and invokes the associated slot or method. On closing the top-level widget of the application, PyQt deletes the widget and performs a clean termination of the application.

In PyQt, any widget can be used as a top-level window. The super().__init__() method invokes the base class constructor from the MyForm class, that is, the constructor of the QDialog class is invoked from MyForm class to indicate that QDialog is displayed through this class is a top-level window.

The user interface design is instantiated by calling the setupUI() method of the class that was created in the Python code (Ui_Dialog). We create an instance of the Ui_Dialog class, the class that was created in the Python code, and invoke its setupUi() method. The **Dialog** widget will be created as the parent of all the user interface widgets and displayed on the screen. Remember, QDialog, QMainWindow, and all of the PyQt's widgets are derived from QWidget.

On running the application, you get two pairs of the **Line Edit** and **Push Button** widgets. On typing text into one **Line Edit** widget, when you click the **Copy** push button, the text will be copied.

Now, on clicking the **Paste** push button, the copied text will be pasted in the second **Line Edit** widget, as shown in the following screenshot:

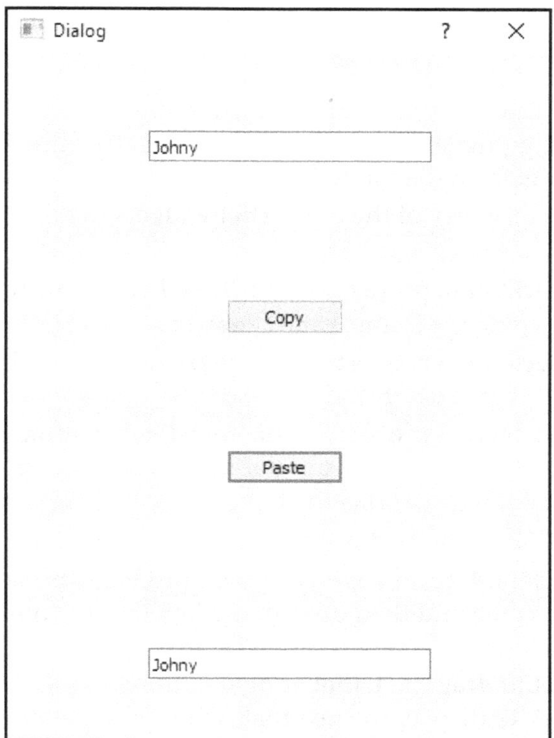

Converting data types and making a small calculator

The most commonly used widget for accepting one-line data is the **Line Edit** widget, and the default data type in a **Line Edit** widget is string. In order to do any computation on two integer values, you need to convert the string data entered in the **Line Edit** widget to the integer data type and then convert the result of computation, which will be a numeric data type, back to string type before being displaying through a **Label** widget. This recipe does exactly that.

How to do it...

To understand how data is accepted by the user and how type casting is done, let's create an application based on the **Dialog without Buttons** template by performing the following steps:

1. Add three `QLabel`, two `QLineEdit`, and one `QPushButton` widget to the form by dragging and dropping three **Label**, two **Line Edit**, and four **Push Button** widgets on the form.
2. Set the **text** property of the two **Label** widgets to `Enter First Number` and `Enter Second Number`.
3. Set the **objectName** property of the three Labels to `labelFirstNumber`, `labelSecondNumber`, and `labelResult`.
4. Set the **objectName** property of the two **Line Edit** widgets to `lineEditFirstNumber` and `lineEditSecondNumber`.
5. Set the **objectName** property of the four **Push Button** widgets to `pushButtonPlus`, `pushButtonSubtract`, `pushButtonMultiply`, and `pushButtonDivide`, respectively.
6. Set the push button's **text** property to `+`, `-`, `x`, and `/`, respectively.
7. Delete the default **text** property of the third label, because the Python script will set the value and then display it when the two numerical values are added.
8. Don't forget to drag the **Label** widget in the designer in order to ensure it is long enough to display the text that will be assigned to it through the Python script.
9. Save the UI file as `demoCalculator.ui`.
10. You can also increase the width of the **Label** widget by setting the **width** property under **geometry** from the **Property Editor** window:

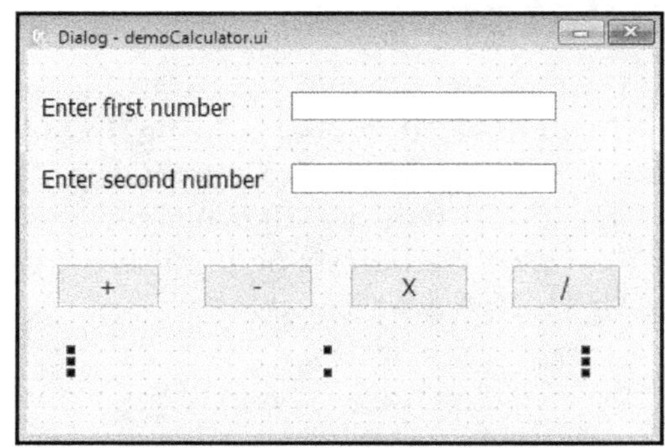

The `.ui` file, which is in XML format, needs to be converted into Python code. The generated Python code, `demoCalculator.py`, can be seen in the source code bundle of this book.

11. Create a Python script named `callCalculator.pyw` that imports the Python code `demoCalculator.py` to invoke a user interface design, and that fetches the values entered in the **Line Edit** widgets and displays their addition. The code in the Python script `callCalculator.pyw` is shown here:

```
import sys
from PyQt5.QtWidgets import QDialog, QApplication
from demoCalculator import *
class MyForm(QDialog):
    def __init__(self):
        super().__init__()
        self.ui = Ui_Dialog()
        self.ui.setupUi(self)
        self.ui.pushButtonPlus.clicked.connect(self.addtwonum)
        self.ui.pushButtonSubtract.clicked.connect
        (self.subtracttwonum)
        self.ui.pushButtonMultiply.clicked.connect
        (self.multiplytwonum)
self.ui.pushButtonDivide.clicked.connect(self.dividetwonum)
        self.show()
    def addtwonum(self):
        if len(self.ui.lineEditFirstNumber.text())!=0:
                a=int(self.ui.lineEditFirstNumber.text())
        else:
                a=0
        if len(self.ui.lineEditSecondNumber.text())!=0:
                b=int(self.ui.lineEditSecondNumber.text())
        else:
                b=0
                sum=a+b
        self.ui.labelResult.setText("Addition: " +str(sum))
    def subtracttwonum(self):
        if len(self.ui.lineEditFirstNumber.text())!=0:
                a=int(self.ui.lineEditFirstNumber.text())
        else:
                a=0
        if len(self.ui.lineEditSecondNumber.text())!=0:
                b=int(self.ui.lineEditSecondNumber.text())
        else:
                b=0
                diff=a-b
        self.ui.labelResult.setText("Substraction: "
```

```
+str(diff))
    def multiplytwonum(self):
        if len(self.ui.lineEditFirstNumber.text())!=0:
                a=int(self.ui.lineEditFirstNumber.text())
        else:
                a=0
        if len(self.ui.lineEditSecondNumber.text())!=0:
                b=int(self.ui.lineEditSecondNumber.text())
        else:
                b=0
                mult=a*b
        self.ui.labelResult.setText("Multiplication: "
+str(mult))
    def dividetwonum(self):
        if len(self.ui.lineEditFirstNumber.text())!=0:
                a=int(self.ui.lineEditFirstNumber.text())
        else:
                a=0
        if len(self.ui.lineEditSecondNumber.text())!=0:
                b=int(self.ui.lineEditSecondNumber.text())
        else:
                b=0
                division=a/b
        self.ui.labelResult.setText("Division: "+str(round
        (division,2)))
if __name__=="__main__":
    app = QApplication(sys.argv)
    w = MyForm()
    w.show()
    sys.exit(app.exec_())
```

How it works...

There are the following four functions used in this code:

- `len()`: This function returns the number of characters in the string
- `str()`: This function converts the argument passed into the string data type
- `int()`: This function converts the argument passed into the integer data type
- `round()`: This function rounds the number passed to the specified decimal digits

The `clicked()` event of `pushButtonPlus` is connected to the `addtwonum()` method to display the sum of the numbers entered in the two **Line Edit** widgets. In the `addtwonum()` method, you first validate `lineEditFirstNumber` and `lineEditSecondNumber` to ensure that if either **Line Edit** is left blank by the user, the value of that **Line Edit** is zero.

The values entered in the two **Line Edit** widgets are retrieved, converted into integers through `int()`, and assigned to the two variables `a` and `b`. The sum of the values in the `a` and `b` variables is computed and stored in the `sum` variable. The result in the variable `sum` is converted into string format through `str` method and displayed via `labelResult`, as shown in the following screenshot:

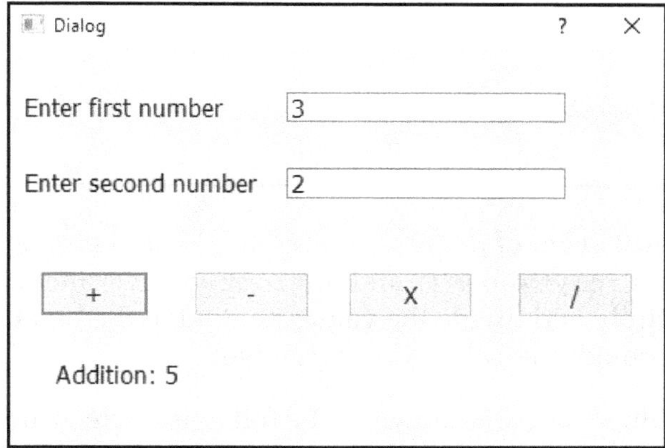

Similarly, the `clicked()` event of `pushButtonSubtract` is connected to the `subtracttwonum()` method to display the subtraction of the numbers entered in the two **Line Edit** widgets. Again, after validation of the two **Line Edit** widgets, the values entered in them are retrieved and converted into integers. Subtraction is applied on the two numbers and the result is assigned to the `diff` variable.

Finally, the result in the `diff` variable is converted into string format through the `str()` method and displayed via `labelResult`, as shown in the following screenshot:

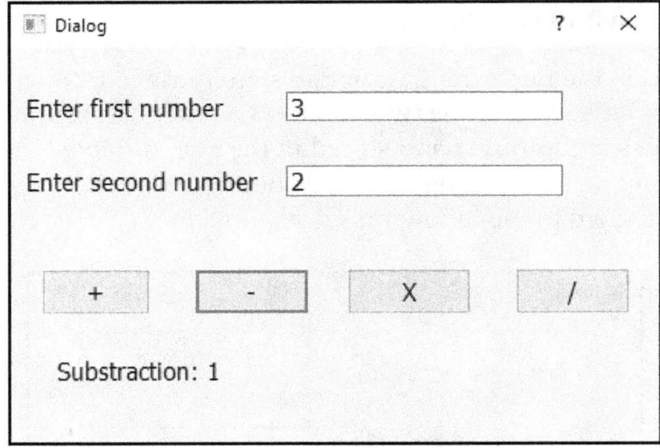

Similarly, the **clicked()** event of `pushButtonMultiply` and `pushButtonDivide` are connected to the `multiplytwonum()` and `dividetwonum()` methods, respectively. These methods multiply and divide the values entered in the two **Line Edit** widgets and display them through the `labelResult` widget.

The result of the multiplication is shown in the following screenshot:

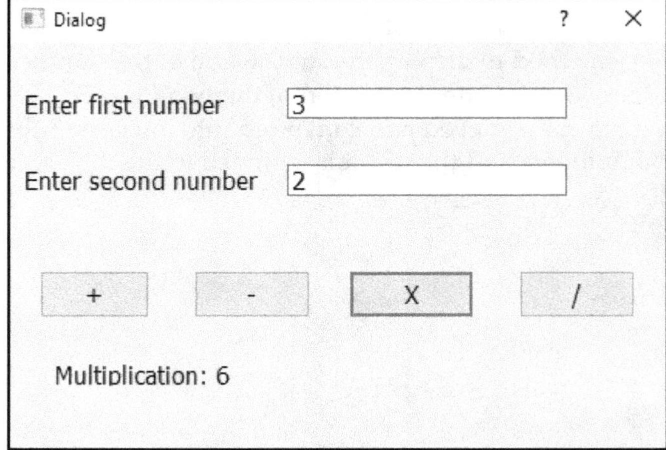

The result of the division is shown in the following screenshot:

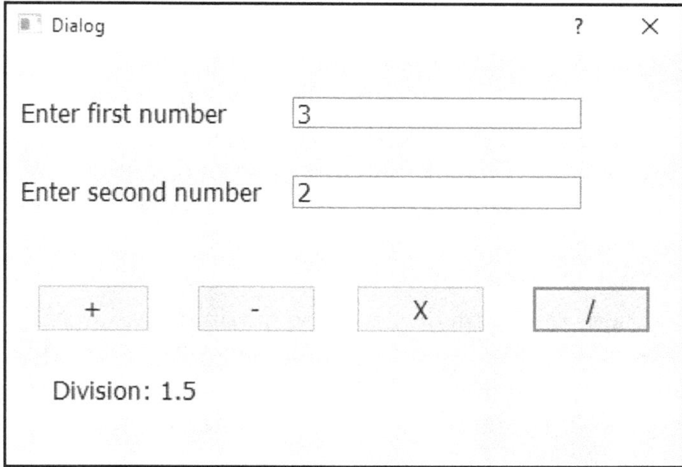

Using the Spin Box widget

The **Spin Box** widget is used for displaying integer values, floating-point values, and text. It applies a constraint on the user: the user cannot enter any random data, but can select only from the available options displayed through **Spin Box**. A **Spin Box** widget displays an initial value by default that can be increased or decreased by selecting the up/down button or up/down arrow key on the keyboard. You can choose a value that is displayed by either clicking on it or typing it in manually.

Getting ready

A **Spin Box** widget can be created using two classes, `QSpinBox` and `QDoubleSpinBox`, where `QSpinBox` displays only integer values, and the `QDoubleSpinBox` class displays floating-point values. Methods provided by `QSpinBox` are shown in the following list:

- `value()`: This method returns the current integer value selected from the spin box.
- `text()`: This method returns the text displayed by the spin box.
- `setPrefix()`: This method assigns the prefix text that is prepended to the value returned by the spin box.

- `setSuffix()`: This method assigns the suffix text that is to be appended to the value returned by the spin box.
- `cleanText()`: This method returns the value of the spin box without a suffix, a prefix, or leading or trailing whitespaces.
- `setValue()`: This method assigns the value to the spin box.
- `setSingleStep()`: This method sets the step size of the spin box. Step size is the increment/decrement value of the spin box, that is, it is the value by which the spin box's value will increase or decrease on selecting the up or down buttons.
- `setMinimum()`: This method sets the minimum value of the spin box.
- `setMaximum()`: This method sets the maximum value of the spin box.
- `setWrapping()`: This method passes the Boolean value true to this method to enable wrapping in the spin box. Wrapping means the spin box returns to the first value (minimum value) when the up button is pressed while displaying the maximum value.

Signals emitted by the `QSpinBox` class are as follows:

- **valueChanged()**: This signal is emitted when the value of the spin box is changed either by selecting the up/down button or using the `setValue()` method
- **editingFinished()**: This signal is emitted when focus is lost on the spin box

The class used for dealing with float values in spin boxes is `QDoubleSpinBox`. All the preceding methods are supported by the `QDoubleSpinBox` class too. It displays values up to two decimal places by default. To change the precision, use `round()`, which displays the values up to the specified number of decimal places; the value will be rounded to the specified number of decimals.

The default **minimum**, **maximum**, **singleStep**, and **value** properties of a spin box are **0**, **99**, **1**, and **0**, and of a double spin box are **0.000000**, **99.990000**, **1.000000**, and **0.000000**, respectively.

Let's create an application that will ask the user to enter a price for a book, followed by the quantity of the books purchased by the customer, and will display the total amount of books. Also, the application will prompt you to enter a price for 1 kg of sugar, followed by the quantity of sugar bought by the user. On entering the quantity of sugar, the app will display the total amount of sugar. The quantity of the books and the sugar will be entered through a spin box and double spin box, respectively.

How to do it...

To understand how integer and float values can be accepted through spin boxes and used in further computation, let's create a new application based on the **Dialog without Buttons** template and follow these steps:

1. Let's begin by dragging and dropping three **Label**, a **Spin Box**, a **Double Spin Box**, and four **Line Edit** widgets.
2. The **text** property of two Label widgets is set to `Book Price value` and `Sugar Price`, and the **objectName** property of the third **Label** widget is set to `labelTotalAmount`.
3. Set the **objectName** property of the four **Line Edit** widgets to `lineEditBookPrice`, `lineEditBookAmount`, `lineEditSugarPrice`, and `lineEditSugarAmount`, respectively.
4. Set the **objectName** property of the **Spin Box** widget to `spinBoxBookQty` and that of the **Double Spin Box** widget to `doubleSpinBoxSugarWeight`.
5. Delete the default **text** property of the third **Label** widget, **TextLabel**, as you will be setting its text in the program to display the total amount.
6. The third **Label** widget will become invisible on deleting its **text** property.
7. Disable the two **Line Edit** widgets, `lineEditBookAmount` and `lineEditSugarAmount`, by unchecking their enabled property from the **Property Editor** window as you want them to display non-editable values.

8. Save the application with the name `demoSpinner.ui`:

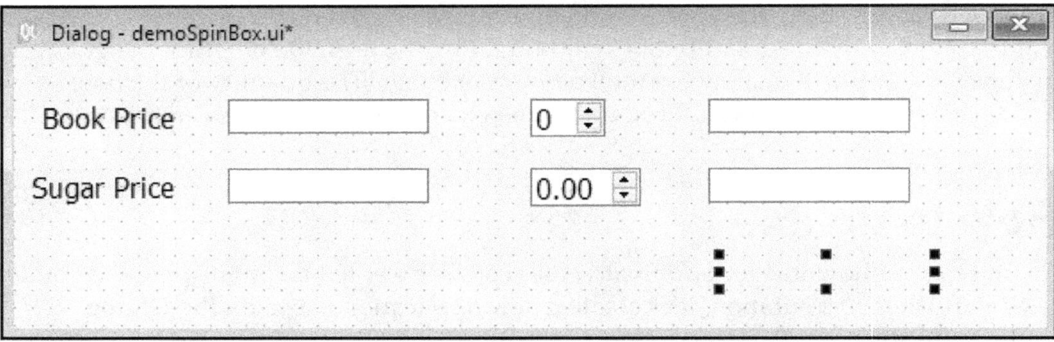

9. On using the `pyuic5` command utility, the `.ui` (XML) file will be converted into Python code. The generated Python code file, `demoSpinner.py`, can be seen in the source code of this book.

10. Create a Python script file named `calldemoSpinner.pyw` that imports the code, `demoSpinner.py`, enabling you to invoke the user interface design that displays the numbers selected through spin boxes and also compute the total book amount and total sugar amount. The `calldemoSpinner.pyw` file will appear as shown here:

```
import sys
from PyQt5.QtWidgets import QDialog, QApplication
from demoSpinBox import *
class MyForm(QDialog):
    def __init__(self):
        super().__init__()
        self.ui = Ui_Dialog()
        self.ui.setupUi(self)
        self.ui.spinBoxBookQty.editingFinished.connect(self.
        result1)
self.ui.doubleSpinBoxSugarWeight.editingFinished.connect
        (self.result2)
        self.show()
    def result1(self):
        if len(self.ui.lineEditBookPrice.text())!=0:
bookPrice=int(self.ui.lineEditBookPrice.text())
        else:
                bookPrice=0
                totalBookAmount=self.ui.spinBoxBookQty.value()
*

                bookPrice
```

```
                    self.ui.lineEditBookAmount.setText(str
                    (totalBookAmount))
        def result2(self):
            if len(self.ui.lineEditSugarPrice.text())!=0:
                    sugarPrice=float(self.ui.lineEditSugarPrice.
                    text())
            else:
                    sugarPrice=0
                    totalSugarAmount=self.ui.
                    doubleSpinBoxSugarWeight.value() * sugarPrice
                    self.ui.lineEditSugarAmount.setText(str(round
                    (totalSugarAmount,2)))
totalBookAmount=int(self.ui.lineEditBookAmount.
                    text())
                    totalAmount=totalBookAmount+totalSugarAmount
                    self.ui.labelTotalAmount.setText(str(round
                    (totalAmount,2)))
if __name__=="__main__":
    app = QApplication(sys.argv)
    w = MyForm()
    w.show()
    sys.exit(app.exec_())
```

How it works...

In this code, you can see that the `editingFinished` signal of the two spin boxes is attached to the `result1` and `result2` functions. It means that when focus is lost on any of the spin boxes, the respective method will be invoked. Focus is lost on a widget when the user moves onto other widgets with the mouse or by pressing the **Tab** key:

- In the `result1` method, you retrieve the integer value for the purchased book quantity from the **Spin Box** widget and multiply it with the book price entered in the `lineEditBookPrice` widget to compute the total book cost. The total book cost is then displayed through the `lineEditBookAmount` widget.

- Similarly, in the `result2` method, you retrieve the floating-point value that is the weight of the sugar purchased from the double spin box and multiply it with the price of the sugar per kg entered in the `lineEditSugarPrice` widget to compute the total sugar cost, which is then displayed through the `lineEditSugarAmount` widget. The total of the book cost and sugar cost is finally displayed through the `labelTotalAmount` widget, as shown in the following screenshot:

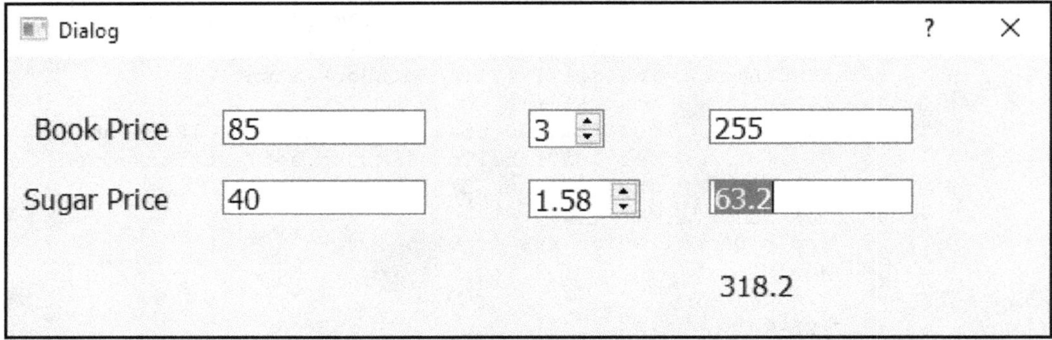

Using scrollbars and sliders

Scrollbars are useful while looking at large documents or images that cannot appear in a limited visible area. Scrollbars appear horizontally or vertically, indicating your current position in the document or image and the size of the region that is not visible. Using the slider handle provided with these bars, you can access the hidden part of the document or image.

Sliders are a way of selecting an integer value between two values. That is, a slider can represent a minimum and maximum range of values, and the user can select a value within this range by moving the slider handle to the desired location in the slider.

Getting ready

Scrollbars are used for viewing documents or images that are larger than the view area. To display horizontal or vertical scrollbars, you use the `HorizontalScrollBar` and `VerticalScrollBar` widgets, which are instances of the `QScrollBar` class. These scrollbars have a slider handle that can be moved to view the area that is not visible. The location of the slider handle indicates the location within the document or image. A scrollbar has the following controls:

- **Slider handle**: This control is used to move to any part of the document or image quickly.
- **Scroll arrows**: These are the arrows on either side of the scrollbars that are used to view the desired area of the document or image that is not currently visible. On using these scroll arrows, the position of the slider handle moves to show the current location within the document or image.
- **Page control**: The page control is the background of the scrollbar over which the slider handle is dragged. When the background is clicked, the slider handle moves towards the click by one page. The amount the slider handle moves can be specified via the **pageStep** property. The page step is the amount by which a slider moves when the user presses the *Page Up* and *Page Down* keys. You can set the amount of the **pageStep** property by using the `setPageStep()` method.

The method that is specifically used to set and retrieve values from scrollbars is the `value()` method, described here.

The `value()` method fetches the value of the slider handle, that is, its distance value from the start of the scrollbar. You get the minimum value of the scrollbar when the slider handle is at the top edge in a vertical scrollbar or at the left edge in a horizontal scrollbar, and you get the maximum value of the scroll bar when the slider handle is at the bottom edge in a vertical scrollbar or at the right edge in a horizontal scrollbar. You can move the slider handle to its minimum and maximum values via the keyboard too, by pressing the *Home* and *End* keys, respectively. Let's take a look at the following methods:

- `setValue()`: This method assigns value to the scrollbar and, as per the value assigned, the location of the slider handle is set in the scrollbar
- `minimum()`: This method returns the minimum value of the scrollbar

- `maximum()`: This method returns the maximum value of the scrollbar
- `setMinimum()`: This method assigns the minimum value to the scrollbar
- `setMaximum()`: This method assigns the maximum value to the scrollbar
- `setSingleStep()`: This method sets the single step value
- `setPageStep()`: This method sets the page step value

`QScrollBar` provides only integer values.

The signals emitted through the `QScrollBar` class are shown in the following list:

- **valueChanged()**: This signal is emitted when the scrollbar's value is changed, that is, when its slider handle is moved
- **sliderPressed()**: This signal is emitted when the user starts to drag the slider handle
- **sliderMoved()**: This signal is emitted when the user drags the slider handle
- **sliderReleased()**: This signal is emitted when the user releases the slider handle
- **actionTriggered()**: This signal is emitted when the scrollbar is changed by user interaction

Sliders are generally used to represent some integer value. Unlike scrollbars, which are mostly used to display large documents or images, the sliders are interactive and an easier way to enter or represent integer values. That is, by moving and positioning its handle along a horizontal or vertical groove, you can make a horizontal or vertical slider to represent some integer value. To display horizontal and vertical sliders, the `HorizontalSlider` and `VerticalSlider` widgets are used, which are instances of the `QSlider` class. Similar to the methods that we saw in scrollbars, the sliders too generate signals such as **valueChanged()**, **sliderPressed()**, **sliderMoved()**, **sliderReleased()**, and many more on moving the slider handle.

The slider handle in scrollbars and sliders represents a value within the minimum and maximum range. To change the default minimum and maximum values, you can change their values by assigning values to the **minimum**, **maximum**, **singleStep**, and **pageStep** properties.

The default values of the **minimum**, **maximum**, **singleStep**, **pageStep**, and **value** properties of sliders are **0**, **99**, **1**, **10**, and **0**, respectively.

Let's create an application consisting of horizontal and vertical scrollbars, as well as horizontal and vertical sliders. The horizontal scrollbar and slider will represent sugar level and blood pressure respectively. That is, on moving the horizontal scroll bar, the sugar level of the patient will be displayed through the **Line Edit** widget. Similarly, the horizontal slider, when moved, will represent blood pressure and will be displayed through the **Line Edit** widget.

The vertical scrollbar and slider will represent the heart rate and cholesterol level, respectively. On moving the vertical scrollbar, the heart rate will be displayed via the **Line Edit** widget and on moving the vertical slider, the cholesterol level will be displayed through the **Line Edit** widget.

How to do it...

To understand the working of the horizontal and vertical scrollbars, and the working of the horizontal and vertical sliders, to understand how scrollbars and sliders generate signals when their values are changed, and the how respective slot or method can be associated to them, perform the following steps:

1. Let's create a new application of the **Dialog without Buttons** template and drag and drop horizontal and vertical scrollbars and sliders onto the form.
2. Drop four **Label** widgets and a **Line Edit** widget to display the value of the scrollbar and slider handle.
3. Set the **text** property of the four **Label** widgets to `Sugar Level`, `Blood Pressure`, `Pulse rate`, and `Cholesterol`, respectively.
4. Set the **objectName** property of the horizontal scrollbar to `horizontalScrollBarSugarLevel`, vertical scroll bar to `verticalScrollBarPulseRate`, horizontal slider to `horizontalSliderBloodPressure`, and vertical slider to `verticalSliderCholestrolLevel`.
5. Set the **objectName** property of the **Line Edit** widget to `lineEditResult`.

6. Save the application with the name `demoSliders.ui`.The form will appear as shown in the following screenshot:

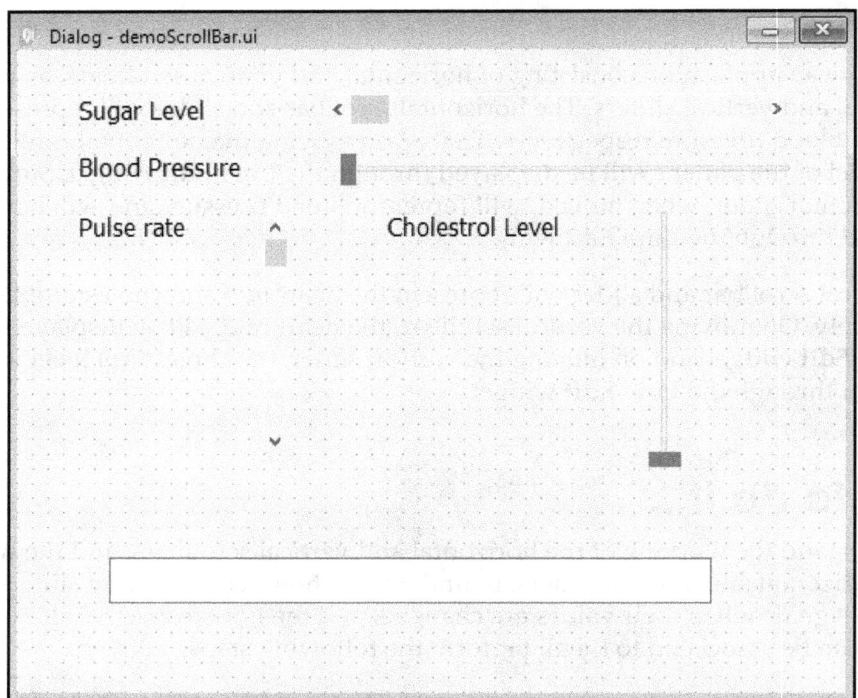

   The `pyuic5` command utility will convert the `.ui` (XML) file into Python code. The generated Python file, `demoScrollBar.py`, can be seen in the source code bundle of this book.

7. Create a Python script file named `callScrollBar.pyw` that imports the code, `demoScrollBar.py`, to invoke the user interface design and synchronizes the movement of the scrollbar and slider handles. The script will also display the value of the scrollbar and slider handle with a **Label** widget. The Python script `callScrollBar.pyw` will appear, as shown here:

```
import sys
from PyQt5.QtWidgets import QDialog, QApplication
from demoScrollBar import *
class MyForm(QDialog):
    def __init__(self):
        super().__init__()
```

```
        self.ui = Ui_Dialog()
        self.ui.setupUi(self)
self.ui.horizontalScrollBarSugarLevel.valueChanged.connect
        (self.scrollhorizontal)
self.ui.verticalScrollBarPulseRate.valueChanged.connect
        (self.scrollvertical)
self.ui.horizontalSliderBloodPressure.valueChanged.connect
        (self.sliderhorizontal)
self.ui.verticalSliderCholestrolLevel.valueChanged.connect
        (self.slidervertical)
        self.show()
    def scrollhorizontal(self,value):
        self.ui.lineEditResult.setText("Sugar Level :
"+str(value))
    def scrollvertical(self, value):
        self.ui.lineEditResult.setText("Pulse Rate :
"+str(value))
    def sliderhorizontal(self, value):
        self.ui.lineEditResult.setText("Blood Pressure :
        "+str(value))
    def slidervertical(self, value):
        self.ui.lineEditResult.setText("Cholestrol Level :
        "+str(value))
if __name__=="__main__":
    app = QApplication(sys.argv)
    w = MyForm()
    w.show()
    sys.exit(app.exec_())
```

How it works...

In this code, you are connecting the `valueChanged()` signal of each widget with the respective functions so that if the scrollbar or slider handle of the widget is moved, the corresponding function is invoked to perform the desired task. For instance, when the slider handle of the horizontal scrollbar is moved, the `scrollhorizontal` function is invoked. The `scrollhorizontal` function displays the value represented by the scrollbar, that is, **Sugar Level**, through the **Label** widget.

Similarly, when the slider handle of the vertical scrollbar or slider is moved, the `scrollvertical` function is invoked and the heart rate, the value of the slider handle of the vertical scrollbar, is displayed through the **Label** widget, as shown in the following screenshot:

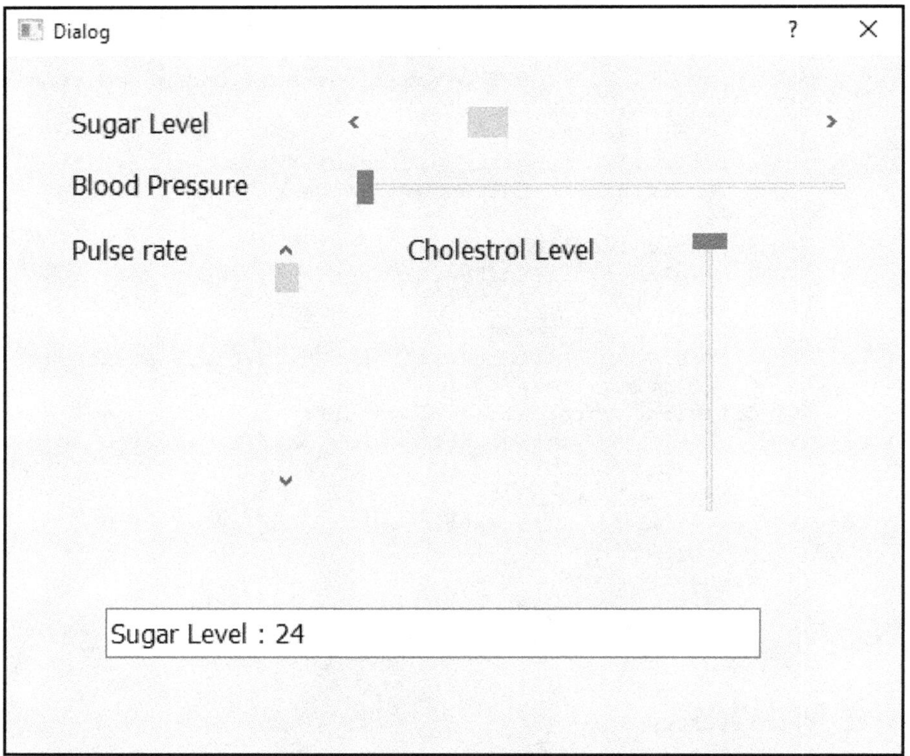

Similarly, when the horizontal and vertical sliders are moved, the blood pressure and cholesterol levels are displayed accordingly, as shown in the following screenshot:

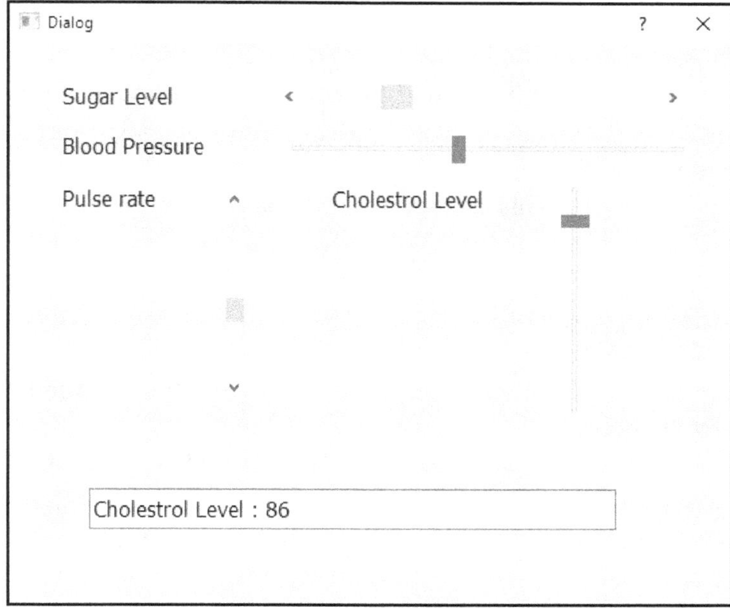

Using List Widget

To display several values in an easier and expandable format, you can use **List Widget**, which is an instance of the `QListWidget` class. **List Widget** displays several items that can not only be viewed, but can be edited and deleted, too. You can add or remove list items one at a time from the **List Widget** item, or collectively you can set list items by using its internal model.

Getting ready

Items in the list are instances of the `QListWidgetItem` class. The methods provided by `QListWidget` are shown in the following list:

- `insertItem()`: This method inserts a new item with the supplied text into **List Widget** at the specified location.

- `insertItems()`: This method inserts multiple items from the supplied list, starting at the specified location.
- `count()`: This method returns the count of the number of items in the list.
- `takeItem()`: This method removes and returns items from the specified row in **List Widget**.
- `currentItem()`: This method returns the current item in the list.
- `setCurrentItem()`: This method replaces the current item in the list with the specified item.
- `addItem()`: This method appends the item with the specified text at the end of **List Widget**.
- `addItems()`: This method appends items from the supplied list at the end of **List Widget**.
- `clear()`: This method removes all items from **List Widget**.
- `currentRow()`: This method returns the row number of the current selected list item. If no list item is selected, it returns the value `-1`.
- `setCurrentRow()`: This method selects the specified row in **List Widget**.
- `item()`: This method returns the list item at the specified row.

Signals emitted by the `QListWidget` class are shown in the following list:

- **currentRowChanged()**: This signal is emitted when the row of the current list item changes
- **currentTextChanged()**: This signal is emitted whenever the text in the current list item is changed
- **currentItemChanged()**: This signal is emitted when the focus of the current list item is changed

How to do it...

So, let's create an application that displays certain diagnostic tests through **List Widget**, and that when the user selects any test from **List Widget**, the selected test is displayed through a **Label** widget. Here is the step-by-step procedure to create the application:

1. Create a new application of the **Dialog without Buttons** template and drag and drop two **Label** widgets and one **List Widget** onto the form.
2. Set the **text** property of the first **Label** widget to `Choose the Diagnosis Tests`.

3. Set the **objectName** property of **List Widget** to `listWidgetDiagnosis`.
4. Set the **objectName** property of the **Label** widget to `labelTest`.
5. Delete the default **text** property of the `labelTest` widget as we will display the selected diagnosis test through this widget via code.
6. To display diagnosis tests through **List Widget**, right-click on it and from the context menu that opens up, select the **Edit Items** option.
7. Add the diagnosis tests one by one, followed by clicking on the **+** button at the bottom after typing every test, as shown in the following screenshot:

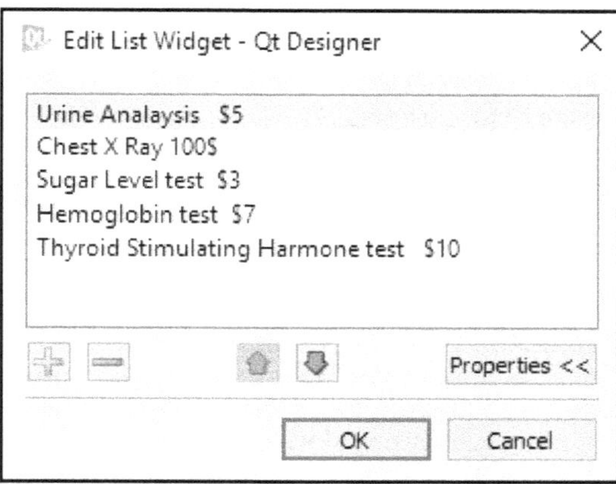

8. Save the application with the name `demoListWidget1.ui`. The form will appear as shown in the following screenshot:

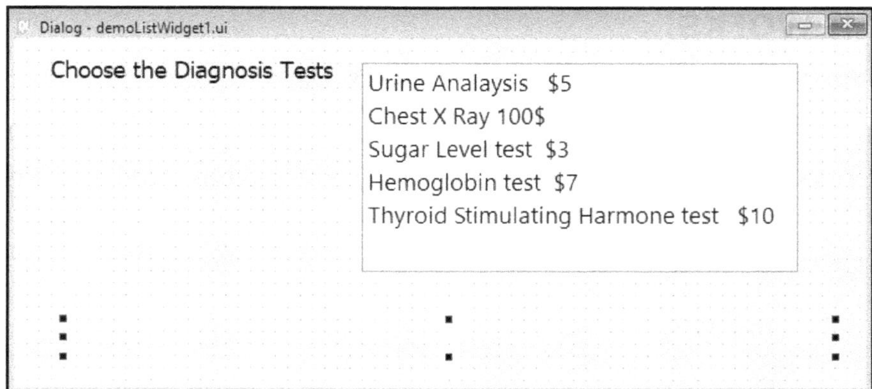

The `pyuic5` command utility will convert the `.ui` (XML) file into Python code. The generated Python code, `demoListWidget1.py`, can be seen in the source code bundle of this book.

9. Create a Python script file named `callListWidget1.pyw` that imports the code, `demoListWidget1.py`, to invoke the user interface design and the code that displays the diagnosis test selected from **List Widget.** The code in the Python script, `callListWidget1.pyw`, is as shown here:

```
import sys
from PyQt5.QtWidgets import QDialog, QApplication
from demoListWidget1 import *
class MyForm(QDialog):
    def __init__(self):
        super().__init__()
        self.ui = Ui_Dialog()
        self.ui.setupUi(self)
        self.ui.listWidgetDiagnosis.itemClicked.connect(self.
        dispSelectedTest)
        self.show()
    def dispSelectedTest(self):
        self.ui.labelTest.setText("You have selected
        "+self.ui.listWidgetDiagnosis.currentItem().text())
if __name__=="__main__":
    app = QApplication(sys.argv)
    w = MyForm()
    w.show()
    sys.exit(app.exec_())
```

How it works...

You can see that the `itemClicked` event of **List Widget** is connected to the `dispSelectedTest()` method. That is, on clicking any of the list items from **List Widget**, the `dispSelectedTest()` method is invoked, which uses the `currentItem` method of **List Widget** to display the selected item of **List Widget** through the label called `labelTest`.

On running the application, you will see **List Widget** showing a few diagnosis tests; on selecting a test from the **List Widget**, the test will appear through the **Label** widget, as shown in the following screenshot:

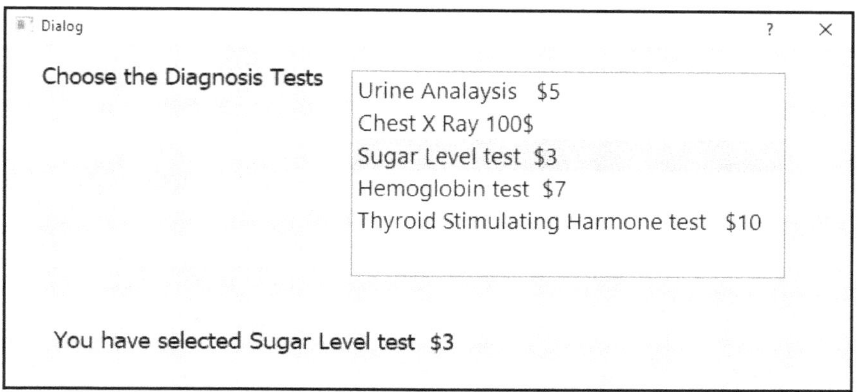

Selecting multiple list items from one List Widget and displaying them in another

In the preceding application, you were selecting only a single diagnosis test from the **List Widget** item. What if I want to do multiple selections from the **List Widget** item? In the case of multiple selections, instead of a **Line Edit** widget, you need another **List Widget** to store the selected diagnosis test.

How to do it...

Let's create an application that displays certain diagnosis tests through **List Widget** and when user selects any test from **List Widget**, the selected test will be displayed in another **List Widget**:

1. So, create a new application of the **Dialog without Buttons** template and drag and drop two **Label** widgets and two **List Widget** onto the form.
2. Set the text property of the first **Label** widget as `Diagnosis Tests` and that of the other to `Selected tests are`.
3. Set the **objectName** property of the first **List Widget** to `listWidgetDiagnosis` and of the second **List Widget** to `listWidgetSelectedTests`.

4. To display diagnosis tests through **List Widget**, right-click on it and from the context menu that opens up, select the **Edit Items** option.
5. Add the diagnosis tests one by one followed by clicking on the **+** button at the bottom after typing every test.
6. To enable multiple selections from **List Widget**, select the `listWidgetDiagnosis` widget and from the **Property Editor** window, change the **selectionMode** property from `SingleSelection` to `MultiSelection`.
7. Save the application with the name `demoListWidget2.ui`. The form will appear as shown in the following screenshot:

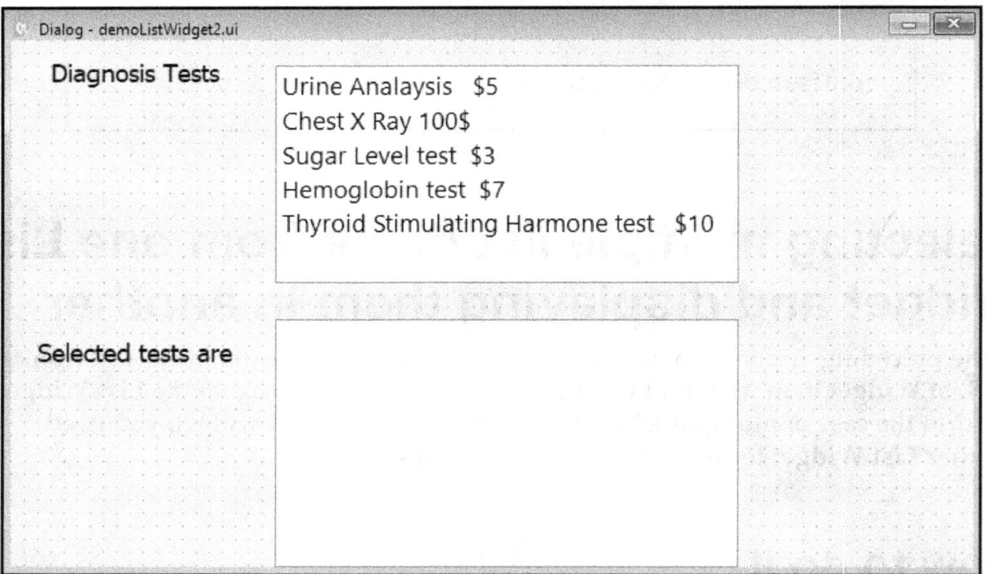

By using the `pyuic5` utility, the XML file `demoListWidget2.ui` will be converted into Python code as the `demoListWidget2.py` file. The generated Python code, from the `demoListWidget2.py` file, can be seen in the source code bundle of this book.

8. Create a Python script file named `callListWidget2.pyw` that imports the code, `demoListWidget2.py`, to invoke the user interface design and the code that displays the multiple selected diagnosis tests selected from **List Widget.** The Python script `callListWidget2.pyw` will appear as shown here:

```
import sys
from PyQt5.QtWidgets import QDialog, QApplication
from demoListWidget2 import *
class MyForm(QDialog):
    def __init__(self):
        super().__init__()
        self.ui = Ui_Dialog()
        self.ui.setupUi(self)
self.ui.listWidgetDiagnosis.itemSelectionChanged.connect
        (self.dispSelectedTest)
        self.show()
    def dispSelectedTest(self):
        self.ui.listWidgetSelectedTests.clear()
        items = self.ui.listWidgetDiagnosis.selectedItems()
        for i in list(items):
            self.ui.listWidgetSelectedTests.addItem(i.text())
if __name__=="__main__":
    app = QApplication(sys.argv)
    w = MyForm()
    w.show()
    sys.exit(app.exec_())
```

How it works...

You can see that the `itemSelectionChanged` event of the first **List Widget** is connected to the `dispSelectedTest()` method. That is, on selecting or unselecting any of the list items from the first **List Widget** item, the `dispSelectedTest()` method is invoked. The `dispSelectedTest()` method invokes the `selectedItems()` method on **List Widget** to get the list of all the selected items. Thereafter, using the `for` loop, all the selected items are added to the second **List Widget** by invoking the `addItem()` method on it.

On running the application, you will see **List Widget** showing a few diagnosis tests; on selecting any number of tests from the first **List Widget**, all the selected tests will appear through the second **List Widget** item, as shown in the following screenshot:

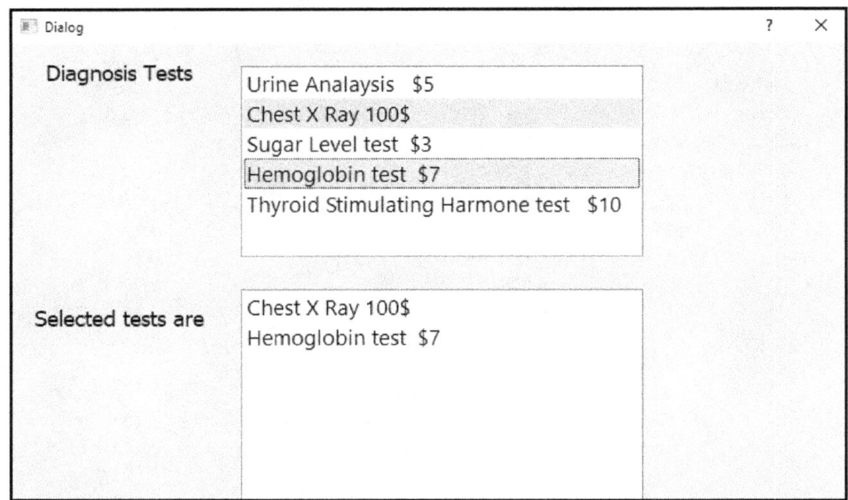

Adding items into List Widget

Although you can add items to the **List Widget** item manually through **Property Editor**, sometimes you need to add items to the **List Widget** item dynamically through code. Let's create an application that explains the process of adding items to **List Widget**.

In this application, you will use **Label**, **Line Edit**, **Push Button**, and **List Widget**. The **List Widget** item will be empty initially, and the user is asked to enter desired food items into **Line Edit** and select an **Add to List** button. The entered food item will then be added to the **List Widget** item. All subsequent food items will be added below the previous entry.

How to do it...

Perform the following steps to know how items can be added to the **List Widget** item:

1. We will begin by creating a new application based on the **Dialog without Buttons** template and dragging and dropping **Label**, **Line Edit**, **Push Button**, and **List Widget** onto the form.
2. Set the **text** property of the **Label** and **Push Button** widgets to `Your favourite food item` and `Add to List`, respectively.
3. Set the **objectName** property of the **Line Edit** widget to `lineEditFoodItem`, that of **Push Button** to `pushButtonAdd`, and that of **List Widget** to `listWidgetSelectedItems`.
4. Save the application with the name `demoListWidget3.ui`. The form will appear as shown in the following screenshot:

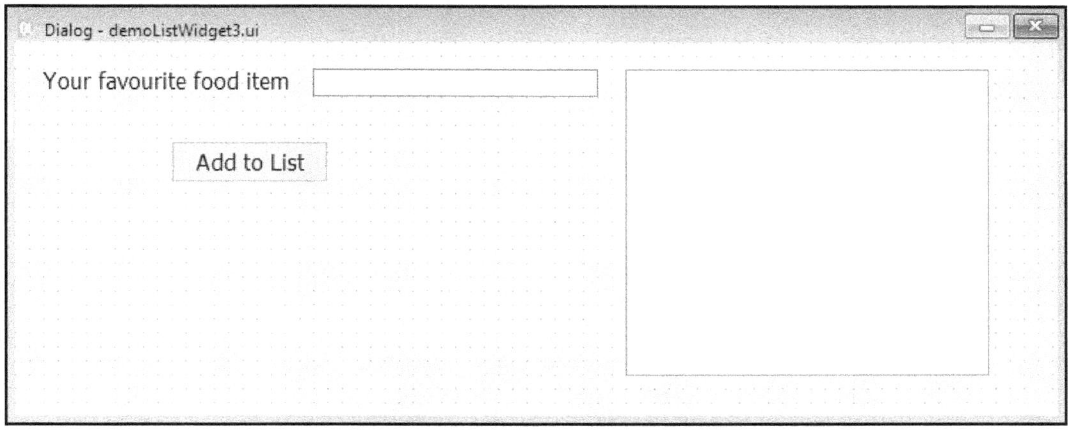

On executing the `pyuic5` utility, the XML file `demoListWidget3.ui` will be converted into Python code as `demoListWidget3.py`. The code of the generated Python file, `demoListWidget3.py`, can be seen in the source code bundle of this book.

5. Create a Python script file named `callListWidget3.pyw` that imports the Python code `demoListWidget3.py` to invoke the user interface design and adds the food items entered by the user in **Line Edit** to **List Widget**. The Python code in the `callListWidget3.pyw` file will appear as shown here:

```
import sys
from PyQt5.QtWidgets import QDialog, QApplication
from demoListWidget3 import *
class MyForm(QDialog):
    def __init__(self):
        super().__init__()
        self.ui = Ui_Dialog()
        self.ui.setupUi(self)
        self.ui.pushButtonAdd.clicked.connect(self.addlist)
        self.show()
    def addlist(self):
        self.ui.listWidgetSelectedItems.addItem(self.ui.
        lineEditFoodItem.text())
        self.ui.lineEditFoodItem.setText('')
        self.ui.lineEditFoodItem.setFocus()
if __name__=="__main__":
    app = QApplication(sys.argv)
    w = MyForm()
    w.show()
    sys.exit(app.exec_())
```

How it works...

The **clicked()** event of the **Push Button** widget is connected to the `addlist` function. Hence, after entering the text to be added to **List Widget** in the **Line Edit** widget, when the user selects the **Add to List** button, the `addlist` function is invoked. The `addlist` function retrieves the text entered in **Line Edit** and adds it to **List Widget**. The text in the **Line Edit** widget is then removed, and the focus is set on it, enabling the user to enter different text.

In the following screenshot, you can see the text entered by the user in the **Line Edit** widget is added to **List Widget** when the user selects the **Add to List** button:

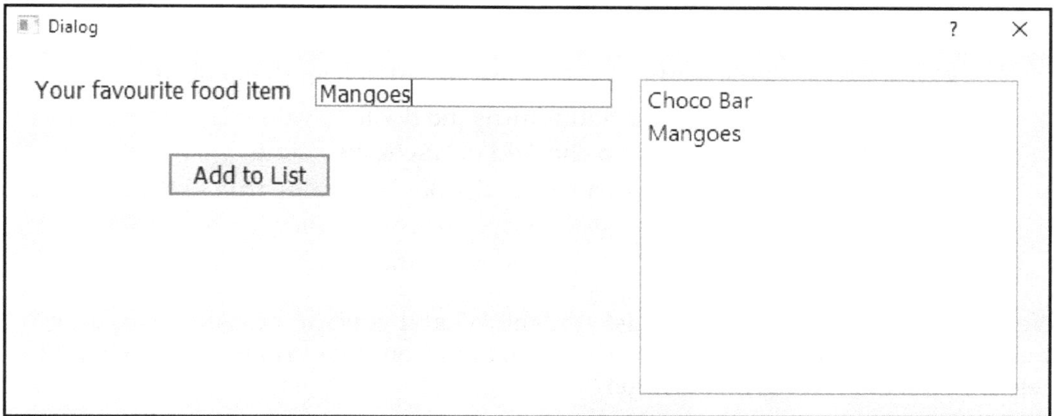

Performing operations in List Widget

In this recipe, you will learn how to perform different operations on list items in **List Widget**. **List Widget** is basically used for showing a collection of similar items, enabling the user to choose the desired items. Consequently, you need to add items to **List Widget**. Also, you might require to edit any item in **List Widget**. Sometimes, you might require to delete an item from **List Widget**. One more operation that you might want to perform on **List Widget** is deleting all items from it, clearing the entire **List Widget** item. Before learning how to add, edit, and delete items from **List Widget**, let's understand the concept of a list item.

Getting ready

List Widget consists of several list items. These list items are instances of the `QListWidgetItem` class. The list items can be inserted into **List Widget** using the `insertItem()` or `addItem()` methods. List items may be in text or icon form and can be checked or unchecked. Methods provided by `QListWidgetItem` are given next.

Methods provided by the QListWidgetItem class

Let's take a look at the following methods provided by the `QListWidgetItem` class:

- `setText()`: This method assigns the specified text to the list item
- `setIcon()`: This method assigns the specified icon to the list item
- `checkState()`: This method returns the Boolean value depending on whether the list item is in a checked or unchecked state
- `setHidden()`: This method passes the Boolean value true to this method to hide the list item
- `isHidden()`: This method returns true if the list item is hidden

We have learned to add items to **List Widget**. What if you want to edit an existing item in **List Widget**, or you want to delete an item from **List Widget**, or you want to delete all the items from **List Widget**?

Let's learn to perform different operations on **List Widget** by creating an application. This application will display **Line Edit**, **List Widget**, and a couple of **Push Button** widgets. You can add items to **List Widget** by entering the text in **Line Edit**, followed by clicking the **Add** button. Similarly, you can edit any item from **List Widget** by clicking an item from **List Widget**, followed by clicking the **Edit** button. Not only this, but you can even delete any item from **List Widget** by clicking the **Delete** button. If you want to clear the entire **List Widget**, simply click on the **Delete All** button.

How to do it....

Perform the following steps to understand how different operations can be applied on the **List Widget** item; how items can be added, edited, and deleted from the **List Widget** item; and how the entire **List Widget** item can be cleared:

1. Open Qt Designer, create a new application based on the **Dialog without Buttons** template, and drag and drop a **Label**, **Line Edit**, four **Push Button**, and **List Widget** widgets onto the form.
2. Set the **text** property of the **Label** widget to `Enter an item`.
3. Set the **text** property of the four **Push Button** widgets to `Add`, `Edit`, `Delete`, and `Delete All`.

4. Set the **objectName** property of the four **Push Button** widgets to `psuhButtonAdd`, `pushButtonEdit`, `pushButtonDelete`, and `pushButtonDeleteAll`.

5. Save the application with the name `demoListWidgetOp.ui`.

   The form will appear as shown in the following screenshot:

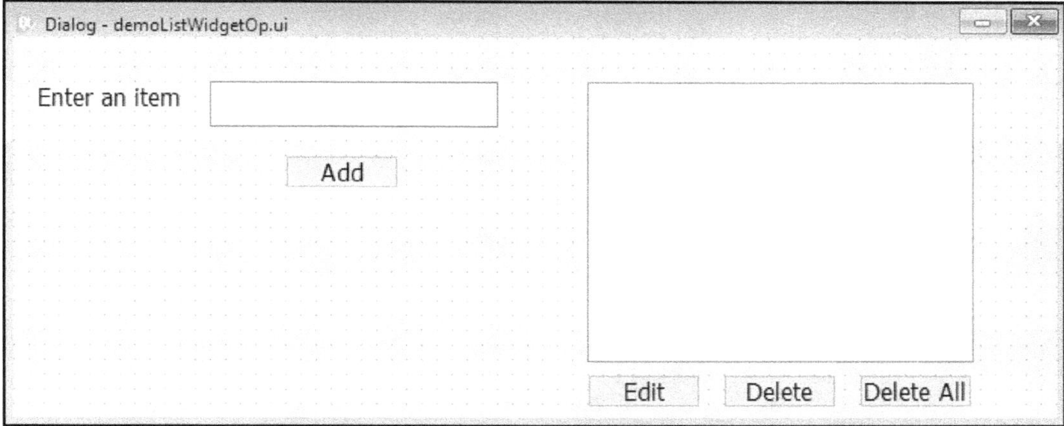

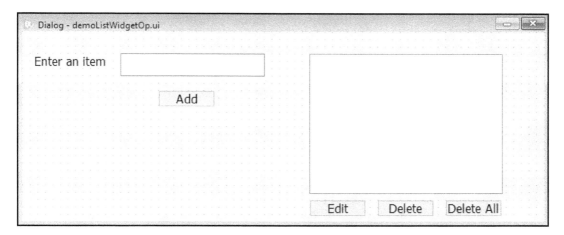

The XML file `demoListWidgetOp.ui` needs to be converted into the Python script by making use of the `pyuic5` command utility. The generated Python file `demoListWidgetOp.py` can be seen in the source code bundle of this book.

6. Create a Python script file named `callListWidgetOp.pyw` that imports the Python code, `demoListWidgetOp.py`, enabling you to invoke the user interface design and add, delete, and edit the list items in **List Widget**. The code in the Python script `callListWidgetOp.pyw` is shown here:

```
import sys
from PyQt5.QtWidgets import QDialog, QApplication,
QInputDialog, QListWidgetItem
from demoListWidgetOp import *
class MyForm(QDialog):
    def __init__(self):
        super().__init__()
        self.ui = Ui_Dialog()
        self.ui.setupUi(self)
        self.ui.listWidget.addItem('Ice Cream')
        self.ui.listWidget.addItem('Soda')
```

```
            self.ui.listWidget.addItem('Coffee')
            self.ui.listWidget.addItem('Chocolate')
            self.ui.pushButtonAdd.clicked.connect(self.addlist)
            self.ui.pushButtonEdit.clicked.connect(self.editlist)
            self.ui.pushButtonDelete.clicked.connect(self.delitem)
            self.ui.pushButtonDeleteAll.clicked.connect
            (self.delallitems)
            self.show()
        def addlist(self):
            self.ui.listWidget.addItem(self.ui.lineEdit.text())
            self.ui.lineEdit.setText('')
            self.ui.lineEdit.setFocus()
        def editlist(self):
            row=self.ui.listWidget.currentRow()
            newtext, ok=QInputDialog.getText(self, "Enter new
    text",
            "Enter new text")
            if ok and (len(newtext) !=0):
    self.ui.listWidget.takeItem(self.ui.listWidget.
                    currentRow())
                    self.ui.listWidget.insertItem(row,
                    QListWidgetItem(newtext))
        def delitem(self):
            self.ui.listWidget.takeItem(self.ui.listWidget.
            currentRow())
        def delallitems(self):
            self.ui.listWidget.clear()
    if __name__=="__main__":
        app = QApplication(sys.argv)
        w = MyForm()
        w.show()
        sys.exit(app.exec_())
```

How it works...

The **clicked()** event of `pushButtonAdd` is connected to the `addlist` function. Similarly, the **clicked()** event of the `pushButtonEdit`, `pushButtonDelete`, and `pushButtonDeleteAll` objects are connected to the `editlist`, `delitem`, and `delallitems` functions, respectively. That is, on clicking any push button, the respective function is invoked. The `addlist` function calls the `addItem` function on the **List Widget** item to add the text entered in the **Line Edit** widget. The `editlist` function uses the `currentRow` method on **List Widget** to find out the list item to be edited.

The `getText` method of the `QInputDialog` class is invoked to prompt the user for the new text or edited text. On clicking the **OK** button in the dialog, the current list item will be replaced by the text entered in the dialog box. The `delitem` function invokes the `takeItem` method on **List Widget** to delete the current row, that is, the selected list item. The `delallitems` function invokes the `clear` method on the**List Widget** item to clear or delete all the list items from the **List Widget** item.

On running the application, you will find an empty **List Widget**, **Line Edit**, and **Add** push button below the **Line Edit** widget. Add any text in the **Line Edit** widget and click on the **Add** button to add that item to **List Widget**. After adding four items to **List Widget,** it might appear as shown in the following screenshot:

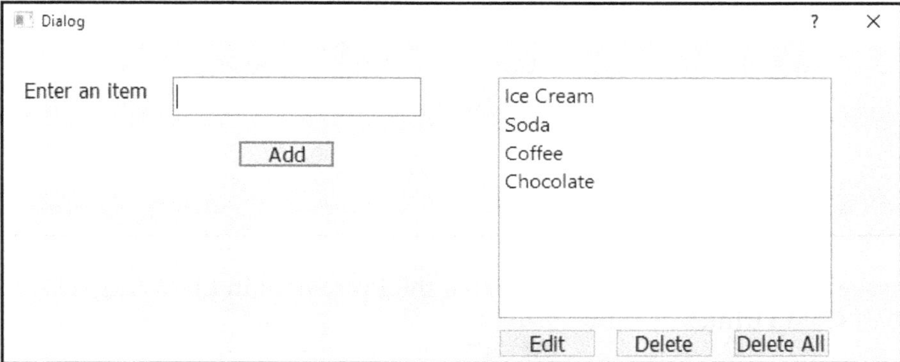

Let's add one more item, Pizza, to **List Widget**. Type `Pizza` in the **Line Edit** widget and click the **Add** button. The **Pizza** item will be added to the **List Widget** item, as shown in the following screenshot:

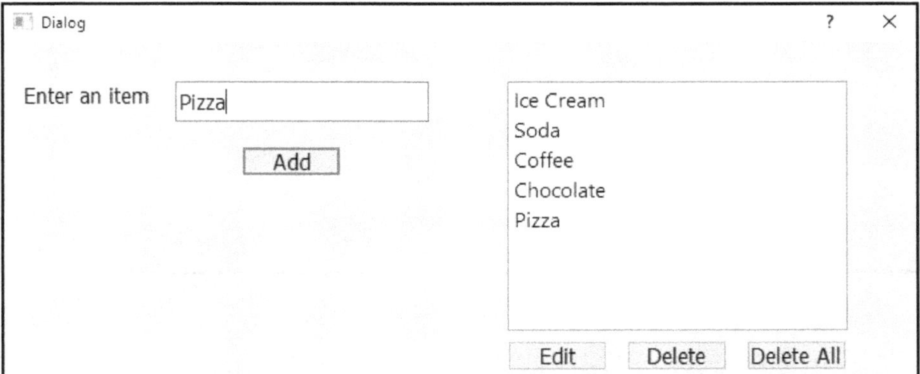

Assuming we want to edit the **Pizza** item from **List Widget**, click the **Pizza** item in **List Widget** and click on the **Edit** button. On clicking the **Edit** button, you get a dialog box prompting you to enter a new item to replace the **Pizza** item. Let's enter `Cold Drink` in the dialog box, followed by clicking the **OK** button, as shown in the following screenshot:

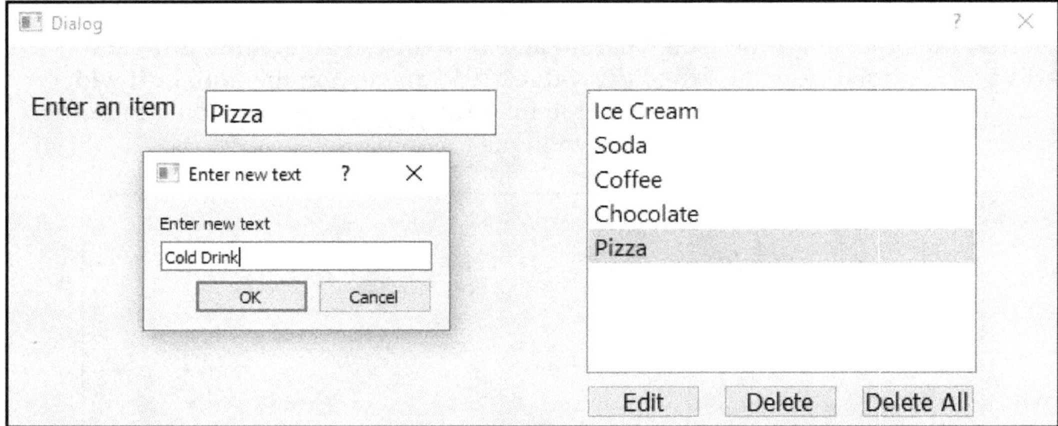

You can see in the following screenshot that the **Pizza** item in **List Widget** is replaced by the text **Cold Drink**:

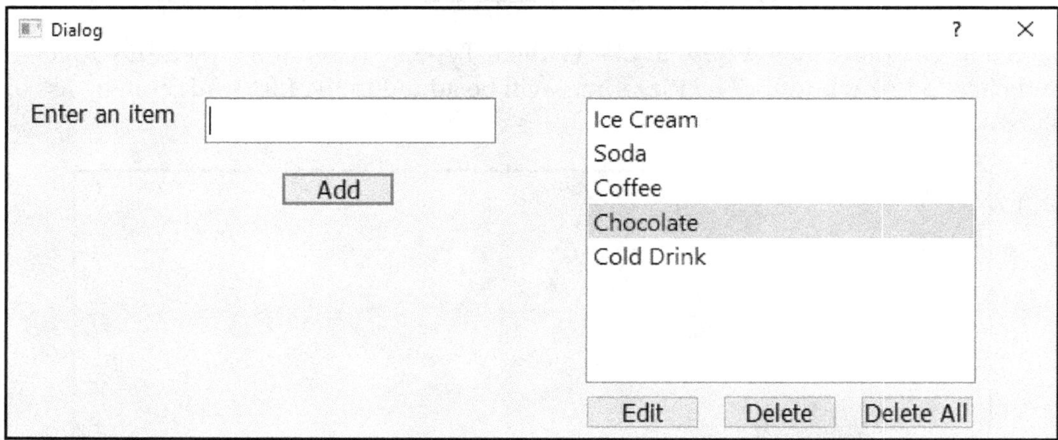

In order to delete any item from **List Widget**, simply click that item from **List Widget**, followed by clicking the **Delete** button. Let's click the **Coffee** item from **List Widget** and click on the **Delete** button; the **Coffee** item will be deleted from **List Widget**, as shown in the following screenshot:

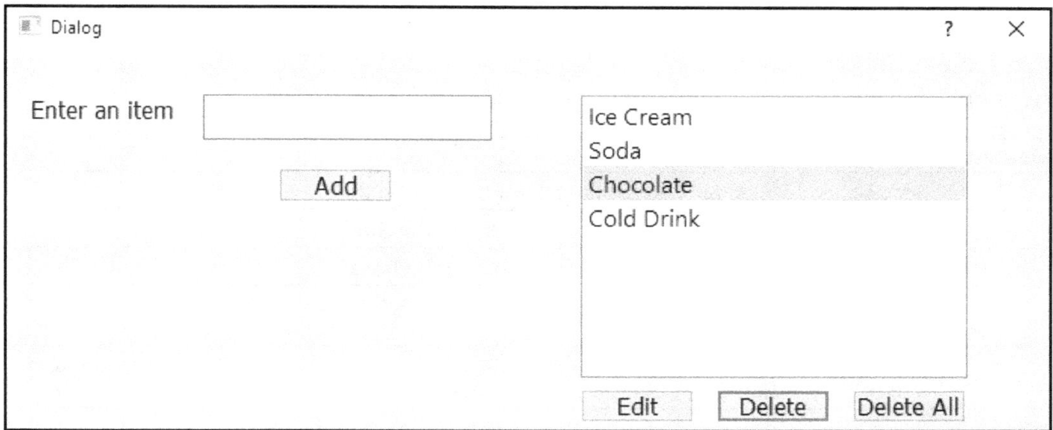

On clicking the **Delete All** button, the entire **List Widget** item will become empty, as shown in the following screenshot:

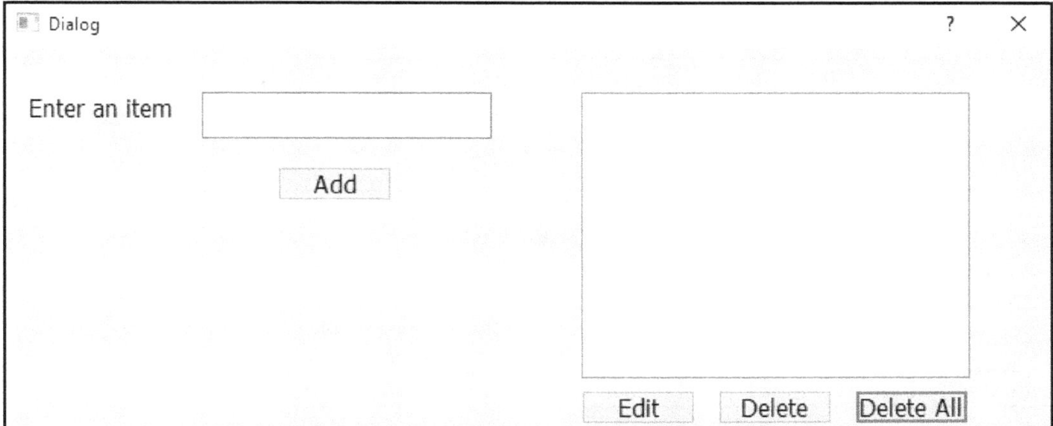

Using the Combo Box widget

Combo boxes are used for getting input from the user with an applied constraint; that is, the user will be shown certain options in the form of a popup list and he/she can only select from the available choices. A combo box takes less space when compared with **List Widget**. The `QComboBox` class is used for displaying combo boxes. Not only can you display text through a combo box, but `pixmaps` too. Here are the methods provided by the `QComboBox` class:

Method	Usage
`setItemText()`	Sets or changes the text of the item in the combo box.
`removeItem()`	Removes the specific item from the combo box.
`clear()`	Removes all items from the combo box.
`currentText()`	Returns the text of the current item, that is, the item that is currently chosen.
`setCurrentIndex()`	Sets the current index of the combo box, that is, it sets the desired item in the combo box as the currently chosen item.
`count()`	Returns the count of the items in the combo box.
`setMaxCount()`	Sets the maximum number of items that are allowed in the combo box.
`setEditable()`	Make the combo box editable, that is, the user can edit items in the combo box.
`addItem()`	Appends the specified content to the combo box.
`addItems()`	Appends each of the strings supplied in the text to the combo box.
`itemText()`	Returns the text at the specified index location in the combo box.
`currentIndex()`	Returns the index location of the currently chosen item in the combo box. If the combo box is empty or no item is currently chosen in the combo box, the method will return `-1` as the index.

The following are the signals that are generated by `QComboBox`:

Signal	Description
currentIndexChanged()	Emitted when the index of the combo box is changed, that is, the user selects some new item in the combo box.
activated()	Emitted when the index is changed by the user.
highlighted()	Emitted when the user highlights an item in the combo box.
editTextChanged()	Emitted when the text of an editable combo box is changed.

To understand the workings of a combo box practically, let's create a recipe. This recipe will display certain bank account types via a combo box and will prompt the user to choose the type of bank account he/she wants to open. The selected bank account type from the combo box will be displayed on the screen through a **Label** widget.

How to do it...

The following are the steps to create an application that makes use of a combo box to show certain options and explains how the selected option from the combo box can be displayed:

1. Create a new application of the **Dialog without Buttons** template, drag two **Label** widgets and a **Combo Box** widget from the **Widget** box, and drop them onto the form.
2. Set the **text** property of the first **Label** widget to `Select your account type`.
3. Delete the default **text** property of the second **Label** widget, as its text will be set through code.
4. Set the **objectName** property of the **Combo Box** widget to `comboBoxAccountType`.
5. The second **Label** widget will be used to display the bank account type that is chosen by the user, so set the **objectName** property of the second **Label** widget to `labelAccountType`.
6. As we want the **Combo Box** widget to display certain bank account types, right-click on the **Combo Box** widget and from the context menu that opens up, select the **Edit Items** option.
7. Add some bank account types to the **Combo Box** widget one by one.
8. Save the application by name as `demoComboBox.ui`.

9. Click the + button displayed at the bottom of the dialog to add a bank account type to the **Combo Box** widget, as shown in the following screenshot:

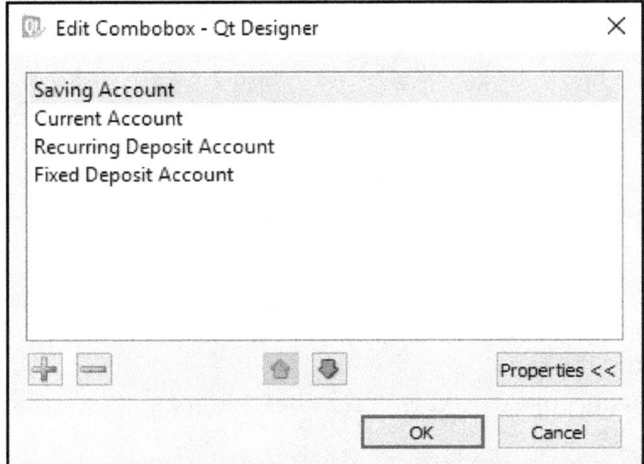

10. After adding the desired bank account types, click on the **OK** button to exit from the dialog. The form will now appear, as shown in the following screenshot:

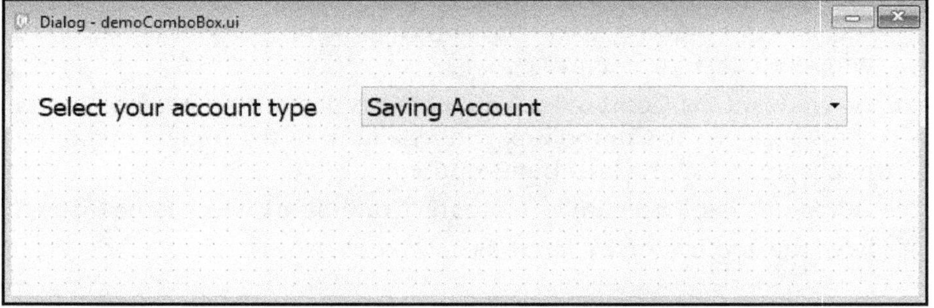

The user interface created with Qt Designer is stored in a `.ui` file, which is an XML file, and needs to be converted to the Python code. The `pyuic5` utility can be used for generating Python code from the XML file. The generated file, `demoComboBox.py`, can be seen in the source code bundle of this book.

11. Treat the `demoComboBox.py` file as a header file, and import it to the file from which you will invoke its user interface design that is you will be able to access the combo box.
12. Create another Python file with the name `callComboBox.pyw` and import the `demoComboBox.py` code into it. The code in the Python script `callComboBox.pyw` is as shown here:

```
import sys
from PyQt5.QtWidgets import QDialog, QApplication
from demoComboBox import *
class MyForm(QDialog):
    def __init__(self):
        super().__init__()
        self.ui = Ui_Dialog()
        self.ui.setupUi(self)
self.ui.comboBoxAccountType.currentIndexChanged.connect
        (self.dispAccountType)
        self.show()

    def dispAccountType(self):
        self.ui.labelAccountType.setText("You have selected
        "+self.ui.comboBoxAccountType.itemText(self.ui.
        comboBoxAccountType.currentIndex()))

if __name__=="__main__":
    app = QApplication(sys.argv)
    w = MyForm()
    w.show()
    sys.exit(app.exec_())
```

How it works...

In the `demoComboBox.py` file, a class with the name of the top-level object is created with `Ui_ prepended`. That is, for the top-level object, `Dialog`, the `Ui_Dialog` class, is created and stores the interface elements of our widget. That class includes two methods, `setupUi` and `retranslateUi`.

The `setupUi` method creates the widgets that are used in defining the user interface in Qt Designer. Also, the properties of the widgets are set in this method. The `setupUi` method takes a single argument, which is the top-level widget of the application, an instance of `QDialog`. The `retranslateUi` method translates the interface.

In the `callComboBox.pyw` file, whenever the user selects any item from the combo box, the `currentIndexChanged` signal will be emitted and the `currentIndexChanged` signal is connected to the `dispAccountType` method, so whenever any item is selected from the combo box, the `dispAccountType` method will be invoked.

In the `dispAccountType` method, you access the currently selected index number by invoking the `currentIndex` method of the `QComboBox` class and passing the fetched index location to the `itemText` method of the `QComboBox` class to get the text of the currently selected combo box item. The currently selected combo box item is then displayed through the **Label** widget.

On running the application, you will find a combo box showing four bank account types: **Saving Account**, **Current Account**, **Recurring Deposit Account**, and **Fixed Deposit Account**, as shown in the following screenshot:

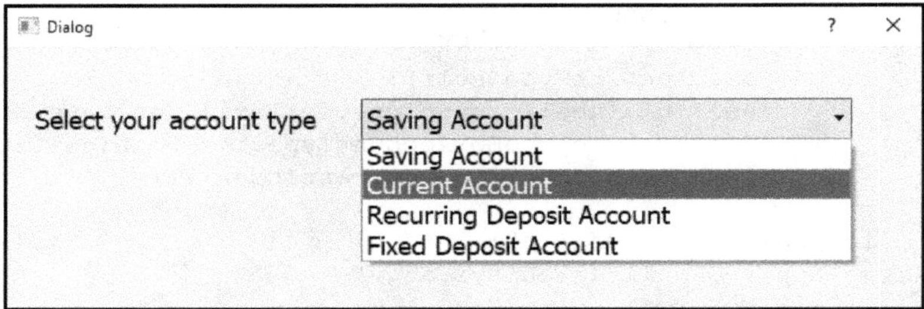

On selecting a bank account type from the combo box, the chosen bank account type will be displayed through the **Label** widget, as shown in the following screenshot:

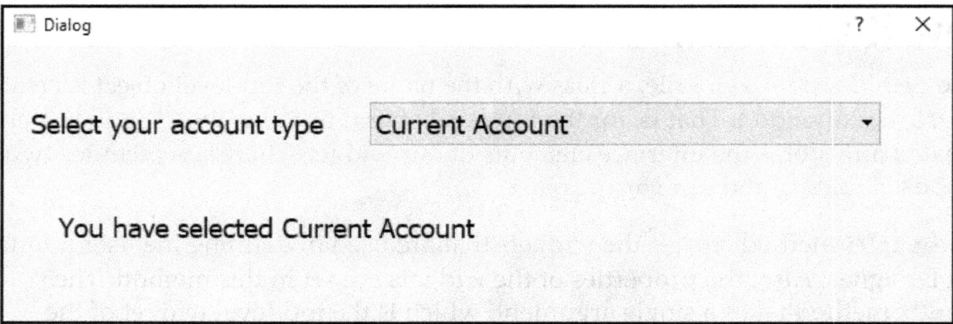

Using the Font Combo Box widget

The **Font Combo Box** widget, as the name suggests, displays a list of font styles to choose from. The chosen font style can be applied to the desired content if required.

Getting ready

To understand the workings of the **Font Combo Box** widget practically, let's create a recipe. This recipe will display a **Font Combo Box** widget and a **Text Edit** widget. The user will be able to type the desired content in the **Text Edit** widget. After typing the text in the **Text Edit** widget, when the user selects any font style from the **Font Combo Box** widget, the selected font will be applied to the content typed into the **Text Edit** widget.

How to do it...

Here are the steps to display an active **Font Combo Box** widget and to apply the selected font to the text written in the **Text Edit** widget:

1. Create a new application of the **Dialog without Buttons** template and drag two **Label** widgets, a **Font Combo Box** widget, and a **Text Edit** widget from the **Widget** box and drop them onto the form.
2. Set the text property of the first **Label** widget to `Select desired font` and that of the second **Label** widget to `Type some text`.
3. Save the application by name as `demoFontComboBox.ui`. The form will now appear as shown in the following screenshot:

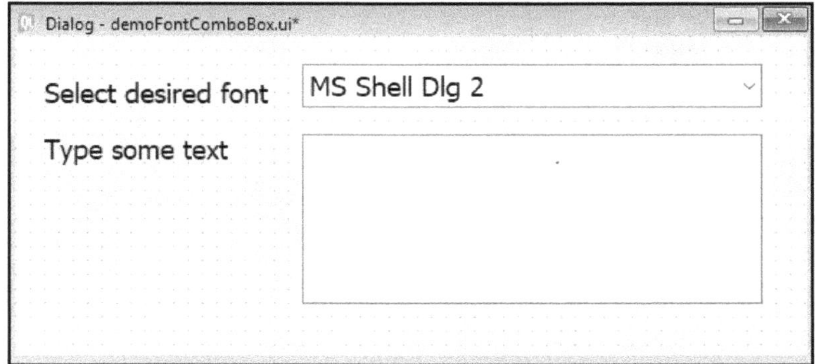

The user interface created with Qt Designer is stored in a `.ui` file, which is an XML file, and needs to be converted to the Python code. On converting to Python code, the generated file, `demoFontComboBox.py`, can be seen in the source code bundle of this book. The preceding code will be used as a header file and is imported into the file in which the GUI is desired, that is, the user interface designed can be accessed in any Python script by simply importing the preceding code.

4. Create another Python file with the name `callFontFontComboBox.pyw` and import the `demoFontComboBox.py` code into it.

The code in the Python script, `callFontComboBox.pyw`, is as shown here:

```
import sys
from PyQt5.QtWidgets import QDialog, QApplication
from demoFontComboBox import *
class MyForm(QDialog):
    def __init__(self):
        super().__init__()
        self.ui = Ui_Dialog()
        self.ui.setupUi(self)
myFont=QtGui.QFont(self.ui.fontComboBox.itemText(self.ui.
        fontComboBox.currentIndex()),15)
        self.ui.textEdit.setFont(myFont)
        self.ui.fontComboBox.currentFontChanged.connect
        (self.changeFont)
        self.show()
    def changeFont(self):
myFont=QtGui.QFont(self.ui.fontComboBox.itemText(self.ui.
        fontComboBox.currentIndex()),15)
        self.ui.textEdit.setFont(myFont)
if __name__=="__main__":
    app = QApplication(sys.argv)
    w = MyForm()
    w.show()
    sys.exit(app.exec_())
```

How it works...

In the `callFontComboBox.pyw` file, whenever the user selects any font style from the **Font Combo Box** widget, the `currentFontChanged` signal is emitted and this signal is connected to the `changeFont` method, so whenever any font style is chosen from the **Font Combo Box** widget, the `changeFont()` method will be invoked.

In the `changeFont()` method, you access the selected font style by invoking two methods. The first method invoked is the `currentIndex()` method of the `QFontComboBox` class, which fetches the index number of the selected font style. The second method invoked is the `itemText()` method, and the index location of the currently selected font style is passed to this method to access the chosen font style. The chosen font style is then applied to the content written in the **Text Edit** widget.

On running the application, you will find a **Font Combo Box** widget showing available font styles in the system, as shown in the following screenshot:

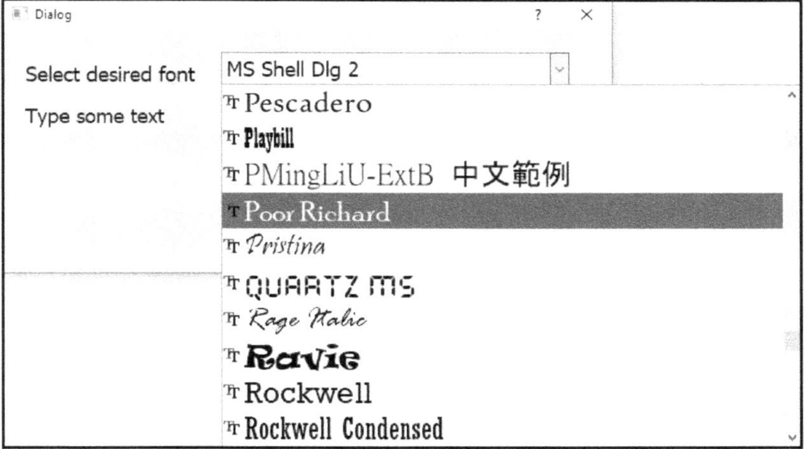

Type some text in the **Text Edit** widget and choose the desired font from the font combo box. The chosen font style will be applied to the text written in the **Text Edit** widget, as shown in the following screenshot:

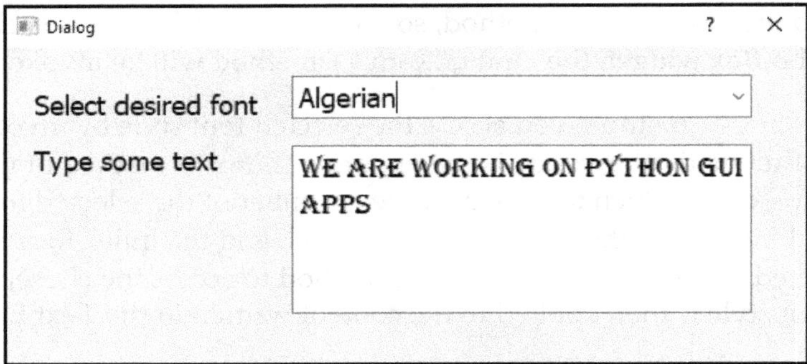

Using the Progress Bar widget

The **Progress Bar** widget is very useful in representing the progress of any task. Whether it is downloading a file from a server, virus scanning on a machine, or some other critical task, the **Progress Bar** widget helps inform the user of the percentage of the task that is done and the percentage that is pending. As the task completes, the **Progress Bar** widget keeps updating, indicating progress in the task.

Getting ready

To understand how the progress bar is updated to show the progress of any task, let's create a recipe. This recipe will display a **Progress Bar** widget, indicating the total time required to download a file. When the user clicks the push button to begin downloading the file, the **Progress Bar** widget will update from **0%** to **100%** gradually; that is, the progress bar will update as the file is being downloaded. The **Progress Bar** widget will show **100%** when the file is completely downloaded.

How to do it...

Initially, the **Progress Bar** widget is at **0%** and to make it go up, we need to make use of a loop. The loop will increment its value as the task represented by the **Progress Bar** widget progresses towards completion. Every increment in the loop value will add to some progress in the **Progress Bar** widget. Here is the step-by-step procedure to show how a progress bar can be updated:

1. Create a new application from the **Dialog without Buttons** template, and drag a **Label** widget, a **Progress Bar** widget, and a **Push Button** widget from the **Widget** box and drop them onto the form.
2. Set the **text** property of the **Label** widget to `Downloading the file` and that of the **Push Button** widget to `Start Downloading`.
3. Set the **objectName** property of the **Push Button** widget to `pushButtonStart`.
4. Save the application by name as `demoProgressBar.ui`. The form will now appear, as shown in the following screenshot:

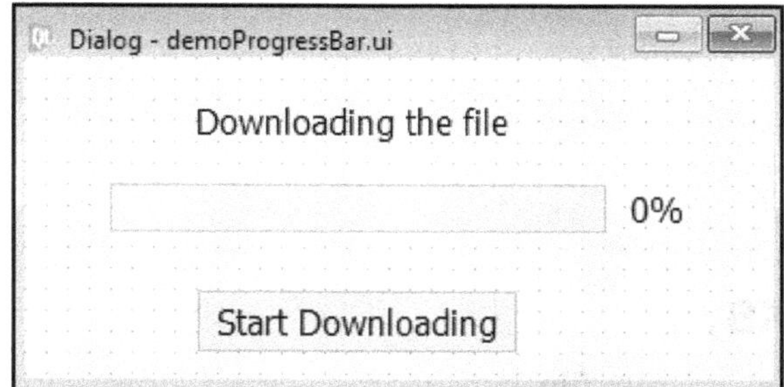

The user interface created with Qt Designer is stored in a `.ui` file, which is an XML file and needs to be converted into Python code. The generated Python code, `demoProgressBar.py`, can be seen in the source code bundle of this book. The preceding code will be used as a header file and is imported into the file in which the GUI is desired; that is, the user interface designed in the code can be accessed in any Python script by simply importing the preceding code.

5. Create another Python file with the name `callProgressBar.pyw` and import the `demoProgressBar.py` code into it. The code in the Python script `callProgressBar.pyw` is as shown here:

```
import sys
from PyQt5.QtWidgets import QDialog, QApplication
from demoProgressBar import *
class MyForm(QDialog):
    def __init__(self):
        super().__init__()
        self.ui = Ui_Dialog()
        self.ui.setupUi(self)
self.ui.pushButtonStart.clicked.connect(self.updateBar)
        self.show()

    def updateBar(self):
        x = 0
        while x < 100:
            x += 0.0001
            self.ui.progressBar.setValue(x)

if __name__=="__main__":
    app = QApplication(sys.argv)
    w = MyForm()
    w.show()
    sys.exit(app.exec_())
```

How it works...

In the `callProgressBar.pyw` file, because we want the progress bar to show its progress when the push button is pressed, the **clicked()** event of the progress bar is connected to the `updateBar()` method, so when the push button is clicked, the `updateBar()` method will be invoked. In the `updateBar()` method, a `while` loop is used that loops from `0` to `100`. A variable, `x`, is initialized to the value `0`. With every iteration of the while loop, the value of `x` is incremented by `0.0001`. The value in the `x` variable is applied to the progress bar when updating it. That is, with every iteration of the while loop, the value of `x` is incremented and the value of `x` is used in updating the progress bar. Hence, the progress bar will begin its progress at **0%** and continue until it reaches **100%**.

On running the application, initially, you will find the **Progress Bar** widget at **0%** along with the push button at the bottom with the caption **Start Downloading** (see the following screenshot). Click the **Start Downloading** push button and you will see that the progress bar begins showing progress gradually. The progress bar keeps going up until it reaches **100%** to indicate that the file is completely downloaded:

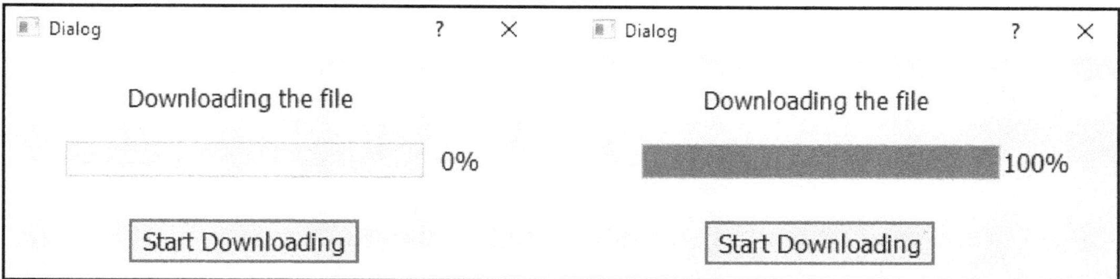

15
Understanding OOP Concepts

In this chapter, we will cover the following topics:

- Object-oriented programming
- Using classes in GUI
- Using single inheritance
- Using multilevel inheritance
- Using multiple inheritance

Object-oriented programming

Python supports **object-oriented programming** (**OOP**). OOP supports reusability; that is, code that was written earlier can be reused for making large applications, instead of starting from scratch. The term object in OOP refers to a variable or instance of a class, where a class is a template or blueprint of a structure that consists of methods and variables. The variables in the class are called **data members**, and the methods are called **member functions**. When instances or objects of a class are made, the objects automatically get access to data members and methods.

Creating a class

The `class` statement is used for creating a class. The following is the syntax for creating a class:

```
class class_name(base_classes):
    statement(s)
```

Here, `class_name` is an identifier to identify the class. After the `class` statement comes the statements that make up the body of the class. The `class` body consists of different methods and variables to be defined in that class.

You can make an individual class or a class that inherits another class. The class that is being inherited is called the **base class**. The `base_classes` parameter after `class_name` in the syntax represents all the base classes that this class will be inheriting. If there is more than one base class, then they need to be separated by commas. The class that is being inherited is called the **super class** or **base class**, and the inheriting class is called a **derived class** or **subclass**. The derived class can use the methods and variables of the base class, and hence implements reusability:

```
class Student:
    name = ""
    def __init__(self, name):
        self.name = name
    def printName(self):
        return self.name
```

In this example, `Student` is a class that contains an attribute called `name` that is initialized to null.

Using the built-in class attributes

A `class` statement automatically assigns certain values to certain fixed class attributes. Those class attributes can be used to fetch information about the class. The list of class attributes are as follows:

- `__name__`: This attribute represents the class name used in the `class` statement
- `__bases__`: This attribute represents the base class names mentioned in the `class` statement
- `__dict__`: The dictionary object that represents other class attributes
- `__module__`: This attribute represents the module name in which the class is defined

A class can have any number of methods, and each method can have any number of parameters. One mandatory first parameter is always defined in a method, and that first parameter is usually named `self` (though you can give any name to this parameter). The `self` parameter refers to the instance of the class that calls the method. The syntax for defining methods in a class is as follows:

```
class class_name(base_classes):
    Syntax:
        variable(s)
    def method 1(self):
        statement(s)
    [def method n(self):
        statement(s)]
```

A class can have the following two types of data member:

- **Class variable**: These are the variables that are shareable by all instances, and changes made to these variables by any one instance can be seen by other instances too. These are the data members that are defined outside of any method of the class.
- **Instance variable**: These variables, which are defined inside a method, only belong to the current instance of the object and are known as **instance variables**. Changes made to instance variables by any instance are limited to that particular instance and don't affect the instance variables of other instances.

Let's see how to create an instance method and how it can be used to access class variables.

Accessing class variables in instance methods

To access class variables, the class variables must be prefixed with the class name. For example, to access the `name` class variable of the `Student` class, you need to access it as follows:

```
Student.name
```

You can see that the `name` class variable is prefixed with the `Student` class name.

Instances

To use the variables and methods of any class, we need to create its objects or instances. An instance of a class gets its own copy of variables and methods. This means the variable of one instance will not interfere with the variable of another instance. We can create as many instances of a class as desired. To create an instance of a class, you need to write the class name followed by arguments (if any). For example, the following statement creates an instance of the `Student` class with the name `studentObj`:

```
studentObj=Student()
```

You can create any number of instances of the `Student` class. For example, the following line creates another instance of the `Student` class:

```
courseStudent=Student()
```

Now, the instance can access the class attribute and method of the class.

You need to specify `self` explicitly when defining the method. While calling the method, `self` is not mandatory because Python adds it automatically.

To define the variables of a class, we get help from the `__init__()` method. The `__init__()` method is like a constructor in traditional OOP languages and is the first method to be executed after the creation of an instance. It is used for initializing the variables of the class. Depending on how the `__init__()` method is defined in the class, that is, with or without parameters, the arguments may or may not be passed to the `__init__()` method.

As mentioned earlier, the first argument of every class method is a class instance that is called `self`. In the `__init__()` method, `self` refers to the newly created instance:

```
class Student:
    name = ""
    def __init__(self):
        self.name = "David"
        studentObj=Student()
```

In the preceding example, the `studentObj` instance is the instance of the `Student` class being created, and its class variable will be initialized to the `David` string.

Even arguments can be passed to the `__init__()` method, as shown in the following example:

```
class Student:
    name = ""
    def __init__(self, name):
        self.name = name
        studentObj=Student("David")
```

In the preceding example, the `studentObj` instance is created and the `David` string is passed to it. The string will be assigned to the `name` parameter defined in the `__init__()` method, which, in turn, will be used to initialize the class variable, `name`, of the instance. Remember, the `__init__()` method must not return a value.

Like the class variables, the methods of the class can be accessed by the instance of the class, followed by the method name, with a period (`.`) in between. Assuming there is a `printName()` method in the `Student` class, it can be accessed via the `studentObj` instance with the following statement:

```
studentObj.printName()
```

Using classes in GUI

The data received from the user through the GUI can be directly processed by making use of simple variables, and the processed data can be displayed through variables only. But to keep the data in a structured format and get the benefits of OOP, we will learn to keep data in the form of classes. That is, the data accessed by the user through the GUI can be assigned to the class variables, processed, and displayed through class methods.

Let's create an application that will prompt the user to enter a name and, on clicking the push button after entering a name, the application will display a hello message along with the entered name. The name entered by the user will be assigned to a class variable and the hello message will also be generated by invoking the class method of the class.

How to do it...

The focus of this recipe is to understand how the data entered by the user is assigned to the class variable, and how the message displayed can be accessed via class methods. Let's create a new application based on the **Dialog without Buttons** template and follow these steps:

1. Drag and drop two **Label** widgets, one **Line Edit**, and one **Push Button** widget onto the form.
2. Set the **text** property of the first **Label** widget to `Enter your name`.

Let's not change the **text** property of the second **Label** widget and keep its **text** property to its default value of **TextLabel**. This is because its **text** property will be set through code to display the hello message.

3. Set the **text** property of the **Push Button** widget to `Click`.
4. Set the **objectName** property of the **Line Edit** widget to `lineEditName`.
5. Set the **objectName** property of the **Label** widget to `labelResponse`.
6. Set the **objectName** property of the **Push Button** widget to `ButtonClickMe`.
7. Save the application with the name `LineEditClass.ui`. The application will appear as shown in the following screenshot:

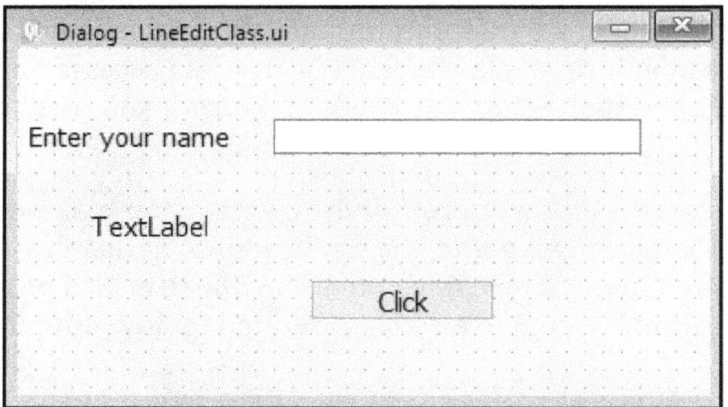

The user interface created with Qt Designer is stored in a `.ui` file, which is an XML file and needs to be converted to Python code.

8. To do the conversion, you need to open a Command Prompt window, navigate to the folder where the file is saved, and issue the following command line:

```
C:\Pythonbook\PyQt5>pyuic5 LineEdit.uiClass -o
LineEditClass.py
```

The generated Python script, `LineEditClass.py`, can be seen in the source code bundle of this book.

9. Treat the preceding code as a header file, and import it into the file from which you will invoke its user interface design.
10. Create another Python file with the name `callLineEditClass.pyw` and import the `LineEditClass.py` code into it:

```
import sys
from PyQt5.QtWidgets import QDialog, QApplication
from LineEditClass import *
class Student:
    name = ""
    def __init__(self, name):
        self.name = name
    def printName(self):
        return self.name
class MyForm(QDialog):
    def __init__(self):
        super().__init__()
        self.ui = Ui_Dialog()
        self.ui.setupUi(self)
self.ui.ButtonClickMe.clicked.connect(self.dispmessage)
        self.show()
    def dispmessage(self):
        studentObj=Student(self.ui.lineEditName.text())
        self.ui.labelResponse.setText("Hello
        "+studentObj.printName())
if __name__=="__main__":
    app = QApplication(sys.argv)
    w = MyForm()
    w.show()
    sys.exit(app.exec_())
```

How it works...

In the `LineEditClass.py` file, a class with the name of the top-level object is created with `Ui_ prepended`. That is, for the top-level object, `Dialog`, the `Ui_Dialog` class is created and stores the interface elements of our widget. That class has two methods, `setupUi()` and `retranslateUi()`. The `setupUi()` method creates the widgets that are used in defining the user interface in Qt Designer. Also, the properties of the widgets are set in this method. The `setupUi()` method takes a single argument, which is the top-level widget of the application, an instance of `QDialog`. The `retranslateUi()` method translates the interface.

In the `callLineEditClass.py` file, you can see that a class is defined called `Student`. The `Student` class includes a class variable called `name` and the following two methods:

- `__init__()`: It is a constructor that takes the mandatory `self` parameter and a `name` parameter, which will be used to initialize the `name` class variable
- `printName`: This method simply returns the value in the name class variable

The `clicked()` event of the **Push Button** widget is connected to the `dispmessage()` method; after entering a name in the **Line Edit** widget, when the user clicks the push button, the `dispmessage()` method will be invoked. The `dispmessage()` method defines the object of the `Student` class by name, `studentObj`, and passes the name entered by the user in the **Line Edit** widget as a parameter. Hence, the constructor of the `Student` class will be invoked and the name entered by the user is passed to the constructor. The name entered in the **Line Edit** widget will be assigned to the class variable, `name`. After that, the **Label** widget called `labelResponse` is set to display the string, `Hello`, and the `printName` method of the `Student` class is invoked, which returns the string assigned to the name variable.

Hence, on clicking the push button, the **Label** widget will be set to display the string, `Hello`, followed by the name entered by the user in the **Line Edit** box, as shown in the following screenshot:

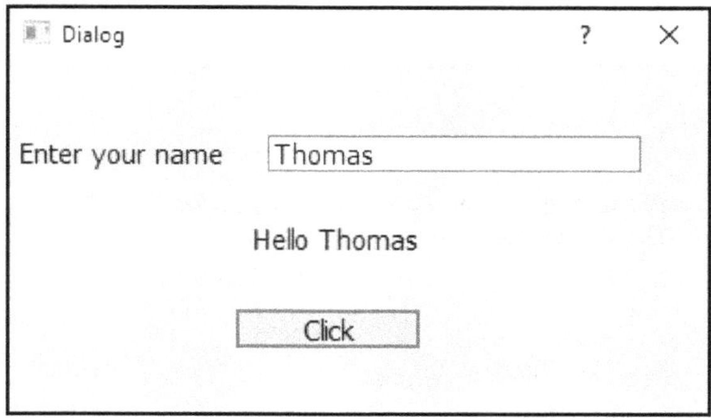

Making the application more elaborate

We can also make use of two or more class attributes in the class.

Let's assume that besides the class name `Student`, we want to also add student's code to the class. In that case, we need to add one more attribute, `code` to the class, and also a `getCode()` method, which will access the student code assigned. Besides the class, the GUI will also change.

We need to add one more **Label** widgets and one **Line Edit** widget to the application and let's save it by another name, `demoStudentClass`. After adding the **Label** and **Line Edit** widgets, the user interface will appear as shown in the following screenshot:

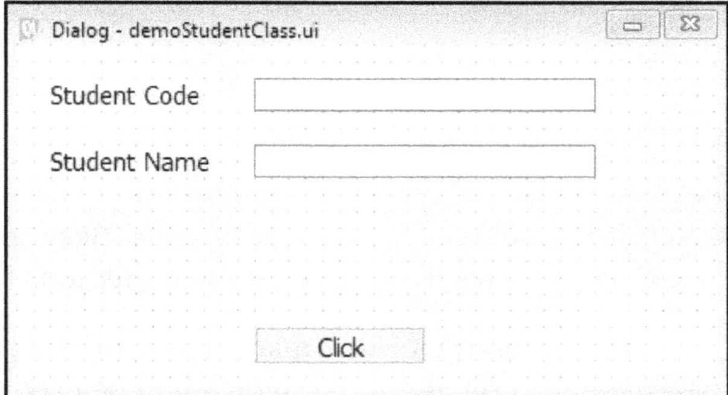

The user interface file, `demoStudentClass.ui`, needs to be converted into Python code. The generated Python script, `demoStudentClass.py`, can be seen in the source code bundle of this book.

Let's create another Python file with the name `callStudentClass.pyw` and import the `demoStudentClass.py` code to it. The code in `callStudentClass.pyw` is as follows:

```
import sys
from PyQt5.QtWidgets import QDialog, QApplication
from demoStudentClass import *
class Student:
    name = ""
    code = ""
    def __init__(self, code, name):
        self.code = code
        self.name = name
    def getCode(self):
        return self.code
    def getName(self):
        return self.name
class MyForm(QDialog):
    def __init__(self):
        super().__init__()
        self.ui = Ui_Dialog()
        self.ui.setupUi(self)
        self.ui.ButtonClickMe.clicked.connect(self.dispmessage)
        self.show()
    def dispmessage(self):
        studentObj=Student(self.ui.lineEditCode.text(),
        self.ui.lineEditName.text())
        self.ui.labelResponse.setText("Code:
        "+studentObj.getCode()+", Name:"+studentObj.getName())
if __name__=="__main__":
    app = QApplication(sys.argv)
    w = MyForm()
    w.show()
    sys.exit(app.exec_())
```

In the preceding code, you see that a class is defined called `Student`. The `Student` class includes the two class variables called `name` and `code`. Besides the two class variables, the `Student` class includes the following three methods too:

- `__init__()`: It is a constructor that takes the mandatory `self` parameter and two parameters, `code` and `name`, which will be used to initialize the two class variables, `code` and `name`

- `getCode()`: This method simply returns the value in the `code` class variable
- `getName()`: This method simply returns the value in the `name` class variable

The `clicked()` event of the **Push Button** widget is connected to the `dispmessage()` method; after entering the code and name in the **Line Edit** widget, when the user clicks the Push Button, the `dispmessage()` method will be invoked. The `dispmessage()` method defines the object of the `Student` class by name, `studentObj`, and passes the code and name entered by the user in the **Line Edit** widgets as parameters. The constructor of the `Student` class, `__init__()`, will be invoked and the code and name entered by the user are passed to it. The code and name entered will be assigned to the class variables code and name, respectively. After that, the **Label** widget called `labelResponse` is set to display the code and name entered by invoking the two methods, `getCode` and `getName`, via the `studentObj` object of the `Student` class.

Hence, on clicking the push button, the **Label** widget will display the code and name entered by the user in two **Line Edit** widgets, as shown in the following screenshot:

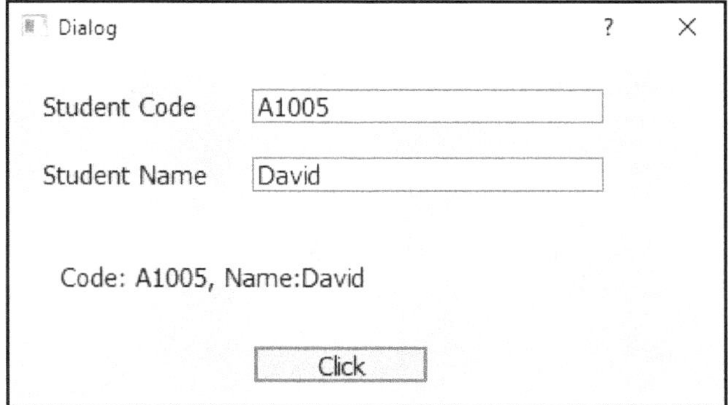

Inheritance

Inheritance is a concept by which the method and variables of an existing class can be reused by another class, without the need for re-coding them. That is, existing code that is tested and run can be reused immediately in other classes.

Types of inheritance

The following are the three types of inheritance:

- **Single inheritance**: One class inherits another class
- **Multilevel inheritance**: One class inherits another class, which in turn is inherited by some other class
- **Multiple inheritance**: One class inherits two or more classes

Using single inheritance

Single inheritance is the simplest type of inheritance, where one class is derived from another single class, as shown in the following diagram:

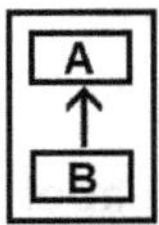

Class **B** inherits class **A**. Here, class **A** will be called the super class or base class, and class **B** will be called the derived class or subclass.

The following statement defines single inheritance where the `Marks` class inherits the `Student` class:

```
class Marks(Student):
```

In the preceding statement, `Student` is the base class and `Marks` is the derived class. Consequently, the instance of the `Marks` class can access the methods and variables of the `Student` class.

Getting ready

To understand the concept of single inheritance through a running example, let's create an application that will prompt the user to enter the code, name, and history and geography marks of a student, and will display them on the click of a button.

The code and name entered by the user will be assigned to the class members of a class called `Student`. The history and geography marks will be assigned to the class members of another class called `Marks`.

To access code and name, along with the history and geography marks, the `Marks` class will inherit the `Student` class. Using inheritance, the instance of the `Marks` class will access and display the code and name of the `Student` class.

How to do it...

Launch Qt Designer and create a new application based on the **Dialog without Buttons** template by performing the following steps:

1. In the application, drag and drop five **Label** widgets, four **Line Edit** widgets, and one **Push Button** widget onto the form.
2. Set the **text** property of the four **Label** widgets to `Student Code`, `Student Name`, `History Marks`, and `Geography Marks`.
3. Delete the **text** property of the fifth **Label** widget, as its **text** property will be set through the code to display the code, name, and history and geography marks.
4. Set the **text** property of the **Push Button** widget to `Click`.
5. Set the **objectName** property of the four **Line Edit** widgets to `lineEditCode`, `lineEditName`, `lineEditHistoryMarks`, and `lineEditGeographyMarks`.
6. Set the **objectName** property of the **Label** widget to `labelResponse` and the **objectName** property of the **Push Button** widget to `ButtonClickMe`.
7. Save the application with the name `demoSimpleInheritance.ui`. The application will appear as shown in the following screenshot:

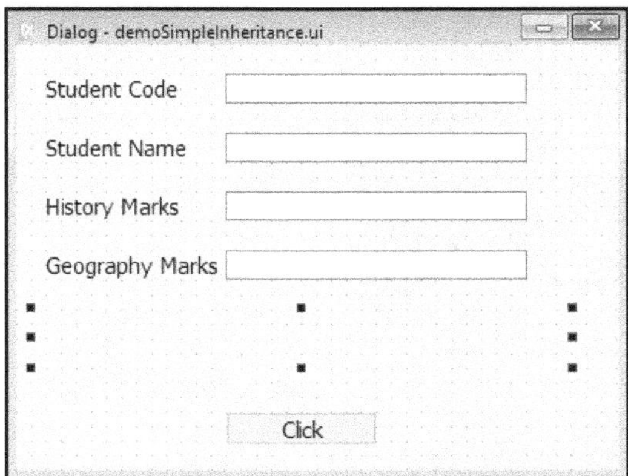

The user interface file, `demoSimpleInheritance.ui`, is an XML file and is converted into Python code using the `pyuic5` utility. You can find the generated Python script, `demoSimpleInheritance.py`, in the source code bundle of this book. The preceding code will be used as a header file, and will be imported in another Python script file, which will invoke the user interface design defined in, `demoSimpleInheritance.py` file.

8. Create another Python file with the name `callSimpleInheritance.pyw` and import the `demoSimpleInheritance.py` code into it. The code in the Python script, `callSimpleInheritance.pyw`, is as given here:

```
import sys
from PyQt5.QtWidgets import QDialog, QApplication
from demoSimpleInheritance import *
class Student:
    name = ""
    code = ""
    def __init__(self, code, name):
        self.code = code
        self.name = name
    def getCode(self):
        return self.code
    def getName(self):
        return self.name
class Marks(Student):
    historyMarks = 0
    geographyMarks = 0
    def __init__(self, code, name, historyMarks,
    geographyMarks):
        Student.__init__(self,code,name)
        self.historyMarks = historyMarks
        self.geographyMarks = geographyMarks
    def getHistoryMarks(self):
        return self.historyMarks
    def getGeographyMarks(self):
        return self.geographyMarks
class MyForm(QDialog):
    def __init__(self):
        super().__init__()
        self.ui = Ui_Dialog()
        self.ui.setupUi(self)
self.ui.ButtonClickMe.clicked.connect(self.dispmessage)
        self.show()
    def dispmessage(self):
        marksObj=Marks(self.ui.lineEditCode.text(),
        self.ui.lineEditName.text(),
```

```
            self.ui.lineEditHistoryMarks.text(),
            self.ui.lineEditGeographyMarks.text())
            self.ui.labelResponse.setText("Code:
            "+marksObj.getCode()+", Name:"+marksObj.getName()+"
            nHistory Marks:"+marksObj.getHistoryMarks()+",
Geography
            Marks:"+marksObj.getGeographyMarks())
if __name__=="__main__":
    app = QApplication(sys.argv)
    w = MyForm()
    w.show()
    sys.exit(app.exec_())
```

How it works...

In this code, you see that a class is defined, called `Student`. The `Student` class includes two class variables called `name` and `code`, along with the following three methods:

- `__init__()`: It is a constructor that takes the mandatory `self` parameter and two parameters, `code` and `name`, that will be used to initialize the two class variables, `code` and `name`
- `getCode()`: This method simply returns the value in the `code` class variable
- `getName()`: This method simply returns the value in the `name` class variable

The `Marks` class inherits the `Student` class. Consequently, an instance of the `Marks` class will not only be able to access its own members, but also that of the `Student` class.

The `Marks` class includes two class variables called `historyMarks` and `geographyMarks`, along with the following three methods:

- `__init__()`: It is a constructor that takes the mandatory `self` parameter and four parameters, `code`, `name`, `historyMarks`, and `geographyMarks`. From this constructor, the constructor of the `Student` class will be invoked and the `code` and `name` parameters will be passed to this constructor. The `historyMarks` and `geographyMarks` parameters will be used to initialize the class members, `historyMarks`, and `geographyMarks`.

- `getHistoryMarks()`: This method simply returns the value in the `historyMarks` class variable.
- `getGeographyMarks()`: This method simply returns the value in the `geographyMarks` class variable.

The `clicked()` event of the Push Button is connected to the `dispmessage()` method. After entering the code, name, and history and geography marks in the **Line Edit** widgets, when the user clicks the push button, the `dispmessage()` method will be invoked. The `dispmessage()` method defines the object of the `Marks` class by name, `marksObj`, and passes the code, name, and history and geography marks entered by the user in the **Line Edit** widgets as parameters. The constructor of the `Marks` class, `__init__()`, will be invoked and the code, name, history, and geography marks entered by the user are passed to it. From the constructor of the `Marks` class, the constructor of the `Student` class will be invoked and `code` and `name` will be passed to that constructor. The `code` and `name` parameters will be assigned to the `code` and `name` class variables, respectively, of the `Student` class.

Similarly, the history and geography marks will be assigned to `historyMarks` and `geographyMarks` class variables, respectively, of the `Marks` class. After that, the **Label** widget called `labelResponse` is set to display the code, name, and history and geography marks entered by invoking the four methods, `getCode`, `getName`, `getHistoryMarks`, and `getGeographyMarks`, via the `marksObj` object. The `marksObj` object of the `Marks` class gets the right to access the `getCode` and `getName` methods of the `Student` class because of using inheritance.

Hence, on clicking the push button, the **Label** widget will display the code, name, history marks, and geography marks entered by the user via the **Label** widget called `labelResponse`, as shown in this screenshot:

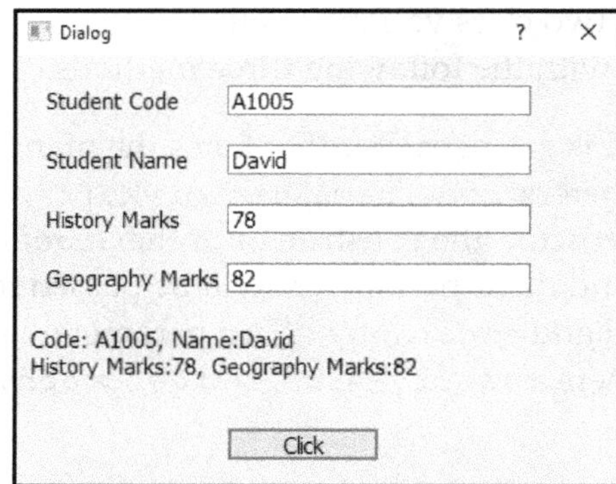

Using multilevel inheritance

Multilevel inheritance is where one class inherits another single class. The inheriting class in turn is inherited by a third class, as shown in the following diagram:

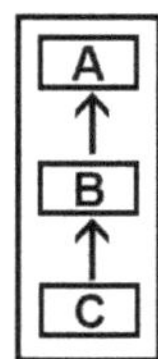

In the preceding diagram, you can see that class **B** inherits class **A** and class **C**, in turn, inherits class **B**.

The following statement defines multilevel inheritance, where the `Result` class inherits the `Marks` class and the `Marks` class, in turn, inherits the `Student` class:

```
class Student:
    class Marks(Student):
        class Result(Marks):
```

In the preceding statement, `Student` is the base class and the `Marks` class inherits the `Student` class. The `Result` class inherits the `Marks` class. Consequently, the instance of the `Result` class can access the methods and variables of the `Marks` class, and the instance of the `Marks` class can access the methods and variables of the `Student` class.

Getting ready

To understand the concept of multilevel inheritance, let's create an application that will prompt the user to enter the code, name, history marks, and geography marks of a student and will display the total marks and percentage on the click of a button. The total marks will be the sum of history marks and geography marks. Assuming the maximum mark is 100, the formula for computing the percentage is: total marks/200 * 100.

The code and name entered by the user will be assigned to the class members of a class called `Student`. The history and geography marks will be assigned to the class members of another class called `Marks`.

To access code and name along with the history and geography marks, the `Marks` class will inherit the `Student` class.

Using this multilevel inheritance, the instance of the `Marks` class will access the code and name of the `Student` class. To calculate total marks and percentage, one more class is used, called the `Result` class. The `Result` class will inherit the `Marks` class. Consequently, the instance of the `Result` class can access the class members of the `Marks` class, as well as those of the `Student` class. The `Result` class has two class members, `totalMarks` and `percentage`. The `totalMarks` class member will be assigned the sum of the `historyMarks` and `geographyMarks` members of the `Marks` class. The percentage member will be assigned the percentage acquired on the basis of the history and geography marks.

How to do it...

In all, there are three classes, named `Student`, `Marks`, and `Result`, where the `Result` class will inherit the `Marks` class and the `Marks` class, in turn, will inherit the `Student` class. Consequently, the members of the `Result` class can access the class members of the `Marks` class as well as those of the `Student` class. Here is the step-by-step procedure to create this application:

1. Launch Qt Designer and create a new application based on the **Dialog without Buttons** template.
2. Drag and drop six **Label** widgets, six **Line Edit** widgets, and one **Push Button** widget onto the form.
3. Set the **text** property of the six **Label** widgets to `Student Code`, `Student Name`, `History Marks`, `Geography Marks`, `Total`, and `Percentage`.
4. Set the **text** property of the **Push Button** widget to `Click`.
5. Set the **objectName** property of the six **Line Edit** widgets to `lineEditCode`, `lineEditName`, `lineEditHistoryMarks`, `lineEditGeographyMarks`, `lineEditTotal`, and `lineEditPercentage`.
6. Set the **objectName** property of the **Push Button** widget to `ButtonClickMe`.
7. Disable the `lineEditTotal` and `lineEditPercentage` boxes by unchecking the **Enable** property from the **Property Editor** window. The `lineEditTotal` and `lineEditPercentage` widgets are disabled because values in these boxes will be assigned through the code and we don't want their values to be altered by the user.

8. Save the application with the name `demoMultilevelInheritance.ui`. The application will appear as shown in the following screenshot:

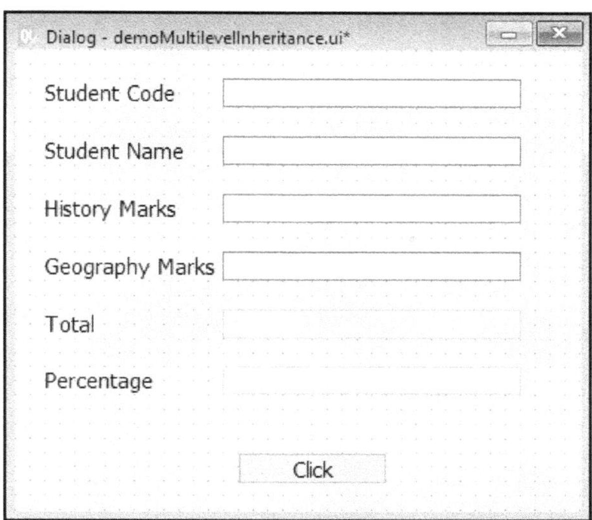

The user interface file, `demoMultilevelInheritance.ui`, is an XML file and is converted into Python code by making use of the `pyuic5` utility. You can see the generated Python script, `demoMultilevelInheritance.py`, in the source code bundle of this book. The `demoMultilevelInheritance.py` file will be used as a header file, and will be imported in another Python script file, which will use the GUI created in `demoMultilevelInheritance.py`.

9. Create another Python file with the name `callMultilevelInheritance.pyw` and import the `demoMultilevelInheritance.py` code into it. The code in the Python script, `callMultilevelInheritance.pyw`, is as shown here:

```
import sys
from PyQt5.QtWidgets import QDialog, QApplication
from demoMultilevelInheritance import *
class Student:
    name = ""
    code = ""
    def __init__(self, code, name):
        self.code = code
        self.name = name
    def getCode(self):
```

```
        return self.code
    def getName(self):
        return self.name
class Marks(Student):
    historyMarks = 0
    geographyMarks = 0
    def __init__(self, code, name, historyMarks,
    geographyMarks):
        Student.__init__(self,code,name)
        self.historyMarks = historyMarks
        self.geographyMarks = geographyMarks
    def getHistoryMarks(self):
        return self.historyMarks
    def getGeographyMarks(self):
        return self.geographyMarks
class Result(Marks):
    totalMarks = 0
    percentage = 0
    def __init__(self, code, name, historyMarks,
    geographyMarks):
        Marks.__init__(self, code, name, historyMarks,
        geographyMarks)
        self.totalMarks = historyMarks + geographyMarks
        self.percentage = (historyMarks +
        geographyMarks) / 200 * 100
    def getTotalMarks(self):
        return self.totalMarks
    def getPercentage(self):
        return self.percentage
class MyForm(QDialog):
    def __init__(self):
        super().__init__()
        self.ui = Ui_Dialog()
        self.ui.setupUi(self)
self.ui.ButtonClickMe.clicked.connect(self.dispmessage)
        self.show()
    def dispmessage(self):
        resultObj=Result(self.ui.lineEditCode.text(),
        self.ui.lineEditName.text(),
        int(self.ui.lineEditHistoryMarks.text()),
        int(self.ui.lineEditGeographyMarks.text()))
        self.ui.lineEditTotal.setText(str(resultObj.
        getTotalMarks()))
        self.ui.lineEditPercentage.setText(str(resultObj.
        getPercentage()))
if __name__=="__main__":
    app = QApplication(sys.argv)
    w = MyForm()
```

```
        w.show()
        sys.exit(app.exec_())
```

How it works...

In the preceding code, in the `callMultilevelInheritance.pyw` file, you can see that a class is defined called `Student`. The `Student` class includes two class variables called `name` and `code`, along with the following three methods:

- `__init__()`: It is a constructor that takes the mandatory `self` parameter and two parameters, `code`, and `name`, that will be used to initialize the two class variables `code` and `name`
- `getCode()`: This method simply returns the value in the `code` class variable
- `getName()`: This method simply returns the value in the `name` class variable

The `Marks` class inherits the `Student` class. Consequently, an instance of the `Marks` class will not only be able to access its own members, but also those of the `Student` class.

The `Marks` class includes two class variables called `historyMarks` and `geographyMarks`, along with the following three methods:

- `__init__()`: It is a constructor that takes the mandatory `self` parameter and four parameters, `code`, `name`, `historyMarks`, and `geographyMarks`. From this constructor, the constructor of the `Student` class will be invoked and the `code` and `name` parameters will be passed to this constructor. The `historyMarks` and `geographyMarks` parameters will be used to initialize the `historyMarks` and `geographyMarks` class members.
- `getHistoryMarks()`: This method simply returns the value in the `historyMarks` class variable.
- `getGeographyMarks()`: This method simply returns the value in the `geographyMarks` class variable.

The `Result` class inherits the `Marks` class. An instance of the `Result` class will not only be able to access its own members, but also those of the `Marks` class and of the `Student` class too.

The `Result` class includes two class variables, called `totalMarks` and `percentage`, along with the following three methods:

- `__init__()`: It is a constructor that takes the mandatory `self` parameter and four parameters, `code`, `name`, `historyMarks`, and `geographyMarks`. From this constructor, the constructor of the `Marks` class will be invoked and the `code`, `name`, `historyMarks`, and `geographyMarks` parameters will be passed to that constructor. The sum of `historyMarks` and `geographyMarks` will be assigned to the `totalMarks` class variable. Assuming the maximum mark for each is 100, the percentage of the history and geography marks will be computed and assigned to the percentage class variable.
- `getTotalMarks()`: This method simply returns the sum of the `historyMarks` and `geographyMarks` class variables.
- `getPercentage()`: This method simply returns the percentage of the history and geography marks.

The `clicked()` event of the **Push Button** widget is connected to the `dispmessage()` method. After entering code, name, history marks, and geography marks in the **Line Edit** widgets, when the user clicks the push button, the `dispmessage()` method will be invoked. The `dispmessage()` method defines the object of the `Result` class by name, `resultObj`, and passes the code, name, history, and geography marks entered by the user in the **Line Edit** widgets as parameters. The constructor of the `Result` class, `__init__()`, will be invoked and the code, name, history marks, and geography marks entered by the user are passed to it. From the `Result` class's constructor, the `Marks` class's constructor will be invoked and code, name, history marks, and geography marks will be passed to that constructor. From the `Marks` class's constructor, the `Student` class constructor will be invoked and the `code` and `name` parameters are passed to it. In the `Student` class's constructor, the `code` and `name` parameters will be assigned to the class variables `code` and `name`, respectively. Similarly, the history and geography marks will be assigned to the `historyMarks` and `geographyMarks` class variables, respectively, of the `Marks` class.

The sum of `historyMarks` and `geographyMarks` will be assigned to the `totalMarks` class variable. Also, the percentage of the history and geography marks will be computed and assigned to the `percentage` class variable.

After that, the **Line Edit** widget called `lineEditTotal` is set to display the total marks, that is, the sum of history and geography marks, by invoking the `getTotalMarks` method via `resultObj`. Also, the **Line Edit** widget called `lineEditPercentage` is set to display the percentage of marks by invoking the `getPercentage` method via `resultObj`.

Hence, on clicking the push button, the **Line Edit** widgets called `lineEditTotal` and `lineEditPercentage` will display the total marks and percentage of history and geography marks entered by the user, as shown in the following screenshot:

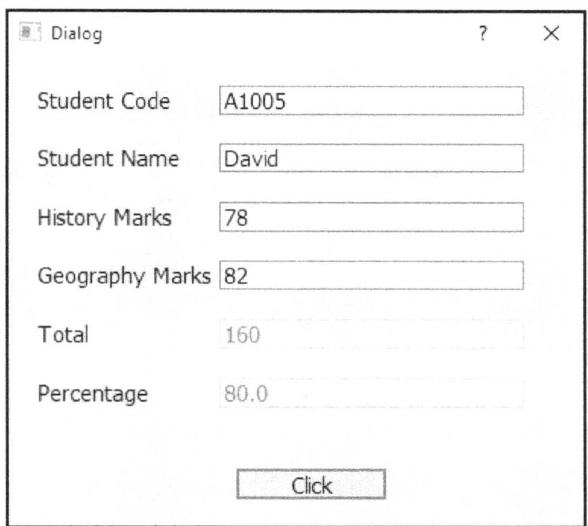

Using multiple inheritance

Multiple inheritance is where one class inherits two or more classes, as shown in the following diagram:

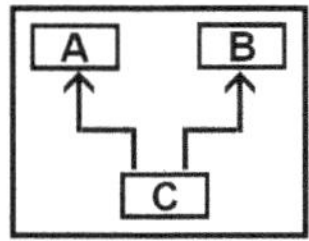

Class **C** inherits both classes, class **A** and class **B**.

The following statement defines multilevel inheritance where the `Result` class inherits the `Marks` class and the `Marks` class in turn inherits the `Student` class:

```
class Student:
    class Marks:
        class Result(Student, Marks):
```

In the preceding statements, `Student` and `Marks` are the base classes and the `Result` class inherits both the `Student` class and the `Marks` class. Consequently, the instance of the `Result` class can access the methods and variables of the `Marks` and `Student` classes.

Getting ready

To understand the concept of multilevel inheritance practically, let's create an application that will prompt the user to enter the code, name, history marks, and geography marks of a student, and will display the total marks and percentage on the click of a button. The total marks will be the sum of history marks and geography marks. Assuming the maximum mark for each is 100, the formula for computing the percentage is: total marks/200 * 100.

The code and name entered by the user will be assigned to the class members of a class called `Student`. The history and geography marks will be assigned to the class members of another class called `Marks`.

To access code and name, along with the history and geography marks, the `Result` class will inherit both classes, the `Student` class as well as the `Marks` class. Using this multiple inheritance, the instance of the `Result` class can access the code and name of the `Student` class, as well as the `historyMarks` and `geographyMarks` class variables of the `Marks` class. In other words, using multiple inheritance, the instance of the `Result` class can access the class members of the `Marks` class, as well as those of the `Student` class. The `Result` class has two class members, `totalMarks` and `percentage`. The `totalMarks` class member will be assigned the sum of the `historyMarks` and `geographyMarks` members of the `Marks` class. The percentage member will be assigned the percentage acquired on the basis of the history and geography marks.

How to do it...

Let's understand through a step-by-step procedure how multilevel inheritance is applied to three classes, `Student`, `Marks`, and `Result`. The `Result` class will inherit both classes, `Student` and `Marks`. These steps explain how the members of the `Result` class can access the class members of the `Student` and `Marks` classes through multilevel inheritance:

1. Launch Qt Designer and create a new application based on the **Dialog without Buttons** template.
2. In the application, drag and drop six **Label** widgets, six **Line Edit** widgets, and one **Push Button** widget onto the form.
3. Set the **text** property of the six **Label** widgets to `Student Code`, `Student Name`, `History Marks`, `Geography Marks`, `Total`, and `Percentage`.
4. Set the **text** property of the **Push Button** widget to `Click`.
5. Set the **objectName** property of the six **Line Edit** widgets to `lineEditCode`, `lineEditName`, `lineEditHistoryMarks`, `lineEditGeographyMarks`, `lineEditTotal`, and `lineEditPercentage`.
6. Set the **objectName** property of the **Push Button** widget to `ButtonClickMe`.
7. Disable the `lineEditTotal` and `lineEditPercentage` boxes by unchecking the **Enable** property from the **Property Editor** window. The `lineEditTotal` and `lineEditPercentage` boxes are disabled because values in these boxes will be assigned through the code, and we don't want their values to be altered by the user.

8. Save the application with the name `demoMultipleInheritance.ui`. The application will appear as shown in the following screenshot:

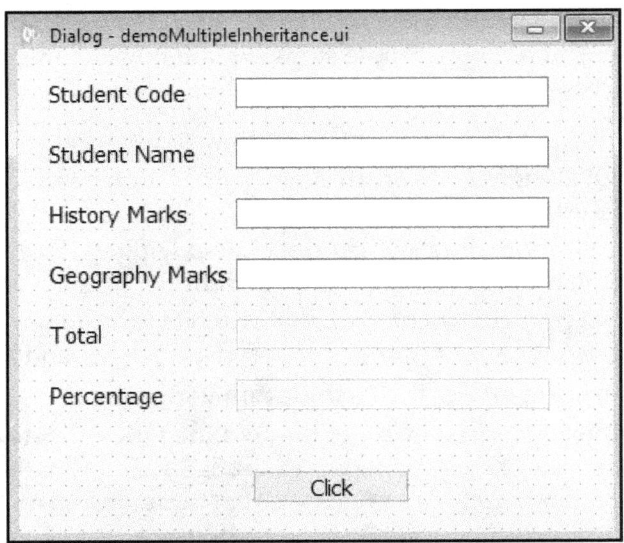

The user interface file `demoMultipleInheritance .ui` is an XML file and is converted into Python code using the `pyuic5` utility. You can find the generated Python code, `demoMultipleInheritance.py`, in the source code bundle of this book. The `demoMultipleInheritance.py` file will be used as a header file and will be imported in another Python script file, which will invoke the GUI created in the `demoMultipleInheritance.py` file.

9. Create another Python file with the name `callMultipleInheritance.pyw` and import the `demoMultipleInheritance.py` code into it:

```
import sys
from PyQt5.QtWidgets import QDialog, QApplication
from demoMultipleInheritance import *
class Student:
    name = ""
    code = ""
    def __init__(self, code, name):
        self.code = code
        self.name = name
    def getCode(self):
```

```
        return self.code
    def getName(self):
        return self.name
class Marks:
    historyMarks = 0
    geographyMarks = 0
    def __init__(self, historyMarks, geographyMarks):
        self.historyMarks = historyMarks
        self.geographyMarks = geographyMarks
    def getHistoryMarks(self):
        return self.historyMarks
    def getGeographyMarks(self):
        return self.geographyMarks
class Result(Student, Marks):
    totalMarks = 0
    percentage = 0
    def __init__(self, code, name, historyMarks,
    geographyMarks):
        Student.__init__(self, code, name)
        Marks.__init__(self, historyMarks, geographyMarks)
        self.totalMarks = historyMarks + geographyMarks
        self.percentage = (historyMarks +
        geographyMarks) / 200 * 100
    def getTotalMarks(self):
        return self.totalMarks
    def getPercentage(self):
        return self.percentage
class MyForm(QDialog):
    def __init__(self):
        super().__init__()
        self.ui = Ui_Dialog()
        self.ui.setupUi(self)
self.ui.ButtonClickMe.clicked.connect(self.dispmessage)
        self.show()
    def dispmessage(self):
        resultObj=Result(self.ui.lineEditCode.text(),
        self.ui.lineEditName.text(),
        int(self.ui.lineEditHistoryMarks.text()),
        int(self.ui.lineEditGeographyMarks.text()))
        self.ui.lineEditTotal.setText(str(resultObj.
        getTotalMarks()))
        self.ui.lineEditPercentage.setText(str(resultObj.
        getPercentage()))
if __name__=="__main__":
    app = QApplication(sys.argv)
    w = MyForm()
    w.show()
    sys.exit(app.exec_())
```

How it works...

In this code, you can see that a class is defined called `Student`. The `Student` class includes two class variables called `name` and `code`, along with the following three methods:

- `__init__()`: It is a constructor that takes the mandatory `self` parameter and two parameters, `code` and `name`, that will be used to initialize the two class variables `code` and `name`
- `getCode()`: This method simply returns the value in the `code` class variable
- `getName()`: This method simply returns the value in the `name` class variable

The `Marks` class includes two class variables, called `historyMarks` and `geographyMarks`, along with the following three methods:

- `__init__()`: It is a constructor that takes the mandatory `self` parameter and two parameters, `historyMarks` and `geographyMarks`. The `historyMarks` and `geographyMarks` parameters will be used to initialize the `historyMarks` and `geographyMarks` class members.
- `getHistoryMarks()`: This method simply returns the value in the `historyMarks` class variable.
- `getGeographyMarks()`: This method simply returns the value in the `geographyMarks` class variable.

The `Result` class inherits the `Student` class as well as the `Marks` class. An instance of the `Result` class will not only be able to access its own members, but also those of the `Marks` class and of the `Student` class too.

The `Result` class includes two class variables called `totalMarks` and `percentage`, along with the following three methods:

- `__init__()`: It is a constructor that takes the mandatory `self` parameter and four parameters, `code`, `name`, `historyMarks`, and `geographyMarks`. From this constructor, the `Student` class constructor will be invoked and the `code` and `name` parameters will be passed to that constructor. Also, from this constructor, the `Marks` class constructor will be invoked and the `historyMarks` and `geographyMarks` parameters will be passed to that constructor. The sum of `historyMarks` and `geographyMarks` will be assigned to the `totalMarks` class variable. Assuming the maximum mark for each is 100, the percentage of the history and geography marks will be computed and assigned to the `percentage` class variable.
- `getTotalMarks()`: This method simply returns the sum of the `historyMarks` and `geography` class variables.
- `getPercentage()`: This method simply returns the percentage of history and geography marks.

The `clicked()` event of the **Push Button** widget is connected to the `dispmessage()` method. After entering code, name, history marks, and geography marks in the **Line Edit** widgets, when the user clicks the push button, the `dispmessage()` method will be invoked. The `dispmessage()` method defines the object of the `Result` class by name, `resultObj`, and passes the code, name, history marks, and geography marks entered by the user in the **Line Edit** widgets as parameters. The constructor of the `Result` class, `__init__()`, will be invoked and the code, name, history marks, and geography marks entered by the user are passed to it. From the `Result` class's constructor, the `Student` class constructor and the `Marks` class constructor will be invoked. The code and name will be passed to the `Student` class constructor, and history and geography marks will be passed to the `Marks` class constructor.

In the `Student` class constructor, the code and name will be assigned to the `code` and `name` class variables, respectively. Similarly, in the `Marks` class constructor, the history and geography marks will be assigned to the `historyMarks` and `geographyMarks` class variables, respectively, of the `Marks` class.

The sum of `historyMarks` and `geographyMarks` will be assigned to the `totalMarks` class variable. Also, the percentage of the history and geography marks will be computed and assigned to the `percentage` class variable.

After that, the **Line Edit** widget called `lineEditTotal` is set to display the total marks, that is, the sum of the history and geography marks, by invoking the `getTotalMarks` method via `resultObj`. Also, the **Line Edit** widget called `lineEditPercentage` is set to display the percentage of marks by invoking the `getPercentage` method via `resultObj`.

Hence, on clicking the push button, the **Line Edit** widgets called `lineEditTotal` and `lineEditPercentage` will display the total marks and percentage of the history and geography marks entered by the user, as shown in the following screenshot:

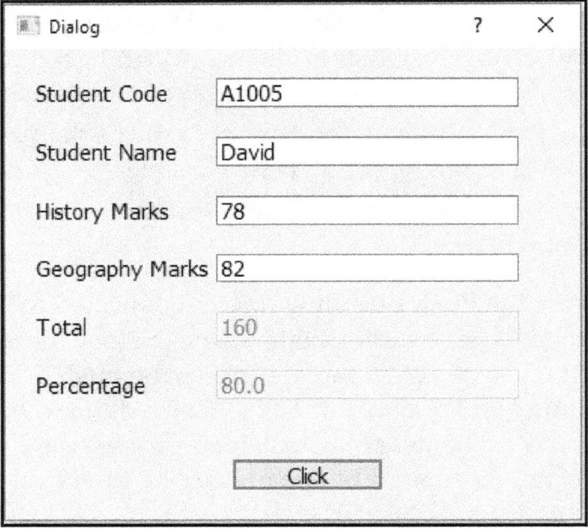

16
Understanding Dialogs

In this chapter, we will learn how to use the following types of dialog:

- The input dialog box
- Using the input dialog
- Using the color dialog
- Using the font dialog
- Using the file dialog

Introduction

Dialogs are required in all applications to get input from the user, and also to guide the user to enter the correct data. Interactive dialogs make the application quite user-friendly too. There are basically the following two types of dialog:

- **Modal dialog**: A modal dialog is a dialog that wants the user to enter mandatory information. This type of dialog doesn't allow the user to use other parts of the application until the modal dialog is closed. That is, the user needs to enter the required information in the modal dialog, and after closing the dialog, the user can access the rest of the application.
- **Non-modal or modeless dialogs**: These are dialogs that enable the user to interact with the rest of the application and dialog box too. That is, the user can continue interacting with the rest of the application while keeping the modeless dialog open. That is why modeless dialogs are usually used for getting non-essential or non-critical information from the user.

The input dialog box

An input dialog box is with the help of the `QInputDialog` class. The `QInputDialog` class provides a dialog to get a single value from the user. The provided input dialog consists of a text field and two buttons, **OK** and **Cancel**. The text field enables us to get a single value from the user, where that single value can be a string, a number, or an item from a list. The following are the methods provided by the `QInputDialog` class to accept different types of input from the user:

- `getInt()`: This method shows a spin box for accepting an integer number. To get an integer from the user, you need to use the following syntax:

  ```
  getInt(self, window title, label before LineEdit widget,
  default value, minimum, maximum and step size)
  ```

  Take a look at the following example:

  ```
  quantity, ok = QInputDialog.getInt(self, "Order Quantity",
  "Enter quantity:", 2, 1, 100, 1)
  ```

  The preceding code prompts the user to enter quantity. If the user does not enter any value, the default value `2` will be assigned to the `quantity` variable. The user can enter any value between `1` and `100`.

- `getDouble()`: This method shows a spin box with a floating point number to accept fractional values. To get a fractional value from the user, you need to use the following syntax:

  ```
  getDouble(self, window title, label before LineEdit widget,
  default value, minimum, maximum and number of decimal places
  desired)
  ```

  Take a look at the following example:

  ```
  price, ok = QInputDialog.getDouble(self, "Price of the
  product", "Enter price:", 1.50,0, 100, 2)
  ```

  The preceding code prompts the user to enter the price of the product. If the user does not enters any value, the default value `1.50` will be assigned to the `price` variable. The user can enter any value between `0` and `100`.

- `getText()`: This method shows a **Line Edit** widget to accept text from the user. To get text from the user, you need to use the following syntax:

  ```
  getText(self, window title, label before LineEdit widget)
  ```

  Take a look at the following example:

  ```
  name, ok = QtGui.QInputDialog.getText(self, 'Get Customer
  Name', 'Enter your name:')
  ```

  The preceding code will display an input dialog box with the title, **Get Customer Name**. The dialog box will also display a **Line Edit** widget allowing user to enter some text. A **Label** widget will also be displayed before the **Line Edit** widget showing the text, **Enter your name:**. The customer's name, entered in the dialog box will be assigned to the `name` variable.

- `getItem()`: This method shows a combo box displaying several items to choose from. To get an item from a drop-down box, you need to use the following syntax:

  ```
  getItem(self, window title, label before combo box, array ,
  current item, Boolean Editable)
  ```

  Here, `array` is the list of items that need to be displayed in the combo box. The `current item` is the item that is treated as the current item in the combo box. `Editable` is the Boolean value, which, if set to `True`, means the user can edit the combo box and enter their own text. When `Editable` is set to `False`, it means the user can only select an item from the combo box but cannot edit items. Take a look at the following example:

  ```
  countryName, ok = QInputDialog.getItem(self, "Input Dialog",
  "List of countries", countries, 0, False)
  ```

  The preceding code will display an input dialog with the title **Input Dialog**. The dialog box shows a combo box showing a list of countries that are displayed via the elements from the countries array. The **Label** widget before the combo box shows the text, **List of countries**. The selected country name from the combo box will be assigned to the `countryName` variable. Users can only choose the country from the combo box but cannot edit any country name from the combo box.

Using the input dialog

The input dialog can accept data of any type, including integer, double, and text. In this recipe, we will learn to get text from the user. We will make use of an input dialog to know the name of the country in which the user lives.

The input dialog box will display a combo box showing different country names. On choosing a country by name, the chosen country name will appear in the textbox.

How to do it...

Let's create a new application based on the **Dialog without Buttons** template by performing the following steps:

1. Since the application will prompt the user to choose the country that he/she lives, via input dialog, so drag and drop one **Label** widget, one **Line Edit** widget, and one **Push Button** widget onto the form.
2. Set the **text** property of the **Label** widget to `Your Country`.
3. Set the **text** property of the **Push Button** widget to `Choose Country`.
4. Set the **objectName** property of the **Line Edit** widget to `lineEditCountry`.
5. Set the **objectName** property of the **Push Button** widget to `pushButtonCountry`.
6. Save the application with the name `demoInputDialog.ui`.

The form will now look as follows:

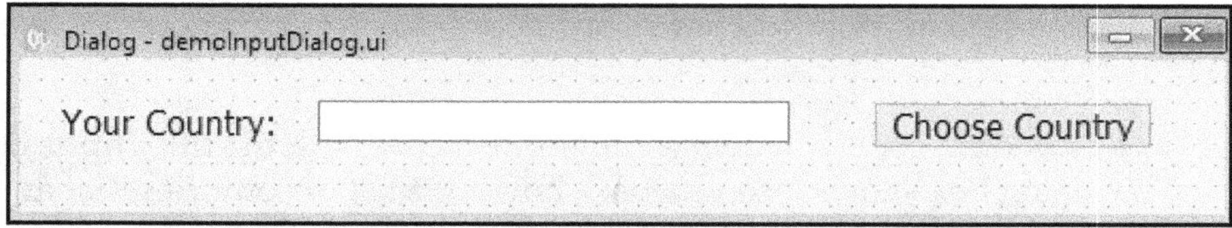

The user interface created with Qt Designer is stored in a `.ui` file, which is an XML file and needs converting to Python code.

7. To do the conversion, you need to open a Command Prompt window, navigate to the folder where the file is saved, and issue the following command line:

```
C:\Pythonbook\PyQt5>pyuic5 demoInputDialog.ui -o
demoInputDialog.py
```

You can find the generated Python script, `demoInputDialog.py`, in the source code bundle of this book.

8. Treat the `demoInputDialog.py` script as a header file, and import it to the file from which you will invoke its user interface design.
9. Create another Python file with the name `callInputDialog.pyw` and import the `demoInputDialog.py` code into it:

```
import sys
from PyQt5.QtWidgets import QDialog, QApplication,
QInputDialog
from demoInputDialog import *
class MyForm(QDialog):
    def __init__(self):
        super().__init__()
        self.ui = Ui_Dialog()
        self.ui.setupUi(self)
self.ui.pushButtonCountry.clicked.connect(self.dispmessage)
        self.show()
    def dispmessage(self):
        countries = ("Albania", "Algeria", "Andorra",
"Angola",
        "Antigua and Barbuda", "Argentina", "Armenia",
"Aruba",
        "Australia", "Austria", "Azerbaijan")
        countryName, ok = QInputDialog.getItem(self, "Input
        Dialog", "List of countries", countries, 0, False)
        if ok and countryName:
            self.ui.lineEditCountry.setText(countryName)
if __name__=="__main__":
    app = QApplication(sys.argv)
    w = MyForm()
    w.show()
    sys.exit(app.exec_())
```

How it works...

In the `demoInputDialog.py` file, a class with the name of the top-level object is created with `Ui_ prepended`. That is, for the top-level object, **Dialog**, the `Ui_Dialog` class is created and stores the interface elements of our widget. That class has two methods, `setupUi()` and `retranslateUi()`.

The `setupUi()` method creates the widgets that are used in defining the user interface in Qt Designer. Also, the properties of the widgets are set in this method. The `setupUi()` method takes a single argument, which is the top-level widget of the application, an instance of `QDialog`. The `retranslateUi()` method translates the interface.

In the `callInputDialog.pyw` file, you can see that the click event of the **Push Button** widget is connected to the `dispmessage()` method that is used to select the country; when the user clicks the push button, the `dispmessage()` method will be invoked. The `dispmessage()` method defines a string array called countries that contains several country names in the form of array elements. After that, the `getItem` method of the `QInputDialog` class is invoked and opens up an input dialog box displaying a combo box. When the user clicks the combo box, it will expand, showing the country names that are assigned to the `countries` string array. When the user selects a country, followed by clicking the **OK** button in the dialog box, the selected country name will be assigned to the `countryName` variable. The selected country name will then be displayed through the **Line Edit** widget.

On running the application, you get an empty **Line Edit** widget and a push button, **Choose Country**, as shown in the following screenshot:

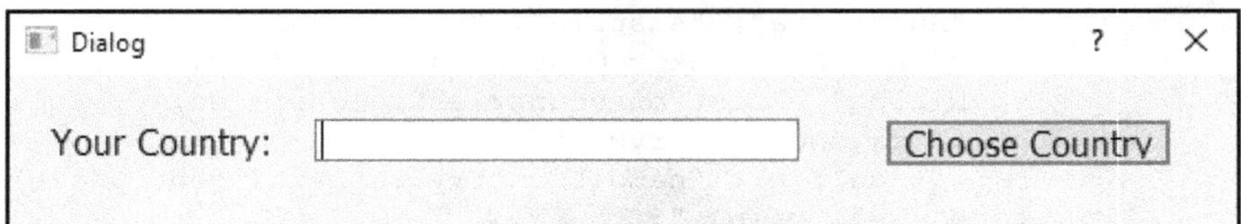

On clicking the **Choose Country** button, the input dialog box will open, as shown in the following screenshot. The input dialog shows a combo box along with two buttons, **OK** and **Cancel**. On clicking the combo box, it will expand to show all the country names, as shown in the following screenshot:

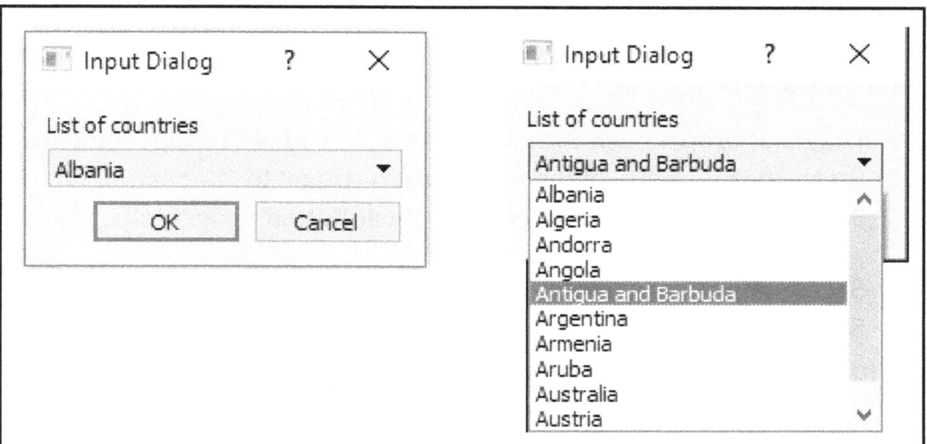

After choosing a country name from the combo box, followed by clicking the **OK** button, the chosen country name will be displayed in the **Line Edit** box, as shown in the following screenshot:

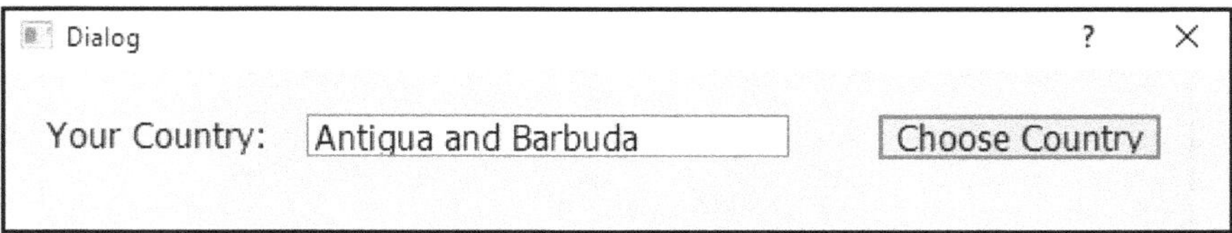

Using the color dialog

In this recipe, we will learn to use color dialog to display a color palette, allowing users to select predefined colors from the palette or create a new custom color.

The application includes a frame, and when the user selects any color from the color dialog, the chosen color will be applied to the frame. Besides this, the hex code of the selected color will also be displayed via a **Label** widget.

In this recipe, we will be making use of the `QColorDialog` class, which provides a dialog widget for selecting color values.

How to do it...

Let's create a new application based on the **Dialog without Buttons** template by performing the following steps:

1. Drag and drop a **Push Button**, a **Frame**, and a **Label** widget onto the form.
2. Set the **text** property of the **Push Button** widget to `Choose color`.
3. Set the **objectName** property of the **Push Button** widget to `pushButtonColor`.
4. Set the **objectName** property of the **Frame** widget to `frameColor`.
5. Set the **Label** widget to `labelColor`.
6. Save the application with the name `demoColorDialog.ui`.

   The form will now look as follows:

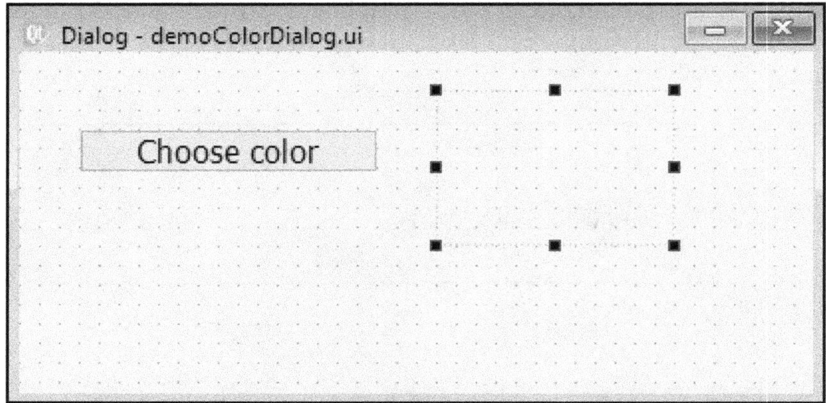

The user interface created with Qt Designer is stored in a `.ui` file, which is an XML file. You can use `pyuic5` utility to convert the XML file into Python code. The generated Python script, `demoColorDialog.py`, can be seen in the source code bundle of this book. The `demoColorDialog.py` script will be used as a header file, and will be imported in another Python script file, which will invoke this user interface design.

7. Create another Python file with the name `callColorDialog.pyw` and import the `demoColorDialog.py` code into it:

```
import sys
from PyQt5.QtWidgets import QDialog, QApplication,
QColorDialog
from PyQt5.QtGui import QColor
from demoColorDialog import *
class MyForm(QDialog):
    def __init__(self):
        super().__init__()
        col = QColor(0, 0, 0)
        self.ui = Ui_Dialog()
        self.ui.setupUi(self)
        self.ui.frameColor.setStyleSheet("QWidget {
background-
        color: %s }" % col.name())
self.ui.pushButtonColor.clicked.connect(self.dispcolor)
        self.show()
    def dispcolor(self):
        col = QColorDialog.getColor()
        if col.isValid():
        self.ui.frameColor.setStyleSheet("QWidget {
background-
        color: %s }" % col.name())
        self.ui.labelColor.setText("You have selected the
color with
        code: " + str(col.name()))
if __name__=="__main__":
    app = QApplication(sys.argv)
    w = MyForm()
    w.show()
    sys.exit(app.exec_())
```

How it works...

In the `callColorDialog.pyw` file, you can see that the **click()** event of the push button is connected to the `dispcolor()` method; that is, when the user clicks the **Choose color** button, the `dispcolor()` method will be invoked. The `dispmessage()` method invokes the `getColor()` method of the `QColorDialog` class, which opens up a dialog showing different colors. Not only can the user choose any predefined basic color from the dialog box, but they can create a new custom color too. After choosing the desired color, when the user clicks the **OK** button from the color dialog, the chosen color will be assigned to the frame by invoking the `setStyleSheet()` method on the **Frame** widget class. Also, the hex code of the chosen color is displayed via the **Label** widget.

On running the application, initially you see a push button, **Choose color**, and a frame that is filled with black by default, as shown in the following screenshot:

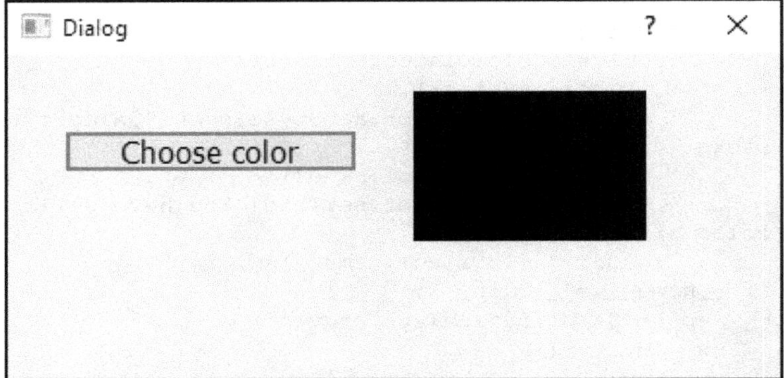

On clicking the **Choose color** button, the color dialog opens up, showing the basic colors shown in the following screenshot. The color dialog also enables you to create your own custom color too:

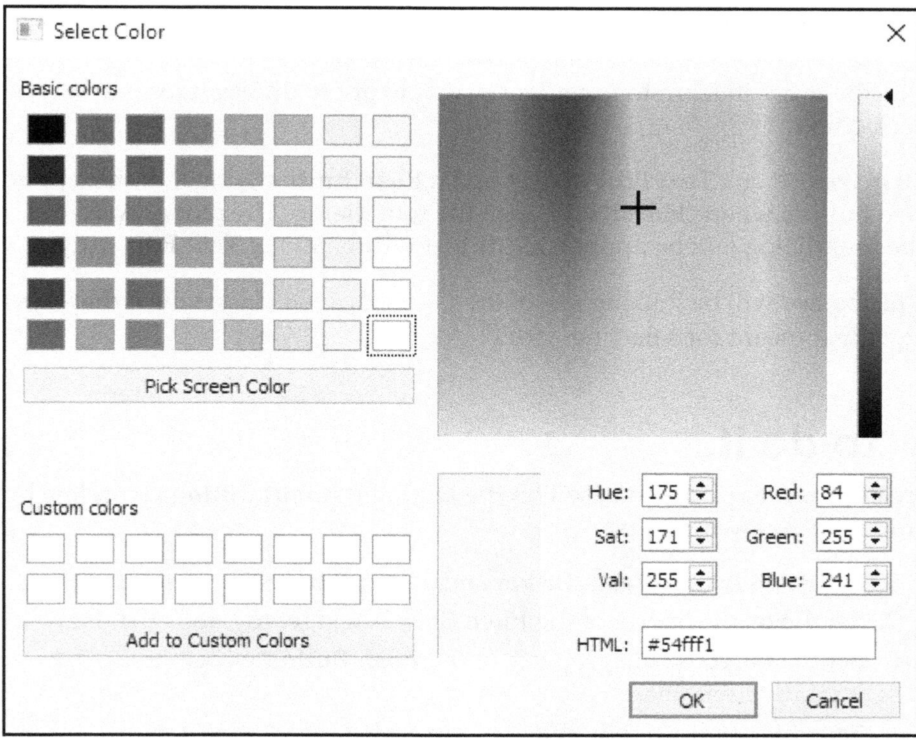

After selecting a color, when you select the **OK** button, the chosen color will be applied to the frame and the hex code of the chosen color will be displayed via the **Label** widget, as shown in the following screenshot:

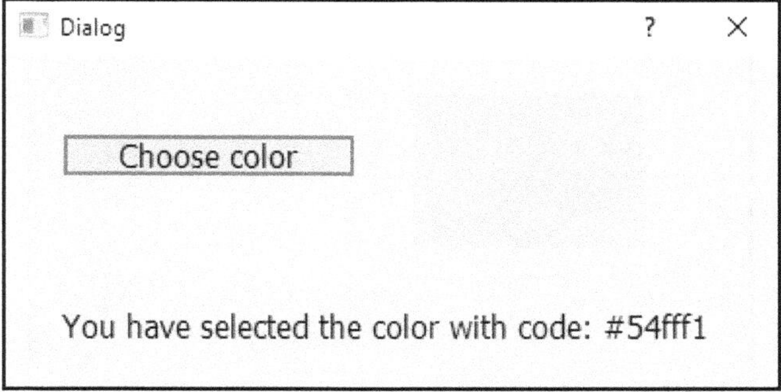

Using the font dialog

In this recipe, we will learn to use a font dialog to apply different fonts and styles to the selected text.

We will make use of a **Text Edit** widget and a **Push Button** widget in this application. The push button, when clicked, will open the font dialog. The font and style selected from the font dialog will be applied to the text written in the **Text Edit** widget.

In this recipe, we will be making use of the `QFontDialog` class, which displays a **Dialog** widget meant for selecting a font.

How to do it...

Let's create a new application based on the **Dialog without Buttons** template by performing the following steps:

1. Drag and drop a **Push Button** and a **Text Edit** widget onto the form.
2. Set the text property of the **Push Button** widget to `Choose Font`.
3. Set the **objectName** property of the **Push Button** widget to `pushButtonFont`.
4. Save the application with the name `demoFontDialog.ui`.
5. After performing the preceding steps, the application will appear as shown in the following screenshot:

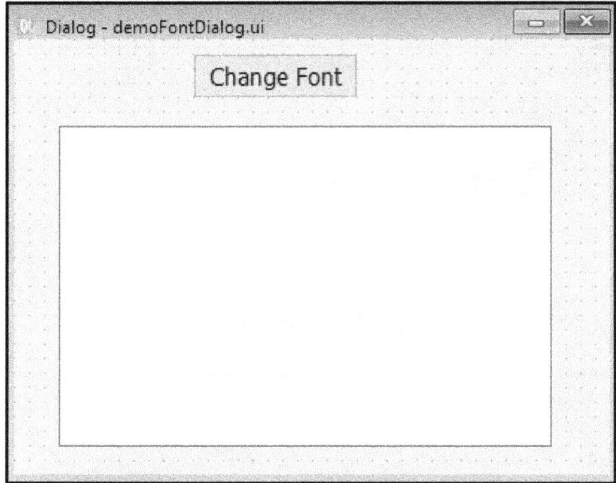

The user interface created with Qt Designer is stored in a .ui file, which is an XML file. Using the pyuic5 command, you can convert the XML file into Python code. The generated Python script, demoFontDialog.py, can be seen in the source code bundle of this book. The demoFontDialog.py script will be used as a header file, and will be imported in another Python script file, which will invoke this user interface design.

6. Create another Python file with the name callFontDialog.pyw and import the demoFontDialog.py code into it:

```
import sys
from PyQt5.QtWidgets import QDialog, QApplication, QFontDialog
from demoFontDialog import *
class MyForm(QDialog):
    def __init__(self):
        super().__init__()
        self.ui = Ui_Dialog()
        self.ui.setupUi(self)
self.ui.pushButtonFont.clicked.connect(self.changefont)
        self.show()
    def changefont(self):
        font, ok = QFontDialog.getFont()
        if ok:
        self.ui.textEdit.setFont(font)
if __name__=="__main__":
    app = QApplication(sys.argv)
    w = MyForm()
    w.show()
    sys.exit(app.exec_())
```

How it works...

In the callFontDialog.pyw file, you can see that the **click()** event of the push button is connected to the changefont() method; that is, when the user clicks the **Choose Font** button, the change() method will be invoked. The changefont() method invokes the getFont() method of the QFontDialog class, which opens up a dialog showing different fonts, font styles, sizes, and effects. On choosing a font, font style, size, or effect, the effect of the choice on the text will be displayed in the **Sample** box. On choosing the desired font, font style, size, and effect, when user clicks the **OK** button, the selected choices will be assigned to the font variable. Subsequently, the setFont() method is invoked on the TextEdit class to apply the chosen font and styles to the text displayed through the **Text Edit** widget.

On running the application, you see a push button, the **Change Font** widget, and the **Text Edit** widget, as shown in the following screenshot:

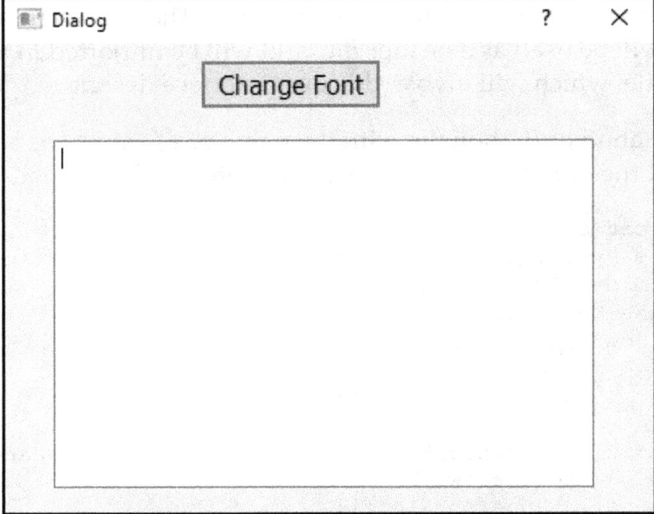

To see the impact of a chosen font from the font dialog, you need to type some text in the **Text Edit** widget, as shown in the following screenshot:

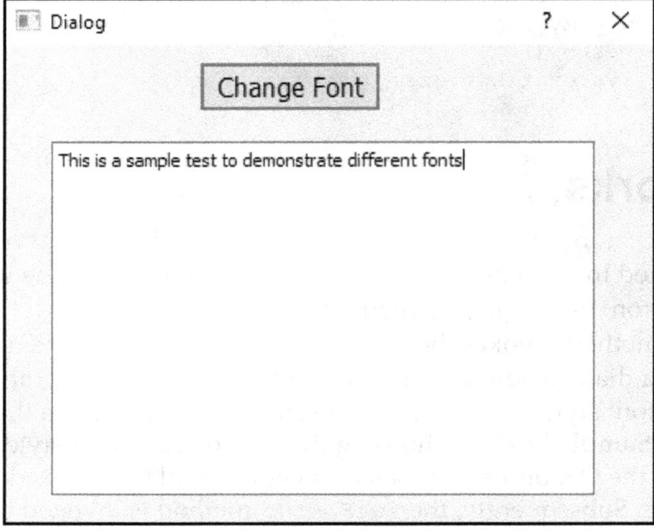

On selecting the **Change Font** button, the font dialog will open up, as shown in the following screenshot. You can see that a different font name will be displayed on the leftmost tab. The middle tab shows different font styles that enable you to make the text appear in bold, italic, bold italic, and regular. The rightmost tab shows different sizes. At the bottom, you can see different checkboxes that enable you to make text appear in underline, strikeout, and so on. Choose the options from any tab and the impact of the chosen font and style can be seen on the sample text shown in the **Sample** box. After selecting the desired font and style, click the **OK** button to close the font dialog:

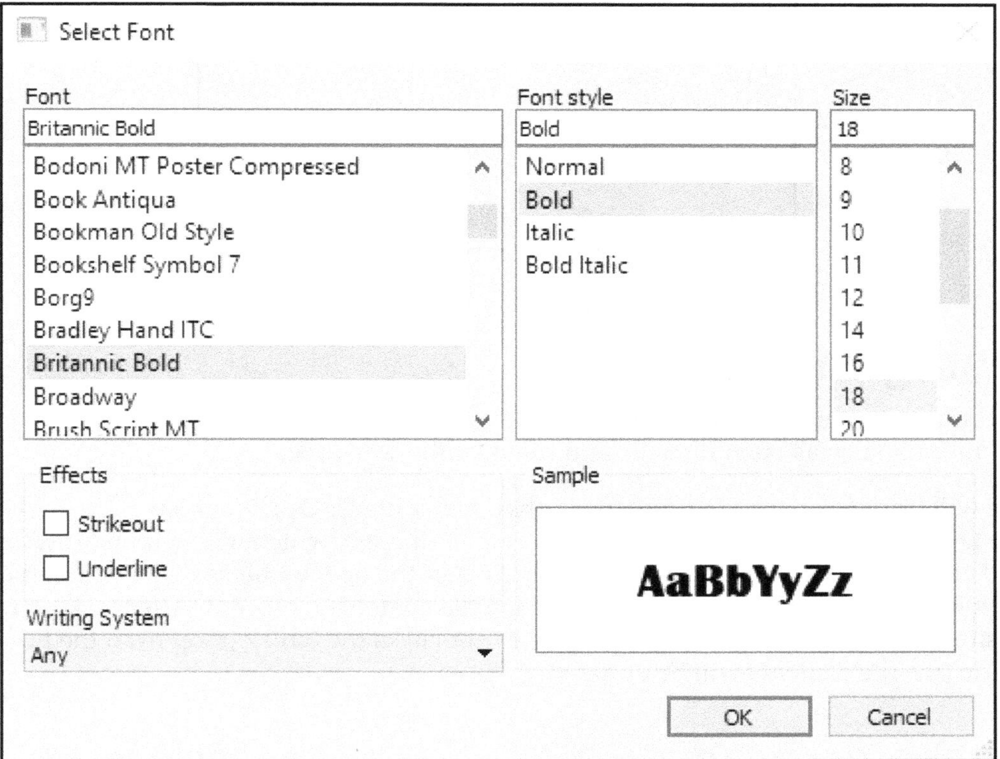

The effect of the chosen font and style will appear on the text written in the **Text Edit** widget, as shown in the following screenshot:

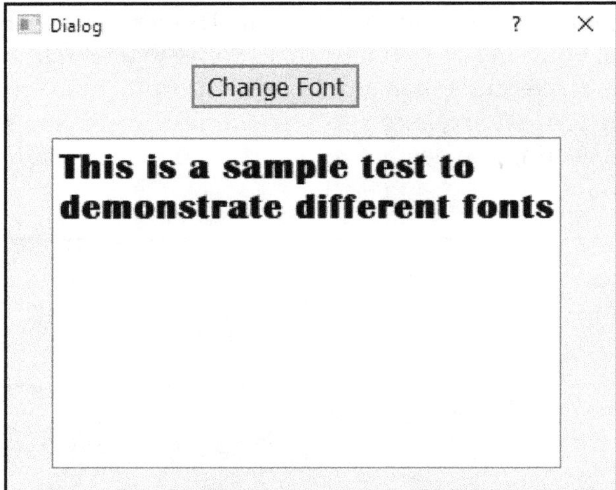

Using the file dialog

In this recipe, we will learn to use a file dialog to understand how different file operations, such as opening a file and saving a file, are done.

We will learn to create a file menu with two menu items, **Open** and **Save**. On clicking the **Open** menu item, the file open dialog box will open, which will help in browsing and choosing the file to open. The file contents of the opened file is displayed in the **Text Edit** box. The user can even update the file contents if desired. After making the desired modifications in the file, when the user clicks the **Save** option from the **File** menu, the file contents will be updated.

Getting ready

In this recipe, we will be making use of the `QFileDialog` class, which displays a dialog that allows users to select files or directories. The files can be selected for both opening and saving.

In this recipe, I will be using the following two methods of the `QFileDialog` class:

- `getOpenFileName()`: This method opens the file dialog, enabling the user to browse the directories and open the desired file. The syntax of the `getOpenFileName()` method is as follows:

  ```
  file_name = QFileDialog.getOpenFileName(self, dialog_title,
  path, filter)
  ```

  In the preceding code, `filter` represents the file extensions; it determines the types of file displayed to open, for example as follows:

  ```
  file_name = QFileDialog.getOpenFileName(self, 'Open file',
  '/home')

  In the preceding example, file dialog is opened that shows all
  the files of home directory to browse from.

  file_name = QFileDialog.getOpenFileName(self, 'Open file',
  '/home', "Images (*.png *.jpg);;Text files (.txt);;XML files
  (*.xml)")
  ```

  In the preceding example, you can see that files from the `home` directory are displayed. The files with the extensions `.png`, `.jpg`, `.txt`, and `.xml` will be displayed in the dialog box.

- `getSaveFileName()`: This method opens the file save dialog, enabling the user to save the file with the desired name and in the desired folder. The syntax of the `getSaveFileName()` method is as follows:

  ```
  file_name = QFileDialog.getSaveFileName(self, dialog_title,
  path, filter, options)
  ```

  `options` represents various options for how to run the dialog, for example, take a look at the following code:

  ```
  file_name, _ =
  QFileDialog.getSaveFileName(self,"QFileDialog.getSaveFileName(
  )","","All Files (*);;Text Files (*.txt)", options=options)

  In the preceding example, the File Save dialog box will be
  opened allowing you to save the files with the desired
  extension. If you don't specify the file extension, then it
  will be saved with the default extension, .txt.
  ```

How to do it...

Let's create a new application based on the **Main Window** template. The **Main Window** template includes a menu at the top by default:

1. We can even use two push buttons to initiate the file open dialog box and file save dialog box, but using the menu items to initiate file operations will give the feel of a real-time application.
2. The default menu bar in the **Main Window** template shows **Type Here** in place of the menu name.
3. The **Type Here** option indicates that the user can type the desired menu name, replacing the **Type Here** text. Let's type `File`, creating a menu in the menu bar.
4. On pressing the *Enter* key, the term **Type Here** will appear as a menu item under the **File** menu.
5. Let's type `Open` as the first menu item in the **File** menu.
6. On pressing the *Enter* key after creating the first menu item, **Open**, the term **Type Here** will appear below **Open**.
7. Replace **Type Here** with the menu item, **Save**.
8. After creating the **File** menu along with two menu items, **Open** and **Save**
9. The application will appear as shown in the following screenshot:

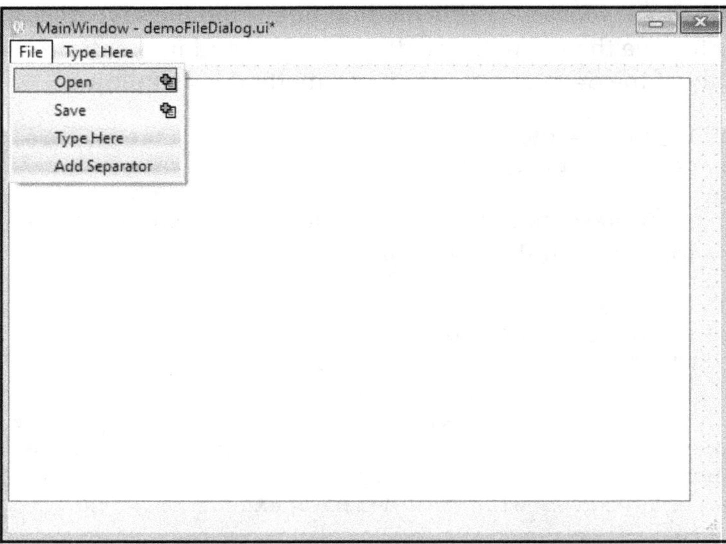

In the **Action Editor** window that is below the **Property Editor** window, you can see that the default object names of the **Open** and **Save** menu items are `actionOpen` and `actionSave`, respectively. The **Shortcut** tab in the **Action Editor** window is currently blank, as no shortcut has yet been assigned to either menu item:

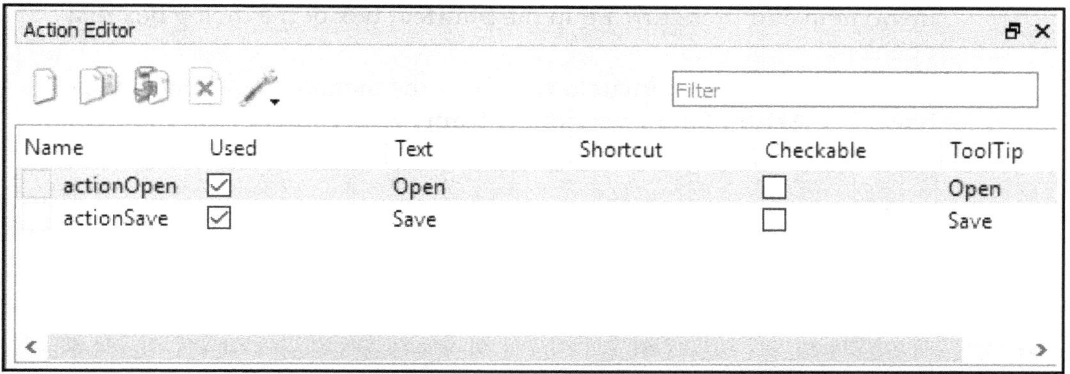

10. To assign a shortcut to the **Open** menu item, double-click on the blank space in the **Shortcut** tab of the `actionOpen` menu item. You get the dialog box, as shown in the following screenshot:

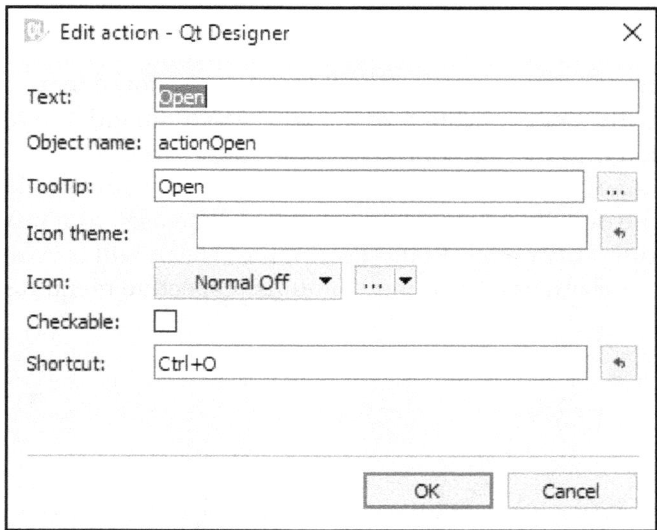

The **Text**, **Object name**, and **ToolTip** boxes are automatically filled with default text.

11. Click on the **Shortcut** box to place the cursor in that box, and press the *Ctrl* and *O* keys to assign *Ctrl* + *O* as a shortcut to the **Open** menu item.
12. Double-click on the blank space in the **Shortcut** tab of the `actionSave` menu item and press *Ctrl* + *S* in the **Shortcut** box of the dialog box that opens up.
13. After assigning the shortcut keys to both the menu items, **Open** and **Save.** The **Action Editor** window will appear as shown in the following screenshot:

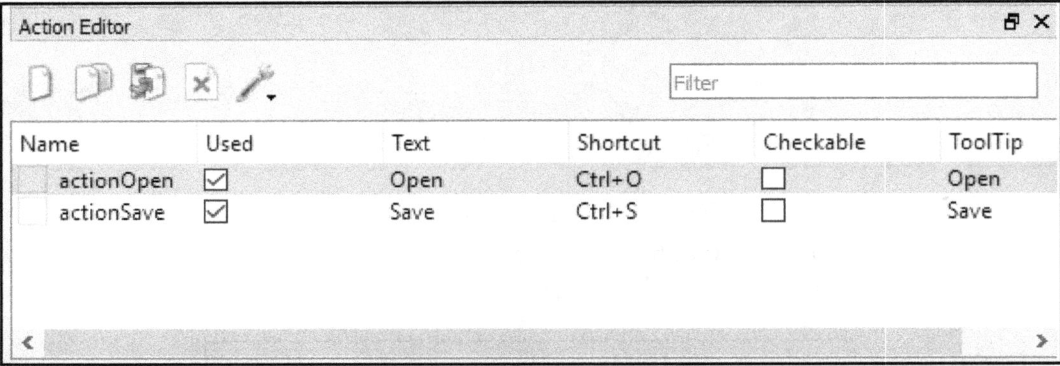

The user interface created with Qt Designer is stored in a `.ui` file, which is an XML file. On application of the `pyuic5` command, the XML file will be converted into Python code. The generated Python script, `demoFileDialog.py`, can be seen in the source code bundle of the book. The `demoFileDialog.py` script will be used as a header file, and will be imported in another Python script file, which will invoke this user interface design, the `File` menu and its respective menu items.

14. Create another Python file with the name `callFileDialog.pyw` and import the `demoFileDialog.py` code into it:

```
import sys
from PyQt5.QtWidgets import QMainWindow, QApplication,
QAction, QFileDialog
from demoFileDialog import *
class MyForm(QMainWindow):
    def __init__(self):
        super().__init__()
        self.ui = Ui_MainWindow()
        self.ui.setupUi(self)
self.ui.actionOpen.triggered.connect(self.openFileDialog)
self.ui.actionSave.triggered.connect(self.saveFileDialog)
        self.show()
    def openFileDialog(self):
        fname = QFileDialog.getOpenFileName(self, 'Open file',
        '/home')
        if fname[0]:
            f = open(fname[0], 'r')
        with f:
            data = f.read()
            self.ui.textEdit.setText(data)
    def saveFileDialog(self):
        options = QFileDialog.Options()
        options |= QFileDialog.DontUseNativeDialog
        fileName, _ = QFileDialog.getSaveFileName(self,
        "QFileDialog.
        getSaveFileName()","","All Files (*);;Text Files
(*.txt)",
        options=options)
        f = open(fileName,'w')
        text = self.ui.textEdit.toPlainText()
        f.write(text)
        f.close()
if __name__=="__main__":
    app = QApplication(sys.argv)
    w = MyForm()
    w.show()
    sys.exit(app.exec_())
```

How it works...

In the `callFileDialog.pyw` file, you can see that the **click()** event of the **Open** menu item with `objectName`, `actionOpen`, is connected to the `openFileDialog` method; when the user clicks the **Open** menu item, the `openFileDialog` method will be invoked. Similarly, the **click()** event of the **Save** menu item with `objectName`, `actionSave`, is connected to the `saveFileDialog` method; when the user clicks the **Save** menu item, the `saveFileDialog` method will be invoked.

In the `openFileDialog` method, the open file dialog is opened by invoking the `getOpenFileName` method of the `QFileDialog` class. The open file dialog enables the user to browse the directories and choose the desired file to open. After selecting the file, when the user clicks the **OK** button, the selected filename is assigned to the `fname` variable. The file is opened in read-only mode and the file contents are read and assigned to the **Text Edit** widget; that is, the file content is displayed in the **Text Edit** widget.

After making the changes in the file contents being displayed in the **Text Edit** widget, when the user clicks the **Save** menu item from the **File** dialog, the `saveFileDialog()` method will be invoked.

In the `saveFileDialog()` method, the `getSaveFileName()` method is invoked on the `QFileDialog` class, which will open the file save dialog box. You can save the file with the same name at the same location, or with some other name. If the same filename is provided at the same location, then, on clicking the **OK** button, you get a dialog box asking whether you want to overwrite the original file with the updated content. On supplying the filename, that file is opened in write mode and the content in the **Text Edit** widget will be read and written into the file. That is, the updated file contents that are available in the **Text Edit** widget are written into the supplied filename.

On running the application, you find a **File** menu with two menu items, **Open** and **Save**, as shown in the following screenshot. You can see the shortcuts of the **Open** and **Save** menu items too:

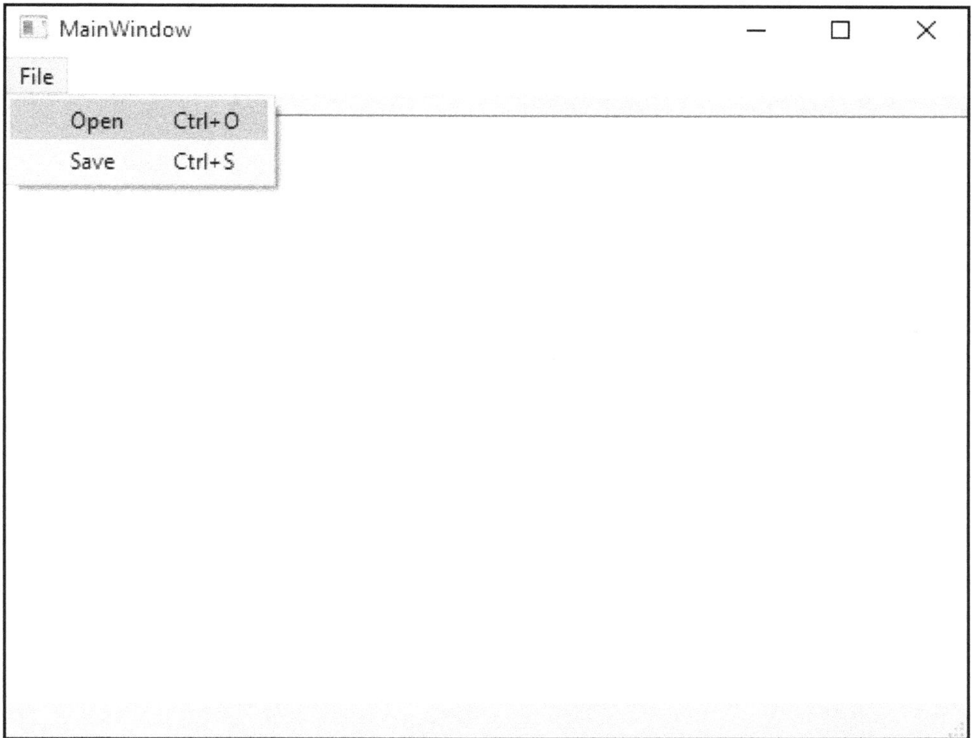

On clicking the **Open** menu item from the **File** menu, or on pressing the shortcut keys *Ctrl* + *O*, you get the **Open** file dialog, as shown in the following screenshot. You can browse the desired directory and select the file to open. After selecting the file, you need to click the **Open** button from the dialog:

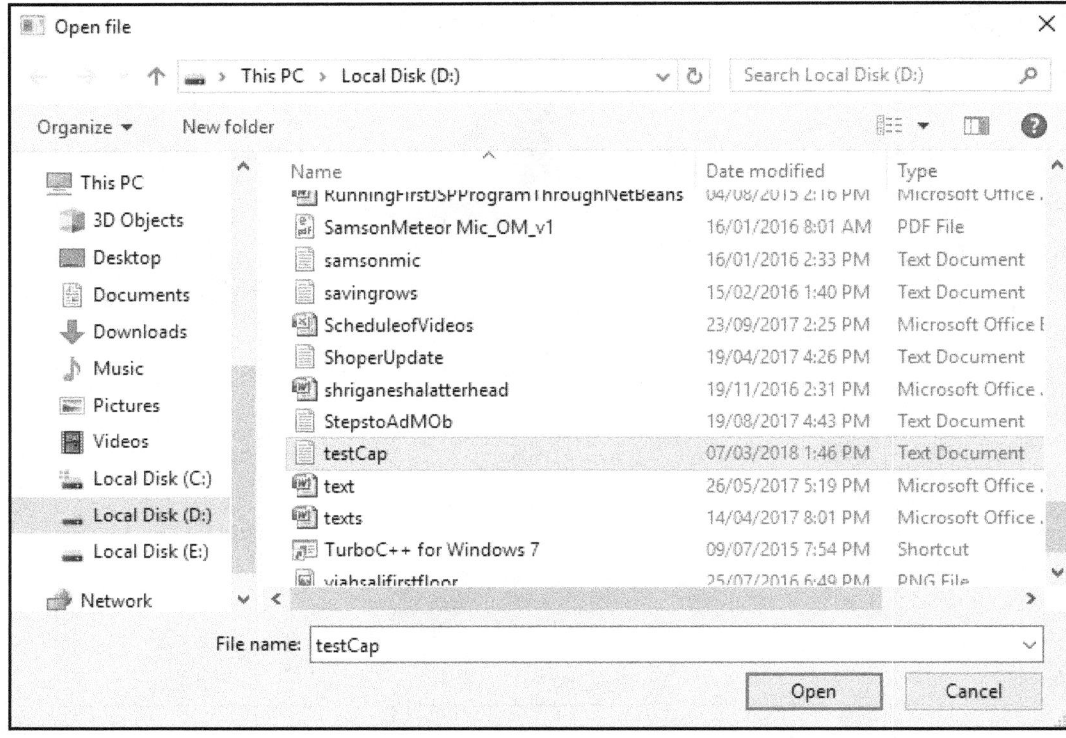

The content of the selected file will be displayed in the **Text Edit** box, as shown in the following screenshot:

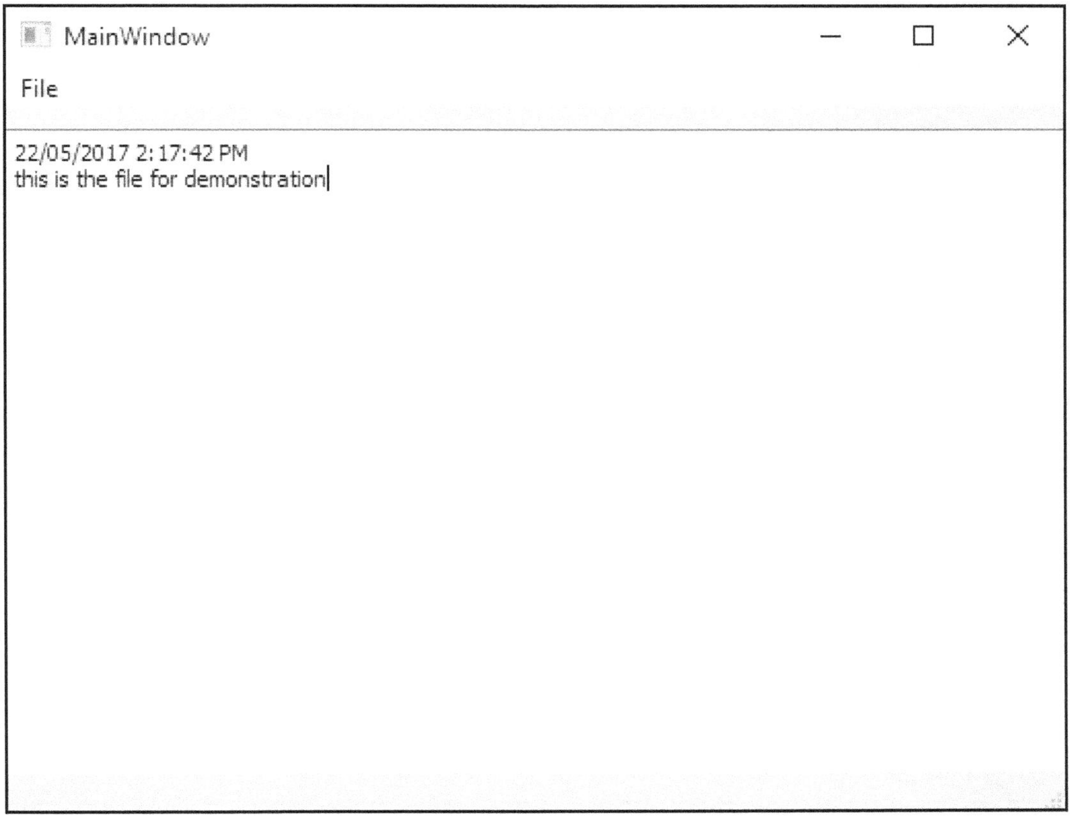

After making modifications in the file contents shown in the **Text Edit** box, when the user clicks on the **Save** menu item from the **File** menu, the `getSaveFileName` method will be invoked to display the save file dialog box. Let's save the file with the original name, followed by clicking the **Save** button, as shown in the following screenshot:

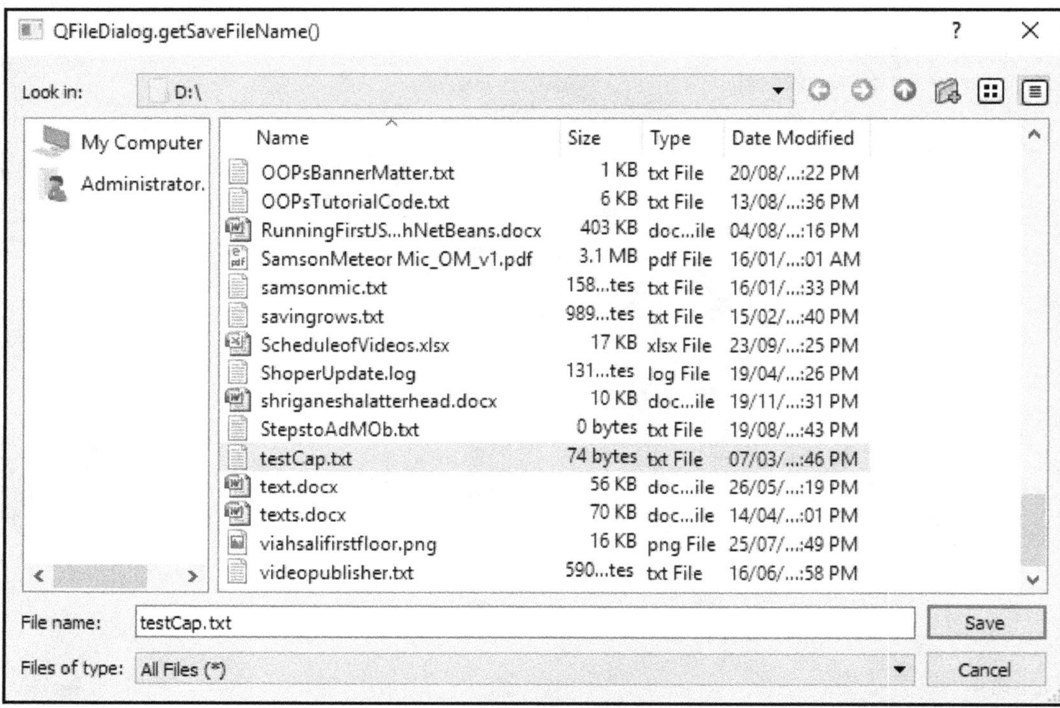

Because the file is being saved with the same name, you will get a dialog box asking for confirmation to replace the original file with the new content, as shown in the following screenshot. Click on **Yes** to update the file with the new content:

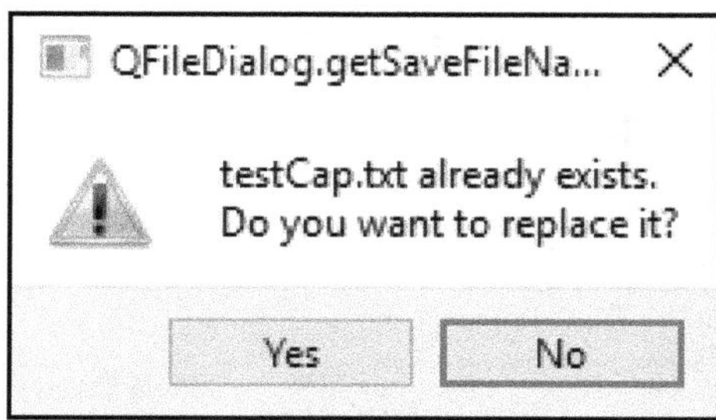

17
Understanding Layouts

In this chapter, we will focus on the following topics:

- Using Horizontal Layout
- Using Vertical Layout
- Using Grid Layout
- Using Form Layout

Understanding layouts

As the name suggest, layouts are used for arranging widgets in the desired format. On arranging certain widgets in a layout, certain size and alignment constraints are applied to the widgets automatically. For example, on increasing the size of the window, the widgets in the layout also increase in size to use up the increased space. Similarly, on reducing the size of the window, the widgets in the layout also decrease in size. The following question arises: how does the layout know what the recommended size of the widget is?

Basically, each widget has a property called **sizeHint** that contains the widget's recommended size. When the window is resized and the layout size also changes, it is through the **sizeHint** property of the widget that the layout managers know the size requirement of the widget.

In order to apply the size constraints on the widgets, you can make use of the following two properties:

- **minimumSize**: If the window size is decreased, the widget will still not become smaller than the size specified in the **minimumSize** property.
- **maximumSize**: Similarly, if the window is increased, the widget will not become larger than the size specified in the **maximumSize** property.

When the preceding properties are set, the value specified in the **sizeHint** property will be overridden.

To arrange widgets in a layout, simply select all the widgets with *Ctrl* + left-click and click **Layout Manager** on the toolbar. Another way is to right-click to open the context menu. From the context menu, you can select the **Layout** menu option, followed by selecting the desired layout from the submenu that pops up.

On selecting the desired layout, the widgets will be laid out in the selected layout, and the layout will be indicated by a red line around the widgets that is not visible at runtime. To see whether the widgets are properly laid out, you can preview the form by selecting **Form**, **Preview**, or *Ctrl* + *R*. To break the layout, select **Form**, **Break Layout**, enter *Ctrl* + *O*, or select the **Break Layout** icon from the toolbar.

The layouts can be nested.

The following are layout managers provided by Qt Designer:

- **Horizontal Layout**
- **Vertical Layout**
- **Grid Layout**
- **Form Layout**

Spacers

In order to control spacing between widgets, horizontal and vertical spacers are used. When a horizontal spacer is kept between the two widgets, the two widgets will be pushed as far left and right as possible. If the window size is increased, the widget sizes will not change and the extra space will be consumed by the spacer. Similarly, when the window size is decreased, the spacer will automatically reduce but the widget sizes will not be changed.

Spacers expand to fill empty space and shrink if the space is decreased.

Let's look at the procedure for arranging widgets in a horizontal box layout.

Using Horizontal Layout

A horizontal layout arranges widgets next to each other in a row that is, widgets are horizontally aligned using **Horizontal Layout**. Let's understand this concept by making an application.

How to do it...

In this application, we will prompt the user to enter an email address and password. The main focus of this recipe is to understand how two pairs of the **Label** and **Line Edit** widgets are horizontally aligned. Here is the step-by-step procedure to create this application:

1. Let's create an application based on the **Dialog without Buttons** template and add two `QLabel`, two `QlineEdit`, and one `QPushButton` widget to the form by dragging and dropping two **Label**, two **Line Edit**, and a **Push Button** widget on the form.
2. Set the **text** property of the two **Label** widgets to `Name` and `Email Address`.
3. Also, set the **text** property of the **Push Button** widget to `Submit`.
4. As the purpose of this application is to understand the layout and nothing else, we won't be setting the **objectName** property of any of the widgets in the application.

The form will now appear as shown in the following screenshot:

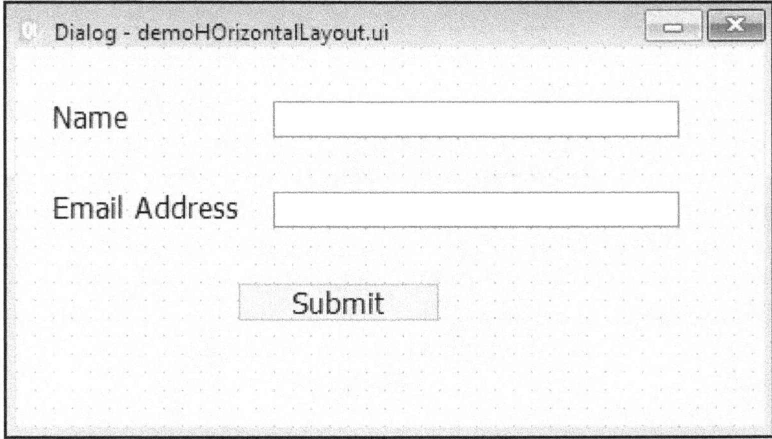

5. We will be applying **Horizontal Layout** on each pair of **Label** and **Line Edit** widgets. So, click on the **Label** widget with the text, `Name`, and, keeping the *Ctrl* key pressed, click on the **Line Edit** widget besides it.

You can select more than one widget by using *Ctrl* + left-click.

6. After selecting the **Label** and **Line Edit** widgets, right-click and select the **Layout** menu option from the context menu that opens up.
7. On selecting the **Layout** menu option, several submenu options will appear on the screen; select the **Layout Horizontally** submenu option. Both the **Label** and **Line Edit** widgets will be aligned horizontally, as shown in the following screenshot:

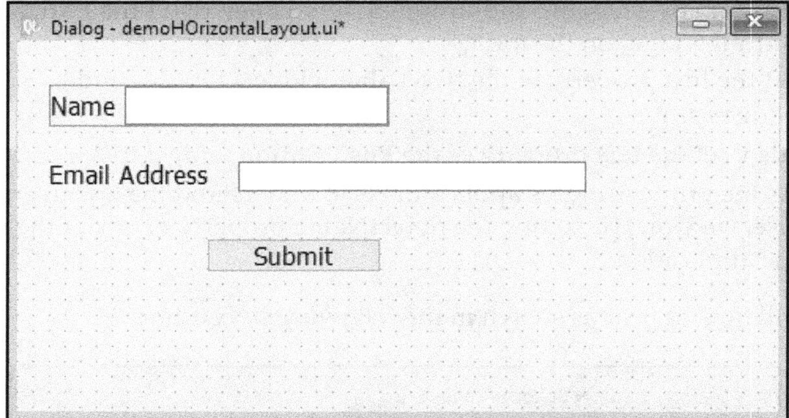

8. What if you want to break the layout? This is very simple: you can break any layout at any time by just selecting the layout and right-clicking on it. The context menu will pop up; select the **Layout** menu option from the context menu, followed by the **Break Layout** submenu option.
9. To horizontally align the second pair of **Label** widgets with the text, `Email Address`, and the **Line Edit** widget beside it, repeat the same procedure as mentioned in steps 6 and 7. This pair of **Label** and **Line Edit** widgets will also be horizontally aligned, as shown in the following screenshot.

You can see that a red rectangle surrounds the two widgets. This red rectangle is the horizontal layout window:

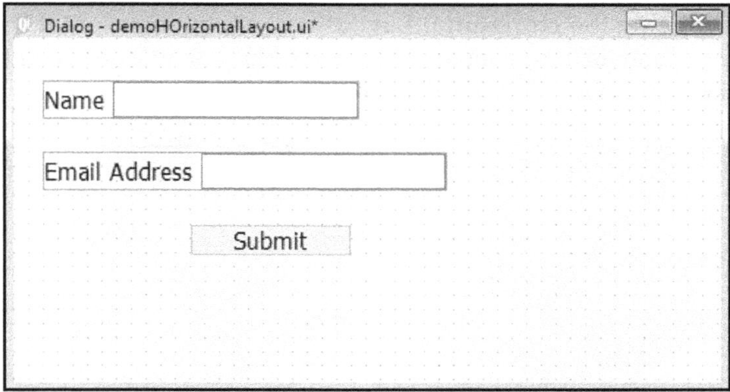

10. To create some space between the first pair of **Label** and **Line Edit** widgets, drag the **Horizontal Spacer** widget from the **Spacers** tab of **Widget Box** and drop it in between the **Label** widget with the text, `Name`, and the **Line Edit** widget beside it.

The **Horizontal Spacer** widget initially takes up the default space between the two widgets. The spacers appear as blue springs on the form.

11. Adjust the size of the horizontal spacer by dragging its nodes to constrain the width of the **Line Edit** widget, as shown in the following screenshot:

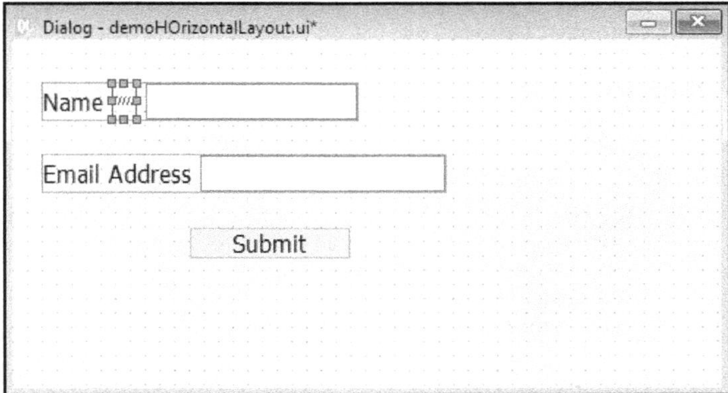

12. Select the red rectangle of the **Horizontal Layout** widget from the first pair of **Label** and **Line Edit** widgets, and drag it to the right so that its width becomes equal to the second pair.
13. On dragging the **Horizontal Layout** widget, the horizontal spacer will increase its width to consume the extra blank space between the two widgets, as shown in the following screenshot:

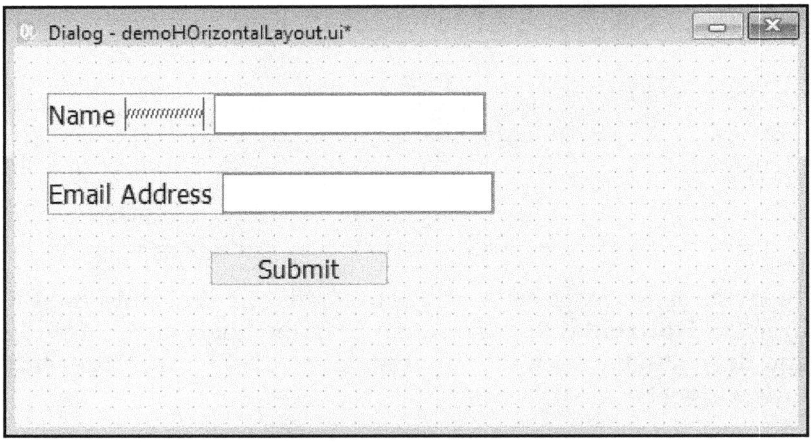

14. Save the application as `demoHorizontalLayout.ui`.

The user interface created with Qt Designer is stored in a `.ui` file, which is an XML file, and we need to convert it to Python code. To do the conversion, you need to open a Command Prompt window and navigate to the folder where the file is saved, then issue the following command line:

```
C:\Pythonbook\PyQt5>pyuic5 demoHorizontalLayout.ui -o
demoHorizontalLayout.py
```

The Python script file `demoHorizontalLayout.py` may have the following code:

```
from PyQt5 import QtCore, QtGui, QtWidgets
class Ui_Dialog(object):
    def setupUi(self, Dialog):
        Dialog.setObjectName("Dialog")
        Dialog.resize(483, 243)
        self.pushButton = QtWidgets.QPushButton(Dialog)
        self.pushButton.setGeometry(QtCore.QRect(120, 130,
111,
        23))
```

```
        font = QtGui.QFont()
        font.setPointSize(12)
        self.pushButton.setFont(font)
        self.pushButton.setObjectName("pushButton")
        self.widget = QtWidgets.QWidget(Dialog)
        self.widget.setGeometry(QtCore.QRect(20, 30, 271, 27))
        self.widget.setObjectName("widget")
        self.horizontalLayout =
QtWidgets.QHBoxLayout(self.widget)
        self.horizontalLayout.setContentsMargins(0, 0, 0, 0)
self.horizontalLayout.setObjectName("horizontalLayout")
        self.label = QtWidgets.QLabel(self.widget)
        font = QtGui.QFont()
        font.setPointSize(12)
        self.label.setFont(font)
        self.label.setObjectName("label")
        self.horizontalLayout.addWidget(self.label)
        spacerItem = QtWidgets.QSpacerItem(40, 20, QtWidgets.
        QSizePolicy.Expanding,QtWidgets.QSizePolicy.Minimum)
        self.horizontalLayout.addItem(spacerItem)
        self.lineEdit = QtWidgets.QLineEdit(self.widget)
        font = QtGui.QFont()
        font.setPointSize(12)
        self.lineEdit.setFont(font)
        self.lineEdit.setObjectName("lineEdit")
        self.horizontalLayout.addWidget(self.lineEdit)
        self.widget1 = QtWidgets.QWidget(Dialog)
        self.widget1.setGeometry(QtCore.QRect(20, 80, 276,
27))
        self.widget1.setObjectName("widget1")
        self.horizontalLayout_2 = QtWidgets.QHBoxLayout(self.
        widget1)
        self.horizontalLayout_2.setContentsMargins(0, 0, 0, 0)
self.horizontalLayout_2.setObjectName("horizontalLayout_2")
        self.label_2 = QtWidgets.QLabel(self.widget1)
        font = QtGui.QFont()
        font.setPointSize(12)
        self.label_2.setFont(font)
        self.label_2.setObjectName("label_2")
        self.horizontalLayout_2.addWidget(self.label_2)
        self.lineEdit_2 = QtWidgets.QLineEdit(self.widget1)
        font = QtGui.QFont()
        font.setPointSize(12)
        self.lineEdit_2.setFont(font)
        self.lineEdit_2.setObjectName("lineEdit_2")
        self.horizontalLayout_2.addWidget(self.lineEdit_2)
        self.retranslateUi(Dialog)
        QtCore.QMetaObject.connectSlotsByName(Dialog)
```

```
    def retranslateUi(self, Dialog):
        _translate = QtCore.QCoreApplication.translate
        Dialog.setWindowTitle(_translate("Dialog", "Dialog"))
        self.pushButton.setText(_translate("Dialog",
"Submit"))
        self.label.setText(_translate("Dialog", "Name"))
        self.label_2.setText(_translate("Dialog", "Email
Address"))
if __name__ == "__main__":
    import sys
    app = QtWidgets.QApplication(sys.argv)
    Dialog = QtWidgets.QDialog()
    ui = Ui_Dialog()
    ui.setupUi(Dialog)
    Dialog.show()
    sys.exit(app.exec_())
```

How it works...

You can see in the code that a **Line Edit** widget with the default **objectName** property, `lineEdit`, and a **Label** widget with the default **objectName** property as **label** are placed on the form. Both the **Line Edit** and **Label** widgets are horizontally aligned using the Horizontal Layout widget. The **Horizontal Layout** widget has the default **objectName** property, `horizontalLayout`. On aligning the **Label** and **Line Edit** widgets, the horizontal space between the two widgets is reduced. So, a spacer is kept between the **Label** and **Line Edit** widgets. The second pair, **Label** with the default **objectName** property `label_2` and the **Line Edit** widget with the default **objectName** property `lineEdit_2`, are horizontally aligned by **Horizontal Layout** with the default **objectName** property, `horizontalLayout_2`.

On running the application, you will find that the two pairs of **Label** and **Line Edit** widgets are horizontally aligned, as shown in the following screenshot:

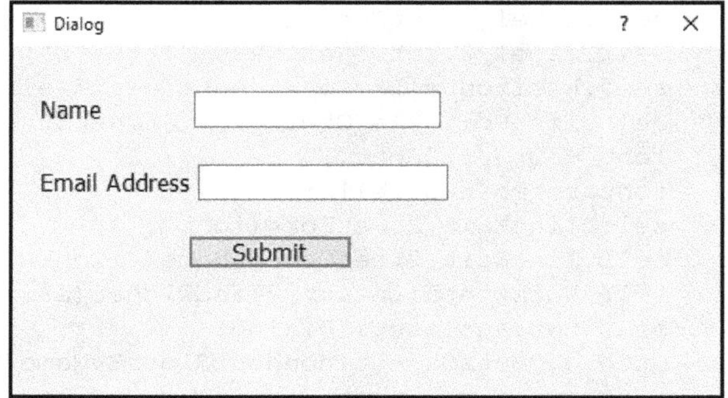

Using Vertical Layout

Vertical Layout arranges the selected widgets vertically, in a column one below the other. In the following application, you will learn the process of laying widgets in a vertical layout.

How to do it...

In this application, we will prompt the user to enter a name and email address. The labels and textboxes for entering names and email addresses, along with the submit button, will be arranged vertically one below the other via **Vertical Layout**. Here are the steps to create the application:

1. Launch Qt Designer and create an application based on the **Dialog without Buttons** template, then add two `QLabel`, two `QlineEdit`, and one `QPushButton` widget to the form by dragging and dropping two **Label**, two **Line Edit**, and one **Push Button** widget onto the form.
2. Set the **text** property of the two **Label** widgets to `Name` and `Email Address`.
3. Set the **text** property of the **Push Button** widget to `Submit`. Because the purpose of this application is to understand the layout and nothing else, we won't be setting the **objectName** property of any of the widgets in the application. The form will now appear as shown in the following screenshot:

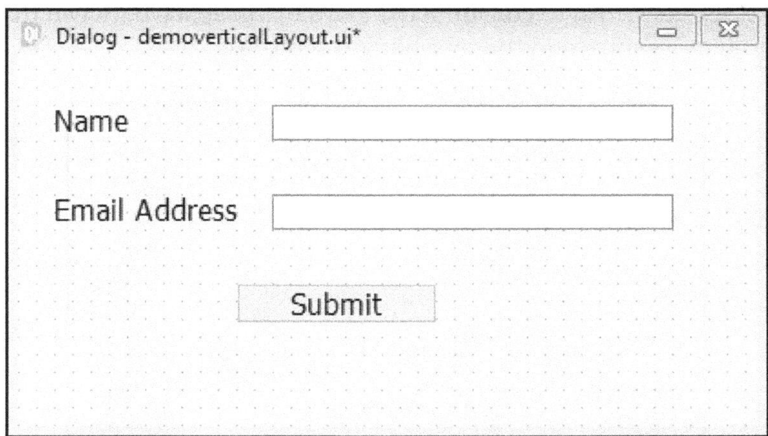

4. Before the application of **Vertical Layout** on the widgets, we need to align the widgets horizontally. So, we will apply the **Horizontal Layout** widget on each pair of **Label** and **Line Edit** widgets. So, click the **Label** widget with the text `Name` and, keeping the *Ctrl* key pressed, click on the **Line Edit** widget besides it.
5. After selecting the **Label** and **Line Edit** widgets, right-click the mouse button and select the **Layout** menu option from the context menu that opens up.
6. On selecting the **Layout** menu option, several submenu options will appear on the screen. Select the **Layout Horizontally** submenu option. Both the **Label** and **Line Edit** widgets will be aligned horizontally.
7. To horizontally align the second pair of **Label** with the text, `Email Address`, and the **Line Edit** widget beside it, repeat the same procedure as mentioned in the previous steps, 5 and 6. You can see that a red rectangle surrounds the two widgets. This red rectangle is the horizontal layout window.
8. To create some space between the first pair of **Label** and **Line Edit** widgets, drag the **Horizontal Spacer** widget from the **Spacers** tab of **Widget Box** and drop it in between the **Label** widget with the text, `Name`, and the **Line Edit** widget besides it. The horizontal spacer will initially take up the default space between the two widgets.
9. Select the red rectangle of the **Horizontal Layout** widget from the first pair of **Label** and **Line Edit** widgets, and drag it to the right so that its width becomes equal to the second pair.
10. On dragging the **Horizontal Layout** widget, the horizontal spacer will increase its width to consume the extra blank space between the two widgets, as shown in the following screenshot:

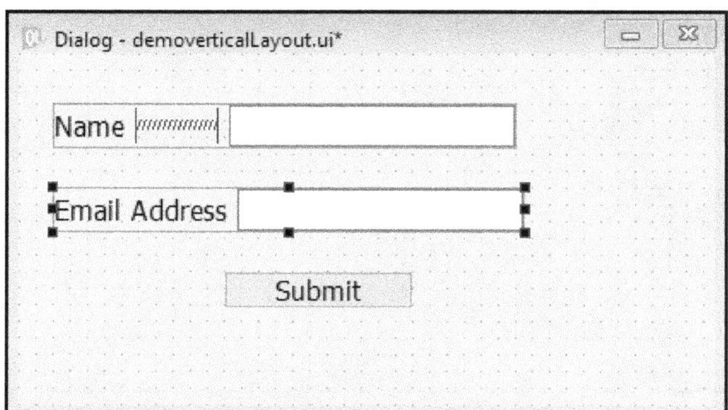

11. Now, select three things: the first **Horizontal Layout** window, the second **Horizontal Layout** window, and the **Submit** button. Keep the *Ctrl* key pressed during these multiple selections.
12. Once these three things are selected, right-click to open the context menu.
13. From the context menu, select the **Layout** menu option, followed by the **Layout Vertically** submenu option. The three items will be aligned vertically, and the width of the **Submit** button will be increased to match the width of the widest layout, as shown in the following screenshot:

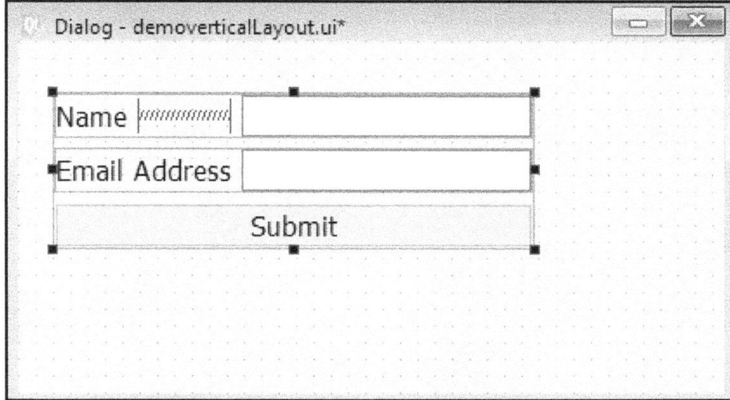

14. You can also select the **Layout Vertically** icon from the toolbar to arrange the widgets in a vertical layout.
15. If you want to control the width of the **Submit** button, you can use the **minimumSize** and **maximumSize** properties of this widget. You will notice that the vertical space between the two horizontal layouts is greatly reduced.
16. To create some space between the two horizontal layouts, drag the **Vertical Spacer** widget from the **Spacers** tab of **Widget Box** and drop it in between the two horizontal layouts.

The vertical spacer will initially take up the default space between the two horizontal layouts

17. To create vertical space between the second horizontal layout and the **Submit** button, drag the vertical spacer and drop it between the second horizontal layout and the **Submit** button.
18. Select the red rectangle of **Vertical Layout** and drag it down to increase its height.
19. On dragging the **Vertical Layout** widget, the vertical spacer will increase its height to consume the extra blank space between the two horizontal layouts and the **Submit** button, as shown in the following screenshot:

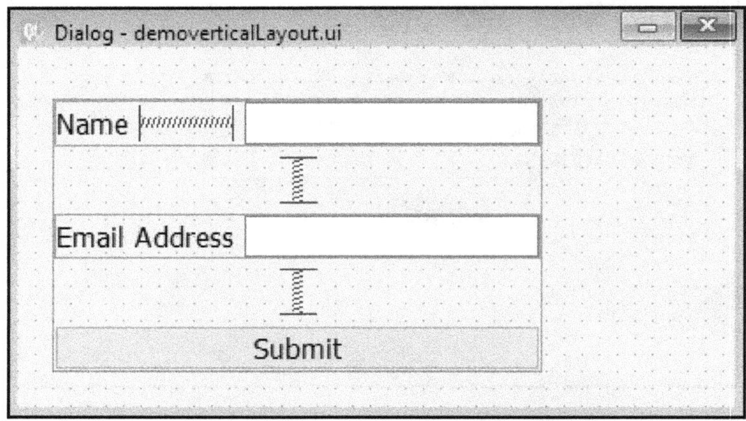

20. Save the application as `demoverticalLayout.ui`.

As we know that the user interface created with Qt Designer is stored in a `.ui` file, which is an XML file, it needs to be converted into Python code. To do the conversion, you need to open a Command Prompt window and navigate to the folder where the file is saved, then issue the following command:

```
C:PyQt5>pyuic5 demoverticalLayout.ui -o demoverticalLayout.py
```

The Python script file, `demoverticalLayout.py`, may have the following code:

```
from PyQt5 import QtCore, QtGui, QtWidgets
class Ui_Dialog(object):
    def setupUi(self, Dialog):
        Dialog.setObjectName("Dialog")
        Dialog.resize(407, 211)
        self.widget = QtWidgets.QWidget(Dialog)
        self.widget.setGeometry(QtCore.QRect(20, 30, 278,
```

```
161))
        self.widget.setObjectName("widget")
        self.verticalLayout =
QtWidgets.QVBoxLayout(self.widget)
        self.verticalLayout.setContentsMargins(0, 0, 0, 0)
        self.verticalLayout.setObjectName("verticalLayout")
        self.horizontalLayout = QtWidgets.QHBoxLayout()
self.horizontalLayout.setObjectName("horizontalLayout")
        self.label = QtWidgets.QLabel(self.widget)
        font = QtGui.QFont()
        font.setPointSize(12)
        self.label.setFont(font)
        self.label.setObjectName("label")
        self.horizontalLayout.addWidget(self.label)
        spacerItem = QtWidgets.QSpacerItem(40, 20, QtWidgets.
        QSizePolicy.Expanding,QtWidgets.QSizePolicy.Minimum)
        self.horizontalLayout.addItem(spacerItem)
        self.lineEdit = QtWidgets.QLineEdit(self.widget)
        font = QtGui.QFont()
        font.setPointSize(12)
        self.lineEdit.setFont(font)
        self.lineEdit.setObjectName("lineEdit")
        self.horizontalLayout.addWidget(self.lineEdit)
        self.verticalLayout.addLayout(self.horizontalLayout)
        spacerItem1 = QtWidgets.QSpacerItem(20, 40, QtWidgets.
        QSizePolicy.Minimum, QtWidgets.QSizePolicy.Expanding)
        self.verticalLayout.addItem(spacerItem1)
        self.horizontalLayout_2 = QtWidgets.QHBoxLayout()
self.horizontalLayout_2.setObjectName("horizontalLayout_2")
        self.label_2 = QtWidgets.QLabel(self.widget)
        font = QtGui.QFont()
        font.setPointSize(12)
        self.label_2.setFont(font)
        self.label_2.setObjectName("label_2")
        self.horizontalLayout_2.addWidget(self.label_2)
        self.lineEdit_2 = QtWidgets.QLineEdit(self.widget)
        font = QtGui.QFont()
        font.setPointSize(12)
        self.lineEdit_2.setFont(font)
        self.lineEdit_2.setObjectName("lineEdit_2")
        self.horizontalLayout_2.addWidget(self.lineEdit_2)
        self.verticalLayout.addLayout(self.horizontalLayout_2)
        spacerItem2 = QtWidgets.QSpacerItem(20, 40, QtWidgets.
        QSizePolicy.Minimum,QtWidgets.QSizePolicy.
        Expanding)
        self.verticalLayout.addItem(spacerItem2)
        self.pushButton = QtWidgets.QPushButton(self.widget)
        font = QtGui.QFont()
```

```
        font.setPointSize(12)
        self.pushButton.setFont(font)
        self.pushButton.setObjectName("pushButton")
        self.verticalLayout.addWidget(self.pushButton)
        self.retranslateUi(Dialog)
        QtCore.QMetaObject.connectSlotsByName(Dialog)
    def retranslateUi(self, Dialog):
        _translate = QtCore.QCoreApplication.translate
        Dialog.setWindowTitle(_translate("Dialog", "Dialog"))
        self.label.setText(_translate("Dialog", "Name"))
        self.label_2.setText(_translate("Dialog", "Email
Address"))
        self.pushButton.setText(_translate("Dialog",
"Submit"))
if __name__ == "__main__":
    import sys
    app = QtWidgets.QApplication(sys.argv)
    Dialog = QtWidgets.QDialog()
    ui = Ui_Dialog()
    ui.setupUi(Dialog)
    Dialog.show()
    sys.exit(app.exec_())
```

How it works...

You can see in the code that a **Line Edit** widget with the default **objectName** `lineEdit` property and the **Label** widget with the default **objectName** `label` property are placed on the form and are horizontally aligned using the horizontal layout with the default **objectName** property, `horizontalLayout`. On aligning the **Label** and **Line Edit** widgets, the horizontal space between the two widgets is reduced. So, a spacer is kept between the **Label** and **Line Edit** widgets. The second pair, the **Label** widget with the default **objectName** `label_2` property and the **Line Edit** widget with the default **objectName** `lineEdit_2` property, are horizontally aligned using the horizontal layout with the default **objectName** `horizontalLayout_2` property. Then, the first two horizontal layouts and the **Submit** button with the default **objectName** `pushButton` property are vertically aligned using the **Vertical Layout** widget with the default `objectName` property, `verticalLayout`. The horizontal space between the first pair of **Label** and **Line Edit** widgets is increased by placing a horizontal spacer between them. Similarly, the vertical space between the two horizontal layouts is increased by placing a vertical spacer called `spacerItem1` between them. Also, a vertical spacer called `spacerItem2` is placed between the second horizontal layout and the **Submit** button to increase the vertical space between them.

On running the application, you will find that the two pairs of **Label** and **Line Edit** widgets, and the **Submit** button, are vertically aligned, as shown in the following screenshot:

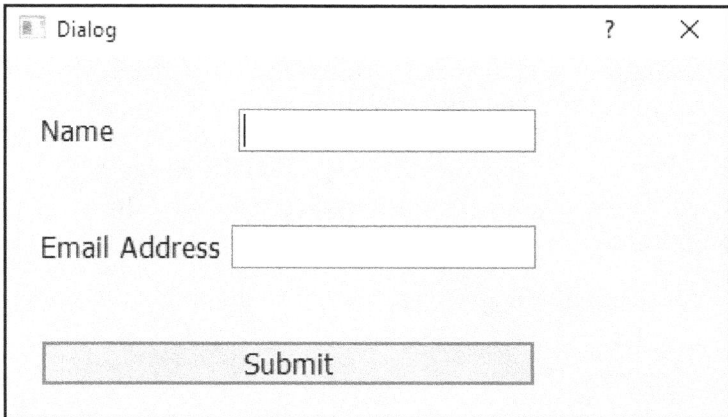

Using Grid Layout

Grid Layout arranges widgets in a stretchable grid. To understand how the **Gird Layout** widget arranges the widgets, let's create an application.

How to do it...

In this application, we will make a simple sign-in form, prompting the user to enter an email address and password, followed by clicking the **Submit** button. Below the **Submit** button, there will be two buttons, **Cancel** and **Forgot Password**. The application will help you understand how these widgets are arranged in a grid pattern. Following are the steps to create this application:

1. Launch Qt Designer and create an application based on the **Dialog without Buttons** template, then add two `QLabel`, two `QlineEdit`, and three `QPushButton` widgets to the form by dragging and dropping two **Label**, two **Line Edit**, and three **Push Button** widgets on the form.
2. Set the **text** property of the two **Label** widgets to `Name` and `Email Address`.

3. Set the **text** property of the three **Push Button** widgets to `Submit`, `Cancel`, and `Forgot Password`.
4. Because the purpose of this application is to understand the layout and nothing else, we won't be setting the **objectName** property of any of the widgets in the application.
5. To increase the vertical space between the two **Line Edit** widgets, drag the **Vertical Spacer** widget from the **Spacers** tab of **Widget Box** and drop it in between the two **Line Edit** widgets. The vertical spacer will initially take up the blank space between the two **Line Edit** widgets.
6. To create vertical space between the second **Line Edit** widget and the **Submit** button, drag the **Vertical Spacer** widget and drop it between them.

   The application will appear as shown in the following screenshot:

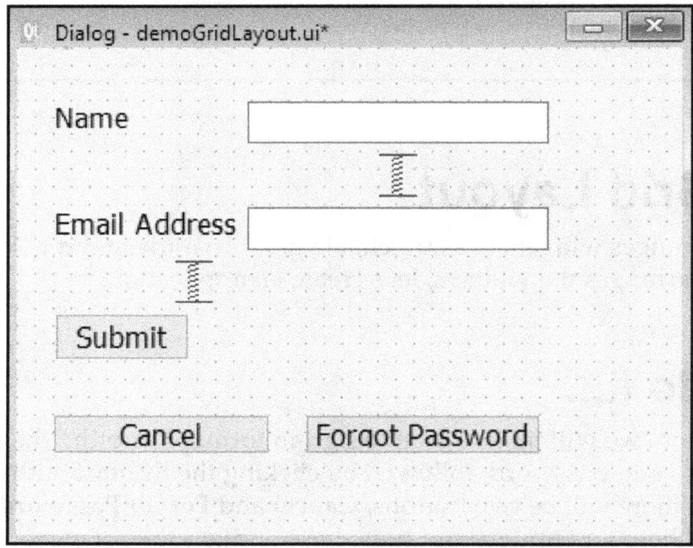

7. Select all the widgets on the form by pressing the *Ctrl* key and clicking all the widgets on the form.
8. After selecting all the widgets, right-click the mouse button to open the context menu.

9. From the context menu, select the **Layout** menu option, followed by selecting the **Layout in a Grid** submenu option.

 The widgets will be aligned in the grid as shown in the following screenshot:

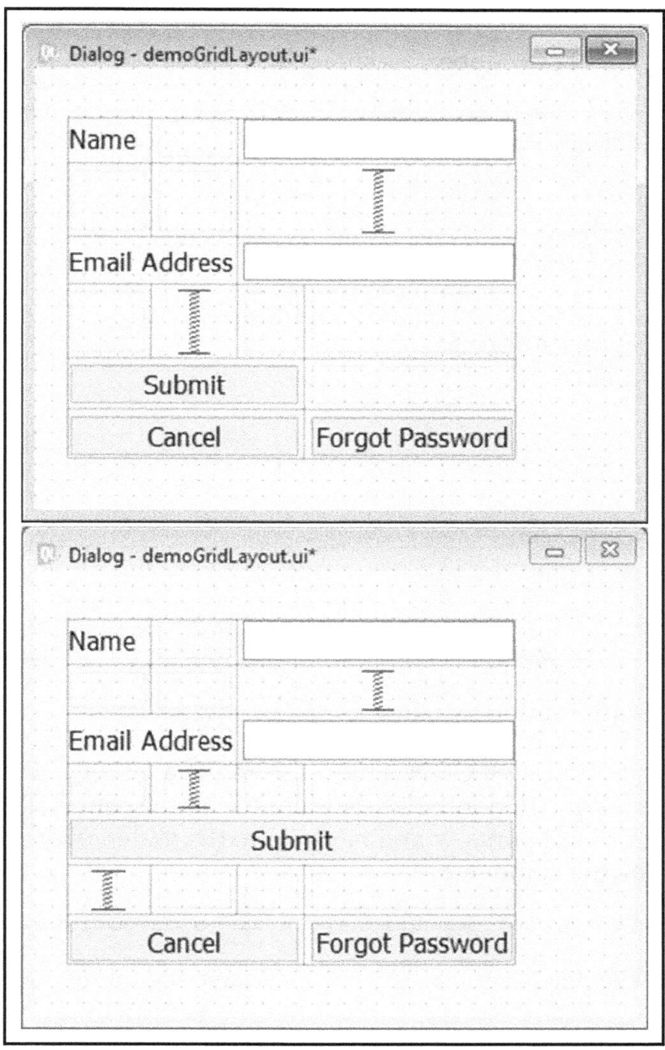

10. To increase the vertical space between the **Submit** and **Cancel** push buttons, drag the **Vertical Spacer** widget from the **Spacers** tab of **Widget Box** and drop it in between them.
11. To increase the horizontal space between the **Cancel** and **Forgot Password** push buttons, drag the **Horizontal Spacer** widget from the **Spacers** tab and drop it in between them.

    The form will now appear as shown in the following screenshot:

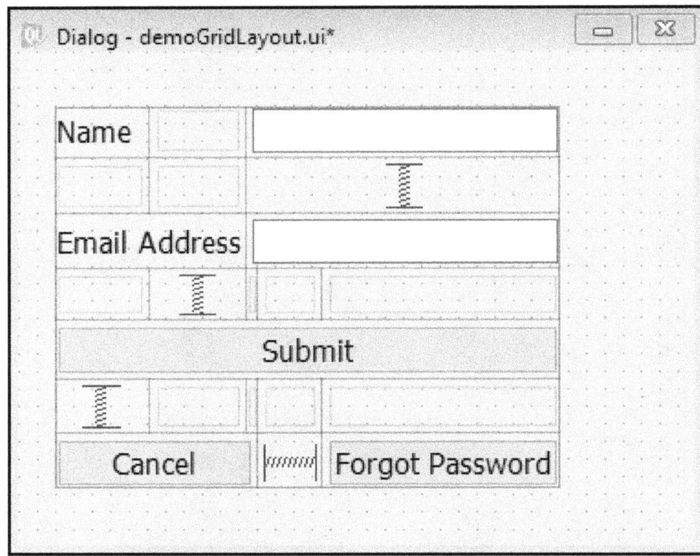

12. Save the application by name as `demoGridLayout.ui`.

The user interface created with Qt Designer is stored in a `.ui` file, which is an XML file, and needs to be converted into Python code. To do the conversion, you need to open a Command Prompt window and navigate to the folder where the file is saved, then issue the following command:

```
C:PyQt5>pyuic5 demoGridLayout.ui –o demoGridLayout.py
```

The Python script file `demoGridLayout.py` may have the following code:

```
from PyQt5 import QtCore, QtGui, QtWidgets
class Ui_Dialog(object):
    def setupUi(self, Dialog):
        Dialog.setObjectName("Dialog")
        Dialog.resize(369, 279)
```

```
        self.widget = QtWidgets.QWidget(Dialog)
        self.widget.setGeometry(QtCore.QRect(20, 31, 276,
216))
        self.widget.setObjectName("widget")
        self.gridLayout = QtWidgets.QGridLayout(self.widget)
        self.gridLayout.setContentsMargins(0, 0, 0, 0)
        self.gridLayout.setObjectName("gridLayout")
        self.pushButton = QtWidgets.QPushButton(self.widget)
        font = QtGui.QFont()
        font.setPointSize(12)
        self.pushButton.setFont(font)
        self.pushButton.setObjectName("pushButton")
        self.gridLayout.addWidget(self.pushButton, 4, 0, 1, 5)
        spacerItem = QtWidgets.QSpacerItem(20, 40, QtWidgets.
        QSizePolicy.Minimum,QtWidgets.QSizePolicy.Expanding)
        self.gridLayout.addItem(spacerItem, 5, 0, 1, 1)
        self.label = QtWidgets.QLabel(self.widget)
        font = QtGui.QFont()
        font.setPointSize(12)
        self.label.setFont(font)
        self.label.setObjectName("label")
        self.gridLayout.addWidget(self.label, 0, 0, 1, 1)
        self.label_2 = QtWidgets.QLabel(self.widget)
        font = QtGui.QFont()
        font.setPointSize(12)
        self.label_2.setFont(font)
        self.label_2.setObjectName("label_2")
        self.gridLayout.addWidget(self.label_2, 2, 0, 1, 2)
        self.lineEdit_2 = QtWidgets.QLineEdit(self.widget)
        font = QtGui.QFont()
        font.setPointSize(12)
        self.lineEdit_2.setFont(font)
        self.lineEdit_2.setObjectName("lineEdit_2")
        self.gridLayout.addWidget(self.lineEdit_2, 2, 2, 1, 3)
        self.lineEdit = QtWidgets.QLineEdit(self.widget)
        font = QtGui.QFont()
        font.setPointSize(12)
        self.lineEdit.setFont(font)
        self.lineEdit.setObjectName("lineEdit")
        self.gridLayout.addWidget(self.lineEdit, 0, 2, 1, 3)
        spacerItem1 = QtWidgets.QSpacerItem(20, 40, QtWidgets.
        QSizePolicy.Minimum,QtWidgets.QSizePolicy.Expanding)
        self.gridLayout.addItem(spacerItem1, 3, 1, 1, 1)
        spacerItem2 = QtWidgets.QSpacerItem(20, 40, QtWidgets.
        QSizePolicy.Minimum,QtWidgets.QSizePolicy.Expanding)
        self.gridLayout.addItem(spacerItem2, 1, 2, 1, 3)
        self.pushButton_2 = QtWidgets.QPushButton(self.widget)
        font = QtGui.QFont()
```

```
        font.setPointSize(12)
        self.pushButton_2.setFont(font)
        self.pushButton_2.setObjectName("pushButton_2")
        self.gridLayout.addWidget(self.pushButton_2, 6, 0, 1,
3)
        self.pushButton_3 = QtWidgets.QPushButton(self.widget)
        font = QtGui.QFont()
        font.setPointSize(12)
        self.pushButton_3.setFont(font)
        self.pushButton_3.setObjectName("pushButton_3")
        self.gridLayout.addWidget(self.pushButton_3, 6, 4, 1,
1)
        spacerItem3 = QtWidgets.QSpacerItem(40, 20, QtWidgets.
        QSizePolicy.Expanding,QtWidgets.QSizePolicy.Minimum)
        self.gridLayout.addItem(spacerItem3, 6, 3, 1, 1)
        self.retranslateUi(Dialog)
        QtCore.QMetaObject.connectSlotsByName(Dialog)
    def retranslateUi(self, Dialog):
        _translate = QtCore.QCoreApplication.translate
        Dialog.setWindowTitle(_translate("Dialog", "Dialog"))
        self.pushButton.setText(_translate("Dialog",
"Submit"))
        self.label.setText(_translate("Dialog", "Name"))
        self.label_2.setText(_translate("Dialog", "Email
Address"))
        self.pushButton_2.setText(_translate("Dialog",
"Cancel"))
        self.pushButton_3.setText(_translate("Dialog",
        "Forgot Password"))
if __name__ == "__main__":
    import sys
    app = QtWidgets.QApplication(sys.argv)
    Dialog = QtWidgets.QDialog()
    ui = Ui_Dialog()
    ui.setupUi(Dialog)
    Dialog.show()
    sys.exit(app.exec_())
```

How it works...

You can see in the code that a **Line Edit** widget with the default **objectName** `lineEdit` property and a **Label** widget with the default **objectName** `label` property are placed on the form. Similarly, a second pair, a **Label** widget with the default **objectName** `label_2` property and a **Line Edit** widget with the default **objectName** `lineEdit_2` property are placed on the form. The vertical space between the two pairs of **Label** and **Line Edit** widgets is increased by placing a vertical spacer called `spacerItem1` between them. A **Push Button** widget with the text, `Submit`, and **objectName**, `pushButton`, is also placed on the form. Again, the vertical space between the second **Label** with **objectName** `label_2` and the **Push Button** widget with **objectName** `pushButton` is increased by placing a vertical spacer called `spacerItem2` between them. Two more push buttons with the default **objectName** properties, `pushButton_2` and `pushButton_3`, are placed on the form. All the widgets are arranged in a stretchable grid layout with the default object name, `gridLayout`. The vertical space between the two push buttons with the object names, `pushButton` and `pushButton_2`, is increased by placing a vertical spacer called `spacerItem3` between them.

On running the application, you will find that the two pairs of **Label** and **Line Edit** widgets, and the **Submit**, **Cancel**, and **Forgot Password** buttons, are arranged in a stretchable grid, as shown in the following screenshot:

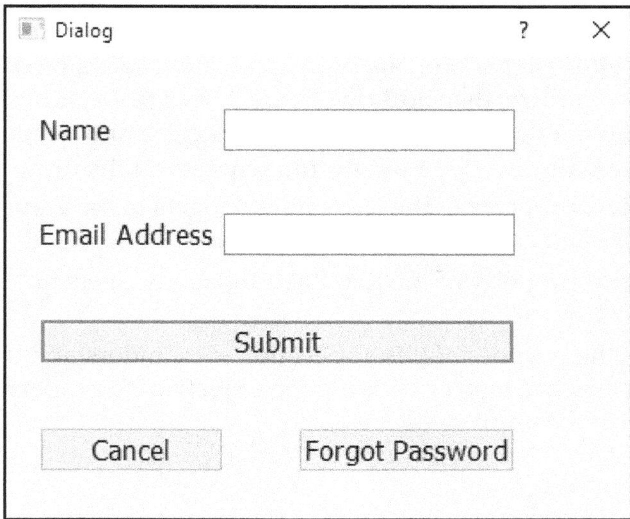

Using Form Layout

Form Layout is considered to be the most demanding layout in almost all applications. This two-column layout is required when displaying products, services, and so on, as well as in accepting feedback or other information from users or customers.

Getting ready

The form layout arranges the widgets in a two-column format. Like a sign-up form of any site or any order form, where the form is divided into two columns, the column on the left shows labels or text and the column on the right shows empty textboxes. Similarly, the form layout arranges the widgets in the left and right columns. Let's understand the concept of **Form Layout** using an application.

How to do it...

In this application, we will make two columns, one for displaying messages and the other column for accepting input from the user. Besides two pairs of **Label** and **Line Edit** widgets for taking input from the user, the application will have two buttons that will also be arranged in the form layout. Here are the steps to create an application that arranges widgets using **Form Layout**:

1. Launch Qt Designer and create an application based on the **Dialog without Buttons** template, then add two `QLabel`, two `QLineEdit`, and two `QPushButton` widgets to the form by dragging and dropping two **Label**, two **Line Edit**, and two **PushButton** widgets on the form.
2. Set the **text** property of the two **Label** widgets to `Name` and `Email Address`.
3. Set the **text** property of the two **Push Button** widgets to `Cancel` and `Submit`.
4. Because the purpose of this application is to understand the layout and nothing else, we won't be setting the **objectName** property of any of the widgets in the application.

The application will appear as shown in the following screenshot:

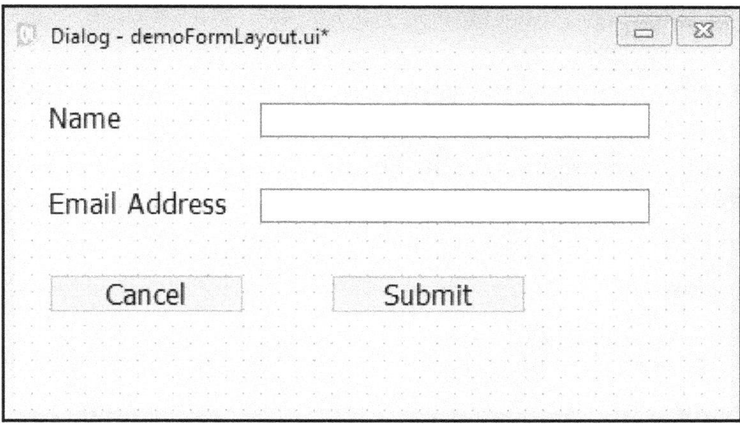

5. Select all the widgets on the form by pressing the *Ctrl* key and clicking all the widgets on the form.
6. After selecting all the widgets, right-click the mouse button to open the context menu.
7. From the context menu, select the **Layout** menu option, followed by selecting the **Layout in a Form Layout** submenu option.

The widgets will be aligned in the **Form Layout** widget, as shown in the following screenshot:

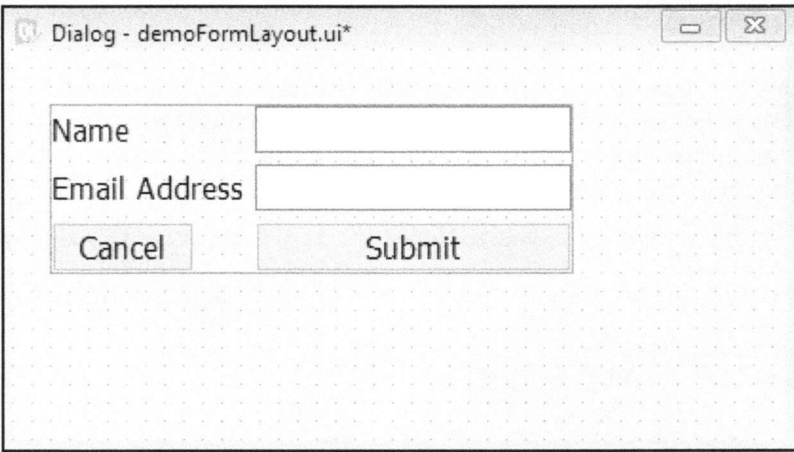

8. To increase the vertical space between the two **Line Edit** widgets, drag the **Vertical Spacer** widget from the **Spacers** tab of **Widget Box** and drop it in between them.
9. To increase the vertical space between the second **Line Edit** widget and the **Submit** button, drag the **Vertical Spacer** widget from the **Spacers** tab and drop it in between them.
10. Select the red rectangle of the **Form Layout** widget and drag it vertically to increase its height. The two vertical spacers will automatically increase in height to use the empty space in between the widgets.

The form will now appear as shown in the following screenshot:

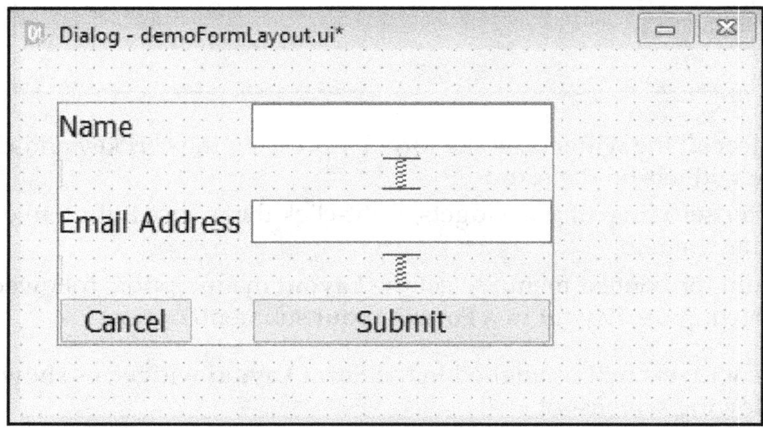

11. Save the application as `demoFormLayout.ui`.

The user interface created with Qt Designer is stored in a `.ui` file, which is an XML file, and needs to be converted into Python code. To do the conversion, you need to open a Command Prompt window and navigate to the folder where the file is saved, then issue the following command:

```
C:PyQt5>pyuic5 demoFormLayout.ui -o demoFormLayout.py
```

The Python script file, `demoFormLayout.py`, may have the following code:

```
from PyQt5 import QtCore, QtGui, QtWidgets
class Ui_Dialog(object):
    def setupUi(self, Dialog):
        Dialog.setObjectName("Dialog")
        Dialog.resize(407, 211)
        self.widget = QtWidgets.QWidget(Dialog)
```

```
        self.widget.setGeometry(QtCore.QRect(20, 30, 276,
141))
        self.widget.setObjectName("widget")
        self.formLayout = QtWidgets.QFormLayout(self.widget)
        self.formLayout.setContentsMargins(0, 0, 0, 0)
        self.formLayout.setObjectName("formLayout")
        self.label = QtWidgets.QLabel(self.widget)
        font = QtGui.QFont()
        font.setPointSize(12)
        self.label.setFont(font)
        self.label.setObjectName("label")
        self.formLayout.setWidget(0, QtWidgets.QFormLayout.
        LabelRole,self.label)
        self.lineEdit = QtWidgets.QLineEdit(self.widget)
        font = QtGui.QFont()
        font.setPointSize(12)
        self.lineEdit.setFont(font)
        self.lineEdit.setObjectName("lineEdit")
        self.formLayout.setWidget(0, QtWidgets.QFormLayout.
        FieldRole,self.lineEdit)
        self.label_2 = QtWidgets.QLabel(self.widget)
        font = QtGui.QFont()
        font.setPointSize(12)
        self.label_2.setFont(font)
        self.label_2.setObjectName("label_2")
        self.formLayout.setWidget(2, QtWidgets.QFormLayout.
        LabelRole,self.label_2)
        self.lineEdit_2 = QtWidgets.QLineEdit(self.widget)
        font = QtGui.QFont()
        font.setPointSize(12)
        self.lineEdit_2.setFont(font)
        self.lineEdit_2.setObjectName("lineEdit_2")
        self.formLayout.setWidget(2, QtWidgets.QFormLayout.
        FieldRole, self.lineEdit_2)
        self.pushButton_2 = QtWidgets.QPushButton(self.widget)
        font = QtGui.QFont()
        font.setPointSize(12)
        self.pushButton_2.setFont(font)
        self.pushButton_2.setObjectName("pushButton_2")
        self.formLayout.setWidget(4, QtWidgets.QFormLayout.
        LabelRole,self.pushButton_2)
        self.pushButton = QtWidgets.QPushButton(self.widget)
        font = QtGui.QFont()
        font.setPointSize(12)
        self.pushButton.setFont(font)
        self.pushButton.setObjectName("pushButton")
        self.formLayout.setWidget(4, QtWidgets.QFormLayout.
        FieldRole,self.pushButton)
```

```
        spacerItem = QtWidgets.QSpacerItem(20, 40, QtWidgets.
        QSizePolicy.Minimum,QtWidgets.QSizePolicy.Expanding)
        self.formLayout.setItem(1,
QtWidgets.QFormLayout.FieldRole,
        spacerItem)
        spacerItem1 = QtWidgets.QSpacerItem(20, 40, QtWidgets.
        QSizePolicy.Minimum,QtWidgets.QSizePolicy.Expanding)
        self.formLayout.setItem(3,
QtWidgets.QFormLayout.FieldRole,
        spacerItem1)
        self.retranslateUi(Dialog)
        QtCore.QMetaObject.connectSlotsByName(Dialog)
    def retranslateUi(self, Dialog):
        _translate = QtCore.QCoreApplication.translate
        Dialog.setWindowTitle(_translate("Dialog", "Dialog"))
        self.label.setText(_translate("Dialog", "Name"))
        self.label_2.setText(_translate("Dialog", "Email
Address"))
        self.pushButton_2.setText(_translate("Dialog",
"Cancel"))
        self.pushButton.setText(_translate("Dialog",
"Submit"))
if __name__ == "__main__":
    import sys
    app = QtWidgets.QApplication(sys.argv)
    Dialog = QtWidgets.QDialog()
    ui = Ui_Dialog()
    ui.setupUi(Dialog)
    Dialog.show()
    sys.exit(app.exec_())
```

How it works...

You can see in the code that a **Line Edit** widget with the default **objectName** `lineEdit` property and a **Label** widget with the default **objectName** `labels` property is placed on the form. Similarly, a second pair, a **Label** widget with the default **objectName** `label_2` property and a **Line Edit** widget with the default **objectName** `lineEdit_2` property are placed on the form. The two push buttons with the object names, `pushButton` and `pushButton_2`, are placed on the form. All six widgets are selected and aligned in a two-column format using the **Form Layout** widget with the default **objectName** `formLayout` property.

On running the application, you will find that the two pairs of **Label** and **Line Edit** widgets, and the **Cancel** and **Submit** buttons, are arranged in a **Form Layout** widget as shown in the following screenshot:

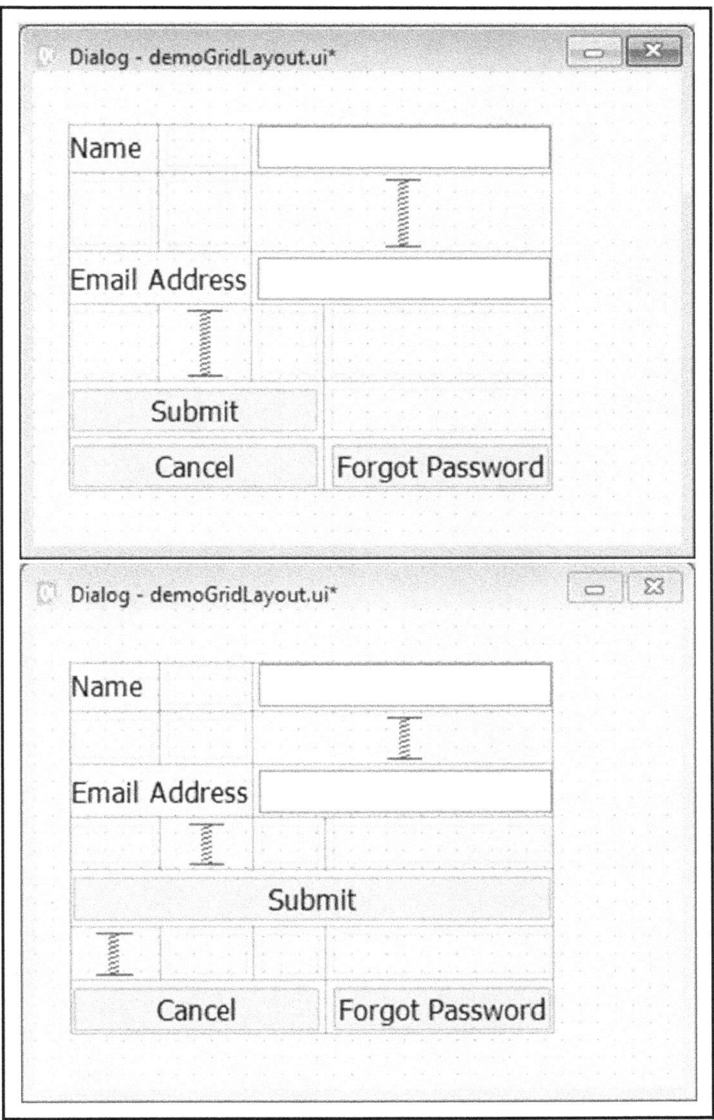

18
Networking and Managing Large Documents

In this chapter, we will learn how to use networking concepts and about how large documents can be viewed in chunks. We will cover the following topics:

- Creating a small browser
- Creating a server-side application
- Establishing client-server communication
- Creating a dockable and floatable sign-in form
- Multiple Document Interface
- Displaying information in sections using Tab Widget
- Creating a custom menu bar

Introduction

Space on a device screen is always limited, but sometimes you come across a situation in which you want to display lots of information or services on the screen. In such a situation, you can either use dockable widgets that can be floated anywhere on the screen; MDI to display multiple documents as and when desired; a **Tab Widget** box to display information in different chunks; or menus to display the required information on the click of a menu item. Also, to better understand networking concepts, you need to understand how clients and servers communicate. This chapter will help you understand all this.

Creating a small browser

Let's now learn a technique to display a web page or the content of an HTML document. We will simply be making use of the **Line Edit** and **Push Button** widgets so that the user can enter the URL of the desired site, followed by clicking on the **Push Button** widget. On clicking the push button, that site will appear in a customized widget. Let's see how.

In this recipe, we will learn how to make a small browser. Because Qt Designer does not includes any widgets specifically, the focus of this recipe is to make you understand how a custom widget can be promoted into `QWebEngineView`, which in turn can be used for displaying a web page.

The application will prompt for a URL and when the user clicks the **Go** button after entering the URL, the specified web page will open in the `QWebEngineView` object.

How to do it...

In this recipe, we will require just three widgets: one for entering the URL, a second for clicking the button, and a third for displaying the website. Here are the steps to creating a simple browser:

1. Create an application based on the **Dialog without Buttons** template.
2. Add the `QLabel`, `QLineEdit`, `QPushButton`, and `QWidget` widgets to the form by dragging and dropping **Label**, **Line Edit**, **Push Button**, and **Widget** onto the form.
3. Set the **text** property of the **Label** widget to `Enter URL`.
4. Set the **text** property of the **Push Button** widget to `Go`.
5. Set the **objectName** property of the **Line Edit** widget to `lineEditURL` and that of the **Push Button** widget to `pushButtonGo`.
6. Save the application as `demoBrowser.ui`.

The form will now appear as shown in the following screenshot:

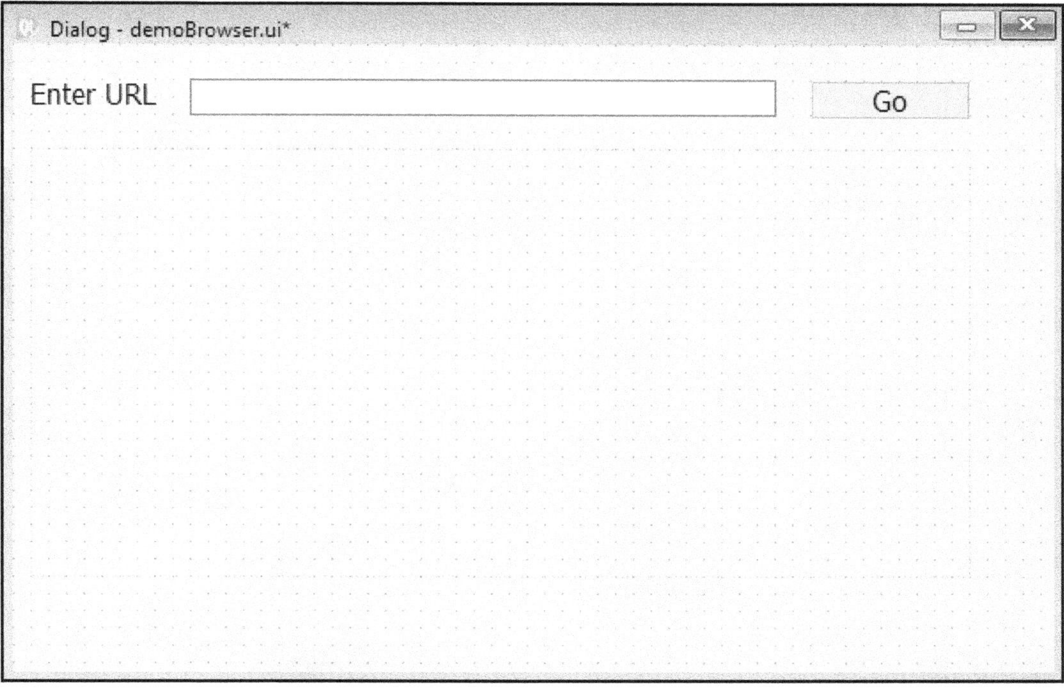

7. The next step is to promote `QWidget` to `QWebEngineView` because, to display web pages, `QWebEngineView` is required.
8. Promote the `QWidget` object by right-clicking on it and selecting the **Promote to ...** option from the menu that pops up.
9. In the dialog box that appears, leave the **Base class name** option as the default, **QWidget**.
10. In the **Promoted class name** box, enter `QWebEngineView` and in the **Header file** box type `PyQt5.QtWebEngineWidgets`.

11. Select the **Promote** button to promote **QWidget** to the `QWebEngineView` class, as shown in the following screenshot:

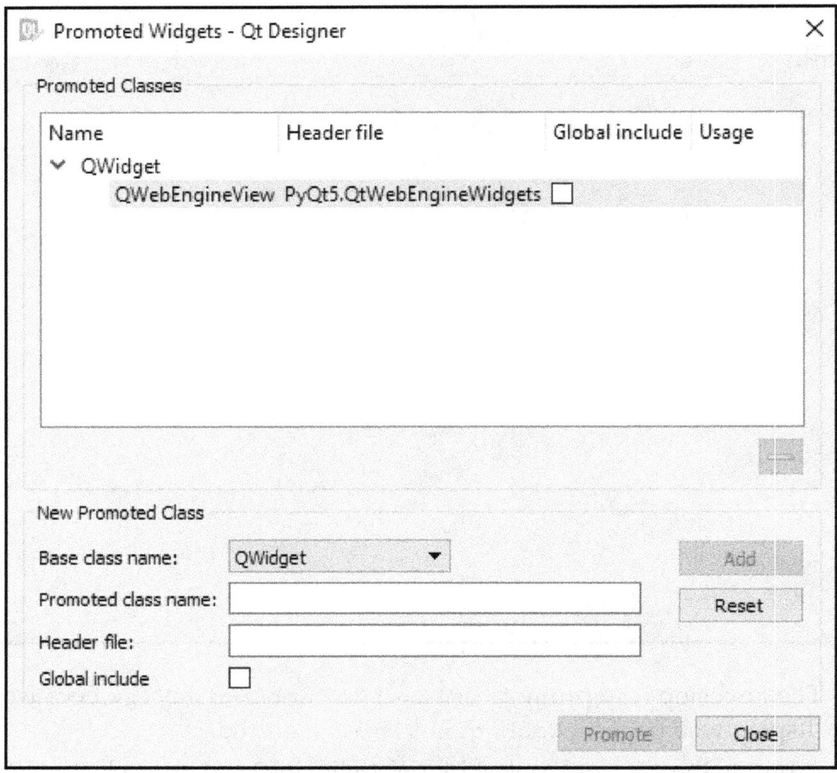

The user interface created with Qt Designer is stored in a `.ui` file, which is an XML file, and needs to be converted into Python code.

12. To do the conversion, you need to open a Command Prompt window and navigate to the folder where the file is saved, then issue the following command:

```
C:\Pythonbook\PyQt5>pyuic5 demoBrowser.ui -o demoBrowser.py
```

You can see the auto-generated Python script file `demoBrowser.py` in the source code bundle of this book.

13. Treat the preceding code as a header file, and import it into the file from which you will invoke its user interface design.

14. Let's create another Python file with the name `callBrowser.pyw` and import the `demoBrowser.py` code into it:

```
import sys
from PyQt5.QtCore import QUrl
from PyQt5.QtWidgets import QApplication, QDialog
from PyQt5.QtWebEngineWidgets import QWebEngineView
from demoBrowser import *
class MyForm(QDialog):
    def __init__(self):
        super().__init__()
        self.ui = Ui_Dialog()
        self.ui.setupUi(self)
        self.ui.pushButtonGo.clicked.connect(self.dispSite)
        self.show()
    def dispSite(self):
        self.ui.widget.load(QUrl(self.ui.lineEditURL.text()))
if __name__=="__main__":
    app = QApplication(sys.argv)
    w = MyForm()
    w.show()
    sys.exit(app.exec_())
```

How it works...

In the `demoBrowser.py` file, a class with the name of the top-level object is created, with `Ui_ prepended`. That is, for the top-level object, `Dialog`, the `Ui_Dialog` class is created and stores the interface elements of our widget. That class includes two methods, `setupUi()` and `retranslateUi()`. The `setupUi()` method creates the widgets that are used in defining the user interface in Qt Designer. Also, the properties of the widgets are set in this method. The `setupUi()` method takes a single argument, which is the top-level widget of the application, an instance of `QDialog`. The `retranslateUi()` method translates the interface.

In the `callBrowser.pyw` file, you see that the **click()** event of the **Push Button** widget is connected to the `dispSite` method; after entering a URL in the **Line Edit** widget, when the user clicks the Push Button, the `dispSite` method will be invoked.

The `dispSite()` method invokes the `load()` method of the `QWidget` class. Recall that the `QWidget` object is promoted to the `QWebEngineView` class for viewing web pages. The `load()` method of the `QWebEngineView` class is supplied with the URL entered in the `lineEditURL` object consequently, the web page of the specified URL opens up or loads in the `QWebEngine` widget.

On running the application, you get an empty **Line Edit** box and a **Push Button** widget. Enter the desired URL in the **Line Edit** widget and click on the **Go** push button, and you will find the web page opens in the `QWebEngineView` widget, as shown in the following screenshot:

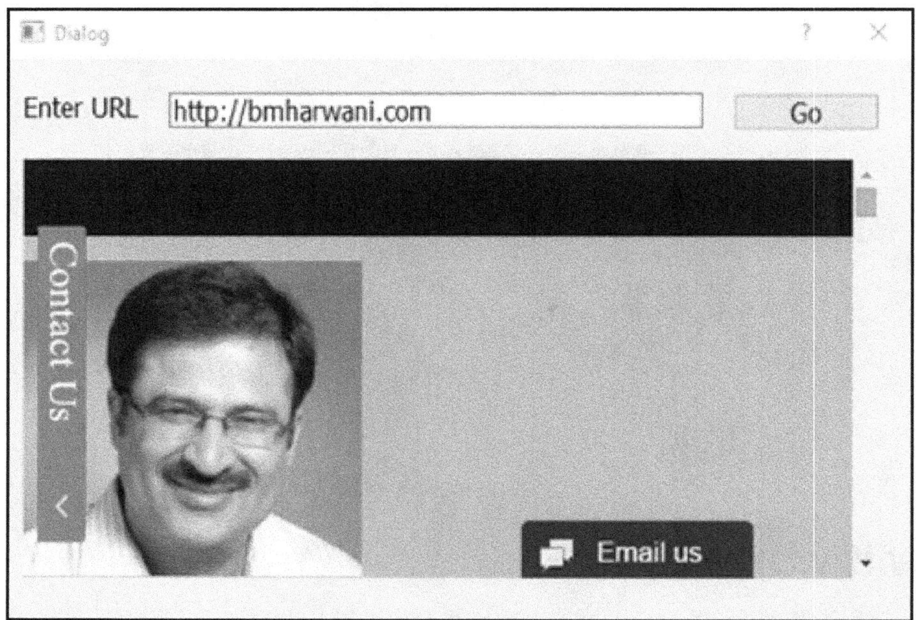

Creating a server-side application

Networking plays a major role in modern life. We need to understand how communication is established between two machines. When two machines communicate, one is usually a server and the other is a client. The client sends requests to the server and the server responds by serving the request made by the client.

In this recipe, we will be creating a client-server application where a connection is established between client and server and each will be able to transfer text messages to the other. That is, two applications will be made and will be executed simultaneously, and the text written in one application will appear in the other.

How to do it...

Let's begin by creating a server application first, as follows:

1. Create an application based on the **Dialog without Buttons** template.
2. Add a `QLabel`, `QTextEdit`, `QLineEdit`, and `QPushButton` to the form by dragging and dropping the **Label**, a **Text Edit**, **Line Edit**, and **Push Button** widgets on the form.

2. Set the **text** property of the **Label** widget to `Server` to indicate that this is the server application.
3. Set the **text** property of the **Push Button** widget to `Send`.
4. Set the **objectName** property of the **Text Edit** widget to `textEditMessages`.
5. Set the **objectName** property of the **Line Edit** widget to `lineEditMessage`.
6. Set the **Push Button** widget to `pushButtonSend`.
7. Save the application as `demoServer.ui`. The form will now appear as shown in the following screenshot:

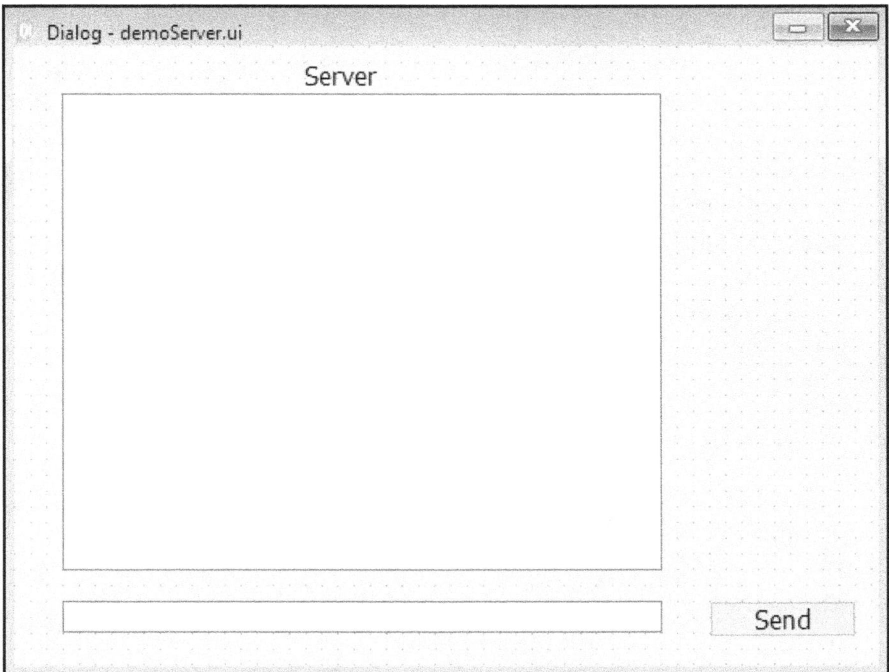

The user interface created with Qt Designer is stored in a `.ui` file, which is an XML file, and needs to be converted into Python code. The code of the generated file, `demoServer.py`, can be seen in the source code bundle of this book.

How it works...

The `demoServer.py` file will be treated as a header file and will be imported into another Python file that will use the GUI of the header file and transmit the data from the server to client and vice versa. But before that, let's create a GUI for the client application. The GUI of the client application is exactly the same as that of the server application, with the only difference that the **Label** widget at the top of this application will display the text **Client**.

The `demoServer.py` file is a generated Python script of the GUI widgets that we dragged and dropped onto the form.

To establish a connection between the server and client, we will require a socket object. To create the socket object, you need to supply the following two arguments:

- **Socket address:** The socket address is represented using certain address families. Each address family requires certain parameters to establish a connection. We will be using the `AF_INET` address family in this application. The `AF_INET` address family needs a pair of (host, port) to establish a connection where the parameter, `host` is the hostname which can either be in string format, internet domain notation, or IPv4 address format and the parameter; `port` is an integer that represents the port number used for communication.
- **Socket type**: The socket type is represented through several constants: `SOCK_STREAM`, `SOCK_DGRAM`, `SOCK_RAW`, `SOCK_RDM`, and `SOCK_SEQPACKET`. We will use the most generally used socket type, `SOCK_STREAM`, in this application.

The `setsockopt()` method is used in the application for setting the value of the given socket option. It includes the following two essential parameters:

- `SOL_SOCKET`: This parameter is the socket layer itself. It is used for protocol-independent options.
- `SO_REUSEADDR`: This parameter allows other sockets to `bind()` to this port unless there is an active listening socket bound to the port already.

You can see in the earlier code that a `ServerThread` class is created, which inherits the `Thread` class of Python's threading module. The `run()` function is overridden where the `TCP_IP` and `TCP_HOST` variables are defined and `tcpServer` is bound with these variables.

Thereafter, the server waits to see whether any client connection is made. For each new client connection, the server creates a new `ClientThread` inside the `while` loop. This is because creating a new thread for each client will not block the GUI functionality of the server. Finally, the threads are joined.

Establishing client-server communication

In this recipe, we will learn to make a client and will see how it can send messages to the server. The main idea is to understand how a message is sent, how the server listens to the port, and how communication is established between the two.

How to do it...

To send messages to the server, we will be making use of the **Line Edit** and **Push Button** widgets. The message written in the **Line Edit** widget will be passed to the server on the click of the push button. Here is the step-by-step procedure for creating a client application:

1. Create another application based on the **Dialog without Buttons** template.
2. Add `QLabel`, `QTextEdit`, `QLineEdit`, and `QPushButton` to the form by dragging and dropping the **Label**, **Text Edit**, **Line Edit**, and **Push Button** widgets on the form.
3. Set the **text** property of the **Label** widget to `Client`.
4. Set the **text** property of the **Push Button** widget to `Send`.
5. Set the **objectName** property of the **Text Edit** widget to `textEditMessages`.
6. Set the **objectName** property of the **Line Edit** widget to `lineEditMessage`.
7. Set the **Push Button** widget to `pushButtonSend`.
8. Save the application by name as `demoClient.ui`.

The form will now appear as shown in the following screenshot:

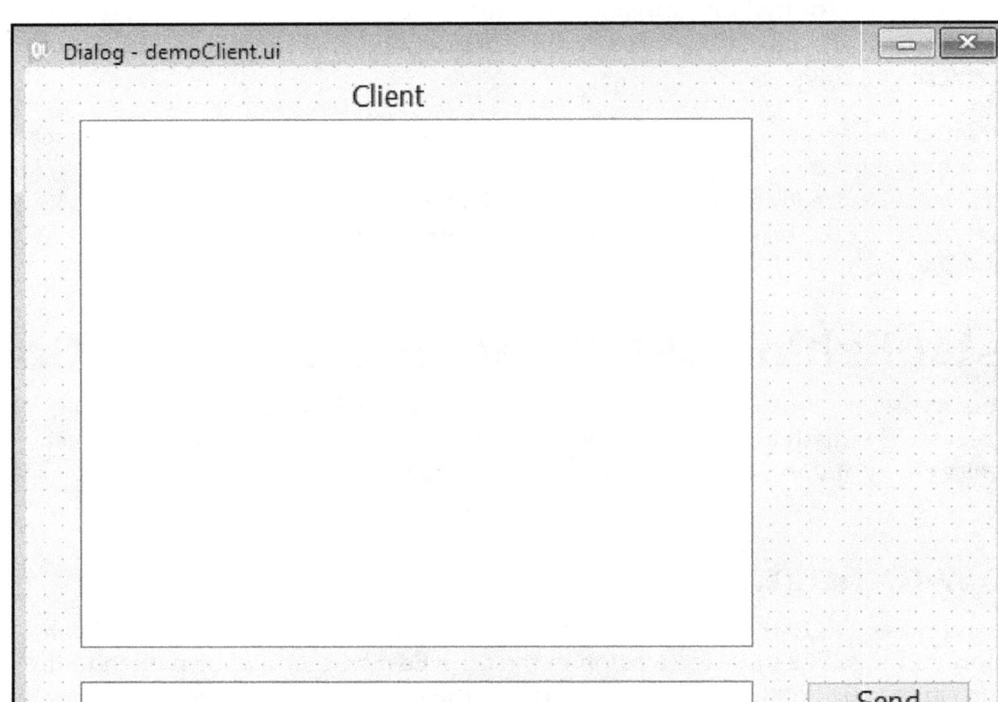

The user interface created with Qt Designer is stored in a `.ui` file, which is an XML file, and needs to be converted into Python code. The code of the autogenerated file, `demoClient.py`, can be seen in the source code bundle of this book. To use the GUI created in the `demoClient.py` file, it needs to be imported into another Python file that will use the GUI and will transmit data from the server to the client and vice versa.

9. Create another Python file with the name `callServer.pyw` and import the `demoServer.py` code into it. The code in the `callServer.pyw` script is as shown here:

```
import sys, time
from PyQt5 import QtGui
from PyQt5 import QtCore
from PyQt5.QtWidgets import QApplication, QDialog
from PyQt5.QtCore import QCoreApplication
```

```
import socket
from threading import Thread
from socketserver import ThreadingMixIn
conn=None
from demoServer import *
class Window(QDialog):
    def __init__(self):
        super().__init__()
        self.ui = Ui_Dialog()
        self.ui.setupUi(self)
        self.textEditMessages=self.ui.textEditMessages
self.ui.pushButtonSend.clicked.connect(self.dispMessage)
        self.show()

    def dispMessage(self):
        text=self.ui.lineEditMessage.text()
        global conn
        conn.send(text.encode("utf-8"))
        self.ui.textEditMessages.append("Server:
        "+self.ui.lineEditMessage.text())
        self.ui.lineEditMessage.setText("")
class ServerThread(Thread):
    def __init__(self,window):
        Thread.__init__(self)
        self.window=window
    def run(self):
        TCP_IP = '0.0.0.0'
        TCP_PORT = 80
        BUFFER_SIZE = 1024
        tcpServer = socket.socket(socket.AF_INET,
        socket.SOCK_STREAM)
        tcpServer.setsockopt(socket.SOL_SOCKET,
        socket.SO_REUSEADDR, 1)
        tcpServer.bind((TCP_IP, TCP_PORT))
        threads = []
        tcpServer.listen(4)
        while True:
            global conn
            (conn, (ip,port)) = tcpServer.accept()
            newthread = ClientThread(ip,port,window)
            newthread.start()
            threads.append(newthread)
        for t in threads:
            t.join()
class ClientThread(Thread):
    def __init__(self,ip,port,window):
        Thread.__init__(self)
        self.window=window
```

```
            self.ip = ip
            self.port = port
        def run(self):
            while True :
                global conn
                data = conn.recv(1024)
                window.textEditMessages.append("Client:
                "+data.decode("utf-8"))

    if __name__=="__main__":
        app = QApplication(sys.argv)
        window = Window()
        serverThread=ServerThread(window)
        serverThread.start()
        window.exec()
        sys.exit(app.exec_())
```

How it works...

In the `ClientThread` class, the `run` function is overridden. In the `run` function, each client waits for data received from the server and displays that data in the **Text Edit** widget. A `window` class object is passed to the `ServerThread` class, which passes that object to `ClientThread`, which, in turn, uses it to access the content written in the **Line Edit** element.

The received data is decoded because the data received is in the form of bytes, which have to be converted into strings using UTF-8 encoding.

The `demoClient.py` file that we generated in the preceding section needs to be treated as a header file and needs to be imported into another Python file that will use the GUI of the header file and transmit data from the client to the server and vice versa. So, let's create another Python file with the name `callClient.pyw` and import the `demoClient.py` code into it:

```
import sys
from PyQt5.QtWidgets import QApplication, QDialog
import socket
from threading import Thread
from socketserver import ThreadingMixIn
from demoClient import *
tcpClientA=None
class Window(QDialog):
    def __init__(self):
        super().__init__()
        self.ui = Ui_Dialog()
```

```
        self.ui.setupUi(self)
        self.textEditMessages=self.ui.textEditMessages
        self.ui.pushButtonSend.clicked.connect(self.dispMessage)
        self.show()
    def dispMessage(self):
        text=self.ui.lineEditMessage.text()
        self.ui.textEditMessages.append("Client:
        "+self.ui.lineEditMessage.text())
        tcpClientA.send(text.encode())
        self.ui.lineEditMessage.setText("")
class ClientThread(Thread):
    def __init__(self,window):
        Thread.__init__(self)
        self.window=window
    def run(self):
        host = socket.gethostname()
        port = 80
        BUFFER_SIZE = 1024
        global tcpClientA
        tcpClientA = socket.socket(socket.AF_INET,
        socket.SOCK_STREAM)
        tcpClientA.connect((host, port))
        while True:
            data = tcpClientA.recv(BUFFER_SIZE)
            window.textEditMessages.append("Server:
            "+data.decode("utf-8"))
            tcpClientA.close()
if __name__=="__main__":
    app = QApplication(sys.argv)
    window = Window()
    clientThread=ClientThread(window)
    clientThread.start()
    window.exec()
    sys.exit(app.exec_())
```

A `ClientThread` class is a class that inherits the `Thread` class and overrides the `run` function. In the `run` function, you fetch the IP address of the server by invoking the `hostname` method on the `socket` class; and, using port `80`, the client tries to connect to the server. Once a connection with the server is made, the client tries to receive data from the server inside the while loop.

On receiving the data from the server, the data is converted into string format from byte format and displayed in the **Text Edit** widget.

We need to run both applications to see client-server communication. On running the `callServer.pyw` file, you get the output shown on the left side of the following screenshot, and on running the `callClient.pyw` file, you get the output shown on the right side. Both are same; only the labels at the top distinguish them:

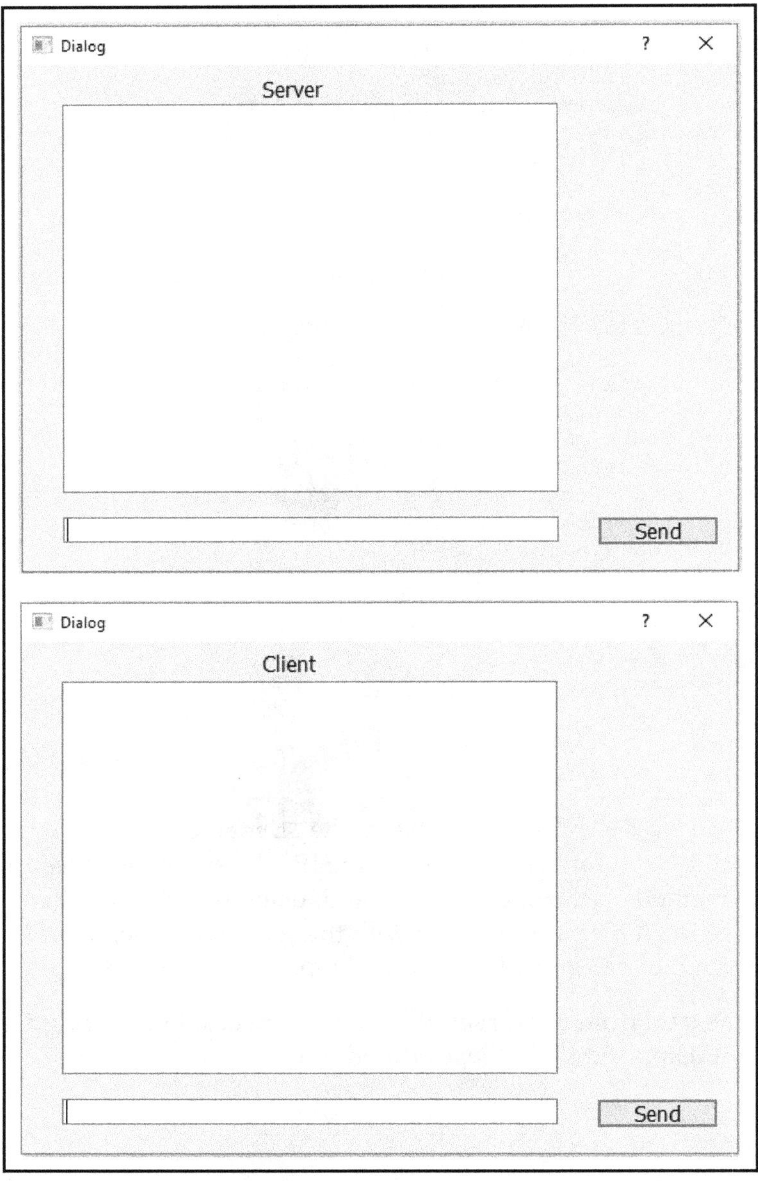

The user can type the text in the **Line Edit** box at the bottom, followed by pressing the **Send** button. On pressing the **Send** button, the text entered in the **Line Edit** widget will appear in the **Text Edit** box of both server and client applications. Text is prefixed with `Server:` to indicate that the text is sent from the server, as shown in the following screenshot:

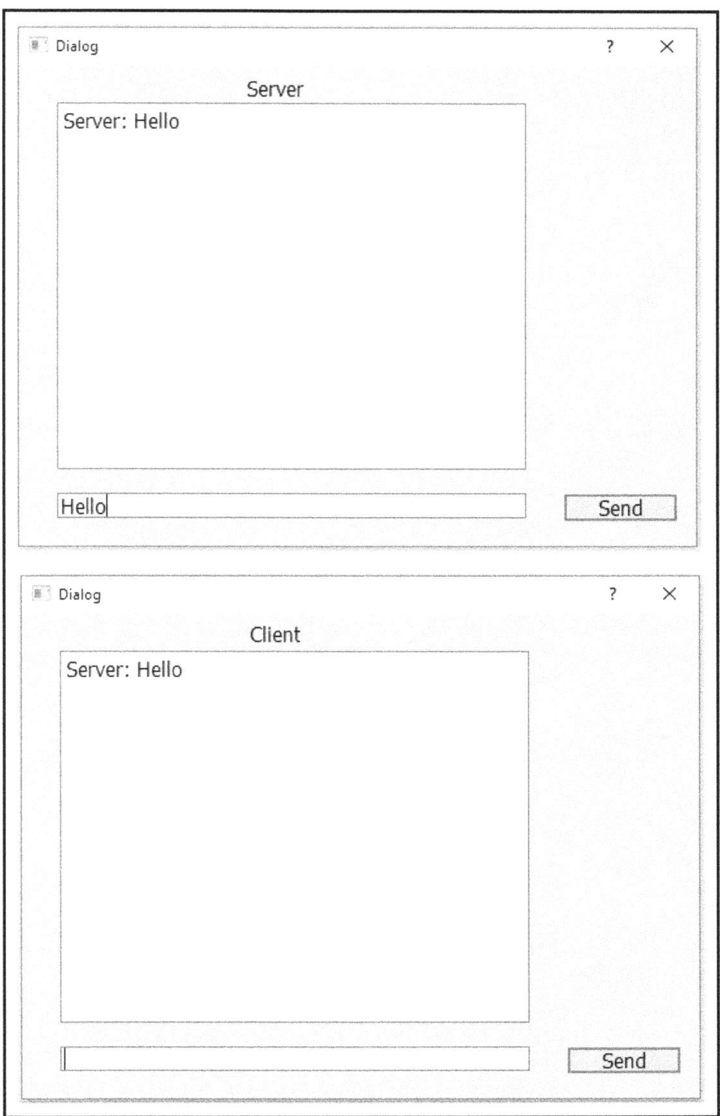

Similarly, if text is written in the **Line Edit** widget of the client application followed by pressing the **Send** button, the text will appear in the **Text Edit** widget of both applications. The text will be prefixed with `Client:` to indicate that the text has been sent from the client, as shown in the following screenshot:

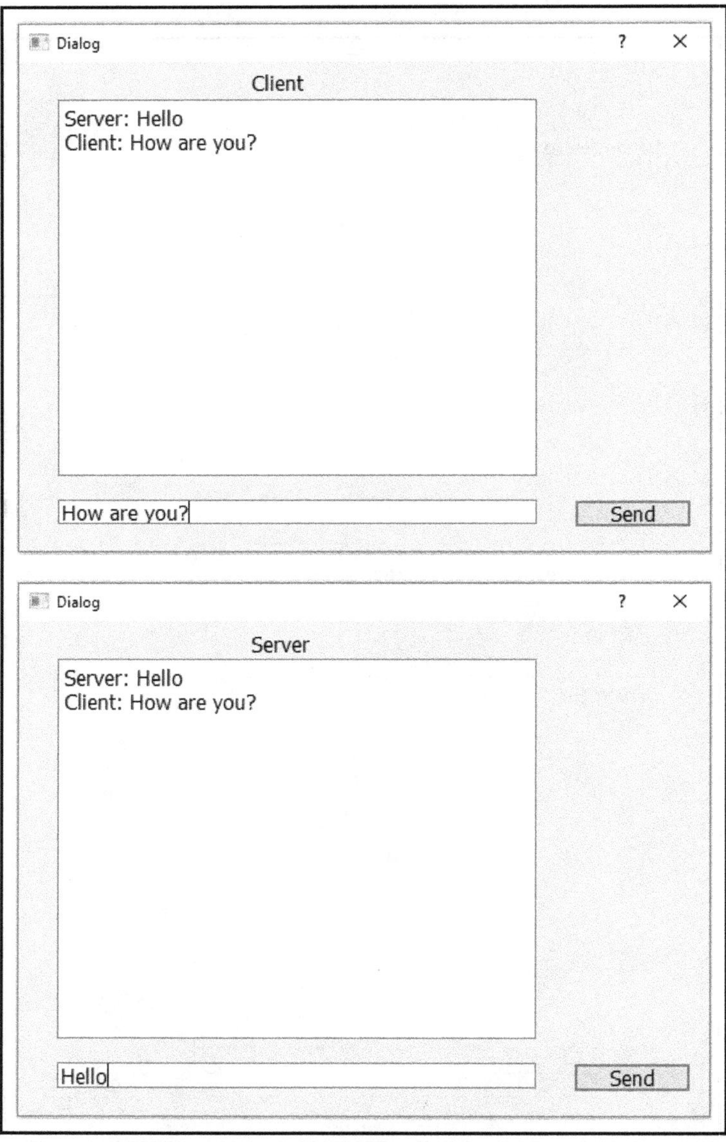

Creating a dockable and floatable sign-in form

In this recipe, we will learn to create a sign-in form that will ask for the email address and password of the user for authentication. This sign-in form is different from the usual sign-in form, in the sense that it is a dockable form. That is, you can dock this sign-in form to any of the four sides of the window—top, left, right, and bottom and can even use it as a floatable form. This dockable sign-in form will be created using the **Dock** widget, so let's get a quick idea about the **Dock** widget.

Getting ready

To create a detachable set of widgets or tools, you need a **Dock** widget. A **Dock** widget is created with the `QDockWidget` class and is a container that has a title bar and buttons at the top to size it. The **Dock** widget, which contains a collection of widgets or tools, can be closed, docked in the dock area, or floated and placed anywhere on the desktop. The **Dock** widget can be docked in different dock areas, such as `LeftDockWidgetArea`, `RightDockWidgetArea`, `TopDockWidgetArea`, and `BottomDockWidgetArea`. The `TopDockWidgetArea` dock area is below the toolbar. You can also restrict the dock areas where the **Dock** widget can be docked. When you do so, the **Dock** widget can be docked to the specified dock areas only. When a **Dock** window is dragged out of the dock area, it becomes a free-floating window.

Here are the properties that control the movement of the **Dock** widget and the appearance of its title bar and other buttons:

Property	**Description**
`DockWidgetClosable`	Makes the **Dock** widget closable.
`DockWidgetMovable`	Makes the **Dock** widget movable between dock areas.
`DockWidgetFloatable`	Makes the **Dock** widget floatable, that is, the **Dock** widget can be detached from the main window and floated on the desktop.
`DockWidgetVerticalTitleBar`	Displays a vertical title bar on the left side of the **Dock** widget.
`AllDockWidgetFeatures`	It switches on properties such as `DockWidgetClosable`, `DockWidgetMovable`, and `DockWidgetFloatable`, that is, the **Dock** widget can be closed, moved, or floated.
`NoDockWidgetFeatures`	If selected, the **Dock** widget cannot be closed, moved, or floated.

In order to make a dockable sign-in form for this recipe, we will be making use of the **Dock** widget and a few more widgets. Let's see the step-by-step procedure for doing this.

How to do it...

Let's make a small sign-in form in the **Dock** widget that will prompt the user for their email address and password. Being dockable, this sign-in form can be moved anywhere on the screen and can be made floatable. Here are the steps to create this application:

1. Launch Qt Designer and create a new **Main Window** application.
2. Drag and drop a **Dock** widget onto the form.
3. Drag and drop the widgets that you want to be available in dock areas or as floating windows in the **Dock** widget.
4. Drag and drop three **Label** widgets, two **Line Edit** widgets, and a **Push Button** widget on the **Dock** widget.
5. Set the **text** property of the three **Label** widgets to `Sign In`, `Email Address`, and `Password`.

6. Set the **text** property of the **Push Button** widget to `Sign In`.
7. We will not set the **objectName** property of the **Line Edit** and **Push Button** widgets and will not provide any code for the **Push Button** widget, because the purpose of this application is to understand how the **Dock** widget works.
8. Save the application as `demoDockWidget.ui`.

The form will appear as shown in the following screenshot:

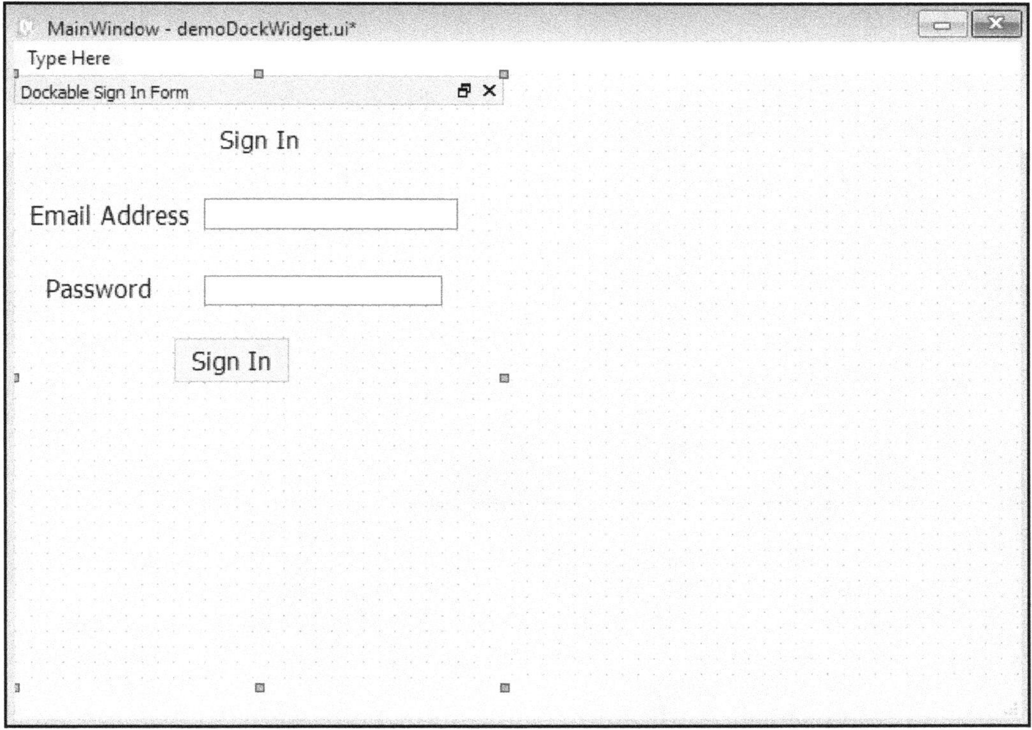

9. To enable all features in the **Dock** widget, select it and check its **AllDockWidgetFeatures** property in the **features** section of the **Property Editor** window, as shown in the following screenshot:

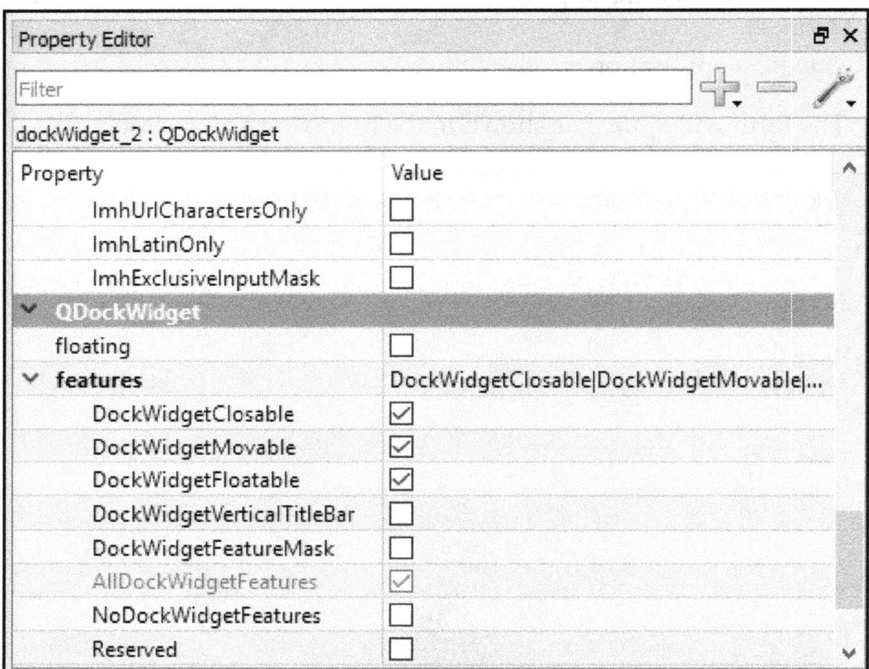

In the preceding screenshot, the **AllDockWidgetFeatures** property is to make the **Dock** widget closable, movable in the dock, and floatable anywhere on the **Desktop**. If the **NoDockWidgetFeatures** property is selected, then all other properties in the **features** section are unchecked automatically. That means all buttons will disappear from the **Dock** widget, and you will not be able to close or move it. If you want the **Dock** widget to appear as floatable on application startup, check the **floating** property just above the **features** section in the **Property Editor** window.

Look at the following screenshot depicting various features and constraints on the **Dock** widget:

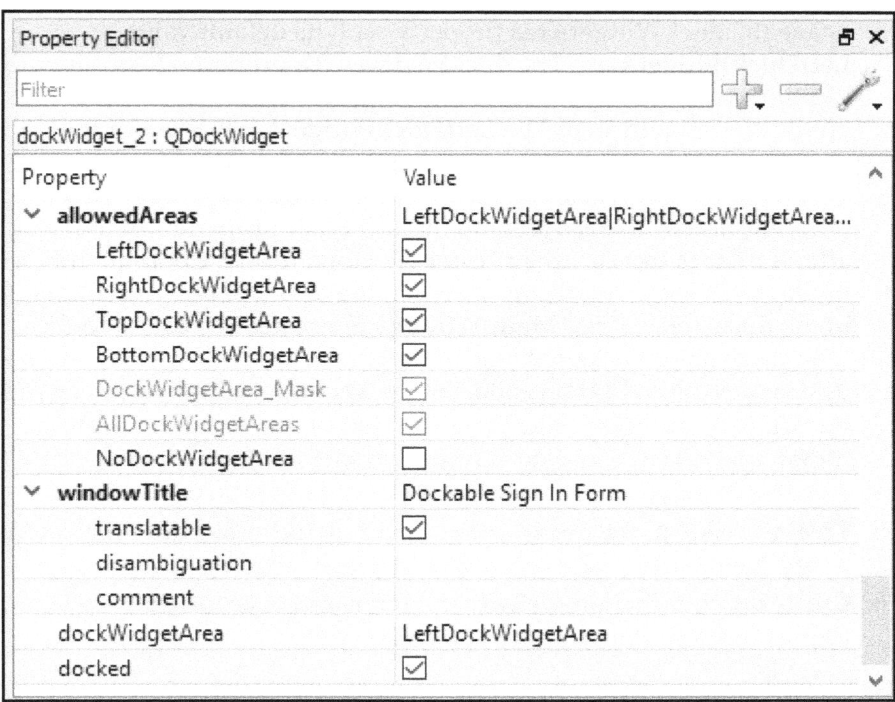

Perform the following steps to apply the desired features and constraints to the **Dock** widget:

1. Check the **AllDockWidgetAreas** option in the **allowedAreas** section to enable the **Dock** widget to be docked in all of the left, right, top, and bottom **Dock** widget areas.
2. Also, by using the **windowTitle** property in the **Property Editor** window, set the title of the dock window to **Dockable Sign In Form**, as shown in the preceding screenshot.

3. Check the **docked** property because it is an essential property to make a **Dock** widget dockable. If the **docked** property is not checked, the **Dock** widget cannot be docked to any of the allowable areas.
4. Leave the **dockWidgetArea** property with its default value, **LeftDockWidgetArea**. The **dockWidgetArea** property determines the location where you want the **Dock** widget to appear as docked when the application is launched. The **LeftDockWidgetArea** value for the **dockWidgetArea** property will make the **Dock** widget first appear as docked in the left **Dock** widget area. If the **NoDockWidgetArea** property is set in the **allowedAreas** section, then all other properties in the **allowedAreas** section are unselected automatically. Consequently, you can move the **Dock** window anywhere on the desktop, but you cannot dock it in the dock areas of the **Main Window** template. The user interface created with Qt Designer is stored in a `.ui` file, which is an XML file, and needs to be converted into Python code. On the application of the `pyuic5` command line utility on the XML file, the generated file is a Python script file, `demoDockWidget.py`. You can see the code of the generated `demoDockWidget.py` file in the source code bundle of this book.
5. Treat the code in the `demoDockWidget.py` file as a header file, and import it into the file from which you will invoke its user interface design.
6. Create another Python file with the name `callDockWidget.pyw` and import the `demoDockWidget.py` code into it:

```
import sys
from PyQt5.QtWidgets import QMainWindow, QApplication
from demoDockWidget import *
class AppWindow(QMainWindow):
    def __init__(self):
        super().__init__()
        self.ui = Ui_MainWindow()
        self.ui.setupUi(self)
        self.show()
if __name__=="__main__":
    app = QApplication(sys.argv)
    w = AppWindow()
    w.show()
    sys.exit(app.exec_())
```

How it works...

As you can see in the preceding code, the necessary modules are imported. An `AppWindow` class is created that inherits from the base class, `QMainWindow`. The default constructor for `QMainWindow` is invoked.

Because every PyQt5 application needs an application object, in the preceding code, an application object was created with the name app by invoking the `QApplication()` method. For passing command line arguments and other external attributes to the application, the `sys.argv` parameter was passed as a parameter to the `QApplication()` method. The `sys.argv` parameter contains command line arguments and other external attributes, if there are any. In order to display the widgets defined in the interface, an instance of the `AppWindow` class was created with the name `w`, and the `show()` method was invoked on it. To exit the application and return the code to Python interpreter that might be used for error handling, the `sys.exit()` method was called.

When the application is executed, you get a **Dock** widget that is docked to the left dockable area by default, as shown in the following screenshot. This is because you have assigned the `LeftDockWidgetArea` value to the `dockWidgetArea` property of the **Dock** widget:

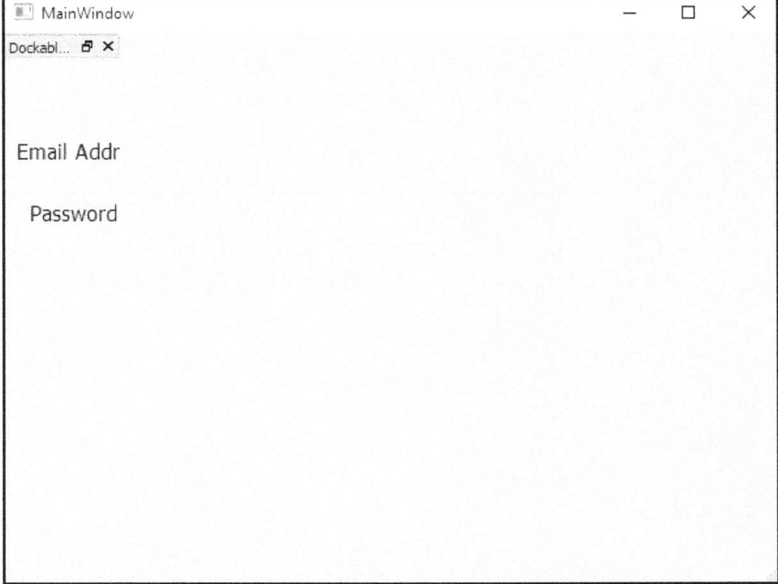

The widgets inside the **Dock** widget are not completely visible, as the default left and dockable areas are narrower than the widgets placed in the **Dock** widget. So, you can drag the right border of the **Dock** widget to make all the contained widgets visible, as shown in the following screenshot:

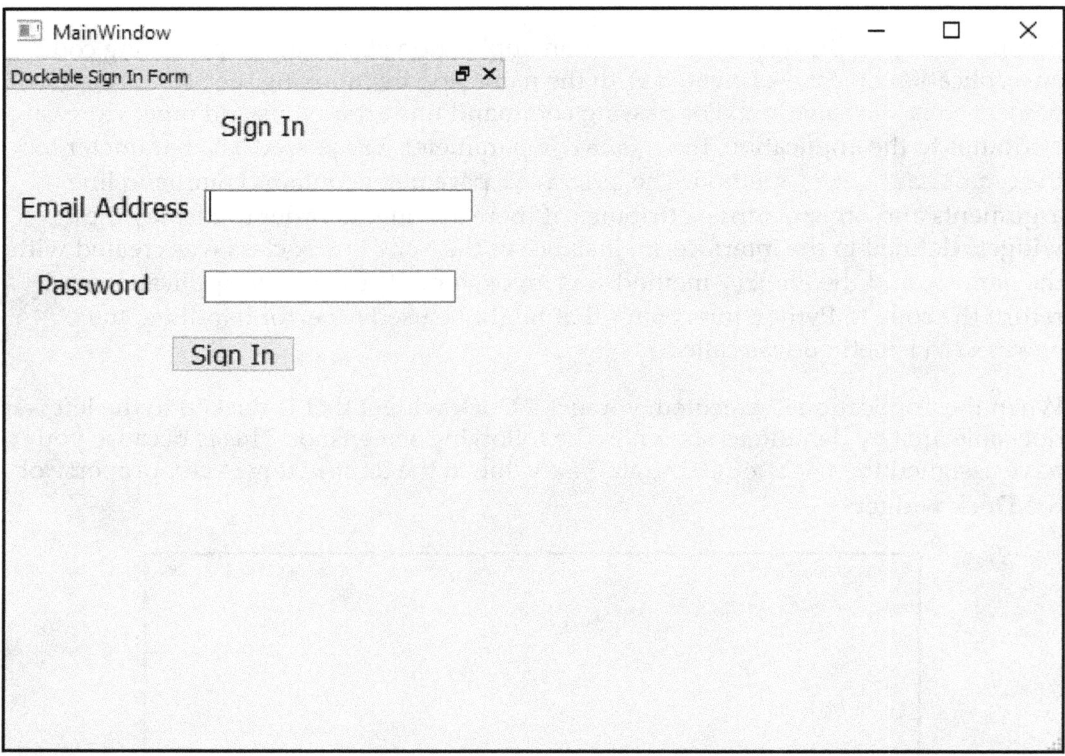

You can drag the widget to any area. If you drag it to the top, it will be docked in the `TopDockWidgetArea` dock area, as shown in the following screenshot:

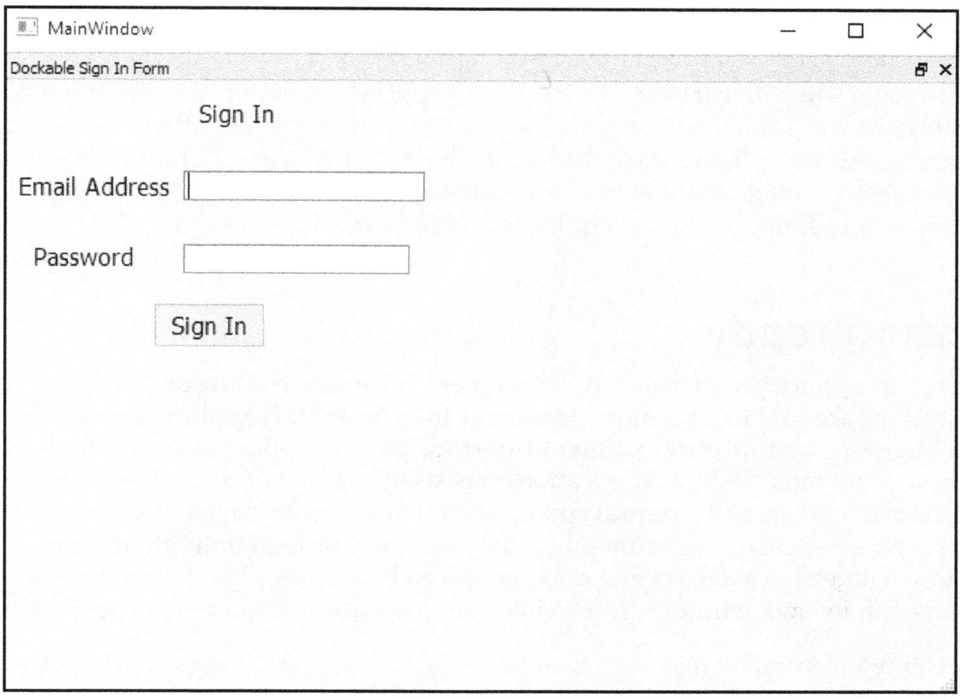

Similarly, when the **Dock** widget is dragged to the right, it will be docked in the `RightDockWidgetArea`

You can drag the **Dock** widget outside the **Main Window** template to make it an independent floating window. The **Dock** widget will appear as an independent floating window and can be moved anywhere on the desktop:

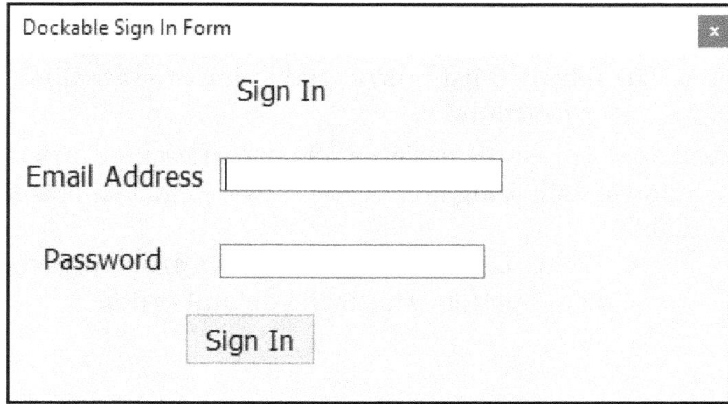

Multiple Document Interface

In this recipe, we will learn how to create an application that will display more than one document at a time. Not only will we be able to manage more than one document, but we will also learn to arrange the documents in different formats. We will be able to manage more than one document using a concept called Multiple Document Interface, so let's see a quick introduction to this.

Getting ready

Usually, an application provides one document per main window and such applications are said to be **Single Document Interface** (**SDI**) applications. As the name suggests, a **Multiple Document Interface** (**MDI**) application is able to display several documents. An MDI application consists of a main window along with a menu bar, a toolbar, and a central space. Several documents can be displayed in the central space, where each document can be managed through individual child window widgets; in MDI, several documents can be displayed and each document is displayed in its own window. These child windows are also known as subwindows.

MDI is implemented by making use of the `MdiArea` widget. The `MdiArea` widget provides an area where child windows or subwindows are displayed. A subwindow has a title and buttons to show, hide, and maximize its size. Each subwindow can display an individual document. The subwindows can be arranged in a cascade or tile pattern by setting the respective property of the `MdiArea` widget. The `MdiArea` widget is an instance of the `QMdiArea` class and the subwindows are instances of `QMdiSubWindow`.

Here are the methods provided by `QMdiArea`:

- `subWindowList()`: This method returns a list of all subwindows in the MDI area. The returned list is arranged in the order that is set through the `WindowOrder()` function.
- `WindowOrder`: This static variable sets the criteria for ordering the list of child windows. Following are the valid values that can be assigned to this static variable:
    - `CreationOrder`: The windows are returned in the order of their creation. This is the default order.

    - `StackingOrder`: The windows are returned in the order in which they are stacked, with the topmost window last in the list.
    - `ActivationHistoryOrder`: The windows are returned in the order in which they were activated.
- `activateNextSubWindow()`: This method sets the focus to the next window in the list of child windows. The current window order determines the next window to be activated.
- `activatePreviousSubWindow()`: This method sets the focus to the previous window in the list of child windows. The current window order determines the previous window to be activated.
- `cascadeSubWindows()`: This method arranges subwindows in cascade fashion.
- `tileSubWindows()`: This method arranges subwindows in tile fashion.
- `closeAllSubWindows()`: This method closes all subwindows.
- `setViewMode()`: This method sets the view mode of the MDI area. The subwindows can be viewed in two modes, **SubWindow View** and **Tabbed View**:
    - **SubWindow View**: This method displays subwindows with window frames (default). You can see the content of more than one subwindow if arranged in tile fashion. It is also represented by a constant value, `0`.
    - **Tabbed View**: Displays subwindows with tabs in a tab bar. Only the content of one subwindow contents can be seen at a time. It is also represented by a constant value, `1`.

How to do it...

Let's create an application that consists of two documents, and each document will be displayed via its individual subwindow. We will learn how to arrange and view these subwindows as desired:

1. Launch Qt Designer and create a new **Main Window** application.
2. Drag and drop a `MdiArea` widget onto the form.
3. Right-click on the widget and select **Add Subwindow** from the context menu to add a subwindow to the `MdiArea` widget.

When the subwindow is added to the `MdiArea` widget, the widget appears as the dark background, as shown in the following screenshot:

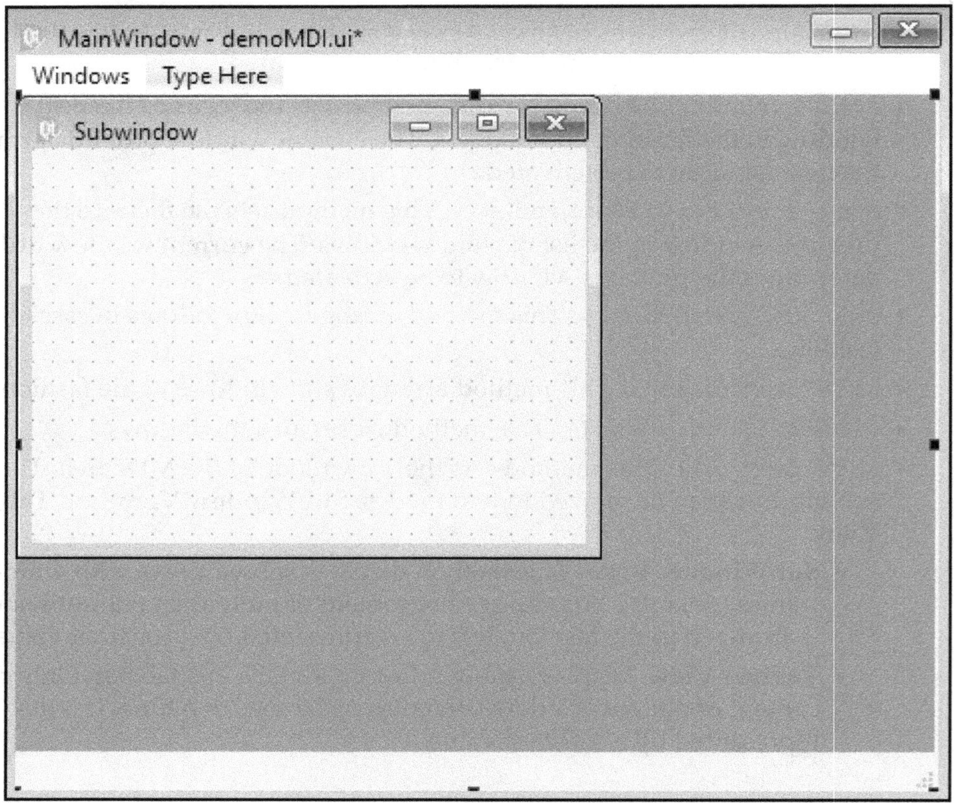

4. Let's, right-click again on the `MdiArea` widget and add one more subwindow to it.
5. To know which one is the first and which one is the second subwindow, drag and drop a **Label** widget onto each subwindow.
6. Set the **text** property of the **Label** widget placed in the first subwindow to `First subwindow`.

7. Set the **text** property of the **Label** widget placed in the second subwindow to `Second subwindow`, as shown in the following screenshot:

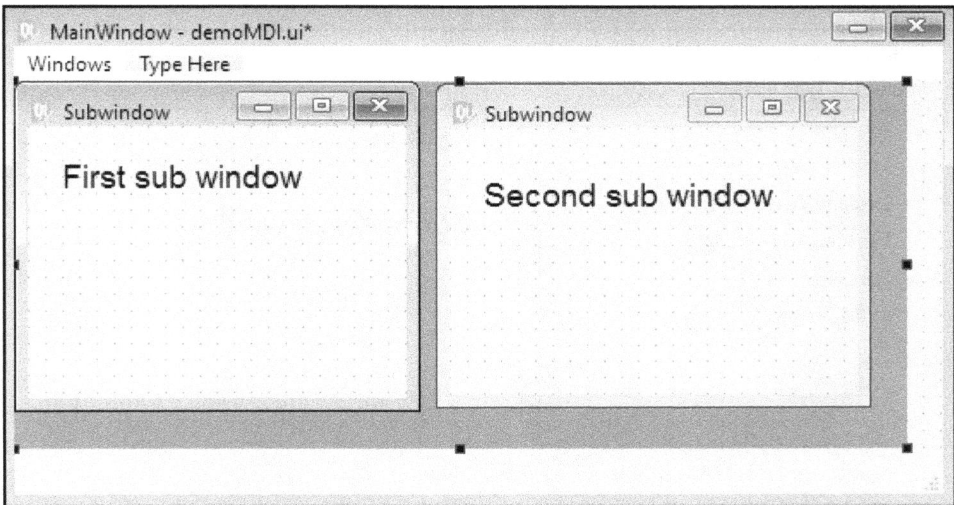

The `MdiArea` widget displays the documents placed in its subwindows in the following two modes:

- **SubWindow View**: This is the default view mode. The subwindows can be arranged in cascade or tile fashion in this view mode. When subwindows are arranged in tile fashion, you can see the content of more than one subwindow simultaneously.
- **Tabbed View**: In this mode, several tabs appear in a tab bar. When a tab is selected, the subwindow associated with it is displayed. Only the content of one subwindow can be seen at a time.

8. To activate the **SubWindow View** and **Tabbed View** modes through the menu options, double-click the **Type Here** placeholder in the menu in the menu bar and add two entries to it: **SubWindow View** and **Tabbed View**.

Also, to see how the subwindows appear when arranged in cascade and tile fashion, add two more menu items, **Cascade View** and **Tile View,** to the menu bar as shown in the following screenshot:

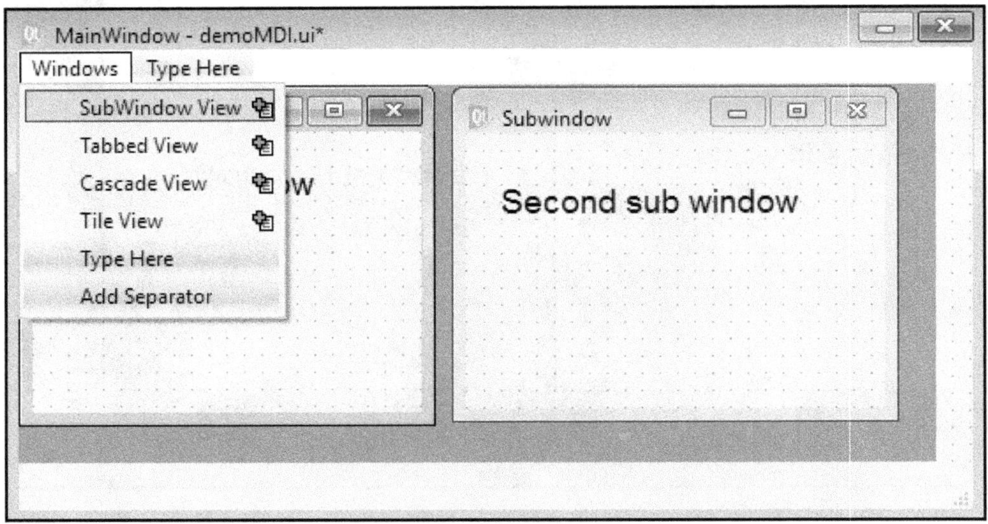

9. Save the application as `demoMDI.ui`. The user interface created with Qt Designer is stored in a `.ui` file, which is an XML file, and needs to be converted into Python code.On the application of the `pyuic5` command line utility, the `.ui` (XML) file will be converted into Python code:

```
C:\Pythonbook\PyQt5>pyuic5 demoMDI.ui -o demoMDI.py.
```

You can see the generated Python code, `demoMDI.py`, in the source code bundle of this book.

10. Treat the code in the `demoMDI.py` file as a header file, and you will import it to the file from which you will invoke its user interface design. The user interface design in the previous code includes `MdiArea` to display the subwindows created in it, along with their respective widgets. The Python script that we are going to create will contain the code for the menu options to do different tasks, such as cascading and tiling the subwindows, changing the view mode from **SubWindow View** to **Tabbed View**, and vice versa. Let's name that Python script `callMDI.pyw` and import the `demoMDI.py` code into it:

```
import sys
```

```
from PyQt5.QtWidgets import QMainWindow, QApplication,
QAction, QFileDialog
from demoMDI import *
class MyForm(QMainWindow):
    def __init__(self):
        super().__init__()
        self.ui = Ui_MainWindow()
        self.ui.setupUi(self)
        self.ui.mdiArea.addSubWindow(self.ui.subwindow)
        self.ui.mdiArea.addSubWindow(self.ui.subwindow_2)
        self.ui.actionSubWindow_View.triggered.connect
        (self.SubWindow_View)
        self.ui.actionTabbed_View.triggered.connect(self.
        Tabbed_View)
        self.ui.actionCascade_View.triggered.connect(self.
        cascadeArrange)
self.ui.actionTile_View.triggered.connect(self.tileArrange)
        self.show()
    def SubWindow_View(self):
        self.ui.mdiArea.setViewMode(0)
    def Tabbed_View(self):
        self.ui.mdiArea.setViewMode(1)
    def cascadeArrange(self):
        self.ui.mdiArea.cascadeSubWindows()
    def tileArrange(self):
        self.ui.mdiArea.tileSubWindows()
if __name__=="__main__":
    app = QApplication(sys.argv)
    w = MyForm()
    w.show()
    sys.exit(app.exec_())
```

How it works...

In the preceding code, you can see that the two subwindows with the default **objectName** properties, `subwindow` and `subwindow_2`, are added to the `MdiArea` widget. After that, the four menu options with objectName properties, `actionSubWindow_View`, `actionTabbed_View`, `actionCascade_View`, and `actionTile_View` are connected to the four methods `SubWindow_View`, `Tabbed_View`, `cascadeArrange`, and `tileArrange` respectively. Hence, when the **SubWindow View** menu option is selected by the user, the `SubWindow_View` method will be invoked. In the `SubWindow_View` method, the **SubWindow View** mode is activated by passing the `0` constant value to the `setViewMode` method of the `MdiArea` widget. The **SubWindow View** displays subwindows with window frames.

Similarly, when the **Tabbed View** menu option is selected by the user, the `Tabbed_View` method will be invoked. In the `Tabbed_View` method, the **Tabbed View** mode is activated by passing the `1` constant value to the `setViewMode` method of the `MdiArea` widget. The **Tabbed View** mode displays tabs in a tab bar and on clicking a tab, the associated subwindow will be displayed.

When the **Cascade View** menu option is selected, the `cascadeArrange` method is invoked, which in turn invokes the `cascadeSubWindows` method of the `MdiArea` widget to arrange subwindows in cascade form.

When the **Tile View** menu option is selected, the `tileArrange` method is invoked, which in turn invokes the `tileSubWindows` method of the `MdiArea` widget to arrange subwindows in tile form.

On running the application, the subwindows initially appear in shrunken mode in the `MdiArea` widget, as shown in the following screenshot. You can see the subwindows along with their titles and minimize, maximize, and close buttons:

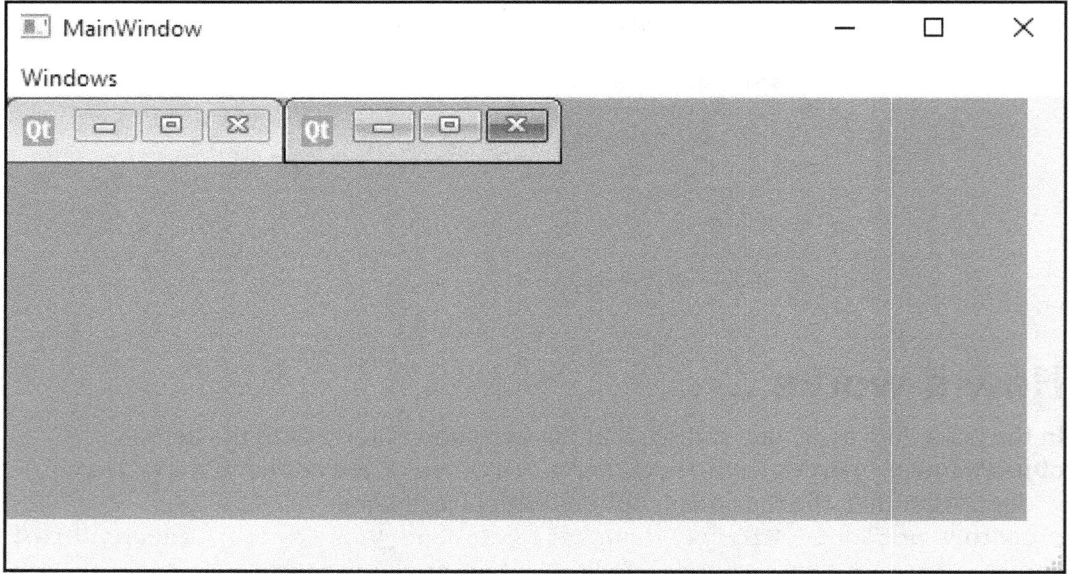

You can drag their borders to the desired size. On selecting the first window from the **Windows** menu, a subwindow becomes active; on selecting the second window, the next subwindow will become active. The active subwindow appears with the brighter title and boundary. In the following screenshot, you can notice that the second subwindow is active. You can drag the boundaries of any subwindow to increase or decrease its size. You can also minimize a subwindow and drag the boundaries of another subwindow to take up the whole width of the `MdiArea` widget. If you select maximize in any subwindow, it will take up all the space of `MdiArea`, making other subwindows invisible:

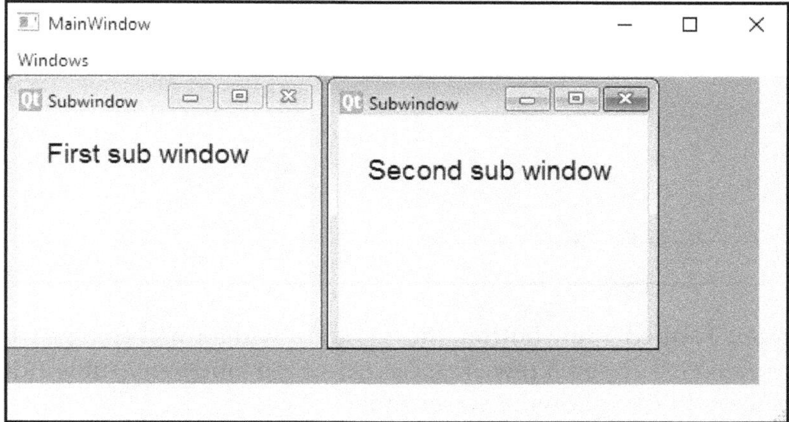

On selecting **Cascade**, the subwindows are arranged in cascade mode, as shown in the following screenshot. If windows are maximized in **Cascade** mode, the top subwindow takes up the whole `MdiArea` widget, hiding other subwindows behind it, as shown in the following screenshot:

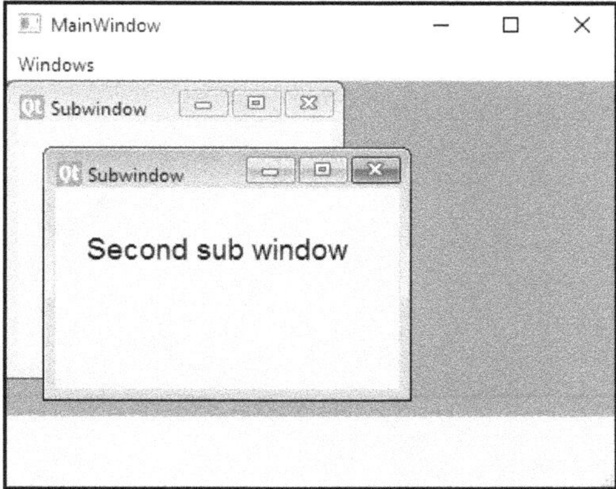

On selecting the **Tile** button, the subwindows are expanded and tiled. Both subwindows expand equally to cover up the entire workspace, as shown in the following screenshot:

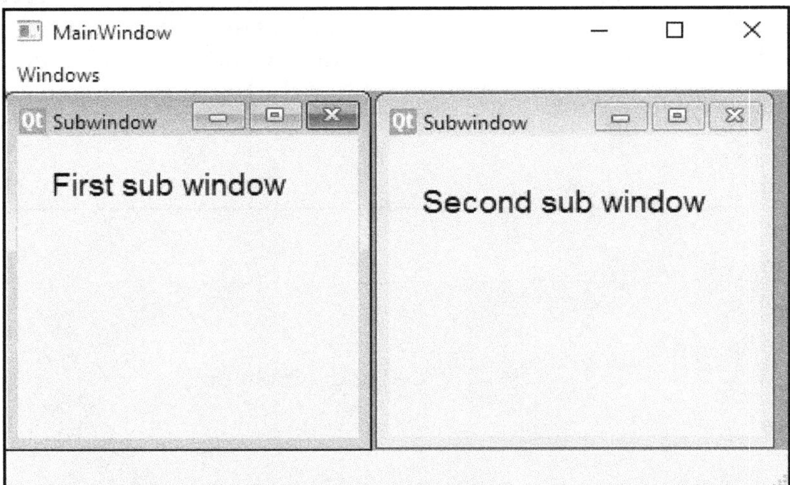

On selecting the **Tabbed View** button, the `MdiArea` widget will change from the **Subwindow** view to **Tabbed View**. You can select the tab of any subwindow to make it active, as shown in the following screenshot:

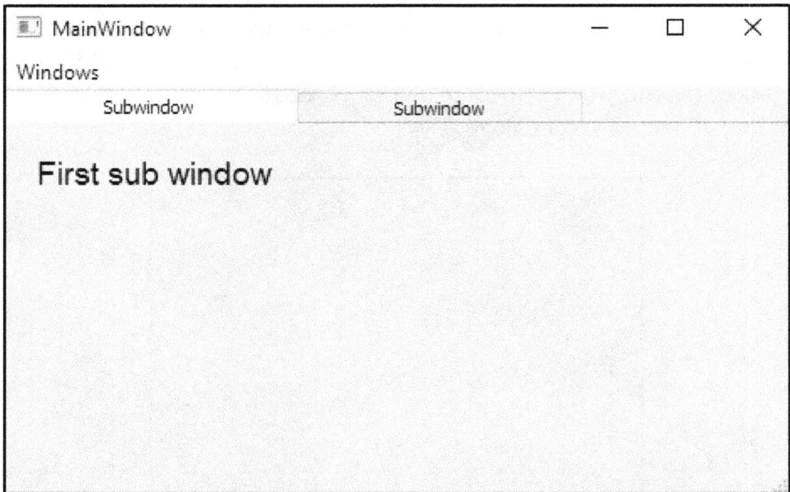

Displaying information in sections using Tab Widget

In this application, we will make a small shopping cart that will display certain products for sale in one tab; after selecting the desired products from the first tab, when the user selects the second tab, they will be prompted to enter the preferred payment option. The third tab will ask the user to enter the address for delivering the products.

We will use **Tab Widget** to enable us to select and fill in the desired information in chunks, so you must be wondering, what is a **Tab Widget**?

When certain information is divided into small sections, and you want to display the information for the section required by the user, then you need to use **Tab Widget**. In a **Tab Widget** container, there are a number of tabs and when the user selects any tab, the information assigned to that tab will be displayed.

How to do it...

Here is the step-by-step procedure to create an application that displays information in chunks using tabs:

1. Let's create a new application based on the **Dialog without Buttons** template.
2. Drag and drop **Tab Widget** onto the form. When you drag **Tab Widget** onto a dialog, it appears with two default tab buttons, labeled **Tab1** and **Tab2**, as shown in the following screenshot:

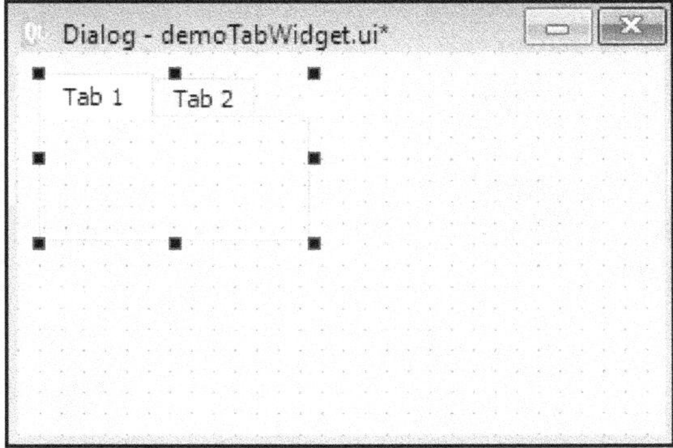

3. You can add more tab buttons to **Tab Widget** and delete existing buttons if you want by adding a new tab button; right-click on either tab button and select **Insert Page** from the menu that pops up. You will see two suboptions, **After Current Page** and **Before Current Page**.

4. Select the **After Current Page** suboption to add a new tab after the current tab. The new tab will have the default text **Page**, which you can always change. The application that we are going to make consists of the following three tabs:

    - The first tab displays certain products along with their prices. The user can select any number of products from the first tab, followed by clicking the **Add to Cart** button.
    - On selecting the second tab, all the payment options will be displayed. The user can choose to pay via **Debit Card**, **Credit Card**, **Net Banking**, or **Cash on Delivery**.
    - The third tab, when selected, will prompt the user for a delivery address: the complete address of the customer along with state, country, and contact number.

The first task that we will do is to change the default text of the tabs:

1. Using the **currentTabText** property of **Tab Widget**, change the text displayed on each tab button.
2. Set the **text** property of the first tab button to `Product Listing` and that of the second tab button to `Payment Method`.
3. To add a new tab button, right-click on the **Payment Method** tab and select **Insert Page** from the context menu that appears.
4. From the two options that appear, **After Current Page** and **Before Current Page**, select **After Current Page** to add a new tab after the **Payment Method** tab. The new tab will have the default text **Page**.
5. Using the **currentTabText** property, change its text to `Delivery Address`.
6. Expand **Tab Widget** by selecting and dragging its nodes to provide a blank space below the tab buttons, as shown in the following screenshot:

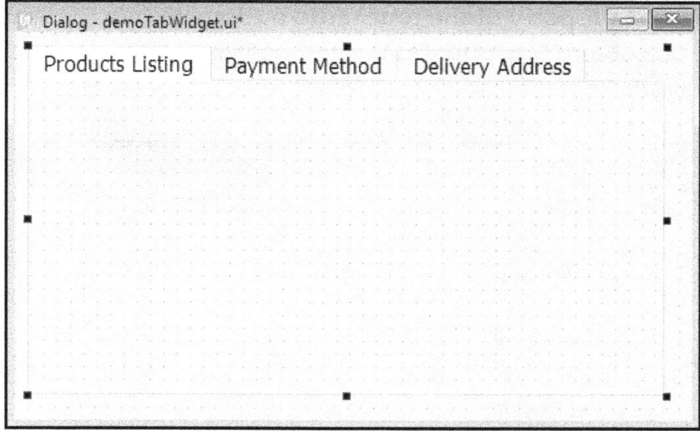

7. Select each tab button and drop the desired widgets into the blank space provided. For example, drop four **Check Box** widgets onto the first tab button, **Product Listing**, to display the items available for sale.
8. Drop a **Push Button** widget on the form.
9. Change the **text** property of the four checkboxes to `Cell Phone $150`, `Laptop $500`, `Camera $250`, and `Shoes $200`.
10. Change the **text** property of the **Push Button** widget to `Add to Cart`, as shown in the following screenshot:

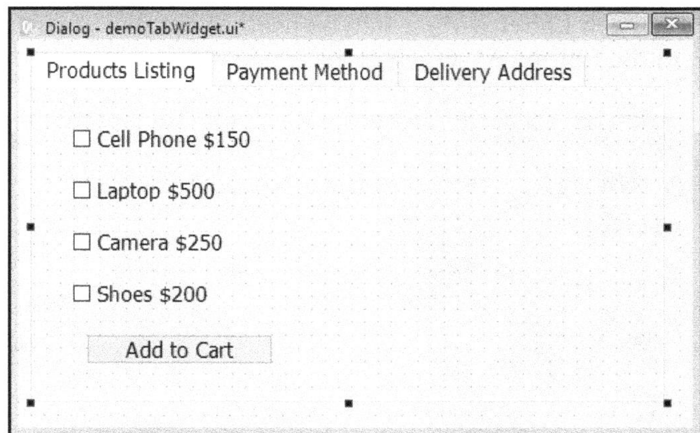

11. Similarly, to provide different payment methods, select the second tab and place four radio buttons in the available space.

12. Set the **text** property of the four radio buttons to `Debit Card`, `Credit Card`, `Net Banking`, and `Cash On Delivery`, as shown in the following screenshot:

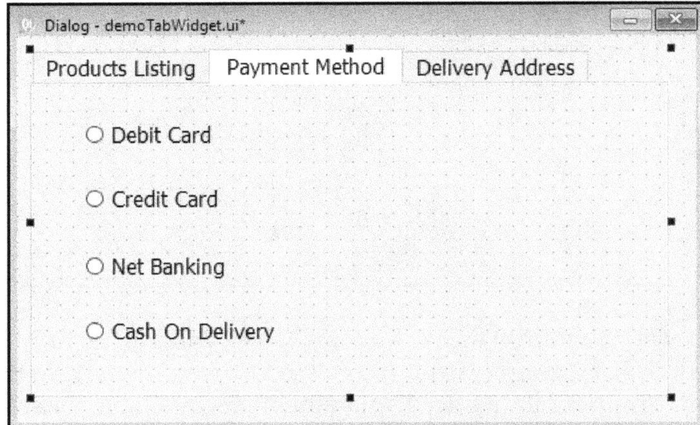

13. Select the third tab and drag and drop few **Line Edit** widgets that prompt the user to provide a delivery address.
14. Drag and drop six **Label** and six **Line Edit** widgets onto the form.
15. Set the **text** property of the **Label** widgets to `Address 1`, `Address 2`, `State`, `Country`, `Zip Code`, and `Contact Number`. The **Line Edit** widgets in front of each **Label** widget will be used to get the address for delivery, as shown in the following screenshot:

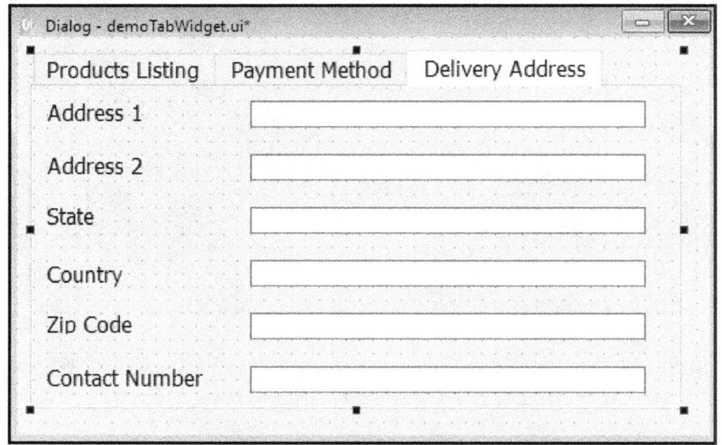

16. Save the application as `demoTabWidget.ui`.

17. The user interface created with Qt Designer is stored in a `.ui` file, which is an XML file, and needs to be converted into Python code. To do the conversion, you need to open a Command Prompt window, navigate to the folder where the file is saved, and issue this command:

```
C:PythonbookPyQt5>pyuic5 demoTabWidget.ui -o demoTabWidget.py
```

The code of the generated Python script file, `demoTabWidget.py`, can be seen in the source code bundle of this book. The user interface design created in the autogenerated code `demoTablWidget.py`, is used by importing it into another Python script.

18. Create another Python file with the name `callTabWidget.pyw` and import the `demoTabWidget.py` code into it:

```
import sys
from PyQt5.QtWidgets import QDialog, QApplication
from demoTabWidget import *
class MyForm(QDialog):
    def __init__(self):
        super().__init__()
        self.ui = Ui_Dialog()
        self.ui.setupUi(self)
        self.show()
if __name__=="__main__":
    app = QApplication(sys.argv)
    w = MyForm()
    w.show()
    sys.exit(app.exec_())
```

How it works...

As you can see in `callTabWidget.pyw`, the necessary modules are imported. The `MyForm` class is created and inherits from the base class, `QDialog`. The default constructor for `QDialog` is invoked.

An application object is created with the name `app` through the `QApplication()` method. Every PyQt5 application must create an application object. The `sys.argv` parameter is passed to the `QApplication()` method while creating the application object. The `sys.argv` parameter contains a list of arguments from the command line and helps in passing and controlling the startup attributes of a script. After this, an instance of the `MyForm` class is created with the name `w`. The `show()` method is invoked on the instance, which will display the widgets on the screen. The `sys.exit()` method ensures a clean exit, releasing memory resources.

When the application is executed, you will find that the first tab, **Products Listing**, is selected by default and the products available for sale specified in that tab are displayed as shown in the following screenshot:

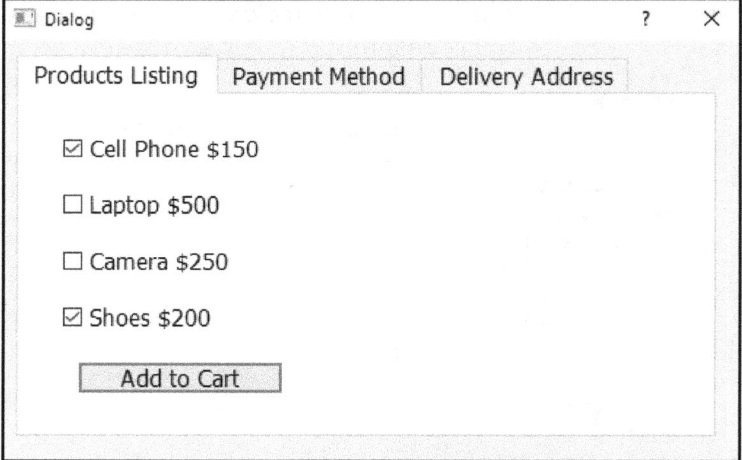

Similarly, on selecting the other tabs, **Payment Method** and **Delivery Address**, you will see the widgets prompting the user to choose the desired payment method and enter a delivery address.

Creating a custom menu bar

A big application is usually broken into small, independent, and manageable modules. These modules can be invoked either by making different toolbar buttons or menu items. That is, we can invoke a module on the click of a menu item. We have seen the **File** menu, the **Edit** menu, and so on in different packages, so let's learn to make a custom menu bar of our own.

In this recipe, we will learn to create a menu bar that shows certain menu items. We will learn to add menu items, add submenu items to a menu item, add separators between menu items, add shortcuts and tool tips to menu items, and much more. We will also learn to add actions to these menu items, so that when any menu item is clicked, a certain action will take place.

Our menu bar will consist of two menus, **Draw** and **Edit**. The **Draw** menu will consist of four menu items, **Draw Circle**, **Draw Rectangle**, **Draw Line**, and **Properties**. The **Properties** menu item will consist of two submenu items, **Page Setup** and **Set Password**. The second menu, **Edit**, will consist of three menu items, **Cut**, **Copy**, and **Paste**. Let's create a new application to understand how to create this menu bar practically.

How to do it...

We will be following a step-by-step procedure to make two menus, along with the respective menu items in each. For quick access, each menu item will be associated with a shortcut key too. Here are the steps to create our customized menu bar:

1. Launch Qt Designer and create a **Main Window** template-based application.

You get the new application with the default menu bar because the **Main Window** template of Qt Designer provides a main application window that displays a menu bar by default. The default menu bar appears as shown in the following screenshot:

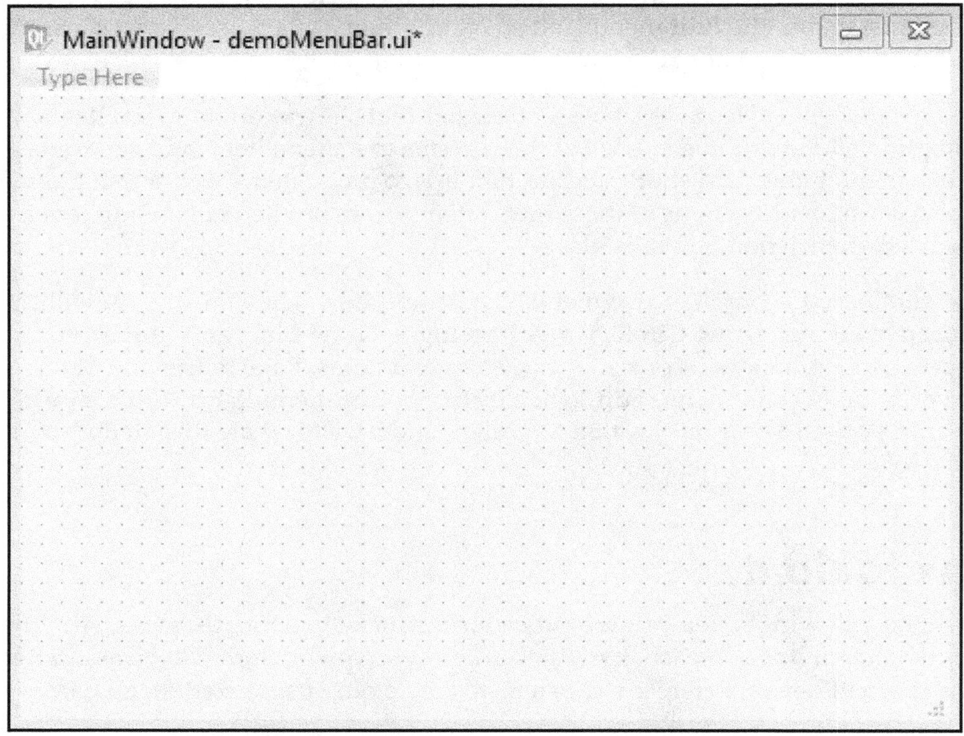

2. We can always remove the default menu bar by right-clicking in the main window and selecting the **Remove Menu Bar** option from the context menu that pops up.
3. You can also add a menu bar later by selecting the **Create Menu Bar** option from the context menu.

The default menu bar contains **Type Here** placeholders. You can replace those with the menu item text.

4. Click the placeholder to highlight it and type to modify its text. When you add a menu item, **Type Here** appears below the new menu item.
5. Again, just single left-click the **Type Here** placeholder to select it and simply type the text for the next menu item.
6. You can delete any menu entry by right-clicking it and, from the context menu that pops up, select the option **Remove Action** action_name.

The menus and menu items in the menu bar can be arranged by dragging and dropping them at the desired location.

While writing menu or menu item text, if you add an ampersand character (`&`) before any character, that character in the menu will appear as underlined and will be treated as a shortcut key. We will also learn how to assign a shortcut key to a menu item later.

7. When you create a new menu item by replacing the **Type Here** placeholders, that menu item will appear as an individual action in the **Action Editor** box, from where you can configure its properties.

Recall that we want to create two menus in this menu bar with text, `Draw` and `Edit`. The **Draw** menu will have three menu items, **Draw Circle**, **Draw Rectangle**, and **Draw Line**. After these three menu items, a separator will be inserted followed by a fourth menu item called **Properties**. The **Properties** menu item will have two submenu items, **Page Setup** and **Set Password**. The **Edit** menu will contain three menu items, **Cut**, **Copy**, and **Paste**.

8. Double-click the **Type Here** placeholder and enter the text for the first menu, `Draw`.

The down arrow key on the **Draw** menu brings up the **Type Here** and **Add Separator** options, as shown in the following screenshot:

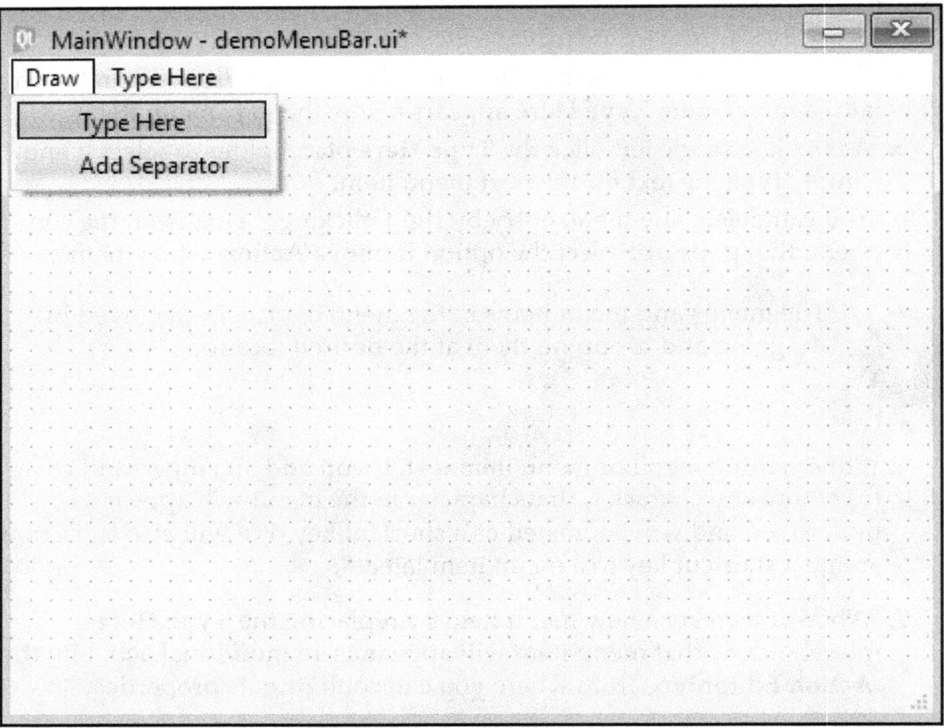

9. Double-click **Type Here** and type `Draw Circle` for the first menu item under the **Draw** menu. The down arrow key on the **Draw Circle** menu provides the **Type Here** and **Add Separator** options again.
10. Double-click **Type Here** and type `Draw Rectangle` for the menu item.
11. Press the down arrow key to get two options, **Type Here** and **Add Separator**.
12. Double-click **Type Here** and type `Draw Line` for the third menu item.
13. On pressing the down arrow key, again you get two options, **Type Here** and **Add Separator**, as shown in the following screenshot:

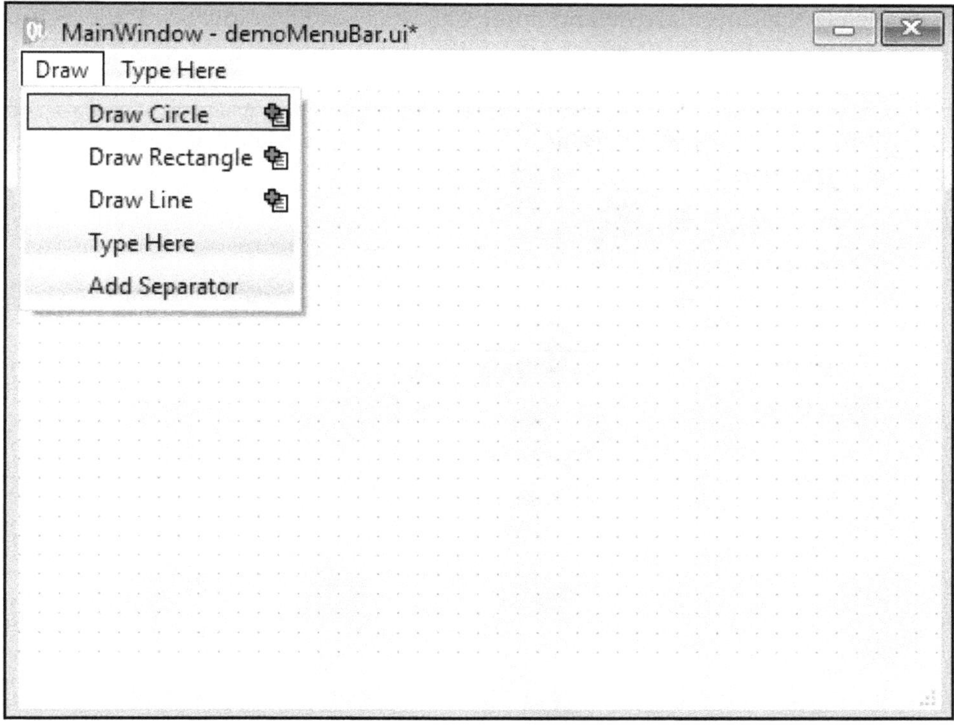

14. Select **Add Separator** to add a separator after the first three menu items.
15. Press the down arrow key after the separator and add a fourth menu item, `Properties`. This is done because we want two submenu items for the **Properties** menu item.
16. Select the right arrow to add submenu items to the **Properties** menu.
17. Press the right arrow key on any menu item to add a submenu item to it. In the submenu item, select **Type Here** and enter the first submenu, `Page Setup`.

18. Select the down arrow and enter `Set Password` below the **Page Setup** submenu item, as shown in the following screenshot:

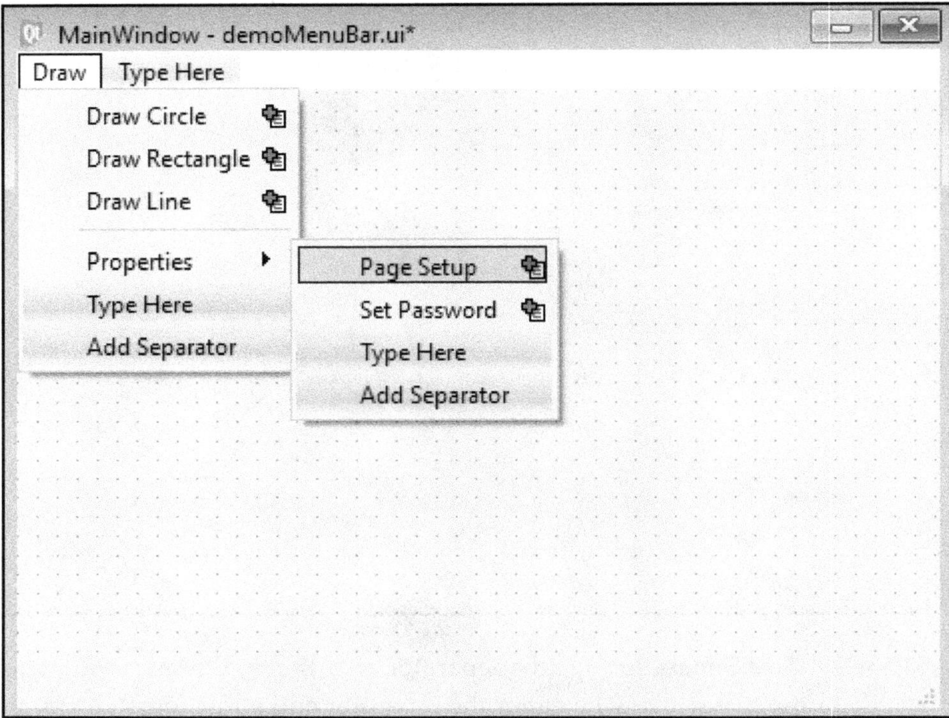

19. The first menu, **Draw**, is complete. Now, we need to add another menu, **Edit**. Select the **Draw** menu and press the right arrow key to indicate that you want to add a second menu to the menu bar.
20. Replace **Type Here** with `Edit`.
21. Press the down arrow and add three menu items, **Cut**, **Copy**, and **Paste**, as shown in the following screenshot:

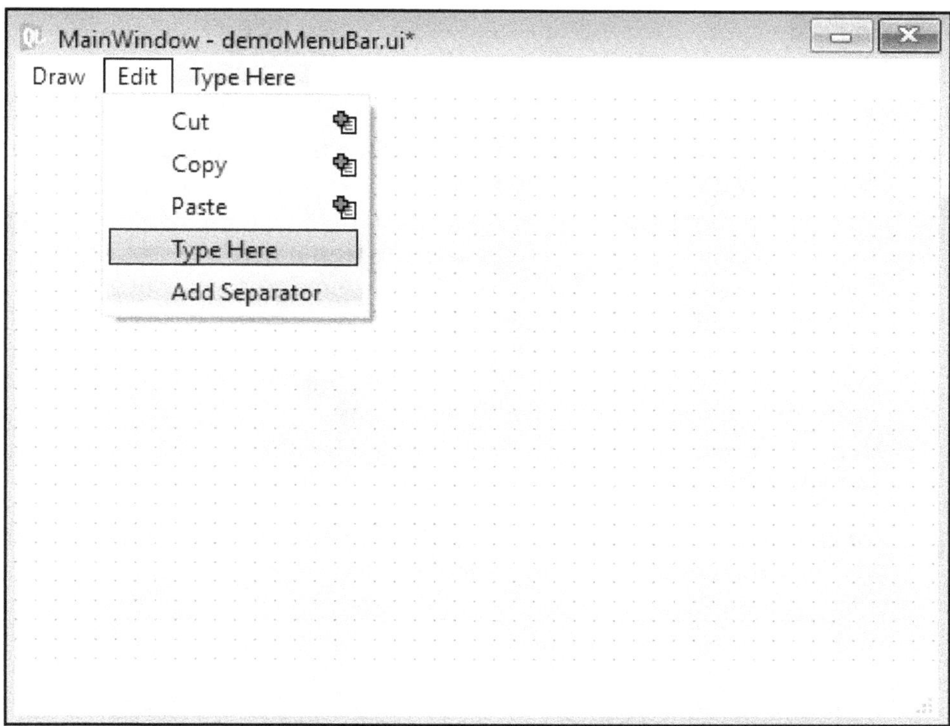

The actions for all menu items will appear in the **Action Editor** box automatically, as shown in the following screenshot:

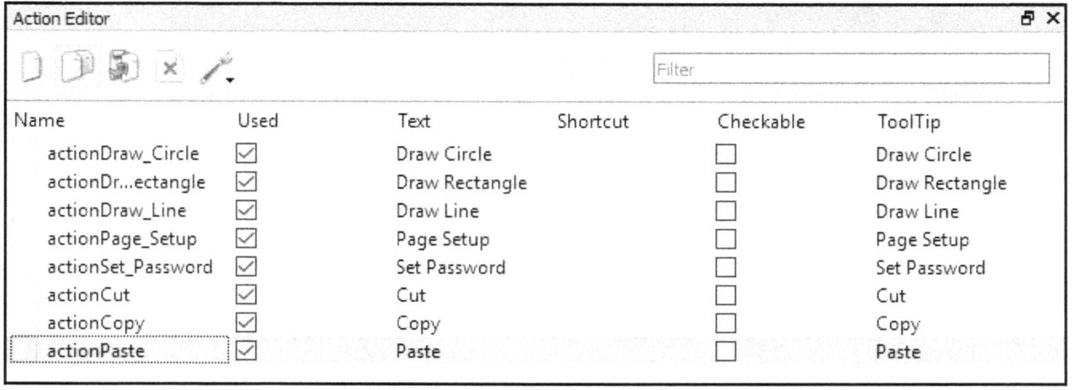

You can see that the action names are generated by prefixing the text action to every menu text and replacing the spaces with underscores. These actions can be used to configure menu items.

22. To add a tooltip message that appears when the user hovers over any menu item, you can use the **ToolTip** property.
23. To assign a tooltip message to the **Draw Circle** menu item of the **Draw** menu, select **actionDraw_Circle** in the **Action Editor** box and set the **ToolTip** property to `To draw a circle`. Similarly, you can assign tooltip messages to all of the menu items.
24. To assign a shortcut key to any menu item, open its action from the **Action Editor** box and click inside the **Shortcut** box.
25. In the **Shortcut** box, press the key combination that you want to assign to the selected menu item.

For example, if you press *Ctrl* + *C* in the **Shortcut** box, **Ctrl+C** appears in the box, as shown in the following screenshot:

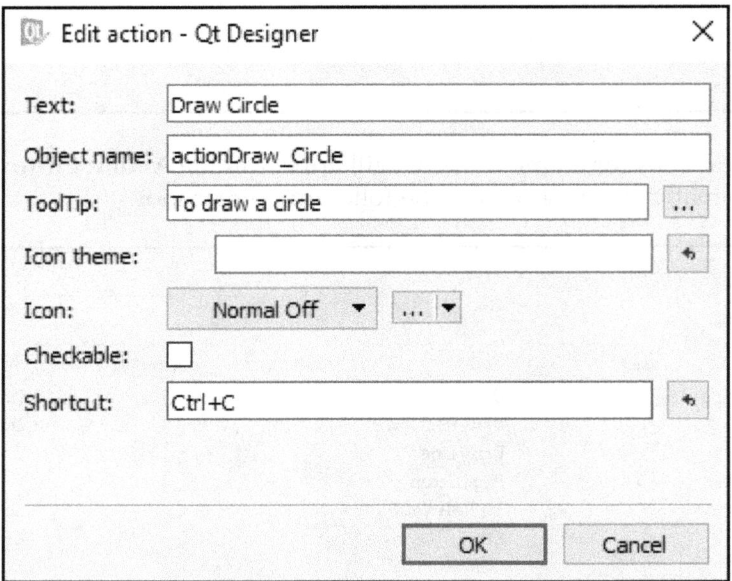

You can have any combination of shortcut keys, such as *Shift* + key, *Alt* + key, and *Ctrl* + *Shift* + key, for any menu item. The shortcut keys will appear automatically with the menu item in the menu bar. You can also make any menu item checkable, that is, you can make it a toggle menu item.

26. To do so, select the action of the desired menu item and check the **Checkable** checkbox. The actions of each menu item, along with its action name, menu text, shortcut keys, checkable status, and tooltip, appear in the **Action Editor** box. The following screenshot shows the action of the **Set Password** submenu item, which confirms that its shortcut key is *Shift* + *P* and it is checkable:

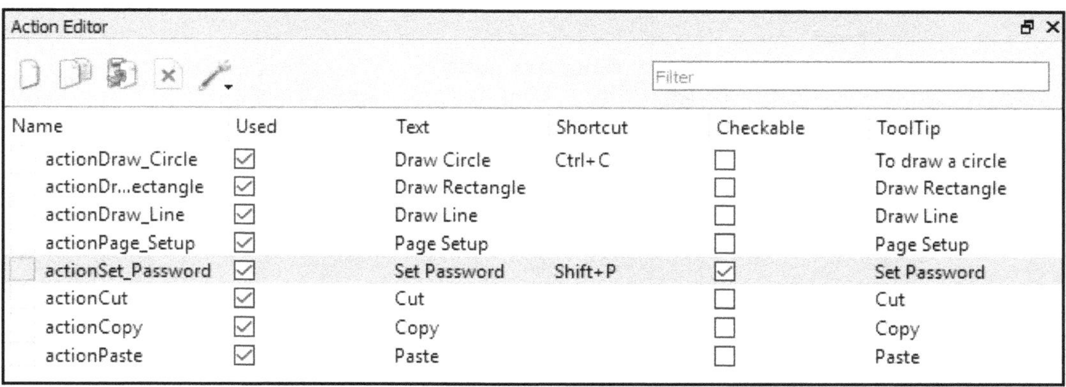

27. For the **Draw Circle**, **Draw Rectangle**, and **Draw Line** menu items, we will be adding code to draw a circle, draw a rectangle, and draw a line respectively.
28. For the rest of the menu items, we want them so that when the user selects any of them, a text message appears on the form indicating which menu item is selected.
29. To display a message, drag and drop a **Label** widget onto the form.
30. Our menu bar is complete; save the application with the name `demoMenuBar.ui`.
31. We use the `pyuic5` command line utility to convert the `.ui` (XML) file into Python code.

The generated Python code, `demoMenuBar.py`, can be seen in the source code bundle of this book.

32. Create a Python script with the name `callMenuBar.pyw` that imports the previous code, `demoMenuBar.py`, to invoke the menu and display the text message with a **Label** widget when a menu item is selected.

You want a message to appear that indicates which menu item is selected. Also, you want to draw a circle, rectangle, and line when the **Draw Circle**, **Draw Rectangle**, and **Draw Line** menu items are selected, respectively. The code in the Python `callMenuBar.pyw` script will appear as shown in the following screenshot:

```
import sys
from PyQt5.QtWidgets import QMainWindow, QApplication
from PyQt5.QtGui import QPainter

from demoMenuBar import *

class AppWindow(QMainWindow):
    def __init__(self):
        super().__init__()
        self.ui = Ui_MainWindow()
        self.ui.setupUi(self)
        self.pos1 = [0,0]
        self.pos2 = [0,0]
        self.toDraw=""
        self.ui.actionDraw_Circle.triggered.connect(self.
        drawCircle)
        self.ui.actionDraw_Rectangle.triggered.connect(self.
        drawRectangle)
self.ui.actionDraw_Line.triggered.connect(self.drawLine)
self.ui.actionPage_Setup.triggered.connect(self.pageSetup)
        self.ui.actionSet_Password.triggered.connect(self.
        setPassword)
        self.ui.actionCut.triggered.connect(self.cutMethod)
        self.ui.actionCopy.triggered.connect(self.copyMethod)
self.ui.actionPaste.triggered.connect(self.pasteMethod)
        self.show()

    def paintEvent(self, event):
        qp = QPainter()
        qp.begin(self)
        if self.toDraw=="rectangle":
            width = self.pos2[0]-self.pos1[0]
            height = self.pos2[1] - self.pos1[1]
            qp.drawRect(self.pos1[0], self.pos1[1], width,
```

```
height)
        if self.toDraw=="line":
            qp.drawLine(self.pos1[0], self.pos1[1],
self.pos2[0],
            self.pos2[1])
        if self.toDraw=="circle":
            width = self.pos2[0]-self.pos1[0]
            height = self.pos2[1] - self.pos1[1]
            rect = QtCore.QRect(self.pos1[0], self.pos1[1],
width,
            height)
            startAngle = 0
            arcLength = 360 *16
            qp.drawArc(rect, startAngle,
            arcLength)
        qp.end()

    def mousePressEvent(self, event):
        if event.buttons() & QtCore.Qt.LeftButton:
            self.pos1[0], self.pos1[1] = event.pos().x(),
            event.pos().y()

    def mouseReleaseEvent(self, event):
        self.pos2[0], self.pos2[1] = event.pos().x(),
        event.pos().y()
        self.update()

    def drawCircle(self):
        self.ui.label.setText("")
        self.toDraw="circle"

    def drawRectangle(self):
        self.ui.label.setText("")
        self.toDraw="rectangle"

    def drawLine(self):
        self.ui.label.setText("")
        self.toDraw="line"

    def pageSetup(self):
        self.ui.label.setText("Page Setup menu item is
selected")

    def setPassword(self):
        self.ui.label.setText("Set Password menu item is
selected")

    def cutMethod(self):
```

```
            self.ui.label.setText("Cut menu item is selected")

        def copyMethod(self):
            self.ui.label.setText("Copy menu item is selected")

        def pasteMethod(self):
            self.ui.label.setText("Paste menu item is selected")

app = QApplication(sys.argv)
w = AppWindow()
w.show()
sys.exit(app.exec_())
```

How it works...

The **triggered()** signal of the action of each menu item is connected to its respective method. The **triggered()** signal of the **actionDraw_Circle** menu item is connected to the `drawCircle()` method, so that whenever the **Draw Circle** menu item is selected from the menu bar, the `drawCircle()` method will be invoked. Similarly, the **triggered()** signal of the **actionDraw_Rectangle** and **actionDraw_Line** menus are connected to the `drawRectangle()` and `drawLine()` methods respectively. In the `drawCircle()` method, the `toDraw` variable is assigned a string, `circle`. The `toDraw` variable will be used to determine the graphics to be drawn in the `paintEvent` method. The `toDraw` variable can be assigned any of the three strings, `line`, `circle`, or `rectangle`. A conditional branching is applied to the value in the `toDraw` variable and the methods to draw a line, rectangle, or circle will be invoked accordingly. The figures will be drawn to the size determined by the mouse, that is, the user needs to click the mouse and drag it to determine the size of the figure.

Two methods, `mousePressEvent()` and `mouseReleaseEvent()`, are automatically called when left mouse button is pressed and released respectively. To store the `x` and `y` coordinates of the location where the left mouse button was pressed and released, two arrays, `pos1` and `pos2`, are used. The `x` and `y` coordinate values of the locations where the left mouse button was pressed and released are assigned to the `pos1` and `pos2` arrays via the `mousePressEvent` and `mouseReleaseEvent` methods.

In the `mouseReleaseEvent` method, after assigning the `x` and `y` coordinate values of the location where the mouse button was released, the `self.update` method is invoked to invoke the `paintEvent()` method. In the `paintEvent()` method, branching takes place on the basis of the string assigned to the `toDraw` variable. If the `toDraw` variable is assigned the `line` string, the `drawLine()` method will be invoked by the `QPainter` class to draw the line between the two mouse locations. Similarly, if the `toDraw` variable is assigned the `circle` string, the `drawArc()` method will be invoked by the `QPainter` class to draw a circle with the diameter supplied by mouse locations. If the `toDraw` variable is assigned the `rectangle` string, then the `drawRect()` method will be invoked by the `QPainter` class to draw the rectangle of the width and height supplied by the mouse locations.

Besides the three menu items, **Draw Circle**, **Draw Rectangle**, and **Draw Line**, if the user clicks any other menu item, a message will be displayed indicating the menu item clicked on by the user. Hence, the **triggered()** signals of the rest of the menu items are connected to the methods that display the message information for the menu item that has been selected by the user through a **Label** widget.

On running the application, you will find a menu bar with two menus, **Draw** and **Edit**. The **Draw** menu will show the four menu items **Draw Circle**, **Draw Rectangle**, **Draw Line**, and **Properties**, with a separator before the **Properties** menu item. The **Properties** menu item shows two submenu items, **Page Setup** and **Set Password**, along with their shortcut keys, as shown in the following screenshot:

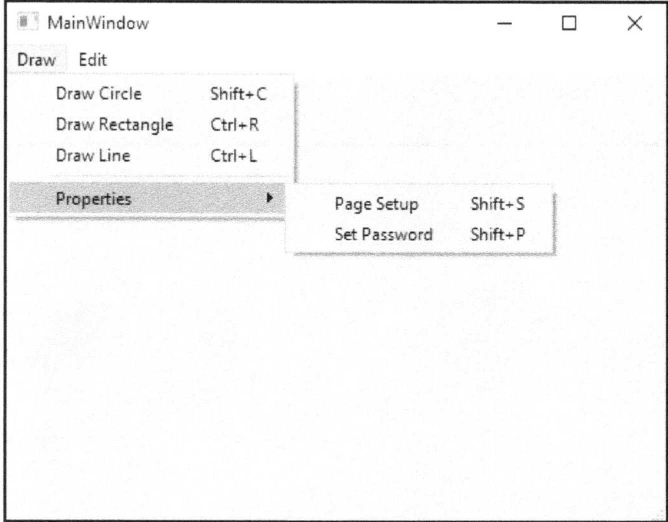

To draw a circle, click on the **Draw Circle** menu item, click the mouse button at a location on the form, and keeping the mouse button pressed, drag it to define the diameter of the circle. On releasing the mouse button, a circle will be drawn between the mouse pressed and mouse released locations, as shown in the following screenshot:

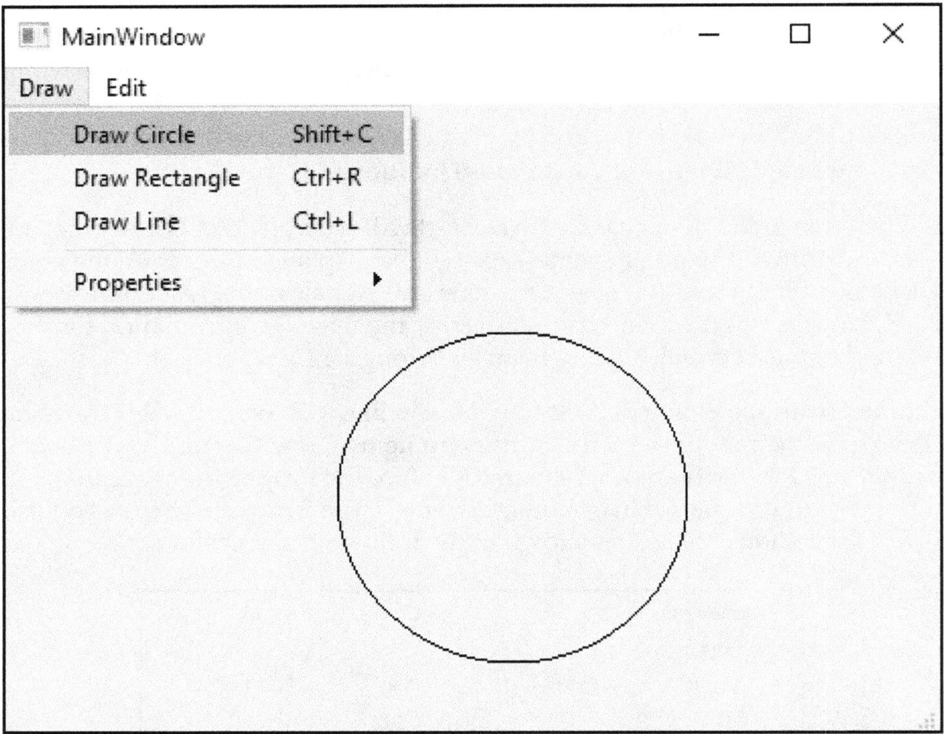

On selecting any other menu item, a message will be displayed, indicating the menu item that is pressed. For example, on selecting the **Copy** menu item, you get a message, **Copy menu item is selected**, as shown in the following screenshot:

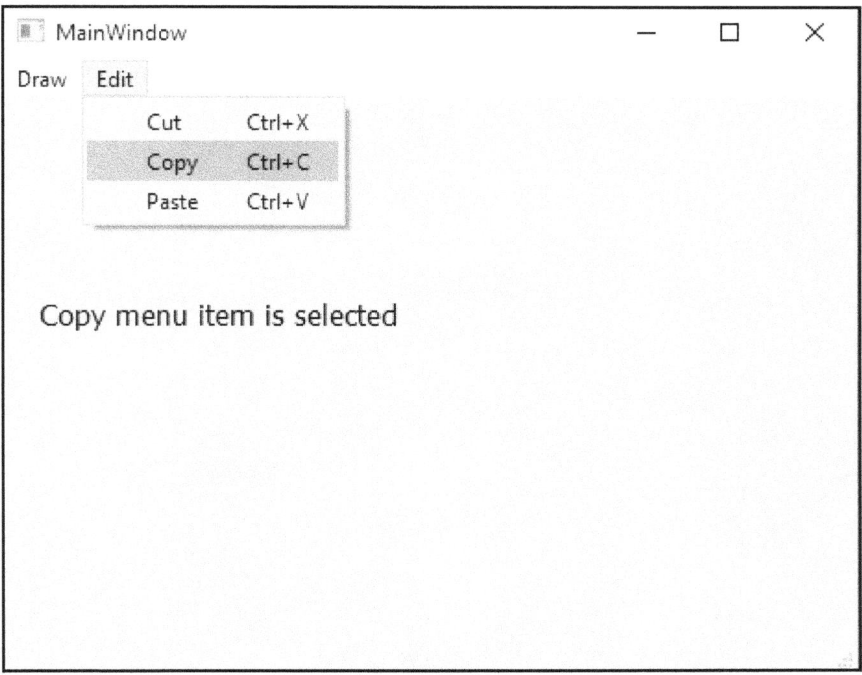

[illegible] selecti[illegible] [illegible] item [illegible] [illegible] [illegible] [illegible] [illegible] [illegible] example [illegible] selecting the [illegible] [illegible] [illegible] [illegible] [illegible] selected, as shown in the following screenshot:

[illegible] item is selected [illegible]

19
Database Handling

Database handling plays a major role in any application as data needs to be stored for future use. You need to store customer information, user information, product information, order information, and so on. In this chapter, you will learn every task that is related to database handling:

- Creating a database
- Creating a database table
- Inserting rows in the specified database table
- Displaying rows in the specified database table
- Navigating through the rows of the specified database table
- Searching a database table for specific information
- Creating a signin form – applying an authentication procedure
- Updating a database table – changing a user's password
- Deleting a row from a database table

We will be using SQLite for database handling. Before we move further into the chapter, let's have a quick introduction to SQLite.

Introduction

SQLite is a very easy-to-use database engine. Basically, it is a lightweight database meant to be used in small applications that can be stored in a single disk file. It is a very popular database used in phones, tablets, small appliances, and instruments. SQLite does not require a separate server process, and does not even require any configuration.

To make this database easy to use in Python scripts, the Python Standard Library includes a module called `sqlite3`. So, to use SQLite in any Python application, you need to import the `sqlite3` module using the `import` statement shown here:

```
import sqlite3
```

The first step to use any database is to create a `connect` object, by means of which you need to establish a connection with the database. The following example establishes a connection to the `ECommerce` database:

```
conn = sqlite3.connect('ECommerce.db')
```

This example will establish a connection to the `ECommerce` database if it already exists. If the database does not already exist, the database will be created first and then the connection established.

You can also create a temporary database in memory, that is, in RAM by using the `:memory:` argument in the `connect` method, as shown here:

```
conn = sqlite3.connect(':memory:')
```

You can also supply the special name `:memory:` to create a database in RAM.

Once the job associated with the database is over, you need to close the connection using the following statement:

```
conn.close()
```

Creating the cursor object

To work with database tables, you need to get a `cursor` object and pass the SQL statements to the `cursor` object to execute them. The following statement creates a `cursor` object called `cur`:

```
cur = conn.cursor()
```

Using the `cursor` object, `cur`, you can execute SQL statements. For example, the following set of statements creates a `Users` table consisting of three columns, `id`, `EmailAddress`, and `Password`:

```
# Get a cursor object
cur = conn.cursor()
cur.execute('''CREATE TABLE Users(id INTEGER PRIMARY KEY, EmailAddress
TEXT, Password TEXT)''')
conn.commit()
```

Remember, you need to commit the changes to the database by invoking the `commit()` method on the connection object, otherwise all the changes made to the database will be lost.

The following set of statements will drop the `Users` table:

```
# Get a cursor object
cur = conn.cursor()
cur.execute('''DROP TABLE Users''')
conn.commit()
```

Creating a database

In this recipe, we will be prompting the user to enter a database name, followed by clicking the push button. Upon clicking the push button, if the specified database does not exist, it is created and, if it already exists, it is connected.

How to do it...

Follow this step-by-step procedure to create a database in SQLite:

1. Let's create an application based on the **Dialog without Buttons** template.
2. Add two `QLabel` widgets, one `QLineEdit` widget, and one `QPushButton` widget to the form by dragging and dropping two **Label** widget, one **Line Edit** widget, and a **Push Button** widget on the form.
3. Set the **text** property of the first **Label** widget to `Enter database name`.
4. Delete the **text** property of the second **Label** widget because this is established.

5. Set the **objectName** property of the **Line Edit** widget to `lineEditDBName`.
6. Set the **objectName** property of the **Push Button** widget to `pushButtonCreateDB`.
7. Set the **objectName** property of the second **Label** widget to `labelResponse`.
8. Save the application by name as `demoDatabase.ui`. The form will now appear as shown in the following screenshot:

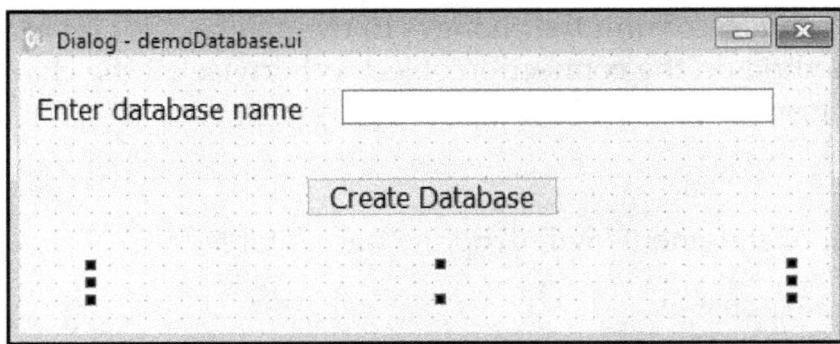

The user interface created with Qt Designer is stored in a `.ui` file, which is an XML file, and needs to be converted into Python code. By applying the `pyuic5` utility, the XML file is converted into Python code. The Python script generated, `demoDatabase.py`, can be seen in the source code bundle of the book.

9. Treat the `demoDatabase.py` script as a header file, and import it into the file from which you will invoke its user interface design.
10. Create another Python file with the name `callDatabase.pyw` and import the `demoDatabase.py` code into it:

```
import sqlite3, sys
from PyQt5.QtWidgets import QDialog, QApplication
from sqlite3 import Error
from demoDatabase import *
class MyForm(QDialog):
    def __init__(self):
        super().__init__()
        self.ui = Ui_Dialog()
        self.ui.setupUi(self)
        self.ui.pushButtonCreateDB.clicked.connect(self.
        createDatabase)
        self.show()
    def createDatabase(self):
        try:
```

```
                conn = sqlite3.connect(self.ui.lineEditDBName.
                text()+".db")
                self.ui.labelResponse.setText("Database is
created")
            except Error as e:
                self.ui.labelResponse.setText("Some error has
                occurred")
            finally:
                conn.close()
if __name__=="__main__":
    app = QApplication(sys.argv)
    w = MyForm()
    w.show()
    sys.exit(app.exec_())
```

How it works...

You can see in the script that the **click()** event of the push button with the **objectName** property `pushButtonCreateDB` is connected to the `createDatabase()` method. This means that, whenever the push button is clicked, the `createDatabase()` method is invoked. In the `createDatabase()` method, the `connect()` method is invoked on the `sqlite3` class and the database name entered by the user in the **Line Edit** widget is passed to the `connect()` method. The `connect()` method will create the database if it does not exist already. If no error occurs in creating the database, the message **Database is created** is displayed via the **Label** widget to inform the user; otherwise, a **Some error has occurred** message is displayed via the **Label** widget to indicate the occurrence of an error.

On running the application, you will be prompted to enter the database name. Suppose we enter the database name as `Ecommerce`. Upon clicking the **Create Database** button, the database will be created and you get the message **Database is created**:

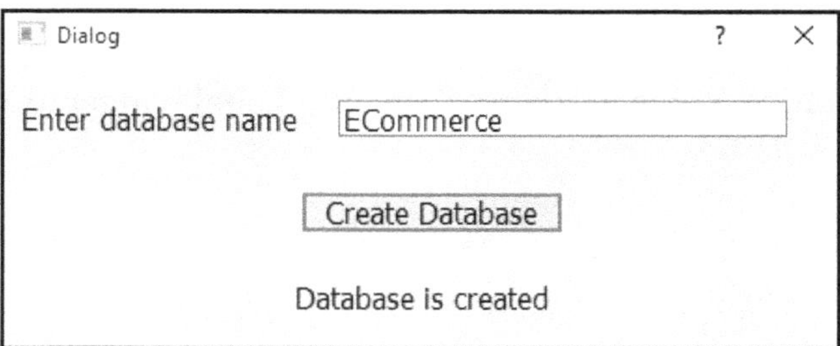

Creating a database table

In this recipe, we will be learning to create a database table. The user will be prompted to specify the database name, followed by the table name that is to be created. The recipe enables you to enter column names and their data types. Upon clicking the push button, the table with the defined columns will be created in the specified database.

How to do it...

Here are the steps to create a GUI that enables the user to enter all the information for the database table to be created. Using this GUI, the user can specify the database name, column names, and choose column types too:

1. Let's create an application based on the **Dialog without Buttons** template.
2. Add five `QLabel`, three `QLineEdit`, one `QComboBox`, and two `QPushButton` widgets to the form by dragging and dropping five **Label**, three **Line Edit**, one **Combo Box**, and two **Push Button** widgets on the form.
3. Set the **text** property of the first four **Label** widgets to `Enter database name`, `Enter table name`, `Column Name`, and `Data Type`.
4. Delete the **text** property of the fifth **Label** widget because this is established through code.
5. Set the **text** property of the two push buttons to `Add Column` and `Create Table`.
6. Set the **objectName** property of the three **Line Edit** widgets to `lineEditDBName`, `lineEditTableName`, and `lineEditColumnName`.
7. Set the **objectName** property of the **Combo Box** widget to `ComboBoxDataType`.
8. Set the **objectName** property of the two push buttons to `pushButtonAddColumn` and `pushButtonCreateTable`.
9. Set the **objectName** property of the fifth **Label** widget to `labelResponse`.

10. Save the application by name as `demoCreateTable.ui`. The form will now appear as shown in the following screenshot:

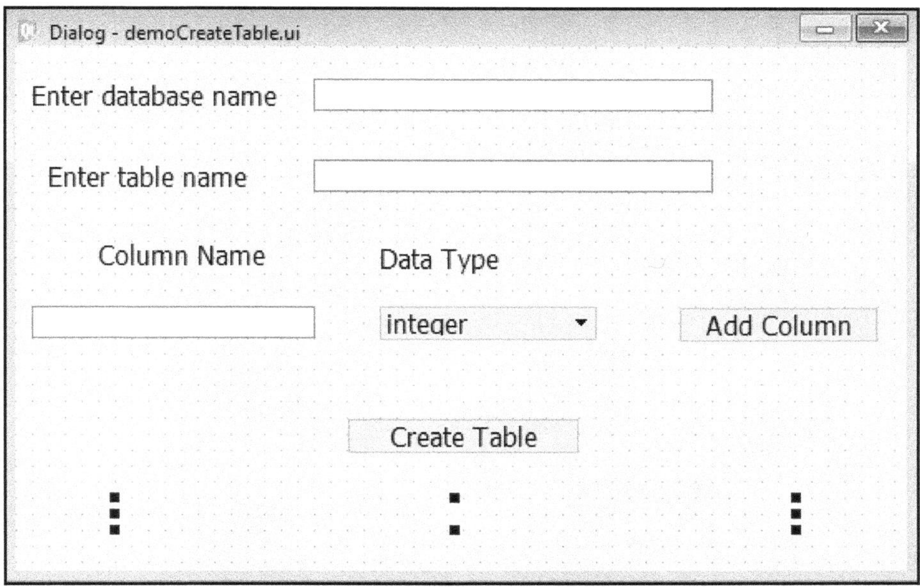

The user interface created with Qt Designer is stored in a `.ui` file, which is an XML file, and needs to be converted into Python code. The `pyuic5` command is used to convert the XML file into Python code. The Python script generated, `demoCreateTable.py`, can be seen in the source code bundle of this book.

11. Treat the `demoCreateTable.py` script as a header file, and import it into the file from which you will invoke its user interface design.

12. Create another Python file with the name `callCreateTable.pyw` and import the `demoCreateTable.py` code into it:

```
import sqlite3, sys
from PyQt5.QtWidgets import QDialog, QApplication
from sqlite3 import Error
from demoCreateTable import *
tabledefinition=""
class MyForm(QDialog):
    def __init__(self):
        super().__init__()
        self.ui = Ui_Dialog()
        self.ui.setupUi(self)
        self.ui.pushButtonCreateTable.clicked.connect(
        self.createTable)
        self.ui.pushButtonAddColumn.clicked.connect(self.
        addColumns)
        self.show()
    def addColumns(self):
        global tabledefinition
        if tabledefinition=="":
            tabledefinition="CREATE TABLE IF NOT EXISTS "+
            self.ui.lineEditTableName.text()+" ("+
            self.ui.lineEditColumnName.text()+"  "+
            self.ui.comboBoxDataType.itemText(self.ui.
            comboBoxDataType.currentIndex())
        else:
            tabledefinition+=","+self.ui.lineEditColumnName
            .text()+" "+ self.ui.comboBoxDataType.itemText
            (self.ui.comboBoxDataType.currentIndex())
            self.ui.lineEditColumnName.setText("")
            self.ui.lineEditColumnName.setFocus()
    def createTable(self):
        global tabledefinition
        try:
            conn = sqlite3.connect(self.ui.lineEditDBName.
            text()+".db")
            self.ui.labelResponse.setText("Database is
            connected")
            c = conn.cursor()
            tabledefinition+=");"
            c.execute(tabledefinition)
            self.ui.labelResponse.setText("Table is
successfully
            created")
        except Error as e:
            self.ui.labelResponse.setText("Error in creating
            table")
```

```
                finally:
                    conn.close()
        if __name__=="__main__":
            app = QApplication(sys.argv)
            w = MyForm()
            w.show()
            sys.exit(app.exec_())
```

How it works...

You can see in the script that the **click()** event of the push button with the **objectName** property `pushButtonCreateTable` is connected to the `createTable()` method. This means that, whenever this push button is clicked, the `createTable()` method will be invoked. Similarly, the **click()** event of the push button with the **objectName** property `pushButtonAddColumn` is connected to the `addColumns()` method. That is, this button, when clicked, will invoke the `addColumns()` method.

In the `addColumns()` method, the `CREATE TABLE SQL` statement is defined, which consists of the column name entered in the **Line Edit** widget and the data type selected from the combo box. The user can add any number of columns to the table.

In the `createTable()` method, first the connection to the database is established, and thereafter the `CREATE TABLE SQL` statement defined in the `addColumns()` method is executed. If the table is successfully created, a message is displayed informing you of the successful creation of the table through the last **Label** widget. Finally, the connection to the database is closed.

On running the application, you will be prompted to enter the database name and table name that you want to create, followed by the columns required in that table. Let's assume you want to create a `Users` table in the `ECommerce` table consisting of two columns, `EmailAddress` and `Password`. Both the columns are assumed to be of the text type.

The first column name, `Email Address`, in the `Users` table can be defined as shown in the following screenshot:

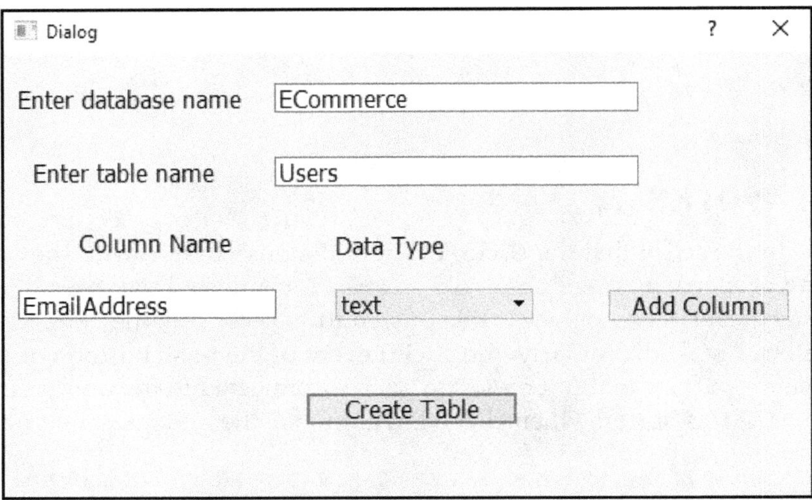

Let's define one more column, called `Password`, of the text type in the `Users` table, followed by clicking the **Create Table** button. If the table is created with the specified number of columns successfully, a message, **Table is successfully created**, is displayed via the last **Label** widget, as shown in the following screenshot:

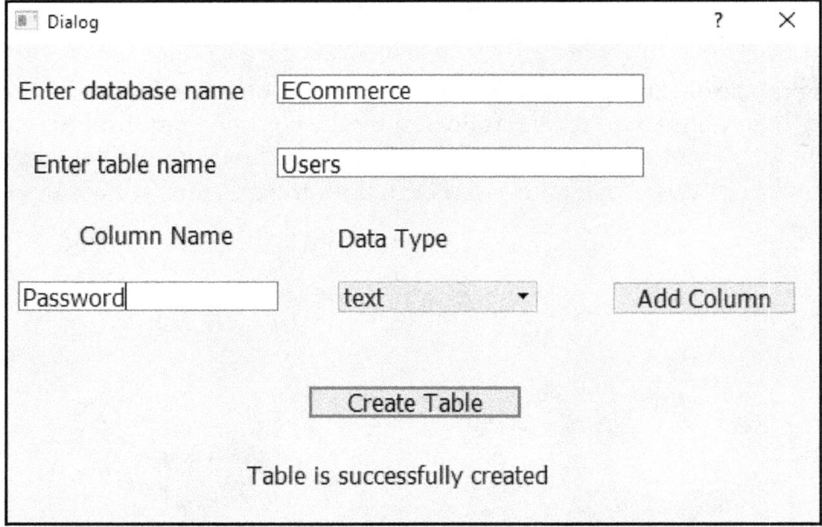

To verify that the table was created, I will be making use of a visual tool that enables you to create, edit, and view the database tables and rows inside them. That visual tool is DB Browser for SQLite, which I downloaded from `http://sqlitebrowser.org/`. On launching DB Browser for SQLite, click the **Open Database** tab below the main menu. Browse and select the `ECommerce` database from the current folder. The `ECommerce` database shows the `Users` table consisting of two columns, `EmailAddress` and `Password`, as shown in the following screenshot, confirming that the database table was created successfully:

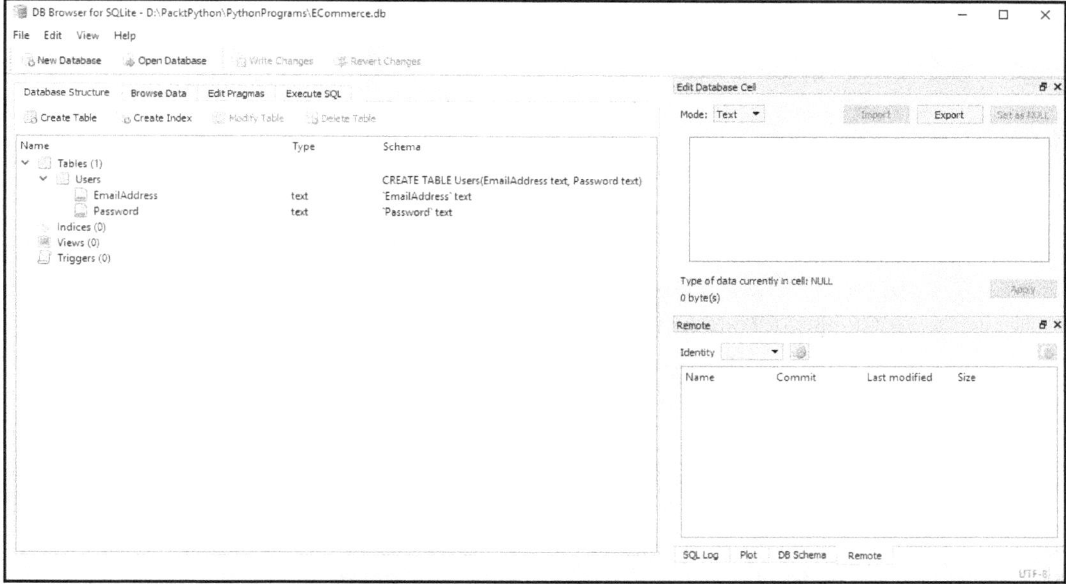

Inserting rows in the specified database table

In this recipe, we will be learning to insert rows into a table. We assume a table called `Users` consisting of two columns, `EmailAddress` and `Password`, already exists in a database called `ECommerce`.

After entering the email address and password in the respective **Line Edit** widgets, when the user clicks the **Insert Row** button, the row will be inserted into the specified database table.

How to do it...

Here are the steps to insert rows into a database table that exists in SQLite:

1. Let's create an application based on the **Dialog without Buttons** template.
2. Add five `QLabel` widgets, four `QLineEdit` widgets, and one `QPushButton` widgets to the form by dragging and dropping five **Label** widgets, four **Line Edit** widgtes, and one **Push Button** widget on the form.
3. Set the **text** property of the first four **Label** widgets to `Enter database name`, `Enter table name`, `Email Address`, and `Password`.
4. Delete the **text** property of the fifth **Label** widget this is established through code.
5. Set the **text** property of the push button to **Insert Row**.
6. Set the **objectName** property of the four **Line Edit** widgets to `lineEditDBName`, `lineEditTableName`, `lineEditEmailAddress`, and `lineEditPassword`.

7. Set the **objectName** property of the **Push Button** widget to `pushButtonInsertRow`.
8. Set the **objectName** property of the fifth **Label** widget to `labelResponse`. As we don't want the password to be displayed, we want asterisks to appear when the user enters their password.
9. To do this, select the **Line Edit** widget that is meant for entering the password and, from the **Property Editor** window, select the **echoMode** property and set it to **Password**, instead of the default **Normal**, as shown in the following screenshot:

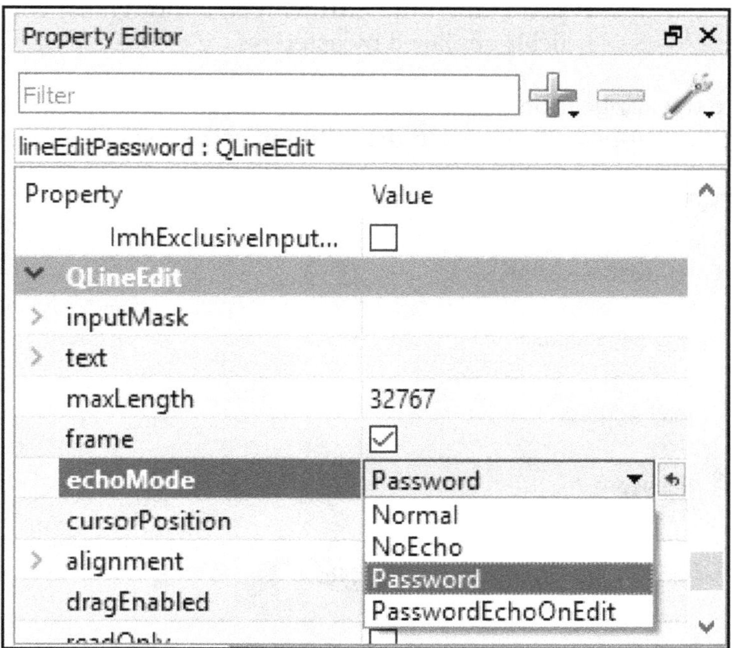

The **echoMode** property shows the following four options:

- **Normal**: It is the default property and it displays characters when typed in the **Line Edit** widget.
- **NoEcho**: It does not display anything when typed in the **Line Edit** widget, that is, you will not even know the length of the text entered.
- **Password**: It is used mostly for passwords. It displays asterisks when typed in the **Line Edit** widget.
- **PasswordEchoOnEdit**: It displays the password while being typed in the **Line Edit** widget, although the content typed is quickly replaced by asterisks.

10. Save the application by name as `demoInsertRowsInTable.ui`. The form will now appear as shown in the following screenshot:

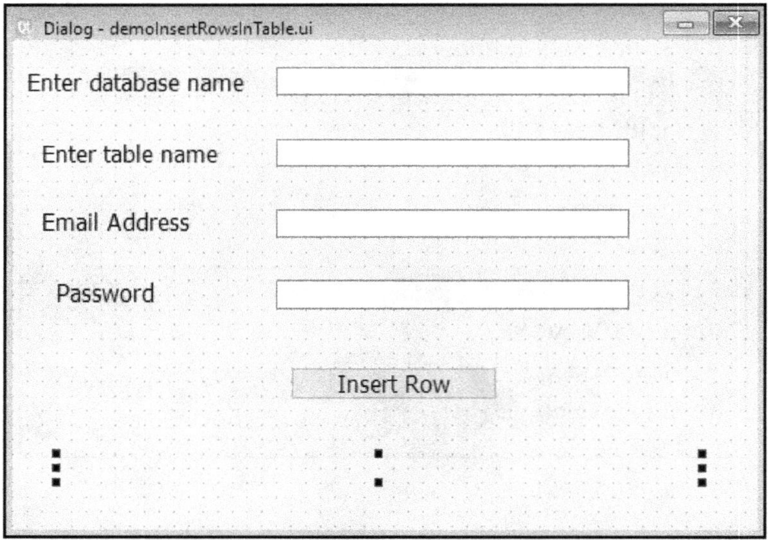

The user interface created with Qt Designer is stored in a `.ui` file, which is an XML file and needs to be converted into Python code. By applying the `pyuic5` utility, the XML file will be converted into Python code. The Python script generated, `demoInsertRowsInTable.py`, can be seen in the source code bundle of the book.

11. Create another Python file with the name `callInsertRows.pyw` and import the `demoInsertRowsInTable.py` code into it. The code in the Python script `callInsertRows.pyw` is as shown here:

```
import sqlite3, sys
from PyQt5.QtWidgets import QDialog, QApplication
from sqlite3 import Error
from demoInsertRowsInTable import *
class MyForm(QDialog):
    def __init__(self):
        super().__init__()
        self.ui = Ui_Dialog()
        self.ui.setupUi(self)
        self.ui.pushButtonInsertRow.clicked.connect(self.
        InsertRows)
        self.show()
    def InsertRows(self):
        sqlStatement="INSERT INTO "+
        self.ui.lineEditTableName.text() +"
        VALUES('"+self.ui.lineEditEmailAddress.text()+"',
        '"+self.ui.lineEditPassword.text()+"')"
        try:
            conn = sqlite3.connect(self.ui.lineEditDBName.
            text()+ ".db")
        with conn:
            cur = conn.cursor()
            cur.execute(sqlStatement)
            self.ui.labelResponse.setText("Row successfully
            inserted")
        except Error as e:
            self.ui.labelResponse.setText("Error in inserting
            row")
        finally:
            conn.close()
if __name__=="__main__":
    app = QApplication(sys.argv)
    w = MyForm()
    w.show()
    sys.exit(app.exec_())
```

How it works...

You can see in the script that the click event of the push button with the **objectName** property `pushButtonInsertRow` is connected to the `InsertRows()` method. This means that, whenever this push button is clicked, the `InsertRows()` method will be invoked. In the `InsertRows()` method, an `INSERT SQL` statement is defined that fetches the email address and password entered in the **Line Edit** widgets. A connection is established with the database whose name is entered in the **Line Edit** widget. Thereafter, the `INSERT SQL` statement is executed, which adds a new row to the specified database table. Finally, the connection to the database is closed.

On running the application, you will be prompted to specify the database name, table name, and the data for the two columns, `Email Address` and `Password`. After entering the required information, when you click the **Insert Row** button, a new row will be added to the table and a message, **Row successfully inserted**, will be displayed, as shown in the following screenshot:

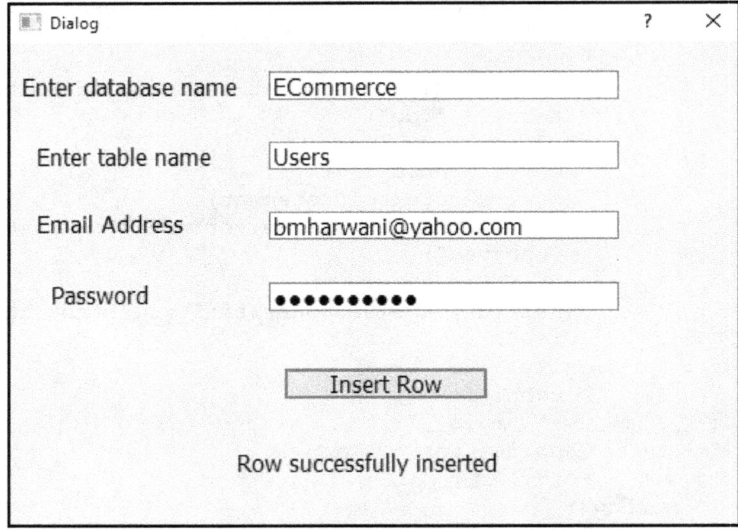

To verify that the row was inserted into the `Users` table, I will be making use of a visual tool called DB Browser for SQLite. It is a wonderful tool that enables you to create, edit, and view the database tables and rows inside them. You can download DB Browser for SQLite from `http://sqlitebrowser.org/`. On launching DB Browser for SQLite, you need to first open the database. To do so, click the **Open Database** tab below the main menu. Browse and select the `Ecommerce` database from the current folder. The `Ecommerce` database shows the `Users` table. Click on the **Execute SQL** button; you get a small window to type the SQL statement. Write an SQL statement, `select * from Users`, and click the Run icon above the window.

All the rows entered in the `Users` table will be displayed in tabular format, as shown in the following screenshot. It confirms that the application made in our recipe is working perfectly well:

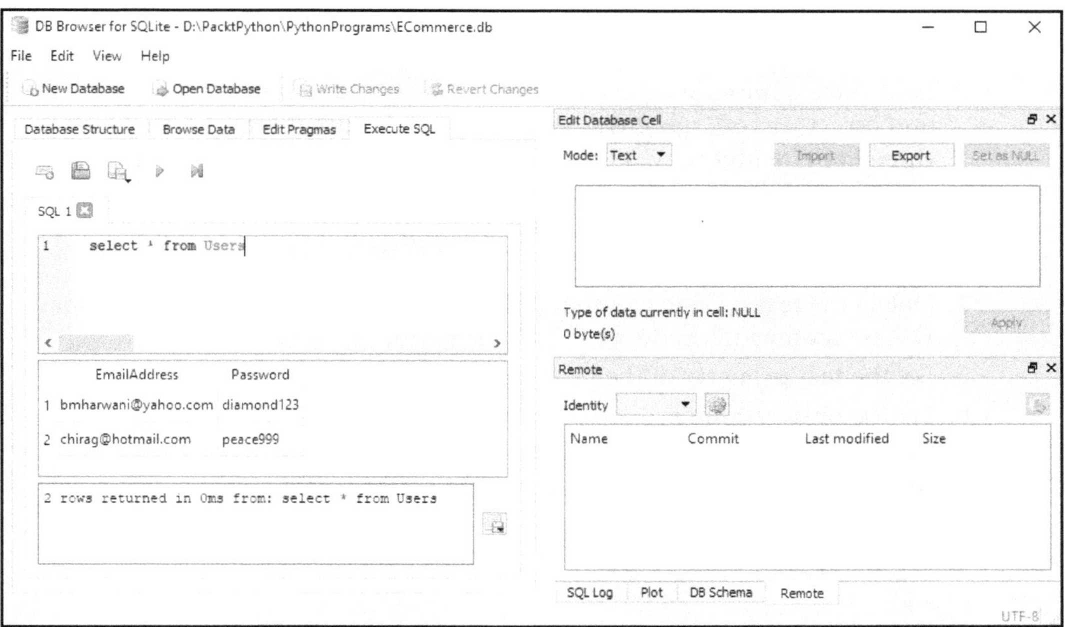

Displaying rows in the specified database table

In this recipe, we will be learning to fetch rows from a given database table and display them in tabular format via the **Table** widget. We assume a table called `Users` consisting of two columns, `EmailAddress` and `Password`, already exists in a database called `ECommerce`. Also, we assume that the `Users` table contains some rows in it.

How to do it...

Follow this step-by-step procedure to access rows from the database table in SQLite:

1. Let's create an application based on the **Dialog without Buttons** template.
2. Add three `QLabel` widgets, two `QLineEdit` widgets, one `QPushButton`, and one `QTableWidget` widget to the form by dragging and dropping three **Label** widgets, two **Line Edit** widgets, one **Push Button** widget, and a **Table** widget on the form.
3. Set the **text** property of the two **Label** widgets to `Enter database name` and `Enter table name`.
4. Delete the **text** property of the third **Label** widget because its **text** property will be set through code.
5. Set the **text** property of the push button to `Display Rows`.
6. Set the **objectName** property of the two **Line Edit** widgets to `lineEditDBName` and `lineEditTableName`.
7. Set the **objectName** property of the **Push Button** widget to `pushButtonDisplayRows`.
8. Set the `objectName` property of the third **Label** widget to `labelResponse`.

9. Save the application by name as `demoDisplayRowsOfTable.ui`. The form will now appear as shown in the following screenshot:

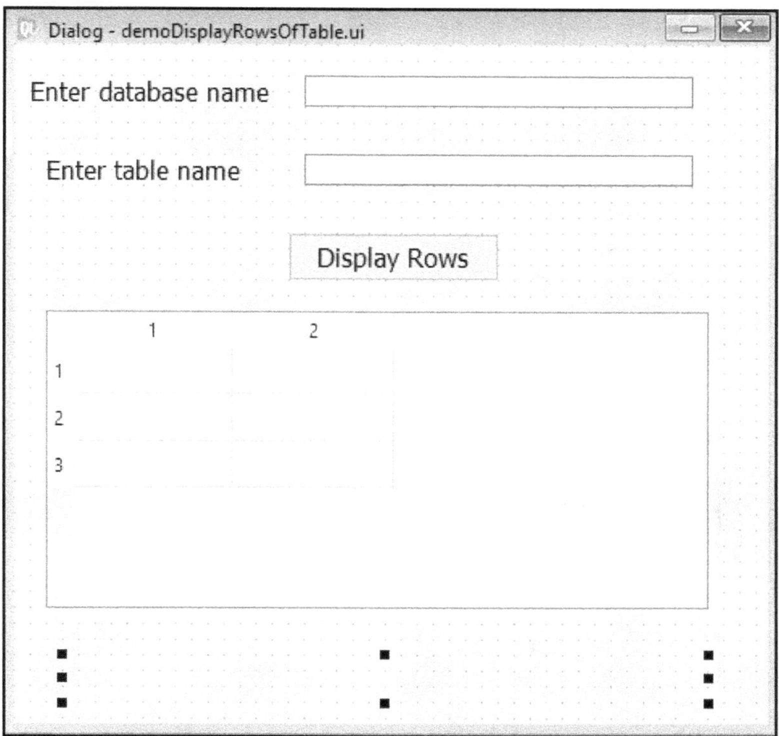

The `Users` table whose rows will be displayed through the **Table** widget consists of two columns.

10. Select the **Table** widget and select its **columnCount** property in the **Property Editor** window.

11. Set the **columnCount** property to `2` and the **rowCount** property to `3`, as shown in the following screenshot:

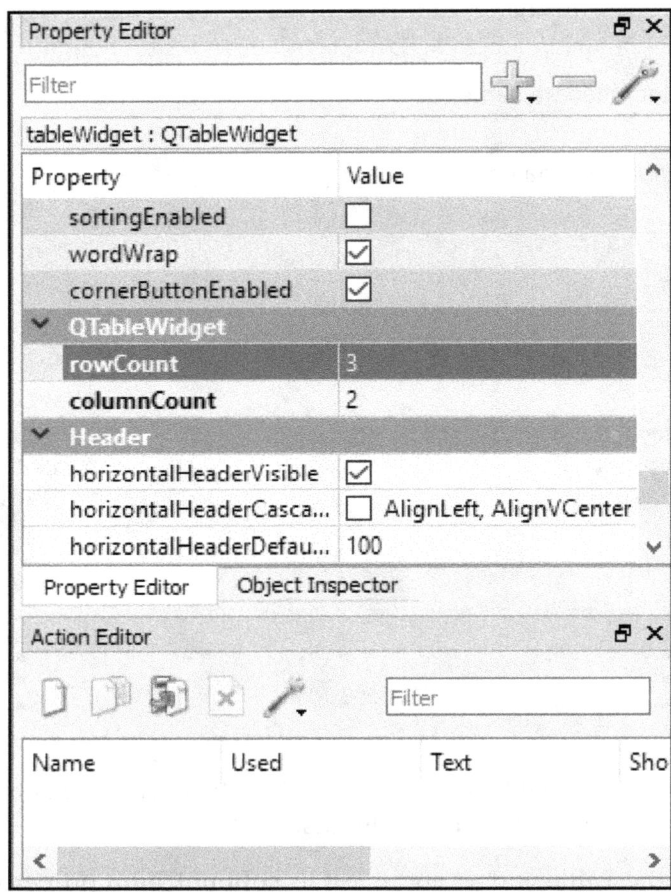

The user interface created with Qt Designer is stored in a `.ui` file, which is an XML file and needs to be converted into Python code. By applying the `pyuic5` utility, the XML file will be converted into Python code. The Python script generated, `demoInsertRowsInTable.py`, can be seen in the source code bundle of this book.

12. Treat the `demoInsertRowsInTable.py` script as a header file, and import it into the file from which you will invoke its user interface design.

13. Create another Python file with the name `callDisplayRows.pyw` and import the `demoDisplayRowsOfTable.py` code into it:

```
import sqlite3, sys
from PyQt5.QtWidgets import QDialog,
QApplication,QTableWidgetItem
from sqlite3 import Error
from demoDisplayRowsOfTable import *
class MyForm(QDialog):
    def __init__(self):
        super().__init__()
        self.ui = Ui_Dialog()
        self.ui.setupUi(self)
        self.ui.pushButtonDisplayRows.clicked.
            connect(self.DisplayRows)
        self.show()

    def DisplayRows(self):
        sqlStatement="SELECT * FROM "+
            self.ui.lineEditTableName.text()
        try:
            conn = sqlite3.connect(self.ui.lineEditDBName.
            text()+ ".db")
            cur = conn.cursor()
            cur.execute(sqlStatement)
            rows = cur.fetchall()
            rowNo=0
        for tuple in rows:
            self.ui.labelResponse.setText("")
            colNo=0
        for columns in tuple:
            oneColumn=QTableWidgetItem(columns)
            self.ui.tableWidget.setItem(rowNo, colNo,
oneColumn)
            colNo+=1
            rowNo+=1
        except Error as e:
            self.ui.tableWidget.clear()
            self.ui.labelResponse.setText("Error in accessing
            table")
        finally:
            conn.close()
if __name__=="__main__":
    app = QApplication(sys.argv)
    w = MyForm()
    w.show()
    sys.exit(app.exec_())
```

How it works...

You can see in the script that the **click()** event of the push button with the **objectName** property `pushButtonDisplayRows` is connected to the `DisplayRows()` method. This means that, whenever this push button is clicked, the `DisplayRows()` method will be invoked. In the `DisplayRows()` method, an `SQL SELECT` statement is defined that fetches the rows from the table whose name is specified in the **Line Edit** widget. Also, a connection is established with the database whose name is entered in the **Line Edit** widget. Thereafter, the `SQL SELECT` statement is executed. The `fetchall()` method is executed on the cursor to keep all the rows that are accessed from the database table.

A `for` loop is executed to access one tuple at a time from the received rows, and again a `for` loop is executed on the tuple to get data in each column of that row. The data accessed in each column of the row is assigned to the **Table** widget for display. After displaying the data in the first row, the second row is picked up from the rows and the procedure is repeated to display the data in the second row in the **Table** widget. The two nested `for` loops are executed until all the rows are displayed through the **Table** widget.

Upon running the application, you will be prompted to specify the database name and table name. After entering the required information, when you click the **Display Rows** button, the content of the specified database table is displayed through the **Table** widget, as shown in the following screenshot:

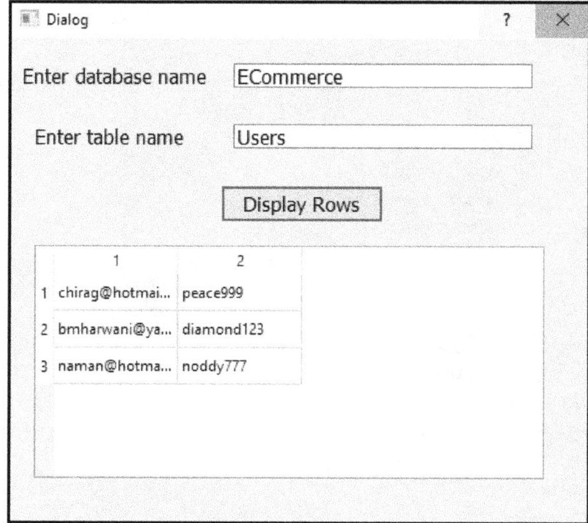

Navigating through the rows of the specified database table

In this recipe, we will be learning to fetch rows from a given database table one at a time. That is, on running the application, the first row of the database table will be displayed. You will be provided with four push buttons in the application, called **Next**, **Previous**, **First**, and **Last**. As the name suggests, upon clicking the **Next** button, the next row in the sequence will be displayed. Similarly, upon clicking the **Previous** button, the previous row in the sequence will be displayed. Upon clicking the **Last** button, the last row of the database table will be displayed and, upon clicking the **First** button, the first row of the database table will be displayed.

How to do it...

Here are the steps to understand how rows from a database table are accessed and displayed one by one:

1. Let's create an application based on the **Dialog without Buttons** template.
2. Add three `QLabel` widgets, two `QLineEdit` widgets, and four `QPushButton` widgets to the form by dragging and dropping three **Label** widgets, two **Line Edit** widgets, and four **Push Button** widgets on the form.
3. Set the **text** property of the two **Label** widgets to `Email Address` and `Password`.
4. Delete the **text** property of the third **Label** widget because its **text** property will be set through code.
5. Set the **text** property of the four push buttons to `First Row`, `Previous`, `Next`, and `Last Row`.
6. Set the **objectName** property of the two **Line Edit** widgets to `lineEditEmailAddress` and `lineEditPassword`.
7. Set the **objectName** property of the four push buttons to `pushButtonFirst`, `pushButtonPrevious`, `pushButtonNext`, and `pushButtonLast`.
8. Set the **objectName** property of the third **Label** widget to `labelResponse`. Because we don't want the password to be displayed, we want the asterisks to appear when the user enters their password.

9. Select the **Line Edit** widget that is meant for entering the password (`lineEditPassword`) and, from the **Property Editor** window, select the **echoMode** property and set it to **Password** instead of the default **Normal**.
10. Save the application by name as `demoShowRecords`. The form will now appear as shown in the following screenshot:

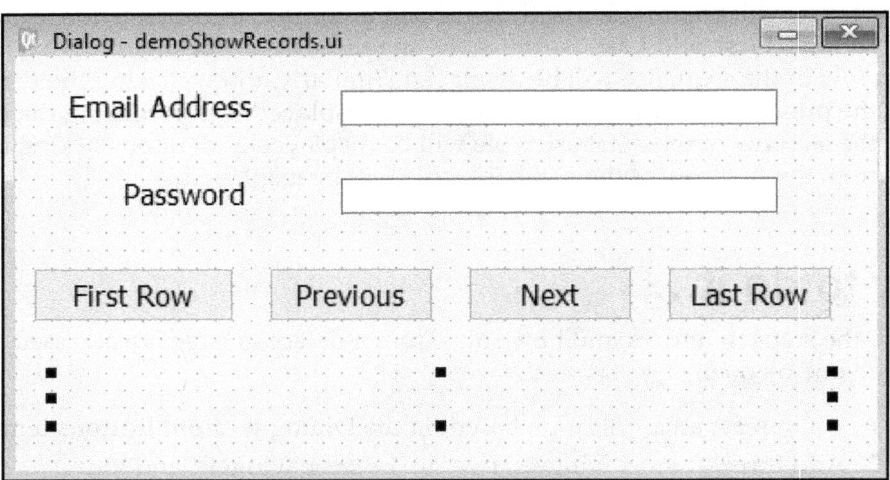

The user interface created with Qt Designer is stored in a `.ui` file, which is an XML file, and on applying the `pyuic5` command, the XML file can be converted into Python code. The Python script generated, `demoShowRecords.py`, can be seen in the source code bundle of the book.

11. Treat the `demoShowRecords.py` script as a header file, and import it into the file from which you will invoke its user interface design.
12. Create another Python file with the name `callShowRecords.pyw` and import the `demoShowRecords.py` code into it.

```
import sqlite3, sys
from PyQt5.QtWidgets import QDialog,
QApplication,QTableWidgetItem
from sqlite3 import Error
from demoShowRecords import *
rowNo=1
sqlStatement="SELECT EmailAddress, Password FROM Users"
conn = sqlite3.connect("ECommerce.db")
cur = conn.cursor()
class MyForm(QDialog):
    def __init__(self):
```

```
        super().__init__()
        self.ui = Ui_Dialog()
        self.ui.setupUi(self)
        cur.execute(sqlStatement)
        self.ui.pushButtonFirst.clicked.connect(self.
        ShowFirstRow)
        self.ui.pushButtonPrevious.clicked.connect(self.
        ShowPreviousRow)
self.ui.pushButtonNext.clicked.connect(self.ShowNextRow)
self.ui.pushButtonLast.clicked.connect(self.ShowLastRow)
        self.show()
    def ShowFirstRow(self):
        try:
            cur.execute(sqlStatement)
            row=cur.fetchone()
        if row:
            self.ui.lineEditEmailAddress.setText(row[0])
            self.ui.lineEditPassword.setText(row[1])
        except Error as e:
            self.ui.labelResponse.setText("Error in accessing
            table")
    def ShowPreviousRow(self):
        global rowNo
        rowNo -= 1
        sqlStatement="SELECT EmailAddress, Password FROM Users
        where rowid="+str(rowNo)
        cur.execute(sqlStatement)
        row=cur.fetchone()
        if row:
            self.ui.labelResponse.setText("")
            self.ui.lineEditEmailAddress.setText(row[0])
            self.ui.lineEditPassword.setText(row[1])
        else:
            rowNo += 1
            self.ui.labelResponse.setText("This is the first
            row")
        def ShowNextRow(self):
            global rowNo
            rowNo += 1
            sqlStatement="SELECT EmailAddress, Password FROM
            Users where rowid="+str(rowNo)
            cur.execute(sqlStatement)
            row=cur.fetchone()
            if row:
                self.ui.labelResponse.setText("")
                self.ui.lineEditEmailAddress.setText(row[0])
                self.ui.lineEditPassword.setText(row[1])
            else:
```

```
                    rowNo -= 1
                    self.ui.labelResponse.setText("This is the
last
                    row")
    def ShowLastRow(self):
        cur.execute(sqlStatement)
        for row in cur.fetchall():
            self.ui.lineEditEmailAddress.setText(row[0])
            self.ui.lineEditPassword.setText(row[1])
if __name__=="__main__":
    app = QApplication(sys.argv)
    w = MyForm()
    w.show()
    sys.exit(app.exec_())
```

How it works...

You can see in the script that the **click()** event of the push button with the **objectName** property `pushButtonFirst` is connected to the `ShowFirstRow()` method, the push button with the **objectName** property `pushButtonPrevious` is connected to the `ShowPreviousRow()` method, the push button with the **objectName** property `pushButtonNext` is connected to the `ShowNextRow()` method, and the push button with the **objectName** property `pushButtonLast` is connected to the `ShowLastRow()` method.

Whenever a push button is clicked, the associated method will be invoked.

In the `ShowFirstRow()` method, an `SQL SELECT` statement is executed that fetches the email address and password columns of the `Users` table. The `fetchone()` method is executed on the cursor to access the first row from the rows that are received on execution of the `SQL SELECT` statement. The data in the `EmailAddress` and `Password` columns is displayed through two **Line Edit** widgets on the screen. If an error occurs when accessing the rows, an error message, `Error in accessing table`, will be displayed through the **Label** widget.

To fetch the previous row, we make use of a global variable, `rowNo`, which is initialized to `1`. In the `ShowPreviousRow()` method, the value of the global variable, `rowNo`, is decremented by `1`. Thereafter, an `SQL SELECT` statement is executed that fetches the `EmailAddress` and `Password` columns of the `Users` table whose `rowid=rowNo`. Because the `rowNo` variable is decremented by `1`, the `SQL SELECT` statement will fetch the previous row in the sequence. The `fetchone()` method is executed on the cursor to access the received row, and the data in the `EmailAddress` and `Password` columns is displayed through two **Line Edit** widgets on the screen.

If the first row is already being displayed, then, upon clicking the **Previous** button, it will simply display a message, **This is the first row**, through the **Label** widget.

We make use of the global variable `rowNo` while accessing the next row in the sequence too. In the `ShowNextRow()` method, the value of the global variable `rowNo` is incremented by `1`. Thereafter, an `SQL SELECT` statement is executed that fetches the `EmailAddress` and `Password` columns of the `Users` table whose `rowid=rowNo`; hence, the next row, that is, the one whose `rowid` is one higher than the current row, is accessed. The `fetchone()` method is executed on the cursor to access the received row and the data in the `EmailAddress` and `Password` columns is displayed through two **Line Edit** widgets on the screen.

If you are looking at the last row in the database table, then, upon clicking the **Next** button, it will simply display a message, **This is the last row**, through the **Label** widget.

In the `ShowLastRow()` method, an `SQL SELECT` statement is executed that fetches the `EmailAddress` and `Password` columns of the `Users` table. The `fetchall()` method is executed on the cursor to access the remainder of the rows in the database table. Using the `for` loop, a `row` variable is moved to the last row from the rows that are received upon execution of the `SQL SELECT` statement. The data in the `EmailAddress` and `Password` columns of the last row is displayed through two **Line Edit** widgets on the screen.

Upon running the application, you will get the first row of the database table displayed on the screen, as shown in the following screenshot. If you click the **Previous** button now, you get the message, **This is the first row**:

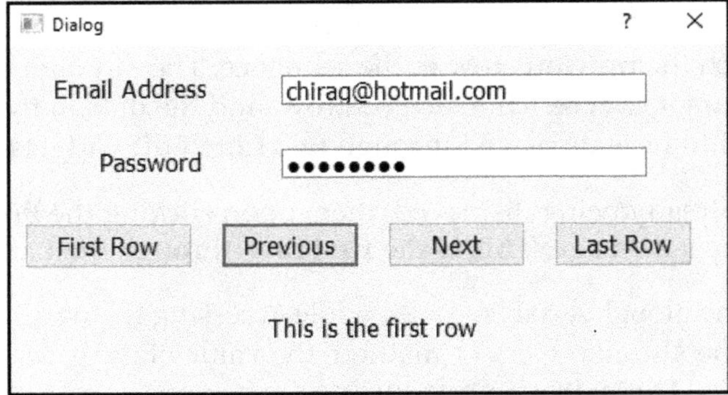

Upon clicking the **Next** button, the next row in the sequence will be displayed on the screen, as shown in the following screenshot:

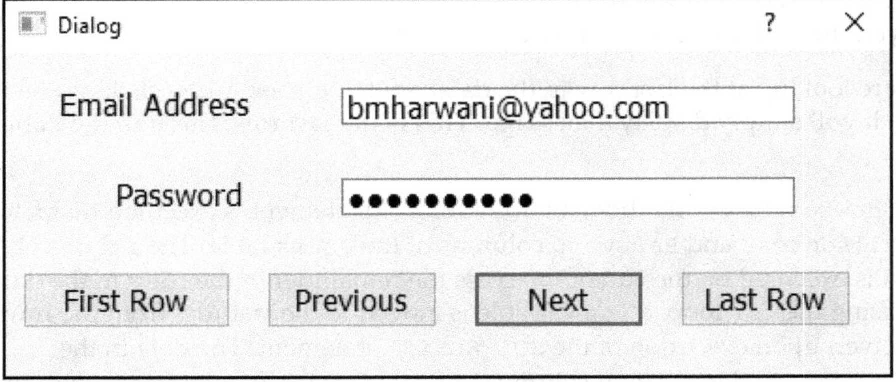

Upon clicking the **Last Row** button, the last row in the database table will be displayed, as shown in the following screenshot:

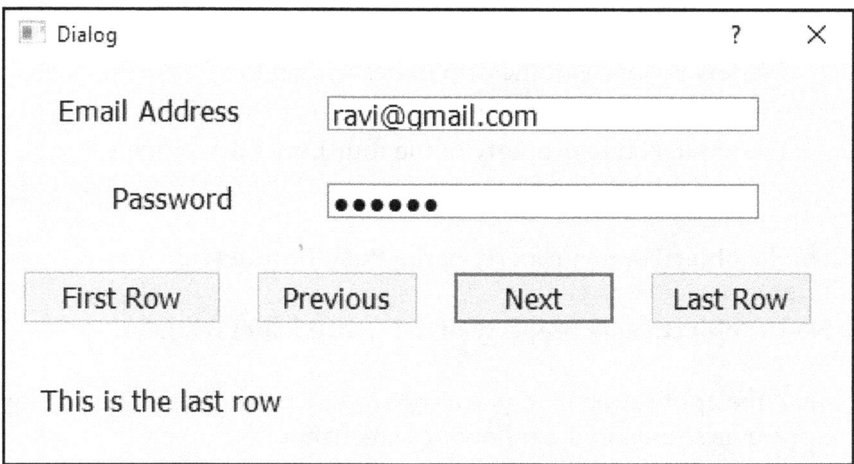

Searching a database table for specific information

In this recipe, we will be learning how searching is performed in a database table to fetch the desired information. We assume that a user has forgotten their password. So, you will be prompted to enter the database name, table name, and email address of the user whose password is required. If any user with the email address supplied exists in the database table, then the password of that user will be searched for, accessed, and displayed on the screen.

How to do it...

Follow these steps to find out how data can be searched for in a database table in SQLite:

1. Let's create an application based on the **Dialog without Buttons** template.
2. Add five `QLabel` widgets, four `QLineEdit` widgets, and one `QPushButton` widget to the form by dragging and dropping five **Label** widgets, four **Line Edit** widgets, and one **Push Button** widget on the form.

3. Set the **text** property of the first three **Label** widgets to `Enter database name`, `Enter table name`, and `Email Address`.
4. Delete the **text** property of the fourth **Label** widget this is established through code.
5. Set the **text** property of the fifth **Label** widget to `Password`.
6. Set the **text** property of the push button to `Search`.
7. Set the **objectName** property of the four **Line Edit** widgets to `lineEditDBName`, `lineEditTableName`, `lineEditEmailAddress`, and `lineEditPassword`.
8. Set the **objectName** property of the **Push Button** widget to `pushButtonSearch`.
9. Set the **objectName** property of the fourth **Label** widget to `labelResponse`.
10. Save the application by name as `demoSearchRows.ui`. The form will now appear as shown in the following screenshot:

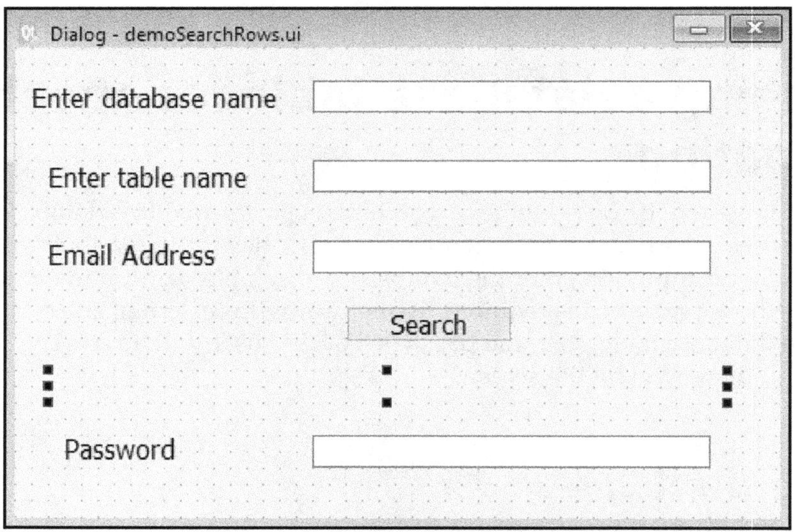

The user interface created with Qt Designer is stored in a `.ui` file, an XML file that needs to be converted into Python code through application of the `pyuic5` command. The generated Python script, `demoSearchRows.py`, can be seen in the source code bundle of the book.

11. Treat the `demoSearchRows.py` script as a header file, and import it into the file from which you will invoke its user interface design.
12. Create another Python file with the name `callSearchRows.pyw` and import the `demoSearchRows.py` code into it:

```
import sqlite3, sys
from PyQt5.QtWidgets import QDialog, QApplication
from sqlite3 import Error
from demoSearchRows import *
class MyForm(QDialog):
    def __init__(self):
        super().__init__()
        self.ui = Ui_Dialog()
        self.ui.setupUi(self)
        self.ui.pushButtonSearch.clicked.connect(self.
        SearchRows)
        self.show()
    def SearchRows(self):
        sqlStatement="SELECT Password FROM
        "+self.ui.lineEditTableName.text()+" where
EmailAddress
        like'"+self.ui.lineEditEmailAddress.text()+"'"
    try:
        conn = sqlite3.connect(self.ui.lineEditDBName.text()+
        ".db")
        cur = conn.cursor()
        cur.execute(sqlStatement)
        row = cur.fetchone()
    if row==None:
        self.ui.labelResponse.setText("Sorry, No User found
with
        this email address")
        self.ui.lineEditPassword.setText("")
```

```
        else:
            self.ui.labelResponse.setText("Email Address Found,
            Password of this User is :")
            self.ui.lineEditPassword.setText(row[0])
        except Error as e:
            self.ui.labelResponse.setText("Error in accessing
row")
        finally:
            conn.close()
if __name__=="__main__":
    app = QApplication(sys.argv)
    w = MyForm()
    w.show()
    sys.exit(app.exec_())
```

How it works...

You can see in the script that the **click()** event of the push button with the **objectName** property `pushButtonSearch` is connected to the `SearchRows()` method. This means that, whenever the push button is clicked, the `SearchRows()` method is invoked. In the `SearchRows()` method, the `connect()` method is invoked on the `sqlite3` class and the database name entered by the user in the **Line Edit** widget is passed to the `connect()` method. The connection to the database is established. An SQL `search` statement is defined that fetches the `Password` column from the table supplied whose email address matches the email address supplied. The `search` SQL statement is executed on the given database table. The `fetchone()` method is executed on the cursor to fetch one row from the executed SQL statement. If the fetched row is not `None`, that is, there is a row in the database table that matches the given email address, the password in the row is accessed and assigned to the **Line Edit** widget with the object name `lineEditPassword` for display. Finally, the connection to the database is closed.

If an error occurs in the execution of the SQL statement, that is, if the database is not found, the table name is incorrectly entered, or the email address column does not exist in the given table, an error message, **Error in accessing row**, is displayed via the **Label** widget with the **objectName** property, `labelResponse`.

Upon running the application, we get a dialog that prompts us for the database name, table name, and column name from the table. Suppose we want to find out the password of the user whose email address is `bmharwani@yahoo.com` in the `Users` table of the `ECommerce` database. After entering the required information in the boxes, when you click on the **Search** button, the password of the user will be accessed from the table and displayed through the **Line Edit** widget, as shown in the following screenshot:

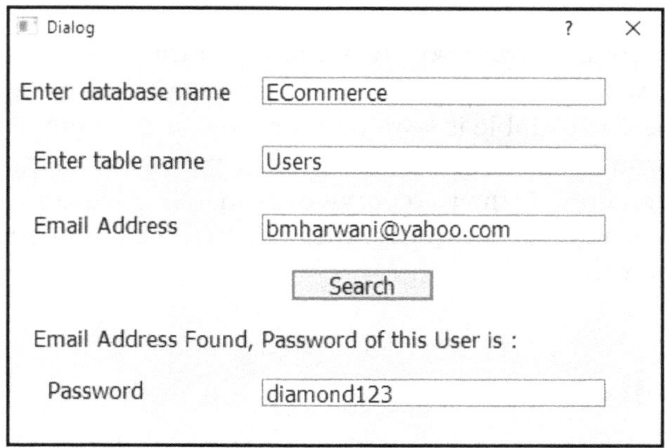

If the email address supplied is not found in the Users table, you get the message "Sorry, No User found with this email address," which is displayed through the Label widget as shown here:

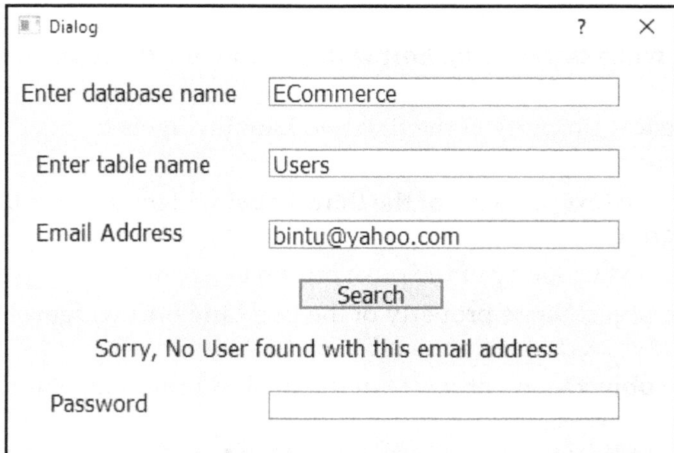

Creating a signin form – applying an authentication procedure

In this recipe, we will be learning how rows can be accessed from a specific table and compared with the information supplied.

We assume that a database called `ECommerce` already exists and a table called `Users` also exists in the `ECommerce` database. The `Users` table consists of two columns, `EmailAddress` and `Password`. Also, we assume that the `Users` table contains a few rows in it. The user will be prompted to enter their email address and password in the signin form. The `Users` table is searched for the specified email address. If the email address is found in the `Users` table, then the password in that row is compared with the password entered. If the two passwords match, a welcome message is displayed; otherwise, an error message indicating that the email address or password don't match is displayed.

How to do it...

Here are the steps to understand how data in a database table can be compared with data entered by the user and authenticate a user:

1. Let's create an application based on the **Dialog without Buttons** template.
2. Add three `QLabel` widgets, two `QLineEdit` widgets, and one `QPushButton` widget to the form by dragging and dropping three **Label** widgets, two **Line Edit** widgets, and one **Push Button** widget on the form.
3. Set the **text** property of the first two **Label** widgets to `Email Address` and `Password`.
4. Delete the **text** property of the third **Label** widget this is established through code.
5. Set the **text** property of the push button to `Sign In`.
6. Set the **objectName** property of the two **Line Edit** widgets to `lineEditEmailAddress` and `lineEditPassword`.
7. Set the **objectName** property of the **Push Button** widget to `pushButtonSearch`.
8. Set the **objectName** property of the third **Label** widget to `labelResponse`.

9. Save the application by name as `demoSignInForm.ui`. The form will now appear as shown in the following screenshot:

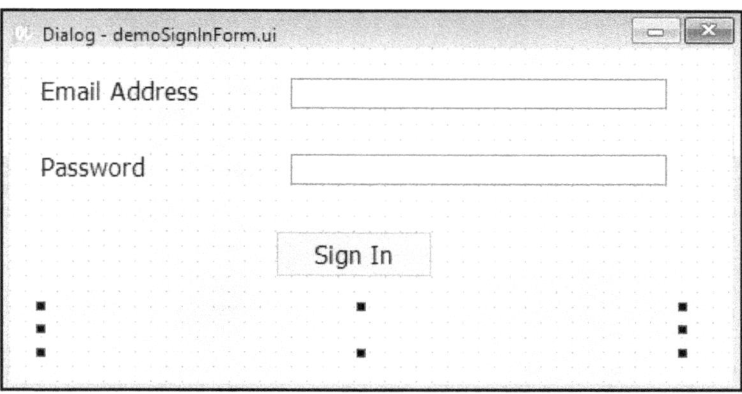

The user interface created with Qt Designer is stored in a `.ui` file, which is an XML file, and needs to be converted into Python code. By applying the `pyuic5` command, the XML file can be converted into Python code. The Python script generated, `demoSignInForm.py`, can be seen in the source code bundle of the book.

10. Treat the `demoSignInForm.py` file as a header file, and import it into the file from which you will invoke its user interface design.

11. Create another Python file with the name `callSignInForm.pyw` and import the `demoSignInForm.py` code into it:

```
import sqlite3, sys
from PyQt5.QtWidgets import QDialog, QApplication
from sqlite3 import Error
from demoSignInForm import *
class MyForm(QDialog):
    def __init__(self):
        super().__init__()
        self.ui = Ui_Dialog()
        self.ui.setupUi(self)
        self.ui.pushButtonSearch.clicked.connect(self.
        SearchRows)
        self.show()
    def SearchRows(self):
        sqlStatement="SELECT EmailAddress, Password FROM Users
        where EmailAddress
like'"+self.ui.lineEditEmailAddress.
```

```
            text()+"'and Password like '"+
    self.ui.lineEditPassword.
            text()+"'"
            try:
                conn = sqlite3.connect("ECommerce.db")
                cur = conn.cursor()
                cur.execute(sqlStatement)
                row = cur.fetchone()
            if row==None:
                self.ui.labelResponse.setText("Sorry, Incorrect
                email address or password ")
            else:
                self.ui.labelResponse.setText("You are welcome ")
            except Error as e:
                self.ui.labelResponse.setText("Error in accessing
                row")
            finally:
                conn.close()
    if __name__=="__main__":
        app = QApplication(sys.argv)
        w = MyForm()
        w.show()
        sys.exit(app.exec_())
```

How it works...

You can see in the script that the click event of the push button with the **objectName** property `pushButtonSearch` is connected to the `SearchRows()` method. This means that, whenever the push button is clicked, the `SearchRows()` method is invoked. In the `SearchRows()` method, the `connect()` method is invoked on the `sqlite3` class to establish a connection with the `ECommerce` database. An SQL `search` statement is defined that fetches the `EmailAddress` and `Password` columns from the `Users` table whose email address matches the email address supplied. The `search` SQL statement is executed on the `Users` table. The `fetchone()` method is executed on the cursor to fetch one row from the executed SQL statement. If the fetched row is not `None`, that is, there is a row in the database table that matches the given email address and password, a welcome message is displayed with the **Label** widget with the **objectName** property, `labelResponse`. Finally, the connection to the database is closed.

If an error occurs in the execution of the SQL statement, if the database is not found, or if the table name is incorrectly entered, or the email address or password columns do not exist in the `Users` table, an error message, **Error in accessing row**, is displayed via the **Label** widget with the **objectName** property, `labelResponse`.

Upon running the application, you will be prompted to enter an email address and password. Upon entering the correct email address and password, when you click the **Sign In** button, you receive the message, **You are welcome**, as shown in the following screenshot:

But if either email address or password is entered incorrectly, you get the message, **Sorry, Incorrect email address or password**, as shown in the following screenshot:

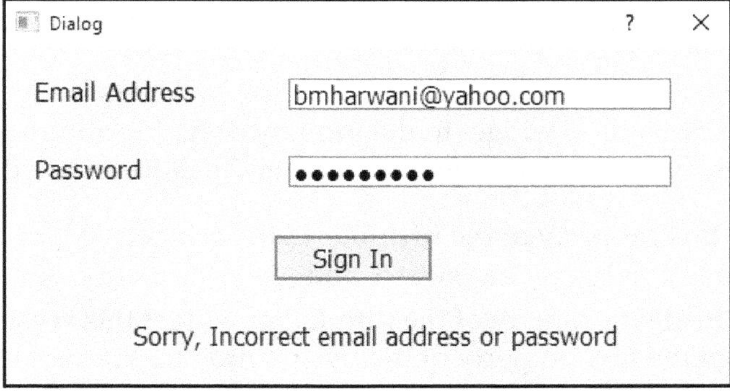

Updating a database table – changing a user's password

In this recipe, you will learn how to update any information in the database. Changing passwords is a very common requirement in almost all applications. In this recipe, we assume that a database called `ECommerce` already exists and a table called `Users` also exists in the `ECommerce` database. The `Users` table consists of two columns, `EmailAddress` and `Password`. Also, we assume that the `Users` table contains a few rows in it. The user will be prompted to enter their email address and password in the form. The `Users` table is searched for the specified email address and password. If a row is found with the specified email address and password, the user will be prompted to enter a new password. The new password will be asked for twice, that is, the user will be asked to enter their new password in both the **New Password** box and the **Re-enter New Password** box. If the passwords entered in the two boxes match, the password will be changed, that is, the old password will be replaced by the new password.

How to do it...

The procedure for deleting data from the database table is very critical, and any mistake in executing such an application can lead to disaster. Here come the steps to delete any row from the given database table:

1. Let's create an application based on the **Dialog without Buttons** template.
2. Add five `QLabel` widgets, four `QLineEdit` widgets, and one `QPushButton` widget to the form by dragging and dropping five **Label** widgets, four **Line Edit** widgets, and one **Push Button** widget on the form.
3. Set the **text** property of the first four **Label** widgets to `Email Address`, `Old Password`, `New Password`, and `Re-enter New Password`.
4. Delete the **text** property of the fifth **Label** widget this is established through code. Set the **text** property of the push button to `Change Password`.

5. Set the **objectName** property of the four **Line Edit** widgets to `lineEditEmailAddress`, `lineEditOldPassword`, `lineEditNewPassword`, and `lineEditRePassword`. Since we don't want the password to be displayed in any of the **Line Edit** widgets that are associated with the password, we want the asterisks to appear when the user enters the password.
6. Select the three **Line Edit** widgets one at a time and from the **Property Editor** window.
7. Select the **echoMode** property and set it to `Password` instead of the default **Normal**.
8. Set the **objectName** property of the **Push Button** widget to `pushButtonChangePassword`.
9. Set the **objectName** property of the fifth **Label** widget to `labelResponse`.
10. Save the application by name as `demoChangePassword.ui`. The form will now appear as shown in the following screenshot:

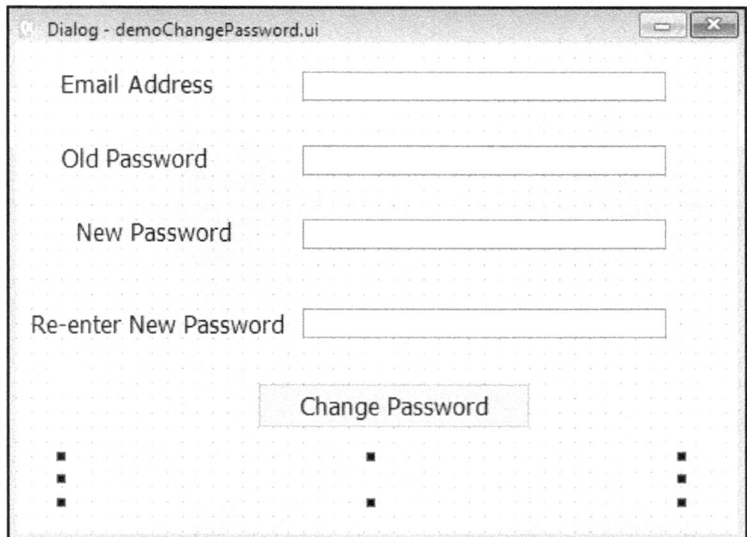

The user interface created with Qt Designer is stored in a `.ui` file, which is an XML file, and needs to be converted into Python code. The `pyuic5` command is used to convert the XML file into Python code. The Python script generated, `demoChangePassword.py`, can be seen in the source code bundle of this book.

11. Treat the `demoChangePassword.py` script as a header file, and import it into the file from which you will invoke its user interface design.
12. Create another Python file with the name `callChangePassword.pyw` and import the `demoChangePassword.py` code into it:

```
import sqlite3, sys
from PyQt5.QtWidgets import QDialog, QApplication
from sqlite3 import Error
from demoChangePassword import *
class MyForm(QDialog):
    def __init__(self):
        super().__init__()
        self.ui = Ui_Dialog()
        self.ui.setupUi(self)
        self.ui.pushButtonChangePassword.clicked.connect(self.
        ChangePassword)
        self.show()
    def ChangePassword(self):
        selectStatement="SELECT EmailAddress, Password FROM
        Users where EmailAddress like '"+self.ui.
        lineEditEmailAddress.text()+"'and Password like '"+
        self.ui.lineEditOldPassword.text()+"'"
        try:
            conn = sqlite3.connect("ECommerce.db")
            cur = conn.cursor()
            cur.execute(selectStatement)
            row = cur.fetchone()
        if row==None:
            self.ui.labelResponse.setText("Sorry, Incorrect
            email address or password")
        else:
        if self.ui.lineEditNewPassword.text()==
          self.ui.lineEditRePassword.text():
            updateStatement="UPDATE Users set Password = '" +
            self.ui.lineEditNewPassword.text()+"' WHERE
            EmailAddress like'"+self.ui.lineEditEmailAddress.
            text()+"'"
        with conn:
            cur.execute(updateStatement)
            self.ui.labelResponse.setText("Password
```

```
successfully
                changed")
            else:
                self.ui.labelResponse.setText("The two passwords
                don't match")
            except Error as e:
                self.ui.labelResponse.setText("Error in accessing
                row")
            finally:
                conn.close()
if __name__=="__main__":
    app = QApplication(sys.argv)
    w = MyForm()
    w.show()
    sys.exit(app.exec_())
```

How it works...

You can see in the script that the **click()** event of the push button with the **objectName** property `pushButtonChangePassword` is connected to the `ChangePassword()` method. This means that, whenever the push button is clicked, the `ChangePassword()` method will be invoked. In the `ChangePassword()` method, the `connect ()` method is invoked on the `sqlite3` class to establish a connection with the `ECommerce` database. An SQL `SELECT` statement is defined that fetches the `EmailAddress` and `Password` columns from the `Users` table whose email address and password matches the email address and password entered in the **Line Edit** widgets. The SQL `SELECT` statement is executed on the `Users` table. The `fetchone()` method is executed on the cursor to fetch one row from the executed SQL statement. If the fetched row is not `None`, that is, there is a row in the database table, then it is confirmed whether the new passwords entered in the two **Line Edit** widgets, `lineEditNewPassword` and `lineEditRePassword`, are exactly the same. If the two passwords are the same, then an `UPDATE` SQL statement is executed to update the `Users` table, changing the password to the new one.

If the two passwords do not match, then no updating is applied to the database table and a message, **The two passwords don't match**, is displayed through the **Label** widget.

If an error occurs in the execution of the SQL `SELECT` or `UPDATE` statement, then an error message, **Error in accessing row**, is displayed via a **Label** widget with the **objectName** property `labelResponse`.

Upon running the application, you will be prompted to enter the email address and password, along with the new password, too. If the email address or password does not match, an error message, **Sorry, Incorrect email address or password**, is displayed via the **Label** widget, as shown in the following screenshot:

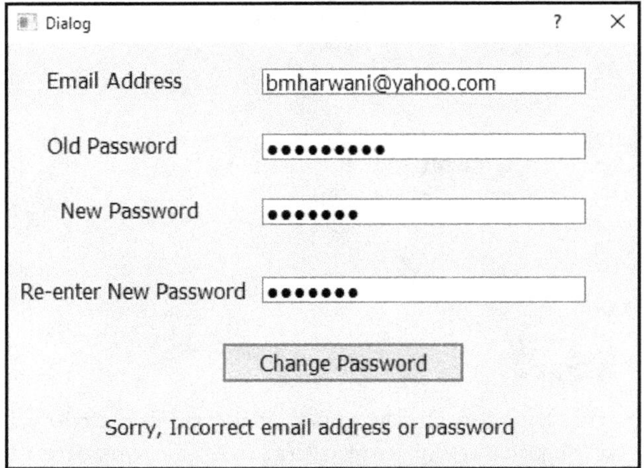

If the email address and password entered are correct, but the new passwords entered in the **New Password** and **Re-enter New Password** boxes do not match, then the message **The two passwords don't match** is displayed on the screen, as shown in the following screenshot:

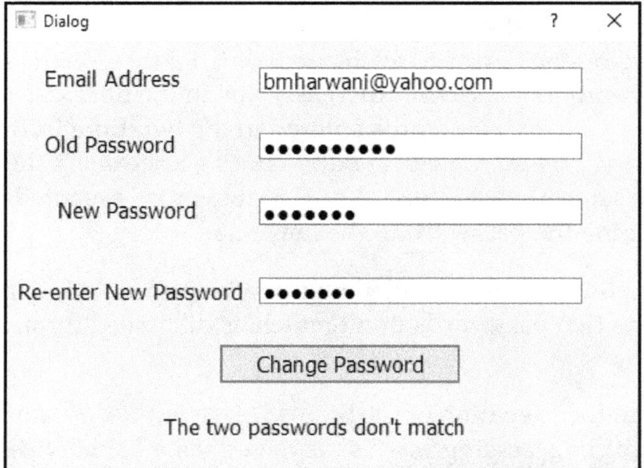

If the email address and passwords are all entered correctly, that is, if the user row is found in the database table and the new passwords entered in the **New Password** and **Re-enter New Password** boxes match, then the `Users` table is updated and, upon successfully updating the table, a message, **Password successfully changed**, is displayed on the screen, as shown in the following screenshot:

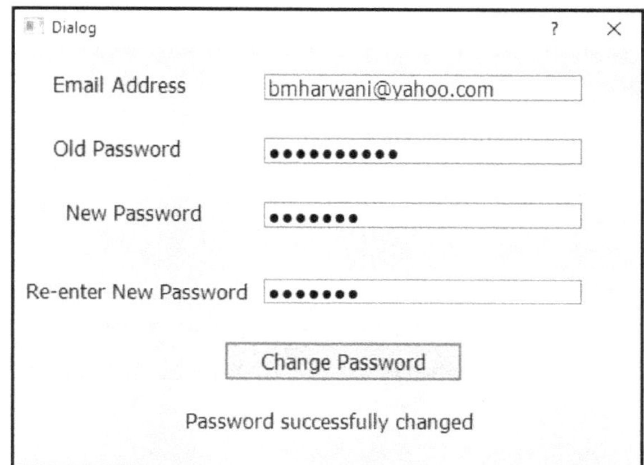

Deleting a row from a database table

In this recipe, we will be learning how to remove a row from a database table. We assume that a database called `ECommerce` already exists and a table called `Users` also exists in the `ECommerce` database. The `Users` table consists of two columns, `EmailAddress` and `Password`. Also, we assume that the `User` table contains a few rows in it. The user will be prompted to enter their email address and password in the form. The `Users` table is searched for the specified email address and password. If any row is found with the specified email address and password in the `Users` table, you will be prompted to confirm whether you are sure that you want to delete the row. If you click on the **Yes** button, the row will be deleted.

How to do it...

The procedure for deleting data from the database table is very critical, and any mistake in executing such an application can lead to disaster. The following are the steps for deleting any row from the given database table:

1. Let's create an application based on the **Dialog without Buttons** template.

2. Add four `QLabel` widgets, two `QLineEdit` widgets, and three `QPushButton` widgets to the form by dragging and dropping four **Label** widgets, two **LineEdit** widgets, and three **Push Button** widgets on the form.
3. Set the **text** property of the first three **Label** widgets to `Email Address`, `Password`, and `Are you Sure?`
4. Delete the **text** property of the fourth **Label** widget this is established through code.
5. Set the **text** property of the three push buttons to `Delete User`, `Yes`, and `No`.
6. Set the **objectName** property of the two **Line Edit** widgets to `lineEditEmailAddress` and `lineEditPassword`.
7. Set the **objectName** property of the three **Push Button** widgets to `pushButtonDelete`, `pushButtonYes`, and `pushButtonNo`.
8. Set the **objectName** property of the fourth **Label** widget to `labelResponse`.
9. Save the application by name as `demoDeleteUser.ui`. The form will now appear as shown in the following screenshot:

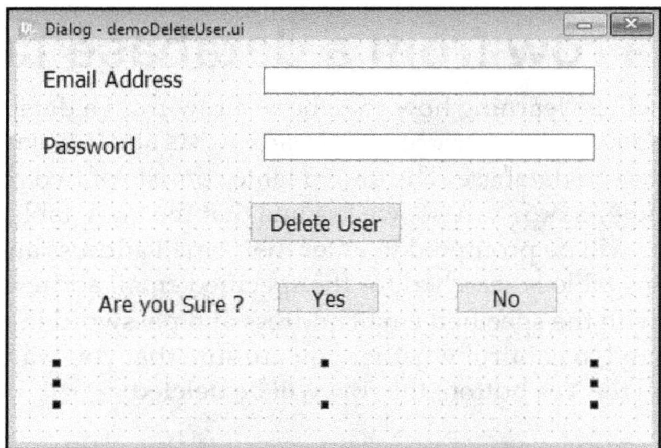

The user interface created with Qt Designer is stored in a `.ui` file, which is an XML file and needs to be converted into Python code. The `pyuic5` command is used for converting the XML file into Python code. The Python script generated, `demoDeleteUser.py`, can be seen in the source code bundle of this book.

10. Treat the `demoDeleteUser.py` script as a header file, and import it into the file from which you will invoke its user interface design.
11. Create another Python file with the name `callDeleteUser.pyw` and import the `demoDeleteUser.py` code into it:

```
import sqlite3, sys
from PyQt5.QtWidgets import QDialog, QApplication
from sqlite3 import Error
from demoDeleteUser import *
class MyForm(QDialog):
    def __init__(self):
        super().__init__()
        self.ui = Ui_Dialog()
        self.ui.setupUi(self)
        self.ui.pushButtonDelete.clicked.connect(self.
        DeleteUser)
        self.ui.pushButtonYes.clicked.connect(self.
        ConfirmDelete)
        self.ui.labelSure.hide()
        self.ui.pushButtonYes.hide()
        self.ui.pushButtonNo.hide()
        self.show()
    def DeleteUser(self):
        selectStatement="SELECT * FROM Users where
EmailAddress
        like'"+self.ui.lineEditEmailAddress.text()+"'
        and Password like '"+ self.ui.lineEditPassword.
        text()+"'"
        try:
            conn = sqlite3.connect("ECommerce.db")
            cur = conn.cursor()
            cur.execute(selectStatement)
            row = cur.fetchone()
        if row==None:
            self.ui.labelSure.hide()
            self.ui.pushButtonYes.hide()
            self.ui.pushButtonNo.hide()
            self.ui.labelResponse.setText("Sorry, Incorrect
            email address or password ")
        else:
            self.ui.labelSure.show()
            self.ui.pushButtonYes.show()
            self.ui.pushButtonNo.show()
            self.ui.labelResponse.setText("")
        except Error as e:
            self.ui.labelResponse.setText("Error in accessing
            user account")
```

```
            finally:
                conn.close()
        def ConfirmDelete(self):
            deleteStatement="DELETE FROM Users where EmailAddress
            like '"+self.ui.lineEditEmailAddress.text()+"'
            and Password like '"+ self.ui.lineEditPassword.
            text()+"'"
            try:
                conn = sqlite3.connect("ECommerce.db")
                cur = conn.cursor()
            with conn:
                cur.execute(deleteStatement)
                self.ui.labelResponse.setText("User successfully
                deleted")
            except Error as e:
                self.ui.labelResponse.setText("Error in deleting
                user account")
            finally:
                conn.close()
if __name__=="__main__":
    app = QApplication(sys.argv)
    w = MyForm()
    w.show()
    sys.exit(app.exec_())
```

How it works...

In this application, the **Label** widget with the text **Are you Sure?** and the two push buttons, **Yes** and **No**, are initially hidden. These three widgets will be displayed only when the email address and password entered by the user are found in the database table. These three widgets enable the user to confirm that they really want to delete the row. So, the `hide()` method is invoked on these three widgets to make them initially invisible. Also, the **click()** event of the push button with the **objectName** property `pushButtonDelete` is connected to the `DeleteUser()` method. This means that whenever the **Delete** button is clicked, the `DeleteUser()` method is invoked. Similarly, the **click()** event of the push button with the **objectName** property `pushButtonYes` is connected to the `ConfirmDelete()` method. This means that when the user confirms deletion of the row by clicking the **Yes** button, the `ConfirmDelete()` method will be invoked.

In the `DeleteUser()` method, you first search to see whether any row exists in the `Users` table that matches the email address and password entered. The `connect()` method is invoked on the `sqlite3` class to establish a connection with the `ECommerce` database. An SQL `SELECT` statement is defined that fetches the `EmailAddress` and `Password` columns from the `Users` table whose email address and password matches the email address and passwords supplied. The SQL `SELECT` statement is executed on the `Users` table. The `fetchone()` method is executed on the cursor to fetch one row from the executed SQL statement. If the fetched row is not `None`, that is, there is a row in the database table that matches the given email address and password, the three widgets, the **Label**, and two push buttons, will be made visible. The user will be shown the message **Are you Sure?** followed by two push buttons with the text **Yes** and **No**.

If the user clicks the **Yes** button, then the `ConfirmDelete()` method is executed. In the `ConfirmDelete()` method, an SQL `DELETE` method is defined that deletes the row that matches the entered email address and password from the `Users` table. After establishing a connection with the `ECommerce` database, the SQL `DELETE` method is executed. If the row is successfully deleted from the `Users` table, a message, **User successfully deleted**, will be displayed through the **Label** widget; otherwise, an error message, **Error in deleting user account**, will be displayed.

Before running the application, we will launch a visual tool called DB Browser for SQLite. The visual tool enables us to create, edit, and view the database tables and rows inside them. Using DB Browser for SQLite, we will first see the existing rows in the `Users` table. After that, the application will run and a row will be deleted. Again, from DB Browser for SQLite, we will confirm the row was really deleted from the `Users` table.

So, launch DB Browser for SQLite and click the **Open Database** tab below the main menu. Browse and select the `Ecommerce` database from the current folder. The `Ecommerce` database shows the `Users` table consisting of two columns, `EmailAddress` and `Password`. Click on the **Execute SQL** button to write an SQL statement. In the window, write the SQL statement `select * from Users`, followed by clicking the Run icon. All existing rows in the `Users` table will be displayed on the screen. You can see in the following screenshot that the `Users` table has two rows:

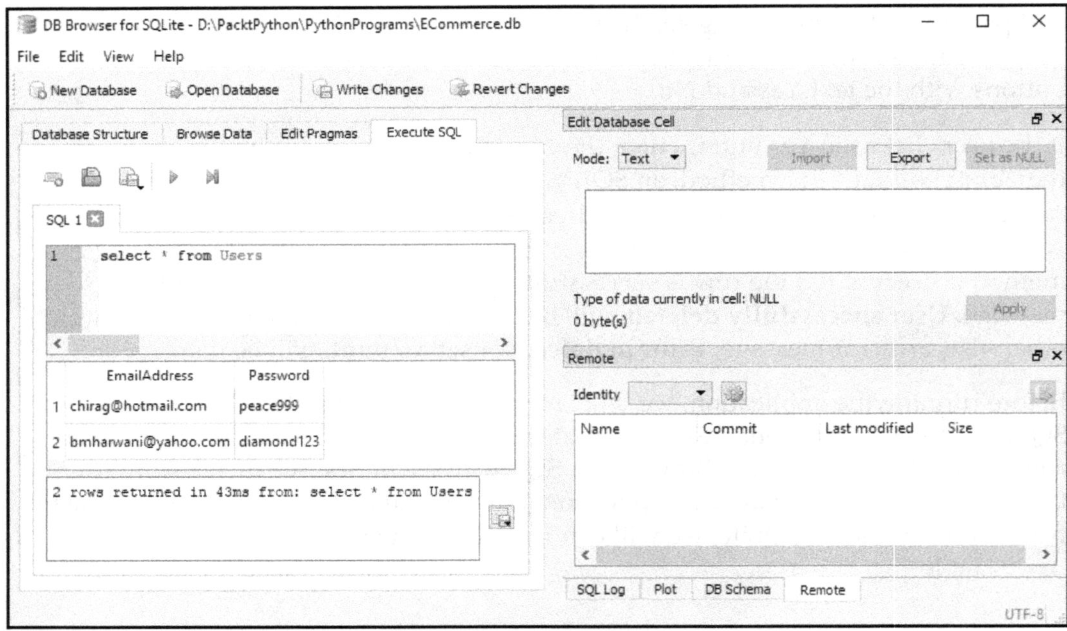

Upon running the application, you will be prompted to enter your email address and password. If you enter the wrong email address and password, you get the message **Sorry, Incorrect email address or password**, as shown in the following screenshot:

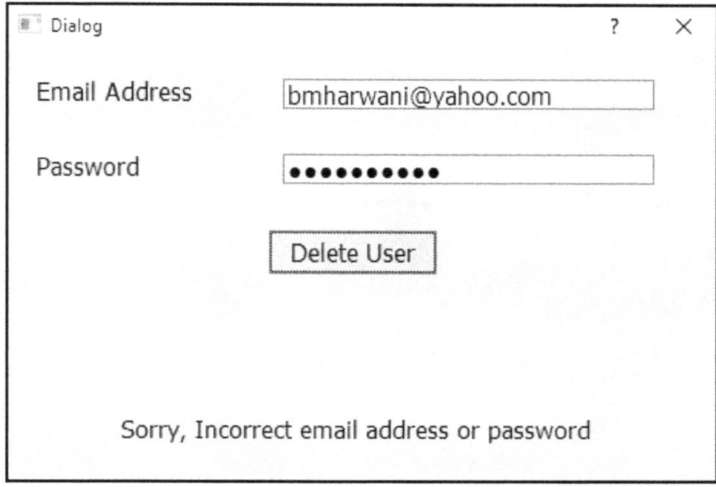

Upon entering the correct email address and password, when you click the **Delete User** button, the three widgets—the **Label** widget and two push buttons, will be made visible, and you get the message **Are you Sure?**, along with the two push buttons, **Yes** and **No**, as shown in the following screenshot:

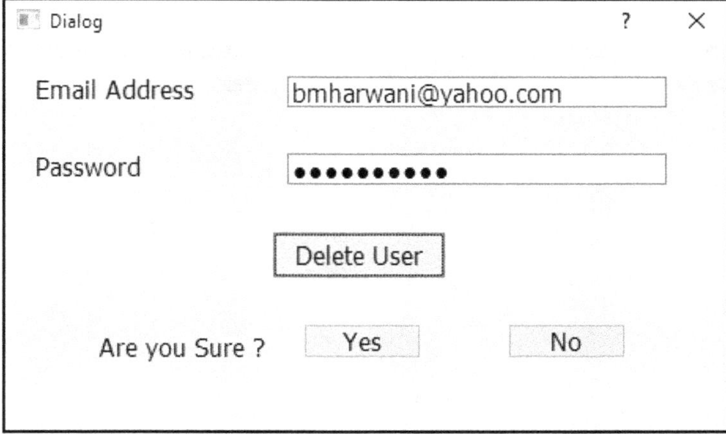

Upon clicking the **Yes** push button, the row in the `Users` table whose email address and password matches the email address and password supplied will be deleted and a confirmation message, **User successfully deleted**, will be displayed through the **Label** widget, as shown in the following screenshot:

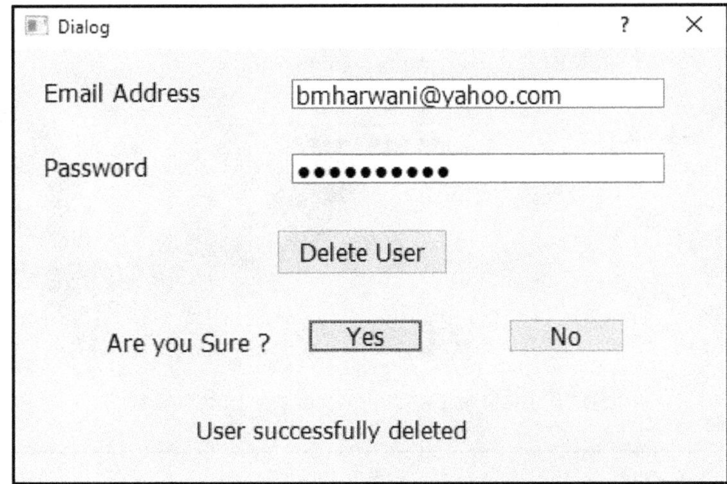

Let's check through the visual tool as to whether the row was actually deleted from the **Users** table. Therefore, launch the DB Browser for SQLite and click the **Open Database** tab below the main menu. Browse and select the `Ecommerce` database from the current folder. The `Ecommerce` database will show the `Users` table. Click on the **Execute SQL** button to write an SQL statement. In the window, write the SQL statement `select * from Users`, followed by clicking the Run icon. All existing rows in the `Users` table will be displayed on the screen.

Before running the application, we saw that there were two rows in the `Users` table. This time, you see only one row in the `Users` table (see the following screenshot), confirming that a row was deleted from the `Users` table:

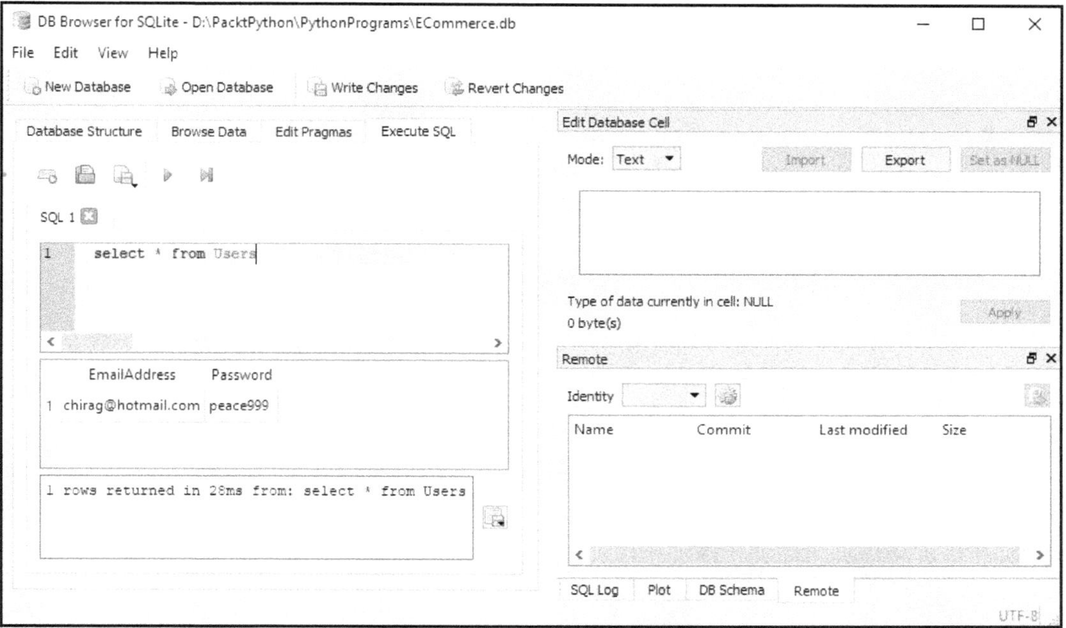

20
Using Graphics

In every application, graphics play a major role in making it more user-friendly. Graphics make concepts easier to understand. In this chapter, we will be covering the following topics:

- Displaying mouse coordinates
- Displaying coordinates where the mouse button is clicked and released
- Displaying a point where the mouse button is clicked
- Drawing a line between two mouse clicks
- Drawing lines of different types
- Drawing a circle of a desired size
- Drawing a rectangle between two mouse clicks
- Drawing text in a desired font and size
- Creating a toolbar that shows different graphics tools
- Plotting a line using Matplotlib
- Plotting a bar using Matplotlib

Introduction

For drawing and painting in Python, we will be making use of several classes. The most important of them is the `QPainter` class.

This class is used for painting. It can draw lines, rectangles, circles, and complex shapes. While drawing with `QPainter`, you can use the `QPainter` class pen to define the color of the drawing; thickness of the pen/brush; style; whether the line is drawn as solid, dotted, or dash-dot; and so on.

Several methods of the `QPainter` class are used in this chapter to draw different shapes. A few of them are listed here:

- `QPainter::drawLine()`: This method is used for drawing a line between two sets of *x* and *y* coordinates
- `QPainter::drawPoints()`: This method is used for drawing a point at a location specified through the supplied *x* and *y* coordinates
- `QPainter::drawRect()`: This method is used for drawing a rectangle between two sets of *x* and *y* coordinates
- `QPainter::drawArc()`: This method is used for drawing an arc from the specified center location, between two specified angles, and with a specified radius
- `QPainter::drawText()`: This method is used for drawing text in a specified font style, color, and size

To understand the different classes and methods required to display graphics practically, let's follow some recipes.

Displaying mouse coordinates

To draw any shape with the mouse, you need to know where the mouse button is clicked, to where the mouse is dragged, and where the mouse button is released. Only after knowing the coordinates where the mouse button is clicked can you go ahead and execute commands to draw different shapes. In this recipe, we will be learning to display the *x* and *y* coordinates to which the mouse is moved on the form.

How to do it...

In this recipe, we will be tracking mouse movement and will be displaying the *x* and *y* coordinates which the mouse is moved on the form. So, in all, we will be using two **Label** widgets in this application, one for displaying a message and the other for displaying mouse coordinates. The complete steps for creating this application are shown here:

1. Let's create an application based on the **Dialog without Buttons** template.
2. Add two `QLabel` widgets to the form by dragging and dropping two **Label** widgets on the form.

3. Set the **text** property of the first **Label** widget to `This app will display x,y coordinates where mouse is moved on`.
4. Delete the **text** property of the second **Label** widget as its **text** property will be set through code.
5. Save the application by name as `demoMousetrack.ui`.

The form will now appear as shown in the following screenshot:

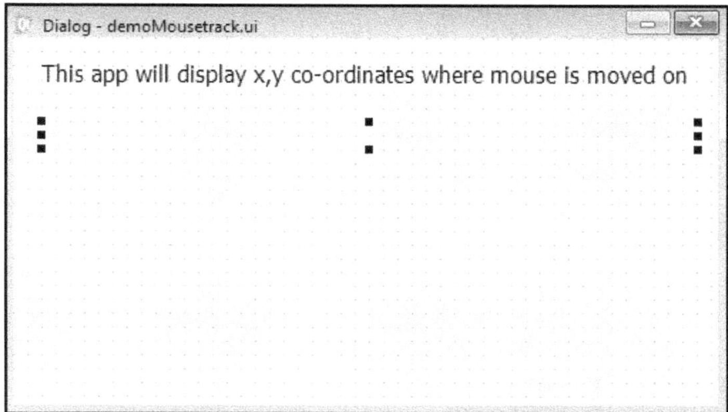

The user interface created with Qt Designer is stored in a `.ui` file, which is an XML file, and needs to be converted into Python code. The `pyuic5` utility is used for converting the XML file into Python code. The generated Python script, `demoMousetrack.py`, can be seen in the source code bundle of the book.

6. Treat the `demoMousetrack.py` script as a header file, and import it into the file from which you will invoke its user interface design.
7. Create another Python file with the name `callMouseTrack.pyw` and import the `demoMousetrack.py` code into it:

```
import sys
from PyQt5.QtWidgets import QDialog, QApplication
from demoMousetrack import *
class MyForm(QDialog):
    def __init__(self):
        super().__init__()
        self.ui = Ui_Dialog()
        self.setMouseTracking(True)
        self.ui.setupUi(self)
```

```
            self.show()
        def mouseMoveEvent(self, event):
            x = event.x()
            y = event.y()
            text = "x: {0}, y: {1}".format(x, y)
            self.ui.label.setText(text)
if __name__=="__main__":
    app = QApplication(sys.argv)
    w = MyForm()
    w.show()
    sys.exit(app.exec_())
```

How it works...

To enable the application to keep track of the mouse, a method, `setMouseTracking(True)`, is used. This method will sense the mouse movement and whenever the mouse is moved, it will invoke the `mouseMoveEvent()` method. In `mouseMoveEvent()`, the `x` and `y` methods are invoked on the `event` object to get the *x* and *y* coordinate values of the mouse's location. The *x* and *y* coordinates are assigned to the `x` and `y` variables respectively. The values in the *x* and *y* coordinates are displayed in the desired format via the **Label** widget.

On running the application, you will get a message that on moving the mouse, its *x* and *y* coordinate values will be displayed. When you move the mouse on the form, the *x* and *y* coordinates of the mouse location will be displayed through the second **Label** widget, as shown in the following screenshot:

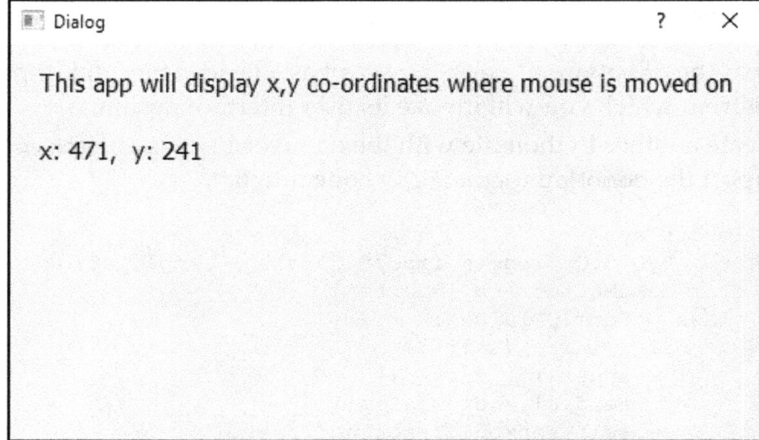

Displaying coordinates where the mouse button is clicked and released

In this recipe, we will be learning to display the *x* and *y* coordinates where the mouse button is clicked, along with the coordinates of where the mouse button is released.

How to do it...

Two methods, `mousePressEvent()` and `mouseReleaseEvent()`, will play major role in this recipe. The `mousePressEvent()` method will be automatically invoked when the mouse is pressed and will reveal the *x* and *y* coordinates when the mouse press event has occurred. Similarly, the `mouseReleaseEvent()` method will be invoked automatically whenever the mouse button is released. Two **Label** widgets will be used in this recipe to display the coordinates where the mouse button is clicked and where the mouse button is released. Here are the steps to create such an application:

1. Let's create an application based on the **Dialog without Buttons** template.
2. Add three `QLabel` widgets to the form by dragging and dropping three **Label** widgets on the form.
3. Set the **text** property of the first **Label** widget to `Displays the x,y coordinates where mouse is pressed and released`.
4. Delete the **text** property of the second and third **Label** widgets, as their **text** properties will be set through code.
5. Set the **objectName** property of the second **Label** widget to `labelPress`, as it will be used for displaying the *x* and *y* coordinates of the location where the mouse button is clicked.
6. Set the **objectName** property of the third **Label** widget to `labelRelease` because it will be used for displaying the *x* and *y* coordinates of the location where the mouse button is released.
7. Save the application by name as `demoMouseClicks.ui`.

The form will now appear as shown in the following screenshot:

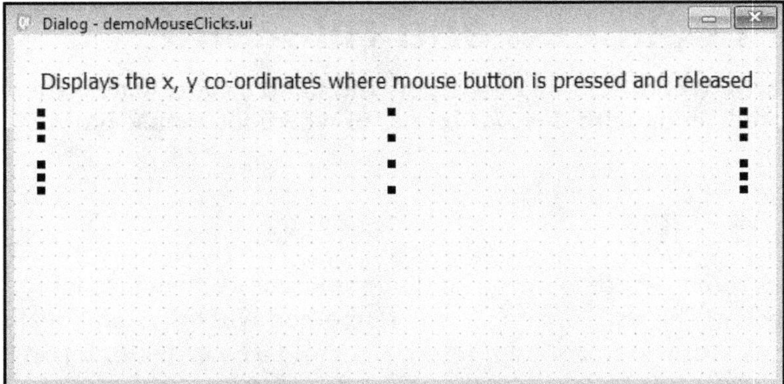

The user interface created with Qt Designer is stored in a `.ui` file, which is an XML file, and needs to be converted into Python code. The `pyuic5` utility is used for converting the XML file into Python code. The generated Python script, `demoMouseClicks.py`, can be seen in the source code bundle of the book.

8. Treat the `demoMouseClicks.py` script as a header file, and import it into the file from which you will invoke its user interface design.
9. Create another Python file with the name `callMouseClickCoordinates.pyw` and import the `demoMouseClicks.py` code into it:

```
import sys
from PyQt5.QtWidgets import QDialog, QApplication
from demoMouseClicks import *
class MyForm(QDialog):
    def __init__(self):
        super().__init__()
        self.ui = Ui_Dialog()
        self.ui.setupUi(self)
        self.show()
    def mousePressEvent(self, event):
        if event.buttons() & QtCore.Qt.LeftButton:
            x = event.x()
            y = event.y()
            text = "x: {0}, y: {1}".format(x, y)
            self.ui.labelPress.setText('Mouse button pressed
at
            '+text)
```

```
        def mouseReleaseEvent(self, event):
            x = event.x()
            y = event.y()
            text = "x: {0}, y: {1}".format(x, y)
            self.ui.labelRelease.setText('Mouse button released at
            '+text)
            self.update()
if __name__=="__main__":
    app = QApplication(sys.argv)
    w = MyForm()
    w.show()
    sys.exit(app.exec_())
```

How it works...

Two methods are automatically invoked when you click the mouse. The `mousePressEvent()` method is invoked when you press the mouse button and the `mouseReleaseEvent()` method is invoked when you release the mouse button. To display the *x* and *y* coordinates of the location where the mouse button is clicked and released, we make use of these two methods. In both the methods, we simply invoke the `x()` and `y()` methods on the `event` object to fetch the *x* and *y* coordinate values of the mouse location. The fetched `x` and `y` values will be assigned to the `x` and `y` variables, respectively. The values in the `x` and `y` variables are formatted in the desired format and displayed through the two **Label** widgets.

On running the application, you will get a message that the *x* and *y* coordinates of the location where the mouse button is clicked and released will be displayed.

When you press the mouse button and release it, the *x* and *y* coordinates of the location where the mouse is pressed and released will be displayed through the two **Label** widgets, as shown in the following screenshot:

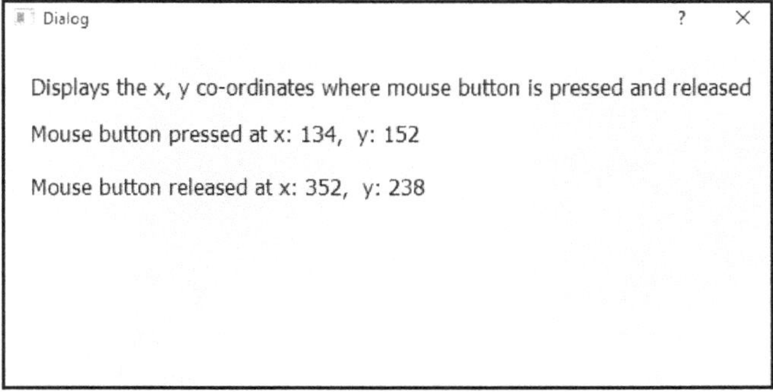

Displaying a point where the mouse button is clicked

In this recipe, we will be learning to display the point where the mouse button is clicked on the form. Point here means a dot. That is, wherever the user presses the mouse, a dot will appear at that coordinate. You will also learn to define the size of the dot too.

How to do it...

The `mousePressEvent()` method will be used in this recipe as it is the method that is automatically invoked when the mouse is pressed on the form. In the `mousePressEvent()` method, we will execute the command to display a dot or point of the desired size. Here are the steps to understand how you can display a point or dot on the form where the mouse button is clicked:

1. Let's create an application based on the **Dialog without Buttons** template.
2. Add a `QLabel` widgets to the form by dragging and dropping a **Label** widget on the form.
3. Set the **text** property of the **Label** widget to `Click the mouse where you want to display a dot.`
4. Save the application by name as `demoDrawDot.ui.`

The form will now appear as shown in the following screenshot:

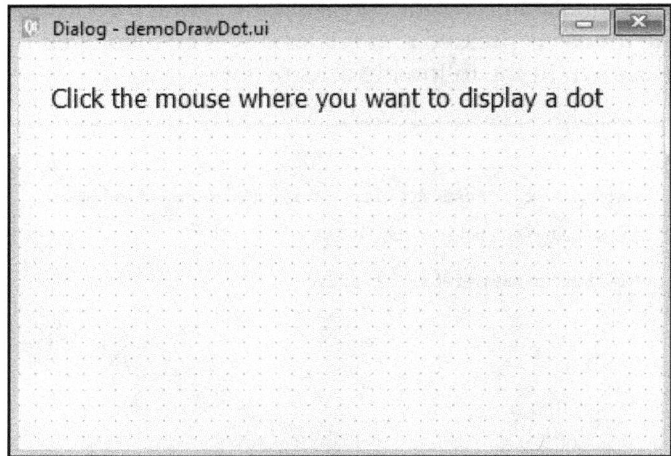

The user interface created with Qt Designer is stored in a `.ui` file, which is an XML file, and needs to be converted into Python code. The `pyuic5` utility is used for converting the XML file into Python code. The generated Python script, `demoDrawDot.py`, can be seen in the source code bundle of the book.

5. Treat the `demoDrawDot.py` script as a header file, and import it into the file from which you will invoke its user interface design.
6. Create another Python file with the name `callDrawDot.pyw` and import the `demoDrawDot.py` code into it:

```
import sys
from PyQt5.QtWidgets import QDialog, QApplication
from PyQt5.QtGui import QPainter, QPen
from PyQt5.QtCore import Qt
from demoDrawDot import *
class MyForm(QDialog):
    def __init__(self):
        super().__init__()
        self.ui = Ui_Dialog()
        self.ui.setupUi(self)
        self.pos1 = [0,0]
        self.show()
    def paintEvent(self, event):
        qp = QPainter()
        qp.begin(self)
        pen = QPen(Qt.black, 5)
        qp.setPen(pen)
        qp.drawPoint(self.pos1[0], self.pos1[1])
        qp.end()
    def mousePressEvent(self, event):
        if event.buttons() & QtCore.Qt.LeftButton:
            self.pos1[0], self.pos1[1] = event.pos().x(),
            event.pos().y()
            self.update()
if __name__=="__main__":
    app = QApplication(sys.argv)
    w = MyForm()
    w.show()
    sys.exit(app.exec_())
```

How it works...

Because we want to display the point where the mouse button is clicked, the `mousePressEvent()` method is used. In the `mousePressEvent()` method, the `pos().x()` and `pos().y()` methods are invoked on the `event` object to fetch the locations of the *x* and *y* coordinates and assign them to the `0` and `1` elements of the `pos1` array. That is, the `pos1` array is initialized to the *x* and *y* coordinate values where the mouse button is clicked. After initializing the `pos1` array, the `self.update()` method is called to invoke the `paintEvent()` method.

In the `paintEvent()` method, an object of the `QPainter` class is defined by name as `qp`. An object of the `QPen` class is defined by name as pen to set the thickness of the pen and its color. Finally, a point is displayed by invoking the `drawPoint()` method at the location whose value is defined in the `pos1` array, that is, where the mouse button is clicked.

On running the application, you will get a message that a dot will be displayed where the mouse button will be clicked. When you click the mouse, a point will appear at that location, as shown in the following screenshot:

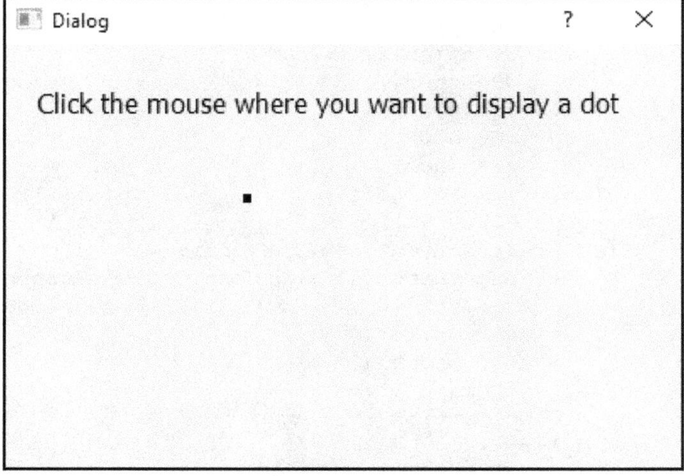

Drawing a line between two mouse clicks

In this recipe, we will learn to display a line between two points, from where the mouse button is clicked till where the mouse button is released on the form. The focus of this recipe is to understand how the mouse press and release events are handled, how the x *a* and *y* coordinates where the mouse button is clicked and released are accessed, and how a line is drawn from the location where the mouse button is clicked to the location where the mouse button is released.

How to do it...

The major players in this recipe are the `mousePressEvent()`, `mouseReleaseEvent()`, and `paintEvent()` methods. The `mousePressEvent()` and `mouseReleaseEvent()` methods are automatically executed whenever the mouse button is clicked or released, respectively. These two methods will be used to access the *x* and *y* coordinates where the mouse button is clicked and released. Finally, the `paintEvent()` method is used to draw a line between the coordinates that were supplied by the `mousePressEvent()` and `mouseReleaseEvent()` methods. Here is the step-by-step procedure to create this application:

1. Let's create an application based on the **Dialog without Buttons** template.
2. Add a `QLabel` widget to the form by dragging and dropping a **Label** widget on the form.
3. Set the **text** property of the **Label** widget to `Click the mouse and drag it to draw the line of desired size.`
4. Save the application by name as `demoDrawLine.ui`.

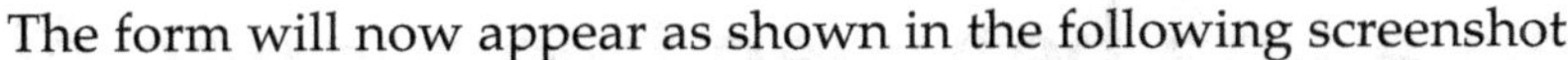

The form will now appear as shown in the following screenshot:

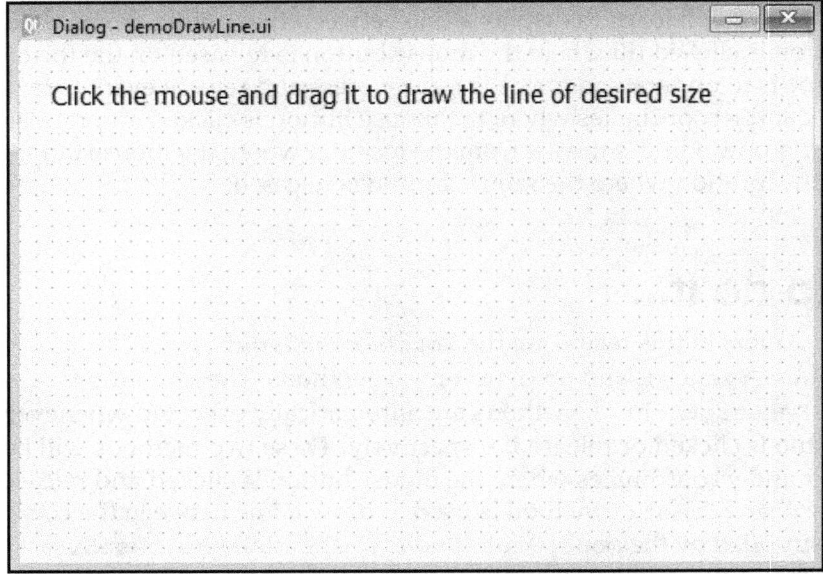

The user interface created with Qt Designer is stored in a `.ui` file, which is an XML file, and needs to be converted into Python code. The `pyuic5` utility is used for converting the XML file into Python code. The generated Python script, `demoDrawLine.py`, can be seen in the source code bundle of the book.

5. Treat the `demoDrawLine.py` script as a header file, and import it into the file from which you will invoke its user interface design.
6. Create another Python file with the name `callDrawLine.pyw` and import the `demoDrawLine.py` code into it:

```
import sys
from PyQt5.QtWidgets import QDialog, QApplication
from PyQt5.QtGui import QPainter
from demoDrawLine import *
class MyForm(QDialog):
    def __init__(self):
        super().__init__()
        self.ui = Ui_Dialog()
        self.ui.setupUi(self)
        self.pos1 = [0,0]
        self.pos2 = [0,0]
```

```
            self.show()
        def paintEvent(self, event):
            qp = QPainter()
            qp.begin(self)
            qp.drawLine(self.pos1[0], self.pos1[1], self.pos2[0],
            self.pos2[1])
            qp.end()
        def mousePressEvent(self, event):
            if event.buttons() & QtCore.Qt.LeftButton:
                self.pos1[0], self.pos1[1] = event.pos().x(),
                event.pos().y()
        def mouseReleaseEvent(self, event):
                self.pos2[0], self.pos2[1] = event.pos().x(),
                event.pos().y()
                self.update()
    if __name__=="__main__":
        app = QApplication(sys.argv)
        w = MyForm()
        w.show()
        sys.exit(app.exec_())
```

How it works...

As we want to display a line between the locations where the mouse button is clicked and released, we will be making use of two methods, `mousePressEvent()` and `mouseReleaseEvent()`. As the name suggests, the `mousePressEvent()` method is automatically invoked when a mouse button is pressed. Similarly, the `mouseReleaseEvent()` method is automatically invoked when the mouse button is released. In these two methods, we will be simply saving the values of the *x* and *y* coordinates where the mouse button is clicked and released. Two arrays are defined in this application, `pos1` and `pos2`, where `pos1` stores the *x* and *y* coordinates of the location where the mouse button is clicked, and the `pos2` array stores the *x* and *y* coordinates of the location where the mouse button is released. Once the *x* and *y* coordinates of the locations where the mouse button is clicked and released are assigned to the `pos1` and `pos2` arrays, the `self.update()` method is invoked in the `mouseReleaseEvent()` method to invoke the `paintEvent()` method. In the `paintEvent()` method, the `drawLine()` method is invoked and the *x* and *y* coordinates stored in the `pos1` and `pos2` array are passed to it to draw a line between the mouse press and mouse release locations.

On running the application, you will get a message to click and drag the mouse button between the locations where the line is required. So, click the mouse button and keeping the mouse button pressed, drag it to the desired location and release the mouse button. A line will be drawn between the locations where the mouse button is clicked and where it is released, as shown in the following screenshot:

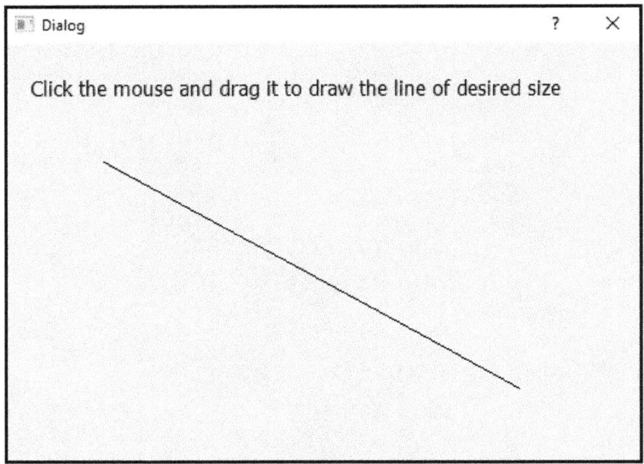

Drawing lines of different types

In this recipe, we will be learning to display lines of different types between two points, from the mouse click location to where the mouse button is released. The user will be shown different line types to choose from, such as solid, dash line, dash-dot line, and so on. The line will be draw in the selected line type.

How to do it...

It is the `QPen` class that is used for defining the size or thickness of the pen used for drawing shapes. The `setStyle()` method of the `QPen` class is used in this recipe to define the style of the line. Here is the step-by-step procedure to draw lines of different styles:

1. Let's create an application based on the **Dialog without Buttons** template.
2. Add a `QLabel` widget to the form by dragging and dropping a **Label** widget on the form.

3. Add a `QListWidget` widget by dragging and dropping a **List Widget** item on the form.
4. Set the **text** property of the **Label** widget to `Select the style from the list and then click and drag to draw a line.`
5. Save the application by name as `demoDrawDiffLine.ui`.
6. The **List Widget** item will be used for showing different types of lines, so right-click on the **List Widget** widget and select the **Edit Items** option to add a few line types to the **List Widget** item. Click the **+** (plus) button at the bottom of the dialog box that opens up and add a few line types, as shown in the following screenshot:

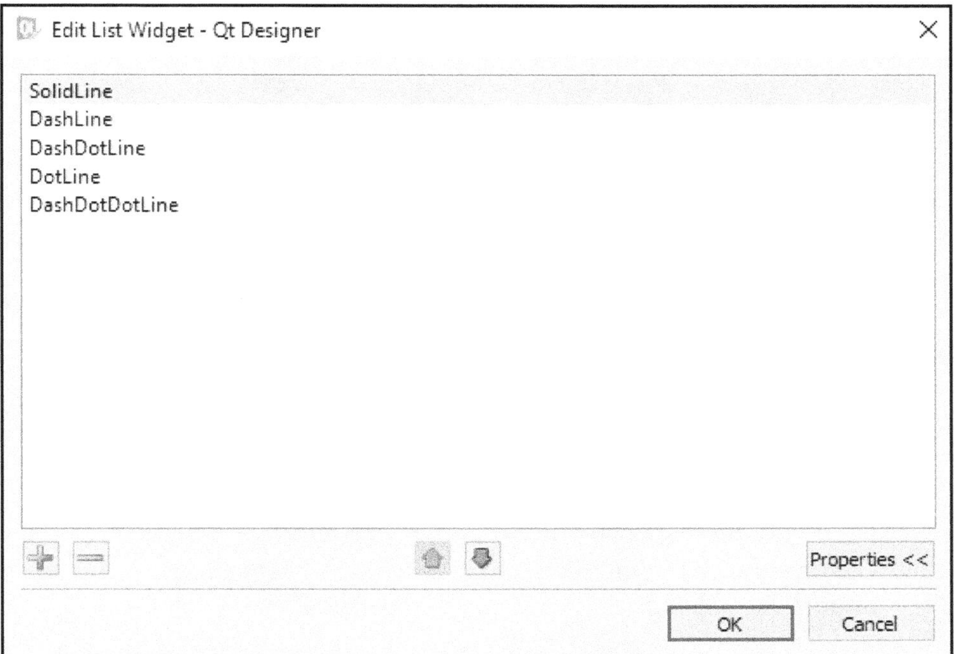

7. Set the **objectName** property of the **List Widget** item to `listWidgetLineType`.

The form will now appear as shown in the following screenshot:

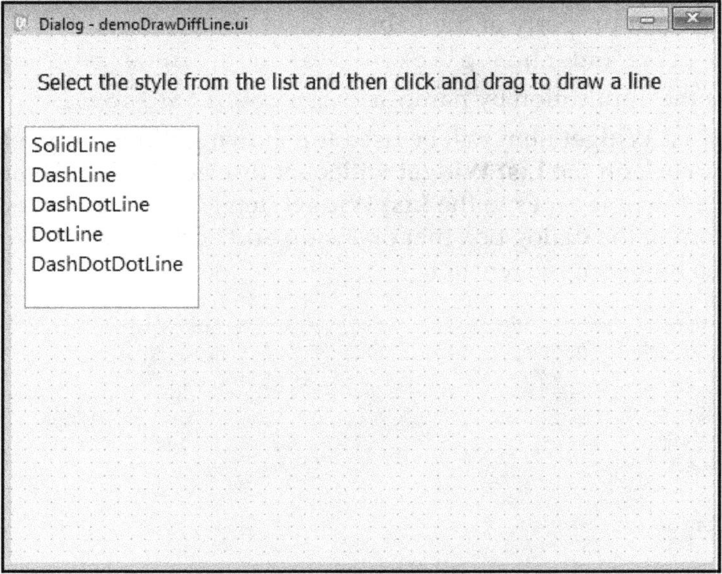

The user interface created with Qt Designer is stored in a `.ui` file, which is an XML file, and needs to be converted into Python code. The `pyuic5` utility is used for converting the XML file into Python code. The generated Python script, `demoDrawDiffLine.py`, can be seen in the source code bundle of the book.

8. Treat the `demoDrawDiffLine.py` script as a header file, and import it into the file from which you will invoke its user interface design.
9. Create another Python file with the name `callDrawDiffLine.pyw` and import the `demoDrawDiffLine.py` code into it:

```
import sys
from PyQt5.QtWidgets import QDialog, QApplication
from PyQt5.QtGui import QPainter, QPen
from PyQt5.QtCore import Qt
from demoDrawDiffLine import *
class MyForm(QDialog):
    def __init__(self):
        super().__init__()
        self.ui = Ui_Dialog()
        self.ui.setupUi(self)
        self.lineType="SolidLine"
```

```
            self.pos1 = [0,0]
            self.pos2 = [0,0]
            self.show()
        def paintEvent(self, event):
            qp = QPainter()
            qp.begin(self)
            pen = QPen(Qt.black, 4)
            self.lineTypeFormat="Qt."+self.lineType
            if self.lineTypeFormat == "Qt.SolidLine":
                pen.setStyle(Qt.SolidLine)
                elif self.lineTypeFormat == "Qt.DashLine":
                pen.setStyle(Qt.DashLine)
                elif self.lineTypeFormat =="Qt.DashDotLine":
                    pen.setStyle(Qt.DashDotLine)
                elif self.lineTypeFormat =="Qt.DotLine":
                    pen.setStyle(Qt.DotLine)
                elif self.lineTypeFormat =="Qt.DashDotDotLine":
                    pen.setStyle(Qt.DashDotDotLine)
                    qp.setPen(pen)
                    qp.drawLine(self.pos1[0], self.pos1[1],
                    self.pos2[0], self.pos2[1])
                    qp.end()
        def mousePressEvent(self, event):
            if event.buttons() & QtCore.Qt.LeftButton:
                self.pos1[0], self.pos1[1] = event.pos().x(),
                event.pos().y()
        def mouseReleaseEvent(self, event):
            self.lineType=self.ui.listWidgetLineType.currentItem()
            .text()
            self.pos2[0], self.pos2[1] = event.pos().x(),
            event.pos().y()
            self.update()
    if __name__=="__main__":
        app = QApplication(sys.argv)
        w = MyForm()
        w.show()
        sys.exit(app.exec_())
```

How it works...

A line has to be drawn between the mouse press and mouse release locations, so we will be making use of two methods in this application, `mousePressEvent()` and `mouseReleaseEvent()`. The `mousePressEvent()` method is automatically invoked when the left mouse button is clicked. Similarly, the `mouseReleaseEvent()` method is automatically invoked when the mouse button is released.

In these two methods, we will be saving the values of the *x* and *y* coordinates where the mouse button is clicked and released respectively. Two arrays are defined in this application, `pos1` and `pos2`, where `pos1` stores the *x* and *y* coordinates of the location where the mouse button is clicked and the `pos2` array stores the *x* and *y* coordinates of the location where the mouse button is released. In the `mouseReleaseEvent()` method, we fetch the line type chosen by the user from the **List** widget and assign the chosen line type to the `lineType` variable. Also, the `self.update()` method is invoked in the `mouseReleaseEvent()` method to invoke the `paintEvent()` method. In the `paintEvent()` method, you define a pen of `4` pixels in **width** and assign it a black color. Also, you assign a style to the pen that matches the line type chosen by the user from the **List** widget. Finally, the `drawLine()` method is invoked and the *x* and *y* coordinates stored in the `pos1` and `pos2` array are passed to it to draw a line between the mouse press and mouse release locations. The line will be displayed in the style that is selected from the **List** widget.

On running the application, you will get a message to select the line type from the list and click and drag the mouse button between the locations where the line is required. So, after selecting a desired line type, click the mouse button and keeping the mouse button pressed, drag it to the desired location and release the mouse button. A line will be drawn between the locations where the mouse button is clicked and where it is released in the style that is chosen from the list. The following screenshot shows the lines of different types:

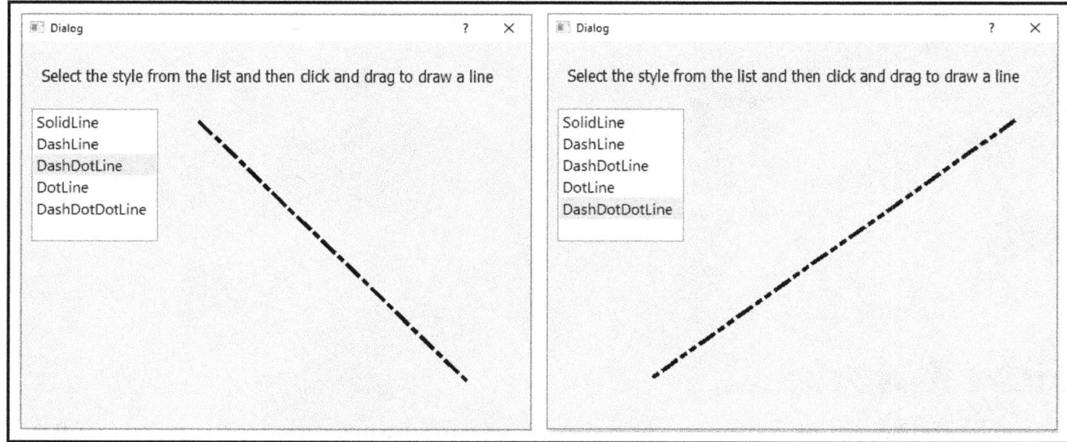

Drawing a circle of a desired size

In this recipe, we will be learning to draw a circle. The user will click and drag the mouse to define the diameter of the circle, and the circle will be drawn at the diameter specified by the user.

How to do it...

A circle is nothing but an arc that is drawn from 0 to 360 degrees. The length of the arc, or you can say the diameter of the circle, is determined by the distance of mouse press event and mouse release events. A rectangle is defined internally from mouse press event until mouse release event, and the circle is drawn within that rectangle. Here are the complete steps to create this application:

1. Let's create an application based on the **Dialog without Buttons** template.
2. Add a `QLabel` widget to the form by dragging and dropping a **Label** widget on the form.
3. Set the **text** property of the **Label** widget to `Click the mouse and drag it to draw a  circle of the desired size.`
4. Save the application by name as `demoDrawCircle.ui`. The form will now appear as shown in the following screenshot:

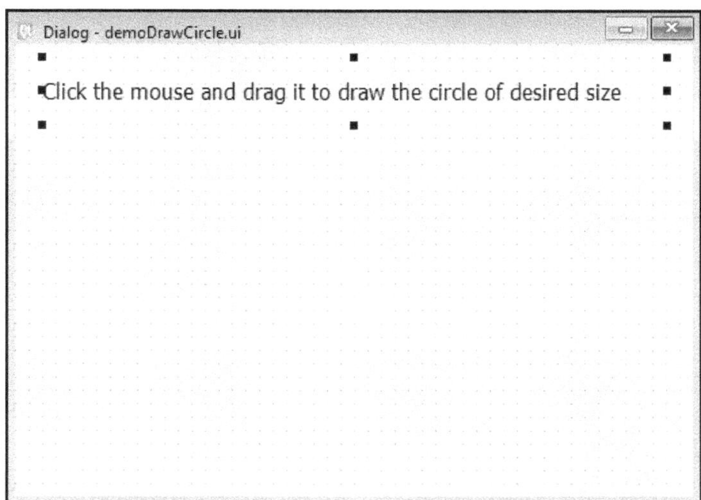

The user interface created with Qt Designer is stored in a `.ui` file and it is an XML file. The XML file is converted into Python code by applying the `pyuic5` utility. You can find the generated Python code, `demoDrawCircle.py`, in the source code bundle of the book.

5. Treat the `demoDrawCircle.py` script as a header file, and import it into the file from which you will invoke its user interface design.
6. Create another Python file with the name `callDrawCircle.pyw` and import the `demoDrawCircle.py` code into it:

```
import sys
from PyQt5.QtWidgets import QDialog, QApplication
from PyQt5.QtGui import QPainter
from demoDrawCircle import *
class MyForm(QDialog):
    def __init__(self):
        super().__init__()
        self.ui = Ui_Dialog()
        self.ui.setupUi(self)
        self.pos1 = [0,0]
        self.pos2 = [0,0]
        self.show()
    def paintEvent(self, event):
        width = self.pos2[0]-self.pos1[0]
        height = self.pos2[1] - self.pos1[1]
        qp = QPainter()
        qp.begin(self)
        rect = QtCore.QRect(self.pos1[0], self.pos1[1], width,
        height)
        startAngle = 0
        arcLength = 360 *16
        qp.drawArc(rect, startAngle, arcLength)
        qp.end()
    def mousePressEvent(self, event):
        if event.buttons() & QtCore.Qt.LeftButton:
            self.pos1[0], self.pos1[1] = event.pos().x(),
            event.pos().y()
    def mouseReleaseEvent(self, event):
        self.pos2[0], self.pos2[1] = event.pos().x(),
        event.pos().y()
        self.update()
if __name__=="__main__":
    app = QApplication(sys.argv)
    w = MyForm()
    w.show()
    sys.exit(app.exec_())
```

How it works...

To draw a circle with the diameter defined between the mouse button pressed and released locations, we will be making use of two methods, `mousePressEvent()` and `mouseReleaseEvent()`. The `mousePressEvent()` method is automatically invoked when a mouse button is pressed and the `mouseReleaseEvent()` method is automatically invoked when the mouse button is released. In these two methods, we will be simply saving the values of the *x* and *y* coordinates where the mouse button is clicked and released. Two arrays, `pos1` and `pos2`, are defined, where the `pos1` array stores the *x* and *y* coordinates of the location where the mouse button is clicked and the `pos2` array stores the *x* and *y* coordinates of the location where the mouse button is released. The `self.update()` method that is invoked in the `mouseReleaseEvent()` method will invoke the `paintEvent()` method. In the `paintEvent()` method, the width of the rectangle is computed by finding the difference between the *x* coordinates of mouse press and mouse release locations. Similarly, the height of the rectangle is computed by finding the difference between the y coordinates of mouse press and mouse release events.

The circle will be created of a size equal to the width and height of the rectangle, that is, the circle will be created within the boundaries specified by the user with the mouse.

Also, in the `paintEvent()` method, the `drawArc()` method is invoked and the rectangle, starting angle of the arc, and length of the arc are passed to it. The starting angle is specified as `0`.

On running the application, you will get a message to click and drag the mouse button to define the diameter of the circle to be drawn. So, click the mouse button and keeping the mouse button pressed, drag it to the desired location and release the mouse button. A circle will be drawn between the locations where the mouse button is clicked and where it is released, as shown in the following screenshot:

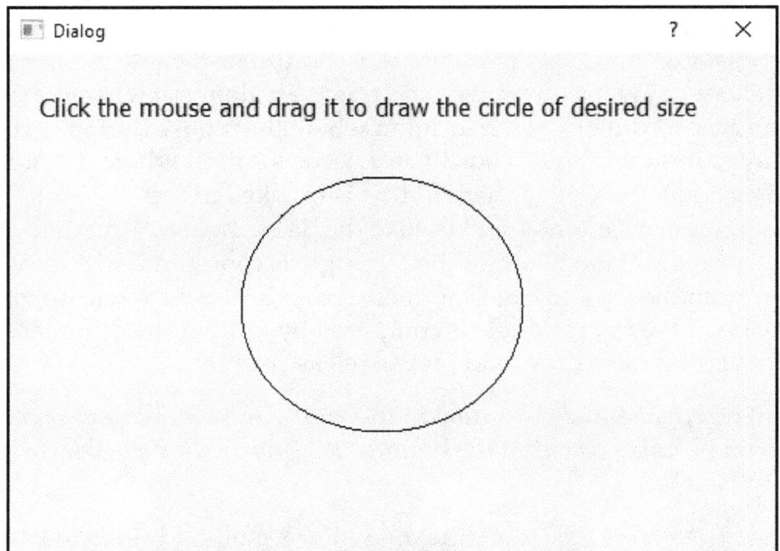

Drawing a rectangle between two mouse clicks

In this recipe, we will be learning to display a rectangle between the two points where the mouse button is clicked and released on the form.

How to do it...

It is a very simple application, where the `mousePressEvent()` and `mouseReleaseEvent()` methods are used to find the *x* and *y* coordinates of the location where the mouse is pressed and released, respectively. Thereafter, the `drawRect()` method is invoked to draw the rectangle from the coordinates where the mouse button is clicked to the coordinates where the mouse button is released. The step-by-step procedure for creating this application is as follows:

1. Let's create an application based on the **Dialog without Buttons** template.
2. Add a `QLabel` widget to the form by dragging and dropping a **Label** widget on the form.
3. Set the **text** property of the **Label** widget to `Click the mouse and drag it to draw a rectangle of the desired size.`
4. Save the application by name as `demoDrawRectangle.ui`. The form will now appear as shown in the following screenshot:

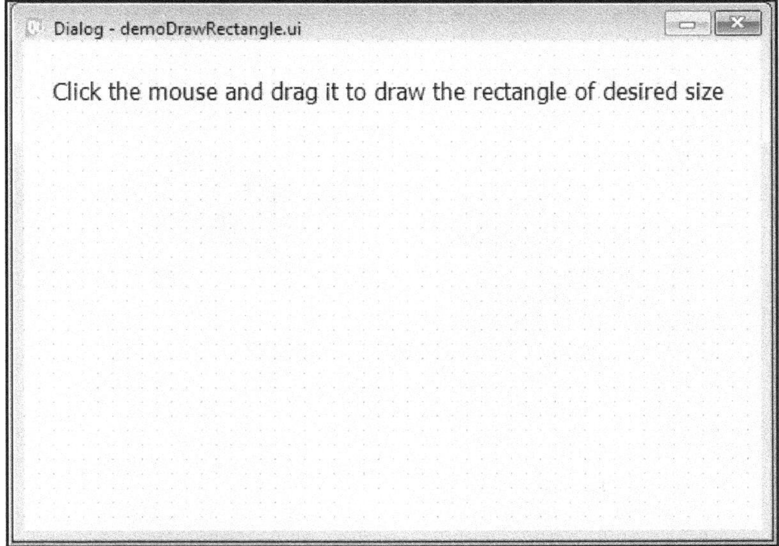

The user interface created with Qt Designer is stored in a `.ui` file, which is an XML file, and needs to be converted into Python code. The `pyuic5` utility is used for converting the XML file into Python code. The generated Python script, `demoDrawRectangle.py`, can be seen in the source code bundle of the book.

5. Treat the `demoDrawRectangle.py` script as a header file, and import it into the file from which you will invoke its user interface design.
6. Create another Python file with the name `callDrawRectangle.pyw` and import the `demoDrawRectangle.py` code into it:

```
import sys
from PyQt5.QtWidgets import QDialog, QApplication
from PyQt5.QtGui import QPainter
from demoDrawRectangle import *
class MyForm(QDialog):
    def __init__(self):
        super().__init__()
        self.ui = Ui_Dialog()
        self.ui.setupUi(self)
        self.pos1 = [0,0]
        self.pos2 = [0,0]
        self.show()
    def paintEvent(self, event):
        width = self.pos2[0]-self.pos1[0]
        height = self.pos2[1] - self.pos1[1]
        qp = QPainter()
        qp.begin(self)
        qp.drawRect(self.pos1[0], self.pos1[1], width, height)
        qp.end()
    def mousePressEvent(self, event):
        if event.buttons() & QtCore.Qt.LeftButton:
            self.pos1[0], self.pos1[1] = event.pos().x(),
            event.pos().y()
    def mouseReleaseEvent(self, event):
        self.pos2[0], self.pos2[1] = event.pos().x(),
        event.pos().y()
        self.update()
if __name__=="__main__":
    app = QApplication(sys.argv)
    w = MyForm()
    w.show()
    sys.exit(app.exec_())
```

How it works...

To draw a rectangle between the mouse button pressed and released locations, we will be making use of two methods, `mousePressEvent()` and `mouseReleaseEvent()`. The `mousePressEvent()` method is automatically invoked when a mouse button is pressed and the `mouseReleaseEvent()` method is automatically invoked when the mouse button is released. In these two methods, we will be simply saving the values of the *x* and *y* coordinates where the mouse button is clicked and released respectively. Two arrays, `pos1` and `pos2`, are defined, where the `pos1` array stores the *x* and *y* coordinates of the location where the mouse button is clicked and the `pos2` array stores the *x* and *y* coordinates of the location where the mouse button is released. The `self.update()` method that is invoked in the `mouseReleaseEvent()` method will invoke the `paintEvent()` method. In the `paintEvent()` method, the width of the rectangle is computed by finding the difference between the *x* coordinates of mouse press and mouse release locations. Similarly, the height of the rectangle is computed by finding the difference between the *y* coordinates of mouse press and mouse release events.

Also, in the `paintEvent()` method, the `drawRect()` method is invoked and the *x* and *y* coordinates stored in the `pos1` array are passed to it. Also, the width and height of the rectangle are passed to the `drawRect()` method to draw the rectangle between the mouse press and mouse release locations.

On running the application, you will get a message to click and drag the mouse button between the locations where the rectangle is required. So, click the mouse button and keeping the mouse button pressed, drag it to the desired location and release the mouse button.

A rectangle will be drawn between the locations where the mouse button is clicked and where it is released, as shown in the following screenshot:

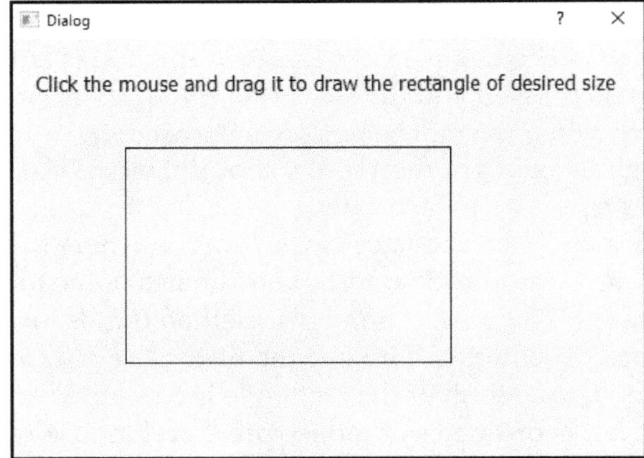

Drawing text in a desired font and size

In this recipe, we will learn to draw text in a specific font and at a specific font size. Four widgets will be required in this recipe such as **Text Edit**, **List Widget**, **Combo Box**, and **Push Button**. The **Text Edit** widget will be used to enter the text that the user wants to display in the desired font and size. The **List Widget** box will display different font names that the user can select from. The **Combo Box** widget will display font sizes that the user can select to define the size of the text. The **Push Button** widget will initiate the action, that is, the text entered in the **Text Edit** widget will be displayed in the chosen font and size on clicking the push button.

How to do it...

The `QPainter` class is the focus of this recipe. The `setFont()` and `drawText()` methods of the `QPainter` class will be used in this recipe. The `setFont()` method will be invoked to set the font style and font size chosen by the user and the `drawText()` method will draw the text written by the user in the **Text Edit** widget in the specified font style and size. Here is the step-by-step procedure to learn how these methods are used:

1. Let's create an application based on the **Dialog without Buttons** template.

2. Add the `QLabel`, `QTextEdit`, `QListWidget`, `QComboBox`, and `QPushButton` widgets to the form by dragging and dropping a **Label** widget, a **Text Edit** widget, a **List Widget** box, a **Combo Box** widget, and a **Push Button** widget on the form.
3. Set the **text** property of the **Label** widget to `Enter some text in leftmost box, select font and size, and click the Draw Text button.`
4. The **List Widget** box will be used for showing different fonts, so right-click on the **List Widget** box and select the **Edit Items** option to add a few font names to the **List Widget** box. Click the **+** (plus) button at the bottom of the dialog box that opens up and add a few font names, as shown in the following screenshot:

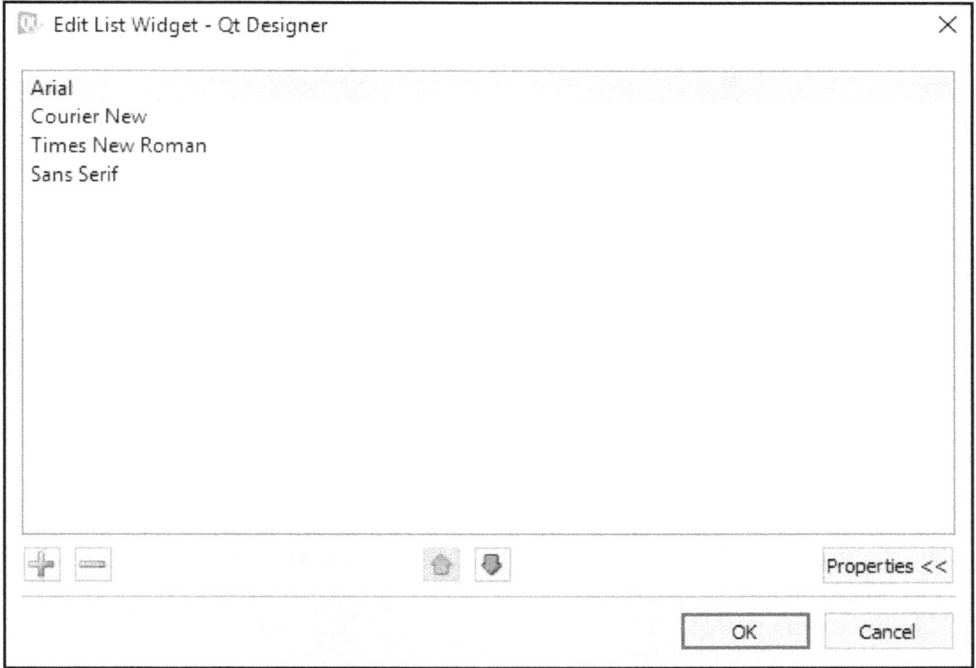

5. The **Combo Box** widget will be used for showing different font sizes, so we need to add certain font sizes to the **Combo Box** widget. Right-click on the **Combo Box** widget and select the **Edit Items** option.

6. Click the **+** (plus) button at the bottom of the dialog box that opens up and add a couple of font sizes, as shown in the following screenshot:

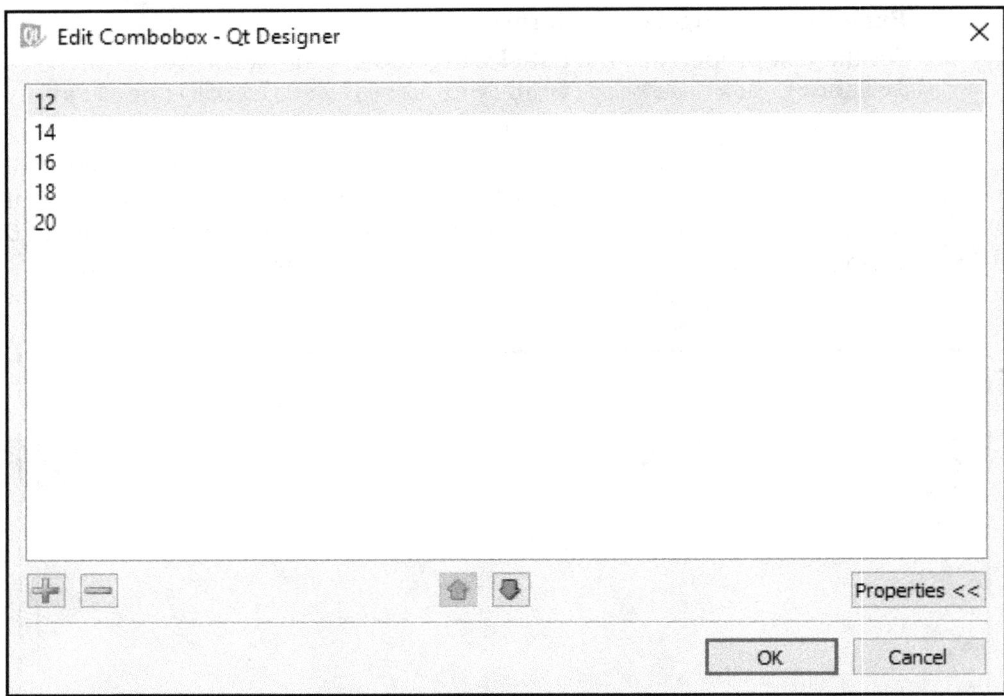

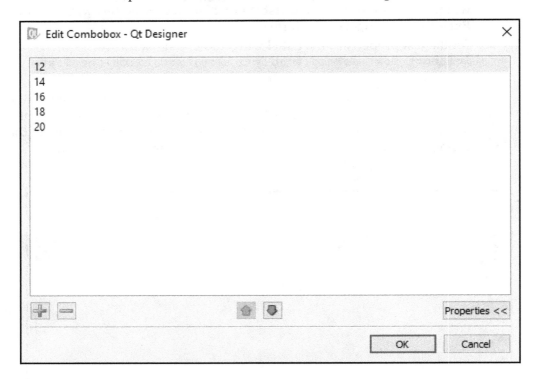

7. Set the **text** property of the **Push Button** widget to `Draw Text`.
8. Set the **objectName** property of the **List Widget** box to `listWidgetFont`.
9. Set the **objectName** property of the **Combo Box** widget to `comboBoxFontSize`.
10. Set the **objectName** property of the **Push Button** widget to pushButtonDrawText.
11. Save the application by name as `demoDrawText.ui`.

The form will now appear as shown in this screenshot:

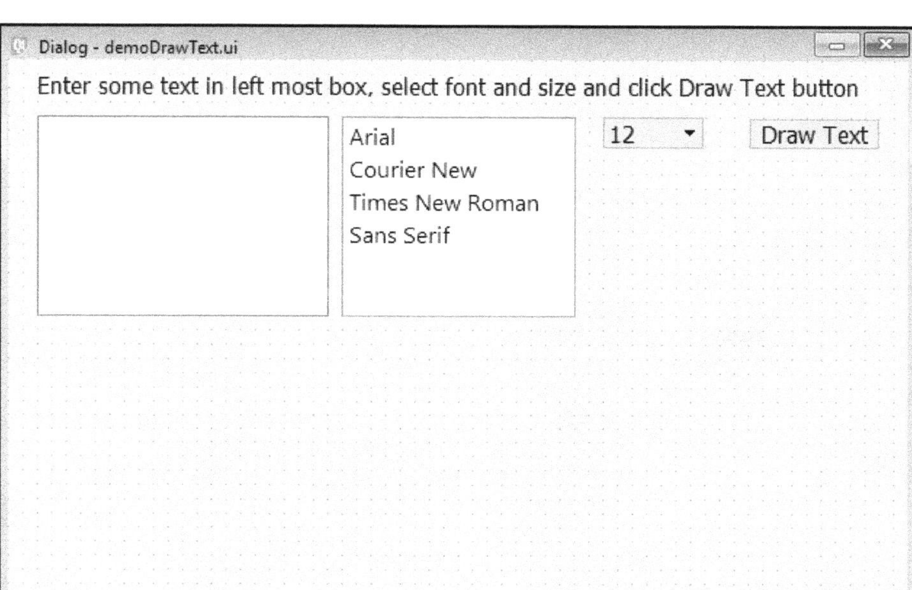

The user interface created with Qt Designer is stored in a `.ui` file and it is an XML file. The XML file is converted into Python code by applying the `pyuic5` utility. You can find the generated Python code, `demoDrawText.py`, in the source code bundle of the book.

12. Treat the `demoDrawText.py` script as a header file, and import it into the file from which you will invoke its user interface design.
13. Create another Python file with the name `callDrawText.pyw` and import the `demoDrawText.py` code into it:

```
import sys
from PyQt5.QtWidgets import QDialog, QApplication
from PyQt5.QtGui import QPainter, QColor, QFont
from PyQt5.QtCore import Qt
from demoDrawText import *
class MyForm(QDialog):
    def __init__(self):
        super().__init__()
        self.ui = Ui_Dialog()
        self.ui.setupUi(self)
        self.ui.pushButtonDrawText.clicked.connect(self.
```

```
            dispText)
            self.textToDraw=""
            self.fontName="Courier New"
            self.fontSize=5
            self.show()
        def paintEvent(self, event):
            qp = QPainter()
            qp.begin(self)
            qp.setPen(QColor(168, 34, 3))
            qp.setFont(QFont(self.fontName, self.fontSize))
            qp.drawText(event.rect(), Qt.AlignCenter,
            self.textToDraw)
            qp.end()
        def dispText(self):
            self.fontName=self.ui.listWidgetFont.currentItem().
            text()
            self.fontSize=int(self.ui.comboBoxFontSize.itemText(
            self.ui.comboBoxFontSize.currentIndex()))
            self.textToDraw=self.ui.textEdit.toPlainText()
            self.update()
if __name__=="__main__":
    app = QApplication(sys.argv)
    w = MyForm()
    w.show()
    sys.exit(app.exec_())
```

How it works...

The **click()** event of the **Push Button** widget is connected to the `dispText()` method, that is, whenever the push button is clicked, the `dispText()` method will be invoked.

In the `dispText()` method, the font name selected from the **List Widget** box is accessed and assigned to the `fontName` variable. Also, the font size selected from the combo box is accessed and assigned to the `fontSize` variable. Besides this, the text written in the **Text Edit** widget is fetched and assigned to the `textToDraw` variable. Finally, the `self.update()` method is invoked; it will invoke the `paintEvent()` method.

In the `paintEvent()` method, the `drawText()` method is called and will draw the text written in the **Text Edit** widget in the font style that is assigned to the `fontName` variable, and in the font size specified in the `fontSize` variable. On running the application, you will find a **Text Edit** widget on the extreme left, font names displayed in the **List Widget** box, and font sizes displayed via the **Combo box** widget. You need to enter some text in the **Text Edit** widget, select a font style from the **List Widget** box and font size from the **Combo Box** widget, and click on the **Draw Text** button. On clicking the **Draw Text** button, the text written in the **Text Edit** widget will be displayed in the selected font and selected font size, as shown in the following screenshot:

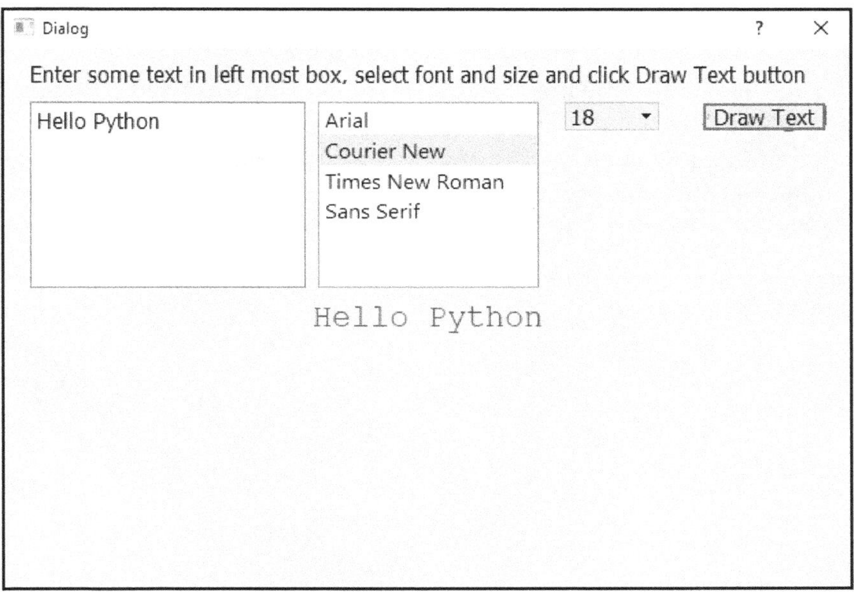

Creating a toolbar that shows different graphics tools

In this recipe, we will learn to create a toolbar that shows three toolbar buttons. These three toolbar buttons show the icons for the line, circle, and rectangle. When the user clicks the line toolbar button from the toolbar, he/she can click and drag the mouse on the form to draw a line between the two mouse locations. Similarly, by clicking on the circle toolbar button, the user can draw a circle on the form by clicking and dragging the mouse.

How to do it...

The focus of this recipe is to help you understand how frequently used commands in an application can be provided to the user via a toolbar, making them easy to access and use. You will learn to create toolbar buttons, define their shortcuts, and their icons too. To define the icons for the toolbar buttons, you will learn to create and use the resource file. The creation and execution of each toolbar button is explained very clearly step by step:

1. Let's create a new application to understand the steps involved in creating a toolbar.
2. Launch Qt Designer and create a main window-based application. You get a new application with the default menu bar.
3. You can remove the menu bar by right-clicking on it and selecting the **Remove Menu Bar** option from the shortcut menu that pops up.
4. To add a toolbar, right-click on the **Main Window** template and select **Add Tool Bar** from the context menu. A blank toolbar will be added below the menu bar, as shown in the following screenshot:

We want to create a toolbar with three toolbar buttons, line, circle, and rectangle. Since the three toolbar buttons will represent three icon images, we assume we have icon files, that is, files with an extension `.ico` for the line, circle, and rectangle.

5. To add tools to the toolbar, create an action in the **Action Editor** box; each toolbar button in the toolbar is represented by an action. The **Action Editor** box is usually found below the **Property Editor** window.
6. If the **Action Editor** window is not visible, select Action Editor from the View menu. The **Action Editor** window appears as shown here:

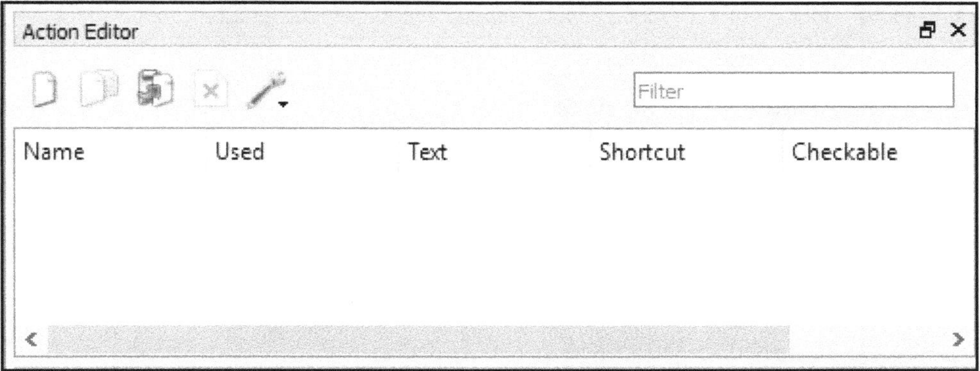

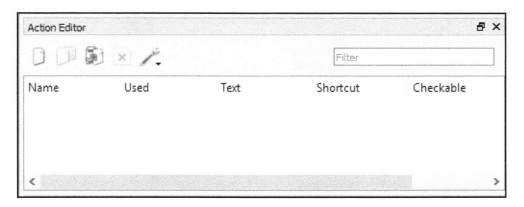

7. In the **Action Editor** window, select the New button to create an action for the first toolbar button. You get the dialog to enter detailed information for the new action.
8. In the **Text** box, specify the name of the action, `Circle`.
9. In the **Object name** box, the name of the action object automatically appears, prefixed with the text `action`.
10. In the **ToolTip** box, enter any descriptive text.

11. In the **Shortcut** box, press *Ctrl* + *C* character to assign `Ctrl + C` as the shortcut key for drawing a circle.
12. The **Icon** drop-down list shows two options, **Choose Resource...** and **Choose File**.
13. You can assign an icon image to the action either by clicking the **Choose File...** option or from the resource file:

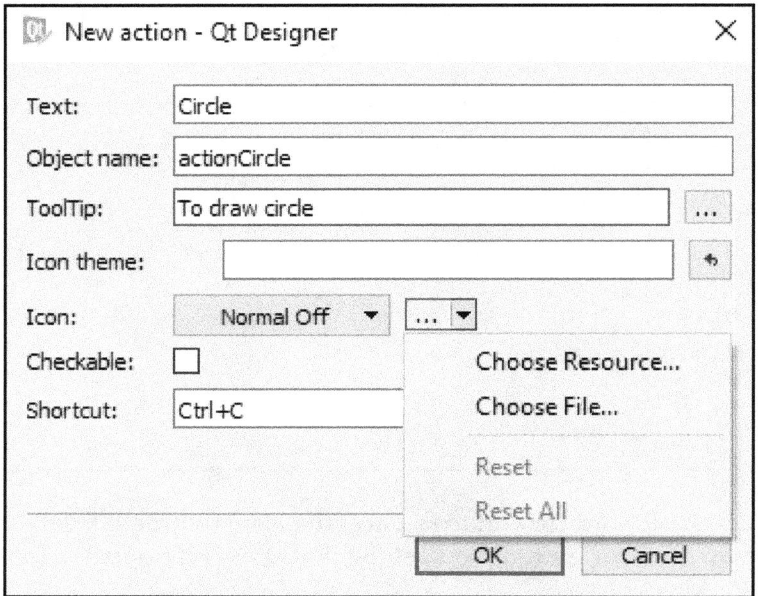

You can select several icons in a resource file and that resource file can then be used in different applications.

14. Select the **Choose Resource...** option. You get the **Select Resource** dialog, as shown in the following screenshot:

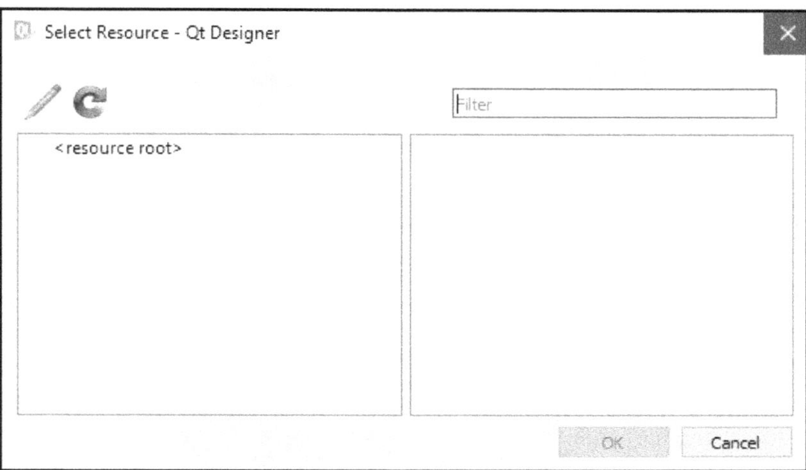

Since no resource has yet been created, the dialog box is empty. You see two icons at the top. The first icon represents Edit Resources and the second icon represents Reload. On clicking the Edit Resources icon, you get the dialog shown here:

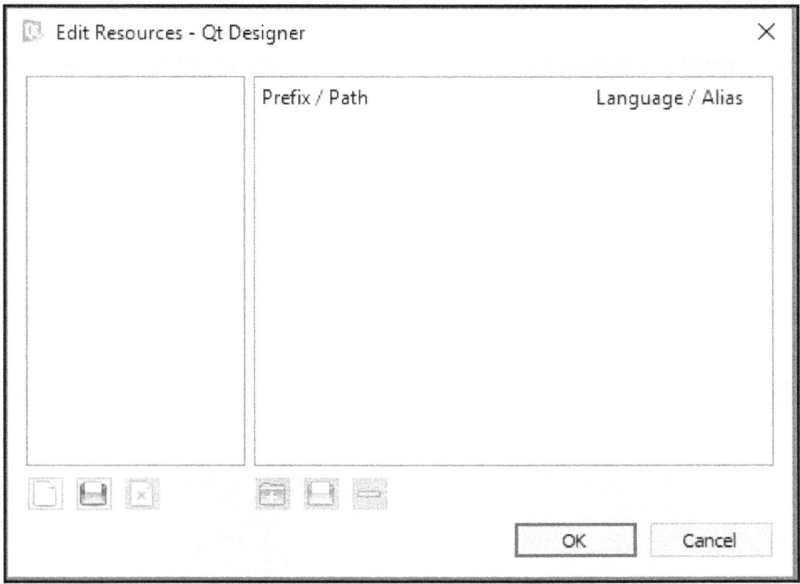

Now let's see how we can create a resource file by performing the following steps:

1. The first step is to create a resource file or load an existing resource file. The first three icons at the bottom represent New Resource File, Edit Resource File, and Remove.
2. Click on New Resource File icon. You will be prompted to specify the name of the resource file.
3. Let's name the new resource file `iconresource`. The file will be saved with the extension `.qrc`.
4. The next step is to add a prefix to the resource file. The three icons below the **Prefix / Path** pane are Add Prefix, Add Files, and Remove.
5. Click on the Add Prefix option, and you will be prompted to enter the prefix name.
6. Enter the prefix as `Graphics`. After adding the prefix, we are ready to add our three icons, circle, rectangle, and line, to the resource file. Recall that we have three icon files with the extension `.ico`.
7. Click the Add Files option to add icons. On clicking the Add Files option, you will be asked to browse to the drive/directory and select the icon files.
8. Select the three icon files one by one. After adding the three icons, the Edit Resources dialog appears as shown here:

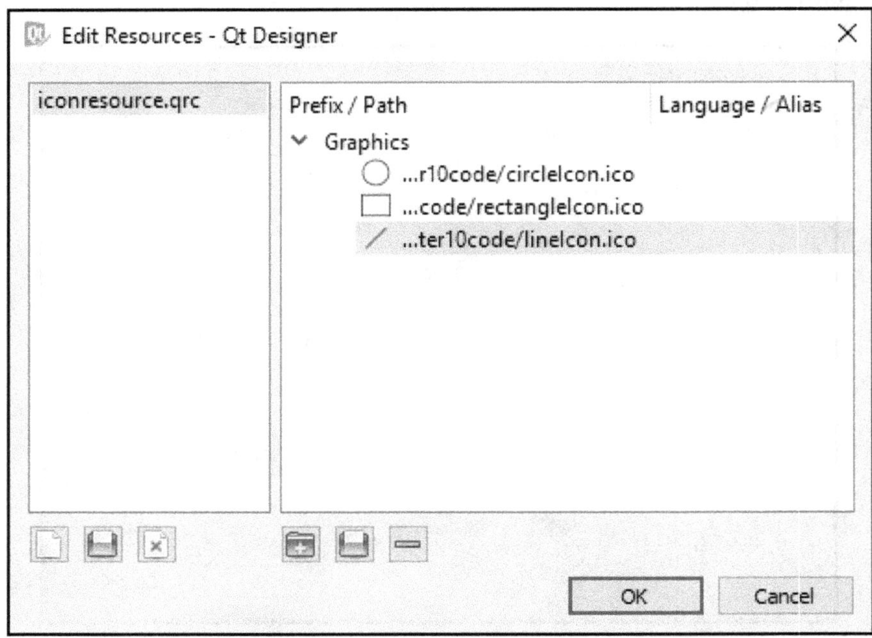

9. On clicking the **OK** button, the resource file will appear, showing the three icons to choose from.
10. Since we want to assign an icon for the circle action, click on the circle icon, followed by clicking the **OK** button:

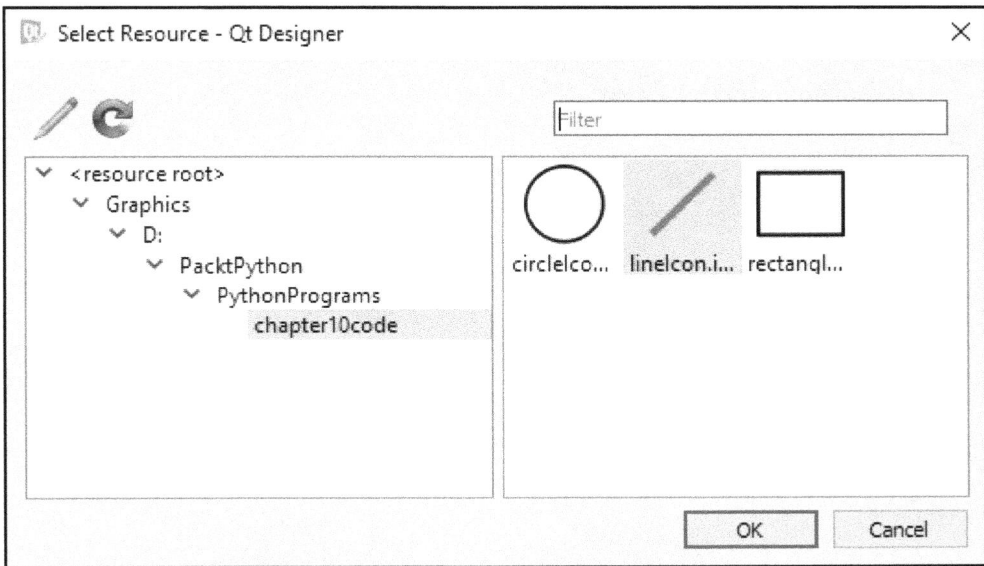

The selected circle icon will be assigned to **actionCircle**.

11. Similarly, create two more actions, `actionRectangle` and `actionLine`, for the rectangle and line toolbar buttons. After adding the three actions, the **Action Editor** window will appear as shown here:

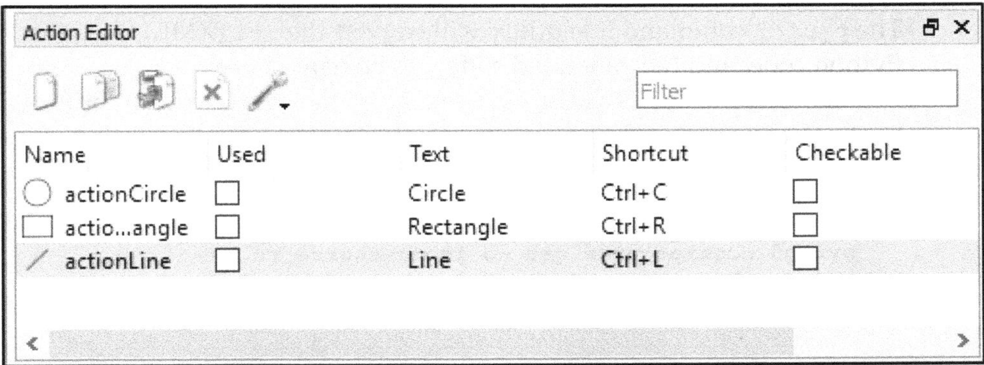

12. To display the toolbar buttons in the toolbar, click one action from the **Action Editor** window and, keeping it pressed, drag it to the toolbar.
13. Save the application with the name `demoToolBars.ui`.

After dragging the three actions to the toolbar, the toolbar will appear as shown here:

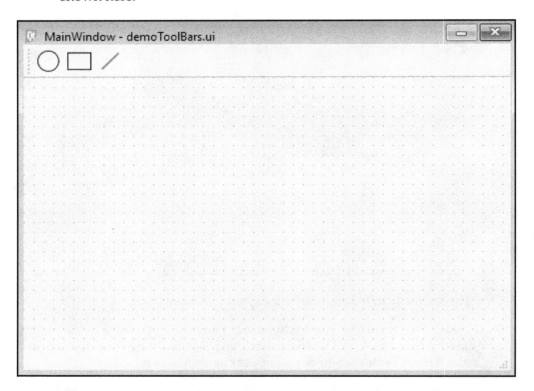

The `pyuic5` command line utility will convert the `.ui` (XML) file into Python code, and the generated code will be named `demoToolBars.py`. You can find the `demoToolBars.py` script in the source code bundle of this book. The `iconresource.qrc` file that we created must be converted into Python format before we move further. The following command line will convert the resource file into a Python script:

```
pyrcc5 iconresource.qrc -o iconresource_rc.py
```

14. Create a Python script named `callToolBars.pyw` that imports the code, `demoToolBar.py`, to invoke the toolbar and to draw the graphic whose toolbar button is selected from the toolbar. The script file will appear as follows:

```
import sys
from PyQt5.QtWidgets import QMainWindow, QApplication
from PyQt5.QtGui import QPainter
from demoToolBars import *

class AppWindow(QMainWindow):
    def __init__(self):
        super().__init__()
        self.ui = Ui_MainWindow()
        self.ui.setupUi(self)
        self.pos1 = [0,0]
        self.pos2 = [0,0]
        self.toDraw=""
self.ui.actionCircle.triggered.connect(self.drawCircle)
        self.ui.actionRectangle.triggered.connect(self.
        drawRectangle)
        self.ui.actionLine.triggered.connect(self.drawLine)
        self.show()

    def paintEvent(self, event):
        qp = QPainter()
        qp.begin(self)
        if self.toDraw=="rectangle":
            width = self.pos2[0]-self.pos1[0]
            height = self.pos2[1] - self.pos1[1]
            qp.drawRect(self.pos1[0], self.pos1[1], width,
            height)
        if self.toDraw=="line":
            qp.drawLine(self.pos1[0], self.pos1[1],
            self.pos2[0], self.pos2[1])
        if self.toDraw=="circle":
            width = self.pos2[0]-self.pos1[0]
            height = self.pos2[1] - self.pos1[1]
            rect = QtCore.QRect(self.pos1[0], self.pos1[1],
            width, height)
            startAngle = 0
            arcLength = 360 *16
            qp.drawArc(rect, startAngle, arcLength)
            qp.end()

    def mousePressEvent(self, event):
        if event.buttons() & QtCore.Qt.LeftButton:
```

```
                self.pos1[0], self.pos1[1] = event.pos().x(),
                event.pos().y()

        def mouseReleaseEvent(self, event):
            self.pos2[0], self.pos2[1] = event.pos().x(),
            event.pos().y()
            self.update()

        def drawCircle(self):
            self.toDraw="circle"

        def drawRectangle(self):
            self.toDraw="rectangle"

        def drawLine(self):
            self.toDraw="line"

app = QApplication(sys.argv)
w = AppWindow()
w.show()
sys.exit(app.exec_())
```

How it works...

The **triggered()** signal of the action of each toolbar button is connected to the respective method. The **triggered()** signal of the **actionCircle** toolbar button is connected to the `drawCircle()` method, so whenever the circle toolbar button is selected from the toolbar, the `drawCircle()` method will be invoked. Similarly, the **triggered()** signal of `actionRectangle` and `actionLine` are connected to the `drawRectangle()` and `drawLine()` methods, respectively. In the `drawCircle()` method, a variable `toDraw` is assigned a string, `circle`. The `toDraw` variable will be used to determine the graphics to be drawn in the `paintEvent()` method. The `toDraw` variable can be assigned any of the three strings, `line`, `circle`, or `rectangle`. A conditional branching is applied on the value in the `toDraw` variable and accordingly, methods to draw a line, rectangle, or circle will be invoked.

How big a line, circle, or rectangle will be drawn is determined by the mouse clicks; the user needs to click the mouse on the form and drag the mouse and release it at the location up to which he/she wants to draw the line, circle, or rectangle. In other words, the length of the line, width and height of the rectangle, and diameter of the circle will be determined by the mouse.

Two arrays, `pos1` and `pos2`, are used to store the *x* and *y* coordinates of the location where the mouse is clicked and the location where the mouse is released, respectively. The *x* and *y* coordinate values are assigned to the `pos1` and `pos2` array via two methods, `mousePressEvent()` and `mouseReleaseEvent()`. The `mousePressEvent()` method is automatically invoked when the mouse button is clicked and the `mouseReleaseEvent()` method is automatically invoked when the mouse button is released.

In the `mouseReleaseEvent()` method, after assigning the *x* and *y* coordinate values of the location where the mouse button is released, the `self.update()` method is invoked to invoke the `paintEvent()` method. In the `paintEvent()` method, branching takes place on the basis of the string assigned to the `toDraw` variable. If the `toDraw` variable is assigned the string `line` (by the `drawLine()` method), the `drawLine()` method will be invoked of `QPainter` class to draw the line between the two mouse locations. Similarly, if the `toDraw` variable is assigned the string `circle` (by the `drawCircle()` method), the `drawArc()` method will be invoked of the `QPainter` class to draw a circle with a diameter supplied by mouse locations. If the `toDraw` variable is assigned the string `rectangle` by the `drawRectangle()` method, then the `drawRect()` method will be invoked of the `QPainter` class to draw a rectangle of the width and height supplied by the mouse locations.

On running the application, you will find a toolbar with three toolbar buttons, circle, rectangle, and line, as shown in the following screenshot (left). Click on the circle toolbar button, then click the mouse button on the form, and, keeping the mouse button pressed, drag it to define the diameter of the circle and release the mouse button. A circle will be drawn from the location where the mouse button is clicked up to the location where the mouse button is released (right):

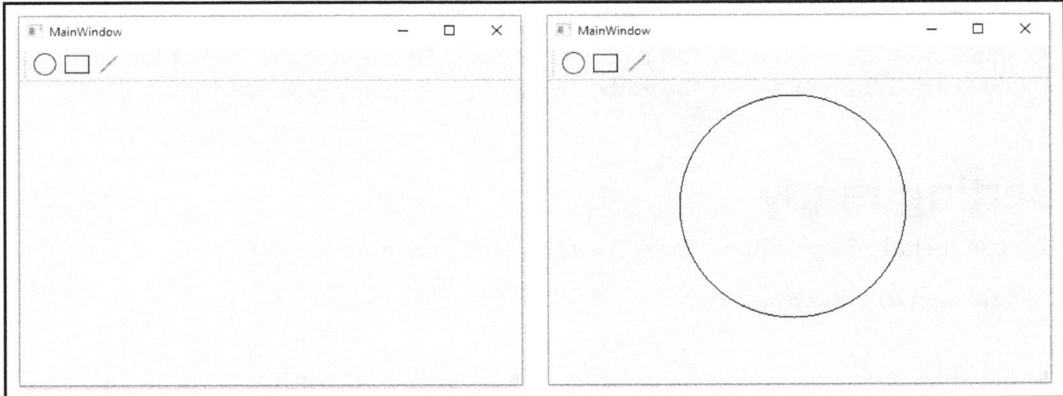

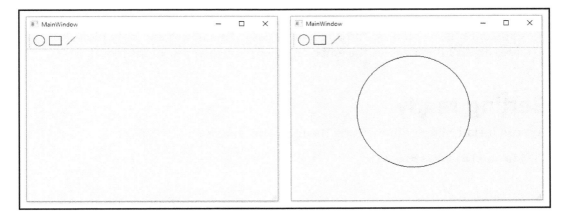

To draw a rectangle, click on the rectangle tool, click the mouse button at a location on the form, and, keeping the mouse button pressed, drag it to define the height and width of the rectangle. On releasing the mouse button, a rectangle will be drawn between the mouse pressed and mouse released locations (left). Similarly, click the line toolbar button and click the mouse button on the form. Keeping the mouse button pressed, drag it up to the location where you want the line to be drawn. On releasing the mouse button, a line will be drawn between the locations where the mouse button is clicked and released (right):

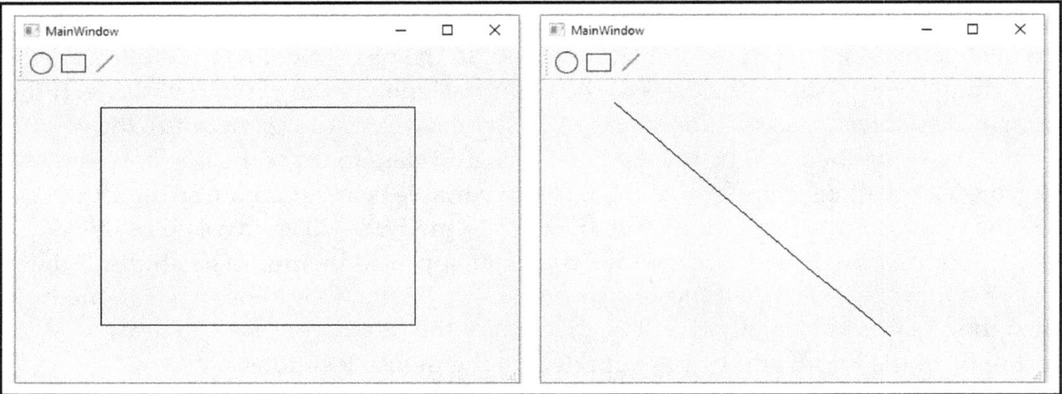

Plotting a line using Matplotlib

In this recipe, we will learn to plot a line using Matplotlib that passes through specific x and y coordinates.

Matplotlib is a Python 2D plotting library that makes the complicated task of plotting lines, histograms, bar charts, and so on quite easy. This library not only plots, but also provides an API that enables the embedding of plots in applications too.

Getting ready

You can install Matplotlib by using the following statement:

```
pip install matplotlib
```

Let's assume that we want to plot a line that uses the following sets of *x* and *y* coordinates:

```
x=10, y=20
x=20, y=40
x=30, y=60
```

On the *x* axis, the value of `x` begins from `0` and increases towards the right and on the *y* axis, the value of `y` is `0` at the bottom and increases as we move up. Because the last pair of coordinates is `30`, `60`, the graph will have the maximum `x` value of `30` and the maximum `y` value of `60`.

The following methods of `matplotlib.pyplot` will be used in this recipe:

- `title()`: This method is used to set the title of the graph
- `xlabel()`: This method is to display the specific text along the *x* axis
- `ylabel()`: This method is to display the specific text along the *y* axis
- `plot()`: This method is used for plotting at the specified *x* and *y* coordinates

How to do it...

Create a Python script with the name `demoPlotLine.py` and write the following code in it:

```
import matplotlib.pyplot as graph
graph.title('Plotting a Line!')
graph.xlabel('x - axis')
graph.ylabel('y - axis')
x = [10,20,30]
y = [20,40,60]
graph.plot(x, y)
graph.show()
```

How it works...

You import `matplotlib.pyplot` in the script and name it graph. Using the `title()` method, you set the title of the graph. Thereafter, the `xlabel()` and `ylabel()` methods are invoked to define the text for the *x* axis and *y* axis, respectively. Because we want to plot a line using three sets of *x* and *y* coordinates, two arrays are defined by name, *x* and *y*. The values of the *x* and *y* coordinates that we want to plot are defined in the two arrays, *x* and *y*, respectively. The `plot()` method is invoked and the two *x* and *y* arrays are passed to it to plot the line using the three *x* and *y* coordinate values defined in the two arrays. The show method is invoked to display the plotting.

On running the application, you find that a line is plotted that passes through the specified *x* and *y* coordinates. Also, the graph will show the specified title, **Plotting a Line !**. Besides this, you can see the designated text being displayed along the *x* axis and *y* axis as shown in the following screenshot:

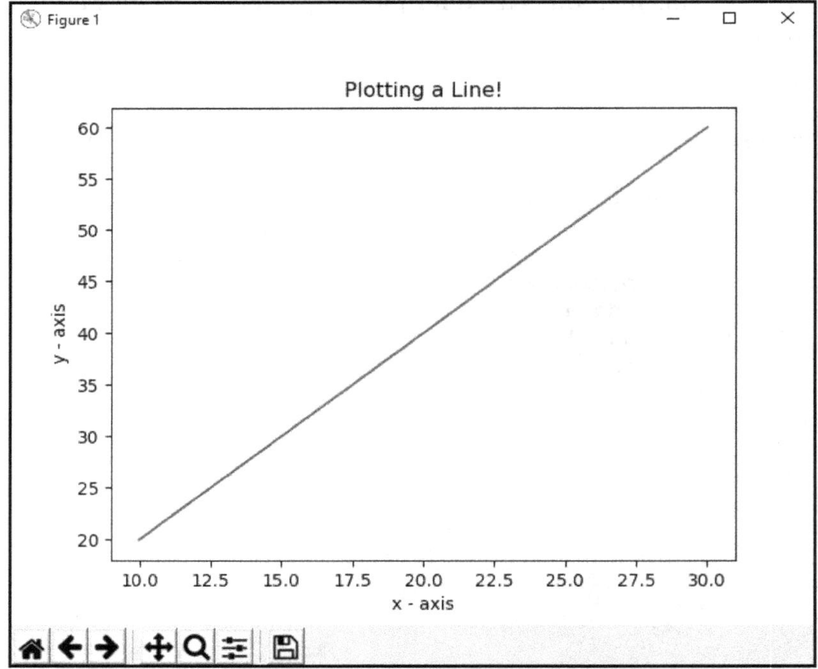

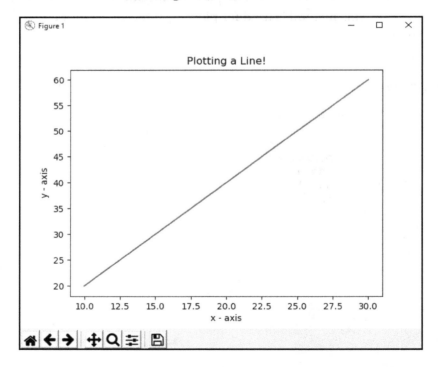

Plotting a bar using Matplotlib

In this recipe, we will learn to plot a bar using Matplotlib that compares the growth of a business over past three years. You will supply the profit percentage in 2016, 2017, and 2018 and the application will show a bar representing the profit percentage in the past three years.

Getting ready

Let's assume that the profit percentage of the organization over the last three years is as follows:

- **2016**: Profit was 70%
- **2017**: Profit was 90%
- **2018**: Profit is 80%

You want to display bars that represent profit percentages and along the *x* axis, and you want the years to be displayed: 2016, 2017, and 2018. Along the *y* axis, you want to display the bar that represent the profit percentage. The value of `y` on the *y* axis will begin from `0` at the bottom and increases while moving toward the top, with the maximum value, `100`, at the top.

The following methods of `matplotlib.pyplot` will be used in this recipe:

- `title()`: This method is used to set the title of the graph
- `bar()`: To plot the bar from the two supplied arrays; one array will represent data for the *x* axis, and the second array will represent data for the *y* axis
- `plot()`: This method is used for plotting at the specified *x* and *y* coordinates

How to do it...

Create a Python script with the name `demoPlotBars.py` and write the following code in it:

```
import matplotlib.pyplot as graph
years = ['2016', '2017', '2018']
profit = [70, 90, 80]
graph.bar(years, profit)
```

```
graph.title('Growth in Business')
graph.plot(100)
graph.show()
```

How it works...

You import `matplotlib.pyplot` in the script and name it graph. You define two arrays, years and profit, where the years array will contain the data for 2016, 2017, and 2018 to represent the years whose profits we want to compare. Similarly, the profit array will contain the values that represent the profit percentages for the last three years. Thereafter, the `bar()` method is invoked and the two arrays, years and profit, are passed to it to display the bar comparing profits in the last three years. The `title()` method is invoked to display the title, **Growth in Business**. The `plot()` method is invoked to indicate the maximum `y` value along the *y* axis. Finally, the `show()` method is invoked to display the bar.

On running the application, you find that a bar is plotted that displays the profits of the organization in the past three years. The *x* axis shows the years and the *y* axis shows the profit percentage. Also, the graph will show the specified title, **Growth in Business** as shown in the following screenshot:

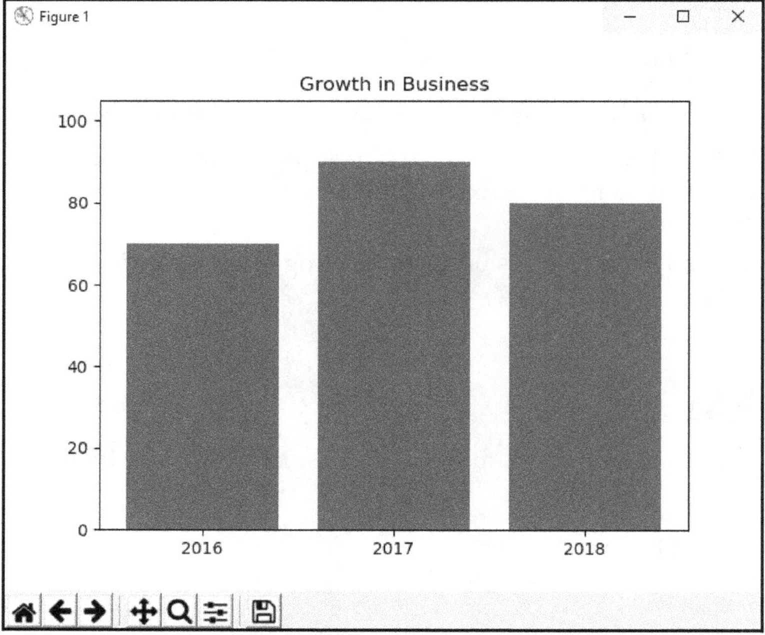

21 Implementing Animation

In this chapter, you will learn how to apply motion to a given graphic image, hence implementing animation. Animations play a major role in explaining the practical workings of any machine, process, or system. In this chapter, we will be covering the following topics:

- Displaying a 2D graphical picture
- Making a ball move down on the click of a button
- Making a bouncing ball
- Making a ball animate as per the specified curve

Introduction

To view and manage 2D graphical items in Python, we need to make use of a class called `QGraphicsScene`. In order to display the contents of `QGraphicsScene`, we need the help of another class, called `QGraphicsView`. Basically, `QGraphicsView` provides a scrollable viewport to display the contents of `QGraphicsScene`. `QGraphicsScene` acts as a container for several graphical items. It also provides several standard shapes, such as rectangles and ellipses, including text items. One more thing: the QGraphicsScene uses OpenGL for rendering the graphics. The OpenGL is very efficient for displaying images and performing multimedia processing tasks. The `QGraphicsScene` class provides several methods that help in adding or removing graphical items from the scene. That is, you can add any graphical item to the scene by calling the `addItem` function. Similarly, to remove an item from the graphics scene, you can call the `removeItem` function.

Implementing animation

To apply animation in Python, we will be making use of the `QPropertyAnimation` class. The `QPropertyAnimation` class in PyQt helps in creating and executing animations in PyQt. The `QPropertyAnimation` class implements animation by manipulating Qt properties such as a widget's geometry, position, and so on. The following are a few of the `QPropertyAnimation` methods:

- `start()`: This method begins the animation
- `stop()`: This method ends the animation
- `setStartValue()`: This method is used to assign the starting value of the animation
- `setEndValue()`: This method is used to assign the ending value of the animation
- `setDuration()`: This method is used to set the duration of the animation in milliseconds
- `setKeyValueAt()`: This method creates a keyframe at the given value
- `setLoopCount()`: This method sets the count of the repetitions desired in the animation

Displaying a 2D graphical image

In this recipe, you will learn to display a 2D graphical image. We assume that you have a graphical image by the name `scene.jpg` on your machine, and you will learn how it is displayed on the form. The focus of this recipe is to understand how the **Graphics View** widget is used to display an image.

How to do it...

The procedure for displaying graphics is very simple. You first need to create an object of `QGraphicsScene`, which in turn makes use of the `QGraphicsView` class to show its contents. Graphical items, including images, are then added to the `QGraphicsScene` class by invoking the `addItem` method of the `QGraphicsScene` class. Here are the steps to display a 2D graphical image on the screen:

1. Create a new application based on the **Dialog without Buttons** template.
2. Drag and drop a **Graphics View** widget onto it.

3. Save the application with the name `demoGraphicsView.ui`. The form will appear as shown in the following screenshot:

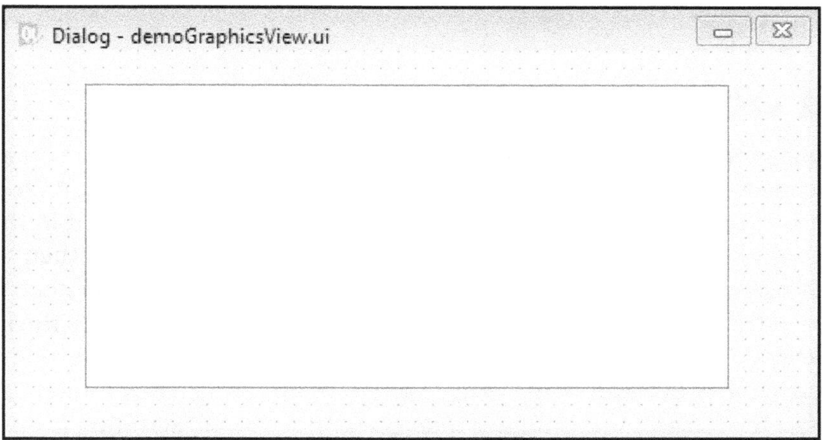

The `pyuic5` command utility converts the `.ui` (XML) file into Python code. The generated Python script, `demoGraphicsView.py`, can be seen in the source code bundle of this book.

4. Create a Python script named `callGraphicsView.pyw` that imports the code, `demoGraphicsView.py`, to invoke the user interface design, loads an image from the disk, and displays it through **Graphics View**. The Python script file, `callGraphicsView.pyw`, will include the following code:

```
import sys
from PyQt5.QtWidgets import QDialog, QApplication,
QGraphicsScene, QGraphicsPixmapItem
from PyQt5.QtGui import QPixmap
from demoGraphicsView import *
class MyForm(QDialog):
    def __init__(self):
        super().__init__()
        self.ui = Ui_Dialog()
        self.ui.setupUi(self)
        self.scene = QGraphicsScene(self)
        pixmap= QtGui.QPixmap()
        pixmap.load("scene.jpg")
        item=QGraphicsPixmapItem(pixmap)
        self.scene.addItem(item)
        self.ui.graphicsView.setScene(self.scene)
if __name__=="__main__":
```

```
app = QApplication(sys.argv)
myapp = MyForm()
myapp.show()
sys.exit(app.exec_())
```

How it works...

In this application, you are using **Graphics View** to display an image. You add a graphics scene to the **Graphics View** widget, and you add `QGraphicsPixmapItem`. If you want to add an image to the graphics scene, you need to provide it in the form of a `pixmap` item. First, you need to represent the image as `pixmap`, and then you make it appear as a `pixmap` item before adding it to the graphics scene. You need to create an instance of `QPixmap` and specify the image that you want to display through its `load()` method. Then, you tag the `pixmap` item as `pixmapitem` by passing `pixmap` to the constructor of `QGraphicsPixmapItem`. `pixmapitem` is then added to the scene via `addItem`. If `pixmapitem` is bigger than `QGraphicsView`, scrolling is enabled automatically.

In the previous code, I used an image with the filename `scene.jpg`. Please replace the filename with an image filename that is available on your disk, or nothing will be displayed on the screen.

The following methods are used:

- `QGraphicsView.setScene`: This method (self, `QGraphicsScene` scene) assigns the scene that is supplied as a parameter to the `GraphicView` instance for display. If the scene is already being viewed, this function does nothing. When a scene is set on a view, the `QGraphicsScene.changed` signal is generated, and the view's scrollbars are adjusted to fit the size of the scene.
- `addItem`: This method adds the specified item to the scene. If an item is already in a different scene, it will first be removed from its old scene and then added to the current scene. On running the application, the `scene.jpg` image will be displayed via the `GrahicsView` widget, as shown in the following screenshot:

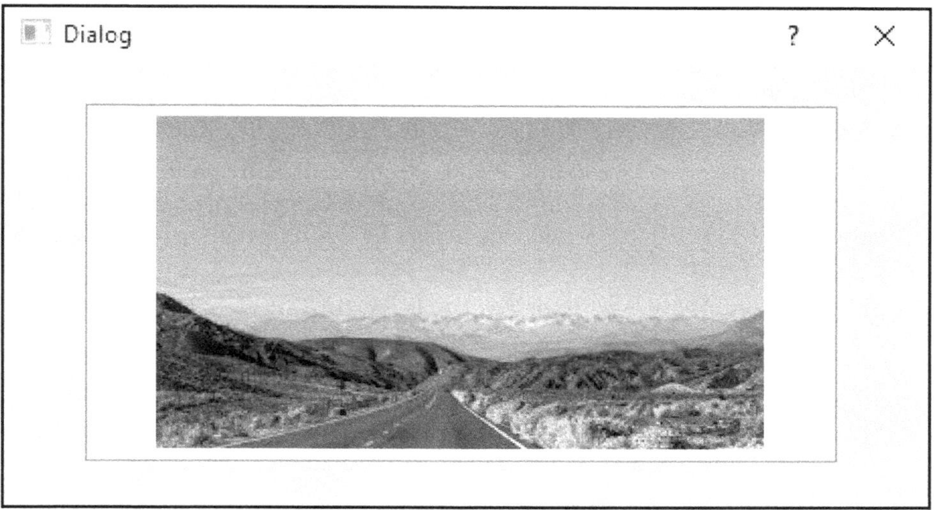

Making a ball move down on the click of a button

In this recipe, you will understand how a basic animation is applied on an object. This recipe will consist of a push button and a ball, and when the push button is pressed, the ball will start animating towards the ground.

How to do it...

To make this recipe, we will be making use of the `QPropertyAnimation` class. The `setStartValue()` and `setEndValue()` methods of the `QPropertyAnimation` class will be used to define the coordinates where the animation needs to start and end, respectively. The `setDuration()` method will be invoked to specify the delay in milliseconds between every animation move. The following is the step-by-step procedure to apply an animation:

1. Create a new application based on the **Dialog without Buttons** template.
2. Drag and drop a **Label** widget and one **Push Button** widget onto the form.

3. Set the **text** property of the **Push Button** widget to `Move Down`. We assume that you have a ball image on your computer with the filename `coloredball.jpg`.
4. Select its **pixmap** property to assign the ball image to the **Label** widget.
5. In the **pixmap** property, out of the two options, **Choose Resource** and **Choose File**, select the **Choose File** option, browse your disk, and select the `coloredball.jpg` file. The image of the ball will appear in place of the **Label** widget.
6. Set the **objectName** property of the **Push Button** widget to `pushButtonPushDown` and that of the **Label** widget to `labelPic`.
7. Save the application with the name `demoAnimation1.ui`. The application will appear as shown in the following screenshot:

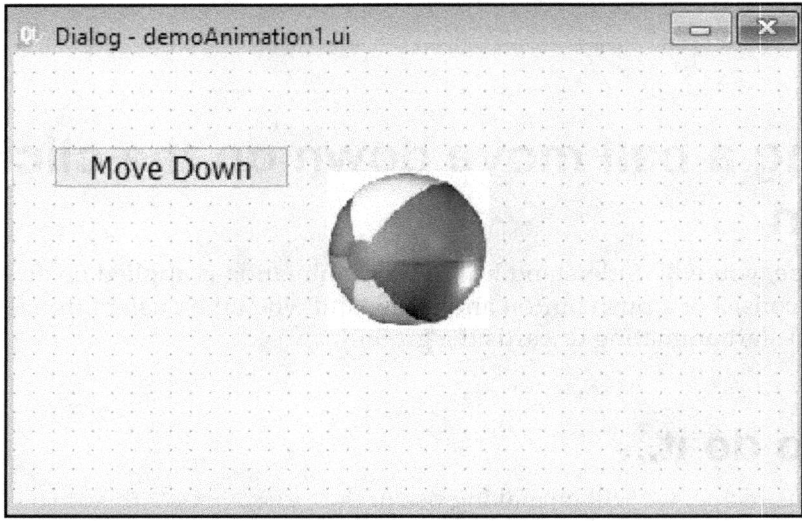

The user interface created with Qt Designer is stored in a `.ui` file, which is an XML file that needs to be converted into Python code. On application of the `pyuic5` command utility, the `.ui` file is converted into a Python script. The generated Python script, `demoAnimation1.py`, can be seen in the source code bundle of this book.

8. Treat the `demoAnimation1.py` script as a header file, and import it into the file from which you will invoke its user interface design.
9. Create another Python file with the name `callAnimation1.pyw` and import the `demoAnimation1.py` code into it:

```
import sys
from PyQt5.QtWidgets import QDialog, QApplication
from PyQt5.QtCore import QRect, QPropertyAnimation
from demoAnimation1 import *
class MyForm(QDialog):
    def __init__(self):
        super().__init__()
        self.ui = Ui_Dialog()
        self.ui.setupUi(self)
        self.ui.pushButtonMoveDown.clicked.connect(self.
        startAnimation)
        self.show()
    def startAnimation(self):
        self.anim = QPropertyAnimation(self.ui.labelPic,
        b"geometry")
        self.anim.setDuration(10000)
        self.anim.setStartValue(QRect(160, 70, 80, 80))
        self.anim.setEndValue(QRect(160, 70, 220, 220))
        self.anim.start()
if __name__=="__main__":
    app = QApplication(sys.argv)
    w = MyForm()
    w.show()
    sys.exit(app.exec_())
```

How it works...

You can see that the **click()** event of the **Push Button** widget with the **objectName** property `pushButtonMoveDown` is connected to the `startAnimation` method; when the push button is clicked, the `startAnimation` method is invoked. In the `startAnimation` method, you create an object of the `QPropertyAnimation` class and name it `anim`. While creating the `QPropertyAnimation` instance, you pass two arguments; the first is the **Label** widget to which you want to apply the animation and the second is the property that defines the object's attribute to which you want to apply the animation to the object's attribute. Because you want to apply an animation to the ball's geometry, you pass `b"geometry"` as the second attribute while defining the `QPropertyAnimation` object. After that, you specify the duration of the animation as `10000` milliseconds, meaning you want to change the geometry of the object after every 10,000 milliseconds. Through the `setStartValue` method, you specify the region that is the rectangular area where you want the animation to start, and by invoking the `setEndValue` method, you specify the rectangular region where you want to stop the animation. By invoking the `start` method, you initiate the animation; consequently, the ball moves down from the rectangular region specified through the `setStartValue` method until it reaches the rectangular region specified through the `setEndValue` method.

On running the application, you will find a push button and a **Label** widget representing the ball image on the screen, as shown in the following screenshot (left). On clicking the **Move Down** push button, the ball starts animating towards the ground and stop its animation at the region specified through the `setEndValue` method, as shown in the following screenshot (right):

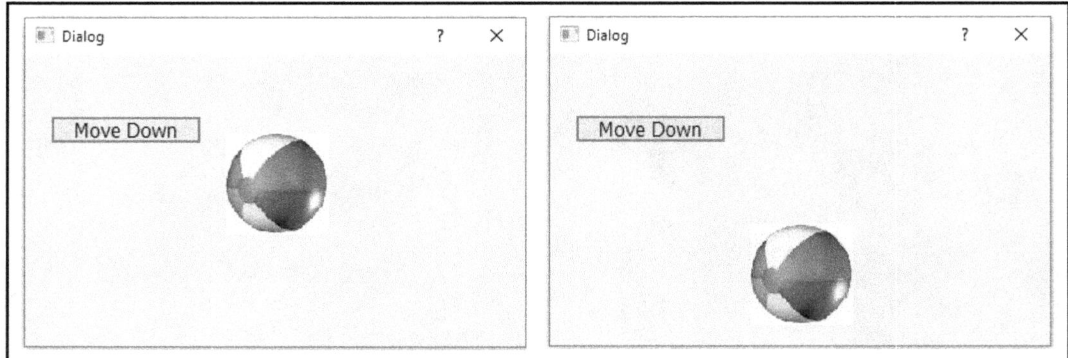

Making a bouncing ball

In this recipe, you will make a bouncing ball; when clicking a button, a ball falls towards the ground and on touching the ground, it bounces back to the top. In this recipe, you will understand how a basic animation is applied on an object. This recipe will consist of a push button and a ball, and when the push button is pressed, the ball will start animating towards the ground.

How to do it...

To make a ball appear to be bouncing, we need to make it first animate towards the ground, and then from the ground up to the sky. To do so, we will be invoking the `setKeyValueAt` method of the `QPropertyAnimation` class three times. The first and second calls to the `setKeyValueAt` method will make the ball animate from the top to the bottom. The third call to the `setKeyValueAt` method will make the ball animate from bottom to top. The coordinates in the three `setKeyValueAt` methods are provided so that the ball bounces in the opposite direction, and not where it came from. The following are the steps to understand how a ball can be animated to appear to be bouncing:

1. Create a new application based on the **Dialog without Buttons** template.
2. Drag and drop a **Label** widget and one **Push Button** widget onto the form.
3. Set the **text** property of the **Push Button** widget to `Bounce`. We assume that you have a ball image on your computer with the filename `coloredball.jpg`.
4. To assign the ball image to the **Label** widget, select its **pixmap** property.
5. In the **pixmap** property, out of the two options, `Choose Resource` and `Choose File`, select the **Choose File** option, browse your disk, and select the `coloredball.jpg` file. The image of the ball will appear in place of the **Label** widget.
6. Set the **objectName** property of the **Push Button** widget to `pushButtonBounce` and that of the **Label** widget to `labelPic`.
7. Save the application with the name `demoAnimation3.ui`.

The application will appear as shown in the following screenshot:

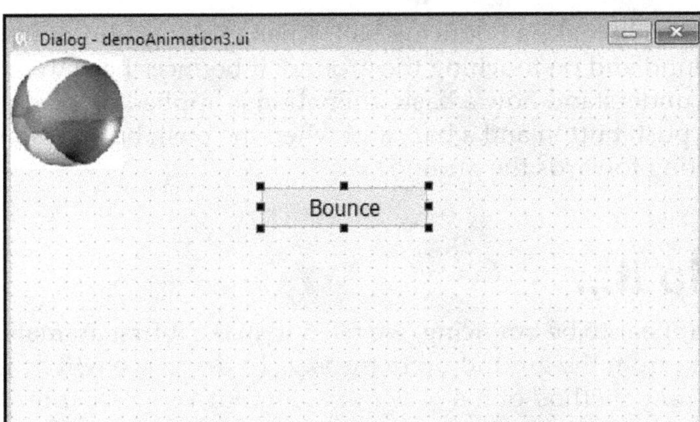

The user interface created with Qt Designer is stored in a `.ui` file, which is an XML file and needs to be converted into Python code. On application of the `pyuic5` command utility, the `.ui` file is converted into a Python script. The generated Python script, `demoAnimation3.py`, can be seen in the source code bundle of this book.

8. Treat the `demoAnimation3.py` script as a header file, and import it into the file from which you will invoke its user interface design.
9. Create another Python file with the name `callAnimation3.pyw` and import the `demoAnimation3.py` code into it:

```
import sys
from PyQt5.QtWidgets import QDialog, QApplication
from PyQt5.QtCore import QRect, QPropertyAnimation
from demoAnimation3 import *
class MyForm(QDialog):
    def __init__(self):
        super().__init__()
        self.ui = Ui_Dialog()
        self.ui.setupUi(self)
        self.ui.pushButtonBounce.clicked.connect(self.
        startAnimation)
        self.show()
    def startAnimation(self):
        self.anim = QPropertyAnimation(self.ui.labelPic,
        b"geometry")
        self.anim.setDuration(10000)
        self.anim.setKeyValueAt(0, QRect(0, 0, 100, 80));
```

```
        self.anim.setKeyValueAt(0.5, QRect(160, 160, 200,
180));
        self.anim.setKeyValueAt(1, QRect(400, 0, 100, 80));
        self.anim.start()
if __name__=="__main__":
    app = QApplication(sys.argv)
    w = MyForm()
    w.show()
    sys.exit(app.exec_())
```

How it works...

You can see that the **click()** event of the **Push Button** widget with the **objectName** property, `pushButtonMoveDown`, is connected to the `startAnimation` method; when the push button is clicked, the `startAnimation` method will be invoked. In the `startAnimation` method, you create an object of the `QPropertyAnimation` class and name it `anim`. While creating the `QPropertyAnimation` instance, you pass two arguments: the first is the **Label** widget to which you want to apply the animation, and the second is the property that defines the object's attribute to which you want to apply the animation to the object's attribute. Because you want to apply an animation to the ball's geometry, you pass `b"geometry"` as the second attribute while defining the `QPropertyAnimation` object. After that, you specify the duration of the animation as `10000` milliseconds, meaning you want to change the geometry of the object after every 10,000 milliseconds. Through the `setKeyValue` method, you specify the region that is the rectangular area where you want the animation to start. You mention the top-left region through this method because you want the ball to fall from the top-left corner towards the ground. Through the second call to the `setKeyValue` method, you supply the region in which you want the ball to fall to the ground. You also specify the angle of the fall. The ball will fall diagonally down towards the ground. By invoking the third `setValue` method, you specify the end value where you want the animation to stop, which in this case is in the top-right corner. Through these three calls to the `setKeyValue` method, you make the ball fall diagonally down towards the ground and then bounce back to the top-right corner. By invoking the `start` method, you initiate the animation.

On running the application, you will find the **Push Button** and **Label** widgets representing the ball image at the top-left corner of the screen, as shown in the following screenshot (left).

On clicking the **Bounce** push button, the ball starts animating diagonally down towards the ground, as shown in the middle screenshot, and after touching the ground, the ball bounces back towards the top-right corner of the screen, as shown on the right:

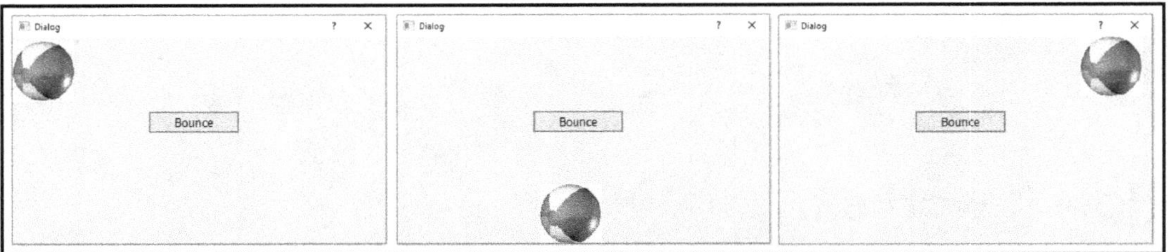

Making a ball animate as per the specified curve

A curve with the desired shape and size is created and a ball is set to move along the shape of the curve on the click of a push button. In this recipe, you will understand how to implement a guided animation.

How to do it...

The `setKeyValueAt` method of the `QPropertyAnimation` class determines the direction of an animation. For guided animation, you invoke the `setKeyValueAt` method in a loop. The coordinates of the curve are passed to the `setKeyValueAt` method in the loop to make the ball animate along the curve. Here are the steps to make an object animate as desired:

1. Create a new application based on the **Dialog without Buttons** template.
2. Drag and drop a **Label** widget and one **Push Button** widget onto the form.
3. Set the **text** property of the **Push Button** widget to `Move With Curve`.
4. Assuming you have a ball image on your computer with the filename `coloredball.jpg`, you can assign this ball image to the **Label** widget by using its **pixmap** property.

5. In the **pixmap** property, you will find two options, **Choose Resource** and **Choose File**; select the **Choose File** option, browse your disk, and select the `coloredball.jpg` file. The image of the ball will appear in place of the **Label** widget.
6. Set the **objectName** property of the **Push Button** widget to `pushButtonMoveCurve` and that of the **Label** widget to `labelPic`.
7. Save the application with the name `demoAnimation4.ui`. The application will appear as shown in the following screenshot:

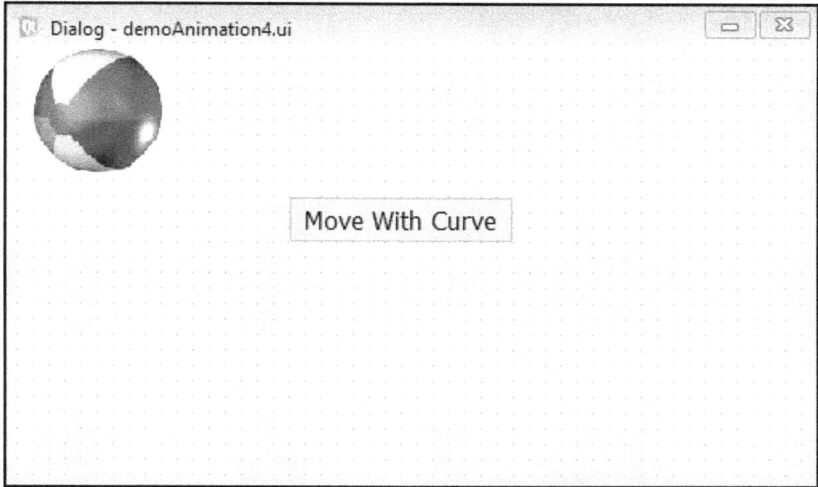

The user interface created with Qt Designer is stored in a `.ui` file and is an XML file. The XML file is converted into Python code by applying the `pyuic5` utility. You can find the generated Python code, `demoAnimation4.py`, in the source code bundle of this book.

8. Treat the `demoAnimation4.py` script as a header file, and import it into the file from which you will invoke its user interface design.

9. Create another Python file with the name `callAnimation4.pyw` and import the `demoAnimation4.py` code into it:

```
import sys
from PyQt5.QtWidgets import QDialog, QApplication
from PyQt5.QtCore import QRect, QPointF, QPropertyAnimation,
pyqtProperty
from PyQt5.QtGui import QPainter, QPainterPath
from demoAnimation4 import *
class MyForm(QDialog):
    def __init__(self):
        super().__init__()
        self.ui = Ui_Dialog()
        self.ui.setupUi(self)
        self.ui.pushButtonMoveCurve.clicked.connect(self.
        startAnimation)
        self.path = QPainterPath()
        self.path.moveTo(30, 30)
        self.path.cubicTo(30, 30, 80, 180, 180, 170)
        self.ui.labelPic.pos = QPointF(20, 20)
        self.show()
    def paintEvent(self, e):
        qp = QPainter()
        qp.begin(self)
        qp.drawPath(self.path)
        qp.end()
    def startAnimation(self):
        self.anim = QPropertyAnimation(self.ui.labelPic,
b'pos')
        self.anim.setDuration(4000)
        self.anim.setStartValue(QPointF(20, 20))
        positionValues = [n/80 for n in range(0, 50)]
        for i in positionValues:
            self.anim.setKeyValueAt(i,
            self.path.pointAtPercent(i))
            self.anim.setEndValue(QPointF(160, 150))
            self.anim.start()
if __name__=="__main__":
    app = QApplication(sys.argv)
    w = MyForm()
    w.show()
    sys.exit(app.exec_())
```

How it works...

First of all, you make the curve appear on the screen. This is the curve that will guide the ball's animation; that is, it will act as a path for the animation. You define an instance of the `QPainterPath` class and name it **path**. You invoke the `moveTo` method of the `QPainterPath` class to specify the starting location of the path or curve. The `cubicTo` method is invoked to specify the curved path for the ball's animation.

You can see that the **click** event of the **Push Button** widget with the **objectName** property `pushButtonMoveCurve` is connected to the `startAnimation` method; when the **Push Button** widget is clicked, the `startAnimation()` method will be invoked. In the `startAnimation` method, you create an object of the `QPropertyAnimation` class and name it `anim`. While creating the `QPropertyAnimation` instance, you pass two arguments: the first is the **Label** widget to which you want to apply the animation, and the second is the property that defines the object's attribute to which you want to apply the animation to the object's attribute. Because you want to apply the animation to the ball's position, you pass `b'pos"` as the second attribute while defining the `QPropertyAnimation` object. After that, you specify the duration of the animation as `4000` milliseconds, meaning you want to change the position of the ball after every `4000` milliseconds. Using the `setStartValue()` method of the `QPropertyAnimation` class, you specify the coordinates from where you want the ball to animate. You set the `for` loop that specifies the values that the ball needs to move along. You specify the path of the ball's animation by invoking the `setKeyValue` method inside the `for` loop. Because the ball needs to be drawn at every point specified in the path, you set the point where the ball needs to be drawn by invoking the `pointAtPercent()` method and passing it to the `setKeyValueAt()` method. You also need to set the location where the animation needs to stop by invoking the `setEndValue()` method.

Shortly after, you specify the start and end locations of the animation, you specify the path of animation, and the `paintEvent()` method is called to redraw the ball at every point of the path.

On running the application, you find the **Push Button** widget and a **Label** widget representing the ball image in the top-left corner of the screen (left side of the screenshot) and on clicking the **Move With Curve** push button, the ball starts animating along the drawn curve and stops where the curve ends (right side of the screenshot):

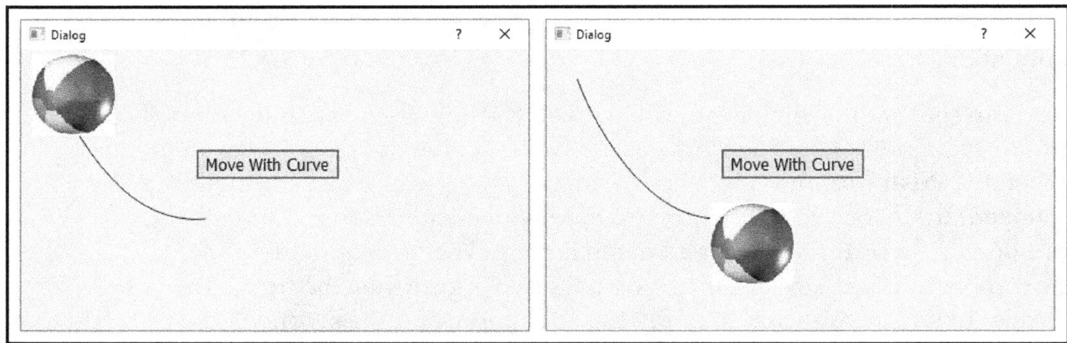

22
Using Google Maps

In this chapter, you will learn to use Google Maps in Python applications and explore the different advantages provided by Google. You will learn to do the following tasks:

- Find out details of a location or landmark
- Get complete information from latitude and longitude values
- Find out the distance between a two locations
- Display a location on Google Maps

Introduction

The Google Maps API is a set of methods and tools that can be used to find out complete information, including longitude and latitude values, for any location. You can use the Google Maps API methods to find distances between two locations or directions to any location; you can even display Google Maps, marking that location, and much more.

More precisely, there is a Python `client` library for Google Maps Services. There are several Google Maps APIs, including the Directions API, Distance Matrix API, Geocoding API, Geolocation API, and many more. To use any Google Maps web services, your Python script sends a request to Google; to serve that request, you need an API key. You need to follow these steps to get an API key:

1. Visit `https://console.developers.google.com`
2. Log in to the console using your Google account
3. Select one of your existing projects or create a new project
4. Enable the API(s) you want to use
5. Copy the API key and use it in your Python script

You need to visit the Google API Console, `https://console.developers.google.com`, and get API keys so that your application is authenticated to work with Google Maps API web services.

API keys help in several ways; first of all, they help identify your application. The API key is included with every request, hence it helps Google monitor your application's API usage, know if your application has consumed its free daily quota, and consequently bill your application too

So, in order to use Google Maps API web services in your Python application, you just need to enable the desired API and get a API key for use in your Python application.

Finding out details of a location or a landmark

In this recipe, you will be prompted to enter a location or landmark whose details you want to know. For example, if you enter `Buckingham Palace`, the recipe will display the city and postal code of the location where the palace is situated, along with its longitude and latitude values.

How to do it...

The search method of the `GoogleMaps` class is the key player in this recipe. The landmark or location entered by the user is passed to the search method. The `city`, `postal_code`, `lat`, and `lng` properties of the object returned from the search method are used to display the city, postal code, latitude, and longitude of the location, respectively. Let's see how it is done through the following step-by-step procedure:

1. Create an application based on the **Dialog without Buttons** template.
2. Add six `QLabel`, a `QLineEdit`, and a `QPushButton` widget to the form by dragging and dropping six **Label**, one **Line Edit**, and a **Push Button** widget onto the form.
3. Set the **text** property of the first **Label** widget to `Find out the City, Postal Code, Longitude and Latitude` and that of the second **Label** widget to `Enter location`.

4. Delete the **text** property of the third, fourth, fifth, and sixth **Label** widgets, because their **text** properties will be set through code; that is, the city, postal code, longitude, and latitude of the entered location will be fetched through code and will be displayed through these four **Label** widgets.
5. Set the **text** property of the **Push Button** widget to `Search`.
6. Set the **objectName** property of the **Line Edit** widget to `lineEditLocation`.
7. Set the **objectName** property of the **Push Button** widget to `pushButtonSearch`.
8. Set the **objectName** property of the rest of the four **Label** widgets to `labelCity`, `labelPostalCode`, `labelLongitude`, and `labelLatitude`.
9. Save the application by name as `demoGoogleMap1.ui`. The form will now appear as shown in the following screenshot:

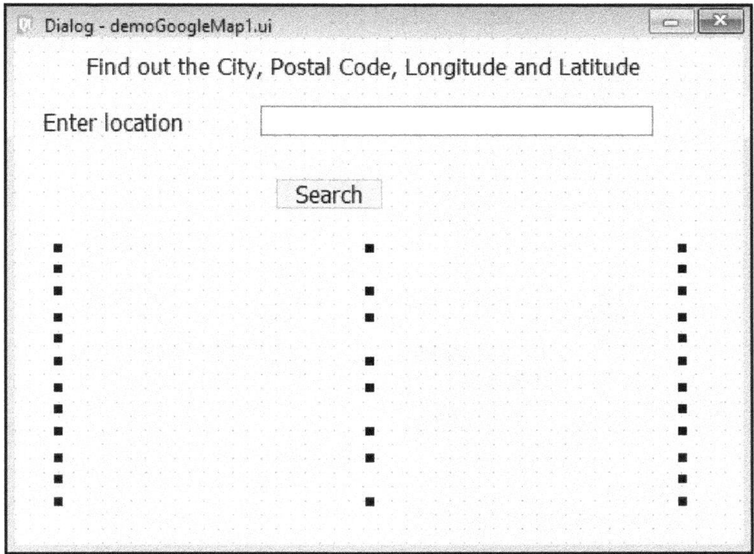

The user interface created with Qt Designer is stored in a `.ui` file and it is an XML file. The XML file is converted into Python code by applying the `pyuic5` utility. You can find the generated Python code, `demoGoogleMap1.py`, in the source code bundle for the book.

10. Treat the `demoGoogleMap1.py` script as a header file, and import it into the file from which you will invoke its user interface design.
11. Create another Python file with the name `callGoogleMap1.pyw` and import the `demoGoogleMap1.py` code into it:

```
import sys
from PyQt5.QtWidgets import QDialog, QApplication
from geolocation.main import GoogleMaps
from demoGoogleMap1 import *
class MyForm(QDialog):
    def __init__(self):
        super().__init__()
        self.ui = Ui_Dialog()
        self.ui.setupUi(self)
        self.ui.pushButtonSearch.clicked.connect(self.
        displayDetails)
        self.show()
    def displayDetails(self):
        address = str(self.ui.lineEditLocation.text())
        google_maps = GoogleMaps(api_key=
        'xxxxxxxxxxxxxxxxxxxxxxxxxxxx')
        location = google_maps.search(location=address)
        my_location = location.first()
        self.ui.labelCity.setText("City:
        "+str(my_location.city))
        self.ui.labelPostalCode.setText("Postal Code: "
        +str(my_location.postal_code))
        self.ui.labelLongitude.setText("Longitude:
        "+str(my_location.lng))
        self.ui.labelLatitude.setText("Latitude:
        "+str(my_location.lat))
if __name__=="__main__":
    app = QApplication(sys.argv)
    w = MyForm()
    w.show()
    sys.exit(app.exec_())
```

How it works...

You can see in the script that the **click** event of the push button with the **objectName** property `pushButtonSearch` s connected to the `displayDetails` method. This means that, whenever the push button is clicked, the `displayDetails` method will be invoked. In the `displayDetails` method, you access the location entered by the user in the **Line Edit** widget and assign that location to the address variable. You define a Google Maps instance by passing the API key that you got on registering with Google. Invoke the `search` method on the Google Maps instance, passing the location entered by the user in this method. The result of the `search` method is assigned to the `my_location` structure. The city member of the `my_location` structure contains the city entered by the user. Similarly, the `postal_code`, `lng`, and `lat` members of the `my_location` structure contain the postal code, longitude, and latitude information of the location entered by the user, respectively. The city, postal code, longitude, and latitude information are displayed via the last four **Label** widgets.

On running the application, you will be prompted to enter a location you want to find information about. Suppose you enter `Taj Mahal` in the location, followed by clicking the **Search** button. The city, postal code, longitude, and latitude information of the Taj Mahal landmark will be displayed on the screen, as shown in the following screenshot:

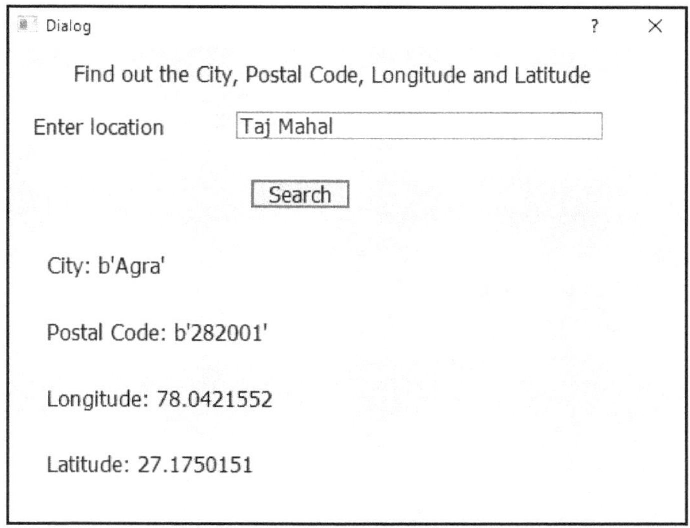

Getting complete information from latitude and longitude values

In this recipe, you will learn how to find out the complete details of a location whose longitude and latitude values you know. This process of converting a point location, that is, latitude and longitude values, into a readable address (the place name, city, country name, and so on) is known as **reverse geocoding**.

The application will prompt you to enter longitude and latitude values, and then it will display the matching location name, city, country, and postal code for that location.

How to do it...

Let's create an application based on the **Dialog without Buttons** template by performing the following steps:

1. Add seven `QLabel`, two `QLineEdit`, and a `QPushButton` widget to the form by dragging and dropping seven **Label**, two **Line Edit**, and a **Push Button** widget onto the form.
2. Set the **text** property of the first **Label** widget to `Find out the Location, City, Country and Postal Code`, that of the second **Label** widget to `Enter Longitude`, and that of the third **Label** widget to `Enter Latitude`.
3. Delete the **text** properties of the fourth, fifth, sixth, and seventh **Label** widgets because their **text** properties will be set through code; that is, the location, city, country, and postal code of the location whose longitude and latitude are entered by the user will be accessed through code and will be displayed through these four **Label** widgets.
4. Set the **text** property of the **Push Button** widget to `Search`.
5. Set the **objectName** property of the two **Line Edit** widgets to `lineEditLongitude` and `lineEditLatitude`.

6. Set the **objectName** property of the **Push Button** widget to `pushButtonSearch`.
7. Set the **objectName** property of the other four **Label** widgets to `labelLocation`, `labelCity`, `labelCountry`, and `labelPostalCode`.
8. Save the application by name as `demoGoogleMap2.ui`. The form will now appear as shown in the following screenshot:

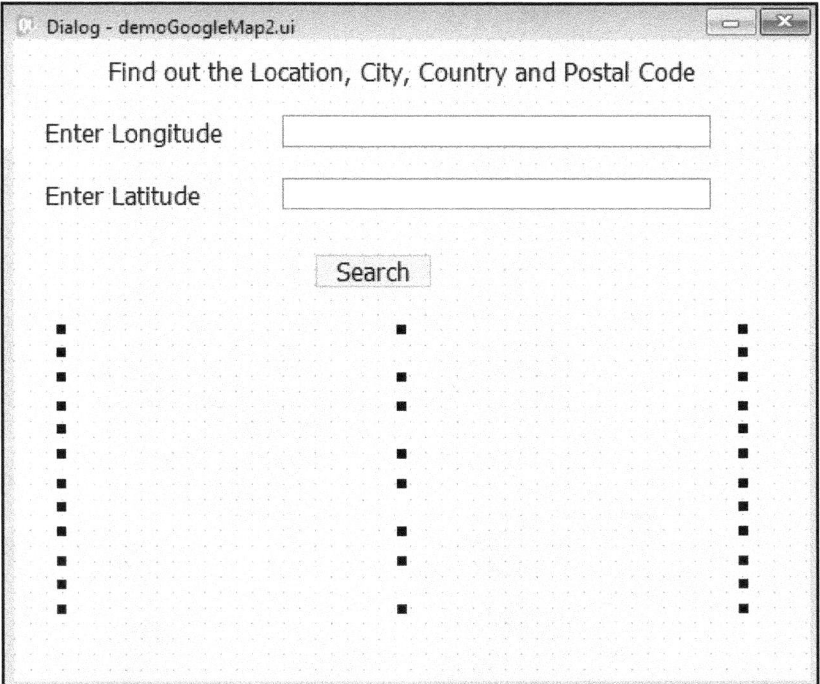

The user interface created with Qt Designer is stored in a `.ui` file, which is an XML file and needs to be converted into Python code. The `pyuic5` utility is used to convert the XML file into Python code. The generated Python script, `demoGoogleMap2.py`, can be seen in the source code bundle for the book.

9. Treat the `demoGoogleMap2.py` script as a header file, and import it into the file from which you will invoke its user interface design.
10. Create another Python file with the name `callGoogleMap2.pyw` and import the `demoGoogleMap2.py` code into it:

```
import sys
from PyQt5.QtWidgets import QDialog, QApplication
from geolocation.main import GoogleMaps
from demoGoogleMap2 import *
class MyForm(QDialog):
    def __init__(self):
        super().__init__()
        self.ui = Ui_Dialog()
        self.ui.setupUi(self)
        self.ui.pushButtonSearch.clicked.connect(self.
        displayLocation)
        self.show()
    def displayLocation(self):
        lng = float(self.ui.lineEditLongitude.text())
        lat = float(self.ui.lineEditLatitude.text())
        google_maps = GoogleMaps(api_key=
        'AIzaSyDzCMD-JTg-IbJZZ9fKGE1lipbBiFRiGHA')
        my_location = google_maps.search(lat=lat, lng=lng).
        first()
        self.ui.labelLocation.setText("Location:
        "+str(my_location))
        self.ui.labelCity.setText("City:
        "+str(my_location.city))
        self.ui.labelCountry.setText("Country:
        "+str(my_location.country))
        self.ui.labelPostalCode.setText("Postal Code:
        "+str(my_location.postal_code))
if __name__=="__main__":
    app = QApplication(sys.argv)
    w = MyForm()
    w.show()
    sys.exit(app.exec_())
```

How it works...

In the script, you can see that the **click()** event of the push button with the **objectName** property `pushButtonSearch` is connected to the `displayLocation` method. This means that, whenever the push button is clicked, the `displayLocation` method will be invoked. In the `displayLocation` method, you access the longitude and latitude entered by the user through the two **Line Edit** widgets and assign them to two variables, `lng` and `lat`, respectively. A Google Maps instance is defined by passing the API key that you got on registering with Google. Invoke the `search` method on the Google Maps instance, passing the longitude and latitude values that were supplied by the user. The `first` method is invoked on the retrieved search and the first location that matches the supplied longitude and latitude values is assigned to the `my_location` structure. The location name is displayed through the **Label** widget. To display the city, country, and postal code of the location, the `city`, `country`, and `postal_code` members of the `my_location` structure are used.

On running the application, you will be prompted to enter longitude and latitude values. The location name, city, country, and postal code related to the supplied longitude and latitude will be displayed on the screen through the four **Label** widgets, as shown in the following screenshot:

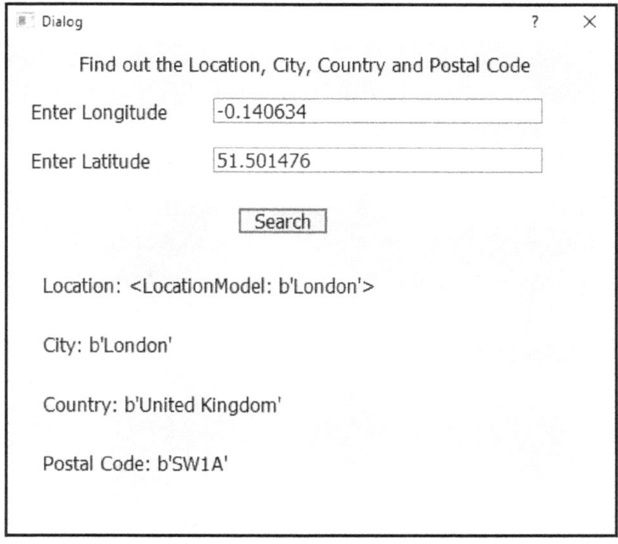

Finding out the distance between two locations

In this recipe, you will learn how to find out the distance in kilometers between the two locations entered by the user. The recipe will simply prompt the user to enter two locations, followed by clicking the **Find Distance** button, and the distance between the two will be displayed.

How to do it...

Let's create an application based on the Dialog without Buttons template by performing the following steps:

1. Add four `QLabel`, two `QLineEdit`, and a `QPushButton` widget to the form by dragging and dropping four **Label**, two **Line Edit**, and a **Push Button** widget onto the form.
2. Set the **text** property of the first **Label** widget to `Find out the distance between two locations`, that of the second **Label** widget to `Enter first location`, and that of the third **Label** widget to `Enter second location`.
3. Delete the **text** property of the fourth **Label** widget because its **text** property will be set through code; that is, the distance between the two entered locations will be computed through code and displayed in the fourth **Label** widget.
4. Set the **text** property of the **Push Button** widget to `Find Distance`.
5. Set the **objectName** properties of the two **Line Edit** widgets to `lineEditFirstLocation` and `lineEditSecondLocation`.
6. Set the **objectName** property of the **Push Button** widget to `pushButtonFindDistance`.
7. Set the **objectName** property of the fourth **Label** widget to `labelDistance`.

8. Save the application by name as `demoGoogleMap3.ui`. The form will now appear as shown in the following screenshot:

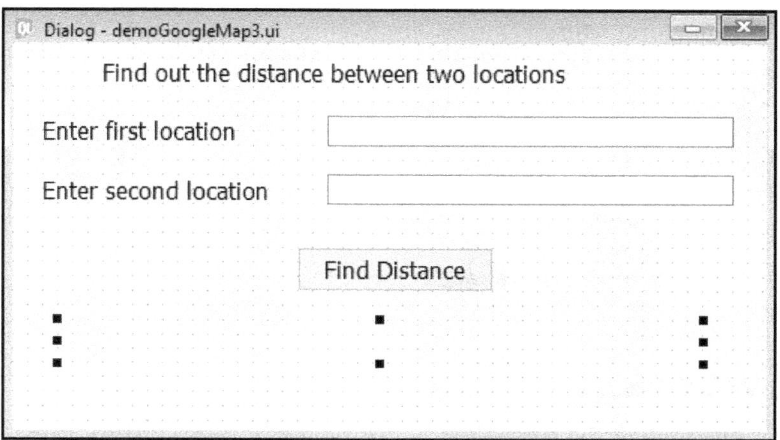

The user interface created with Qt Designer is stored in a `.ui` file and it is an XML file. The XML file is converted into Python code by applying the `pyuic5` utility. You can find the generated Python code, `demoGoogleMap3.py`, in the source code bundle for the book.

9. To use the GUI created in the `demoGoogleMap3.py` file, we need to create another Python script and import `demoGoogleMap3.py` file in that script.
10. Create another Python file with the name `callGoogleMap3.pyw` and import the `demoGoogleMap3.py` code into it:

```
import sys
from PyQt5.QtWidgets import QDialog, QApplication
from googlemaps.client import Client
from googlemaps.distance_matrix import distance_matrix
from demoGoogleMap3 import *
class MyForm(QDialog):
    def __init__(self):
        super().__init__()
        self.ui = Ui_Dialog()
        self.ui.setupUi(self)
        self.ui.pushButtonFindDistance.clicked.connect(self.
        displayDistance)
        self.show()
    def displayDistance(self):
        api_key = 'xxxxxxxxxxxxxxxxxxxxxxxxxxxxxxxxxxxxxx'
        gmaps = Client(api_key)
```

```
            data = distance_matrix(gmaps,
            self.ui.lineEditFirstLocation.text(),
            self.ui.lineEditSecondLocation.text())
            distance = data['rows'][0]['elements'][0]['distance']
            ['text']
            self.ui.labelDistance.setText("Distance between
            "+self.ui.lineEditFirstLocation.text()+"
            and "+self.ui.lineEditSecondLocation.text()+" is
            "+str(distance))
if __name__=="__main__":
    app = QApplication(sys.argv)
    w = MyForm()
    w.show()
    sys.exit(app.exec_())
```

How it works...

You create an instance of the `Client` class and name it `gmaps`. While creating the `Client` instance, you need to pass the API key that you got on registering with Google. The **click()** event of the push button with **objectName**, `pushButtonFindDistance`, is connected to the `displayDistance` method. This means that, whenever the push button is clicked, the `displayDistance` method will be invoked. In the `displayDistance` method, you invoke the `distance_matrix` method, passing the `Client` instance and the two locations entered by the user, to find out the distance between them. The `distance_matrix` method returns a multidimensional array that is assigned to the data array. From the data array, the distance between the two locations is accessed and assigned to the `distance` variable. The value in the `distance` variable is finally displayed through the **Label** widget.

On running the application, you will be prompted to enter the two locations whose intervening distance you want to know. After entering the two locations, when you click the **Find Distance** button, the distance between the two locations will be displayed on the screen, as shown in the following screenshot:

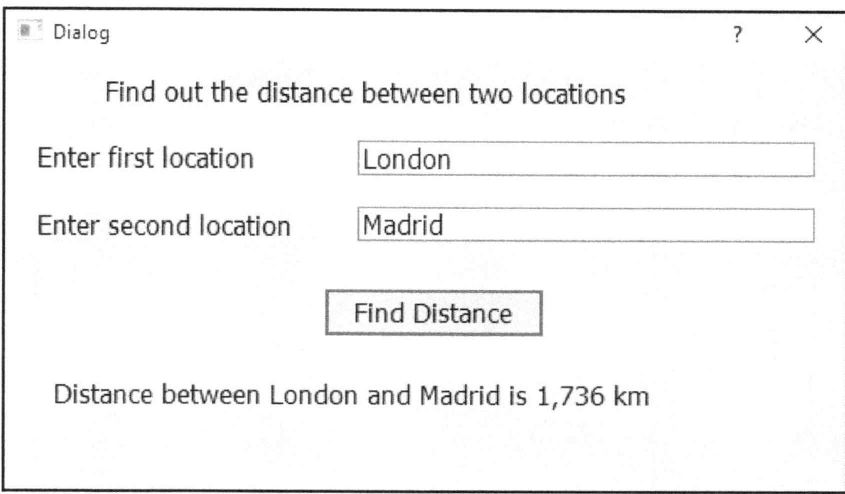

Displaying location on Google Maps

In this recipe, you will learn how to display a location on Google Maps if you know the longitude and latitude values of that location. You will be prompted to simply enter longitude and latitude values and, when you click the **Show Map** button, that location will appear on Google Maps.

How to do it...

Let's create an application based on the **Dialog without Buttons** template by performing the following steps:

1. Add two `QLabel`, two `QLineEdit`, a `QPushButton`, and a `QWidget` widget to the form by dragging and dropping two **Label**, two **Line Edit**, a **Push Button**, and a **Widget** container onto the form.

2. Set the text property of the two **Label** widgets to `Longitude` and `Latitude`.
3. Set the **text** property of the **Push Button** widget to `Show Map`.
4. Set the **objectName** property of the two **Line Edit** widgets to `lineEditLongitude` and `lineEditLatitude`.
5. Set the **objectName** property of the **Push Button** widget to `pushButtonShowMap`.
6. Save the application by name as `showGoogleMap.ui`. The form will now appear as shown in the following screenshot:

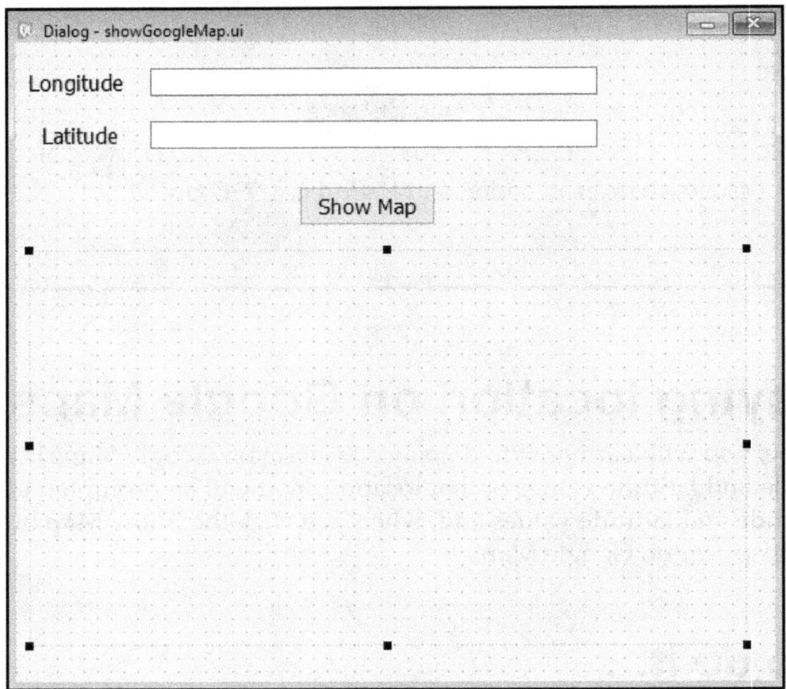

7. The next step is to promote the `QWidget` widget to `QWebEngineView` because, to display Google Maps, `QWebEngineView` is required. Because Google maps is a web application, we need a QWebEngineView to display and interact with Google maps.

8. Promote the `QWidget` widget by right-clicking on it and selecting the **Promote to ...** option from the menu that pops up. In the dialog box that appears, leave the **Base class name** option as the default, **QWidget**.
9. In the **Promoted class name** box, enter `QWebEngineView` and, in the header file box, type `PyQT5.QtWebEngineWidgets`.
10. Click on the **Promote** button to promote the `QWidget` widget to the `QWebEngineView` class, as shown in the following screenshot:

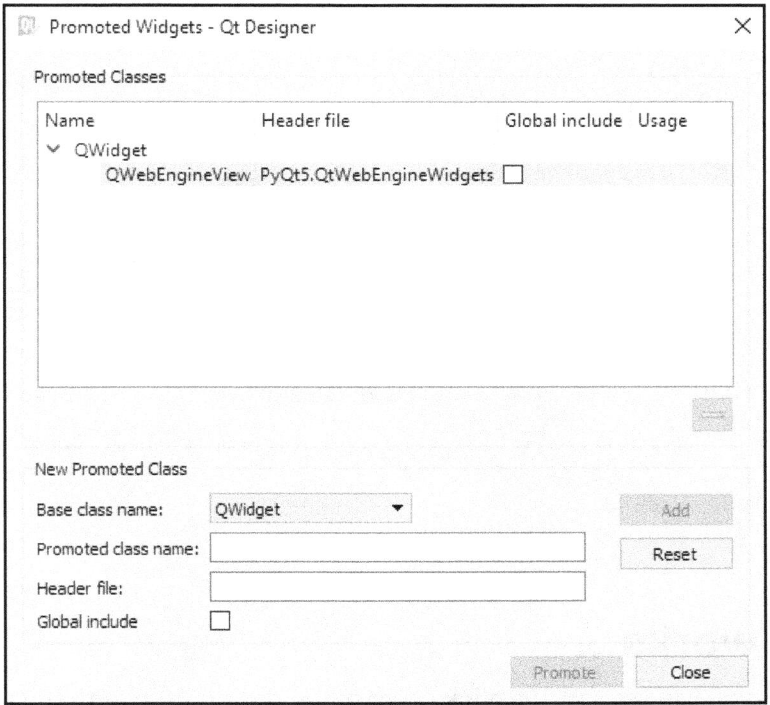

11. Click on the **Close** button to close the **Promoted Widgets** dialog box. The user interface created with Qt Designer is stored in a `.ui` file, which is an XML file and needs to be converted into Python code. The `pyuic5` utility is used to convert the XML file into Python code. The generated Python script, `showGoogleMap.py`, can be seen in the source code bundle for the book.

12. Treat the `showGoogleMap.py` script as a header file, and import it into the file from which you will invoke its user interface design.
13. Create another Python file with the name `callGoogleMap.pyw` and import the `showGoogleMap.py` code into it:

```
import sys
from PyQt5.QtCore import QUrl
from PyQt5.QtWidgets import QApplication, QDialog
from PyQt5.QtWebEngineWidgets import QWebEngineView
from showGoogleMap import *
class MyForm(QDialog):
    def __init__(self):
        super().__init__()
        self.ui = Ui_Dialog()
        self.ui.setupUi(self)
self.ui.pushButtonShowMap.clicked.connect(self.dispSite)
        self.show()
    def dispSite(self):
        lng = float(self.ui.lineEditLongitude.text())
        lat = float(self.ui.lineEditLatitude.text())
        URL="https://www.google.com/maps/@"+self.ui.
        lineEditLatitude.text()+","
        +self.ui.lineEditLongitude.text()+",9z"
        self.ui.widget.load(QUrl(URL))
if __name__=="__main__":
    app = QApplication(sys.argv)
    w = MyForm()
    w.show()
    sys.exit(app.exec_())
```

How it works...

In the script, you can see that the **click** event of the push button with the **objectName** property `pushButtonShowMap` is connected to the `dispSite ()` method. This means that, whenever the push button is clicked, the `dispSite()` method will be invoked. In the `dispSite ()` method, you access the longitude and latitude entered by the user through the two **Line Edit** widgets, and assign them to two variables, `lng` and `lat`, respectively. Thereafter, you create a URL that invokes Google Maps from `google.com` and passes the latitude and longitude values entered by the user.

The URL is initially in text form and is typecast to a `QUrl` instance and passed to the widget that is promoted to `QWebEngineView` to display the website. The `QUrl` is a class from Qt that provides several methods and properties to manage URLs. Google Maps, with the specified latitude and longitude values, is then displayed via the `QWebEngineView` widget.

On running the application, you will be prompted to enter the longitude and latitude values of the location you want to see on Google Maps. After entering the longitude and latitude values, when you click on the **Show Map** button, Google Maps will display that location, as shown in the following screenshot:

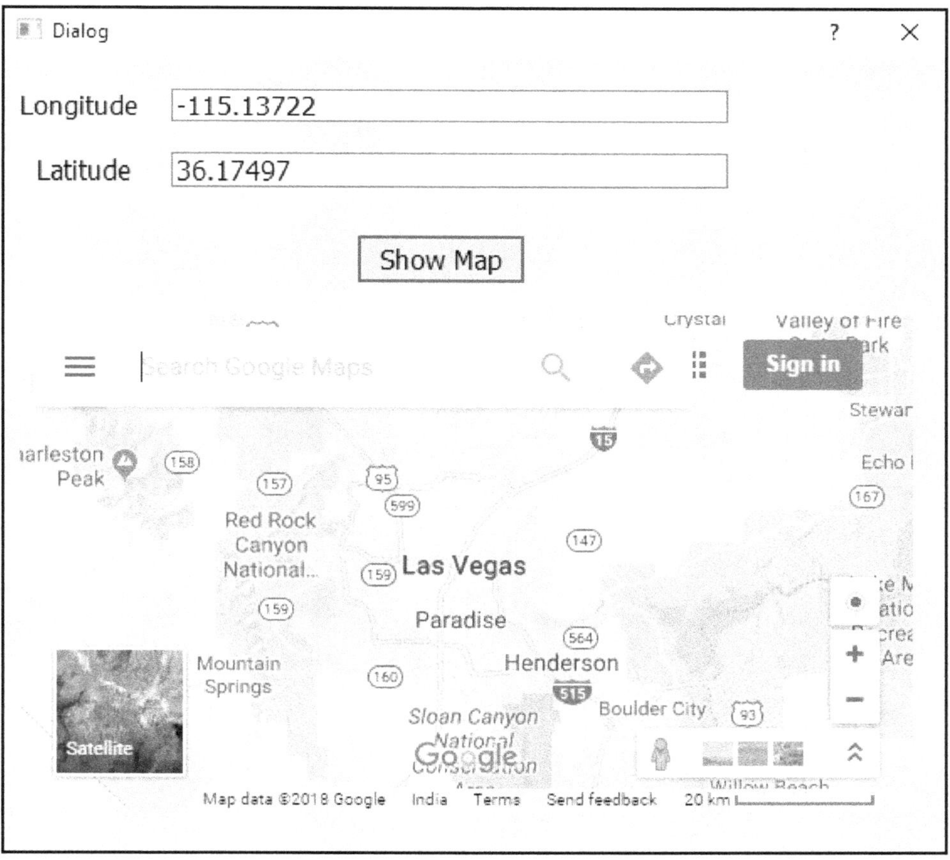

Other Books You May Enjoy

If you enjoyed this book, you may be interested in these other books by Packt:

Tkinter GUI Application Development Cookbook
Alejandro Rodas de Paz

ISBN: 978-1-78862-230-1

- Add widgets and handle user events
- Lay out widgets within windows using frames and the different geometry managers
- Configure widgets so that they have a customized appearance and behavior
- Improve the navigation of your apps with menus and dialogs
- Apply object-oriented programming techniques in Tkinter applications
- Use threads to achieve responsiveness and update the GUI
- Explore the capabilities of the canvas widget and the types of items that can be added to it
- Extend Tkinter applications with the TTK (themed Tkinter) module

Tkinter GUI Programming by Example
David Love

ISBN: 978-1-78862-748-1

- Create a scrollable frame via the Canvas widget
- Use the pack geometry manager and Frame widget to control layout
- Learn to choose a data structure for a game
- Group Tkinter widgets, such as buttons, canvases, and labels
- Create a highly customizable Python editor
- Design and lay out a chat window

Leave a review - let other readers know what you think

Please share your thoughts on this book with others by leaving a review on the site that you bought it from. If you purchased the book from Amazon, please leave us an honest review on this book's Amazon page. This is vital so that other potential readers can see and use your unbiased opinion to make purchasing decisions, we can understand what our customers think about our products, and our authors can see your feedback on the title that they have worked with Packt to create. It will only take a few minutes of your time, but is valuable to other potential customers, our authors, and Packt. Thank you!

Index

2

A

H

I

J

L

Q

R

S

T

U

V

W

www.ingramcontent.com/pod-product-compliance
Lightning Source LLC
Chambersburg PA
CBHW060632060326
40690CB00020B/4378

* 9 7 8 1 8 3 8 9 8 8 4 7 0 *